Jesus and Identity

MATRIX
The Bible in Mediterranean Context

Richard L. Rohrbaugh
The New Testament in Cross-Cultural Perspective

∞∞∞

Forthcoming volumes in the series

Pieter F. Craffert
*The Life of a Galilean Shaman:
Jesus of Nazareth in Anthropological–Historical Perspective*

Douglas E. Oakman
Jesus and the Peasants

Stuart L. Love
*Jesus and Marginal Women:
Healing in Matthew's Gospel*

EDITORIAL BOARD

John H. Elliott   John S. Kloppenborg
Anselm Hagedorn   Douglas E. Oakman
K. C. Hanson   Gary Stansell

Jesus and Identity
Reconstructing Judean Ethnicity in Q

MARKUS CROMHOUT

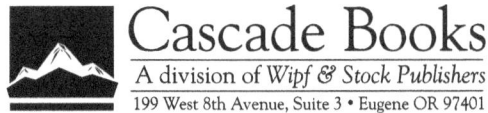

JESUS AND IDENTITY
Reconstructing Judean Ethnicity in Q

Matrix: The Bible in Mediterranean Context, Volume 2

Copyright © 2007 Markus Cromhout. All rights reserved. Except for brief quotations in critical publications or reviews, no part of this book may be reproduced in any manner without prior written permission from the publisher. Write: Permissions, Wipf & Stock, 199 W. 8th Ave., Eugene, OR 97401.

Cascade Books
A Division of Wipf and Stock Publishers
199 W. 8th Ave., Suite 3
Eugene, OR 97401

ISBN 13: 978-1-55635-103-7

Cataloging-in-Publication data:

Cromhout, Markus.
Jesus and identity : reconstructing Judean ethnicity in Q / Markus Cromhout.

xiv + 390 p.; 23 cm.

Matrix: The Bible in Mediterranean Context, Volume 2

ISBN 13: 978-1-55635-103-7 (alk. paper)

1. Ethnicity – Biblical teaching. 2. Bible. N.T. Gospels—Criticism, interpretation, etc. 3. Q hypothesis (source criticism). I. Title. II. Series.

BS2555.2 C75 2007

Manufactured in the U.S.A.

Contents

Preface vii
Abbreviations ix

   Introduction 1

1 Identifying the Problem 9

2 A Socio-Cultural Model of Judean Ethnicity 67

3 Judean Ethnicity in the First Century CE 117

4 Who Were the Galileans? 231

5 Judean Ethnicity in Q 257

Bibliography 381

Preface

THE WORK presented in the following pages is a revised version of my Ph.D. dissertation titled: *The Reconstruction of Judean Ethnicity in Q*, prepared under the supervision of Professor Andries Van Aarde for the Faculty of Theology, University of Pretoria, and which was accepted May 2006. Since then I refined, and hopefully, improved my approach to ethnicity theory and its broader application to the work presented here. It is encouraging to see that more and more work is appearing on the important—but mostly neglected—aspect of ethnic identity. It is unfortunate that the more recent work could not be sufficiently incorporated here, but it is my hope that this volume will make a positive contribution to the debate.

My indebtedness to the various scholars whose work is utilized here, of course, needs to be acknowledged. Whether I at times agree or disagree, the arguments presented here would simply not have been possible without their research, which must be the culmination of thousands of hours of work. Where would we be without the learning and insight of others? My sincere gratitude also goes to Professors Bill Domeris (South African Theological Seminary) and Patrick Hartin, (Gonzaga University) who have endorsed the publication of this work. So too Professor John Kloppenborg (University of Toronto) and Dr. K. C. Hanson at Wipf and Stock Publishers, whose support and encouragement made it all possible.

On a more personal note, the following people have also in various ways contributed. There is Adri Goosen at the faculty office, whose friendly assistance makes working with her a pleasure. To Johann Kitching I owe much, having opened doors of opportunity for me and whose encouragement and support was demonstrated in many ways. Thanks to him the dissertation could be finished in a shorter time than usual. To my parents I say thank you for everything, for their support in all aspects of my life, too numerous to mention here. I would not be where I am today if it was not for their love and involvement. And a special thank you to my soul mate, Joy, who patiently endured my many hours of research, typing up, and refining this work. Her unconditional love, support and understanding goes beyond description. Lastly, a special mention is in order for Professor Andries van Aarde. At the time when the dissertation was prepared, he had to contend with serious illness. Even so, this work benefited greatly from hours of discussion and his vast insight made this a journey of wonderful discovery. His support, that extends even to the present, is worthy of my heartfelt and deepest gratitude. This work I dedicate to him: Εὐλογήσαι σε κύριος καὶ φυλάξαι σε.

Markus Cromhout
Johannesburg, 14 December 2006

Abbreviations

Apocrypha

2 Ezra	2 Ezra
4 Ezra	4 Ezra
Tob	Tobit
Jdt	Judith
AddEsth	Additions to Esther
WisSol	Wisdom of Solomon
Sir	Sirach
1 Bar	1 Baruch
LetJer	Letter of Jeremiah
PrAzar	Prayer of Azariah
Sus	Susanna
Bel	Bel and the Dragon
1 Macc	1 Maccabees
2 Macc	2 Maccabees

Pseudepigrapha

Ap. Ab.	*Apocalypse of Abraham*
T. Ab.	*Testament of Abraham*
Ap. Adam	*Apocalypse of Adam*
T. Adam	*Testament of Adam*
L.A.E.	*Life of Adam and Eve*
Let. Aris.	*Letter of Aristeas*
2 Bar.	*2 (Syriac) Baruch*
3 Bar.	*3 (Greek) Baruch*
4 Bar.	*4 Baruch*
Ap. Dan.	*Apocalypse of Daniel*
1 En.	*1 (Ethiopic) Enoch*
2 En.	*2 (Slavonic) Enoch*
Ezek. Trag.	*Ezekiel the Tragedian*
Hist. Rech.	*History of the Rechabites*

T. Isaac	Testament of Isaac
AscenIs	Ascension of Isaiah
T. Jac.	Testament of Jacob
JanJam	Jannes and Jambres
T. Job	Testament of Job
Jos. Asen.	Joseph and Asenath
Jub.	Jubilees
L.A.B.	Liber antiquitatum biblicarum
3 Macc	3 Maccabees
4 Macc	4 Maccabees
Pr. Man.	Prayer of Manasseh
Ap. Mos.	Apocalypse of Moses
T. Mos.	Testament of Moses
Liv. Pro.	Lives of the Prophets
Sib. Or.	Sibylline Oracles
Pss. Sol.	Psalms of Solomon
T. Sol.	Testament of Solomon
T. 12Patr.	Testaments of the Twelve Patriarchs
T. Reu.	Testament of Reuben
T. Sim.	Testament of Simeon
T. Levi	Testament of Levi
T. Jud.	Testament of Judah
T. Iss.	Testament of Issachar
T. Zeb.	Testament of Zebulun
T. Dan	Testament of Dan
T. Naph.	Testament of Naphtali
T. Gad	Testament of Gad
T. Ash.	Testament of Asher
T. Jos.	Testament of Joseph
T. Benj.	Testament of Benjamin

Dead Sea Scrolls

CD	Damascus Document
1QH	Thanksgiving Hymns
1QS	Rule of the Community
1QM	War Scroll (4Q471^a)
1QpHab	Habakkuk Pesher
1QpMic	Micah Pesher
3Q15	The Copper Scroll
4QMMT	More Works of the Torah
4QpIsa^d	Isaiah Pesher 1
4QTest	Testimonies
4QpsDan	Pseudo Daniel

4Q381	Non-canonical Psalms
4Q512	Purification Ritual
4Q521	Messianic Apocalypse
11QTemple	Temple Scroll
11QMelch	Melchizedek

Philo

Abraham	On Abraham
Creation	On the Creation of the World
Decal	On the Decalogue
Embassy	The Embassy to Gaius
Flaccus	Against Flaccus
Hyp	Hypothetica
MigAbraham	On the Migration of Abraham
Moses	The Life of Moses
Omnis Probus	Quod Omnis Probus Liber Sit (That Every Good Person Is Free)
PreStudies	On the Preliminary Studies
Providence	On Providence
Rewards	On Rewards and Punishments
SpecLaws	On the Special Laws
Virtues	On the Virtues
QExodus	Questions and Answers on Exodus
QGenesis	Questions and Answers on Genesis

Josephus

Ant.	Jewish Antiquities
Apion	Against Apion
Life	Life of Josephus
War	Jewish Wars

New Testament Apocrypha and Related Texts

2 Clem.	2 Clement
Did.	Didache
GEbion	Gospel of the Ebionites
EgerGos	Egerton Gospel
GThom	Gospel of Thomas
Herm. Man.	Shepherd of Hermas, Mandate(s)
POxy	Papyrus Oxyrhynchus

Early Fathers

H.E.   Eusebius, *Historica ecclesiastica*
Pr. Ev.   Eusebius, *Praeparatio evangelica*

Rabbinic Writings

Ab.	Abot
Arak.	Arakhin
A.R.N.	Abot de-Rabbi Nathan
A.Z.	'Abodah Zarah
b.	Babylonian Talmud
B.B.	Baba Batra
Ber	Berakot
Bikk	Bikkurim
B.M.	Batei Midrashot
Dem.	Demai
'Eduy.	'Eduyyot
'Erub.	'Erubin
Exod. Rab.	Šemot Rabbah
Giṭṭ.	Giṭṭin
Hor.	Horayot
Kel.	Kelim
Ker.	Keritot
Ket.	Ketubot
Kid.	Kiddushin
LamR	Ekah Rabbah
m.	Mishnah
Maas.	Maaserot
Meg.	Megillah
Mik.	Mikwa'ot
Ned.	Nedarim
Nid.	Niddah
Par.	Parah
Pes.	Pesaḥim
P.R.E.	Pirke de-Rabbi Eliezer
Sanh.	Sanhedrin
Shab.	Shabbat
Sheb.	Shebiit
Sheq.	Sheqalim
Sif. Deut.	Sifre Deuteronomy
Sif. Num.	Sifre Numbers
Soṭ.	Soṭah
Sukk.	Sukkah

t.	Tosephta
Taʿan.	Taʿanit
Tg. Cant.	Targum Canticles
Tg. Ezk.	Targum Ezekiel
Tg. Isa.	Targum Isaiah
Tg. Jon.	Targum Jonathan
Tg. Neof.	Targum Neofiti
Tg. Num.	Targum Numbers
Tg. Onq.	Targum Onqelos
Tg. Yer.	Targum Yerushalmi
Tg. Ps.-J.	Targum Pseudo-Jonathan
Ter.	Terumot
y.	Jerusalem Talmud
Yeb.	Yebamot
Yom.	Yoma

Roman Authors

Hist.	Tacitus, *Histories*
Sat.	Juvenal, *Satire*

Modern

BAR	*Biblical Archaeology Review*
BDAG	Frederick W. Danker, reviser and editor, *A Greek-English Lexicon of the New Testament and Other Early Christian Literature*. 3d ed. Chicago: University of Chicago Press, 2000
BibIntSer	Biblical Interpretation Series
BR	*Bible Review*
BTB	*Biblical Theology Bulletin*
CBQ	*Catholic Biblical Quarterly*
DJSS	Duke Judaic Studies Series
ERS	*Ethnic and Racial Studies*
HTS	*Hervormde Teologiese Studies*
JBL	*Journal of Biblical Literature*
JSJSup	Journal for the Study of Judaism Supplements
JSNT	*Journal for the Study of the New Testament*
JSNTSup	Journal for the Study of the New Testament Supplements
JSOTSup	Journal for the Study of the Old Testament Supplements
NovTSup	Novum Testamentum Supplements
NTS	*New Testament Studies*
NTTS	New Testament Tools and Studies

SBEC	Studies in the Bible and Early Christianity
SBT	Studies in Biblical Theology
SNTSMS	Society for New Testament Studies Monograph Series
WUNT	Wissenschaftliche Untersuchungen zum Neuen Testament

Introduction

A FRIEND OF mine, who performs missionary work among the Zulus of KwaZulu-Natal, recently told me of the realities he encounters. Even congregations that have long been established, he said, tenaciously cling onto traditions that are incompatible with Christian theology. The Zulus are a very proud people, and especially those in the rural areas foster ancestral traditions as part of their culture. This in itself poses no problem, but they—like many peoples in Southern Africa—have a strong tradition about making contact and seeking guidance from their ancestors. On special days they make sacrifices to them, all based on the view that the ancestors, believed to be close to God, are sort of "demigods" themselves possessing powers that can have a major impact on the quality of one's life here. You must make the ancestors happy and seek their blessing in all areas of your life. They do all this, despite the fact that they would regard themselves as Christians. His experiences illustrate that even today ethnic identity is many times inseparable from religious identity. How much more must it have been the case for the Israelites or Judeans ("Jews") of Palestine who lived in the time of Jesus, including the Messianists ("Christians")? David Sim's point is certainly no exaggeration; speaking of the first century,

> the various traditions which comprised [Judeanism] took very seriously the notion of ethnicity, and the messianic movement associated with Jesus of Nazareth was no exception to this rule. So important was this issue that it threatened to tear apart the early church [*sic*] in the first few decades of its existence. (Sim 1996:171)

In this study I investigate the question of Judean ethnicity in further detail. Our focus will eventually shift to the people presupposed by the hypothetical source known as Q. As this study progresses, hopefully it will become clear that without a better understanding of first-century

Judean ethnicity and all the dynamics that it entails, a more comprehensive understanding of Jesus and the movements that he spawned is not possible.

Judean and Judeanism versus Jew and Judaism

As this investigation is focussed on the question of ethnic identity, it would be appropriate to discuss why it is preferred to use the terms *Judean* and *Judeanism*, instead of *Jew* and *Judaism*. Is it proper to refer to "Jews" and "Judaism" when speaking of the people and religion of first-century Palestine? Pilch argued that it is anachronistic to speak of "Jews" in the biblical period, and the Greek word Ἰουδαῖοι should be translated as *Judean*, a designation which the Israelites accepted during the Second Temple period (520 BCE–70 CE). The religion of that period (in all its diversity) is also properly called Judean or Judaic, and "Judaism" is not a proper term for it did not yet exist. Only from the sixth century can we speak of rabbinic "Judaism" and from when it is proper to use the term "Jews" (Pilch 1997). In similar vein, BDAG (2000) argued consistently that "Judean" and "Judeanism" is the best translation.

Let us first address the term *Judean*. The term *Judean* (Ἰουδαῖος) begins as a way to identify someone from Judea (Ἰουδαία) (Josephus, *Ant.* 11.173). According to Dunn, for its early usage Ἰουδαῖος should be translated as "Judean," rather than "Jew." He basically follows the argument of Cohen (1999:70–136; cf. 1990:204–23) who stated that prior to the Hasmonean period Ἰουδαῖος should always be translated "Judean," never as "Jew." But there was a shift from purely an ethno-geographical term to one of a more "religious" significance, first evident in 2 Macc 6:6 and 9:17. Here Ἰουδαῖος for the first time can be properly translated as "Jew." In Greco-Roman writers Ἰουδαῖος was first used as a religious term at the end of the first century. Dunn (2003:262–63) basically rejects the BDAG terminology—by implication, that of Pilch as well—as he argues that it does not take into consideration the shift in reference as outlined by Cohen. But is the argument justified?

To switch from "Judean" to "Jew" based on a so-called shift to a more "religious" significance is arbitrary at best. Dunn's objection (and Cohen's argument) cannot be accepted since for first-century Judean ethnicity—here particularly ethno-geographical identity—was inseparable from religious identity, something which Dunn himself suggests[1]

---

1. As will be shown throughout this book, there is a lot of agreement with Dunn's

(since Judea was a temple state). Esler points out that in antiquity it was common practice to name ethnic groups in relation to the territory from which they came. Speaking of the Greeks and Romans he writes that one "would expect them to connect ['Ιουδαῖοι] with the territory called 'Ιουδαία that this people inhabited, and that is what we usually find" (Esler 2003:63). The attachment between the people and the land is even closer in Judean sources (cf. Esler 2003:64–65). Dunn (2003:262–63) himself admits that "even in later usage, referring, for example, to Jews long settled in the diaspora, the basic sense of 'the Jews' as the nation or people identified with the territory of Judea is still present." Esler (2003:70) also states that Cohen "seems to assume that from the first century BCE onward it is possible to speak of 'religion' existing as a realm of human experience distinct from other realms such as kinship, politics, and economics in a manner similar to modern understandings of religion," but "in the Mediterranean world of the first century CE the features that we refer to as 'religious' ideas and institutions were primarily embodied in structures of the political and domestic realms." Perhaps this critique misses the thrust of Cohen's approach,[2] but what particularly convinced Esler to translate 'Ιουδαῖοι as "Judeans"

work in terms of content, but here one must disagree with him on the matter of terminology, and what he sees as "ambivalence" between ethno-geographical identity and religious identity by the use of the term 'Ιουδαῖος (Dunn 2003:263). He argues this ambivalence and shift to a more religious significance allowed for non-Judeans to become (religious) "Jews," such as in the case of Izates, king of Adiabene, without the need for circumcision (Josephus, *Ant.* 20.38–46). But this was a unique and exceptional case, and Izates was eventually required to undergo circumcision anyway. In a technical sense, his circumcision was an affirmation of what his religious status really implied—ethnically he became a Judean, irrespective of the attempts to "mask" it by him not having to undergo circumcision. As Sim (1996:176) mentions the "importance of this narrative lies in the fact that circumcision as the normal rite of entrance into [Judeanism] is taken for granted." The point is this: at that time there was basically no (complete) religious conversion to Judeanism apart from a complete ethnic conversion, involving the performance of all Judean customs and allegiance to the temple in Jerusalem.

2. Apart from the preference for "Jew," Cohen argues that 'Ιουδαϊσμός analogous to Hellenism developed to become a function of religion and culture; the religious definition supplemented the traditional ethnic definition. "Jewishness" (which he proposes as a translation for 'Ιουδαϊσμός) became an "ethno-religious identity." This is despite the fact that he knows that 'Ιουδαϊσμός as a term refers to more than just religion, as religion is but one of many aspects that make a group or culture distinctive (Cohen 1999:7–8, 137). The approach taken here is in line with the latter, in that it is better to regard 'Ιουδαϊσμός (Judeanism) as a summary term for an entire cultural system, where "religion" must not be preferred above other cultural aspects. As such, Judeanism was a term for a cultural system *that already existed*, being territorially rooted in Judea. Its practitioners are therefore properly called Judeans.

is a passage from Josephus (*War* 2.43ff; cf. *Ant.* 17.254), which describes that "the people," that is Galileans, Idumeans, Pereans, *and people from Judea itself* (ὁ γνήσιος ἐξ αὐτῆς Ἰουδαίας λαός) came to Jerusalem in response to the actions of Sabinus, the Roman procurator of Syria, an event dated to 4 BCE. Esler (2003:67) argues that the "critical point in this passage is that the existence of a segment of this people who lived in Judea itself was irrelevant to the fact that all those of its members who came to Jerusalem were Ἰουδαῖοι." Josephus, Esler (2003:72) suggests, distinguishes this group of Judeans from others with the use of a periphrastic explanation, literally "the people by physical descent from Judea itself" although Esler prefers to translate it as "the membership of the people from Judea itself."

What is argued against Dunn with regard to the term *Judean* is also true for the term *Judeanism* (Ἰουδαϊσμός). Here the translation of the BDAG will be followed, instead of the usual "Judaism." The Greek term Ἰουδαϊσμός appears first in 2 Maccabees in three passages (2:21; 8:1; 14:38). It also appears in 4 Macc 4:26 and Paul himself boasts how he had excelled in Judeanism beyond many of his peers (Gal 1:13–14). Dunn noted, in the earliest phase of its usage, there is no evidence for its use by Gentiles (Dunn refers to "Judaism" as such). Judeanism started as a Judean self-reference, reflecting the perspective of Hellenistic Judeanism. Be that as it may, in 2 Maccabees Ἰουδαϊσμός is coined to counter Ἑλληνισμός ("Hellenism"; 2 Macc 4:13) and ἀλλοφυλισμός ("foreignness"; 2 Macc 4:13; 6:24). So the term *Judeanism* was used as a self-definition to mark out the character of belief and practice that distinguished its participants from the surrounding culture and ethos (cf. Dunn 2003:261). To put it differently, it was a summary term for an entire cultural system that reacted to Hellenism.

So here the terms *Judean* and *Judeanism* will be used throughout whether they are used as "insider" or "outsider" designations. This means that "Jew(s)" and "Judaism" will also deliberately be replaced with "Judean(s)" and "Judeanism" when referring to or quoting from the work of scholars (when quoted, the replacement will appear in square brackets). This is by no means intended to be an anachronistic distortion of their positions. It should be remembered that they speak of "Jews" and "Judaism." The replacement serves as a necessary economy and to illustrate that what these scholars wrote in reference to "Jews" and "Judaism" also holds true for what is argued here in reference to "Judeans" and "Judeanism." For our purposes therefore a Judean refers to an "Israelite" inhabitant of Judea (and Palestine generally), a person who was a Judean by religion and culture and therefore had ethnic connections to Judea and allegiance to its state religion (cf. Duling 2005). The entire cultural system of Judeans is also properly called "Judeanism."

Messianist and Messianism versus Christian and Christianity

As Pilch (1997) argued that it is anachronistic to speak of "Jews" in the biblical period, so he argued that it is anachronistic to speak of "Christians" in the biblical period. He argues that first-century "Yahwism" consisted of various groups: Pharisaic, Messianic (called Christian), Sadducaic, Essene, among others. Again his argument is accepted as having merit, and for our purposes we will call the early followers of Jesus 'Messianists.' The form of Judeanism they belonged to was therefore Messianism. As we shall see, the Judeanism of Q was a radically redefined "covenantal nomism."

The Approach

In chapter 1, the approach at first glance will appear to be somewhat unorthodox. To end up investigating Judean ethnicity in Q, we will begin by utilising scholarship on the historical Jesus. The reason is simple. It is often claimed that Jesus was this or that kind of "Jew," or rather, Judean, but Jesus scholarship lacks an overall interpretive framework within which to understand what kind of Judean Jesus was. Chapter 1 is dedicated to expose this shortcoming, as an overview will be done of the work of two important scholars in this field: John P. Meier and John Dominic Crossan.

Chapter 2 will be dedicated to the task of developing a Socio-Cultural Model of Judean Ethnicity. It will be important to understand that the approach taken here to Judeanism varies from the norm, in that it is understood primarily as an *ethnic identity*, not as a "religious system" as such. The proposed model will be a synthesis of the following: Sanders' notion of covenantal nomism; Berger and Luckmann's theories on the sociology of knowledge; Dunn's "four pillars of Second Temple Judeanism ('Judaism')," combined with the insights gained from his "new perspective" on Paul; the insights of cultural anthropology, with the focus on modern ethnicity theory; and lastly, Duling's own proposal for a Socio-Cultural Model of Ethnicity, taking note that the latter is a more generic model. The proposed model will be termed "covenantal nomism." It will be a pictorial and abstract representation of the Judean social construction of reality, or the Judean "symbolic universe." It will also be argued that first-century Judeanism as an ethnic identity was *essentially* primordialist.

In chapter 3 I will elaborate upon the model by giving it the relevant and appropriate content. We will look at the importance of historical links to the past via a shared historical tradition and a common ancestry. The battle with Hellenism will be discussed and related to this, the adoption of the Greek language by Judeans and the infiltration of Hellenistic religious thought. We will then investigate aspects of Judean religion and customs applicable to the temple, the synagogue, and the home. Millennial hopes too are very important, as they were a driving force of Judeanism in the first century, and it will be argued that it primarily had to do with the independent control and ownership of the land. Judean kinship patterns will be investigated as well, and finally, an overview of Judean-Gentile relations will end the chapter.

Chapter 4 will investigate the ethnic identity of Galileans, as Q has plausibly been located in Galilee. Based on archaeological excavations and literary evidence it will be demonstrated that there existed a fundamental continuity between the people of Judea and Galilee. They had a common culture and both lived on the ancestral land of Israel. Judeanism was not some foreign import into Galilee that contested with local traditions. Galileans shared the same "symbolic universe" as the people of Judea. In effect, the Galileans were ethnic Judeans.

The hypothetical source Q will be the focus of chapter 5. An approach will be adopted where Q will consist of two stratums, therefore modifying Kloppenborg's own approach of three stratums. Each stratum will be investigated on its own and the findings of the analyses will be explained. As a preliminary thesis the following will be stated: *Q presupposes a community whose Judean ethnicity was in (re)construction. Most of the cultural features demonstrate a strong element of discontinuity with traditional Judean identity (= covenantal nomism)*. The Q people were given an *eschatological Judean identity*, based on their commitment to Jesus and the requirements of the kingdom/reign of God. This proved to be an identity that necessitated the polemical and apologetic strategy of the main redaction.

As the journey now begins in earnest, it is hoped that a realization will take shape how *critically important* the matter of *ethnic identity* was to Judeans in the first century. Surrounded by a Gentile world filled with idolatry, the emperor cult and economic exploitation of the land, the Judeans were a unique people that for greater part, held their ethnic identity intact, even though their "symbolic universe" was not. The foreigner was in the house. Nevertheless, they were people of the covenant, the one Creator of the world's special and chosen people, living on the land given to them by Yahweh. They were committed to their ethnic identity by doing God's will. This Judean self-understanding, it is hoped, even applicable to the Q people, will become clearer as this investigation unfolds.

CHAPTER 1

Identifying the Problem

Introduction

WHAT DID it *really* mean to be Judean in the first century CE? Biblical scholarship may have a general idea of what Judean ethnic identity involved, but this chapter is dedicated to introduce a particular problem—biblical scholarship generally, does not grasp or have a full appreciation of what informed the *entire process* of Judean ethnic identity formation in the first century, or at any period for that matter. A holistic picture, or at least some analytical framework and background to what ethnicity entails is lacking and this is a problem that needs to be addressed.

This problem is quite acute in scholarship on the historical Jesus. The reason for this is that in the so-called "Third Quest," a lot of attention is drawn to Jesus' "Jewishness." Scholars do recognize today that Jesus was a "Jew," or rather what we prefer to call him, a Judean, who must be understood within his Judean context. The problem is, however, what it meant to be a Judean is something vague. A sufficient interpretive apparatus of what it really meant to be Judean is not in place.

Bearing in mind the lack of this interpretive framework, a preliminary question therefore is: As scholars now see it, what kind of Judean was Jesus? A second but related question is: As scholars now see it, what kind of Judean was Jesus relative to his co-ethnics? What continuities or discontinuities exist? How and why was Jesus similar or different? For our present purposes, we will concentrate on two reconstructions of the historical Jesus which are representative examples of a more "traditional" or "alternative" approach; first, John P. Meier's *A Marginal Jew: Rethinking the Historical Jesus*; and second, John Dominic Crossan's *The Historical Jesus: The Life of a Mediterranean Jewish Peasant*; although the latter does really fit in with the supposed character of the "Third Quest" bearing in mind that Crossan fully appreciates that Jesus was a Judean ("Jew"). But to clarify, this chapter does not make an attempt to do a detailed study of Jesus' ethnic identity anew. The aim is to provide an overview of Meier and Crossan's reconstructions to find out what content—explicitly or implicitly—do they assign to Jesus' ethnic identity? Based on their reconstructions, what kind of Judean was Jesus? The eventual focus will be on Q, so later it will be attempted to answer that question applicable to the Q people.

In analysing their reconstructions the deliberate choice has been made to be guided by the insights of social or cultural anthropology. *Ethnicity theory* has broadly recognized several cultural features that are important for ethnic identity. The cultural features include the following:

1. *name*, a corporate name that identifies the group
2. *myths of common ancestry*, the group claims to be descendents of a particular person or group/family
3. *shared "historical" memories*, the group points to common heroes and events of the past
4. *land*, the group has actual or symbolic attachment to an ancestral land
5. *language*, or local dialect
6. *kinship*, members of the group belong to family units which in turn, demonstrate communal solidarity with the local community or tribe, and with the group as a national entity
7. *customs* identifiable with that group
8. *religion*
9. *phenotypical features*, which points to genetic features (Duling 2005:127–28; Esler 2003:43–44).

With the exception of the last feature, which does not come into play (as Judeans basically looked like everybody else in the Roman-Hellenistic world), those cultural features that are affected in the reconstructions of Meier and Crossan will be mentioned.

Admittedly, the above approach has its problems. The analysis to follow might include aspects of their work that was originally never intended to illuminate what kind of Judean Jesus was. But at the same time, by using the cultural features listed above it will expose the reality that often scholars write about Jesus without realising that they unconsciously say something about what kind of Judean Jesus was. The same is true also of those things that scholars *do not say*, or omit, from their reconstructions of the historical Jesus. This negative feature of biblical scholarship will be fully exposed in chapter 2. Another problem is that by using the cultural features a guide, we are also slightly anticipating the form of the model that will be adapted from the work of Duling (2005). But any investigation into the Judeanness of Jesus will have to see how these cultural features receive treatment in various reconstructions. So what will concern us here is what Meier and Crossan regard as authentic Jesus tradition, and how this tradition affects the cultural features already listed. In their view, what kind of Judean was Jesus? What content, be it explicitly or implicitly, do they assign to Jesus' Judean ethnic identity? This chapter is therefore also a useful way to introduce the various cultural features and biblical texts that impact the question of ethnic identity. We will first analyse the work of Meier.

John P. Meier—Jesus, a Marginal "Jew"

Meier interprets Jesus as an eschatological prophet continuing in the eschatological tradition of John the Baptist, but with a different emphasis. Where John announced imminent judgment, Jesus announced the imminent arrival of the "kingdom (= rule or reign) of God." This entailed participation for all Israel—including sinners—and Jesus understood that God's reign was already partly present in his own ministry and miracle working. So in preparation for the kingdom proper, Jesus set out to restore the twelve tribes of Israel. Meier's work on the historical Jesus is not yet finished, since a fourth (and presumably final) volume of his work is yet to come. This section, therefore, concentrates on the first three volumes on which the brief summary given above is also based. The investigation will naturally focus only on that which clarifies Meier's view on Jesus and the question of his ethnic identity.

Jesus' Background: His Family and Upbringing

Initially, Meier draws attention to the names of Jesus and his family—here it specifically pertains to the cultural features of *myths of common ancestry*, *shared "historical" memories*, and to a lesser extent, *religion*. In the case of Jesus himself, our English form of Jesus' name is derived from the Hebrew name *Yešu* (Meier 1991:205–7). This is the shortened form of the more correct *Yešua*, which in turn was a shortened form of the name of the biblical hero Joshua, in Hebrew *Yehošua*. The latter, in keeping with usual ancient Hebrew names, was a theophoric name that originally meant "Yahweh helps or "May Yahweh help."The later popular etymology had the name to mean "Yahweh saves" or "May Yahweh save" (cf. Matt 1:21). Jesus' name may signify something else within the context of first-century Galilee. When we come to the family of Jesus it is probably not by accident that like Jesus himself, his family members have names that hark back to the patriarchs, the exodus from Egypt, and entrance into the promised land. Jesus' putative father was Joseph,[1] who had the name of one of the twelve sons of Jacob/Israel and who was the progenitor, through Ephraim and Manasseh, of two of the twelve tribes. His mother was Mary, in Hebrew Miriam, the name of Moses' sister. His four brothers were named after the patriarchs who fathered the twelve sons/tribes of Israel (James = Jacob) and after three of the twelve sons (Joses = Joseph, Simon = Simeon, and Jude = Judah). Jesus also had at least two, but unnamed, sisters.[2] For most of the Old Testament period Israelites were not named after the great patriarchs mentioned in Genesis and Exodus. A change seemingly occurred after the exile and accelerated around the time of the Maccabean revolt against the Seleucid king Antiochus IV Epiphanes (reigned 175–164/163 BCE) who attempted to Hellenize Judeans and suppress Judean religious and ethnic customs. It was especially Judeans in rural areas and small towns of Palestine that reacted towards the Seleucid persecution with

---

1. Of course, the question of Jesus' *ancestry* through Joseph (according to Matthew and Luke the putative or legal father) may also come into play. Meier accepts attestation of Jesus' Davidic descent as early and widespread in various strands of New Testament tradition and it should not be quickly dismissed as a *theologoumenon* (Meier 1991:216–19). Meier will discuss any possible claims of Davidic sonship/messiaship by Jesus himself only in his fourth volume. Therefore it need not concern us further here.

2. For an investigation on the family of Jesus, see Bauckham (2000). James became the head of the Church in Jerusalem after Peter left (Acts 15:13; 21:18 with 12:17; cf. 1 Cor 15:7; Gal 2:12). According to Julius Africanus, who lived in Emmaus in the early third century, the relatives of Jesus were missionaries (as suggested by Paul; 1 Cor 9:5) and known as the *desposunoi*, "those who belong to the master." He notes they had a family genealogy and writes: "From the [Judean] villages of Nazareth and Kokhaba, they travelled around the rest of the land and interpreted the genealogy they had and from the Book of Days [viz. Chronicles] as far as they could trace it" (cited in Eusebius, *H. E.* 1.7.14). What this probably means is that Jesus' family travelled around Israel preaching the Gospel to their fellow Judeans, while using a family genealogy to defend the claim that Jesus was the messianic son of David. If this report is authentic, it indicates that besides Jerusalem, Nazareth and Kokhaba (in Galilee) were also significant centres for the early Messianists in Palestine.

escalating native-religious feeling. So it may be around this time that the custom of naming children after past heroes became increasingly common (Meier 1991:207). Meier then asserts:

> The custom may have struck an especially responsive chord in Galilee, where Judaism [?] for centuries had had to live side by side with strong pagan influence; it was only after the victories of the Maccabees that a vigorous [Judean] presence could again assert itself in "Galilee of the Gentiles."[3] Most likely, therefore, the fact that all of Jesus' immediate family bear "patriarchal" and "matriarchal" names betoken the family's participation in this reawakening of [Judean] national and religious identity, an identity that looked to the idyllic past of the patriarchs for definition. (Meier 1991:207–8)

Meier (1991:208) also states that it "may not be too farfetched to suggest that we hear an echo of this theme of national restoration [of Israel] years later when the adult Jesus chooses precisely twelve men to be his inner group of disciples. The number twelve was probably meant to conjure up the idea of the twelve patriarchs, the twelve tribes, and hence the restoration of all Israel by Joshua/Jesus of Nazareth." We will return to the issue of Jesus' restoration of Israel and the twelve disciples later, but based on Meier's reconstruction, Jesus' home environment was conducive for fostering a strong national and "religious" identity. Meier's reconstruction, however, puts misplaced emphasis on "Judaism" as a *religious* identity, something that will be pointed out again later. First-century Judaism was not a religious system as such, *it was an ethnic identity*. Viewed from this perspective it can be said that Jesus, from a young age, would have had a strong Judean self-awareness which in adult life translated into a mission of Israel's national restoration.

Language

The matter of Jesus' *language* is what Meier (1991:255–68) discusses next.[4] Most researchers are today convinced that Aramaic was the

---

3. Meier is correct that a strong "Jewish/Judean" presence asserted itself in Galilee during the time of the Hasmoneans. But archaeological evidence does not support his view that "Judaism" for centuries lived side by side with pagan influence. After the Assyrian invasion Galilee was virtually empty of Israelite inhabitants. This changed when the Hasmoneans expanded their territory to the north (Reed 1999; 2000; Chancey 2002).

4. For a more detailed discussion of language in first century Palestine, see chapters 3 and 4. These chapters also involve an overview of other aspects that were important

normal everyday language spoken by the average first-century Judean in Israel. As a teacher who directed his message at ordinary Judean peasants whose everyday language was Aramaic, he basically spoke to and taught his fellow Judeans in Aramaic. Some traces of it remain embedded in the text of the Greek Gospels (Mark 5:41; 7:34; 14:36; 15:34). The Aramaic that Jesus used has been identified as a Galilean version of western Aramaic, which was distinct in some ways from the Aramaic spoken in Judea. Apart from Aramaic, however, Jesus would also have known some Hebrew and Greek. Jesus' habit of preaching in the synagogues and debating with scribes and Pharisees on scriptural matters makes it likely that he had some knowledge of biblical Hebrew. Jesus would have learned Hebrew in the Nazareth synagogue or a nearby school. In addition, in his woodworking establishment, Meier speculates, Jesus may have had opportunities to also pick up enough Greek to strike bargains and write receipts. This must be seen in combination with regular pilgrimages by his family to Jerusalem, which was exposed to Hellenistic culture, where the young Jesus would have been exposed to Greek culture and language. So it might be that Jesus was able to speak enough Greek to speak directly with Pilate at his trial.[5] But it is unlikely that Jesus attained "scribal literacy," or enough command of and fluency in Greek to teach at length. So Meier is doubtful that any of Jesus' teachings existed from the very beginning in Greek that needed no translation as it was collected in the Greek Gospels.[6]

So overall, when it comes to the cultural feature of *language*, Jesus was pretty much like the average Judean. But the average Judean lived in an environment where especially the Greek language penetrated into the fabric of society and where more and more Judeans spoke Greek as a second or even a first language. The world of Judeanism was seeing some significant change in this regard.

for Judean ethnic identity and so will not be treated at length here.

5. Cf. Porter (1994:148–53), who refers to four passages where Jesus would have the highest likelihood of speaking in Greek (Mark 7:25–30; John 12:20–28; Matt 8:5–13 = Luke 7:2–10; Mark 15:2–5 = Matt 27:11–14 = Luke 23:2–5 = John 18:29–38). The overall evidence of inscriptions and papyri "have persuaded some scholars that bilingualism was widespread in [Judean] Palestine in the first century [CE], and that it is quite proper to ask whether Jesus and his immediate disciples could speak Greek" (Schürer et al. 1979:79). Could Jesus speak Greek? Fitzmyer (1992) argues the answer is most certainly yes.

6. As Hengel (1989) has pointed out, however, the Jesus tradition would have been available in Greek from the earliest stages of the Jesus movement due to the presence of many Judean ("Jewish") Greek speakers in Palestine, particularly in Jerusalem.

Literacy

A related matter is literacy: was Jesus literate?[7] This matter may pertain to four cultural features, namely *shared "historical" memories*, *language*, *customs*, and *religion*. Meier states that for "all the differences among various groups of [Judeans], the narratives, laws, and prophecies of their sacred texts gave them a corporate memory and a common ethos. The very identity and continued existence of the people Israel were tied to a corpus of written and regularly read works in a way that simply was not true of other peoples in the Mediterranean world of the 1st century." Furthermore, to be able "to read and explain the Scriptures was a revered goal for religiously minded [Judeans]. Hence literacy held special importance for the [Judean] community" (Meier 1991:274, 275). It should not be taken to mean that all Judean men learned to read—women rarely had the opportunity. But in the case of Jesus himself, Meier suggests, it is reasonable to suppose that Jesus' religious formation, either through his father or a more learned Judean at the synagogue, was immense and that it included instruction in reading biblical Hebrew, including the ability to expound it—by implication, Jesus would also have had literacy in Aramaic (Meier 1991:276–78). Meier's argument is based on characteristics of Jesus' adult life. He became intensely focussed on the Judean religion, and according to the gospels he engaged in learned disputes over Scripture and halakah with students of the Law. He was accorded the respectful title of "teacher" (or *rabbi*), and the gospels present him as preaching and teaching in the synagogues, and "his teaching was strongly imbued with the outlook and language of the sacred texts of Israel" (Meier 1991:276). So according to Meier, it is probable that Jesus, based on the piety of his father and the possible existence of a local synagogue, received an "elementary" education learning the religious traditions and texts of Judeanism.[8] He argues thus:

> The circumstantial evidence from archaeology points to a Nazareth that was a thoroughly [Judean] settlement. Granted, then, that Nazareth was a village of close to 2,000 people, practically all of whom were [Judeans], the existence of a synagogue with some educational program for [Judean] boys is a likely

---

7. Generally, literacy (at various levels) is estimated at around 10 percent for the ancient population, including Judeans. Millard (2003) has argued, however, that based on the archaeological evidence, although not everyone could read and write, these skills were widely practiced in the Palestine of Jesus' day.

8. Cf. Evans (2001:19): "Jesus' teaching in the synagogues is not easily explained if he were unable to read and had not undertaken study of Scripture."

hypothesis. Especially if Jesus' family shared the resurgence of religious and national sentiment among Galilean [Judean] peasants, this hypothesis of some formal education in the local synagogue is well grounded. (Meier 1991:277)

Importantly, Meier also alludes to the type of Judeanism of the Galilean peasants. In what follows, the cultural features of *name, myths of common ancestry, shared "historical" memories, land, customs*, and *religion* are affected. According to Meier, it was a Judeanism that was fiercely loyal to basics like Mosaic Torah, circumcision, observance of Sabbath, observance of kosher food laws, main purity rules, and pilgrimages to the Jerusalem temple for the great feasts. It was conservative in nature and would not be attracted to what they considered the novelties of the Pharisees or the theoretical details debated by the elite (Meier 1991:277; 1994:1039; 2001:617). At the end of his second volume Meier also mentions that Galilean Judeans were surrounded "by a fair number of Gentiles and a fair amount of Hellenistic culture" present within Sepphoris and so "would cling tenaciously to the basics of their religion as 'boundary symbols' reinforcing their identity" (Meier 1994:1039–40). Meier also makes mention that their popular, mainstream Judeanism held to certain key beliefs that were articulated in a dramatic story of origins. For the Judeans, the story was the national myth of God and Israel:

> [T]he one true God . . . had chosen Israel as his special people, freed it from slavery by the exodus from Egypt, given it the covenant and the Torah at Mt. Sinai, and led it into the promised land of Palestine as its perpetual inheritance. [After Israel's unfaithfulness and exile] he had mercifully brought them back to their land and given them the hope of a full, glorious renewal at some future date. (Meier 2001:617)

Meier can be commended for mentioning important elements that contributed towards Judean identity (see also the discussion on *kinship* below), but again his emphasis on Judeanism as a religion must be questioned.[9] This is due to the methodological flaw of Meier's research in that it does not do justice to all the dynamics that were involved with first-century CE Judean identity. Religion was but one aspect of identity, and it must not be preferred or elevated above the other aspects of iden-

---

9. Cf. Esler (2006:27), who states that "to focus on 'Jews' as representatives of a religion 'Judaism' is both anachronistic and grossly reductionist and does little justice to the identity of first century Judeans."

tity. Meier approaches Judeanism too much according to the modern and secularized interpretive paradigm, where "religion" is an area that can be treated on its own. The Tanak, and the Torah in particular, should rather be approached as the constitution of Judean *ethnic identity*, not so much that it contains "religious" information. *Literacy, and adhering to mainstream Judeanism therefore gives insight into what it meant to be Judean (= covenant membership), not into what it meant to be "religious."* Apart from these comments, however, it becomes clear that based on Meier's reconstruction of Jesus' Galilean and family background, Jesus grew up in an environment that was conducive to fostering a strong Judean ethnic identity.[10] Jesus would have had a strong awareness of Israel's God, its history, basic covenant obligations, and attachment to the land.

The Family

Now we will shift our attention to the matter of *kinship*. Meier says that being the firstborn son, Jesus would have received special attention from Joseph, so that in addition to teaching him religious traditions, Joseph would also have taught Jesus his own trade. Meier interprets τέκτων (Mark 6:3; cf. Matt 13:55) to mean "woodworker" (not "carpenter" as such), which in the context of the gospels would mean that Jesus had a fair amount of technical skill in constructing parts of houses (e.g., doors, door frames, etc.) and making furniture (e.g., beds, tables, etc.) (Meier 1991:276, 280–85, 317). As an aside, Meier also questions the idea that Jesus would have applied his trade in Sepphoris where he would have been exposed to urban culture in a strong Hellenistic city. His ministry, as pictured by the gospels, was restricted to traditional Judean villages and towns, and this "general picture of Jesus' activity in Galilee . . . does not favour early and influential contact with Hellenistic centers like Sepphoris" (Meier 1991:284). So when it comes to the "interim" years of Jesus' life, he would have spent it almost entirely as a citizen of Nazareth in Galilee plying his father's trade as a woodworker.

When it comes to Jesus' relationship with his immediate family, Meier points to the fact that in the ancient world the individual was part of a larger social unit. "The extended family," Meier explains, together with the village or town "imposed identity and social function on

10. Cf. Evans (2001:21): "The context, family and formation of Jesus point in every way to an extensive exposure to a Torah-observant [Judean] way of life. Jesus was raised in a [Judean] Galilee that embraced the faith of the Fathers and the teaching of Scripture, a Galilee that resisted [non-Judean] influences, sometimes violently."

the individual in exchange for the communal security and defence the individual received from the family. The break Jesus made with these ties to his extended family and village, after so many years of an uneventful life in their midst, and his concomitant attempt to define a new identity and social role for himself, no doubt left deep scars that can still be seen in the Gospel narratives [e.g., Mark 3:21, 31–35; 6:1–6; John 7:3–9]" (Meier 1991:317). Meier (1991:350) argues that Jesus' father probably died before he embarked on his public ministry, compared with his mother, brothers, and sisters. It is these family members that survived, the evangelists tell us, who thought that Jesus was mad (Mark 3:21), or that his brothers did not believe in him (John 7:5), or were refused a request to see him (Mark 3:31–35).

Another matter related to *kinship* is the demands made by Jesus to follow him.[11] A Q tradition has a candidate disciple ask Jesus for permission to bury his father before devoting himself fully to follow him (Matt 8:21–22 // Luke 9:59–60; cf. Luke 9:61–62). Jesus declines the request quite harshly and says: "Let the dead bury their dead." "This demand," Meier (2001:50, 68) explains, "to ignore a basic obligation of piety to a dead parent . . . is shockingly discontinuous from the fundamental morality that both [Judeans] and [Messianists] held dear . . . Jesus' imperious command to follow posed a grave challenge to a traditional society where reverence for one's parents . . . was a sacred obligation enshrined in the Ten Commandments."[12] Further, following Jesus

11. Cf. Duling (2001) who understands the recruitment style of Jesus in the Synoptic Gospels as akin to a "faction type of coalition" which is also an ego-centered network, for which Duling also develops a model. The attractional leader or ego personally recruits followers which form his "intimate network" (cf. Mark 1:16–20; 3:13–14, 16–18; 6:7). Where the commitment must be total, recruitment will take place publicly and directly, aimed more likely at strangers or casual acquaintances. Then beyond that are the recruits of the "effective network" and "extended network," or wider group of followers (cf. Mark 3:7; 5:24; 8:34; 10:32, 52; 11:9; 14:51; 15:41). Commenting on Mark 4:10, Duling (2001:158) says that it "clearly mirrors the concentric circle model of Ego-centered faction—Ego, intimate network, and effective network. The members of the intimate network are usually portrayed as leaving, or being requested to leave, their kin, friends, and worker groups. The resulting faction is a surrogate family, a fictive family."

12. As the father had obligations towards his son, so the son had obligations towards his father, something which came to prominence at funerary rites (Guijarro 2001). Under normal circumstances, Jesus' "imperious command" would be "shockingly discontinuous" with basic morality, but refusal to bury parents (and fellow Judeans) was not something new to Judeanism. According to Fletcher-Louis (2003:66–67), non-burial of Judeans by fellow Judeans was on occasion "a self-conscious act of piety to leave other [Judeans]—'apostates'—unburied as a deliberate declaration of divine punishment and excommunication." The apostates, as outsiders, were also regarded as "spiritually dead."

Identifying the Problem 19

as a disciple entailed leaving behind home, parents, and livelihood, and doing so was not a temporary appointment (Meier 2001:54–55). This was an ethos quite contrary to that expected by Ben Sirach, who made a son's obligations to father and mother paramount and recommended the enjoyment of one's wealth (e.g., Sir 3:1–16; 7:27–28; 14:11–16; 31:8–11). But those called upon as disciples were to experience and proclaim the kingdom of God, risking danger and hostility, and to "turn back from that call—or, equivalently, to turn back from following Jesus—was to show oneself unfit for the kingdom" (Meier 2001:55).

As a result, one may face hostility from one's own family. Meier explains the following within the context of the Mediterranean world:

> What one trusts, relies upon, and contributes to willingly is one's extended family, the primary safety net in peasant society. Ancient Mediterranean society was largely a society of "dyadic personality," where one's identity was formed and maintained in relation to other individuals in one's social unit—the usual unit being the extended family. To bid farewell for an indefinite period to the bonds of emotional and financial support, to spurn the only "opinion group" whose opinion daily affected one's life, to take the shameful path of deserting one's family and work in an honor-shame society—all this was no easy choice for the ordinary [Judean] peasant of Galilee. (Meier 2001:67)

Indeed, Jesus spoke to his disciples about the domestic cost of following him. There dissolution of family ties will bring them rich reward (Mark 10:28–30 par.). A saying in Q illustrates the shocking price of following Jesus; you have to turn your back on your family and "hate" them (Matt 10:37 // Luke 14:26). Here "hate" refers to the "necessity of preferring Jesus unreservedly when one's family opposes the commitment of discipleship or makes rival claims on the would-be disciple" (Meier 2001:68). So Jesus' call to discipleship would occasion fierce family division, something that Jesus predicted (Matt 10:34–36 // Luke 12:51–53; John 7:5). In a sense, Jesus was simply asking them to replicate his own experience (Mark 3:20–35) (Meier 2001:69–71). Those who do the Father's will is Jesus' brother, sister, and mother (cf. Luke 11:27–28), so a radical alternate kinship pattern, we may add, is emerging in Jesus' life and teaching. Of course, this included women followers

---

The saying in Q 9:60 appears to make the same judgment on those who do not follow Jesus, both on the living and on the dead. It also points to the fact that the fictive kinship patterns formed around Jesus used burial practices to define the boundary of the new family of God.

who were not in name referred to as *disciples* (Meier 2001:73–80) and the stay-at-home *supporters* or *adherents* of Jesus (Meier 2001:80–82). But this radical ethos Jesus required of his disciples, unheard of in the Greco-Roman world, did not require stringent borders. Such borders were made clear at the common meals of religious and philosophical groups, such as the Pharisees and Essenes, which were closed to outsiders. In contrast Jesus' group (and his supporters) were radically open to outsiders in their table-fellowship. It was only the acceptance of Jesus and his message that defined the borders of the whole group of his disciples/adherents (Meier 2001:72–73).

Based on Meier's reconstruction, in terms of *kinship* we can see that Jesus' own life and demands on others who follow/support him was in strong discontinuity with Judeanism. Meier neglects to explain, however, what impact this could have had on the patriarchal family as an institution. But Jesus' alternative kinship pattern subverted Judean ethnic identity applicable to any period, since, for example, Jesus sets children against parents and visa versa, and does not allow a potential follower to bury his father. This went against the requirements of the Torah. It went against being a respectable Judean, or Jesus is radically redefining what Judean ethnicity or covenant membership requires.

Jesus and John the Baptist

Before Jesus set out on his public ministry, the enigmatic figure of John the Baptist comes into play. First, there is the character of John's own ministry. John announces the coming wrath of God and instructs his listeners to change their minds and hearts for the better (i.e. undergo heart-felt repentance or μετάνοια) and change their outward life accordingly (Matt 3:7–12; Luke 3:7–9, 15–18). The change to good deeds are the "fruit(s) worthy [i.e., corresponding to and manifesting prior] repentance" (Meier 1994:29). John is facing the difficult task of convincing this "brood of vipers" that mere physical descent from Abraham ("We have Abraham as our father"—Matt 3:9) will not serve as protection on the day of judgment. To claim physical descent from Abraham, Meier explains, "bespeaks a collective consciousness as the chosen people that was meant to instil trust in God's covenant-promises but which instead could breed smug complacency. It is to shatter that complacency that the Baptist shatters the significance of a biological link with Abraham. The omnipotent Creator can make children of Abraham out of the stones lying at the audience's feet just as easily as he can give the status to people . . ." (Meier 1994:29).[13] It may be added here that the status of being children of Abraham, God's chosen people, that is, being Judean by birth (an ethnic identity), becomes somewhat meaningless on its own in view of the imminent judgment. Meier (1994:29) insists, however, that with the threatening speeches of John and Jesus to Israel they do, like Amos and Jeremiah, as Israelite prophets working within and for Israel. Jesus was a committed Israelite "seeking to wake up his own people to what he discerns as imminent danger threatening the covenant community." But it is clear, based on Meier's understanding, that John is subverting or in a radical way is redefining Judean ethnic identity. What we have here is the "abrogation of claims based on salvation history," but Meier says the threats of judgment are not "empty rhetoric," for John means "this abrogation to be taken seriously. As with Jesus, so with John, we have here a notable element of discontinuity with much of the [Judeanism] of John's own time" (Meier 1994:29). Meier sees the thrust of John's message (Matt 3:7–12; Luke 3:7–9) as the following:

> [I]n the face of an imminent fiery judgment, in the face of God's holy wrath, blazing forth and threatening to consume his apparently holy but actually unholy people, even the ostensibly devout are in danger [Meier can be paraphrased here by saying that even those who are *profoundly Judean* are in danger]. There must be confession of sin, not only of one's own individual sins, but also of the corporate sins of the people of God who have gone astray and have therefore lost their assurance of salvation on the day of judgment. Hence not all members of the empirical society called Israel will be part of the eschatological Israel saved by God. Only the swift decision to accept John's baptism and to combine it with a profound change of both inner attitude and external conduct can rescue the individual [Judean] from the fire soon to come. (Meier 1994:30)

Meier further argues that John, in a situation of perceived crisis, claims direct intuitive knowledge of God's will and plans. This knowledge was not mediated through the normal channels of law, temple, priesthood, or scribal scholarship. Yet, John spoke of a shadowy "stronger one" who will accomplish the outpouring of God's spirit on the true Israel, some-

---

13. As Esler points out, appeal or reference to Abraham was a way for Judeans to assert their ethnic identity (we can add here to assert their covenant status). "It has cognitive, emotional and evaluative connotations. Abrahamic descent is thus a way of describing the glorious status of being a Judean" (Esler 2006:27).

thing that the prophets had promised for the last days. Who this figure exactly was may have been unclear to John (Meier 1994:40).

But how did the "dissolution of those ties of salvation history and biological peoplehood [= ethnic identity] that gave Israel confidence" (Meier 1994:30) affect Jesus? Since John's message and baptism was highly subversive of Judean ethnic identity, Jesus' relationship to John is appropriate to the cultural features of *myths of common ancestry*, *shared "historical" memories*, *customs* and *religion*. Meier argues that around 28 CE, Jesus' coming to John for baptism says something particular about his religious state at that time. The baptism indicates that Jesus knew and agreed with John's eschatological message. To recapitulate very briefly, John's message was that Israel, nearing the end of its current history in view of imminent judgment, had apostatized, and the only way to escape God's wrath as sinful children of Abraham was to undergo a basic change of mind and heart accompanied by a change in one's way of living, which had to be sealed by a special, once-and-for-all ritual immersion (Meier 1994:109). Jesus' own ministry may have been a way of making John's call to all Israel for a religious transformation more concrete. It is also implicit that Jesus accepted John as *a* or *the* eschatological prophet. In addition, "Jesus' acceptance of John's baptism means that Jesus saw himself very much as part of the people of Israel—which in John's vision of things means part of a sinful people threatened with divine destruction. Jesus accepted John's baptism of repentance as the divinely appointed means of passage from this sinful Israel to a group of Israelites promised salvation on the day of judgment" (Meier 1994:110). What we have here also is Jesus' feeling of communal solidarity or *kinship* with his fellow Judeans. For Meier, however, this has the following interesting corollary relevant to us. Jesus accepted an unofficial, "charismatic" ritual—John's ritual immersion—as necessary for salvation. This new rite, which John and Jesus centred their religious lives upon (at least in 28 CE), lacked the sanction of tradition and the temple authorities. The introduction of a new type of ritual "implicitly called into question the sufficiency of temple and synagogue worship [for our purposes read "the sufficiency of traditional Judean ethnic identity"] as then practiced" (Meier 1994:110)—although in his third volume, Meier says that there is no tradition that Jesus throughout his public ministry shunned the temple and refused to participate in its festivals. Jesus was basically in unison with "mainstream" Judeans who revered the temple as the one sacred place chosen by God for lawful sacrifice (Meier 2001:499–500).[14]

Meier's reconstruction leaves us with a real paradox. Jesus illustrates continuity with traditional Judean ethnic identity in that he sees himself as part of the people of Israel and joins them to undergo John's baptism. Jesus along with other Judeans also revered the temple as a divine institution. On the other hand, by accepting John's eschatological message and undergoing his baptism, Jesus agrees that traditional ethnic status, being "children of Abraham," will mean nothing at the judgment, and that John's immersion is necessary *for all* Judeans for salvation. This contradicts the tradition of the Torah and temple worship, which implies that ethnic status as required/maintained in both the Torah and temple worship has become insufficient. Put in another way, the ethnic identity of the day was on the one hand revered, while on the other regarded as inadequate, subverted, or we can say radically redefined. Maintenance of covenant status, that is, maintenance of Judean ethnic status, has moved beyond the received Torah and the temple currently operating.

Indeed, Jesus most probably continued this redefinition of ethnic status if we are to take Meier's reconstruction to its logical conclusion. Meier says Jesus was probably a disciple of John where after he continued the practice of *John's* baptism in his own ministry, a baptism that Jesus thought was divinely inspired (John 3:22–30; cf. 4:1–2; Mark 11:27–33) (Meier 1994:123, 163–67). Thus John's message, life, and baptism are to be seen as a vital and indispensable part of Jesus' own ministry. Jesus also proclaims an eschatological message, similar to John's, and "he symbolizes acceptance of his message by conferring on his disciples a ritual washing or baptism, he addresses his ministry to all Israel but undertakes no overt mission aimed directly at Gentiles . . ." (Meier 1994:124). So Jesus had a high regard for John the Baptist even though Jesus' proclamation about the kingdom of God, the new "field of force," had a member of the kingdom as "greater than he [i.e. John]" (Matt 11:7–11; Luke 7:24–28). Nevertheless, Jesus also grouped himself with John over and against their fellow Judeans who did not heed their message, here speaking of the parable of the children in the market place (Matt 11:16–19; Luke 7:31–35). The parable deals with "this generation," a pejorative term Jesus uses for those Judeans who

---

14. Cf. Tomson (2001:40): "Jesus was a devout [Judean] who felt intimately attached to the Temple in Jerusalem as the place of God's holy presence."

do not believe in him (cf. Deut 32:5, 20; Ps 12:8; 78:8; Jer 7:29).[15] Here "generation" reveals Jesus' view of solidarity in sin, and that he is aiming his message at the whole Judean people. Meier claims that "we hear an echo of the program of the Baptist," and the rhetorical questions at the beginning of the parable "introduce material that places John and Jesus side by side" (Meier 1994:145). The people rejected the ascetic prophet from the desert's call to repentance, who ate only locusts and wild honey (he "came neither eating nor drinking"), since he must be mad ("He has a demon"). Jesus did the exact opposite (he "came eating and drinking") and issued a different call to repentance and extended table-fellowship to religious outcasts of Judean society to offer a joyous way for people to enter the kingdom. Meier explains:

> With a sudden burst of puritanism, this generation felt no hallowed prophet sent from God would adopt such a freewheeling, pleasure-seeking lifestyle, hobnobbing with religious lowlife and offering assurances of God's forgiveness without demanding the proper process for reintegration into [Judean] religious society. How could this Jesus be a true prophet and reformer when he is a glutton and a drunkard, a close companion at meals with people who robbed their fellow [Judeans] (the toll collectors) or who sinned willfully and heinously, yet refused to repent (sinners). Thus, for opposite but equally convenient reasons, this generation . . . rejects the call to repentance of both the excessively ascetic John and the excessively jolly Jesus. The result is spiritual paralysis and an apparent frustration of God's saving plan to rescue his chosen people in this last hour of their history. (Meier 1994:149)

The issue of Jesus' relationship with sinners appears in other texts that Meier regards as possibly having historical basis (Matt 21:31–32; Luke 7:29–30; cf. Luke 3:10–14). These are stray M and L traditions wherein it is said that some religiously and socially marginal tax collectors and prostitutes accepted John's message and baptism, while the Judean leaders rejected it. While sinful, therefore marginal Judeans came to the ascetic John for baptism, Jesus on the other hand undertook an itinerant ministry throughout Galilee, parts of Judea, as well as Perea and the Decapolis, and maybe areas to the north of Galilee going as far

15. The phrase "this (evil) generation" occurs only twice in the Tanak, speaking about the generation of Noah (Gen 7:1) and once of the time of Moses (Deut 1:35). These two generations became types of the last generation (*Jub.* 23:14, 15, 16, 22; *1 En.* 93:9; 1QpHab 2:7; 1QpMic). The *evil* generation in the wilderness is referred to in Deut 1:35; Num 32:13; cf Pss 94:10 and 78:8 (Allison 2000:59).

as Tyre and Sidon, not forgetting several journeys to Jerusalem. Jesus was consciously reaching out to all Israel in its last hour, moving away from John's stress on repentance in the face of imminent judgment, yet not entirely abandoning John's eschatological call, with emphasis now on the joy of salvation the repentant sinner could experience in the already present but yet to come kingdom of God (Meier 1994:167–70).

So it appears that side by side, both John and Jesus were in the process of redefining Judean ethnic identity. Their call went to all Israel (no overt mission to Gentiles exists), but this new identity would include the repentant sinners, the marginal of Judean society, not those who would have regarded themselves as righteous Judeans and who by all accounts were properly living within the guidelines of the present ethnic-religious system. Jesus set himself with John over and against the "this generation" since Judean ethnicity as it was defined in the first century is to a degree abandoned by them. The tax collectors and prostitutes came to John for baptism. Jesus alike enjoys table-fellowship with sinners. So baptism, a disregard for purity and food laws, the idea of sinners regaining their ethnic status as righteous Judeans without following the normal processes required by the Torah (via the temple), plus the exclusion of "this generation"—all of this turned traditional Judean ethnic identity on its head. Being a traditional Judean (= having traditional covenant membership) was simply no longer good enough.

Another text that Meier looks at merits discussion, as it pertains specifically to the cultural features of *shared "historical" memories, customs*, and *religion*. Meier tentatively accepts Matt 11:12–13 (= Luke 16:16) as authentic (or at least, Jesus' own viewpoint) when restored to what seems to be its earliest form. Meier's (1994:160) hypothetical reconstruction of this Q saying is as follows:[16]

> 16a The law and the prophets [lasted?] until John;
> 16b From then on,
>   the kingdom of God suffers violence,
>   and the violent plunder it.

Meier's treatment of this passage is quite significant in view of our present purposes. He explains that all of Israel's history until the time of the Baptist is placed under the rubric of Israel's scriptures, explained as the Law and the prophets. In that is God's instruction about the founding events of Israel's existence and the instruction about the

---

16. The IQP reconstructs the Q saying pretty much the same way (Robinson et al. 2002:141).

proper response in worship and daily life. The prophets also entail a further impression upon the mind of duties under the covenant plus promises of punishment yet final restoration. "But in some sense," Meier (1994:160) says, "that holds true only 'up until John.' From the time of John onwards, a new state of affairs [i e the kingdom of God] has broken in on the scene." Meier clarifies his position by stating that "John was *pivotal* to the process by which the time of the law and the prophets came to an end and the time of the kingdom commenced" (Meier 1994:162–63; and see 403–4).

Meier can be paraphrased by saying that John was pivotal to the process by which traditional Judean ethnic identity came to an end. What has defined Judean ethnicity up until that moment has now, by being on its own, become irrelevant. Judean ethnic identity is now defined by the requirements of the kingdom. Many other gospel texts (Matt 11:2–19 par.; Matt 12:28 // Luke 11:20 and Mark 3:24–27 par.; Luke 17:20–21; Mark 1:15; Matt 13:16–17 // Luke 10:23–24; Mark 2:18–20) also speak of the kingdom as present (Meier 1994:398–506) and it was already suffering violent opposition (Matt 11:12–13 // Luke 16:16) (Meier 1994:403–4). The kingdom of God had taken on concrete, visible form in the words and deeds of Jesus. This is also true of the eschatological banquet. Jesus was questioned why his disciples did not fast (Mark 2:18–20), an honored practice among devout Judeans and in the early church. Jesus, however, places a general prohibition on voluntary fasting as the "eschatological banquet of salvation, promised in the near future to many coming from east and west [i.e. Gentiles—Matt 8:11–12 // Luke 13:28–29], was in some way already available to those who shared Jesus' joy at mealtime . . . [I]n some way the kingdom is already present . . ." (Meier 1994:448).

So based on Jesus' message, it can be said that the kingdom requires the participation of a different kind of Judean, for the Torah, the constitution of Judean ethnic identity, in combination with customary practices, are qualified by or surpassed by the kingdom.

Jesus and the Kingdom of God

Jesus and the Gentiles

The first passage concerning the question of Jesus and ethnicity that will be discussed—here again relevant to the cultural features of *land*, *customs*, and *religion*—most likely comes from the Q source (Matt 8:11–12 // Luke 13:28–29). Meier (1994:314) reconstructs the primitive tradition behind the text as follows that he believes would have been close to Matthew's version:[17]

> Many [or: they] from east and west shall come
>
> and shall recline [at table]
>
> with Abraham and Isaac and Jacob
>
> in the kingdom of God.
>
> But you shall be thrown out.
>
> In that place there shall be weeping and grinding of teeth.

In the Old Testament and the pseudepigrapha numerous prophecies are made where Gentiles are involved in the drama of the end-time. They will worship the one true God or come to Israel, specifically Jerusalem, when the end-time arrives (cf. Isa 2:1–4; 25:6–8; 51:4–6; 59:19; Mic 4:1–4; Zech 14:16; Mal 1:11; Tob 13:11; 14:6 on the Gentiles). But the way that the Gentiles are involved varies from writer to writer. It is either viewed in a positive way where the Gentiles are devout pilgrims, joining Israel in its worship of Yahweh. On the other hand, the Gentiles are viewed negatively where they are defeated and made to bow down before a victorious Israel. Meier (1994:314) argues that since "such ideas about the Gentiles were often connected with the hope that all Israel would be regathered to the Promised Land and Zion, and since Jesus seems to have shared this hope for a regathered or reconstituted Israel, there is nothing impossible or anachronistic about the historical Jesus speaking of the coming of the Gentiles in the context of the kingdom of God." Meier (1994:315) therefore thinks it is more likely that the "many" refer to Gentiles than to Diaspora Judeans,[18] but in addition, he argues

> this depiction of their [viz. the Gentiles] coming to salvation *only* at the final banquet in the kingdom does not fit the situ-

---

17. Here Meier's reconstruction of the Q saying again accords pretty well with that of the IQP (Robinson et al 2002:133).

18. This view is not supported by the various texts. The directions from "Sunrise/East and Sunset/West" occur in texts in connection with *the return of Judeans* to the land of Israel (Zech 8:7–8; 1 Bar 4:37; 5:5; *Pss. Sol.* 11:2; *1 En.* 57:1). Allison (1997:179–80) states that his research has not turned up a single text where the expression refers to the eschatological ingathering of Gentiles. There are parallel expressions where it is described that the exiles will return from Assyria/Babylon and Egypt (Isa 27:12–13; Hos 11:11; Zech 10:10). For Luke's longer version that includes "from north and south"; cf. Isa 43:5–6; Zech 2:10 (LXX); *Pss. Sol.* 11:2–3.

ation of the early church, which conducted a lively mission to
the Gentiles in the decades after Jesus' crucifixion. On the other
hand, a prophecy that the Gentiles would come to salvation *only*
at the final banquet [not within ordinary human history] would
fit the situation of the historical Jesus, who did not view either
himself or his disciples as charged with the task of undertaking
a mission to the Gentiles while this present world ran its course.
(Meier 1994:315)

Meier insists that Jesus understood his mission (and that of the *Twelve*) as only directed to his own people, namely, Israel.[19] That is why the mission to Gentiles in this present world was such a strong departure for the early church and caused so much controversy in the first Messianist generation. "Neither the actions nor the words of the historical Jesus had given precise and detailed instructions for such an initiative" (Meier 1994:315). The words of Matt 8:11–12 // Luke 13:28–29 presuppose the opposite; the Gentiles will join the saved Israelites only at the final banquet in the kingdom, while some of his Judean contemporaries (i.e. the "you") will be "thrown out." But "the idea of the Gentiles streaming into the kingdom of God to be joined by the long-dead but now obviously living patriarchs of Israel surely brings us beyond any political kingdom of this present world, including a mere reconstitution of the kingdom of David on a grander scale" (Meier 1994:317; cf. 2001:438–39).

---

19. The relevant texts here are Matt 15:24 and 10:5–6. At first, Meier did not want to judge on their authenticity, although he stated that the two texts reflect accurately the entire picture of Jesus' mission derived from the Gospels. This is indirectly supported by the distinction Paul makes in Rom 15:8–9: "For I tell you that Christ has become a servant of the Jews on behalf of God's truth, to confirm the promises made to the patriarchs so that the Gentiles may glorify God for his mercy . . . ." Paul does not claim that Christ ever ministered directly to Gentiles, even though it would have aided his cause (cf. Rom 1:6) (Meier 1994:374, 660). Later on, Meier judged Matt 15:24 as being Matthew's own creative redaction and 10:5–6 to be the product of some first generation Messianists who opposed the proclamation of the Gospel to non-Judeans. Nevertheless, Meier (2001:543–44) still regarded Matt 10:5–6 as reflecting accurately what happened during the public ministry of Jesus. Many scholars have accepted Matt 10:5 as authentically representing Jesus' words or outlook (e.g., Enslin 1961:160; Harnack 1962:40; Jeremias 1971:14; Vermes 1973:49; 2000:140–43, 156–57). Otherwise there are various nuances in interpretation. The prohibition designates geographical boundaries (Jeremias 1967:20) which nevertheless is an extension of Jesus' own mission that was concentrated in Galilee. Alternatively, Jesus during his lifetime basically focused or limited both his own activity and that of his disciples to Israel (Hahn 1965:29, 544–55; Jeremias 1967:19, 25; Richardson 1969:66). There is also the position that the prohibition was part of a strategy to gather Israel so as to enable it to be a source of salvation to the Gentiles (Manson 1964:21; LaGrand 1995:138).

Identifying the Problem 29

Based on Meier's reconstruction above, again we can say that there is both continuity and discontinuity between Jesus and Judean ethnic identity. Jesus shares a hope for a reconstituted Israel and aims his message at all Israel symbolized by the Twelve disciples. But when this kingdom arrives, some Judeans of his generation will be left out and Gentiles will join the patriarchs for the final banquet. This is not a future kingdom where Judean ethnicity will be celebrated via a political kingdom. In fact, the metaphor of a banquet where Gentiles *eat* with the patriarchs illustrates little sympathy for concerns of Judean exclusiveness, purity and food laws, or religious-political nationalism. Yet exactly what kind of Judean does Jesus envision for this future period? This is a question that Meier needs to answer with greater clarity.

A related issue is Jesus' relationship with the Samaritans.[20] As with the Gentiles, Meier (2001:549) argues the gospels agree that Jesus undertook no mission to the Samaritans. But both Luke (9:52–53; 10:30–37; 17:11–19) and John (4:4–42) indicate that Jesus had positive, but passing contact with Samaritans, and that Jesus differed from the typical negative view of Judeans in that he had a benign view of them. What is of interest to us is that Meier prefers to treat the Samaritans from a religious viewpoint, instead of an ethnic one. Meier (2001:541) states that both "Samaritanism and [Judeanism] were latter-day forms of the ancient religion of Israel" that "experienced various traumas, transformations, and developments under the assaults and influences of the Assyrian, Babylonian, Persian, and Hellenistic empires." This is despite the fact that he also makes reference to various Judean texts

---

20. 2 Kgs 17:24–41 relates that the Assyrians settled various peoples in Samaria among them those from Cuthah, which according to Josephus gave the inhabitants of Samaria their new name of Cuthites (*Ant.* 9.288; 11.88). The sentiment towards Samaritans was one of hostility (Sir 50:25–26), to which the Samaritans responded in kind (cf. Luke 9:52–3; *Ant.* 18.29–30; 20.118ff.; *War* 2.232–233). The negative characterizations of the Samaritans by Judeans should not be taken at face value, however. They shared with Judeans monotheism, circumcision, Sabbath and festivals and the Torah, with the main difference being that their centre of worship was not in Jerusalem, but Mount Gerizim (Schürer et al. 1979:17). It was their refusal to worship in Jerusalem that was a principal cause for Judean prejudice against them. In effect, Samaritans were potential Judeans. For an alternative understanding of the Judeans and Samaritans, Hjelm (2000:284) suggests that the Law of Moses that Ezra was supposed to have brought to Jerusalem could well refer to the Samaritan Pentateuch "that had been adopted in Jerusalem [e.g., it suppressed the Gerizim and Schechem traditions] to establish identity and legitimacy for the nationalistic movement of the Maccabees, as well as to legalize the policy of conquest." Thus Judeanism, which unsuccessfully attempted to incorporate the Samaritans, was established on borrowed traditions.

that more than suggests that the Judeans regarded the Samaritans as a different ἔθνος (2 Kgs 17; Josephus, *Ant.* 9.277–291; Sir 50:25–26; 2 Macc 6:2; cf. 5:23).

Turning our attention back to the Gentiles, Meier also regards other eschatological traditions as having historical basis which are relevant to us. Meier (2001:442) argues that Jesus in various ways (the texts are discussed below) referred to the general resurrection of the dead. Besides the tradition of the many that will come from east and west that will eat with the patriarchs in the eschatological banquet (Matt 8:11–12 // Luke 13:28–29), is the tradition where Jesus declares woes on Chorazin, Bethsaida and Capernaum (Matt 11:21–24 // Luke 10:13–15), even stating that the Gentiles of Tyre and Sidon will suffer a less grievous fate at the final judgment (Meier 2001:439–40). There is also another Q tradition where Jesus compares his unresponsive Judean contemporaries with responsive Gentiles (Matt 12:41–42 // Luke 11:31–32). Here, the Gentiles—the queen of Sheba and the Ninevites—will not merely fare better than Jesus' Judean contemporaries at the final judgment, in fact, they will witness against and condemn them (Meier 2001:440–41). It may be added that this eschatological reversal went entirely against the purpose of being God's chosen people, that is, having Judean ethnic identity. To balance this out, however, is Jesus' argument against the Sadducees over the resurrection (Mark 12:18–27). Jesus explains that the God of Abraham, Isaac and Jacob is a God of the living, that is why there will be a resurrection. Meier argues that Jesus believed "past generations would rise from the dead and that faithful Israelites would share in a new type of life similar to that of the angels," and further, the "God of creation and covenant, the God of Abraham, Isaac, and Jacob, would fulfil his deepest commitment to the people of Israel . . . even beyond death" (Meier 2001:443). So, it seems that for Meier the covenant status of the faithful of past generations is secure as far as Jesus is concerned. But the present unrepentant generation's covenant status, that is, their ethnic status as a chosen people, is very uncertain.

Jesus' Mission to Israel

Be that as it may, it was mentioned already that Meier sees that Jesus understood his mission as solely aimed at Israel and chose twelve disciples to help him. Indeed, Jesus shared the hope of the regathering or reconstitution of the tribes of Israel in the end-time. This is relevant to the cultural features of *name* (Israel), *myths of common ancestry, shared "historical" memories, land, kinship* and *religion*. Meier in particular draws

Identifying the Problem

attention to the Q tradition where Jesus promises his disciples that they will sit on twelve thrones judging the twelve tribes of Israel (Matt 19:28 // Luke 22:30). Meier argues this makes sense within the context of Jesus' eschatological proclamation. This proclamation was not addressed indiscriminately to the world but to Israel in its promised land. The Twelve reflected Jesus' own mission to Israel in the end-time "whose very number symbolized, promised, and ... began the regathering of the twelve tribes," hence Jesus promised the Twelve that they "would share in the governance (or judgment?)[21] of the reconstituted Israel" (Meier 2001:137). As a result Jesus did not address himself on equal terms to both Judean and Gentile, and personal encounters with Gentiles are rare. Jesus stands in continuity with mainstream Israelite tradition in that there can be no complete kingdom of God without a complete Israel (Meier 2001:152–53).[22] Meier explains the significance of Matt 19:28 // Luke 22:30 in the following way:

> "You [that is, you Twelve who symbolize and embody the eschatological Israel right now] will sit on twelve thrones judging the twelve tribes of Israel [when the kingdom fully comes and the twelve tribes are restored]" ... The creation of the Twelve thus coheres perfectly with Jesus' eschatological, people-centered message and mission: God is coming in power to gather and rule over all Israel in the end time. (Meier 2001:153–54)

Thus Jesus' concern for Israel is a clear indication of his communal solidarity with his co-ethnics, a special group that was established by God's covenant with an elect people. Jesus wants Israel restored, but somewhat paradoxically, it is a Judean ethnicity that will need redefi-

---

21. In this regard Horsley (1987:201–7; 1995:38; 1999:69, 105, 263) has persistently argued that the "judging (κρίνοντες) of the twelve tribes of Israel" in Q 22:30 has a positive meaning. Like the Hebrew *šapat*, the Greek points to grace and deliverance. So in Q 22:28–30 the Twelve/Q people (?) are portrayed not as judging (negatively) but as "liberating or establishing justice" for the twelve tribes (cf. *Pss. Sol.* 17:28–32; 1QS 8:1–4; *T. Jud.* 24–25). "In Israelite tradition, God does not 'judge' but 'delivers' ('liberates/saves/effects justice for') the orphan, widow, poor, oppressed" or "even the whole people."

22. Yet, should Jesus' "positive, but passing contact with Samaritans" (see above) not perhaps be seen as part of the restoration of Israel? Some Judean texts of the first century looked forward to the future ingathering of scattered Israel, including the ten lost tribes (cf. 2 Macc 1:27–28; 2:18; Tob 13:13; *Pss. Sol.* 8:28. On the ten lost tribes, see Ecc 36:11; 48:10; 1QM 2:1–3; 4QpIsa[d] line 7; 11QTemple 57:5–6; *4 Ezra* 13:32–50; *2 Bar.* 78:1–7; *Sib. Or.* 2:170–73). Josephus gives evidence of speculation as to the number and whereabouts of the lost ten tribes (*Ant.* 11.133).

nition under the circumstances of God's kingdom. Later on, Gentiles (and presumably Samaritans as well?) will be present in the sacred land, and will also eat with Judeans, a radical departure from the ethos of the day. So again it must be asked: Just what kind of Judean does Jesus envision for this future period? Does he expect the Judean community to become universally inclusive? Will these Gentiles be expected to convert to Judeanism or will they participate in God's kingdom *as Gentiles*? How does the vision of a "complete Israel"—and the future role of the Twelve—exactly relate to these Gentiles and matters of Torah observance[23] and possession of the land?[24] The restoration of Israel and the future kingdom asks some serious questions about traditional Judean ethnic identity—how will it survive as is in the future kingdom?

Another important feature for our consideration that Meier discusses was Jesus' unorthodox table-fellowship with toll collectors and sinners, a practice that was not continued by the early Messianist community. It along with other festive meals of Jesus "was meant to foreshadow the final eschatological banquet and to give a foretaste of that banquet even during his public ministry [cf. Matt 8:11–12 // Luke 13:28–29; Mark 14:25 par.]" (Meier 1994:966). This behavior was regarded as scandalous by some (Mark 2:15–17 par.; cf Luke 15:1–2; 19:1–10; Matt 11:18–19 // Luke 7:33–34). Now in terms of the "sinners," Meier (1994: 1036, 1037) explains why, since they were "non-observant [Judeans] who had broken with the covenant community of Israel and were considered equivalent to Gentiles" and it "is a very broad term that includes anyone who was viewed by [Judean] society in general to be living a life antithetical to God's will as expressed in the Law. In particular, it may refer to those [Judeans] who had abandoned practice of the Law and lived like Gentiles." For our purposes we can simply say that Jesus sometimes behaved like a Gentile, disregarded purity and dietary laws when having table-fellowship with sinners in order to redeem them, and so at times lived outside the bounds of what the Torah required. By the general standards of the day, this made Jesus very un-Judean.[25]

---

23. Meier argues that Jesus at times gave startling interpretations of the Mosaic Law (1994:454). But the question of the Law Meier will only discuss at length in his fourth volume.

24. The importance of the land to Judean ethnic identity can hardly be overemphasized. Brueggemann (2002:3) even contends that land "is a central, if not *the central theme* of biblical faith" (emphasis original).

25. As Dunn (1990:193) has argued, the laws on clean and unclean foods (Lev

Identifying the Problem 33

Jesus' Miracles

At the end of Meier's treatment of Jesus and the kingdom of God, Meier gives a summary of his conclusions and understanding of Jesus thus far:

> [Jesus is] a 1st-century [Judean] eschatological prophet who proclaims an imminent-future coming of God's kingdom, practices baptism as a ritual of preparation for that kingdom, teaches his disciples to pray to God as [*'abba*] for the kingdom's arrival, prophesies the regathering of all Israel . . . and the inclusion of the Gentiles when the kingdom comes—but who at the same time *makes the kingdom already present for at least some Israelites* by his exorcisms and miracles of healing. Hence in some sense he already mediates an experience of the joyful time of salvation, expressed also in his freewheeling table-fellowship with toll collectors and sinners and his rejection of voluntary fasting for himself and his disciples. To all this must be added his—at times startling—interpretation of the Mosaic Law. (Meier 1994:454; emphasis added)

The above serves as a recap of Meier's position but the emphasized text also serves to draw attention to the following. Meier accepts at least one miracle tradition involving a Gentile as having historical basis, while another acceptable tradition might possibly have a Gentile involved (both are discussed below). As an aside, it will be mentioned that he regards the story of the Syrophoenician woman[26] whose possessed daughter is healed (Mark 7:24–30; Matt 15:21–28) as a creation of first-generation Messianists therefore it merits no discussion (Meier 1994:659–61).[27] But can we then say that *some* Gentiles (those who re-

---

11:1–23; Deut 14:3–21) took on increasing importance in Judean folklore and self-understanding from the period of the Maccabees. On the importance for Judeans and proselytes to observe Judean customs, see Josephus (*War* 7.50; *Ant.* 20.100 [on apostasy]; *Ant.* 20.17, 41 [on conversion]) and Philo (*Virtues* 102–8).

26. Jackson has suggested that Matthew specifically turns Mark's story of the Syrophoenician woman into a conversion formula for entrance into the Judean community. Matthew uses the Psalms, the story of the Moabite Ruth, and a formula for conversion based on the rabbi's interpretation of that story. It entails that a potential convert must go through a four-time request, three-time rejection, and finally a period of acceptance to become a member of the Judean community. So in the hands of Matthew, Jesus is not necessarily being rude to her, but he is testing her resolve to join the community of faith (Jackson 2002; 2003).

27. Meier's discussion of other miracles regarding Gentiles/Samaritans or those miracles affecting issues of ritual purity or the forgiveness of sins we will not discuss

ceived healing and to a degree their families as well) already experienced the future but already present kingdom in some way? Meier does not really say anything to this effect and he merely states that the gospels agree that in a few exceptional cases "the future offer of salvation to the Gentiles is foreshadowed by the symbols of healing and exorcism" (Meier 1994:660). It is to two of those traditions we now will turn.

These miracles again are of relevance to the cultural features of *customs* and *religion* (since it points towards Gentiles participating in God's kingdom and contact with Gentiles affect status of ritual purity), and the first miracle tradition that will be discussed is the Gerasene Demoniac (Mark 5:1–20). Jesus was in the "region of the Gerasenes," one of the mostly pagan cities of the Decapolis, Gerasa itself situated around 53 km (33 miles) southeast of the Sea of Galilee. Here Jesus exorcises a man from a demon (called "Legion"). Meier follows the work of Franz Annen, who suggested that a plausible life setting is first-generation Messianist Judeans who favored a mission to Gentiles. They were involved in a controversy with conservative Messianists who opposed such a mission. Those who favored the mission to Gentiles used the story of the Gerasene demoniac as an argument against their opponents, in that they are only continuing what Jesus began. This argument would only have been effective if both groups of Messianist Judeans knew and accepted the fact that Jesus did perform an exorcism in the region of Gerasa. Meier accepts this life setting as a possibility and he inclines towards the view that an exorcism performed by Jesus near Gerasa lies at the basis of the narrative (Meier 1994:653).

The second miracle we will look at is the story of the healing (at a distance) of the centurion/royal official's servant (or boy) derived from Q (Matt 8:5–13 // Luke 7:1–10) and John (4:46–54—the story of the royal official's son in John is according to Meier held by most scholars as a variant of the Q tradition). Q presents the centurion as a Gentile,[28] while the story in John implicitly presents the royal official as a Judean, so the ethnic origin of the centurion/royal official is ambiguous. As a "centurion" he must not be understood as a member of the Roman army, since Galilee was not under direct control of a Roman prefect. Antipas maintained and controlled his own army that included both Judeans and Gentiles. Meier (1994:726) summarizes his view simply: while Jesus was in or approaching Capernaum, an official or officer of Herod

either since it adds little to our understanding of Meier's view of Jesus and the question of ethnicity.

28. See pp. 340–41 for a more detailed discussion on Q 7:1–10.

Identifying the Problem 35

Antipas, "possibly a centurion stationed at Capernaum, asked Jesus for the cure of a 'boy' in his household—whether the 'boy' was a slave or a son is not clear. Jesus acceded to the request by healing the 'boy' at a distance."

Jesus and other Judean Groups

Jesus and the Pharisees

How did Jesus relate to other Judean groups of his day? The first significant group Meier discusses is the Pharisees,[29] and in what is to follow concerns the cultural features of *myths of common ancestry*, shared *"his-*

---

29. According to Sanders (1992:380–451), although some Pharisees had high social and economic status, most of them were laymen and had full-time jobs that tied them down (e.g, shopkeeping and farming); so most were of modest means but with a regular income—they did not form an aristocratic group. He also argues against the common opinion that the Pharisees had control of Judeanism, for example, such as the synagogue institution. For most of their history they did desire power but did not have it, the exception being the time when Salome Alexandra ruled. Since they were well educated in the law, they had some time to study, being neither leisured nor destitute. A few priests and Levites were Pharisees. Many people respected their piety and learning, and scrupulous observance of the law (cf. *War* 1.108–9). During the revolt they attained to positions of leadership and thereafter they led the reconstruction of Judeanism. Generally the Pharisees broadly operated within the realm of covenantal nomism by sharing with common Judeanism a zeal for the law. They did not think of themselves as the only true Israel (or as the only ones within the covenant) and they were not a separatist group such as the Dead Sea Sect/Essenes. They did aspire to a level of purity above the ordinary (e.g. by attempting to avoid corpse and *midras* impurity), but below that of the priests. Here Sanders also rejects the idea that the Pharisees thought that they were always eating meals in priestly purity (cf. Neusner 1973). Dunn (1991:110–11) has argued, however, that table-fellowship (along with hand-washing) was an important identity marker and boundary for Pharisees. Otherwise Sanders points out that they had some laws particular to themselves, such as hand-washing (but mainly to protect the priests food from impurity; cf. Dunn's objection above), *'eruvin* (the construction of doorposts and lintels that "fused" several houses into one, so that dishes could be carried from one to the other on the Sabbath), and *demai*-produce (a legal category invented for food that was acquired from others who may not have tithed it). According to Baumgarten, membership in sects was a minority activity and they were more likely to have come from the economic, social and educational elite who could afford the "luxury" to be heavily involved in spiritual affairs, seeing themselves as standing above society as a whole. "They were not an alienated and underemployed intelligentsia, searching for a place in society," they were, however, "elitist" (Baumgarten 1997:51, see with 43–66). This according to him raises a question over the understanding of Pharisees in particular as a "retainer class" in service of the ruling groups (Saldarini 1988). We may add this also raises a question regarding the suggestion of Sanders that the Pharisees were generally of *modest* means with a regular income.

torical" memories, *kinship*, *land*, *customs* and *religion*. Meier understands the Pharisees' program as follows:

> In the face of a perceived threat to the continued existence of [Judeans] as a distinct ethnic, cultural, and religious entity in the ancient Near East, the Pharisees emphasized the zealous and detailed study and practice of the Mosaic Law, the careful observance of legal obligations in concrete areas of life such as tithing, purity laws (especially concerning food, sexual activity, and the proper treatment of the dead), the keeping of Sabbath, marriage and divorce, and temple ritual ... [T]hey possessed a normative body of traditions [of the elders] which went beyond the written Mosaic Law but which was (or at least should be) incumbent on the whole people of Israel. (Meier 2001:330)

Meier goes on to explain that these legal obligations "expressed concretely the response of Israel, God's holy people, to the holy God who had given Israel the Law to mark it out from all the peoples of the earth" (Meier 2001:330). Fidelity to the Law will ensure you will have a share in the world to come. The wicked and the apostates will have no share in the world to come. So it can be said that for the Pharisees, the matter of Judean ethnic identity was critically important. Your life (both present and future) literally depended on it! It is unfortunate, however, that Meier does not explain what the existence of Judeans as a "distinct ethnic, cultural, and religious entity" really means in *all* its facets.

According to Meier, Jesus interacted more with the Pharisees than any other Judean party. He shared with them a consuming desire to bring all Israel to the complete doing of God's will set out in the Law and the prophets (although this aspect of Meier's reconstruction is highly ambiguous taking into account Jesus' own behavior and approach to the Torah). Jesus would also have shared with them the belief in God's election of Israel, his gift of the Law and the requirement of wholehearted response to its demands, God's faithful guidance of Israel through history to a future end that involved the restoration of Israel, a final judgment, resurrection, and perhaps a shared belief in an eschatological figure as God's agent in the end-time (Meier 2001:338).

So in some instances, Jesus appears to be as profoundly Judean as the Pharisees. Yet, there were inevitable disagreements. Relevant to us are issues of halakah, particularly the neglect or rejection of various familial and purity rules (such as Jesus refusing a potential follower the time to bury his father, and possibly a lack of concern regarding food laws) (Meier 2001:338). Unfortunately, Meier reserves a full discussion of Jesus' attitude towards the Law—that was a common concern of "mainstream" Judeanism—to his fourth volume. For the moment Meier argues that when Jesus "addressed such topics and especially when he proclaimed new, startling, and disturbing rules governing such topics, he was addressing and potentially upsetting the lives of all pious [Judeans], not just Pharisees" (Meier 2001:340) and that "Jesus' stance vis-à-vis the Law poses a notable enigma" (Meier 2001:645). Nevertheless, Meier also maintains that as "a Palestinian [Judean] of the 1st century, Jesus takes the Mosaic Law for granted as the normative expression of God's will for Israelite conduct" (Meier 2001:525).

So compared with the Pharisees, Jesus stands both in continuity and discontinuity with Judean ethnic identity. Jesus shares with them the belief in the divine election of Israel, and God's guidance through history to its eschatological restoration. Jesus shares with the Pharisees a desire to bring all Israel in obedience with God's will as revealed by the Torah and prophets and takes it as the normative expression of God's will—although it was pointed out earlier that the Law and prophets is for Jesus only relevant up until the time of John, to be replaced by the demands of the kingdom. Jesus also stands aloof from the Pharisees on matters of law, also "mainstream" Judeanism—Jesus makes new or disturbing rules, and shows neglect or rejection of various familial and purity regulations. It is difficult to reconcile this Jesus with the one that wants to bring all of Israel to obedience to the Torah. Alternatively, Jesus' understanding of what it meant to be Judean or Torah obedient was in many ways peculiar to himself. Is Jesus becoming a different kind of Judean?

JESUS AND THE ESSENES

The discussion on the Essenes of Qumran[30] will affect the cultural features of *kinship*, *customs*, and *religion*. Meier maintains that Jesus believed

---

30. The general consensus is that the Qumran community was part of the Essene movement or a stricter group within it. The group formed under the leadership of a "Teacher of Righteousness," identified as a Zadokite priest, although according to Josephus and Philo the Essenes lived in isolated communities all over Palestine. The archrival of the teacher was the "Wicked Priest," generally identified as Jonathan Maccabees, who attained the high priesthood from the Seleucid Alexander Balas. This suggests that the Essenes were a break-away group in opposition to the temple operation run by the Hasmoneans in Jerusalem. Membership within the group required a two or three year probationary period, where after the initiate's possessions were permanently absorbed into the common fund (1QS 6.13–23), swore an oath of loyalty and was allowed to participate in the community meal. Some peculiar features of the group

in the general resurrection of the dead at the end-time (Mark 12:18–27). Yet, unlike Qumran, Jesus included some Gentiles in the eschatological banquet with the risen patriarchs, while some Israelites will be excluded (Matt 8:11–12). In Qumran's view, however, all Gentiles and all Israelites outside the Essene community will perish (Meier 2001:494). We can say that the Qumranites were doing a serious redefinition of Judean ethnic status of their own.

Jesus also differed from the Qumranites' view of the temple. In all the gospels Jesus is represented as going to the temple, teaching there and eating the Passover lamb that was slain in the temple. There is no tradition that Jesus throughout his public ministry shunned the temple and refused to participate in its festivals. Here Jesus was in unison with "mainstream" Judeans since he revered the temple as the one sacred place chosen by God for lawful sacrifice and he followed the festal calendar observed by the temple's priests (Meier 2001:499–500, 529). This attitude of Jesus, is also supported by other sayings of Jesus that took the temple and its ritual for granted and as obligatory (Mark 1:44; Matt 23:23 // Luke 11:42; Matt 5:23–24; 23:16–21; Luke 18:9–14; John 4:22, 18:20). Although all these sayings may not be authentic, there is enough evidence that Jesus accepted the temple in his own day. This is unlike the Qumranites who thought that the temple in Jerusalem was defiled and who looked forward to its restoration (Meier 2001:499–500). But Meier emphasizes that Jesus accepted the temple, which was ordained by God in the Torah, "*as part of the present order of things*" that "will soon come to an end" (Meier 2001:500, 501; emphasis original). At the coming of God's kingdom, the current temple will be done away with based on Jesus' prophetic action in the temple and sayings about its destruction (Mark 11:15–17; 14:58; Matt 23:37–38 // Luke 13:34–35; Luke 19:41–44; John 2:13–17, 19). It must be remembered that John's baptism, something that Jesus continued with in his own ministry, was regarded as necessary for salvation. It implicitly called into question the sufficiency of temple worship as then practiced. Whether Jesus expected a better or new temple to replace it is unclear, but there are different ver-

---

included their strictness in purity (4Q512; 4Q381 46.5–6) that was accompanied by a strict hierarchy, observation of the solar calendar (as opposed to the standard lunar calendar), their apparent teaching on hatred of outsiders (1QS 1.4, 10), their asceticism and celibacy (although some resident outside of Qumran did get married), and they adhered to deterministic view of the world (1QS 3.15–16) (see Charlesworth 1992: xxxi–xxxvii, 1–74; Campbell 1996:57–104; Vermes 1998:26–90).

sions of a saying that indicate some sort of new temple would be built (Mark 14:58; John 2:19) (Meier 2001:501).

Also relevant to our concerns is the matter of ritual purity. Because of the Qumranites' eschatological radicalism, they were extremely vigorous in matters of ritual purity and observance of the Sabbath, which is "glaringly different from Jesus' relative laxity on the same issues" (Meier 2001:502). For example, they underwent frequent lustrations, adhered to dietary laws that went beyond the requirements of the Torah so that their communal meals were subject to strict control (Meier 2001:525, 528). Indeed, in the eyes of most Judeans they displayed an extreme observance of the Law. In matters of halakah, Jesus was not interested in development of details. Jesus was far from being obsessed with purity rules in that he easily dines with sinners and toll collectors (Mark 2:13–17; Luke 19:1–10; Matt 11:19 // Luke 7:34), physically touches lepers (Mark 1:40–45; Luke 17:11–19; Matt 11:5 par.), and shows no concern over purity issues that would have arisen due to the unchaperoned women that accompanied him during his ministry (Luke 8:1–3). As the eschatological prophet sent to gather all Israel in the end-time, he actively sought out the religiously and socially marginalized and in dramatic fashion celebrated their inclusion in the end-time Israel by enjoying table-fellowship with them. Jesus also had a lenient view regarding the Sabbath rest (Matt 12:11 // Luke 14:5) that was in contradiction with the Essene's strict requirements (Meier 2001:524–29).

In addition, Qumran promoted hatred for those outside the community, based on their worldview that was strongly dualistic. The outsiders were the "sons of darkness," consisting of both Gentiles and those Judeans who did not accept the views and practices of the Qumranites, the "sons of light." In contrast, Jesus' worldview did not develop into an extreme exclusionary view where all Gentiles and all Judeans outside his group were automatically heading towards eternal destruction. Jesus reached out to all Israel and envisaged that many Gentiles would take part in the eschatological banquet (Meier 2001:529). Further, Jesus in his teaching, parables and praxis stressed the message of love, compassion and mercy, including the love of enemies and persecutors.[31] "This inclusive thrust of Jesus . . . stands in stark contrast to the exclusive sectarianism of Qumran, which saw itself alone as the true Israel" (Meier

---

31. Meier refers to the following texts: Mark 2:1–12, 13–17; 11:25; 12:28–34; Matt 5:21–26, 38–48; 6:12, 14–15; 18:10–14, 15, 21–35; Luke 7:36–50; 9:51–55; 10:25–37; 15:1–32; 19:9–14; 19:1–10; cf. John 8:1–11.

2001:530). The latter can be paraphrased as follows: The Qumranites saw only themselves as being truly Judean.

In comparison with the Qumranites, we see again elements of continuity and discontinuity in Meier's understanding of Jesus. The Essenes of Qumran were the pinnacle expression of Judean exclusivity and suspicion of others, even avoiding the temple. Jesus, however, shared with "mainstream" Judeanism a high regard for the temple and followed its festivals. But he also regarded the temple as part of the present order of things. Jesus' prophetic actions and sayings about the temple's destruction clearly went against the structure of Judean ethnic identity in his day—even more so if he did not say anything about the temple being rebuilt. But if baptism is necessary for salvation—even for the devout—does this not make the temple as a place of "lawful sacrifice" already somewhat superfluous in various ways, particularly when it comes to the biblical "guilt" offerings (cf. Lev 4–6)? Again in matters of halakah, such as ritual purity and Sabbath observance, Jesus was very relaxed; but even ordinary Judeans would have regarded the Qumranites' observance as extreme. Nevertheless, Jesus was inclusive, and wanted to gather all Israel in preparation for the end, and said some Gentiles will also participate in the eschatological banquet. He even had table-fellowship with religiously and socially marginalized Judeans. This went against the general tendencies of the day where Judean ethnic identity was pre-occupied with exclusiveness, purity and food laws and which was taken to the extreme by the sectarianism of Qumran who "hated" their enemies. Jesus' inclusiveness placed emphasis on love (even of enemies and persecutors), compassion and mercy.

Overall, Meier intimates that it is hardly surprising that Jesus showed less concern for detailed rules of purity and Sabbath observance. Circumstances did not really allow for Galileans to be engaged with Jerusalem based scholasticism and politics developed in the halakah of the rival Pharisees, Sadducees (and Essenes). "The Nazareth apple had not fallen far from the Galilean tree" (Meier 2001:618). This remark, however, is somewhat suspect. The adult life of Jesus, based on Meier's own reconstruction, suggests that he in various ways was different in behavior and outlook when compared with the average Galilean.

Summary: John P. Meier—Jesus a Marginal "Jew"

Overall, Meier can be commended for the detailed nature of his work. This becomes evident in that all the cultural features listed at the beginning are represented to various degrees. It is Meier's interpretive paradigm of Judeanism as a religious identity that needs to be adjusted. These remarks aside, in Meier's reconstruction of the historical Jesus, we consistently find a pattern of continuity and discontinuity with traditional Judeanism. Guided by the insights of ethnicity theory, Jesus appears to be very Judean and un-Judean in the same breath. We will first have a look at what is continuous between Jesus and Judean ethnicity.

If we look at the names of Jesus and his family, they are all derived from the time of the patriarchs, the Exodus and entrance into the promised land. This suggests that Jesus' family participated in the reawakening of Judean national and religious feeling in Galilee. Jesus would have spoken Aramaic, as most Judeans of Palestine would have, but would also have learned Hebrew and acquired some literacy from Joseph or someone in the local synagogue. Jesus would have been able to read the Hebrew Scriptures and expound it. His religious formation was immense and received an "elementary" education learning the religious traditions and texts of Judeanism. But Jesus would also have acquired limited skill in Greek, but many Judeans, both of Palestine and the Diaspora, would have known Greek. Jesus' Galilean background was generally conservative in nature, and surrounded by Gentiles, Galileans clinged to the basics of their religion and culture to reinforce their identity (Torah, circumcision, Sabbath observance, purity and food laws and pilgrimage to the temple). The type of Judeanism they followed also held onto certain key beliefs. As the one true God's chosen people, he led them out of slavery during the exodus, made a covenant with them and gave them the land as a perpetual inheritance. After the exile, he also gave them a promise of a future and glorious renewal. Jesus would have received special attention from his putative father Joseph, and in addition to seeing to Jesus' religious education, would also have taught him his own trade as a woodworker. Overall, the childhood circumstances of Jesus in Galilee were conducive to fostering a strong Judean ethnic identity.

The adult Jesus went to John the Baptist and received his once-off ritual immersion in water, something he saw as divinely inspired. This implies that Jesus accepted John's eschatological message and saw himself as part of sinful Israel. Both Jesus and John the Baptist worked as prophets within and for Israel. Jesus chose a circle of twelve intimate disciples, something that symbolized Jesus' hope for a regathered and reconstituted Israel. Jesus saw his mission as only directed at Israel, and had but passing contact with Gentiles and Samaritans. For Jesus, there can be no kingdom of God without a complete Israel. God will also honor his commitment to Israel and the covenant since the patriarchs and faithful Israelites will through the resurrection share in a life similar to the angels.

Jesus shared with the Pharisees a consuming desire to bring all Judeans to a faithful obedience of the Torah. Jesus takes the Mosaic Law for granted as the normative expression of God's will. Jesus also shared with them (by implication Judeans in general) a belief in Israel's divine election, and God's faithful guidance in history to its eschatological restoration. Along with mainstream Judeanism Jesus also revered the temple as the one holy place chosen by God for lawful sacrifice, and followed its annual festivals—but the temple is according to Jesus, part of the present order of things.

This brings us to those aspects where Jesus stood in discontinuity with traditional Judeanism. When Jesus went on his itinerant mission, Jesus broke away from his family. He defined a new identity and social role for himself. Jesus also made stringent demands on his followers—obligations to home and parents, the social unit that formed and maintained your identity, they must be willing to leave behind. Commitment to Jesus is more important. It is those who do the Father's will who are Jesus' family: his brother, sister, and mother. This alternative kinship pattern caused family divisions, but Meier unfortunately does not explain what impact this could have had on the patriarchal family as an institution.

By accepting John's message and baptism, Jesus accepts that physical descent from Abraham—even for the devout—will mean nothing at the coming judgment. It is only by a confession of sin, baptism, and a profound change of heart and conduct that one will be saved. This salvation is available outside the normal channels of Judeanism (the Law, temple and priesthood, etc.), which brings into question its sufficiency, as well as the sufficiency of ethnic status as it operated then. Covenant status and divine election has moved beyond traditional Judean ethnic identity.

In his own ministry, Jesus continued with John's baptism. He also grouped himself along with John over and against their Judean contemporaries ("this generation"), and condemns them for not heeding their message. The Law and the prophets functioned up until John, but from then onwards it was the kingdom that had broken onto the scene. What has usually defined Judean ethnicity has now on its own become irrelevant, and is appropriated towards the demands of the kingdom.

When the kingdom of God will fully come, Gentiles will also sit and eat with the patriarchs at the eschatological banquet, while some of Jesus' contemporaries will be thrown out. Gentiles will therefore be present within the Israelite ancestral land. This also illustrates that the kingdom will go beyond a political kingdom reserved for Judeans. At the judgment, the Queen of Sheba and the Ninevites will witness against and condemn that generation. Meier does not explain what kind of Judean Jesus envisions for this future period. Meier's Jesus does not see the future kingdom as a celebration of Judean ethnic identity. Also, the implications for Law observance and ownership of the land Meier does not explain.

This future kingdom is in a sense already present through Jesus' healings and table-fellowship. Jesus does not fast, and enjoys having table-fellowship with Israelites, including tax collectors and sinners, the religious outcasts of Judean society, to enact participation in God's salvation for all Israelites. The sinners especially qualified to be regarded as being outside that privileged realm of Judean identity, and here Jesus shows little regard for purity and food laws. Jesus has a very inclusive approach and is not interested to set up boundaries between his own group and other Judeans. Combined with Jesus' shocking behavior around the meal table, Jesus ignored rules concerning the family, and sometimes gave new and startling laws. He also touches lepers while healing. It is difficult to reconcile this Jesus with one that had a consuming desire (along with the Pharisees) to bring all Israel to a complete obedience of the Law. In some exceptional cases, Jesus also performed miracles for Gentiles, pointing to the future offer of salvation for them. And lastly, Jesus acted and said something about the temple's that implied its destruction—it is not clear whether Jesus thought it would be rebuilt in some way.

Does the above analysis qualify Jesus as a "marginal Judean"? And how can the eschatological prophet of Israel, the fulfilment of all Israel's hopes and expectations be "marginal" to begin with? This constitutes a profound paradox. But overall, the element of discontinuity, pervasive in Meier's reconstruction of the historical Jesus, needs a more comprehensive explanation than him merely being "marginal." This aspect of Meier's reconstruction will be returned to after a proposed analytical framework or model has been put into place (see chapter 2).

John Dominic Crossan— Jesus, a Mediterranean "Jewish" Peasant

Crossan's approach to the historical Jesus is heavily influenced by the social sciences or the insights of cultural anthropology. Crossan puts Jesus and first century Palestine into the larger context of the "Brokered (Roman) Empire," which entailed the normal features of honor and shame, patronage and clientage. Jesus himself broke away from John the Baptist's eschatological message and announced the brokerless kingdom of God available to all in the present. Indeed, for Crossan, the heart of the Jesus movement was a shared egalitarianism of spiritual and material resources. But based on Crossan's reconstruction, how did Jesus relate to first-century Judean ethnicity?

Jesus, Nazareth, and Sepphoris

The first matter that will be investigated is Crossan's treatment of Nazareth. What follows concerns the cultural feature of *customs* and general cultural identity. Archaeological investigations have uncovered tombs, the vast majority of which are chambers with a number of shafts cut horizontally into the walls in order that the body could be placed inside head first. The burial shafts or niches were called *loculi* graves in Latin and *kokim* graves in Hebrew. These kind of burial chambers are important since they virtually became the standard type of Judean tomb from about 200 BCE. A conclusion Crossan (1991:16) draws from this is that "Nazareth was a very [Judean] village in the Roman era." Other archaeological findings also suggest that the principle activity of villagers was agriculture. Crossan argues, however, that three qualifications must be added to the picture of Nazareth as a Judean agricultural hamlet in the early Roman period.

First, there is the consideration of regional topography. The differences between Upper and Lower Galilee must be taken into account and the location of Nazareth in the southern most part of Lower Galilee. Compared to Upper Galilee, where the Meiron range reaches a height of almost four thousand feet, the four ranges of Lower Galilee reach heights of over one thousand feet. Lower Galilee would not have been as isolated as Upper Galilee. A rural agricultural Judeanism would have been more characteristic of those living in the north, while some negative comments of later rabbis and clichés in the New Testament might suggest an accommodation to Hellenism in Lower Galilee. Nevertheless, Nazareth itself was located at an elevation of over one thousand feet on the southernmost hill of Galilee that "isolated the village off the beaten track" (Crossan 1991:17).

The second qualification that Crossan employs is political geography. A major city contains within its region various smaller cities that in turn serves a region with towns, each of which is surrounded by villages. The key factors that determine this settlement pattern are commerce and administrative functions. Crossan explains this hierarchy of settlement in Lower Galilee "was represented by Bethshan/Scythopolis as its *major city*, Sepphoris and Tiberias as its *smaller cities*, Capernaum and Magdala/Tarichaeae as its *towns*. Nazareth, clearly a *village*, is closest, not to one of those towns, but, at three or four miles distance, to Sepphoris, a smaller city" (Crossan 1991:17; emphasis original). The main west-east road through Galilee ran from Ptolemais on the Mediterranean coast through Sepphoris and Tiberias. Ptolemais itself was on the Via Maris, "that most ancient Palestinian highway of international commerce and conquest that opened Sepphoris and its environs to cosmopolitan influence" (Crossan 1991:18). Sepphoris was also the end point for the north-south road from Jerusalem, meaning that two roads carrying different types of influence converged there. Nazareth may have been off the beaten track but it was not far off a fairly well beaten track. So Nazareth must be understood in terms of its "relationship to an urban provincial capital" that amongst other things contained courts, a fortress, a theater,[32] a palace, a colonnaded street atop the acropolis, a royal bank and a population of around 30,000 (Crossan 1991:18–19).[33]

Third, there is possibly the most important qualification, which comes from comparative demography. There was an unusually large number of urban and larger village centres in lower Galilee that made it one of the most densely populated regions of the Roman Empire. One is never more than a day's walk from anywhere in lower Galilee and hence any village could not escape the effects and ramifications of urbanization. Life in lower Galilee was as urbanized as any other part of the Roman Empire, but geographical proximity and demographic density also entailed cultural continuity. Any hostilities that existed between Sepphoris and Tiberias on the one hand, and rural areas on

---

32. It is doubtful that the theater was built in Jesus' time. The theater probably dates to the late first or early second century CE (Chancey and Meyers 2000:24; Chancey 2002:75).

33. Reed (2000:80, 82) estimates that Sepphoris had a population of around 8,000 to 12,000 inhabitants.

the other, were based on political disputes and not on a cultural split. A cultural continuum existed from city to country.

Based on the three considerations mentioned above Crossan concludes that the peasants of Nazareth "lived in the shadow of a major administrative city, in the middle of a densely populated urban network, and in continuity with its hellenized cultural traditions" (Crossan 1991:19).[34] One cannot think of Jesus as a Galilean peasant as isolated, a "good old country boy," since the lives of Galileans were influenced by the all-pervasive presence of the Roman city. The significance of this Crossan does not develop here but it must be seen in connection with his argument that Jesus must be seen within the context of inclusive Hellenistic Judeanism, a matter that will be addressed later.

Jesus and the Brokerless Kingdom

Now we shift our attention at first to Jesus' relationship with John the Baptist. Crossan accepts Jesus' baptism by John as one of the surest things we can know about both of them. Jesus, in submitting himself to John's baptism, initially accepted his apocalyptic expectation but thereafter changed his view of John's mission and message. From originally accepting John's message to await the coming of God as a repentant sinner, Jesus developed his own distinctive message and movement: it was now a question of being in the kingdom (Crossan 1991:232–38). To be more exact, it was a "brokerless kingdom" available in the present. The kingdom of God must be understood as people living under divine rule. It refers to a way of life or mode of being, not a nation or empire (human power) dependent on place (Crossan 1991:266). Of course, this affects the cultural features of *land*, *customs*, and *religion*. Particularly in terms of the *land*, Judean identity was inseparable from its relationship to the land. The gift of the land was a primary reason for Israel's existence and was part of God's covenant agreement with his people. So for the average Judean, his/her relationship with God, indeed, his/her very identity was very much dependent on place. Here Jesus' understanding of the kingdom of God would be vastly different when compared with other Judeans. But how did this "landless" brokerless kingdom give ex-

---

34. Here the remarks of Hengel are ever important. What is meant by "Hellenistic" should be defined more precisely; for example, does it refer to oriental syncretism, or does "it refer to technology, art, economics, politics, rhetoric and literature, philosophy or religion?" What was impossible was a Judean pagan cult, the denial of monotheism, the failure to observe the Torah and the desecration of the temple (Hengel 1989:54).

Identifying the Problem 47

pression to itself? Through magic and open commensality. And it is to these aspects of Crossan's reconstruction that we will turn next.

Jesus the Magician

Following the lead of Geza Vermes, Crossan places Jesus within the tradition of miracle-working stemming from Elijah and Elisha, who apart from Jesus, were also given contemporary expression in the figures of Honi and Hanina. In contrast to Vermes, however, Crossan argues that "the title *ḥasid* is not appropriate, since ultra-strict observance of the law does not seem at all part of the constitutive identity of these wonder workers" and Crossan (1991:157) does not restrict the later development of the tradition to a northern (Galilean) provenance. Further, we are dealing "with a type of wonder worker who operates with certain and secure divine authority not mediated through or dependent on the normal forms, rituals, and institutions through which that divine power usually operates" and the dichotomy is that of "magician as personal and individual power against priest or rabbi as communal and ritual power" (Crossan 1991:157). To be more specific, before the temple's destruction, "it was magician against Temple" and "magicians implicitly challenge the *legitimacy* of spiritual power" (Crossan 1991:157, 158; emphasis original). Hence, Crossan specifically deals with Jesus' miracles/magic as religious banditry. Crossan (1991:305) proposes that "magic is to religion as banditry is to politics" and "magic is unofficial and unapproved religion." Here we will deal with three miracles that Crossan regards as historical and which more directly pertains to the issue of Judean ethnicity.[35] Specifically, it affects the cultural features of *customs* and *religion*.

The first tradition we will discuss is Jesus' curing of a leper (EgerGos 2b [35–47]; Mark 1:40–45 par.; Luke 17:11–19). The leper petitions Jesus, if the latter so wishes, to make him clean ("if you will"), and Jesus' response is "I will." Here Jesus' authority is set on par or even above that of the temple, since Jesus cannot only heal, but declare someone healed ("clean") as well. But there is also the injunction to submit to the legal purity regulations of the temple (Lev 12–14). Jesus both is

---

35. The miracles that according to the Gospels Jesus performed for Gentiles at a distance (Luke 7:1–2 // Matt 8:5–10, 13; cf. John 4:46–53 and Mark 7:24–30; Matt 15:21–23, 25–28) Crossan regards as "programmatic defenses of the later Gentile mission, as Jesus' proleptic initiation of that process . . . Early [Messianist] communities symbolically retrojected their own activities back into the life of Jesus" (Crossan 1991:328).

and is not an obedient observer of levitical purity regulations. Crossan (1991:322) argues that a common source behind the tradition "already reversed and rectified the image of Jesus as an alternative to or negation of Mosaic purity regulations by that terminally appended injunction to legal fidelity." The Egerton Gospel intensified the vision of Jesus as a law observant teacher. Mark, on the other hand, intensifies the thrust of the *original* story. He has a leper as deeply reverential to Jesus, "has Jesus actually touch the leper, and qualifies the fulfilment of the purity regulations with the confrontation challenge 'as a witness to (against) them,' namely the priests ... For Mark, then, Jesus is precisely *not* a law-observant [Judean]" (Crossan 1991:323; emphasis original). Crossan accepts the possibility that the "touch" of the leper was a traditional part of the story; hence Jesus would have showed little respect or concern for purity regulations.

The other two traditions also deal with Jesus subverting the temple monopoly. First, Jesus heals a paralytic and also declares his sins forgiven. Besides the differences in place and detail, Crossan sees that behind John 5:1–9 and Mark 2:1–12 par. is a single traditional event. Here the conjunction between sickness and sin involves a terrible irony, especially in first-century Palestine. Excessive taxation, Crossan explains,

> could leave poor people physically malnourished or hysterically disabled. But since the religiopolitical ascendancy could not blame excessive taxation, it blamed sick people themselves by claiming that their sins had led to their illnesses. And the cure for sinful sickness was, ultimately, in the Temple. And that meant more fees, in a perfect circle of victimization. When, therefore, John the Baptist with a magical rite or Jesus with a magical touch cured people of their sickness, they implicitly declared their sins forgiven or nonexistent. They challenged not the medical monopoly of the doctors but the religious monopoly of the priests. All of this was religiopolitically subversive. (Crossan 1991:324)

The same is basically true of the third tradition where Jesus heals a blind man (John 9:1–7; Mark 8:22–26). Here Jesus as the Sent One uses spittle, and he sends the blind man to Siloam (meaning "Sent") to consummate the healing. For Crossan (1991:326), "a physical event for one man becomes a spiritual process for the world."

The implications are that the religious authority of the temple is undermined and concerns over ritual purity are ignored. Jesus touches the leper, short-circuits the priests in the temple and declares him as "clean,"[36] and through healing he implicitly declares all the beneficiaries' sins as forgiven.[37] Jesus engages in religious banditry, in opposition to the priests as representatives of communal and ritual power. He subverts traditional Judean ethnic identity in more than one respect. Jesus' authority is set on an equal or even higher level than that of the temple, a source of victimization, and he serves as an alternative or negation of Mosaic purity regulations, and therefore, aspects of the Torah itself. So for Jesus, the temple and priesthood do not appear to be divinely appointed institutions in need of restoration. They were not a necessary means whereby covenant membership (= Judean ethnic identity) could be maintained/restored as prescribed in the Torah. The role of the temple and priests, also that of traditional covenant membership, becomes superfluous. So overall, Jesus subverts traditional Judean ethnic identity in more than one respect. Jesus the wonderworker like Elijah and Elisha, Honi and Hanina, was not interested to observe the Law strictly. He was hardly Judean in this respect.

Jesus and Open Commensality

Another expression of the brokerless kingdom was the nature of Jesus' table-fellowship. This affects the cultural features of communal solidarity or *kinship, customs,* and *religion*. Based on various traditions (Mark 2:18–20; Luke 7:31–35 // Matt 11:16–19; Luke 11:14–15, 17–18 // Matt 12:22–26; Matt 9:32–34; Mark 3:22–26), Crossan (1991:260) takes it to mean that John the Baptist lived an apocalyptic asceticism and that Jesus did the opposite. Jesus was accused of gluttony and drunkenness and of keeping bad company. But what exactly did Jesus do? Crossan finds an answer in the Parable of the Feast (GThom 64:1–2; Luke 14:15–24 // Matt 22:1–13). The various evangelists interpreted and applied the parable to their own situations but behind them all is a common structural plot. The parable concerns a person who gives an unannounced feast, sending friends to invite friends, who did not accept the invitation and who were then replaced by anyone off the streets. This "anyone" is very important to Crossan since it

---

36. The notions of the sacred and the profane, of the pure/clean and impure/unclean, were important aspects of the Judean worldview. It was especially the role of the priests to distinguish (*badal*) between the two (Lev 10:10) and which had to be taught to the people (Ezek 44:23) (Schmidt 2001:91).

37. Forgiveness of sins was normally obtained through the sacrificial cult ("guilt offerings") of the temple. See Lev 4–6.

negates the very social function of table, namely, to establish a social ranking by what one eats, how one eats, and with whom one eats. It is the random and open commensality of the parable's meal that is the most startling element. One could, in such a situation, have classes, sexes, ranks, and grades all mixed up together. The social challenge of such egalitarian commensality is the radical threat of the parable's vision ... And the almost predictable counteraccusation to such open commensality is immediate: Jesus is a glutton, a drunkard, and a friend of tax collectors and sinners. He makes, in other words, no appropriate distinctions and discriminations. (Crossan 1991:262)

By making no appropriate distinctions and discriminations with whom he eats, we can say that Jesus was being very un-Judean compared with the average demands of contemporary Judeanism. Similar accusations against Jesus are found elsewhere (POxy 1224, 2.5.1, lines 1–5; Mark 2:13–17 par.; GEbion 1c; Luke 15:1–2). Crossan clusters seven other traditions around the ideal of open or egalitarian commensality, four of which that will be discussed. First, there are two traditions that negate any value to food taboos or table rituals (GThom 14:3; Mark 7:14–15; Matt 15:10–11; Acts 10:14; 11:8 and GThom 89; Luke 11:39–41 // Matt 23:25–26). Together they also insist that the inside and what comes from the inside out are more important than the outside and what comes from the outside in. Jesus was not aiming here exclusively at the developed table rituals of the Pharisees though. Crossan (1991:262) explains that an "open table and an open menu offend alike against any cultural situation in which distinctions among foods and guests mirror social distinctions, discriminations, and hierarchies." But Jesus' viewpoint did offend the Pharisees. Jesus' accusations against the Pharisees in two traditions (GThom 39:1 and POxy 655; GThom 102; Luke 11:52 // Matt 23:13 and Luke 11:43 // Matt 23:6–7; Mark 12:38–40 parr) when seen in conjunction highlights the parallelism between food regulations and social hierarchy (Crossan 1991:262–63). So was Jesus for or against the ritual laws of Judeanism? Crossan (1991:263) explains:

> His position must have been, as it were, unclear. I propose ... that he did not care enough about such ritual laws either to attack or to acknowledge them. He ignored them, but that, of course, was to subvert them at a most fundamental level. Later, however, some followers could say that, since he did not attack them, he must have accepted them. Others, contrariwise, could

Identifying the Problem 51

say that, since he did not follow them, he must have been against them. Open commensality profoundly negates distinctions and hierarchies between female and male, poor and rich, Gentile and [Judean].

Importantly, if Jesus does not really care about ritual laws (he ignores them), then he did not care about certain aspects of the Torah, the "constitution" so to speak of Judean ethnic identity (= covenant membership). And if Jesus subverted ritual laws at their most fundamental level, then likewise did he subvert Judean ethnic identity at its most fundamental level. What Crossan also implies is that open commensality profoundly negates distinctions and hierarchies between the ritually pure and unclean, between those who observe food laws and those who do not (sinners and Gentiles). But ritual purity and food laws were primary ethnic identity markers for the cultural situation of Judeans of the first century, including those that lived in Galilee. The average Judean keeping to the basic food and purity laws would not eat with sinners, much less with Gentiles—both were "impure." Here, at times, Jesus ignored the dietary and purity laws and pretty much behaved like a sinner or Gentile, in other words, as one who was outside the realm of the covenant, outside the realm of common Judean ethnicity. The kinship pattern of Jesus appears to be universal—any person is welcome to eat at his table, no matter what or how they eat.

But there was more to Jesus' association with undesirables. Jesus announced a kingdom for those who are like children. A "kingdom of children is a kingdom of nobodies" (Crossan 1991:269). Crossan finds corroboration for this picture in Jesus' following saying: "Blessed are you poor (πτωχοὶ) for yours is the kingdom of God" (Luke 6:20 // Matt 5:3; GThom 54; cf Jas 2:5). Crossan (1991:272) brings attention to the fact that the Greek term πτωχός is a word that suggests "one who crouches," and so a "begger."[38] The πτωχός was somebody that lost his/her family and social ties. He/she was a wanderer, a foreigner to others, somebody who could not tax for any length of time the resources of a group to which he/she could contribute very little or anything at all. Based on the stratification of agrarian societies "Jesus spoke

---

38. Cf Stegemann & Stegemann (1999:199–203), who regard πένητες as denoting the relatively poor and πτωχοὶ as the absolutely poor. For the time of their nomadic existence, Jesus and his disciples (some of whom were fishermen) belonged to the latter—although, under normal circumstances, the τέκτων Jesus and his initial disciples as ἁλιεῖς could also have been very poor. For the dynamics of the fishing industry in Galilee, see Hanson (1997; also Hanson & Oakman 1998:106–10).

of a Kingdom not of Peasant or Artisan classes but of the Unclean, Degraded, and Expendable classes," put in another way, a "Kingdom of the Destitute" (Crossan 1991:273). Jesus likened this Kingdom to the spread of weeds (mustard and darnel) as seen from the angle of the landless poor, a Kingdom of undesirables. But the Kingdom of God needs the recognition of the Kingdom as present. "For Jesus," Crossan (1991:283) maintains, "a Kingdom of beggars and weeds is a Kingdom of here and now."

Magic and Meal Coming Together

One of the most crucial aspects in Crossan's (1991:332–48) reconstruction is Jesus' mission charge to his disciples. He finds in three texts what he understands to be the place where one can see the heart of the Jesus movement (GThom 14:2; Luke 10:(1), 4–11 = Matt 10:7, 10b, 12–14; Mark 6:7–13 = Matt 10:1, 8–10a, 11 = Luke 9:1–6): this entails mission, dress, place, commensality, healing, the Kingdom, and lastly itinerancy. It involves Jesus' instruction to his followers/disciples. They must go to people and share healing and the Kingdom in exchange for a meal. It entails the "conjunction of magic and meal, miracle and table, compassion and commensality" (Crossan 1991:332).

Of concern to us here is Jesus' instruction to them on how they should be dressed. This is relevant to the cultural feature of *customs*, but its aim affects *religion* as well. Crossan focuses on four items that is present in more than two independent sources: money/purse, sandals, bag, and bread. These items the disciples are not to take with them on their journey, although Mark allows the sandals which Crossan regards as a development in the tradition. In terms of these items Crossan (1991:338) says one immediately "notices a very striking anomaly precisely against the general background of Greco-Roman Cynicism."[39] The recognizable dress of the counter-cultural Cynics included a cloak, wallet/bag (πήρα) and a staff, and their life typically included barefoot itinerancy (Crossan 1991:81). The *pera*'s function was especially to denote their self-sufficiency. But Crossan finds in Jesus' instructions the opposite; the disciples must carry no bag, no bread, that is, no food for their journey. Crossan (1991:339) proposes the bag's prohibition "goes back to Jesus and that it must be explained in terms of the functional symbolism of the social movement he was establishing." The reason why there is no bag is because the missionaries were not to be self-sufficient.

---

39. For an alternative understanding of the disciples' dress, see pp. 362–63 below.

Crossan explains the missionaries will "share a miracle and a Kingdom" to "receive in return a table and a house." It is here, that Crossan (1991:341) suggests, where one can find "the heart of the original Jesus movement, a shared egalitarianism of spiritual and material resources... it concerns the longest journey in the Greco-Roman world, maybe in any world, the step across the threshold of a peasant stranger's home." The point of the exercise was commensality, not alms wages, charges or fees.

> For Jesus ... commensality was not just a strategy for supporting the mission ... Commensality was, rather, a strategy for building or rebuilding peasant community on radically different principles from those of honor and shame, patronage and clientage. It was based on egalitarian sharing of spiritual and material power at the most grass-roots level. For this reason, dress and equipment appearance was just as important as house and table response. (Crossan 1991:344)

Now what exactly are the implications for Jesus' ethnicity? One might say that combining "magic and meal" to enact the unbrokered Kingdom, to use Crossan's own words, would have a double impact on the subversion of the temple authority, and on purity and food regulations, thus, on aspects of the Torah itself. Combined with the peculiar dress code (for example, does Crossan have itinerant Jesus and his disciples walking around barefoot?—and if so, what does it mean?), Judean ethnic identity as defined and lived out in the first century stood under fierce attack. What we have here is a basic disregard for what covenant membership normally required. Both the "brokered" Judean temple-state and the social and religious discrimination Jesus opposes was part of mainstream Judeanism and generally sanctioned by the Torah. The Judean ethnicity Jesus now envisages—a community of equals—has no need of hierarchy or discrimination of any sort. Jesus and his disciples are permanent and willful "apostates" in this regard, since Crossan (1991:349) presumes "that dress and itinerancy, miracle and table, healing and commensality, characterized Jesus as much as his missionaries and that they characterized them not just once but all the time. 'Mission' is thus much more than a single one-time sending of some set group." But it must be mentioned that Crossan places these counter-cultural features of Jesus' "mission" within a context of peasant society just as much over and against the ethos of the Greco-Roman world as he does his Judean social world.

As already suggested, this radical "mission" of Jesus happened to bring him into conflict with the temple as institution. John the Baptist also offered an alternative to the temple but from another fixed location, from desert and Jordan rather from Zion and Jerusalem. Crossan (1991:346) sees in the itinerancy of Jesus' movement a radical nature because it is a symbolic representation of unbrokered egalitarianism. Jesus was

> atopic, moving from place to place, he coming to the people rather than they to him. This is an even more radical challenge to the localized univocity of Jerusalem's Temple, and its itinerancy mirrored and symbolized the egalitarian challenge of its protagonist. No matter, therefore, what Jesus thought, said, or did about the Temple, he was its functional opponent, alternative, and substitute: his relationship with it does not depend, at its deepest level, on this or that saying, this or that action. (Crossan 1991:355)

For Crossan, however, Jesus did symbolically enact and say something about the temple's destruction (GThom 71; Mark 14:55–59 par.; Mark 15:29–32 par.; Acts 6:11–14; John 2:18–22). Crossan (1991:359) proposes that the earliest recoverable stratum involved an action that symbolically destroyed the temple (Mark 11:15–16; John 2:14–16), accompanied by a saying announcing what was happening, "I will destroy this house utterly beyond repair" (GThom 71). Crossan proposes that poor Galilean peasants did not go up and down regularly to the temple feasts. Crossan (1991:360) thinks

> it quite possible that Jesus went up to Jerusalem only once and that the spiritual and economic egalitarianism he preached in Galilee exploded in indignation at the Temple as the seat and symbol of all that was nonegalitarian, patronal, and even oppressive on both the religious and the political level. His symbolic destruction simply actualized what he had already said in his teachings, effected in his healings, and realized in his mission of open commensality.

Crossan explains in conclusion that the symbolic destruction was but the logical extension of the miracle and table conjunction, of open healing and open eating.

Naturally, this conjunction of open healing and open eating, that culminates in opposition to the temple, places Jesus and his followers in discontinuity with common Judeanism of their day. They become

Identifying the Problem

like Mediterranean peasant philosophers, who, within the context of Judeanism, offer healing and forgiveness, acting as substitutes or opponents of the temple, indeed, as opponents of a patronal, brokered, hierarchical, and exclusive Judeanism. Jesus also symbolically destroys the temple with no vision to rebuild it. As mentioned already, the temple and priesthood were not a necessary means whereby covenant membership (= Judean ethnic identity) could be maintained/restored as prescribed in the Torah. Further, there would be no need for pilgrimage festivals. So much for remembering God's deliverance at Passover, or bringing agricultural offerings in thankfulness of God's generous provision through the land (this also affects the cultural features of *shared "historical" memories* and *myths of common ancestry*). Jesus and his disciples give no credence to dietary and purity laws, honor and shame, and offer healing and the kingdom in exchange for a meal, an extension of their open commensality. Overall they are ignoring certain requirements of the Torah and what Judean ethnicity of the day required. Indeed, be it by accident or design, the borders are shifted whereby "sinners" and Gentiles can be included within the fellowship. Jesus and his followers are redefining Judean ethnic identity based on a spiritual, social and economic egalitarianism, that could potentially even include the traditional "outsiders."

Jesus and the Patriarchal Family

So how does radical egalitarianism affect the family? Of course, this concerns the cultural feature of *kinship*. Crossan initially refers to two traditions to answer this question (GThom 79:1–2; Luke 11:27–28; John 13:17; Jas 1:25 and GThom 99; Mark 3:19–21, 31–35 par.; *2 Clem.* 9:11; GEbion 5). It is not the womb who carried Jesus who is blessed, but those who do the will of God. Jesus further declares that it is his followers who are his real family (1991:299). Crossan also alludes to the tradition that Jesus said he was to bring not peace, but a sword (GThom 16; Luke 12:51–53 // Matt 10:34–36). Jesus was to bring division within families. But Crossan (1991:300) argues the point of this tradition is not about those who believe in Jesus and those who do not. "It is, just as in Micah 7:6, the normalcy of familial hierarchy that is under attack." The strife is between generations and in both directions. "Jesus will tear the hierarchical or patriarchal family in two along the axis of domination and subordination"[40] and "even more significant, is that the

---

40. Crossan (1991:262–63) understands egalitarianism as the elimination of all so-

division imagined cuts across sex and gender." The same point is made

cial distinctions (or ranking/class), discriminations and hierarchies. Here it is applied to the family. Borg understands Jesus along similar lines. One aspect of Borg's (1994:151) understanding of the historical Jesus is that he was a teacher of an "alternative wisdom." One area of that alternative wisdom undermined the conventional wisdom of the patriarchal family. Indeed, Jesus' anti-family sayings illustrate that Jesus was no champion of (patriarchal) family values. Borg (1994:107) maintains the "invitation was to break with the patriarchal family—an oppressive hierarchical structure mirroring the society as a whole."

Elliott has responded to such arguments, in particular against Crossan, that such an egalitarian reading of Jesus towards the family (and egalitarianism in general) is an idealist fallacy. It is an interpretation that appears more eisegesis than exegesis, an anachronistic reading of modern notions into the biblical texts (something which Crossan pre-emptively denied, as he claims egalitarianism was deeply rooted in peasant society). Jesus' invitation to abandon family, property, possessions, occupations, and protection, Elliott maintains, says nothing about the family as an institution in itself. It is simply the re-ordering of conventional priorities. "In these sayings Jesus issues no condemnation of the family as such. He only declares the biological family to be of secondary significance or indifference in light of the imminent commencement of God's reign" (Elliott 2002:78–79). Jesus did not require the elimination of loyalty to one's family altogether. Jesus and his disciples were offered hospitality by supporters located in stable, conventional households. "Many, if not most, did not renounce their homes, property, and possessions, but rather put them at the disposal of those on the move" (Elliott 2002:79). Jesus had a positive conception of the family as an institution, gave positive attention to it, and he used it as a model to define life under God's reign (cf Guijarro 2004:118) and overall, differences of age, gender, class and ethnicity remained as demarcations of identity and status and Jesus "urged conduct that would relativise but not eliminate such disparities" (Elliott 2002:85–86). The hallmark of the reign of God, the heavenly patriarch, was a "radical inclusivity" that "relativized all conventional lines of discrimination and exclusion," not a "radical egalitarianism" where the family and its structure of authority disappears (Elliott 2002:87). Jesus' formation of a surrogate family had a profound impact since it was the same model of communal life that was adopted by his followers after his death (Elliott 2003; cf Guijarro 2004:120).

So the essential difference between Crossan and Elliott is as follows: Crossan sees Jesus as eliminating authority and hierarchy, while for Elliott, these typical features remained—otherwise, their assessments have a lot in common actually; Jesus worked against social discrimination of various kinds. Guijarro brings another angle to the reason why Jesus broke ties with the family. Jesus and his disciples broke their family ties not to criticize patriarchal structures but to assume the lifestyle conditions of the peasantry, particularly landless peasantry. By becoming wandering beggars themselves, Guijarro (2004:117) suggests, they, as coming from a higher class, would have seemed more credible to peasants that lived in a similar situation in society where poverty meant the lack of family support. Guijarro (2004:116) also argues that the "success that Jesus' preaching had among peasant masses that followed him would be very difficult to explain if he had a clearly anti-familial attitude. The family was not only the basis of Israelite society, but also the main source of identity among individuals, so that an attack on the family would be interpreted as an attack on traditional societal values and on the Israelite religion."

Identifying the Problem

in the tradition about hating one's family (GThom 55:1–2; 101; Luke 14:25–26 // Matt 10:37). Thus by being against the patriarchal family Jesus' egalitarian vision extends to the family as well.

In Jesus' teaching against divorce (1 Cor 7:10–11; Luke 16:18 // Matt 5:31–32; Mark 10:10–12 par.; *Herm. Man.* 4.1:6, 10) sharp focus is brought to the honor of a wife. In Judean law at the time of Jesus, a wife was not allowed to initiate divorce proceedings, but more to the point, Jesus says against the norm that a man *can* commit adultery against the wife. The honor of the wife is to be as much protected as that of the husband. So it was not merely a teaching against divorce but an attack on androcentric honor. Its negative effects went far beyond divorce for it was the basis of the dehumanization of women, children, and non-dominant males. For Crossan (1991:302), "Jesus sets parents against children and wife against husband, sets, in other words, the Kingdom against the Mediterranean. But not just against the Mediterranean alone."

The breakdown of the patriarchal family also comes into play when Crossan's treats Jesus' relationship with his own hometown (Nazareth) and his family, especially his brothers (GThom 31 & POxy 1.31; Mark 6:1–6 par.; Luke 4:16–24; John 4:44). A prophet does not get honor from his own hometown and relatives. But Crossan does not see the tension as about belief in Jesus; it is about brokerage. Here we simply have Jesus' own experience of what he said about bringing division in families. Crossan (1991:347) argues that if Jesus "was a well-known magician, healer, or miracle worker, first, his immediate family, and, next, his village, would expect to benefit from and partake in the handling of that fame and those gifts. Any Mediterranean peasant would expect an expanding ripple of patronage-clientage to go out from Jesus ...in turning his back on Nazareth and on his family [Jesus repudiated] such brokerage...."

For our purposes, Crossan's interpretation allows for Jesus to be seen as again subverting or redefining Judean ethnic identity. For example, obligations to parents was a divine command. Kinship patterns, here the patriarchal family, crucial to social and ethnic identity, stands to be obliterated. If Crossan is understood correctly, a brokerless kingdom involves not a brokered ethnic family, but a brokerless spiritual family where all are regarded as equals.

Jesus and Inclusive Judeanism

Crossan (1991:417–18) insists that Jesus must be understood within his contemporary "Judaism," or rather, contemporary Judeanism. But as far as he is concerned, there was in the time of Jesus only one sort of Judeanism, namely Hellenistic Judeanism.[41] It was a Judeanism that responded to Greco-Roman culture. Crossan further distinguishes between *exclusive* and *inclusive* Judeanism, or between exclusive and inclusive reactions to Hellenism. By inclusive Judeanism Crossan understands a Judeanism "seeking to adapt its ancestral customs as liberally as possible with maximal association, combination, or collaboration with Hellenism on the ideological level" but he also admits that inclusivity "at its extreme, can mean abdication, betrayal, and disintegration" (Crossan 1991:418). Crossan also brings attention to the writings of Judeans and Gentiles and what they had to say about one another—it was not always nice reading, in both directions, but at times it was positive. It is on the latter that Crossan focuses on, specifically on two ideological issues, the understanding of God and the question of morality. Only the Judean writings that Crossan refers to will be discussed.

Crossan explains that in the *Letter of Aristeas* (latter second century BCE), it is explained that Judeans and pagans worship the same God, although under different names. And an unknown Judean, writing probably in Alexandria somewhere between 30 BCE and 40 CE, writes about adultery, homosexuality, and infanticide. The *Sentences of Pseudo-Pholyclides* speaks against those three issues, but for Crossan the Sentences are based on a more inclusive vision of Judeanism and paganism. Why? It presumes a superior ethic not only from exclusively Judean revelation but from natural law commonly available to all (Crossan 1991:419–20). Now Crossan proceeds by asking the following three intriguing questions:

> First, left to itself, what would have happened to the dialectic of exclusive and inclusive [Judeanism]? Second, left to itself, would [Judeanism] have been willing to compromise on, say, circumcision, in order to increase missionary possibilities among Greco-Roman pagans? Or, again, if paganism conceded on divinity and morality, could [Judeanism] have conceded on intereating and intermarrying? Third, left to itself, could [Judeanism] have converted the Roman Empire? . . . Moot questions because, of course, the process was not left to itself. Within sixty-five years, first in 70–73, next in 113–115, and finally in 132–135 C.E.,

---

41. For an overview of the influence and conflict with Hellenism, see chapter 3.

[Judeanism] in, respectively, Palestine, Egypt and its environs, and Palestine again, rose against Rome. (Crossan 1991:420)

The effects of these were of course the destruction of the temple in Jerusalem and Judea was proscribed to Judeans, and eventually, rabbinical Judeanism/Judaism emerged along with the ascendancy of exclusive over inclusive Judeanism/Judaism.

Now of relevance to us is that Crossan regards the questions he posed as important, since he interprets Jesus "against the background of inclusive rather than exclusive [Judeanism]," "a peasant, oral and popular praxis of what might be termed . . . a [Judean] Cynicism" (Crossan 1991:421). Crossan (1991:421) continues by saying it "involved practice and not just theory, life-style and not just mind-set in opposition to the cultural heart of Mediterranean civilization, a way of looking and dressing, of eating, living, and relating that announced its contempt for honor and shame, for patronage and clientage. They were hippies in a world of Augustan yuppies. Jesus and his followers . . . fit very well against *that* background" (emphasis original). Jesus was also closest to a magician-type figure, and in consequence, Crossan argues we are forced to bring together two disparate elements: healer and Cynic, magic and meal.

> The historical Jesus was, then, a *peasant [Judean] Cynic*. His peasant village was close enough to a Greco-Roman city like Sepphoris that sight and knowledge of Cynicism are neither inexplicable nor unlikely . . . His strategy, implicitly for himself and explicitly for his followers, was the combination of free healing and common eating, a religious and economic egalitarianism that negated alike and at once the hierarchical and patronal normalcies of [Judean] religion and Roman power . . . He was neither broker nor mediator . . . Miracle and parable, healing and eating were calculated to force individuals into unmediated physical and spiritual contact with God and unmediated physical and spiritual contact with one another. He announced, in other words, the brokerless kingdom of God. (Crossan 1991:421–22; emphasis original)

Crossan (1991:422) also argues that "Jesus, as a peasant [Judean] Cynic, was already moving, but on a popular level, within the ambience of inclusive [Judeanism's] synthesis of [Judean] and Gentile tradition." Unfortunately, Crossan does not give a comprehensive explanation of what inclusive or exclusive Judeanism involves. Was the former limited to matters of God and morality? And how did inclusive or exclusive

Judeanism actually operate in the real world, particularly in Galilee, and by whom?[42] And did both approaches qualify to be *equally* Judean in the first century? Crossan's reconstruction appears to estrange Jesus from first-century Judean ethnic identity in a dramatic way. Although Judeanism was influenced by Hellenism, it was very much geared at achieving the opposite than a synthesis of Judean and Gentile tradition (particularly when it came to crucial matters of *land, kinship, customs,* and *religion*). If Jesus' egalitarianism "negated alike and at once the hierarchical and patronal normalcies of [Judean] religion" then Jesus negated important aspects of Judean ethnic identity. Jesus is counter-cultural to various aspects of what the God of Israel traditionally required for covenant membership. The "Judean constitution," the Torah, Yahweh's gift to his people, is under attack. But Crossan's understanding of the situation of Nazareth here allows for an opposite conclusion. It was in proximity to a Greco-Roman city like Sepphoris, thereby locating Jesus within the ambience of an *inclusive* Judeanism. Jesus was socialized to become, ideologically, an inclusive Judean, not to be Torah-obedient as such. Jesus in a sense appears to be more "universally spiritual" and less Judean. Jesus does not want to fix what was "broken"[43]—he abandons primary Judean institutions altogether. He was a product of cultural continuity between rural and urban areas of Lower Galilee, itself part of the larger sea of Hellenism and the Roman Empire that gave opportunity for a synthesis between Judean and Gentile Hellenistic tradition.

Summary: John Dominic Crossan— Jesus, A Mediterranean "Jewish" Peasant

Crossan's reconstruction had very little that connected Jesus with traditional Judean ethnicity in the first century. (Of course, Crossan's

---

42. Crossan's understanding here of the cultural dynamics of Nazareth and Sepphoris and its "hellenized cultural traditions" is not strongly supported by the archaeological evidence. Sepphoris was certainly Hellenized in terms of its public architecture, form of government, and use of the Greek language. Public architecture is, of course, more instructive as to the ruler's cultural orientation than that of the ordinary people (Reed 2000:43). And generally, archaeological investigations have revealed that Sepphoris was overwhelmingly inhabited by Judeans (Chancey 2001; 2002:79–80). Reed (2000:135) also argues that theories of Greek education or Cynic philosophical schools at Sepphoris are implausible since the city was not home to a significant number of Romans or Greeks.

43. This statement must be understood quite liberally. It points to Jesus' apparent lack of willingness to be a reformer *within* Judean society and remaining *within* the Judean institutional order.

historical Jesus would stand in continuity with his notion of inclusive Hellenistic "Judaism.") Jesus appeared more as a peasant Mediterranean philosopher than a peasant Judean prophet or sage, and his Judean background is stretched very thin over the ethos of the Roman-Hellenistic empire. Where continuity exists is Jesus' faith in God, but not the God peculiar to Israel as such, since Greeks and Romans can also know God albeit under different names. Nazareth was also a Judean village, but it must be seen as in cultural continuity with Sepphoris and its Hellenized traditions. In addition, Jesus illustrates a strong community solidarity with socially marginalized Judeans, but one gets the impression this is ideologically not reserved for Judeans alone. There is an openness that could potentially even include the "sinners" and the Gentiles.

Besides the above, after Jesus was baptized by John, Jesus broke away from his eschatological message and concerned himself with the brokerless kingdom of God that is available in the present. It involves those people who place themselves under divine rule—it is not dependent on a nation or place. Jesus obviously had no concern of Judean hopes for ownership of the land.

Jesus challenged the legitimacy of the temple's spiritual power and engages in religious banditry. For Crossan, Jesus was a magician, personal and individual power in opposition to priest or rabbi as communal and ritual power. Through Jesus' healings/magic, he is placed on par or even above the authority of the temple, and he implicitly forgives the beneficiaries their sins. He touches lepers and makes them "clean," and so serves as an alternative or negation of the Mosaic purity regulations. The temple is seen as a source of victimization. For Jesus, the temple and priesthood are not divinely appointed institutions in need of restoration or the neccesary means by which covenant membership (= Judean ethnic identity) can be restored as prescribed in the Torah.

Overall, Jesus ignores purity rules. In his open commensality, Jesus shows he has no interest in making appropriate distinctions and discriminations. He negates the value of food taboos and table rituals. Judeans of different classes and sexes are free to eat together, their ritual status being irrelevant. In various ways, Jesus did not care about some aspects of the Law, which can be understood for our purposes as the "constitution" of Judean ethnic identity. Hence Jesus subverted Judean ethnic identity on more than one level.

When magic and meal come together, the "mission" of Jesus (and his followers) to enact the brokerless kingdom requires a peculiar dress code, in some ways similar (yet different) to Greco-Roman Cynicism.

Jesus and his followers are (barefoot?) itinerants as opposed to the localized temple. Jesus serves as the temple's functional opponent, alternative and its substitute—by implication, also to the Torah in some respects. When Jesus was in Jerusalem he symbolically destroyed it and said he would destroy it beyond repair. Jesus, therefore, saw no need for pilgrimage festivals, and commemorating the Exodus, Passover or other agricultural feasts, all in some way celebrating the redemptive history of Israel. The open commensality of Jesus also demonstrates that Jesus and his followers were redefining Judean ethnic identity based on a spiritual, social and economic egalitarianism.

Jesus was also against the brokered and patriarchal family. He brought division between the generations, and set a wife against her husband—similar tension Jesus experienced with his own family. Jesus sets up an alternative kinship pattern based on egalitarian principles.

Lastly, Jesus moved within the ambience of inclusive Hellenistic Judeanism's synthesis of Judean and Gentile tradition, a popular praxis that might be termed a Judean Cynicism. Unfortunately, Crossan does not give a detailed picture of what inclusive as opposed to exclusive Judeanism involved. In the very least, inclusive Judeanism recognized that it had common ground with some Gentile traditions, such as the understanding of God and questions of morality. Overall, Jesus is a peasant Judean Cynic, who sets the kingdom—a religious, social and economic egalitarianism not dependent on place or nation—in opposition to the Mediterranean and Judean ethos of honor and shame, patronage and clientage. The egalitarianism of Jesus negated at once the hierarchichal and patronal normalcies of Judean religion. The Judean "constitution," the Torah, particularly its ritual aspects, is under attack. Jesus appears to be "universally spiritual" and less Judean as such.

So if Jesus was a peasant Judean Cynic, a counter-cultural figure, what does that mean for Jesus' ethnic identity? Crossan by no means denies that Jesus was a Judean, yet his reconstruction with a very strong element of discontinuity with traditional Judeanism, does have some strong implications for Jesus' Judean identity. This we will investigate in further detail in chapter 2. A counter-cultural and Hellenized figure such as Jesus, in opposition to a hierarchical and brokered Judeanism as he was, needs to be analysed in terms of an overall interpretive framework or a guideline that more or less gives guidelines for a common Judeanism. If such a guideline is in place, only then will it be possible to determine what kind of Judean Crossan's Jesus really was.

Identifying the Problem

The problems identified above with Meier and Crossan's reconstructions exist generally in the so-called "Third Quest." As already mentioned, it is supposed that one of the characteristic traits of the "Third Quest" is to place emphasis on the "Jewishness," or rather Judeaness of Jesus. It also generally wants to place Jesus *within* Judeanism and to view him as properly integrated into the Judeanism of his day. Thus the "Third Quest" emphasizes the *continuity* between Jesus and his environment and assumes him to be an integral part of it (Du Toit 2001:100–109; Harrington 1987). Holmén (2001:150) explains that the "Third Quest" is distinguished from earlier phases of Jesus research "by viewing Jesus as profoundly [Judean], properly integrated into the [Judeanism] of his time." But he also notes that on closer examination, such a view "reveals that there are some intricate difficulties involved here." He is especially referring to the view that has developed over the past few decades that there was no orthodox Judeanism in Jesus' day. Judeanism was formative, or dynamic, and there was an almost unlimited diversity and variety, or that pluralism was commonplace. Holmén (2001:152–53) has noted the paradox: "We can actually determine what is 'profoundly [Judean]' only if we use some kind of 'normative [Judeanism]' as a yardstick." He further argues the "*crucial problem of the 'Third Quest' seems to be that it is not the least clear what [*Judeanness'*] means*. Indeed, judged on the basis of different scholarly pictures of Jesus it can mean almost anything" (Holmén 2001:154; emphasis added). So to talk about Jesus' Judeanness has become widespread, but it is something quite void of real meaning. It is "not much more than a slogan which leaves the impression of representing something good and enlightened but under the veil of which many things can happen" (Holmén 2001:157). Harrington (1987:8) has also argued that our increased understanding of Judeanism's diversity "has made it even more difficult to be sure precisely what kind of [Judean] Jesus was and against which historical background we should try to understand him."

Holmén (2001:158–59) suggests that it is possible to focus the analysis of the data on different elements, namely, on "what is common and what unites, and what is different and what separates." By utilising these two features, "*we arrive at different definitions of [Judeanism] not to be seen as mutually exclusive but as complementary and purpose-orientated*" (emphasis original). Holmén then draws attention to the strategies of "nominalism" and "essentialism." Nominalism accounts for the differences on Judeanism. Essentialism looks at common characteristics of Judeanism, such as core belief and foundational metaphor, monotheism, covenant and ethnic exclusivism, and so on. Holmén (2001:160) suggests that for Jesus-of-history research, "essentialism" is the appropriate strategy, although he does not find the term all that satisfying. He refers to scholars who in their own way have attempted to set some guidelines for something like basic or common Judeanism; i.e. Dunn (the "four pillars"—see next chapter), Sanders ("covenantal nomism"— see next chapter) and Wright ("mainline," explained through the study of worldview, beliefs and hope). Holmén goes on to explain:

> The guidelines for basic or common [Judeanism] would not question the diversity of first-century [Judeanism], neither would they question Jesus' [Judeaness]. But the guidelines would enable us meaningfully to evaluate just how he was [Judean] by justifying the positing of pictures of Jesus varying from the commonly [Judean] to the marginally [Judean]. We could again assess whether Jesus was, for example, profoundly [Judean] or a 'different kind of [Judean].' (Holmén 2001:161)

Following Holmén's lead we will have a look at Dunn and Sanders' attempts at establishing guidelines for a "common Judaism," or rather, "common Judeanism," and eventually their work will be integrated into a proposed model, drawing inspiration from Duling's (2005) Socio-Cultural Model of Ethnicity. Duling's generic model, amongst other things, lists the cultural features to look out for when analysing the ethnic identity of a particular group of people (i.e. *name, myths of common ancestry, shared "historical" memories, phenotypical features, land, language, kin, customs,* and *religion*).

There are scholars who are of the opinion that we cannot even speak of a "common Judaism/Judeanism." We should rather speak of "Judaisms"/Judeanisms. For example, Chilton and Neusner (1995) argue that there was no single orthopraxy or law that governed life of all "Jews." The work such as produced by Dunn and Sanders is also criticized in that it focuses only on a small selection of theological elements that are claimed to be constitutive of "Jewish" identity. The argument for a "common Judeanism" is developed in the next chapter, but for now it can be asked is the absolute insistence on "Judaisms"/Judeanisms not taking the ancient data to an unnecessary extreme?[44] It is agreed that

---

44. We can elaborate on this by making the following contrast. One can speak of "Judaisms/Judeanisms" as you can speak of "Christianities." Perhaps it is possible then to speak of a "common Christianity," as Christians share many common beliefs and

the approaches of Dunn and Sanders are limited, something which they themselves admit (see next chapter), but it is argued here that their aim is warranted and their different approaches which concentrate on a few "theological" issues and on what is common and what unite are a step in the right direction. Ethnicity theory informs us that religion is one cultural feature that contributes towards ethnic identity. In addition, in pre-modern eras a distinctive religion or vision of a world religion proved to be a very strong force in the persistence of ethnic identity (Smith 1994:716). The notions of Israel's God (monotheism), his election of Israel and gift of the Law, adherence to the temple and the requirement to obey so as to maintain covenant status, elements variously emphasized by Dunn and Sanders respectively, most certainly qualify as a distinctive religion or vision of a religion. These elements were widely shared and Judeans for the greater part had far more in common than what divided them (cf. Stegemann & Stegemann 1999:149–50).

The above suggests that if we approach first century Judaism, or rather, first century *Judeanism* as an *ethnic identity* (cf. Cohen 1999:7; Stegemann 2006), not merely as a loose collectivity of differing religious persuasions, the potential does exist that we can speak of a "common Judaism/Judeanism." In this respect the more "theological" even if limited approach of Dunn and Sanders give us a good starting point. This does not eliminate the reality of diversity within "Judaism"/Judeanism. Even so, the overwhelming majority of "Jews"/Judeans (being peasant farmers living in villages and towns) were not members of any religious sect and would have adhered to the basics of "Jewish"/Judean religion

practices. By contrast, however, first century "Judaism"/Judeanism was something that present day Christianity is not—it was an *ethnic identity*, a unique cultural entity in addition to being a religious identity. And what Chilton and Neusner write of a particular "Judaism" can equally apply to "Judaism"/Judeanism as an ethnic identity. They speak of three necessary components of a religious system, e.g. of a specific "Judaism": 1) way of life; 2) worldview; and 3) a theory of the social entity. So when it comes to "a Judaism," "a Judaic theory of the social order will always call its social entity 'Israel,' invariably will appeal to the Torah, and inevitably will link the main propositions of the theory to the Torah, whether through explicit, verbal exegesis, or through gestures or actions or rites that mirror or mimic those of the Torah, or through other media of cultural continuity ... The way of life of a Judaism finds its critical task in mediating between a way of living deemed natural and broadly accepted [!] and the special traits of the distinct social entity, that is, in defining 'we' as against 'they'" (Chilton & Neusner 1995:42–43). But we must ask why this cannot be applied to all or most "Jews"/Judeans as a distinct social entity, whose participants in most respects had "a way of living deemed natural and broadly accepted" and a common worldview derived from the Torah, and who would call their social entity Israel. Ethnicity theory (see pp. 81–88 below) in this regard also speaks of a "we" *aggregative* self-definition (and a "we-they" *oppositional* self-definition).

and culture common to all. But be they priests, Pharisees, Essenes, Sadducees, or peasant farmers, their wives and children included, they all would have been recognized—both from without and within—as "Jews"/Judeans, whether they had marginal status or not. We are speaking here of a collectivity of people who expressed their identity through a widely shared religion, but in addition to this, also a shared ancestry and history, customs, kinship, and attachment to the ancestral land of Israel.

The focus will therefore now shift to develop a socio-cultural model of Judean ethnicity where the above mentioned elements will feature prominently. It is proposed that by developing a model, it can shed some light on what "common Judeanism" actually constituted. This is also essential to the thesis presented here since the eventual aim is to analyse the Judean ethnicity of Jesus' early followers as presupposed by the source Q. How did being a follower of Jesus affect your Judean ethnic identity? And how did they compare to the "common" or "essentialist" ethnic identity of the greater mass of Judeans of their day? We can also gain better insight into what kind of Judean Jesus was himself. As Holmén points out, there is not really a clear idea of what being "Jewish"/Judean meant in the first century, and it is on this important issue that we will focus our energy in the next chapter.

CHAPTER 2

A Socio-Cultural Model of Judean Ethnicity

Introduction

DENNIS DULING (2005) recently developed a Socio-Cultural Model of Ethnicity (see pp. 93–98 below). This model serves as a guide in two ways: 1) it lists what cultural features to look out for and 2) defines the processes that are behind ethnic identity formation. Both aspects illuminate our understanding of what a particular ethnic identity may involve. This chapter is dedicated to adapting Duling's generic model in order for it to serve as a guide when assigning content to *Judean* ethnic identity. In other words, the model must help us answer: What did it mean, broadly speaking, to be Judean? This model, it is suggested here, will help in some way as to what "common Judeanism" involved. This "common Judeanism" serves as a point of centre so to speak, to which any form of deviance or differentiation can be compared (e.g., the Pharisees, Essenes, and Sadducees; cf. Josephus, *Ant.* 18.11–25; *War* 2.119–66). In particular, the model can also help us understand Messianist Judean identity, as it developed, was lived out and expressed by the early followers of Jesus. Later on, we will specifically concentrate on the community presupposed by Q. So as already intimated, a model of Judean ethnicity can be helpful on various levels. It can be used as a guide for understanding mainstream or common Judean ethnic identity, while it may also be used to investigate or compare the ethnic identity of various forms sectarian Judeanism.

Attempts have already been made to help define what was essential to Judeanism. At first we will have a look at Sanders' "covenantal nomism," and then at Dunn's "four pillars of Second Temple Judaism/Judeanism." In what is to follow the aim will be to demonstrate that although both these approaches tell us a lot about Judeanism, they do not tell us everything about what it meant to be a Judean. They in particular lack the insights of ethnicity theory (which will be discussed later) and generally focus more on the "religious" aspects, while other aspects of ethnic identity—such as *land, kinship, myths of common ancestry,* and *shared "historical" memories*—are not given the same prominence it deserves.

Covenantal Nomism

Arguably, Sanders' notion of covenantal nomism has revolutionized our understanding of Palestinian "Judaism" (hereafter "Judeanism"). For a first-century "Jew" (hereafter "Judean"), Israel's covenant relationship with God was basic, basic that is to the Judean's sense of national identity and the understanding of his/her religion. Sanders (1992:262) explains that "covenant" stands for God's grace in election ("getting in"), and "nomism" stands for the requirement of obedience to the law ("staying in"). Otherwise, Sanders explains covenantal nomism as follows: "(1) God has chosen Israel and (2) given the law. The law implies both (3) God's promise to maintain the election and (4) the requirement to obey. (5) God rewards obedience and punishes transgression. (6) The law provides for means of atonement, and atonement results in (7) maintenance or re-establishment of the covenantal relationship. (8) All those who are maintained in the covenant by obedience, atonement and God's mercy belong to the group which will be saved." He adds: "An important interpretation of the first and last points is that election and ultimately salvation are considered to be God's mercy rather than human achievement" (Sanders 1977:422). Importantly, the emphasis is on *maintaining* your covenant relationship with God—obedience to the Law was not thought of as a means of *entering* or *attaining* a special relationship with God. Dunn (1990:186) quotes Sanders' work in the following convenient manner in that covenantal nomism

> is the view that one's place in God's plan is established on the basis of the covenant and that the covenant requires as the proper response of man his obedience to its commandments, while providing means of atonement for transgression ... *Obedience maintains one's position in the covenant, but it does not earn God's grace as such* ... Righteousness in [Judeanism] is a term which implies the maintenance of status among the group of the elect. (Sanders 1977:75, 420, 544)

Viewed from the perspective of ethnic identity, we can paraphrase/modify the above quote as follows: Covenantal nomism is the view that one's place in God's plan is established on the basis of the covenant, a covenant which in itself established Judean (or Israelite) ethnicity (= status of divine election). The covenant requires as the proper response from a Judean his/her obedience to the commandments, which will maintain his/her position as a (righteous) Judean within the covenant. Alternatively, the covenant provides also for means of atonement for transgression to maintain his/her status as a (righteous) Judean within the covenant. Righteousness in Judeanism is a term which implies the maintenance of status as a Judean among fellow Judeans who are the elect people of God.

Thus in broad terms one may suggest that covenantal nomism properly explains who is an ethnic Judean and who is not, and how it came to be that way. Here it is understood primarily in *religious* terms, however, since covenantal nomism is equivalent to divine election or "righteousness," or the maintenance of status in the sight of Yahweh. At the same time, Sanders admits that covenantal nomism does not cover the entirety of Judean theology or the entirety of Judeanism.

> It deals with the theological understanding of the constitution of God's people: how they get that way, how they stay that way. In terms of [Judeanism] as a religion, this leaves out a lot of details of what people did, though it requires analysis of why they thought that they *should* do what they did . . . What it covers . . . is crucial for understanding [Judeanism], which is a national religion and way of life, focused on the God of Israel and the people of Israel: God called them; being [Judean] consists of responding to that call. (Sanders 1992:262–63; emphasis original)

From all of the above we can infer that covenantal nomism involves the existence of a two-way relationship. God called a particular people and in that process established a constitution or charter (= covenant as expressed through the Torah) of Judean ethnic identity. The people elected must respond to that call, and so give expression to that ethnic identity through obedience to the constitution. Differently put, God established Judean ethnic identity. A group of people respond(ed) by being Judean, in whatever way was deemed necessary. For our purposes therefore it seems appropriate to redefine covenantal nomism as an *ethnic descriptor*. Seen from this view, we can speak of covenantal nomism as defining a "common Judeanism," where its religious or theological aspects become part of a greater whole. This also avoids the pitfall of "Judaisms/Judeanisms." Thus covenantal nomism, when redefined as an ethnic descriptor, can be understood as encapsulating the Judean "symbolic universe," containing more or less everything that typified Judean ethnic identity. Covenantal nomism was the Judean social construction of reality, a reality that took shape over several centuries of development. In the chapters to follow the focus will be on how covenantal nomism *as an ethnic identity* was interpreted and understood and what the "popular opinion" dictated in terms of how it should be given expression in every day life. The point is this: the redefined covenantal nomism as outlined above called into being, contained, shaped and defined Judean ethnicity. Also, on an anthropological and more concrete level, covenantal nomism *is* Judean ethnic identity—certain people translated that symbolic universe into everyday living. For the present purposes redefined covenantal nomism and Judean ethnicity are virtually synonymous in meaning.

Covenantal Nomism as a "Symbolic Universe"

The notion of the "symbolic universe" is drawing on the insights of Berger & Luckmann (1966). To begin with, human beings exist within a social order, but it is a result of human production in the course of ongoing human externalization. This process occurs within the context of social interaction. All human activity is subject to habitualization. Habitualized actions produce institutions, which typify both individual actors and individual actions. As such, it forms "knowledge." As these institutions or knowledge are passed on from generation to generation, it acquires an objective quality: "This is the way that things are done," or, put in another way, it becomes the social construction of reality. This objective reality confronts the individual and into which a child is socialized into. As such it is perceived an external reality that exists outside of the individual.

> An institutional world, then, is experienced as an objective reality. It has a history that antedates the individual's birth and is not accessible to his biographical recollection. It was there before he was born, and it will be there after his death. (Berger & Luckmann 1966:60)

The important thing, however, is "that the relationship between man, the producer, and the social world, his product, is and remains a dialectical one . . . The product acts back upon the producer" (Berger

& Luckmann 1966:61). Thus externalization and objectification is followed by internalization. "*Society is a human product. Society is an objective reality. Man is a social product*" (Berger & Luckmann 1966:61; emphasis original). In this manner "objective truths," which were established based on historical processes, are passed on from generation to generation in the course of socialization and so becomes internalized as subjective reality.

> Externalization is the ongoing outpouring of human being into the world, both in the physical and the mental activity of men. Objectification is the attainment by the products of this activity (again both physical and mental) of a reality that confronts its original producers as a facticity external to and other than themselves. Internalization is the reappropriation by men of this same reality, transforming it once again from structures of the objective world into structures of the subjective consciousness. It is through externalization that society is a human product. It is through objectification that society becomes a reality *sui generis*. It is through internalization that a man is a product of society. (Berger 1973:14)

The institutional order requires legitimation if it is to be transmitted to a new generation. "Legitimation not only tells the individual why he *should* perform one action and not another; it also tells him why things *are* what they are. In other words, 'knowledge' precedes 'values' in the legitimation of institutions" (Berger & Luckmann 1966:94; emphasis original). One means of legitimation is where the entire institutional order is placed within a "symbolic universe." A symbolic universe is where

> *all* the sectors of the institutional order are integrated in an all-embracing frame of reference, which now constitutes a universe in the literal sense of the word, because *all* human experience can now be conceived of as taking place *within* it. The symbolic universe is conceived of as the matrix of *all* socially objectivated and subjectively real meanings; the entire historic society and the entire biography of the individual are seen as events taking place *within* this universe. (Berger & Luckmann 1966:96; emphasis original)

This universe is constructed by the means of social objectivations, "yet its meaning bestowing capacity far exceeds the domain of social life, so that the individual may 'locate' himself within it even in his most solitary experiences" (Berger & Luckmann 1966:96).

The commonalities between the redefined notion of covenantal nomism *as an ethnic identity* and the idea behind the symbolic universe can immediately be perceived. Judeanism was quite distinct in its worldview. As Sanders (1992:50) explains: "It attempted to bring the entirety of life under the heading, 'Divine Law' [for our purposes read: it attempted to bring all human experience into a Judean symbolic universe or covenantal nomism]. As a religion, it was not strange because it included sacrifices, but because it included ethical, family and civil law as well." Having been spared the modern reality of secularization, all aspects of Judean life were permeated with the divine and had a deeper significance. All aspects of life were under God and should be lived in accordance with God's will (cf. Josephus, *Apion* 2.170–73). For Judeans, there was no differentiation between "ritual" and "ethics," between religious, social and economic dynamics of life, as God gave all the commandments and obedience to his will required equal obedience to all. For example, the treatment of one's neighbor[1] was just as important as eating food accidentally that should have gone to the priest or altar (cf. Sanders 1992:194–95). When seen within the context of covenantal nomism as a symbolic universe, for some Roman rule (and control of the temple hierarchy) was intolerable; others accepted it as long as the temple rites were not interfered with beyond a reasonable point.

Importantly, symbolic universes are social products with a history. "If one is to understand their meaning, one has to understand the history of their production" (Berger & Luckmann 1966:98). For first-century Palestinian Judeanism, the character of its symbolic universe was primarily shaped by Israel's relationship with the *land*. They lost the land through the Babylonian exile. They regained it, but only partially, as they remained under foreign domination for most of their history. But it was the Babylonian exile that provided the background for the shaping of the Torah, the primary reference for the Judean symbolic universe. The land was theirs as a perpetual inheritance, but it was the sins of Israel that caused them to lose control of it. Obedience and holiness was required, and along with hopes of restoration, as given through the prophets, it existed as important parts of that universe. The Judean symbolic universe could only become complete by Israel's obedience, restoration and ownership of the land.

---

1. One can mention here the importance that alms-giving was supposed to have had in our period (Ps 112:9 cited in 2 Cor 9:9; Dan 4:27; Sir 29:12; 40:24; Tob 4:10; 12:9; 14:10–11) (cf. Dunn 1991:129).

The symbolic universe is also nomic, or ordering in character. Everything is placed into its proper place, which also facilitates the formation of individual identity. This identity is dependant on the person's relationship with significant others, and the identity "is ultimately legitimated by placing it within the context of a symbolic universe" (Berger & Luckmann 1966:100). The latter is a "sheltering canopy" wherein both the institutional order and individual biography can be placed. It also provides the delimitation of social reality. It sets the limits to what is relevant in terms of social interaction. "The symbolic universe assigns ranks to various phenomena in a hierarchy of being, defining the range of the social within this hierarchy" (Berger & Luckmann 1966:102). Now in Judean society, this hierarchy of being was objectified in things such as the patriarchal family (cf. Guijarro 2001) and the purity order which was symbolized by the temple's architecture (Schmidt 2001:32–33). In terms of the latter, the priests who function in the temple have the highest degree of purity, then comes the laity and proselytes. These, however, contracted various forms impurity which nevertheless could be removed. At the bottom are those permanently "impure" (e.g., sinners and those with various bodily defects or ailments), and entirely outside of this order are the Gentiles. Berger & Luckmann (1966:103) also explain that the

> symbolic universe also orders history. It locates all collective events in a cohesive unity that includes past, present and future. With regard to the past, it establishes a "memory" that is shared by all the individuals socialized within the collectivity. With regard to the future, it establishes a common frame of reference for the projection of individual actions. Thus the symbolic universe links men with their predecessors and their successors in a meaningful totality ... All the members of a society can now conceive of themselves as *belonging* to a meaningful universe, which was there before they were born and will be there after they die (emphasis original).

Naturally, once symbolic universes come into being, they require to be maintained. Various universe-maintenance procedures can be used. This is especially necessary when a society is confronted with another society with its own history. Here an alternative symbolic universe comes into focus, with its own official traditions, which may judge your own universe as ignorant, mad or the like. "The alternative universe presented by the other society must be met with the best possible reasons for the superiority of one's own" (Berger & Luckmann 1966:108). As we shall see in the next chapter, this is especially true of Judeanism in its confrontation with Hellenism. Universe-maintenance can employ mythology, or more developed mythologies develop into more systematic theologies—Judeanism case in point!

Universe-maintenance also employs therapy and nihilation.

> Therapy entails the application of conceptual machinery to ensure that actual or potential deviants stay within the institutionalized definitions of reality, or, in other words, to prevent the 'inhabitants' of a given universe from 'emigrating' . . . This requires a body of knowledge that includes a theory of deviance, a diagnostic apparatus, and a conceptual system for the 'cure of souls.' (Berger & Luckmann 1966:113)

One is reminded here of the Judean sacrificial cult and the practice of ritual immersion, where any form of deviance (sin or impurity) can be rectified. In this manner Judeans could maintain their position within the covenant, or the Judean symbolic universe. "Nihilation, in its turn," is to "liquidate conceptually everything outside the same universe . . . nihilation denies the reality of whatever phenomena or interpretations of phenomena [that] do not fit into that universe" (Berger & Luckmann 1966:114). There are two ways in which this can be done. First, the phenomena are afforded a negative ontological status. It is regarded as inferior and should not be taken seriously. Second, deviant phenomena are grappled with theoretically in terms of concepts belonging to your own universe. Both these examples of nihilation are evident in Judeanism and are mutually complimentary. Gentile ways are regarded as inferior. They are guilty of idolatry and sexual immorality, in short, of "lawlessness." They are not part of the Judean symbolic universe, not divinely elected, ignorant of God's law, impure,[2] and in some texts described as bereft of the truth.

The last element of the symbolic universe we will discuss here is its maintenance by "experts." As more complex forms of knowledge appear, "they claim ultimate jurisdiction over that stock of knowledge in its totality." These universal experts "claim to know the ultimate significance of what everybody knows and does" (Berger & Luckmann 1966:117). Now one of the consequences "is a strengthening of traditionalism in the institutionalized actions thus legitimated, that is, a strengthening of

---

2. Gentiles originally were not rated according to the degrees of purity, but as things developed, they were afforded an "impure status" due to their presence within the ancestral land of Israel. For more on this, see chapter 3.

the inherent tendency of institutionalization toward inertia" (Berger & Luckmann 1966:117). The Judean parallel is obvious in the existence of the priesthood and their control of the temple and scribal training in the law. Other "expert groups" also appeared, such as the Pharisees and Essenes for example.

The above was to illustrate how easily the redefined understanding of covenantal nomism can be understood as the Judean symbolic universe. It was the Judean social construction of reality that had to be maintained in the face of historical developments and Hellenistic and Roman ideology. Covenantal nomism was therefore also the legitimation of Judean ethnic identity, where all Judean institutions, practices and beliefs were placed within the context of an all-embracing frame of reference. Within this universe people were told why they *should* do the things they did and why things *are* what they are. It bestowed meaning onto its "inhabitants," ordered reality into its proper place, and connected the "inhabitants" with its history, ancestors, and future generations and events.

The Four Pillars of Second Temple Judeanism

Another attempt at establishing a "common Judeanism," or to identify what was essential to Judeanism, was formulated by Dunn. Dunn (2003:281) takes into account the factionalism that existed in first-century Judeanism, but he also says "there was a common foundation of practice and belief which constituted the . . . common factors unifying all the different particular forms of first-century [Judeanism] and on which they were built." Dunn (1991:18–36; 2003:287–92) in particular speaks, using our own terminology, of the "four pillars of Second Temple Judeanism." These include the temple, God, election, and Torah, although Dunn admits that this is not a complete characterization of Judeanism. Here follows Dunn's proposal in abbreviated form.

Temple

The land of Israel was focused in the temple. Dunn (2003:287) maintains that there "can be no doubt that the temple was the central focus of Israel's national and religious life prior to its destruction in 70 CE. Judea was a temple state." The temple was 1) a *political* center, the basis for the high priest and high priestly families; 2) an *economic* center, where the daily sacrifices and offerings were made and which required the payment of the annual temple tax. It was also the focal point of the three main pilgrimage festivals; and 3) a *religious* center, the place where God had chosen to put his name, the focal point for an encounter between the divine and the human, as well as the sacrificial cult on which human well-being and salvation depended (Dunn 1991:31–35). As Dunn (2003:287) observes, it was "a primary identity marker of Israel the covenant people." In the Roman period "Jew," or rather Judean, was as much a religious identifier as an ethnic identifier since it focused identity in Judea, the state that depended on the status of Jerusalem as the location of the temple. The disputes and renunciations relating to the temple attest to its importance on how it should function correctly.

God

"Belief in God," Dunn (2003:288) explains, "as one and in God's unimage-ableness was certainly fundamental to the first-century [Judean]." The *Shema* was probably said by most Judeans on a regular basis (Deut 6:4, 7) testifying to the unity of God (*Ant.* 5.1, 27, 112). Little of this is apparent upon the surface of late Second Temple Judeanism simply because it was not a matter for controversy and so could be taken for granted. Judeans were exclusive monotheists and Judean literature gives testimony of strong attacks on pagan, or rather Gentile idolatry (e.g., WisSol 11–15; *Sib. Or.* 3:8–45). We need to recall Josephus' report of violent reaction from the people when Pilate brought in standards regarded as idolatrous into Jerusalem (*Ant.* 18.55–59) and the attempt of Caligula to have a statue of himself set up within the temple (*Ant.* 18.261–72).

Election

Election points to two features in particular: Israel as a covenant people and the promised land. "Equally fundamental was Israel's self-understanding of itself as the people of God specially chosen from among all the nations of the world to be his own" (Dunn 2003:289). This selection formed a mutual attachment between God and Israel through the covenant. This conviction was already there in pre-exilic times where the ancient stories recall the choice of Abraham and the promise of the land (Gen 12:1–3; 15:1–6; 17:1–8; Deut 7:6–8; 32:8–9), a promise that was fulfilled by the rescue from Egypt (Deut 6:20–25; 26:5–10).

Election became a central category of self-definition in the post-exilic period onwards (Ezra 9–10). It was the foundational motivation to resist Hellenistic syncretism in the Maccabean crisis, and "it constantly came to expression in the compulsive desire to maintain distinct and separate identity from the other nations" (cf. *Jub.* 15:30–32; 22:16) (Dunn 2003:289). So opposed to Hellenism stood "Judeanism" (Ἰουδαϊσμός; 2 Macc 2:21; 8:1; 14:38), a term that made its appearance around the time of the Maccabean revolt, and it "bears a clear overtone from its first usage of a fierce nationalistic assertion of Israel's election and of divine right to religious (if not national) freedom in the land given it by God" (Dunn 1991:22). This separation from the nations lies behind the everyday preoccupation with purity, which is also attested by the more than 300 ritual baths (*miqva'ot*) dating from the Roman period uncovered by archaeology in Judea, Galilee and the Golan. Related to this are the strict laws of clean and unclean at the meal table (Lev 20:24–26; Acts 10:10–16, 28). Thus election was closely linked to the other pillars, since "it expressed itself in fear of contamination by Gentile idolatry, and in the conviction that the holiness of Israel (land and people) was dependent on the holiness of the Temple (hence the prohibition which prevented Gentiles from passing beyond the court of Gentiles in the Temple area)" (Dunn 2003:290).

Torah

The Torah was the focus of the covenant. The Torah (the first five books of Moses) had been given to Israel as a mark of God's favor and choice of Israel. It was an integral part of God's covenant with Israel, to show its people how to live as the people of God (Deuteronomy), or to put it in another way, the commandments spell out Israel's covenant obligations. They were the people of the law/covenant, an identity that was at stake during the Maccabean crisis (1 Macc 1:57; 2:27, 50; 2 Macc 1:2–4; 2:21–22; 5:15; 13:14). So understandably the watchword for national resistance during that period was "zeal for the law" (1 Macc 2:26–27, 50, 58; 2 Macc 4:2; 7:2, 9, 11, 37; 8:21). So too in the period following the Maccabean crisis, the close relationship between election, covenant and law remained a fundamental theme of Judean self-understanding (Sir 17:11–17; 39:8; *Jub.* 1:4–5; 2:21; 6:4–16; 15; 22:15–16; 23:19; *Pss. Sol.* 10:4; *L.A.B.* 9:7–8; 23:10; 30:2; 35:2–3). So generally there was a common pattern of "covenantal nomism" characteristic of Judeanism in our period (Dunn 1991:24–25).

Because of the law, great emphasis was placed on Israel's *distinctiveness* as a chosen people. It was also the Torah that served as the boundary separating Israel from other nations (*Jub.* 22:16; *Let. Aris.*

139, 142; Philo, *Moses* 1.278) by its insistence on the maintenance of the purity code (Lev 20:24–26; cf. Dan 1:8–16)—it served as an "identity marker." The Gentiles were "without the law, outside the law," and so were equated with being "sinners" (1 Macc 2:44, 48; Tob 13:6 [LXX 8]; *Jub.* 23:23–4; *Pss. Sol.* 1:1; 2:1–2; 17:22–5). With this sense of distinctiveness came a sense of *privilege*; the Judeans were the nation specially chosen by God and were favored by the gift of the covenant and law. With this came a somewhat exaggerated pride, as Gentiles were attracted to Judean customs (Philo, *Moses* 2.17–25; Josephus, *Apion* 2.277–286) and the law was understood to be the embodiment of divine Wisdom. This sense of privilege gave rise to perplexity as *4 Ezra* (3:28–36; 4:23–4; 5:23–30; 6:55–9) could not understand how God can spare the sinful nations yet be so harsh with his law-keeping people (Dunn 1991:25–28).

The Torah, the definitive element of the Scriptures, also served as both school textbook and law of the land so "we may assume a substantial level of respect and observance of its principal regulations within common [Judeanism]" (Dunn 2003:291). It is also important not think of the Torah as exclusively religious documents since we have to recognize the interlocking nature of Israel as a religio-national entity. Because of the centrality of the Torah, it would also feature in the divisions within Judeanism, a competitive dispute as to what it meant in practice (i.e. how to calculate feast days, the right maintenance of purity, food laws and Sabbath were the usual flash points). So all would have agreed that they need to live according to the principles of "covenantal nomism," and any group's claim that it alone was doing so effectively denied that others did (Dunn 2003:292).

Judean Customs as Covenantal Praxis

In addition to the four pillars discussed above, it is to Dunn's credit that he realized the importance of customs or ritual practices to Judean self-understanding. In his studies on Paul's attitude towards the Law in Galatians, Dunn has drawn on Sanders' notion of covenantal nomism and developed what is known now as a "new perspective." Paul, as Dunn explains, was not opposing a legalistic works-righteousness (e.g., see Ridderbos 1975:139–40) when some Judean Messianists insisted on Gentiles undergoing circumcision or when they withdrew from having table-fellowship with them (Gal 2). Paul was opposing specific covenant works, or "works of the law," namely circumcision and food laws. Why? Because "*these observances were widely regarded as characteristically and distinctively [Judean]*. Writers like Petronius,[3] Plutarch,[4] Tacitus[5] and Juvenal[6] took it for granted that, in particular, circumcision, abstention from pork, and the Sabbath, were observances which marked out the practitioners as [Judeans], or as people who were very attracted to [Judean] ways" (Dunn 1990:191–92; emphasis original). Dunn (1990:192) continues in that

> these observances in particular functioned as identity markers, they served to identify their practitioners as [Judean] in the eyes of the wider public, they were peculiar rites which marked out the [Judeans] as that particular people … These identity markers identified [Judeanness] because they were seen by the [Judeans] themselves as fundamental observances of the covenant. They functioned as badges of covenant membership.[7]

We can paraphrase that last sentence to say that these observances, or examples of Judean customs, were badges of Judean ethnic identity. That is why Peter and Barnabas withdrew from table-fellowship with Gentiles. They could not resist that strong appeal to national identity

---

3. Cf. Petronius, *Satyricon* 102.14; *Fragmenta* 37 on circumcision.

4. Cf. Plutarch, *Quaestiones Conviviales* 4.5; where he has a discussion on why Judeans do not eat pork.

5. Cf. Tacitus (*Hist.* 5.4) on the Sabbath. Tacitus writes on circumcision: "They adopted circumcision to distinguish themselves from other peoples by this difference" (*Hist.* 5.5.2). That Tacitus understands circumcision to be quite characteristic of Judeans should be noted for many other peoples (Samaritans, Arabs and Egyptians) also practiced circumcision.

6. Cf. Juvenal (*Sat.* 6.160; 14.98) on abstention from pork and on the Sabbath (*Sat.* 14.96–106).

7. Smiles (2002) has criticized Dunn's understanding of the Judean "zeal" for the Law in that he places too much emphasis on "Israel's distinctiveness" and the Law's social function as an "identity" and "boundary" marker, that is, too keep Gentiles out. What Paul primarily opposes was not "separatism," but "activism," the belief that law-observance is constitutive of the covenant. "Separatism was for the sake of obedience [to the Law]; the reverse was never true" (Smiles 2002:298). It must be said that Dunn does not neglect to mention that zeal or law-observance was important for participation in the covenant. But attention needs to be drawn to the following: "activism" and "separatism" were more often than not opposite ends of the same coin. Ethnic identity (see below) is usually both *oppositional* in nature (= "separatism") and about internal cultural content (= "activism"). This is especially true in circumstances of cultural contact between two groups or cultures, and especially where the one culture is under threat. Since Judeanism was under threat for most of its history, obedience to the Law was as much for the sake of separatism as the reverse was true.

and covenant faithfulness. These customs defined the boundaries of the covenant people (or Judean ethnic identity), that is why one could hardly claim to be a good Judean without observing these minimal observances. As Dunn explains, for a typical Judean of the first century CE, "*it would be virtually impossible to conceive of participation in God's covenant* [or read *Judean ethnic identity*], *and so in God's covenant righteousness, apart from these observances, these works of the law*" (1990:193; emphasis original). So what Paul was opposing was something like Sanders' notion of covenantal nomism, understood as where God's grace extends only to those who wore those badges that marked out God's people. For Paul "the covenant is no longer to be identified or characterized by such distinctively [Judean] observances as circumcision, food laws, and Sabbath. *Covenant* works had become too closely identified as [*Judean*] observances, *covenant* righteousness as *national* righteousness" (Dunn 1990:197; emphasis original).

Against the background of the redefined understanding of covenantal nomism, Dunn's explanation of Paul's polemic becomes even clearer. Paul opposes a rigid attachment to covenantal nomism, an ethnic identity, but in the sense that God's mercy is no longer restricted to those who perform Judean customs that marked out that identity. What Paul also expected from his fellow Judean Messianists was for them to sacrifice important elements of their identity. It is like asking black Christians in many parts of Africa to distance themselves from the traditional roles of the ancestors. But the important thing for our work lies in the highly prominent place that customs had in Judeanism as is evident in the polemics of the early Messianist movement and the Judean literature of the period. Judeanism as a religion was more a matter of *doing* things than theology or faith. Ancient Judeanism had no creeds. Judean customs are important for they were related to covenant membership. It therefore seems appropriate, from here on, to refer to Judean customs as *covenantal praxis*. Covenantal praxis was a way to assert your covenant membership or ethnic identity, a way to affirm your participation in covenantal nomism, the Judean symbolic universe. Cohen explains that for Judeans and Gentiles

> the boundary line between [Judeanism] and paganism was determined more by [Judean] observances than by [Judean] theology. Josephus defines an apostate as a [Judean] who "hates the customs of the [Judeans]" or "does not abide by the ancestral customs." He defines a convert to [Judeanism] as a gentile who through circumcision "adopts the ancestral customs of the

[Judeans]"[8] ... For Philo too the essence of conversion is the adoption of the way of life of the [Judeans].[9] (Cohen 1987:61)

Schmidt expresses a similar viewpoint:

> More than beliefs, multiple and debated, it is *rites* that weave the protective web of [Judean] identity. The rites classify and identify. They separate those who practise from those who do not. They trace the dividing line between [Judeans] and Gentiles, between those who join the community and those who are cast out. They form a bond between all the subgroups, all the constituents of the [Judean] community. (Schmidt 2001:25; emphasis original)

Not surprisingly it is also more practices, not theology, which determined the boundary lines *within* the Judean community (Cohen 1987:61). Judean debates centres in matters of law. Qumranites criticized fellow Judeans' way of life, their observance of the calendar, purity, and administration of the temple. Although Judeanism "was defined more by its practices than its beliefs" (Cohen 1987:103), Judeanism certainly had a theological element to it, however. Proper action was ultimately grounded in proper belief. Nevertheless, if we want to understand Judean ethnic identity better, we will always have to remember that Judean identity, an ethnic identity which was in many ways "religious," yes, was most visibly expressed through covenantal praxis. Covenantal praxis was covenantal nomism in action—it was simply being a Judean, and it had very little, if anything to do with "legalistic works-righteousness."

Ethnicity Theory

The insights gained from the work of Sanders, Dunn, Berger and Luckmann, helpful as they are, need to be complimented with the insights of social or cultural anthropology, particularly ethnicity theory. Ethnicity theory is a relatively new form of science. The term "ethnicity" was not used until 1941, and only from the 1960s did it become a major social-scientific concept (Duling 2005:126). The French word for an ethnic group, *ethnie*, is also used in English and is mainly found in social-scientific literature (Esler 2003:40). Ethnicity theory is a burgeoning enterprise due to the reality of modern ethnic conflict and resurgence in ethnic affiliation in most parts of the world. But what is

---

8. Cf. *War* 7.50; *Ant.* 20.100 (on apostasy); *Ant.* 20.17, 41 (on conversion).
9. Cf. *Virtues* 102–8.

ethnicity? There appears to be no universal definition as to what ethnicity (or "ethnic identity") is, although in some writings, a degree of overlap is discernable.[10] To give a somewhat abridged definition here, ethnicity is a form of social identity, referring to a collectivity of individuals who ascribe to themselves and/or by others, a sense of belonging and a common cultural tradition. The cultural tradition may in various combinations make use of and/or be dependent on a common name, a shared ancestry, a shared historical tradition, having common phenotypical or genetic features, a link to a specific territory, a shared language or dialect, kinship patterns, customs, and a shared religion (cf. Duling 2005). Jenkins (1997:165) has proposed a "basic social anthropological model" of ethnicity, which is as follows:

- Ethnicity is about cultural differentiation [it involves the communication of similarity and difference];

- Ethnicity is concerned with culture—shared meaning—but is also rooted in, and the outcome of, social interaction;

- Ethnicity is no more fixed than the culture of which it is a component, or the situations in which it is produced and reproduced;

- Ethnicity is both collective and individual, externalized in social interaction and internalized in personal self-identification.

From the above it may be inferred that ethnicity is essentially about cultural differentiation. As shall be explained below, however, ethnic-

---

10. It has been variously described as the "social organization of culture difference" (Barth 1969); or an "ethnic group is a self-perceived group of people who hold in common a set of traditions not shared by others with whom they are in contact. Such traditions typically include 'folk' religious beliefs and practices, language, a sense of historical continuity, and common ancestry or place of origin ... [T]he ethnic identity of a group of people consists of their subjective symbolic or emblematic use of any aspect of culture, in order to differentiate themselves from other groups" (De Vos 1975:9, 16); or "ethnic identity can best be defined as a feeling of belonging and continuity-in-being (staying the same person(s) through time) resulting from an act of self-ascription, and/or by others, to a group of people who claim both common ancestry and a common cultural tradition" (Roosens 1994:84); or as a last example, ethnic communities may be defined "as named human populations with shared ancestry, myths, histories and cultures, having an association with a specific territory and a sense of solidarity" (Smith 1986:32).

ity is a more complicated social phenomenon, particularly in terms of exactly how it is formed and maintained.

Primordialism vs. Constructionism

So exactly how are ethnic groups formed and maintained? Initially, two major theoretical approaches to ethnicity were proposed; namely, Primordialism and Constructionism (Duling 2005:126–27).

Primordialism, associated with Edward Shils (1957a; 1957b) and Clifford Geertz (1963), stresses that "ethnic groups are held together by 'natural affections.' These are bonds so compelling, so passionate, so 'coercive,' and so overpowering, that they are fixed, *a priori*, involuntary, ineffable, even as 'sacred.' These bonds are deeply rooted in family, territory, language, custom, and religion" (Duling 2005:126). They are, in a word, "primordial."[11] In this instance one's ethnic identity "may not be so much a matter of choice, still less rational choice, but of tradition and emotions provoked by a common ancestry" (Esler 2003:45).

Now some reactions to the primordialist approach are based on a misunderstanding of what Shils and Geertz were explaining, and are purely dismissive. Primordialism is criticized in that it regards ethnicity as "fixed," "natural," "pre-social" or the like, and incapable of changing (as opposed to the constructionist view that ethnicity is *fluid* and socially *constructed*—see below). It is agreed here that without a proper psychological explanation, a primordialist approach on its own can tend to be somewhat vague and deterministic. Ethnicity then becomes an abstract natural phenomenon that is explained on the basis of "human nature," with little attention being given to the social and historical contexts in which ethnic groups are formed (Jones 1997:68–70). But these elements which have come to typify the primordialist approach (i.e. it regards ethnicity as "natural," "pre-social" etc) neither Shils nor Geertz argued in the first place. As Jenkins points out, Geertz, for example, recognizes the role that culture plays in defining primordial bonds and that it varies in intensity in different societies and different time periods. Further, for Geertz "what matters analytically is that ties of blood, language and culture are *seen* by actors to be ineffable and obligatory; that they are *seen* as natural" (Jenkins 1997:45; emphasis original). Shils and Geertz

---

11. Fenton (2003:83) points out, however, that neither Shils nor Geertz themselves were defining *ethnicity*. They merely pointed out that some relationships (family, religion, language, customs etc) had a distinctive—primordial—quality when compared with others, such as your relationship with the state.

merely described what these primordial attachments were like for the social actors themselves (cf. Scott 1990:150; Fenton 2003:80–84).

On a more sensible level, it is thought that individuals acquire such primordial bonds "through early processes of socialization" and "such attachments have an overwhelming power because of a universal, human, psychological need for a sense of belongingness and self-esteem" (Jones 1997:66). Particularly important here is the role of the family or kinship patterns in identity formation, and particularly in a context where ethnic differentiation is prominent (Jenkins 1997:47, 58–59).[12] Fenton (2003:89–90) also explains:

> [T]o "think out of existence" primordiality is somehow to turn one's back on affect, the powerful influence of familiarity and customariness in social life, and the diffuse sense of attachment that flows from circumstances of birth and socialization, use of language and ingrained habits of thought and social practice ... It is simply to acknowledge that this kind of familiarity exists, that habits of thought do become ingrained and are often associated with early life, place, the family, and wider grouping or regions.

So although some have attempted to argue away the merits of primordialism (Eller & Coughlan 1993; Denzey 2002), one can hardly deny its abiding importance for ethnicity. Primordial attachments (particularly formed within the context of kinship and ancestry relations) contain meaning for their participants. It is the stuff of history, tradition, habit, and an individual sense of belonging (cf. Scott 1990:163; Grosby 1996:55). This approach emphasizes the view of the participant, or how ethnic groups themselves understand reality (i.e. an insider or emic perspective).[13] From an etic (or outsider) perspective, however,

---

12. Jenkins, however, avoids using the term "primordial." Where ethnic identity is sufficiently salient to be internalized during early primary socialization, ethnicity can be characterized as a *primary*—not primordial—dimension of individual identity (Jenkins 1997:47).

13. According to Esler primordial attachments is a notion where "we are able to draw the standard anthropological distinction between the emic (insider or indigenous) and the etic (outsider or social-scientific) points of view" (Esler 2003:46). What Esler points to here is the need for an etic apparatus set at a reasonably high level of abstraction, yet the definition of ethnicity is plagued by the nature of ethnicity itself: "Are ethnic groups based on shared 'objective' cultural practices and/or socio-structural relations that exist independently of the perceptions of the individuals concerned, or are they constituted primarily by the subjective processes of perception and derived social organization of their members?" (Jones 1997:57).

primordialism brings to attention the emotional and psychological strength of ethnic affiliation.

Constructionism or the self-ascriptive approach to ethnicity[14] associated with Frederik Barth (1969; cf. Barth 1994:12), became the major alternative to primordialism (others would say it is instrumentalism—see below). Barth initially argued that the "cultural stuff," although important for social boundaries, is "not as important as the act *of social boundary marking itself*" (Duling 2005:127; emphasis original). Constructionists took this further and argued that "ethnic identity is not inherent, fixed, or natural; rather, it is *fluid, freely chosen*, and thus can be seen to be *perpetually constructed, that is, continually reconstructed*" (Duling 2005:127; emphasis original). The emphasis shifted to *how* and *why* ethnic groups create and maintain their group boundaries. In this case the boundary between an ethnic group and outsiders is more of a process than a barrier, thus "cultural features of the ethnic group are the visible and variable manifestation, but not the cause, of an ethnic boundary and identity.... [C]ultural indicia might change over time and yet the ethnic group could still retain a sense of its own distinctiveness" (Esler 2003:42–43). Therefore, in this approach it is important to remember that cultural features do not constitute, but *signal* ethnic identity and boundaries. An ethnic identity is maintained but with *no necessary relation to specific cultural content*—the ethnic identity is self-ascriptive, continuously renewed and renegotiated through social practice (Esler 2003:42, 47). Constructionists also claim that groups construct their ethnic boundaries in two major ways: firstly "in relation to like-minded, like-practiced peers, a 'we' *aggregative* self-definition" and secondly, "in relation to *others*, a 'we-they' *oppositional* self-definition." The latter is usually ethnocentric (Duling 2005:127).

A major development based on constructionism is instrumentalism, where an ethnic group's self-construction is rational and self-interested and deliberately mobilized in an attempt to further its own political-economic agenda (Duling 2005:127; Esler 2003:46).

---

14. Variants or developments of this approach in reaction to primordialism are referred to as "circumstantialist" (which incorporates the "situationalist"/"instrumentalist" approach), and "transactionalist." The circumstantialist approach views ethnic identity is important in some contexts, while not important in others. The identity is constant but circumstances determine whether it matters (Fenton 2003:84). At times circumstances lead to the *rational strategic selection* of ethnic identity, as a means to achieve desired political, economic, and other social ends (i.e., the situationalist/instrumentalist approach) (Scott 1990:148).

Another approach to ethnicity, which is also relevant here, is ethnosymbolism. This approach analyses how an ethnic group's nostalgia about its perceived past—expressed through cosmogonic myths, election myths, memories of a golden age, symbols—shapes the group's ability to endure, but also to change and adapt (Duling, 2005:127). This can be seen in Judean literature (e.g., *Jubilees* and *L.A.B.*) where past traditions are used creatively for the Judean struggle against Hellenism and the maintenance of the Judean symbolic universe. As Gruen (2002) has demonstrated, much of Judean literature was written to boost Judean self-esteem.

As with primordialism, constructionalism, and instrumentalism also has its critics. Instrumentalists have been criticized "for defining interests largely in material terms, for failing to take seriously the participant's sense of the permanence of their *ethnies* (which might be termed 'participant's primordialism'), and, above all, for underplaying the affective dimensions of ethnicity" (Hutchinson & Smith 1996:9). With regards to the "boundary" issue, according to Roosens (1994), the construction of a boundary does not constitute identity. The boundary can only express, add to or play down an ethnic identity which already exists. "Ethnic identity can take its drive and pattern from an interplay of oppositions with outsiders, but it mostly combines this source of differentiation with an internal source of identification" (Roosens 1994:84). So any ethnicity is logically and ontologically prior to any boundary between "us" and "them." Roosens (1994:85–87) even goes on to say that concrete interaction with a specific outgroup is not even required, and he brings to focus the role that kinship/the family and ancestry (genealogy) plays in this regard. What also binds the family is a sense of origin and history, shared virtues, loyalty to tradition and personal honor (Roosens 1994:90–93). So ethnicity is dependent on the "internal cultural stuff" that is independent of, and that exists before any external boundary. Smith (1986:49) and Fenton (2003:74–75) express similar viewpoints. Fenton also explains, however, that Barth did not discount the importance of cultural differences: "where groups follow particular customs, adopt a familiar dress, and speak their own language, these things needed to be studies and understood" (Fenton 2003:111). Jenkins (1997:45) also explains that Barth "has never neglected the power and stability of ethnic identifications . . . [H]is argument was that in certain, not uncommon, circumstances ethnic change *can* happen, not that it *must*" (emphasis original). Jenkins also points out that Barth has recently explored "the importance of ongoing and historically relatively stable 'streams of tradition' or 'universes of discourse', within the constraints of which ethnic identities are produced and reproduced in practice" (cf. Jenkins 1996:812; 1994:198).

Overall, the constructionist (or self-ascriptive) approach has become the dominant theoretical perspective on ethnicity, even though most people regard their cultural practices as deeply rooted in antiquity (Avruch 2003:72; Jenkins 1996:814). Jones (1997:84) explains that

> from the late 1960s onwards the dominant view within "western" social scientific traditions has been that ethnic groups are "self-defining systems" and consequently particular ethnic groups have been defined on the basis of self-identification and identification by others. Such a definition has largely been set within a theoretical framework focusing on the construction of ethnic boundaries in the context of social interaction and their organizational properties. Ethnicity has been regarded as essentially a consciousness of identity *vis-à-vis* other groups; a "we"/ "they" opposition.

Duling (2005:127) also explains that most theorists agree that people ascribe their ethnicity to themselves (constructionism), but there is still great interest in the "cultural stuff." There is also still wide disagreement on whether self-constructed ethnicity is "irrational and ineffable" (primordialist) or "rational and self-interested" (instrumentalist).[15] This brings us to another important dimension in the debate. As can be seen from the above discussion, primordialism and constructionism/instrumentalism were basically regarded as mutually exclusive, exaggerating the differences between Geertz and Barth in particular. Hence the reaction to primordialism: ethnicity is not "fixed," or "pre-social" and it is subject to change; hence the reaction to constructionism/instrumentalism: ethnic attachments are sometimes stubborn and also exists before any boundary between "us" and "them." But as Jenkins points out, the approaches of Geertz and Barth have as much in common as what separates them (Jenkins 1997:45, 48; 1994:812–13). So although it is universally agreed that ethnic identity is socially constructed (i.e. it is not "natural," "pre-social" or rooted in human biology), there appears to be a growing recognition among ethnicity theorists that some form

---

15. In this regard Esler (2003:48) argues that "either option [i.e. instrumentalism or primordialism] is possible but that local and individual circumstances will affect which mode is in action at any particular time ... [W]e need to be open to the possible stubbornness of ethnic affiliation, while not underestimating the power of individuals and groups to modify ethnic identity for particular social, political, or religious ends."

of reconciliation or intermediate position is necessary between the constructionist approach on the one hand (particularly its emphasis on the *fluid* and *free* transactional nature of ethnicity across the "boundary"), and on the other, the primordial dimensions of ethnicity and/or the importance of cultural content (Hutchinson & Smith 1996:9; Fenton 2003:111, 194–95; Jenkins 1997:121–22). There have been attempts to integrate the various approaches (e.g., Scott 1990) and it is also suggested that both perspectives are continuously present, but to varying degrees (Jones 1997:80). For our purposes here, primordialism and constructionism/instrumentalism are therefore not seen as mutually exclusive in line with recent approaches. The interaction across the "boundary" cannot be separated from the cultural contents of ethnicity (Jenkins 1997:121–22) and/or its "primordial" dimensions (Scott 1990:149). Either position cannot explain ethnicity on its own. Fenton (2003:90) also explains that it is "perfectly possible to have a conception of ethnic identity which allows us to see them ... as being constituted by elements which are civic, instrumental, circumstantial and primordial." Perhaps it is better to conclude that the social and historical context of an ethnic group will dictate how we approach their ethnic identity. At times ethnicity is more fluid and changing. At times ethnic attachments are more stubborn. At times ethnicity is important; at times it is not. Within the same group, any combination of these dynamics can also be present at the same time.

Ethnicity as Grounded in the *Habitus*

Jones (1997:87–105) has attempted a theoretical approach which she suggests overcomes the primordialist and instrumentalist dichotomy. Her own approach thus falls in line with the broad consensus where constructionism is the underlying perspective. At the outset she draws attention to Bourdieu's theory of practice which develops a concept known as the *habitus*:

> The structures constitutive of a particular type of environment ... produce *habitus*, systems of durable, transposable *dispositions*, structured structures predisposed to function as structuring structures, that is, as principles of generation and structuring of practices and representations which can be objectively "regulated" and "regular" without any way being the product of obedience to rules. (Bourdieu 1977:72; emphasis original)

The *habitus* therefore is made up of durable dispositions (or "unreflexive habit" [Jenkins 1994:203; 1997:58; 2003:64]), that produce certain perceptions and practices that "become part of an individual's sense of self at an early age, and which can be transposed from one context to another ... As such, the *habitus* involves a process of socialization whereby new experiences are structured in accordance with the structures produced by past experiences, and early experiences retain a particular weight" (Jones 1997:88). But interestingly, the *habitus* are both "structuring structures" and "structured structures," which shape, and are shaped by social practice (Jones 1997:89). Jones then draws attention to the work of Bentley, who builds on Bourdieu's theory of practice to develop a *practice theory of ethnicity*, which for Jones (1997:90) provides an objective grounding for ethnic subjectivity:

> According to the practice theory of ethnicity, sensations of ethnic affinity are founded on common life experiences that generate similar habitual dispositions ... It is commonality of experience and of the preconscious habitus it generates that gives members of an ethnic cohort their sense of being both familiar and familial to each other. (Bentley 1987:32–33)

Thus, "it can be argued that the intersubjective construction of ethnic identity is grounded in the shared subliminal dispositions of the *habitus* which shape, and are shaped by, objective commonalities of practice ... The cultural practices and representations that become objectified as symbols of ethnicity are derived from, and resonate with, the habitual practices and experiences of the people involved, as well as reflecting the instrumental contingencies and meaningful cultural idioms of a particular situation" (Jones 1997:90). Hence the cultural features employed by an ethnic group are neither purely primordialist (irrational and ineffable) nor purely instrumentalist (rational and self-interested), but a combination of both.

It needs to be mentioned that Jenkins also brings into focus that the "sense of self," located in the *habitus*, is much influenced by categorization. "Entering into ethnic identification during childhood is definitively a matter of categorization: we learn who we are because, in the first instance, other people—whether they be co-members or Others—tell us. Socialization *is* categorization" (Jenkins 1997:166; emphasis original). Where ethnicity is important, a child will not only learn she is an "X," but also what it means: "in terms of her esteem and worth in her own eyes and in the eyes of others; in terms of appropriate and inappropriate behaviour; and in terms of what it means *not* to be an 'X' . . ." (Jenkins 1997:59; emphasis original). This "sense of self" may continue into adulthood. This would be particularly relevant to the first-century personality where the individual would always see himself or herself through the eyes of others (Malina 2001). Malina speaks of honor as a grant of reputation by others. It is nothing other than your conscience. At the same time the individual is also a group-orientated personality. The "dyadic" person is essentially a "group-embedded and group-orientated person . . . Such persons internalize and make their own what others say, do, and think about them because they believe it is necessary, for being human, to live out the expectation of others" (Malina 2001:62). Important is the interaction between the individual and "person-sustaining groups" such as the family, village, city and nation. The insights of Malina can certainly be appropriated to an individual's sense of ethnic identity. If so, ethnicity is not complicated by the social phenomena of individualism and social mobility as encountered in the modern western world (cf. Fenton 2003). If it existed, it was the exception and not the norm. For our purposes here, the "sense of self" and group-orientated personality, and the reciprocal relationships and categorization that it implies, should form important elements of the *habitus*.

Returning to Jones (1997:93–99), she continues by adapting Bentley's theory, as far as we can identify, in three major ways. First, a shared *habitus* does not necessarily lead to feelings of ethnic affinity. The opposite is also true. Differences in *habitus* do not exclude identification. What is important here is the role that the "ethnic others" play in the construction of ethnicity—ethnicity is essentially a consciousness of difference vis-à-vis others, not merely a recognition of similarities. Thus loosely affiliated groups of people who nevertheless have commonalities of practice and experience may band together in opposition to outside cultures. European colonialization of African peoples is a case in point (Jones 1997:93–95). A second, but related issue is that in "some situations there may be a high degree of contiguity between ethnicity and the *habitus*, whereas in other situations characterized by social dislocation and subordination there may appear to be very little" (Jones 1997:97). So ethnic identities also encode relations of power. Ethnicity can form the basis of political mobilization and resistance. Here subordinated minority ethnic groups of diverse origins can for example form a collectivity as a result of large scale urban migration. With time cultural realties and relationships of inequality will lead "to their incorporation as part of the structured dispositions of the *habitus*" (Jones 1997:97; cf. Stein 2004). Third, the manifestation of a particular ethnic identity may also vary in different social and historical contexts. "For instance, the institutionalization of ethnicity in the modern nation-state and its representation in national politics, is likely to be qualitatively different from the activation of ethnicity in the processes of interaction between members of a local community or neighbourhood" (Jones 1997:99).

Thus the concept of the *habitus* is overall broadened by Jones. Bentley's notion of the *habitus* draws on the theory of Bourdieu, which reflects the situation of a highly integrated and uniform system of dispositions characteristic of a small scale society. Yet, this does not properly explain highly differentiated and complex societies. "Ethnicity is a multidimensional phenomenon constituted in different ways in different social domains. Representations of ethnicity involve the dialectical opposition of situationally relevant cultural practices . . . Consequently there is rarely a one-to-one relationship between representations of ethnicity and the entire range of cultural practices and social conditions associated with a particular group." What we end up with, from a bird's eye view that is, is "one of overlapping ethnic boundaries constituted by representations of cultural difference, which are at once transient, but also subject to reproduction and transformation in the ongoing processes of social life" (Jones 1997:100). To summarize, Jones' (1997:128–29) approach to ethnicity, it can be paraphrased as follows:

- The construction of ethnicity is grounded in the *habitus* —the shared subliminal dispositions of social agents— which shape, and are shaped by, objective commonalties of practice. The *habitus* provides the basis to recognize common sentiments and interests, and to perceive and communicate cultural affinity and difference.

- As a result, the primordialist and instrumentalist dichotomy can be overcome. The cultural practices that become objectified as symbols of ethnicity both derive from and resonate with habitual practices and experiences of the people in question, but also reflects the instrumental contingencies of a particular situation.

- Ethnicity is not always congruent with the *habitus* or the cultural practices of a group. Very importantly, ethnic identity involves an objectification of cultural practices in the recognition and communication of difference in opposition to others. The extent to which ethnicity is grounded in a pre-existing *habitus* or cultural realities is highly variable and dependent on prevailing social conditions, that is, the nature of interaction and the power relations between groups of people.

- So cultural practices that communicate the "same" identity may vary in different social contexts subject to different social conditions. Rarely will there be a one-to-one relationship between representations of ethnicity and the entire range of cultural practices and social conditions relevant to a particular ethnic group. One finds rather the pattern of overlapping ethnic boundaries, which are produced by context-specific representations of cultural difference. The latter are transient, but also subject to reproduction and transformation in the ongoing processes of social life.

There is a lot of the above that explains first-century Palestinian Judeanism, but not everything. For example, it can be questioned whether the broadening of the *habitus* and the idea of "overlapping ethnic boundaries" is *that* applicable. Admittedly, such a distinction is relevant when taking into account that Judeans lived in Judea, Galilee and the Diaspora, in both rural and urban settings, and that a minority of Judeans belonged to sectarian groups. These diverse social contexts are offset, however, by the nature of Judeanism itself. This is where we need to draw attention to Berger's notion of the "symbolic universe," which nevertheless, shows much affinity with the approach of Jones outlined above. Just as human beings both shape, and is shaped by an objective society (= institutions derived from habitual actions), so the *habitus* (subliminal and habitual dispositions) both shape, and is shaped by objective common cultural practices. But Berger's notion of the symbolic universe adds important dimensions, however. It involves the human search for *meaning*, combined with the theory that the institutional order is *integrated into an all-embracing frame of reference*, first century Judeanism being exemplary of such an approach. The point is this: the overwhelming majority of Judeans, here focussing on those who lived in Palestine in particular, were informed and shaped by the same symbolic universe, indeed similar *habitus*, relevant to every social and historical context due to the all-encompassing and permanent nature of the covenant. Admitting certain peculiarities, their beliefs and cultural practices, were, to a large degree, homogenous. Judeanism can be understood as a more "vertical" ethnic group, where "a single ethnic culture permeates in varying degrees most strata of the population ..." (Smith 1986:77). The same identity was *communicated by similar beliefs and cultural practices in different social and historical contexts*. Most certainly the dimensions of belongingness and self-esteem also come into play here. And of course, Judeans were ethnically exclusive, so ethnicity was important! The implications are that Judeanism is understood as a highly integrated and uniform system of dispositions, but more about Judean ethnicity later when the proposed model is explained.

Jones can also be seen as perhaps regarding ethnicity too much as *oppositional* in nature. Her approach nevertheless allows for the following contingencies: Ethnicity is the result of socialization and categorization. At times ethnicity can be more fluid and changing; at times ethnic attachments can be more stubborn. At times ethnicity can be important and at other times not. These various dynamics of ethnicity can be present at the same time. It therefore can take into account the "internal" content and the primordial dimensions of ethnicity, as well as the interaction across the "boundary." Overall, it is a good working theory from which to work, and to adapt to the circumstances of first-century Judeanism.

Socio-Cultural Model of Ethnicity

Ethnicity theory has broadly recognized several cultural features that are important for ethnic identity, although not all of them are required for ethnic formation. The various featured proposed has quite logically been summarized by Duling (2005:127–28) to include the following: 1) *name*, a corporate name that identifies the group; 2) *myths of common ancestry*, the group claims to be descendents of a particular person or group/family; 3) *shared "historical" memories*, the group points to common heroes and events of the past; 4) *land*, the group has actual or symbolic attachment to an ancestral land; 5) *language*, or local dialect; 6) *kinship*, members of the group belong to family units which in turn, demonstrate communal solidarity with the local community or tribe, and with the group as a national entity; 7) *customs* identifiable with that group (dress, food, sport etc); 8) the cultural feature of *religion*;

and 9) *phenotypical features*, which point to genetic features (cf. Esler 2003:43–44).

Duling in turn developed a model that lists these key representative socio-cultural features that could influence an ethnic group's values, norms and behavior. He describes it as an outsider's model (etic model) that is "imposed" on the available data. Duling (2005:127) further describes it as a "socio-cultural umbrella" that highlights "cultural stuff" but the broken lines and temporal arrow (see graphic) attempt to allow for the dominant constructionist approach in ethnicity theory. Duling's model, he admits, runs the risk of oversimplifying distinctive historic or local ethnographic information, but Duling regards his model as heuristic; it is open to criticism and modification or, if necessary, even reconstruction. Meanwhile, any discussions of ethnicity can look out for such features in ancient literature (Duling 2005:127). It is also important to note that the most widespread of these features are kinship relations and myths of common ancestry, and some connection with a homeland is not far behind (Duling 2005:127; cf. Esler 2003:44). Duling's (2005:128) model is as follows on the next page.

Ethnicity in Antiquity

Are these cultural features found in Duling's model evident in ancient literature? The answer is "yes." Duling (2005:127–29) points to several texts where it becomes evident that ancient peoples were recognized by their name, language, ancestry, customs and religion to name but a few (cf. Esler 2003:55–56). These texts will be quoted to bring attention to the relevant cultural features mentioned. First is a quotation from Herodotus:

> For there are many great reasons why we [i.e. those in Greece] should not do this [i.e. desert to the Persians], even if we so desired; first and foremost, the burning and destruction of the adornments and temples of our gods, whom we have constrained to avenge to the utmost rather than make pacts with the perpetrator of these things, and next the kinship of all Greeks in blood and speech [*name, kinship, phenotypical features* and *myths of common ancestry* (?), *language*], and the shrines of gods and the sacrifices that we have in common [*religion*, with *shared "historical" memories* inferred], and the likeness of our way of life [*customs*], to all of which it would not befit the Athenians [*land* (?)] to be false (Herodotus, *Histories* 8.144.2).

A Socio-Cultural Model of Judean Ethnicity

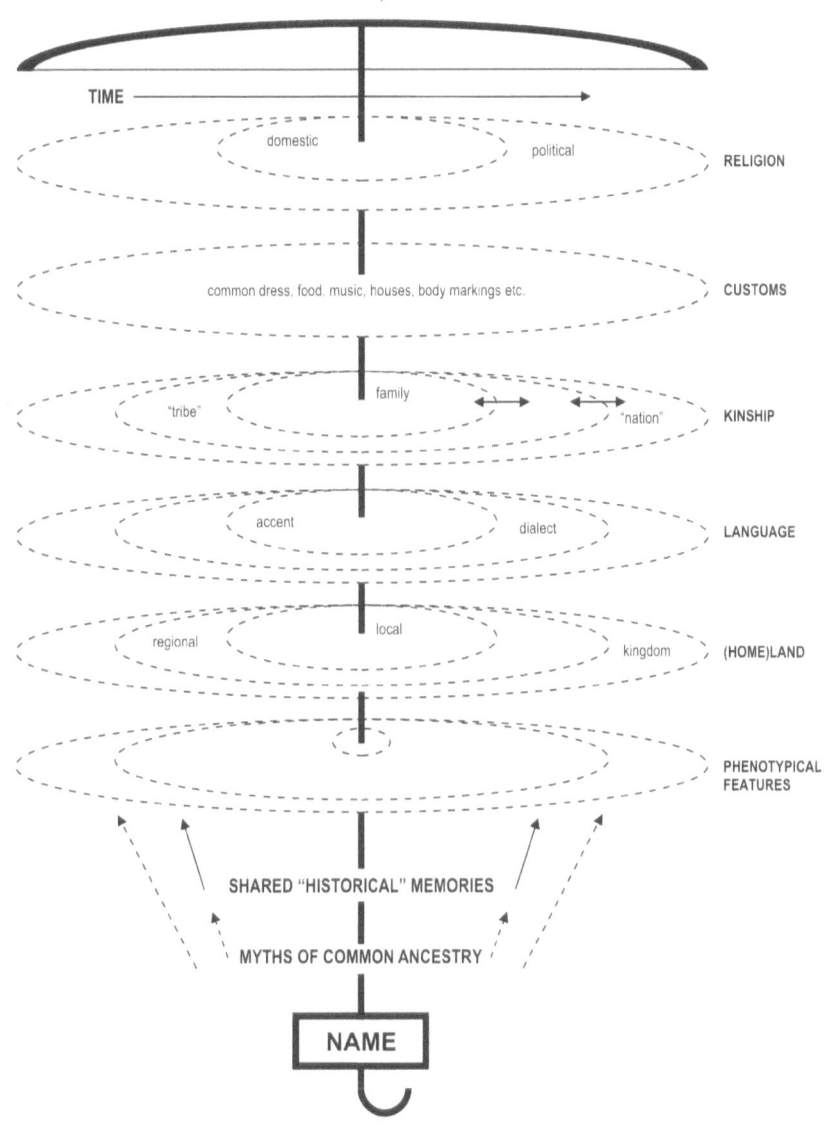

D C Duling's Socio-Cultural Model of Ethnicity

Second is a text from the geographer Strabo:

> For the *ethnos* of the Armenians and that of the Syrians and Arabians betray a close affinity, not only in their language, but in their mode of life [*customs*], and in their bodily build [*phenotypical*

features], and particularly wherever they live as close neighbours [*land*] (Strabo, *Geography* 1.2.34).

Our third text comes from the Tanak:

> He also said, "Blessed be the LORD, the God of Shem! [*religion*] May Canaan be the slave of Shem ... These are the sons of Shem [*myths of common ancestry*] by their clans [*kinship*] and *languages*, in their territories [*land*] and nations (ἔθνεσιν). (Gen 9:26; 10:31, NIV)

Here the various cultural features and *ethnoi* of Shem is contrasted with that of Ham, the father of the Canaanites. It becomes evident that ancient peoples were recognized by their name, language, ancestry, customs and religion to name but a few. So it is by no means inappropriate to apply modern ethnicity theory, with the necessary caution, to ancient peoples (Duling 2005:127–29; Esler 2003:53). According to Smith (1986:32–46; 1997) ethnic communities played an active part in human society from at least the third millennium BCE. What helped to shape ethnic groups were (1) *sedentarization and nostalgia*, where peoples gave up their pastoral and nomadic lifestyle and formed small village settlements, which formed oases of folk culture and local ties, to which was attached a nostalgia for the past; (2) *organized religion*, where, for example, the origin myths of the ethnic group and their religious beliefs about creation are interrelated, and the role that religion played in the communication of ethnic myths and symbols; and (3) *inter-state warfare*, particularly those between different kinds of political authority. Smith (1986:46) concludes that "ethnicity provides one of the central axes of alignment and division in the pre-modern world, and one of the most durable."

It can also be mentioned that people were often recognized as displaying characteristic features. The ancients observed that Ethiopians were dark-skinned and Germans were pale skinned. The ancient world also had its version of ethnocentricism, where your own people and culture were regarded as superior to others. Different nations were seen to have different moral characteristics as well, whether good or bad. The Egyptians were superstitious, inhospitable, and intemperate; Arabs are thieves; Greeks are fast-talkers and tricksters (Cohen 1987:48; Esler 2003:53). Esler (2003:52–53) also explains that

The Romans thought the Greeks[16] were characterized by *levitas*, that is, flightiness, lack of determination and grit. They found the Judeans antisocial, and hence misanthropic, especially because of their refusal to participate in imperial feast days. The Greeks found the Romans vulgar and lacking in taste.

The evidence that a people was identified as an ethnic group analogous to today's understanding is complimented by the ancient usage of ἔθνος in certain instances (already evident in the last two quoted texts above). To begin with, in Greek antiquity, the word ἔθνος had a much broader semantic range than our modern understanding of the term "ethnicity" (Duling 2005:129; cf. Saldarini 1994:59–60). In early writings the singular ἔθνος could refer to any kind of group of almost any size; a flock of birds, a swarm of bees, bands of warriors and young men, or groups of the dead. It could refer to the gender categories of men and women, or alternatively, the inhabitants of a small village, a city, several cities, an entire region, or a number of people living together. Migrants from different geographical regions could be referred to as an ἔθνος, while the term was also made applicable to a guild or trade association. It is also used of an ethnic tribe with its own proper name. Ἔθνος also acquired the meanings of "people" and "nation," referring "to a group of people with cultural, linguistic, geographical, or political unity" (Saldarini 1994:59).

This broad semantic range continued into the Hellenistic period, and a social class of people or a caste can be called an ἔθνος. Orders of priests were referred to as the holy ἔθνη, and ἔθνη can mean rural folk, in contrast to city people. Ἔθνη or ἐθνικός can be used to refer to "others," in contrast to one's own group. But the Greeks were increasingly referring to other peoples as ἔθνος. The plural form τὰ ἔθνη (also γένη) was even more used of other peoples, usually having the ring of ethnocentric stereotyping (Duling 2005:129; Esler 2003:55).

What about ancient Judean literature? Duling draws on the work of Muthuraj, who has argued that in ancient Judean literature, ἔθνος and τὰ ἔθνη (Hebrew *goy* and *goyim*) refers mostly to "people(s)" or "nation(s)" of the world in a positive or neutral sense (Muthuraj 1997:3–36). English translations (i.e. the use of "Gentiles," "pagans," "heathen"), Muthuraj maintains, are too loaded with bias towards outsiders by modern Jewish or Christian monotheists. Duling states this

16. The Greeks can of course also be referred to as the "Hellenes" (Ἕλληνές). The word "Greek" is derived from the Roman word for them: the *Graeci*, who came from *Graecia* (Esler 2003:55).

provides an important insight since ἔθνος could still be used to describe Israelites.¹⁷ He points out, however, that there are clear examples where τὰ ἔθνη in the LXX are oppositional terms for outsiders, as does the Hebrew it translates (Duling 2005:129). In the Maccabean literature for example, it says that there were those who had themselves uncircumcised, forsaking the covenant, and they "joined with the ἔθνη and sold themselves to do evil (1 Macc 1:15; cf. 2 Macc 10:4). According to Duling, similar nuances appear with regards to the adjective ἐθνικός and the adverb ἐθνικῶς. So one can conclude that in Judean literature, whether one thinks of Gentiles in a neutral, negative or positive sense will depend on the context.

In summary then and to reaffirm, ancient writers identified different groups of people in a similar way as anthropologists do today by way of reference to cultural features. In some cases, ἔθνος and ἔθνη could refer to a specific *ethnic* group or groups (similar to a modern ethnie or ethnies), in addition to its various other meanings. The singular could refer to your own or to an outside people. The plural was used even more to refer to other peoples. Both ἔθνος and the plural τὰ ἔθνη could be used in a positive or neutral sense, while the latter could also take on a negative ethnocentric meaning. The literary context will always have to be taken into account.

The Socio-Cultural Model of Judean Ethnicity: A Proposal

At this stage, all of the above can be put together into a proposal on how a more comprehensive understanding of the dynamics of Judean ethnic identity can be achieved. The proposed model below is a synthesis of covenantal nomism when redefined as an ethnic descriptor, Berger & Luckmann's notion of a "symbolic universe," Dunn's "four pillars" and his "new perspective" on Paul, the insights of ethnicity theory, and Duling's Socio-Cultural Model of Ethnicity. It must also be understood that the proposed model is attempting at establishing guidelines for a *mainstream* or *common Palestinian* Judeanism. The proposed model looks as follows:

---

17. 1 Macc 8:23; 10:25; 11:30; 12:3; 13:36; 14:28; 15:1–2; 2 Macc 11:27; Philo, *Decal.* 96.

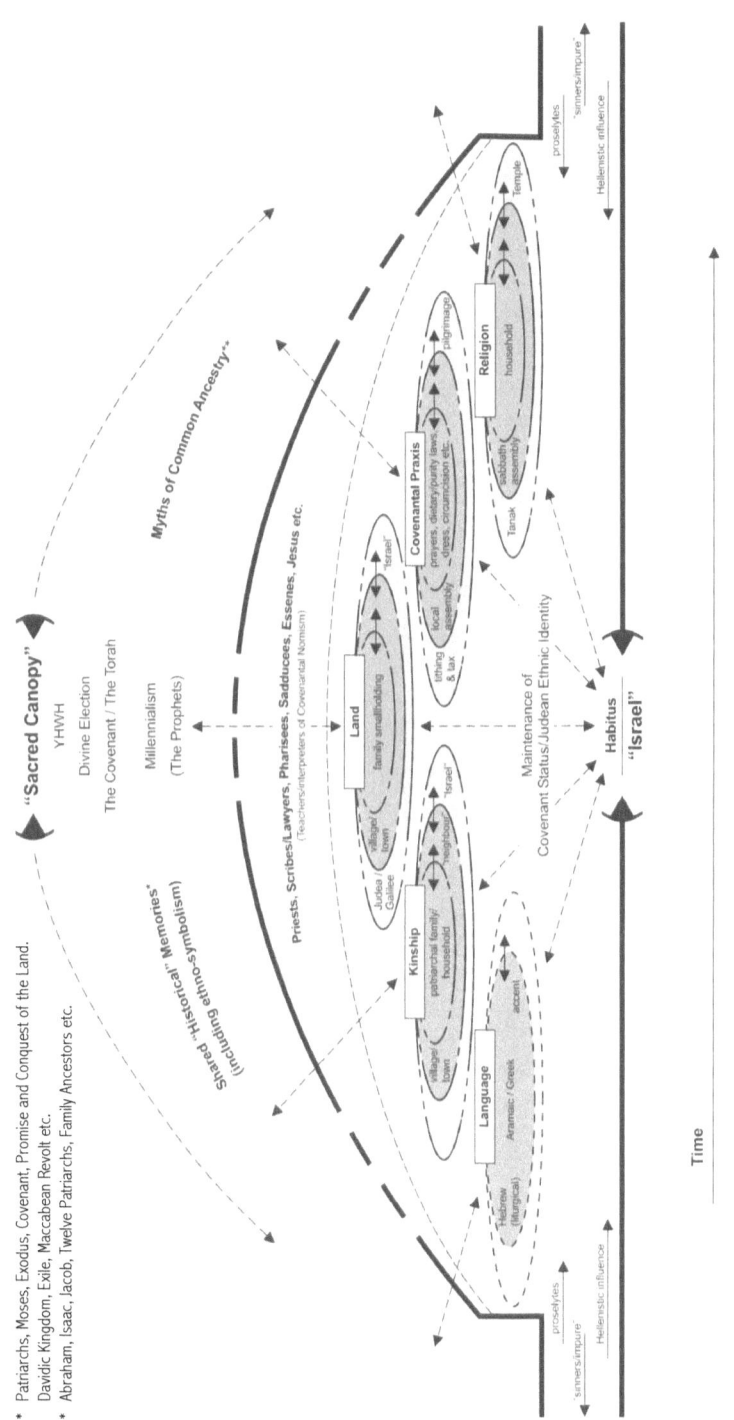

Covenantal Nomism:
An Amendment of D C Duling's Socio-Cultural Model of Ethnicity

The Socio-Cultural Model of Judean Ethnicity admittedly is a modern construct, as Duling put it, "imposed" on the available data. The model bears the appropriate name of "Covenantal Nomism." The name and model describes the entire process of Judean ethnic identity formation, how a group of people become Judean, and how they stay that way. It does *not* describe a "religious" system, but a group of people, Judeans, who lived an ethnic identity. It therefore at the same time also functions as a pictorial representation of the Judean social construction of reality, or their "symbolic universe." Admittedly, it entailed a relatively high degree of abstraction. In other words, the model is also a "container," where it is used as a theoretical device wherein all the elements of the Judean "world" can be placed. It is another way to understand Judean identity, for within this "world" one finds an ethnic identity, a way of being, of doing, and knowing (cf. Fishman 1996).

The model consists mainly of two areas, namely, the "Sacred Canopy" and the "Habitus/Israel." The "Sacred Canopy" is primarily the dimension in the model dealing with God who established (in the past), and continues to prescribe (in the present), Judean ethnicity through his divine election, the covenant, and gift of the Torah ("getting in"). The "Habitus/Israel" (which extends to include more tangible cultural features), refers to a group of people, Israel, responding to that call by being Judean ("staying in"). We will first discuss the Habitus/Israel in further detail. (It should be noted here that in what is to follow also draws on the insights gained from the next chapter, where a more comprehensive investigation into the various aspects of Judean ethnicity is performed.)

The *Habitus*/Israel

Judean ethnicity is the result of socialization. First, it is grounded in the *habitus*, the shared habitual dispositions of Judean social agents, or in short, "Israel," which shape and are shaped by objective common cultural practices. Here we enter the realm of affect, the powerful influence of familiarity and customariness in social life, and the strong attachments that result from ingrained habits of thought and social practice (cf. Fenton 2003:89–90). Second, within the *habitus* the "sense of self" is internalized through categorization, be it through the family, the village/town, or through society as a whole. In this regard, the identity of the individual as a group-orientated personality, and his/her sense of belongingness and self-esteem form important elements. Here we enter the realm of origins and history, tradition, shared values and meaning.

The Habitus/Israel primarily constitutes the dialectical interrelationship between the *habitus* and the more tangible institutions or cultural features of Judean ethnicity, which collectively, is contained within the thick black lines. This interrelationship is dominated by the endeavor to respond to God's divine election and to maintain covenant status or Judean ethnic identity ("staying in"). Being grounded in the *habitus*, the interrelationship produces Judean ethnic identity, which involves the objectification of cultural practices in the recognition and communication of affinity *and* difference *vis-à-vis* other peoples.

As already mentioned, ethnicity theory explains that most widespread of the cultural features are kinship relations and myths of common ancestry and some connection with a homeland. Some prominence is given to the cultural feature of *land* in the model, as it always was a primary feature of Judean ethnicity, and is related to the very strong hopes of restoration that Judeans had (i.e. "Millennialism"). Land is flanked by *kinship* and *covenantal praxis* (which stands in close association with *religion*), which in their own way were also primary sources of identity. But overall, the Habitus/Israel points to Judeans living on their land, circumcising their sons, eating food according to the laws of *kashrut*, going on pilgrimage, their family ties and communal solidarity, and attending the Sabbath assembly and so on. It points to covenantal nomism in action.

The above explains the dialectic relationship between the Habitus/Israel, and the immediate cultural features that gave expression to that ethnic identity. The argument is also made here that the predominant constructionist approach in Duling's model, represented by the broken lines, does not properly explain first-century Palestinian Judeanism. His broken lines is replaced by a predominantly primordialist approach, represented by the more solid lines. It is argued therefore that Judean ethnicity was *essentially* primordialist, meaning, it was made up of elements that for the greater part can be described as "primordial attachments." Most constructionist elements are secondary, and in fact, are based on or derived from a primordialist approach to ethnicity. Esler (2003:69) has argued, however, that the period from the 530s BCE to 100 CE the Judeans "maintained a strong sense of identity in relation to outsiders in spite of *radical changes* in the cultural features by which that separation was expressed" (emphasis added). Unfortunately, Esler does not explain what the "radical changes" in the cultural features are.

Not denying that there were some constructionist elements to Judean ethnicity (see below) we must ask is the argument for radical change not, perhaps, exaggerating the evidence? Esler appears to be guided here solely by the constructionist position that emphasizes that the cultural features of an ethnic group are *fluid* and *freely* chosen. There are two important reasons why Judean ethnicity is understood as essentially primordialist.

First, Judeanism was primordial, not in the sense that it was deterministic, "natural" or "pre-social," but it was conditioned, or "determined" by the inherent nature of covenantal nomism itself. The Judean symbolic universe only had one mandate: Perpetually regenerate thyself! It was argued earlier that Judeanism could be understood as a highly integrated and uniform system of dispositions. For this reason, Judean ethnicity was highly congruent with the *habitus* and established cultural practices. Differently put, covenantal nomism reproduced covenantal nomism. The reason for this is that socialization and the objectification of cultural practices (be they "internal" or "external") were governed by the requirements of the covenant and Torah. So it was not simply a matter of habitual dispositions or the role of affect, or a sense of history and tradition, it was also about being obedient to God's will. Judeans did not have the "freedom" to construct their culture as other ethnic groups had. Being God's elect people therefore had its restrictions, relevant to all social contexts and opposing interactions. So the extreme constructionist idea that "cultural features of the ethnic group are the visible and variable manifestation, but not the cause, of an ethnic boundary and identity" (Esler 2003:42) is hardly applicable to Judeanism. Judean cultural features were basically "permanent" and therefore inseparable from Judean ethnic identity. So in themselves, Judean cultural features were the cause of a rigid and tenacious ethnic boundary and identity in addition to the aspect of social organization.

Second, Judeanism formed part of the Roman Empire, hence it was the victim of political and economic oppression and exploitation. A related feature is that Judeanism was under pressure from Hellenism—at one stage it was even persecuted and forced to adopt Hellenistic culture (Maccabean revolt). Judeanism was fighting back to preserve its identity and distinctiveness. The literature of the period makes varied use of ethno-symbolism to help the Judean people endure and to help them remember who they are; people of the covenant, and a people who are called to obedience to God's commandments. Esler (2003:46) himself noted that "members of an ethnic group, particularly one under threat, are far more likely to adhere to a primordialist view of ethnicity" than to an interactive and self-ascriptive (the extreme constructionist) approach, and even less to an instrumentalist one. In this regard Scott has argued that that primordial sentiments will become greater the greater the amount of *opposition* experienced by that group. He explains further "with respect to the *content* of ethnic identity, the primordial sentiments will also attach to the symbols against which the greatest opposition is expressed, whether language, territory, heroes, music, dance, cuisine, or clothing, such that they will become even more salient in the individual's reckoning of his or her ethnicity" (Scott 1990:163; emphasis original). And the greater the opposition experienced by the group, the greater its ethnic solidarity becomes, which according to Scott (1990:166), also tends to increase the lower the person's socio-economic status. It must further be recalled that ethnic identities also encode relations of power. Judean ethnicity encoded an identity in which reality conflicted with the ideal, in which a dominated people longed for divine deliverance.

Where a constructionist approach is relevant, three examples will be discussed. First, the laws on clean and unclean foods do not hold such a central place in the Torah (Lev 11:1–23; Deut 14:3–21). From the time of the Maccabees, however, they took on increasing importance in Judean folklore and Judean self-understanding (Dunn 1990:193). For the devout, one had to avoid the impure food of Gentiles or non-observant Judeans at all cost. Second, in post-exilic Israel Gentiles could convert to Judeanism while intermarriage was prohibited. For a Gentile woman, marriage with a Judean man was a de facto equivalent of conversion (Cohen 1987:51, 54). The latter can be regarded as part of the defensive marriage strategy of post-exilic Judeanism as outlined by Malina (2001:136–43). But generally, conversion required the severing of all your previous ethnic and religious roots. These two examples, however, corroborate the suggestion that any constructionist element to Judeanism had its basis in primordialism. It self-explanatory that these two developments in various ways were more a result of compelling and passionate bonds "deeply rooted in family, territory, language, custom, and religion" (Duling 2005:126).

The third example is an exception to the above. It concerns the cultural feature of *language*. When viewing the model, it will be seen that it is the only cultural feature that is represented by broken lines, indicating it was a cultural feature in (re)construction. It is commonly accepted that Aramaic was the everyday spoken language of Palestinian Judeans, but based on the available evidence more and more Judeans spoke Greek as a second, or even as a first language. The use of Hebrew, the Judean language proper, was surprisingly not that widespread as the other languages at all. The adoption of the Greek language was in no way a reinforcement of primordialism, but even here, some form of primordialism existed as the Judean scriptures were translated into Greek, and often Judean authors wrote their works in Greek as well. At the same time it must be said that speaking the Greek language did not seem to undermine your ethnic identity. Thus the cultural feature of language was not an important factor for determining Judean ethnicity.

A convenient way of analyzing an ethnic group is also by differentiating between the varying perspectives of those involved with the group. These processes of ethnic identity formation can also be modeled on three separate though connected levels of abstraction: micro, median, and macro (Barth 1994; cf. Esler 2003:48–49). Briefly, the micro level is concerned with processes that affect the ordinary members of the group. Its focus is on individual persons and interpersonal interaction. It has to do with "the management of selves in the complex context of relationships, demands, values and ideas; the resultant experiences of self-value, and the embracements and rejections of symbols and of social fellowships that are formative of the person's consciousness of ethnic identity" (Barth 1994:21). The median level is concerned with entrepreneurship, leadership and rhetoric. In this instance processes create and mobilize groups and intervene to constrain or compel people's expression and action on the micro level. Lastly, the macro level concerns itself with outsiders with power over the group. It involves state policies (whether legal or ideological) that allocates rights and obligations, which may involve the use of force and the control and manipulation of public information. These processes of ethnic identity formation are represented in the model, where the micro and median levels are indicated by the darker grey areas, and the macro level by the lighter grey areas. These areas broadly correspond to Malina's "person-sustaining groups." By representing the micro and median level with the same color, it attempts to show how closely connected these two levels are in Judean society.

Lastly, there were those Judeans, predominantly the priesthood, who along with others acted as teachers or interpreters of covenantal nomism. They were the "experts" whose main task was the maintenance of the Judean symbolic universe, in other words, they were the guardians of Judean ethnic identity. Smith (1994:712) explains that the close links between organized religion and ethnicity can be seen in the overlap between their respective myths of origin and creation, in the role of sectarian communities, and above all in the personnel and channels of communication in each case. In fact, priests and scribes, their sacred scriptures, rituals and liturgies have often emerged as the primary guardians and conduits of ethnic distinctiveness.

One can see the same is true of first century Judeanism and the important role that the priesthood, scribes and the other "experts" (e.g., Pharisees, Essenes) played in the preservation of the Judean way of life. They were the link between the Sacred Canopy and the Habitus/Israel. The historical Jesus operated here as well.

The Sacred Canopy

The second main part of our model is the "Sacred Canopy." For a lack of a better description, it constitutes the Judean "religion" or "theology." The *habitus* not only shape, and are shaped by common cultural practices, but they also shape and are shaped by Israel's common beliefs; i.e. the "Sacred Canopy." Not to be forgotten is the role of categorization. This dialectical interrelationship primarily has to do with the belief that Yahweh established/prescribes Judean ethnicity ("getting in"). It therefore also involves the recognition and communication of affinity *and* difference vis-à-vis other peoples. But the sacred canopy represents the more "intangible" aspects of Judean ethnicity, or the furthest reach of Judean self-externalization (cf. Berger 1973:37).

> Religion legitimates social institutions by bestowing upon them an ultimately valid ontological status, that is, by *locating* them within a sacred and cosmic frame of reference . . . Israel legitimated its institutions in terms of the divinely revealed law throughout its existence as an autonomous society . . . Religious legitimation purports to relate the humanly defined reality to ultimate, universal and sacred reality. The inherently precarious and transitory constructions of human activity are thus given the semblance of ultimate security and permanence. (Berger 1973:42, 44; emphasis original)

The sacred canopy is that part of covenantal nomism under which all of that system or identity we call Judeanism took shape. It is under which the entire Judean institutional order is integrated into an all-embracing and sacred frame of reference. It was that externalization that informed the overall Judean self-concept. And importantly, the "religious enterprise of human history profoundly reveals the pressing urgency and intensity of man's quest for meaning. The gigantic projections of religious consciousness ... constitute the historically most important effort of man to make reality humanly meaningful, at any price" (Berger 1973:106–7).

From the perspective of ethnicity theory, first-century Judeanism can be understood as a "totalizing ethnicity," where "ethnic organization and ethnic attributions of meaning pervade all or almost all spheres of life. Under these circumstances ethnic identity is totalizing or summative—it draws in to itself everything else" (Fenton 2003:115). Fishman (1996:66, 68) also says that ethnicity "is a *Weltanschauung* that helps to explain origins, clarify eternal questions, rationalize human destiny, and purports to offer an entre to universal truths ... [Ethnicity] is an experience of deeply rooted, intimate and eternal belonging." What Fenton and Fishman describe is similar to what the proposed socio-cultural model of Judean ethnicity attempts to depict graphically.

Importantly, in pre-modern eras a distinctive religion or vision of a world religion proved to be a very strong force in the persistence of ethnic identity. The sacred canopy points first and foremost to Yahweh, the God of Israel and his election of that people, the covenant and gift of the Torah. Inseparable from this, however, are *shared "historical" memories* and the rich ethno-symbolism contained therein, and the *myths of common ancestry*. All of these together are an example of a communal *mythomoteur*, or constitutive political myth of an ethnie (see Smith 1986:61–68; 1994:716). The community is endowed with sacred qualities, "which may generate an almost messianic fervour in times of crisis, particularly when allied to a heightened sense of superiority and a myth of ethnic election" (Smith 1994:716).

The last element of the furthest reach of Judean self-externalization is Millennialism. As inspired by the prophets, and no doubt contemporary reality, Israel was awaiting God's intervention on their behalf. The future restoration of Israel primarily referred to Israel's independent control and ownership of the land. Through divine intervention the Judean symbolic universe was to be made complete.

Summary

So the above is the proposed model and a basic explanation of the rationale behind it. The Socio-Cultural Model of Judean Ethnicity is a pictorial and abstract representation of the Judean symbolic universe, which is termed covenantal nomism. It consists of the Habitus/Israel, which stand in a close interrelationship with the more tangible Judean cultural features. The *habitus*, or habitual dispositions of Judean social agents, both shape and are shaped by objective common cultural practices. The "sense of self" is also influenced here through categorization. Here Judeans are responding to Yahweh's divine election, by being Judean, by maintaining their covenant status or Judean ethnic identity ("staying in"). The Sacred Canopy is the furthest reach of Judean self-externalization, under which all Judean institutions or cultural features are placed within a sacred and all-embracing frame of reference. The *habitus* also shape and are shaped by common beliefs, including a common history and ancestry. Here is the Judean belief that Yahweh established/prescribes Judean ethnicity ("getting in"). There is also a future element, in that Israel was hoping for future restoration. Collectively, being grounded in the *habitus*, the two dialectic interrelationships produce Judean ethnic identity, which involves the objectification of cultural practices in the recognition and communication of affinity *and* difference vis-à-vis other peoples.

The model as outlined and explained above is not regarded as definitive or final. As with Duling, it must be regarded it as heuristic; it should be changed or reconstructed as needed. It therefore also runs the risk of oversimplifying historic or local ethnographic information. It is suggested, however, that it will serve as a useful guideline to determine mainstream or common Judean ethnicity, and to determine where Judeans are "deviant" from the norm. If this model can be accepted, bearing in mind that it is still a work in progress, we can return to the issue of the historical Jesus, being left unfinished in the previous chapter.

So What Kind of Judean Was Jesus?

The question is now how did Jesus operate within and relate to the realm of covenantal nomism as explained above? With the help of the proposed model, I provide here an overview of Meier and Crossan's work to see how they are understood to have answered that question. Whether they would endorse this assessment is a matter altogether different, but it is the intention to as objectively as possible take their reconstructions to its logical conclusion. It must be emphasized that not any claims with regards to the historical Jesus are made here. The analysis below is based on their *interpretations* of the historical Jesus.

John P. Meier—Jesus, a Marginal "Jew"

So where does Meier's Jesus fit on the scale mentioned by Holmén from the commonly Judean to the marginally Judean? Meier's Jesus appears to be profoundly Judean in some respects while being a different kind of Judean in others. We must bear in mind that Meier's work is yet to be completed, but here is what can be gathered from his work thus far.

Jesus and the *Habitus*/Israel

A few general remarks can be made first. As will be recalled, the names of Jesus and his family hark back to the patriarchs, the Exodus, and conquest of the promised land. This means that his family participated in the reawakening of national and religious feeling. Galilee was conservative in nature, and surrounded by Gentile territories, Galileans clinged to the basics of Israelite religion to reinforce their identity. Jesus himself received some basic training, and had the ability to read Hebrew and expound the Scriptures. All of these combine to suggest that Jesus was socialized from a young age into finding his identity as a Judean, and that his sense of belongingness and self-esteem was dependent on how he operated within the Judean symbolic universe. Overall, Jesus grew up in an environment that would have fostered a strong Judean ethnic identity. To put it differently, the social environment of Jesus was essentially primordialist, that is, it was dominated by "primordial attachments" in order for the Judeans to differentiate themselves culturally from the surrounding Gentiles.

Language: Apart from Hebrew, Jesus would have spoken Aramaic as his everyday language, but had some knowledge of Greek as well although he never attained scribal literacy. Overall, language did not play that of an important role in establishing Judean identity, as many Judeans living in Palestine would have spoken Greek.

Religion: *Primordialist tendencies*: Jesus shared with the Pharisees a consuming desire to bring all Judeans to faithful obedience to God's will as set out in the Torah. The Mosaic law is taken for granted as the normative expression of God's will.

Jesus also revered the temple as the one holy place chosen by God for lawful sacrifice. Jesus followed its festivals, although he regarded the temple as belonging to the present order of things.

(Re)constructionist tendencies: The Law and the prophets functioned up to John the Immerser, from which time the kingdom of God had broken onto the scene. What has defined Judean ethnic identity

has now on its own become irrelevant, and is appropriated towards or qualified by the demands of the kingdom. In this regard Jesus gives new and startling laws. He also through his own teaching and demands on his followers undermines the Law with regards to the family, but also the food and purity laws are undermined through his inclusive table-fellowship and healings. In various ways the kingdom of God stands in tension with the traditional Torah.

The actions and sayings of Jesus pointed to the temple's destruction, but it is not clear whether he thought it would be rebuilt some day.

Kinship: *Primordialist tendencies:* Jesus operated as a prophet within and for sinful Israel. The mission of Jesus was exclusively aimed at Israel and he had but passing contact with Gentiles and Samaritans. By accepting John's immersion, he demonstrated communal solidarity with a sinful Israel.

(Re)constructionist tendencies: Jesus might have followed his father's trade as a woodworker, but Jesus broke with his family to define a new role and social identity for himself. He made the same demands on some of his followers. Jesus establishes an alternative kinship pattern; those who do the Father's will is Jesus' real family, his mother, brother and sister. Any notion of biological peoplehood based on family and ancestry collapses and is replaced by a spiritual kinship. The Judean symbolic universe is redefined, where faithful Israel (i.e. those who heed Jesus' message) is opposed to unfaithful Israel.

Jesus has open table-fellowship, and this inclusive approach demonstrates no interest to set up boundaries between his own group and other Judeans.

Covenantal Praxis: *Primordialist tendencies:* See "religion" above.

(Re)constructionist tendencies: Jesus received the immersion of John, and so saw himself as part of a sinful Israel. Jesus must have accepted John's message—it is only through confession of sin and baptism, and a profound change of heart and conduct that Israelites will be saved. This was required even of the devout (i.e. the profoundly Judean). This brings into question the sufficiency of the Judean symbolic universe and Judean ethnic identity as it operated at the time. Covenant status, divine election, indeed ethnic identity, has moved beyond traditional Judeanism. Jesus continued with John's baptism in his own ministry, thereby extending the eschatological dimension of John's message.

In enacting the presence of the kingdom of God, Jesus enjoys table-fellowship with various Israelites, including tax collectors and sinners. Here Jesus demonstrates little concern for purity laws. The kingdom of God represents an alternative symbolic universe, where the socially marginalized are restored into a correct relationship with God through inclusive fellowship and following Jesus—this occurs outside the traditional channels of Torah, priesthood, and temple.

Land: *Primordialist tendencies*: For Jesus, there can be no complete kingdom without a complete Israel. The Twelve disciples symbolized a regathered and reconstituted Israel.

(Re)onstructionist tendencies: The future kingdom of God envisages the participation of Gentiles. It will not be a political kingdom reserved for Judeans alone, while unfaithful Israel, even the supposed devout, will be thrown out of the kingdom. The future kingdom will therefore consist of people who heeded the message of Jesus, regardless of their ethnic identity.

Jesus and the Sacred Canopy

Primodialist tendencies: Jesus shared the belief in Israel's divine election and God's gift of the Torah. In terms of Millennialism, there can be no kingdom of God without a complete Israel. God will show his faithfulness to Israel and the covenant as the patriarchs and faithful Israelites will share in the resurrection.

(Re)constructionist tendencies: When the kingdom of God is established in full, Gentiles will also sit and eat with the patriarchs at the eschatological banquet, while some of Jesus' contemporaries, including the devout, will be thrown out of the kingdom. The Queen of Sheba and the Ninevites will be present and condemn that generation. On occasion, Jesus also performed miracles for Gentiles, which pointed to the future offer salvation for them. The future aspect of the kingdom therefore envisages a symbolic universe where ethnic identity is not a determining factor.

Shared "Historical" Memories and Myths of Common Ancestry: *Primordialist tendencies*: Jesus chose Twelve disciples, employing this example of ethno-symbolism to point to a regathered and reconstituted Israel. There can be no kingdom of God without a complete Israel.

Jesus referred to the patriarchs participating in the resurrection, and the symbolism behind the Twelve disciples imply that Jesus ascribed positive value to Israel's epic history. Jesus further shares the belief in God's faithful guidance of Israel through history.

(Re)constructionist tendencies: By accepting the immersion of John, Jesus accepts that physical descent from Abraham, even for the devout,

will mean nothing on its own at the coming judgement. Here any notion of ethno-symbolism is used to confront the present understanding of covenant membership and salvation history. Here ethno-symbolism is not used to maintain the status quo, or to help Judeans endure in the current situation. It is used in view of the demands of the future yet present kingdom of God in a challenging way.

CONCLUSIONS

Jesus' ethnic identity is therefore a curious and perplexing mixture of primordialism and constructionism. The constructionist element, however, given its content by the demands of the (future yet present in some way) kingdom of God, dominates. There are *elements of discontinuity in every cultural feature*, besides language, which anyhow does not really play an important role here in terms of our assessment of Meier's historical Jesus. Thus the balance of the evidence makes us understand Meier's historical Jesus as a different kind of Judean. Jesus is an eschatological prophet, who announces the arrival of the kingdom (= rule or reign) of God, an alternative symbolic universe that builds on traditional covenantal nomism, but in some respects undermines it in the process. It will not even have room for those who are according to the traditional system devout (profoundly Judean). The kingdom requires the participation of a different kind of Judean. Particularly the future vision requires different expectations and ways of doing things accustomed to. This kingdom envisages no celebration of Judean ethnic identity exclusive of complete Gentile participation. *Covenantal nomism, thus Judean ethnic identity, is in (re)construction*, and this process will gather momentum when the kingdom is fully established. In all of this, to call Jesus a "Marginal Judean" is being kind. Jesus somehow outgrew the primordialism of contemporary Judeanism. Jesus already in some ways stood aloof from the Judean symbolic universe but nevertheless retained a close contact. Indeed, the *Judean* symbolic universe is already in the process of being transformed into a *universal* symbolic universe, which paradoxically, will still focus on geographical Israel.

John Dominic Crossan—
Jesus, a Mediterranean "Jewish" Peasant

On that scale mentioned by Holmén between the commonly Judean and the marginally Judean, Jesus definitively leans heavily towards the marginal side of the scale. Again, we will do a brief overview of the most salient features.

Jesus and the *Habitus*/Israel

Jesus grew up in Nazareth, but as a Judean village, it must be seen in cultural continuity with Sepphoris and its Hellenized traditions. Overall Jesus moved within the ambience of inclusive Hellenistic Judeanism and its synthesis of Judean and Gentile tradition. Jesus was therefore socialized into an environment that was not inclined to be primordialist.

Religion: *(Re)constructionist tendencies*: Jesus challenged the legitimacy of the temple's spiritual power. In fact, he engages in religious banditry in this regard and sees the temple as a source of victimization. Through his healings/magic, which fell in line with the traditions of Elijah and Elisha, he is placed on par or even above the authority of the temple. He declares the leper as "clean" and so serves as an alternative or negation of Mosaic purity laws. In the process, the beneficiaries of his magic implicitly receive the forgiveness of sins.

The itinerant mission of Jesus and his followers are in opposition to the localized temple. Jesus serves as the temple's functional opponent and its substitute. By implication, Jesus opposes aspects of the Torah as well. When Jesus was in Jerusalem, he symbolically destroyed the temple and said he would destroy it beyond repair.

Kinship: *(Re)constructionist tendencies*: Jesus demonstrated a strong communal solidarity with marginalized Judeans, but one gets the impression that ideologically, it was not reserved for Judeans alone.

Jesus opposes the brokered and patriarchal family in line with Micah 7:6. He establishes an alternative kinship pattern based on egalitarian principles.

Covenantal Praxis: *(Re)constructionist tendencies*: Jesus was baptized by John, but thereafter he moved away from John's eschatological message to proclaim the brokerless kingdom of God available in the present.

Jesus ignores purity laws. He negates the value of food taboos and table rituals. According to Jesus, Judeans of different classes and ranks are free to eat together. Their ritual status is irrelevant.

When magic and meal come together in Jesus' itinerant mission to enact the brokerless kingdom, he and his followers adopt a peculiar dress code somewhat similar yet different to Greco-Roman Cynicism.

Land: *(Re)constructionist tendencies*: Jesus preached a non-eschatological message of the brokerless kingdom that is available in

A Socio-Cultural Model of Judean Ethnicity 113

the present. It concerns a mode of being. People place themselves under divine rule but it is not dependent on nation or place. Indeed, there is a very strong universal element to Jesus' teaching.

Jesus and the Sacred Canopy

Jesus evidently had a profound faith in God, but not necessarily the God peculiar to Israel, for even Gentiles know God albeit different names. As for the rest, not much can be said here. Evidently Jesus did not give any priority to the notions of a common ancestry and a shared historical and religious tradition, or the hopes of Israel's future restoration.

Conclusions

Jesus' ethnic identity is therefore overwhelmingly constructionist. There are *elements of discontinuity in every cultural feature* when it comes to Jesus. The balance of the evidence makes us understand Crossan's historical Jesus most definitively as a different kind of Judean. When compared with Crossan's other work on Jesus and early Christianity/Messianism, Jesus may be said to stand in continuity with the Tanak's theology of redistributive justice (cf. Crossan 1999; Crossan & Reed 2001). As for the rest, Crossan's Jesus practically obliterates Judean ethnic particularity. Jesus is a peasant Judean Cynic, who sets the kingdom over and against the brokered and hierarchical Mediterranean, of which Judeanism was a part as well. But overall, the immediate social background of Jesus is stretched very thin over the larger Greco-Roman world. There is very little, if any cultural particularity in the historical Jesus. As can be seen the cultural features of *shared "historical" memories* and *myths of common ancestry* does not really function in Crossan's reconstruction. Although Jesus' magic is placed in the tradition of Elijah and Elisha, and Jesus' attack on the family hierarchy is similar to Mic 7:6, there is no explicit connection that Jesus makes with the past. Ethno-symbolism is virtually non-existent in Jesus' frame of reference. Nothing is said of God's divine election of Israel, or his gift of the Torah, or covenant membership. Evidently Jesus has no concern for the future fate of Israel with regards to its restoration. *Had Jesus any notion of covenantal nomism, or Judean ethnic identity, it was in the process of radical (re)construction.* If Meier's Jesus in some ways stood aloof from the Judean symbolic universe, Crossan's Jesus is off the radar. He appears more to be a peasant Mediterranean philosopher-like figure, oh, who by the way, happens to be Judean. The present and brokerless kingdom of God involves a counter-cultural lifestyle with a strong egalitarian social vision, which by accident or design, may potentially involve any person of whatever ethnic background. The symbolic universe in which Jesus operated was truly universal in its scope, which according to this analysis, obliterates ethnic identity altogether.

Summary

It is interesting to compare Meier's and Crossan's reconstructions. Jesus' discontinuity or his (re)constructionist tendency is either explained by his eschatological perspective regarding the future but also present kingdom (Meier) or by Jesus moving within the realm of a counter-cultural inclusive Hellenistic Judeanism (Crossan). But both agree that Jesus to a greater or lesser extent stood in discontinuity with covenantal nomism when compared with the proposed model. As a reminder, the model represents an understanding that covenantal nomism (= Judean ethnic identity) of our period was essentially primordialist. In terms of Jesus' discontinuity, the three cultural features normally regarded as the most widespread or important for ethnic groups are quite telling. Jesus had no pre-occupation for an exclusive and independent political homeland, although "Israel" was where Jesus focussed his mission. Jesus developed an alternative kinship pattern. Belief in a common ancestry was in one respect revered, while on the other subverted since covenant status was no longer dependent on *biological* ancestry (Meier only).

In terms of covenantal praxis (or customs), again has Jesus at times as straying from the accepted norm. Jesus in (at least some) situations (healing and eating) showed little regard for purity and food laws. Lastly, when it came to religion, in word and deed Jesus anticipated the destruction of the temple and generally the Torah observance of Jesus in some respects is scandalous by the norms of the day. On these last two cultural features in particular, Meier and Crossan share what seems to be a broad agreement on Jesus' actions (cf. Borg 1983; 1987; Horsley 1987;[18] Sanders 1985; 1993; Becker 1998). So in particular instances, when compared with the proposed model in all its aspects, the Jesus produced by historical reconstruction can hardly be described as being profoundly Judean. What both Meier and Crossan suggest in their own unique way is the following: Jesus of Nazareth—and at that moment *within* Judeanism itself—was covenantal nomism or Judean ethnic

---

18. Horsley, however, argues that Jesus did not recruit or specially welcome social outcasts such as tax collectors, sinners, prostitutes, beggars, cripples, and the poor. These traditions come from the early Messianist communities. Jesus restored the healed to normal social interaction in their communities.

identity in (re)construction. Jesus defined a new way of being Judean. He undermined traditional Judean ethnic identity in the process. Importantly, this process of ethnic identity formation was a move in the opposite direction of mainstream Judean ethnicity which was essentially primordialist in character, being dominated by the requirements of the covenant and Torah and the need for cultural differentiation from the Gentiles.[19] This can potentially help to explain "of how it could be that Jesus lived within [Judeanism] and yet became the origin of a movement that eventually broke with it?" (Paget 2001:151).

---

19. See the analysis of first-century Judeanism in the next chapter.

CHAPTER 3

Judean Ethnicity in the First Century CE

Introduction

IN THE previous two chapters, several characteristics pertaining to Judean ethnic identity have been identified. This chapter will be devoted to investigate this matter in further detail in order to give our model the necessary and relevant content. It is not the aim here to do an intensive historical overview of Judeanism around the turn of the era, but more to identify in broader detail what would have been *typical* of first century Judean identity, even if it was not necessarily applicable to *all* Judeans. The methodology employed here is primarily based on three approaches. First, if some or other Judean practice or view is repeated in various texts across different periods, we can be reasonably confident that it formed part of the common stock of knowledge and practice. Second, the archaeological findings of our period will be brought into view. Third, some things of course might also be simply taken for granted and not explicitly explained, and this is where we will turn to the research of various scholars. These approaches outlined here are not mutually exclusive and so will often be integrated.

The "Sacred Canopy"

Before we proceed to investigate the more tangible aspects of Judean ethnicity, a few words will be used to describe the sacred canopy in further detail. A lot has been said about it already when we investigated Dunn's "four pillars," so the treatment below must be seen as complimentary. Faith in the God of Israel is axiomatic—it is hardly necessary to belabor this point.¹ Equally taken for granted is the notion of divine election. Israel is God's special and chosen people.² God says that when Israel is restored that "everyone will know that I am the God of Israel and the father of all the children of Jacob and king upon Mount Zion forever and ever" (*Jub.* 1:28). Israel is the "portion and inheritance of God" (*Pss. Sol.* 14:5). In the Psalms of Solomon the following moving passage is found:

> And now, you are God and we are the people whom you have loved; look and be compassionate, O God of Israel, for we are yours, and do not take away your mercy from us, lest they set upon us. For you chose the descendants of Abraham above all the nations, and you put your name upon us, Lord, and it will not cease forever. You made a covenant with our ancestors concerning us, and we hope in you when we turn our souls toward you. May the mercy of the Lord be upon the house of Israel forevermore. (*Pss. Sol.* 9:8–11)

This passage is but one of many that illustrate how Judean religion was intimately connected with the cultural features of *shared "historical" memories* and *myths of common ancestry*. With the notion of divine election came a sense of privilege as well: "I will give a light to the world and illumine their dwelling places and establish my covenant with the sons of men and glorify my people above all nations. For them I will bring out the eternal statutes that are for those in the light but for the ungodly a punishment" (*L.A.B.* 11:1). The Judeans are a "sacred race of pious men" (*Sib. Or.* 3:573). This was due to the covenant and the gift of Torah (otherwise described as the covenants, statutes, ordinances, judgements and commandments), something else simply taken for granted by the various texts.³ The Law is the "foundation of understanding that God

---

1. E.g., the worship of one God is a major theme in *2 Enoch* (e.g., *2 En.* 9:1; 10:6; 33:8; 34:1; 36:1; 47:3; 66:4–5). Some admonishments to avoid idolatry (e.g., *L.A.B.* 29:3; 34; 36:3–4; 38; 39:6; *Liv. Pro.* 3:2; 21:8; 22:2) illustrates that the temptation existed nevertheless.

2. Cf. *T. Mos.* 4:2; *Jub.* 1:17, 21; 12:24; 15:30, 32; 16:17–18; *L.A.B.* 19:8; 20:4; 23:12; 24:1; 30:2; 32:1; 35:2; 39:7; 49:2–3; *3 Macc* 2:6, 17; *4 Ezra* 5:23–27; 6:56–59.

3. In the Apocrypha the law, statutes, etc. appears approximately 260 times: Tob (17); Jdt (3); AddEsth (4); WisSol (13); Sir (57); 1 Bar (10); PrAzar (2); PrMan (1); Sus (4); 1 Macc (42); 2 Macc (36); 2 Ezra (30); *4 Ezra* (41). It is equally numerous in the pseudepigrapha, appearing in various contexts; e.g., *1 En.* 5:4; 99:2; 108:1–2; *2 En.* 2:2[J]; 7:3; 31:1; 34:1; 65:5; 71:25; *Sib. Or.* 3:256–57, 275–76; 573–80; *Ap. Zeph.* 3:4; *T. Reu.* 3:9; 6:8; *T. Levi* 9:6; 13:1–3; 14:4; 16:2; 19:1–2; *T. Jud.* 16:3; 18:3; 23:5; 26:1; *T. Iss.* 5:1; 6:1; *T. Zeb.* 10:2; *T. Dan* 5:1; 6:9–10; 7:3; *T. Naph.* 2:6; 3:2; *T. Gad* 3:1; 4:7;

had prepared from the creation of the world" (*L.A.B.* 32:7). Collectively, Yahweh, divine election, the covenant and the requirements of the Law were of the primary elements that gave *the overwhelming majority* of Judeans their collective identity and recognition of similarities as well as a consciousness of difference vis-à-vis other peoples, related to the we/they opposition. Schmidt (2001:23) writes that a collective consciousness, which would be common to all Judeans, "implies a minimal consensus," and at the very least, the sacred canopy embodies such a minimal consensus. Josephus boasts, and not without justification, that "Unity and identity of religious belief, perfect uniformity in habits and customs, produce a very beautiful concord in human character." It is particularly the Law that

> above all we owe our admirable harmony . . . Among us alone will be heard no contradictory statements about God . . . among us alone will be seen no difference in the conduct of our lives. With us all act alike, all profess the same doctrine about God. (*Apion* 2.179–81)

Here we can see again how every aspect of Judean life was subsumed under the sacred canopy: the institutional order is naturally seen as integrated into an all-embracing sacred and cosmic frame of reference. And for people like Josephus, to be a Judean is not to confess a personal faith. "It is first of all a declaration of . . . solidarity with a community" (Schmidt 2001:20). Part of the sacred canopy would be Israel's hope for future restoration, but this will be discussed in further detail later on.

As already stated above, part and parcel of the sacred canopy are the cultural features of *shared "historical" memories* (including ethno-symbolism) and *myths of common ancestry*. Various scribal groups creatively retold the history of Israel in various works where the events, ancestors and heroes of the past are held up as an inspiration or corrective reminder for present behavior and attitude. In this regard it can be mentioned that ethnicity is a social identity where commitment is primarily, but not exclusively, orientated to the past (De Vos 1975:17–19).[4] A shared cultural heritage derived from the past influences present

T. Ash. 6:3; 7:5; *T. Jos.* 11:1; 18:1; *T. Benj.* 3:1; 10:3, 5, 11; *T. Mos.* 9:4, 6; *Let. Aris.* 15, 45; *Jub.* 1:9–10, 14, 24; 2:31; 20:7; 21:5, 23; 23:16, 19; 24:11; *Vita* 34:1; 49:2; *L.A.B.* 9:8; 11:1–5, 7, 12:2; 13:3, 10; 16:5; 19:1, 6, 9; 21:7, 9–10; 22:5–6; 23:2, 10; 24:3; 28:2; 29:4; 30:1–2, 5; 35:3; 39:6; *Liv. Pro.* 2:18; 3:16; 17:1; 3 Macc 1:3; 3:4; 7:10–12; 4 Macc 1:17; 2:6, 8–10, 23; 4:19, 24; 5:16ff.; *Pss. Sol.* 4:8; 14:2.

4. De Vos also speaks of "present" and "future" commitments. Present commitments

behavior, and at the same time, ethnicity is concerned with the future survival of that group. In a sense, the surival of the group ensures your own survival (cf. Nash 1996:27). Ethnicity "makes every human a link in an eternal bond from generation to generation—from past ancestors to those in the future. Ethnicity is experienced as a guarantor of eternity" (Fishman 1996:63).

Being rooted in the past, Judean ethnicity celebrated the covenant and the Law given to the ancestors, combined with those memories that recall the events leading up to and the founding of Israel. In the literature of our period, frequent mention is made of the Law of the fathers (3 Macc 1:23), or the "covenant with/of our fathers" (*L.A.B.* 9:4; 19:2; 23:11; 30:7; 1 Macc 2:20, 50; 4:10; *4 Bar.* 6:21) which was mediated through Moses (*T. Mos.* 1:14), a "genius" according to one text (*Let. Aris.* 312). God will have mercy on Israel because of the fathers (*L.A.B.* 35:3; 2 Macc 8:15). To renounce the Law is to abandon ancestral beliefs (3 Macc 1:3; 4 Macc 16:16), or the customs of the fathers (2 Macc 11:25; 4 Macc 18:5). The link to the ancestors and the past was as axiomatic as the faith in Yahweh and his divine election of Israel.[5] Eleazar exclaims: "I will not violate the solemn oaths of my ancestors to keep the Law, not even if you gouge out my eyes and burn my entrails" (4 Macc 5:29; cf. 9:1–2, 29). Israel is also admonished: "O offspring of the seed of Abraham, children of Israel, obey this Law and be altogether true to your religion" (4 Macc 18:1). Daniel supposedly said: "Far be it from me to leave the heritage of my fathers and cleave to the inheritances of the uncircumcised" (*Liv. Pro.* 4:16). Other texts may be quoted:

> Woe to you who reject the foundations and the eternal inheritance of your forefathers! (*1 En.* 99:14)

> Happy—who preserves the foundations of his most ancient fathers, made firm from the beginning. Cursed—he who breaks down the institutions of his ancestors and fathers. (*2 En.* 52:9–10 [J])

---

are where your primary loyalty is directed to your country, or an occupation. Future commitments may involve loyalty to a revolutionary or a universalist religious movement.

5. In the Apocrypha, the (fore)fathers are mentioned approximately 84 times: Tob (6); Jdt (6); AddEsth (1); WisSol (7); Sir (4); 1 Bar (9); PrAzar (3); Bel (1); 1 Macc (17); 2 Macc (10); 2 Ezra (11); PrMan (1); 4 Ezra (7). See also *T. Levi* 10:1; 15:4; *T. Mos.* 9:4; *L.A.B.* 32:13; 3 Macc 6:3, 28, 32; 4 Macc 13:17; *Pss. Sol.* 17:4; 18:3.

The most popular figures referred to are Abraham, Isaac, and Jacob.⁶ Similarly frequent mention is made of the "God of my/our/their fathers,"⁷ or the God of Abraham (AddEsth 14:18) or even "Jacob's God" (*Pss. Sol.* 15:1). Abraham is referred to as "our/your father" or Israelites are identified as "children of Abraham" (*T. Levi* 8:15; *Jub.* 36:6; 4 Macc 9:21; 18:23).⁸ To be a child of Abraham is to have an elevated status, that is, to have the glorious status of being a Judean. It is this Judean self-understanding that Paul opposes in Galatians 3 (Esler 2006). Otherwise Judeans are the "seed of Jacob" (*4 Ezra* 8:16; *Jub.* 19:23) or "descendents of Jacob" (*4 Ezra* 9:30).⁹

The above is sufficient to conclude that the memories of the past, and the symbolic and biological link with the ancestors were an important part of the Judean sacred canopy. Your identity as a Judean in the present had everything to with the relationship that the God of Israel had with your ancestors. Being an upstanding Judean would also require you to honor the memory of your ancestors through your faith and obedience, and your participation in the Judean way of life. With this being explained, from now on this chapter is dedicated to elucidate the Habitus/Israel, while giving some relevant historical background as well.

What's in a Name?

Three names were used in the past for the region (and people) under discussion; Palestine, Judea and Israel. *Palaistine* is the Greek name that literally designated the land of the Philistines. The designation also referred to the place where the Phoenicians lived, but also the coastal strip stretching down to Egypt and the hinterland located south of Syria (Schmidt 2001:28–29, 31). This term, however, does not appear

6. Tob 4:12; Jdt 8:26; Sir 44:22; 1 Bar 2:34; 2 Macc 1:2; PrMan 1:1, 7; 4 Ezra 1:39; 6:8–9; *Ap. Zeph.* 9:4; *T. Levi* 15:4; 18:6, 14; *T. Jud.* 25:1; *T. Dan* 7:2; *T. Ash.* 7:7; *T. Benj.* 10:4, 6; *T. Mos.* 3:9; *Jub.* 1:7; *4 Bar.* 4:10; 6:21; 4 Macc 7:19; 13:17; 16:25; *Ezek. Trag.* 104–105; and the object of special attention in Jubilees.

7. *2 En.* 71:30; *T. Mos.* 9:6; *Jub.* 36:6; Tob 8:5; Jdt 7:28; 10:8; WisSol 9:1; PrAzar 1:3, 29; 2 Ezra 1:50; 4:62; 8:25; 9:8; PrMan 1:1; *L.A.B.* 27:7; 4 Macc 12:17.

8. Abraham is also mentioned in *T. Levi* 9:12; *T. Jos.* 6:8; *L.A.B.* 18:5; *4 Macc* 6:17, 23; 14:20; 15:28; 17:6; AdEsth 14:18; Sir 44:19; 1 Macc 2:52; 12:21; *4 Ezra* 3:13; 7:36; 3 Macc 6:3.

9. Jacob is also mentioned in *T. Jud.* 25:5; *T. Job* 1:5; *Jub.* 1:28; 19:23; 22:10ff; 23:23; *L.A.B.* 18:6; Sir 23:12; 24:8, 23; 36:11; 45:5, 17; 46:14; 47:22; 48:10; 49:10; 1 Bar 3:36; 4:2; 1 Macc 1:28; 3:7, 45; 5:2; *4 Ezra* 3:16, 19; 9:30; 12:46; 3 Macc 6:3; *Pss. Sol.* 7:10; 15:1.

in the Septuagint, other Judean literature or the New Testament, and is only rarely found in rabbinical literature. As such, it did not form part of Judean self-understanding and was used by Gentiles to refer to the Judean community. The term will be used here, however, as a matter of convenience when referring to the entire region where Judean influence was present.

"Judea" and "Israel" merits further discussion, as these terms were used by the Judeans themselves. As argued in the introductory chapter, it is agreed with the suggestion that the people of first-century Judea, and all those connected with its cultural and religious identity should be properly called Judeans. The culture they adhered to was Judeanism (in opposition to Hellenism). Josephus remarks that those who returned from Babylon were called "Judeans" (Ἰουδαῖοι), literally "those of the tribe of Judah," and the country itself took its name from the tribe that first settled there (*Ant.* 11.173). Indeed, the region was given the name *Yehudah*, which was translated Ἰουδαία in the Septuagint (Schmidt 2001:29). So "Judean" was an ethnic, religious and geographic reference. Yet Israel/Israelite continued to be used alongside Judea/Judean, whether referring to the geographical region or to the people itself. According to Dunn, Israel was used as the preferred self-designation, as opposed to "Jew(s)," or rather "Judean(s)," which was used by others to distinguish them from other ethnic and religious groups. So "Israel(ite)," denotes self-understanding and is used by the insider or participant (with reference to its internal history, election, and as heirs of the promise made to the patriarchs), whereas "Judean" denotes an outsider or spectator view, which was nevertheless used by Judeans themselves (Dunn 2003:263–64; 1991:145). Schmidt (2001:30) explains that when the rebels of the first and second Judean revolt inscribed "Israel" and not "Judea" on their coins, they "did more than declare the independence of their territory; they asserted themselves as heirs of the ancestral and sacred land." "Israel" is rich with symbolism as it "designates the land where the people maintain privileged relations with their God" (Schmidt 2001:31). Therefore Judea/Judean(s), as opposed to Israel, does not capture the essence of Judean identity. In Judean literature it is therefore hardly surprising that "Israel" occurs more frequently—this is especially true in the pseudepigrapha.[10]

---

10. "Israel" appears approximately 235 times in the Apocrypha: Tob (3), Jdt (47), AddEsth (6), Sir (18), 1 Bar (18), PrAzar (2), Sus (3), 1 Macc (56), 2 Macc (4), 2 Ezra (58), *4 Ezra* (17). "Israelites" appears about 10 times in the Apocrypha: Jdt 6:14; 1 Bar 3:4; 1 Macc 1:43, 53, 58 plus 5 other texts. "Israel" is the overwhelmingly favorite

The implications for the model are clear as everything converges on the *habitus*, embodied by the people "Israel." It is by no means an exaggeration to understand the people "Israel" (which also refers to the land) as constituting a collective of habitual dispositions, and the place where the "sense of self" as being part of Israel is internalized through categorization.

Judeanism Encounters Hellenism

In 587 BCE many citizens of the kingdom of Judah were exiled to Babylonia. The Persians conquered Babylonia in 539 BCE, and the Judeans were permitted by Cyrus the Great to return to their homeland. At least two waves of Babylonian Judeans returned to Judea in the 530s and 520s. Alexander the Great in turn conquered Persia, introducing the Hellenistic Age, "bringing with it completely new customs and a substantially different view of the universe" (Soggin 1993:301). After the unexpected death of Alexander in 323 BCE, his empire was fought over and divided by his generals, known as the Diadochi ("successors"). After years of wars, in around 301 BCE, Judea became part of the kingdom of Egypt (Ptolemies). In 200 BCE Judea was in turn conquered by the kings of Syria (Seleucids). But after Alexander's death "all the cultures of the East began to contribute to the new creation we call Hellenism. Hellenistic culture was not merely a debased version of the culture of classical Athens. Its substrate was Greek and its language of expression was Greek, but it absorbed ideas and practices from all the cultures with which it came into contact, thereby assuming many and diverse forms" (Cohen 1987:36). In non-Judean regions of Palestine, the penetration of Hellenistic culture is most evident in religion. Sometimes Hellenistic elements were fused with indigenous cults and at other times Greek cults totally took over. The worship of Apollo was common in Philistine cities (Raphia, Gaza, Ashkelon), probably promoted by Seleucid influ-

designation in the pseudepigrapha. Here follows a representative list: *T. Reu.* 1:10; 6:8; *T. Sim.* 6:5; *T. Levi* 4:4; 7:3; 8:16; *T. Jud.* 22:1–2; *T. Iss.* 5:8; *T. Zeb.* 9:5; *T. Dan* 1:9; 5:4, 13; 6:2, 6–7; 7:3; *T. Naph.* 7:1; 8:1–3; *T. Jos.* 1:2; *T. Benj.* 10:11; *T. Mos.* 3:7; 10:8; *Jub.* 1:28; 15:28; 30:5ff; 49:14, 22; 50:5; *L.A.B.* 9:4; 27:13; 32:8; 34:5; 35:3; 39:9; *Liv.Pro.* 3:12; 22:2; 3 Macc 2:6, 17; 4 Macc 17:22; *Pss. Sol.* 7:8ff.; 9:1ff; 10:5 et al. "Judea" appears approximately 81 times in the Apocrypha: Tob (1), Jdt (9), AddEsth (1), 1 Macc (46), 2 Macc (9), 2 Ezra (15). "Judeans" is used about 119 times: AddEsth (3), Sus (1), 1 Macc (41), 2 Macc (62), 2 Ezra (12); the singular "Judean" about 6 times: AddEsth 11:3; Bel 1:28; 2 Macc 6:6; 9:17; 3:11, 27. In other texts "Judea" (*Sib. Or.* 5:329), "Judeans" (*Hist. Rech.* 9:2; 3 Macc 2:28; 3:3; 4:21; 5:3, 6, 20, 31, 35 et al; 4 Macc 5:7) and "Judean" (3 Macc 1:3; 3:2, 6) only appear on a handful of occasions.

ence. Apollo was considered as the divine ancestor of the Seleucids as Dionysus was believed to be the divine ancestor of the Ptolemies (Schürer et al. 1979:29, 35).

Resistance to and Influence of Hellenistic Culture

How were the Judeans affected by Hellenism? It is said that Moses

> surrounded us with unbroken palisades and iron walls to prevent our mixing with any of the other peoples in any matter, being thus kept pure in body and soul, preserved from false beliefs, and worshipping the only God omnipotent over all creation . . . So, to prevent our being perverted by contact with others or mixing with bad influences, he hedged us in on all sides with strict observances connected with meat and drink and touch and hearing and sight, after the manner of the Law. (*Let. Aris.* 139–42)

So the symbolic universe of Judeanism is represented here quite idealistically as something quite impervious to foreign influence. According to Cohen (1987:37), however, all forms of Judeanism—of both the Diaspora and in the land of Israel—were Hellenized; there was no "pure" Judeanism. "'To Hellenize or not to Hellenize' was not a question the [Judeans] of antiquity had to answer. They were given no choice. The questions that confronted them were 'how?' and 'how far?' . . . How far could [Judeanism] go in absorbing foreign ways and ideas before it was untrue to itself and lost its identity?" (Cohen 1987:45). How Judeanism answered these questions is the subject matter we will focus on next.

The Maccabean Revolt

When Palestine was under the control of the Ptolmies of Egypt, Judean religion and customs were allowed to continue pretty much without interference. During 202–198 BCE, the Seleucid, Antiochus III, took control of Palestine supported by the high priest Simon II, a Zadokite. It is probably this Simon who is eulogized by Ben Sira (50:1–11) and the text also indicates that the high priest enjoyed autonomy and presented the sacrifices to God on behalf of the people, and conferred God's blessing on the people in return (Sir 50:18–21). Ben Sira 50:24 (Hebrew version) wishes for Simon the son of Onias to be blessed and that his offspring may continue to rule as priests. Ben Sira "regarded [Judean] life as it existed under the reign of Simon as the virtually complete embodiment of the nation's highest aspirations" (Baumgarten 1997:27). Those who wanted to emphasize the separation between Israel and the nations also achieved much when Antiochus III (ca 200 BCE) issued a decree on request of the priest. The decree, cited by Josephus (*Ant.* 12.145–46), states that foreigners are not allowed to enter the enclosure of the temple,[11] neither Judeans, except those who purify themselves before hand. These demands are nowhere explicitly mentioned in the Tanak. In Gentile temples, all those who purified themselves were allowed to enter, be they natives or foreigners. In Jerusalem, however, foreigners were permanently banned (Baumgarten 1997:82). The Hellenizing priests—descendants of Simon II—believed that regulations individually catering for Judeans and Gentiles were a source of disaster (1 Macc 1:11). "Perhaps these regulations were especially vulnerable to criticism, because crucial aspects of these rules were not found in the Bible. They could thus easily be represented as innovations, subject to reform" (Baumgarten 1997:83).

A "reform" was attempted which took on various dimensions. Just before 175 BCE there was a split in the Judean aristocracy, that is, between the Zadokite high priest Onias III and his brother Jason. The latter was in favor of Hellenization, or more succinctly, the adoption of Greek education, athletics and dress. The attempt was further made to transform Jerusalem into a Greek polis, or at least, for the citizens to be called "Antiochenes." Jason, the "ungodly wretch, and no high priest" (2 Macc 4:13) was appointed and had support from Antiochus IV Epiphanes ("God revealed") who came to power in Syria in 175. First Maccabees describes that there were "wicked men" in Israel who wanted to make a covenant with the ἐθνῶν, and who was granted permission by the king to observe Gentile ordinances (1 Macc 1:11–13). Having obtained permission, they returned to Jerusalem where they built a gymnasium at the foot of the temple. According to 2 Macc 4:9 Jason also asked for a training centre to be built. In this manner a process was initiated whereby the Hellenistic spirit could be instilled in young Judean men. It is claimed that Antiochus further encouraged young Judean men to reject the ancestral law: "Share in the Greek style, change your mode of living, and enjoy your youth" (4 Macc 8:8).

Particularly in the gymnasium the "curious" feature of Judean ethnic identity became all too visible—the circumcision of the male foreskin, since exercises were conducted in the nude. Some Judeans underwent an epispasm by which the foreskin was restored, and so was said to have forsaken the "holy covenant" (1 Macc 1:15). No wonder the gymnasium

11. In the Tanak a sacrifice may be offered by a Gentile (Lev 22:25; cf. 1 Kgs 8:41–43).

was regarded as one of the most important abominations of Hellenism (1 Macc 1:14–15; 2 Macc 4:9–17). Jubilees 3:31 also says Adam and Eve covered their genitals, unlike the Gentiles. According to Cohen (1987:52; cf. Schmidt 2001:34), there are passages in the Tanak that speak of the importance of circumcision (Gen 17; 34; Exod 4:24–26; 12:43–49; Josh 5:2–11; Jer 9:24–25) but the Bible "as a whole generally ignores it and nowhere regards it as the essential mark of [Judean] identity or as the sine qua non for membership in the [Judean polity]. It attained this status only in Maccabean times." But circumcision was a primary requirement for covenant membership for males, or to put it differently, for Judean ethnic identity. Genesis 17:10–14 makes this quite clear, where God speaks to Abraham in the following terms:

> This is my covenant with you and your descendants after you, the covenant you are to keep: Every male among you shall be circumcised. You are to undergo circumcision, and it will be the sign of the covenant between me and you . . . Any uncircumcised male, who has not been circumcised in the flesh, will be cut off from his people; he has broken my covenant. (NIV)

To remove your circumcision was from a traditional Judean perspective wholly unthinkable (cf. *T. Levi* 6:3–6; *T. Mos.* 8:1–3; Theodotus in Eusebius, *Pr. Ev.* 9.22.4–9; Sir 44:20).[12] Even the angels are created as circumcised (*Jub.* 15:27) and so are able to participate with Israel in its rites, feasts, and Sabbath days (*Jub.* 2:18). Also Moses was born "in the covenant of God and the covenant of the flesh" (*L.A.B.* 9:13), that is, he was born circumcised (cf. *b. Sot.* 12a; *Exod. Rab.* 1:24). In postbiblical Hebrew "covenant" had become a technical term for circumcision (Harrington 1985:316, n. o). The importance of circumcision is emphasized in *Jub.* 15:25–32, and the failure to perform the rite, presumably the procedure of epispasm as well, is regarded as an "eternal error" (*Jub.* 15:33–34). It should not come as a surprise that circumcision (along with food laws) became a major issue when Gentiles were incorporated into the Messianist community (Acts 15:1–29; Gal 2:1–10).

---

12. Cf. *m. Ned.* 3:11, where circumcision virtually realizes a state of human ontological perfection: "Great is circumcision, for despite all the commandments which Abraham our father carried out, he was called complete and whole only when he had circumcised himself as it is said, *Walk before me and be perfect*" (Gen 17:1). The same passage regards the foreskin as "disgusting," and also states that was it not for circumcision (which also points to the covenant), God would not have created the world (Jer 33:25) (Neusner 1988:412).

The influence of Hellenism, however, had impact in other areas as well. New fashions included the wearing of a Greek hat, according to 2 Macc 4:12, the extreme height of Hellenism. The hat in question is the *petasos*, the Greek broad-rimmed hat associated with Hermes. So the objection was mainly aimed at a Gentile religious symbol (Rubens 1973:16). One can contrast the Essenes who wore plain clothes and ate plain food (Baumgarten 1997:101). Overall, Hellenism presented a new problem for devout Judeans.

> Hellenism presented itself as an alternative world-view, in the face of which it was necessary to make choices: either to remain a [Judean] or to embrace the new way of living and thinking, thus imperilling the faith. The Hellenists among the [Judeans] thought they could do both, while remaining within the bounds of good faith; according to the orthodox they had in fact chosen Hellenism and denied [Judeanism]. (Soggin 1993:317)

One can say that Hellenism presented an alternative symbolic universe. The presence of a gymnasium in Jerusalem and the Hellenizing priests initiated a process whereby Judean identity came under siege. But things under Antiochus IV became worse. After a failed campaign in Egypt, he besieged Jerusalem and occupied the temple. The following year, in 167 he apparently issued decrees which aimed at the compulsory Hellenization of Judea (1 Macc 1:29; 2 Macc 5:24). According to Jagersma (1986:52) these measures should rather be attributed to those Judeans in Jerusalem in favor of Hellenization and the changes were aimed at giving Judean worship a more Hellenistic form. Under the high priest Menelaus, the temple itself was transformed into a sanctuary dedicated to Zeus Olympius, instead of the "Lord of heaven," the usual designation for God. A second altar, or perhaps a stone on the existing altar was set up, the "abomination of desolation" (βδέλυγμα ἐρημώσεως; Hebrew *šiqquṣ mešomem* (1 Macc 1:54; Dan 9:27; 11:31; 12:11; cf. *T. Mos.* 5:3–4). This happened on 15 December 167 BCE and apparently on 25 December sacrifices were offered to Sol Invictus, the unconquered sun (Soggin 1993:322). This new form of temple cult was extended throughout Judea. Judeans were instructed to build altars (and sacred shrines for idols?) and to sacrifice pigs and unclean animals (1 Macc 1:47, 54; 2 Macc 6:4–9, 21; 7:1). If one takes 1 and 2 Maccabees at face value, many forms of Judean worship were also banned. Antiochus IV banned sacrifices (1 Macc 1:45; cf. *Jub.* 32:4–22); profaned the Sabbath and festival days (1 Macc 1:46; cf. *Jub.* 23:19; 6:37); prohibited circumcision (1 Macc 1:47; cf. *Jub.* 15:24–29); and burnt books (1 Macc 1:56; cf. Jub. 45:16). It is said that many Judeans conformed to these measures be it through pressure or threats, while some chose martyrdom instead (1 Macc 1:57–64; 2 Macc 6:18–19; 7:1ff.; *Ant.* 12.253ff.). According to Jagersma (1986:52–53) the pro-Hasmonean 1 Maccabees would have exaggerated the persecution to bolster the Maccabean claim to the high priesthood so we must assume that the persecution was a limited one.

Whatever the scale of forced Hellenization and the persecution that ensued, the decrees, whether they came from Antiochus or Judean Hellenists, took direct aim at those practices that separated Judeans from Gentiles (1 Macc 1:44–50). The revolt that inevitably followed was spearheaded by the Hasmonean family, beginning with the priest Mattathias, who was neither a Zadokite nor an aristocrat. The "Hasmonean" family is called after an ancestor, Hashmon, but also the Maccabees, due to a nickname, "the hammerer" (*Ant.* 12.365ff.) that was given to Judas, the third son of Mattathias (Sanders 1992:17). In Modein Mattathias was requested to make a pagan sacrifice (to sacrifice a pig to Zeus Olympius?), but refused, choosing to "walk in the covenant of our fathers" thereby not abandoning the Law and ordinances (1 Macc 2:20–21). A Judean who attempted to make a pagan sacrifice at Modein enraged Mattathias and was killed by the latter on the altar. Subsequently Mattathias called upon those who were "zealous for the law," and who "maintain the covenant" (1 Macc 2:27) to join forces with him, and so many went to the wilderness. Many were later killed, as they refused to fight on the Sabbath (1 Macc 2:34–38), a decision that was later reversed (v. 41). Mattathias was soon joined by Hasideans, those who were willing to offer themselves for the sake of the Law (1 Macc 2:42). The word "Hasidean" reflects the Hebrew *ḥasidim*, "pious," referring to a "group of people who wished to resist Hellenization and who were willing to fight and die" (Sanders 1992:18). Collectively their activity was principally aimed at fellow Judeans, killing "sinners" and "lawless men" (1 Macc 2:44). They also destroyed pagan altars and forcefully circumcised Judean children (1 Macc 2:45–46). Mattathias died in 166, but the call to "be zealous for the law" and to "give your lives for the covenant of your fathers" (1 Macc 2:50) was continued through his sons (Judas, Jonathan, and Simon). All in all, we have to do here with Maccabean propaganda, but it must have resonated strongly with popular opinion.

The Hasmonean campaign was eventually successful. Jerusalem was captured (except for the Acra) and on 25 Chislev (around 15 December) 164 BCE the temple was cleansed and rededicated by Judas, an event still celebrated as the feast of Hanukkah, "dedication" (1 Macc 4:59) (Soggin 1993:325). Judas also erected a wall around Mount Zion to keep the Gentiles out (1 Macc 4:60–61)—so Gentiles were not even allowed access to the Court of Gentiles that existed at the time. The Judeans eventually received religious freedom from Antiochus V (164–162 BCE) though attempts at reform probably continued in Jerusalem. In 160 the high priest, Alcimus, began to tear down the wall of the inner court of the Sanctuary. According to 1 Maccabees Alcimus was prevented from finishing his intentions by divine intervention (1 Macc 9:54–56). Thus he, like the other Hellenists, might have endeavored to remove the barrier between Judeans and Gentiles (Baumgarten 1997:83; Schmidt 2001:105).

It is evident that the Maccabean revolt led to several questions being asked about Hellenization, the Law, the high priesthood and military control (Sanders 1992:20–21). Nevertheless, under the leadership of Judas Maccabees, the Judeans had military success against the Seleucids and the internal strife in Syria allowed the Maccabees in time to extend their powers. Judas' brother and successor, Jonathan, was appointed high priest by Alexander Balas in 152 who contended for the Syrian throne (1 Macc 10:18–20). In response, Demetrius I offered Jonathan exemption from taxes (1 Macc 10:26–33). Jonathan received more favors from Demetrius II but was killed in 143 BCE. His brother, Simon, obtained further, yet not complete independence for the Judeans (cf. Gruen 2002), and was appointed as high priest by Demetrius II (1 Macc 10:31–31). He was the one that occupied the fortress Acra (141 BCE), and so the last stronghold of the Hellenizers and their Syrian supporters were captured (1 Macc 13:51). Sanders (1992:22) explains:

> The fall of the Acra terminated any lingering hopes that the Hellenizers had. [Judean] distinctiveness would be maintained, circumcision would be kept, and the Mosaic law would be enforced. Simon and his successors acted very much like other Hellenistic kings . . . but there would be no further effort to break down the barriers between [Judeanism] and the rest of the Graeco-Roman world.

We can see from the above that zeal for the law was equivalent to remaining faithful to the covenant of the forefathers; it was remaining faithful to the symbolic universe of covenantal nomism, or Judean ethnic identity. The Maccabean revolt can be described as a form of *ethnicism*, "a collective movement, whose activities and efforts are aimed at resisting perceived threats from outside and corrosion within, at renewing a community's forms and traditions, and at reintegrating a community's members and strata which have become dangerously divided by conflicting pressures ... [E]thnicism has manifested three broad aims in antiquity ... territorial restoration, genealogical restoration and cultural renewal" (Smith 1986:50–51). Further, Smith (1986:55–56) explains that ethnicism is fundamentally defensive, provoked by military threat, socio-economic challenges, and cultural contact. All these things in various ways describe the situation around the Maccabean revolt, as well as the revolts that followed. Also, persistent interstate warfare promotes ethnic unity for agrarian folk cultures (cf. Smith 1994:710–11), but this can be said for inter-cultural warfare as well.

Be Careful What You Eat

The persecution of Judean customs and religion brought one aspect of Judean identity into focus—the Judean attitude towards food. The laws on clean and unclean foods do not hold such a central place in the Torah (Lev 11:1–23; Deut 14:3–21). Even Jacob's sons ate Gentile food with Gentiles (Gen 43:32). From the time of the Maccabees, however, food laws took on increasing importance in Judean folklore and Judean self-understanding (Dunn 1990:193). The Judeans were supposedly forced to eat pork (1 Macc 1:47–48; 2 Macc 6:18–21; 7:1), but some preferred to die in order not to profane the covenant (1 Macc 1:62–63). Food not defiled by Gentiles and permissible to eat was according to 2 Macc 5:27 very limited. Alternatively, on a practical level the "loyalists had to take extreme steps, from armed revolt to restricting the sources of their food in order to avoid defilement" (Baumgarten 1997:84). So 2 Macc 5:27 explains that Judah and his companions escaped to the wilderness and ate wild food so that they might not share in the defilement (cf. 1 Macc 1:62–63; Dan 1:8). Sometime around 160 BCE, *1 En.* 91:9 used as its slogan: "all that which is (common) with the heathen shall be sundered." *Jubilees* (which perhaps quotes *1 En.* 91–108 in *Jub.* 4:18), in the wake of the Maccabean revolt encourages Judeans: ". . . keep the commandments of Abraham, your father. Separate yourself from the gentiles, and do not eat with them ... Because their deeds are defiled, and all their ways are contaminated, and despicable, and abominable" (*Jub.* 22:16). Here is a classic example of the maintenance of your symbolic universe through nihilation.

The Maccabean martyrs were further remembered for their fidelity to the covenant. Similarly the heroes of popular stories such as Daniel, Tobit, Judith, Esther and Joseph all showed their faithfulness to God, that is, they maintained their Judean identity by refusing to eat "the food of Gentiles" (Dan 1:8–16; 10:3; Tob 1:10–13; Jdt 10:5; 12:1–20; AddEsth 14:17; *Jos. Asen.* 7:1; 8:5), and no Judean abiding by the Torah eats at a Gentile table (*Jub.* 22:16; cf. Acts 11:3; Gal 2:12). These people were heroes because they are faithful Judeans, examples to emulate. The resulting pre-occupation with food has direct bearing on the constructionist approach of ethnicity theory. As a result of the Maccabean crisis, Judean ethnicity was in part (re)constructed around an intensified effort to observe food and purity laws more strictly. But overall, this is representative of a primordialist approach to ethnicity as primordial sentiments attached themselves to existing cultural practices and were intensified to sharpen that consciousness of difference vis-à-vis the nations.

This aspect of universe maintenance continued unabated. Josephus speaks of priests who were imprisoned in Rome, who survived only on figs and nuts (*Life* 3.14). The eating habits of Judeans were also well known among Gentile authors. For example, Tacitus writes scathingly of Judeans and their supposed hatred of the rest of the world: "they eat separately, they sleep separately . . ." (*Hist.* 5.5). Sextus Empiricus (second century CE) commented that Judeans would rather die than eat pork (Sanders 1992:239). According to Philo, when his delegation was in conversation with Emperor Caligula, they were interrupted with the abrupt and irrelevant question: "Why do you refuse to eat pork?" (*Embassy* 361).

The separation between Judeans and Gentiles was made stronger based on the belief that Gentiles were unclean since they did not observe the purity laws. Although Judean purity laws were not really applicable to Gentiles they were treated as impure and any contact could lead to defilement (Acts 10:28) (cf. Sanders 1992:72–76). Their houses and possessions were potential targets of ritual uncleanness, hence were regarded as impure (Schürer et al. 1979:83). A number of Gentile objects could not be used by Judeans since Judeans laws were not observed during its production. Much of the most ordinary foods coming from Gentiles were forbidden to Judeans, but they were allowed to make a profit from buying and selling things such as milk, bread and oil (Schürer et al. 1979:83–84).

Judeanism versus Hellenism

"Judeanism" (Ἰουδαϊσμός) as a term appears for the first time in the literature of this period in reaction to the influence of Hellenism. It speaks of those who fought bravely for Judeanism (2 Macc 2:21) and that their supporters continued in Judeanism (2 Macc 8:1). One Razis, "a lover of his countrymen," was accused of Judeanism and risked his life for it (2 Macc 14:38). Lastly, 4 Macc 4:26 speaks of Antiochus' attempt to force Judeans to eat forbidden food and so renounce Judeanism. Second Maccabees 4:13 speaks of an ἀκμή τις Ἑλληνισμοῦ ("a climax of attempts at Hellenization") during the time of Jason. Here Ἑλληνισμός is for the first time used in a cultural sense as the equivalent of ἀλλοφυλισμός, or "foreignness" (2 Macc 4:13; 6:24) (Hengel 1989:22). Lieu (2002:305) also points out that 2 Maccabees subverts the usual Greek/barbarian antithesis by saying that the fight for Ἰουδαϊσμός is against the "*barbaric* hordes" (2 Macc 2:21). "Foreignness" was also identifiable to the Greeks as akin to the barbarian. Similar language is found in 1 Maccabees (ἀλλόφυλος; ἀλλογενής; ἀλλότριος). But the point is that battle lines were being drawn between Judeanism and Hellenism. Judeanism is that system that is opposed to anything foreign, and that in any way detracts from being Judean. If we may adapt Dunn's explanation:

> [Judeanism] is the summary term for that system embodying national and religious identity which was the rallying point for the violent rejection by the Maccabees of the Syrian attempt to assimilate them by the abolition of their distinctive practices [particularly circumcision and food laws; cf. 1 Macc 1:60–63; 4 Macc 4:26]. From the beginning, therefore [Judeanism] has a *strongly nationalistic overtone* and denotes a powerful integration of religious and national identity which marked [Judeanism] out in its *distinctiveness* from other nations and religions. (Dunn 2003:261; emphasis original).

If we may paraphrase Dunn's explanation, Judeanism is a summary term for that system that embodied Judean ethnicity. It requires "zeal for the law" (1 Macc 2:26, 27, 50, 58; 2 Macc 4:2; cf. Gal 1:13–14). In other words, it requires zeal for being Judean, for the tradition of the forefathers, not zeal for what we understand today in a secularized world as being "religious." According to ethnicity theory, this is what you call primordialism.

The Judean Sects

After the Maccabean Revolt, Judeanism experienced the rise of various sects. Cohen defines that a "sect asserts that *it alone embodies the ideals of the larger group*. In [Judean] terms this means that a sect sees itself as the true Israel ... *it alone understands God's will*" (Cohen 1987:126, 127; emphasis original). Baumgarten has a different but complimentary approach to sectarianism. He "would define a sect as a *voluntary association of protest, which utilizes boundary marking mechanisms—the social means of differentiating between insiders and outsiders—to distinguish between its own members and those otherwise normally regarded as belonging to the same national or religious entity*. Ancient [Judean] sects, accordingly, *differentiated between [Judeans] who were members of their sect and those not*" (Baumgarten 1997:7; emphasis original). But why did Judean sects come to flourish in this period?

In the pre-Maccabean period no Judean faithful ever organized themselves into a socially significant movement to separate themselves from other Judeans. Josephus mentions Pharisees, Sadducees and Essenes for the first time in a comment that concerns the reign of Jonathan. During this period there were a few rapid changes in Judean life: 1) the encounter with Hellenism; 2) the persecutions of Antiochus IV; 3) the cooperation of at least a few traditional leaders with those persecutions; 4) the successful revolt against Antiochus IV; 5) the rise of a new dynasty of high priests, that was soon followed by the acquisition of political independence. The last four events on the list took place over a time span of around twenty-five years (Baumgarten 1997:26).

For Cohen, sectarianism is a culmination of the democratization of Judeanism. It wanted to bridge gap between humanity and God "through constant practice of the commandments of the Torah and total immersion in the contemplation of God and his works. Sectarian piety supplants or supplements the temple cult through prayer, scriptural study, and purifications, and rejects or dilutes the power of the priesthood" (Cohen 1987:172). Baumgarten has another approach and will be the one that will be followed here. Although there were antecedents and forerunners to Judean sects, such as is illustrated in *1 Enoch* and *Jubilees* who focus on social action in response to Hellenism, Baumgarten proposes that "the decisive moment, which brought about the full fledged phenomenon [of sectarianism], came with the victory of the Hasmonean dynasty and their claim for the restoration of traditional rule. The successful revolt of the Maccabees, their assumption of the high priesthood, and the eventual achievement of independence, all raised hopes for a reimposition of boundaries between [Judeans] and [non-Judeans], restrictions which had suffered so much damage in the preceding decades, in particular" (Baumgarten 1997:86). Maccabean propaganda claimed that these expectations of separation were met. It explains that Judas had fortified Mount Zion with high walls and strong towers in order to keep the Gentiles out (1 Macc 4:60). Simon worked to achieve similar ends. He established peace and in his time there were no Gentiles to make the Judeans afraid (1 Macc 4:60). The decree that affirmed Simon's rule stated that he had "put the Gentiles out of the country," and he expelled the men from the citadel of Jerusalem who used to defile the areas of the temple and so undermined its purity (1 Macc 14:36). Indeed, Simon built the walls of Jerusalem higher (1 Macc 14:37) and so continued Judas' program of keeping Gentiles out. Indeed, "zealous hatred of gentiles" pervades 1 Maccabees as a whole (Baumgarten 1997:86), since they are void of true spirituality as they gave up their own religions to follow those decreed by the king (1 Macc 1:41–43; 2:19).

Yet, the Maccabees were inconsistent in their policy towards the surrounding culture. To a degree they opposed practices associated with Gentile culture, but "the needs of government playing the international game of politics, required paying the price of adapting to the surrounding culture" (Baumgarten 1997:87). This tension is very obvious in the fact that Jonathan accepted the high priesthood from Alexander Balas as expressed in the same decree that affirmed his rule. This decree was further "formulated in Greek style, and was based on the political ideology and practice of Greek democracy" (Baumgarten 1997:88). Jonathan's appointment as high priest by the Seleucid Alexander Balas, was the first accommodation of many to foreign culture that was to cause the flourishing of Judean sects. The Seleucids similarly appointed his brother Simon as high priest. It is also claimed by 1 Maccabees that the Judeans and their priests decided that Simon should be their "high priest for ever" (1 Macc 14:41–43), meaning that he and his descendants would be high priests, unless a prophet would arise and declare otherwise. So the rights of the family of Zadok, in charge of the temple for centuries, have been revoked (Sanders 1992:22). Jonathan and Simon's acceptance of this post from Gentile rulers was wholly illegitimate. This led to Onias IV, a Zadokite priest, establishing a temple in Leontopolis in Egypt. The importance of the Zadokite priests in the Dead Sea sect lends support that the "Teacher of Righteousness" was a member of that family; perhaps the Sadducees also claimed the authority of the Zadokite priesthood (Sanders 1992:23–25).

Just after Simon came to power, he built a mausoleum in Hellenistic style in honor of his fathers and brothers (Hengel 1989:31). Aristobulus I even adopted the nickname φιλέλλην, "lover of Greeks" (*Ant.* 13.318). Thus the Maccabean success in various ways undermined the borders that they were supposed to have maintained. There were many expectations when the Maccabees came to power, but their actions provoked disappointment. Baumgarten proposes that it was "in response to this sense of disillusionment, *of a mixture of blessing and curses*, that sectarianism became fully mature. With the old national perimeter facing a new sort of danger ... sects flourished which established new voluntary boundaries of their own against other [Judeans]" (Baumgarten 1997:88; emphasis original). The Damascus Document (CD) gives expression to this and explains the rulers will pay the price for their sins and the Gentile kings they imitated will also be the source of their destruction (CD 8.3–21b). The walls erected by the Maccabees were found wanting, merely "daubed with plaster" (CD 8 alluding to Ezek 13:10). A real fortress was to be found in the Qumran community (1QH 6.25–27). Now those excluded are not only Gentiles, but also Judeans whose defiling presence must be avoided. The Essenes/Qumran Covenanters had sectarian "brothers" that were more important than "natural" brothers (*War* 2.120, 122, 127, 134; Philo, *Omnis Probus* 79; *Hyp.* 11.2; 1QH 9.35–36; 1QS 6.10, 22; CD 6.20; 7.1–2). The new kinship patterns simply superseded or supplanted natural ties (Baumgarten 1997:61–62, 90–91).

Another aspect of history is important to the understanding of the flourishing of Judean sects. In the pre-Maccabean period, Judeanism was constantly at the mercy of imperial power. Dissident Judeans who disagreed on points of *halakah*, particularly how the temple was run, had very few options to bring about reform. This state of affairs changed, however, after independence was achieved. Now dissident voices attempted to realize their agendas, while millenarian hopes provided further impetus (Baumgarten 1997:191–92).

The Judean sects emphasized various things in their polemics. For average Judeans the temple was the main centre of loyalty and the most important focus of identity. As a result, the temple would have been a perfect subject for sects to squabble over. For example, it could involve the detailed points of law concerning proper temple ritual (Baumgarten 1997:68–69). According to Cohen (1987:127–34) in Judeanism the principle objects of sectarian polemics were three: law (marriage,

Sabbath and festivals, temple and purity), (inadequacy of priests in the) temple, and (the correct interpretation of) scripture.

The *boundary marking* of ancient Judean sects concentrated on issues such as dress, marriage, commerce and worship, with basically all groups having regulations on food. But as Baumgarten (1997:7–8) explains, ordinary Judeans "employed boundary marking mechanisms in realms of life such as food, marriage, and worship to distinguish between themselves and [non-Judeans] . . . Ordinary [Judeans], in sum, observed purity regulations more or less strictly" (cf. 1 Macc 1:44–50). In the Second Temple period, the burgeoning use of ritual baths and stone vessels found all over Palestine is further evidence of concern to maintain a life of purity (Sanders 1992:222–29). Priests were born into their status and kept themselves apart from other Judeans to keep their sacred status—they did this with the full consent of society. In other respects Judeans were equal and the levitical rules of defilement did not endorse any form of social stratification. Sectarians, however, *chose* their way of life. Secondly, "they turned the means of marking separation normally applied against [non-Judeans] against those otherwise regarded as fellow [Judeans]" as a means of protest against them/Judean society and as "a result of these actions all [Judeans] were no longer on the same footing: *sectarian [Judeans] treated other [Judeans] as outsiders of a new sort*" (Baumgarten 1997:9; emphasis original).

Distinctions between sectarians and others also came about in the usage of personal names. Based on names of the earliest Pharisees and Qumran members, which are mostly Semitic, Baumgarten suggests "that those involved in sectarian activities were taken from among those less rapidly acculturated in the changing world after the conquests of Alexander" (Baumgarten 1997:46). This stands in contrast with the double names, Hebrew and Greek, of the Maccabean rulers from the time of John Hyrcanus, which is further evidence of their accommodation to influence of the outside world.

The approach to sects is helped with social scientific theory. Baumgarten follows Wilson's (1973:18–26) distinctions between "reformist" and "introversionist" sects. One can classify Sadducees and Pharisees as reformists, the Qumran Covenanters as introversionist. Reformists have hopes of reforming the larger society and has not renounced it totally, still thinking of themselves as part of the whole. Introversionists, on the other hand, have renounced society as a whole and turned in on their own movement completely and regards those outside as irredeemable (Baumgarten 1997:13). How much of the population did the sectarians represent? It is suggested that the total known membership of sects (Pharisees, Sadducees, Essenes/Qumran Covenanters, and the Messianists) do not reach twelve thousand. The Judean population of the time has been estimated to be at least five hundred thousand people, some estimates going as high as two million (Baumgarten 1997:43–44).

Important for our purposes here, Baumgarten explains the sectarians *"were more extreme in their devotion to what they believed to be the proper way to be [Judean] than other members of their contemporary society"* (Baumgarten 1997:200; emphasis added). We can say they had earnest programs of their own to maintain the Judean symbolic universe in opposition to Hellenism. Smith (1986:43) makes the important observation that in pre-modern eras, "what we grasp as religious competition may equally well be understood as ethnic competition for the monopoly of symbolic domination and communication in a given population, whose 'ethnic' profile is as much *shaped* by priestly and scribal activities as it is reinforced" (emphasis original). So the priests, Pharisees, Essenes, Zealots, even the first Messianists, could be approached in a way that understands that each group had their own particular ideas of what it meant to be Judean. Each group attempted to shape Judean ethnicity in their own way, especially those of the more "reformist" bend. But as we have seen, most Judeans were not attached to any particular sect, and certainly they were also interested in living a life according to which they believed was the proper way to be Judean. According to Cohen, the average Judean

> observed the Sabbath and the holidays, heard the scriptural lessons in synagogue on Sabbath, abstained from forbidden foods, purified themselves before entering the temple precincts, circumcised their sons on the eighth day, and adhered to the 'ethical norms' of folk piety. Whatever they may have thought of the priests and the temple, they went on pilgrimage to the temple a few times per year and probably relied on priesthood to propitiate the deity through a constant and well-maintained sacrificial cult. If the 'average' [Judean] of antiquity was anything like the 'average' citizen of every other time and place, he or she was more concerned about rainfall and harvests than about theology and religion. For this 'average' [Judean] the primary benefit of the democratisation of religion [e.g., the development of the synagogue and regular Torah study] was that it provided an additional means for serving God and thereby ensuring divine blessing. (Cohen 1987:172–73)

What Cohen describes above are a people who lived out their ethnic identity. A few amendments are in order, however. First, the Judeans were not necessarily like average persons of every other time and place, and had particular reason to be interested in their ancestral religion or traditions in particular. What is at issue here is the question of the threat to their identity posed by Hellenism, or anything foreign. The memory of the Maccabean revolt would have been strong, even though the Hasmonean rulers themselves were suspect as far as keeping foreign influences out. The encroachment of foreigners on the land—especially after the Romans invaded Palestine—with their religion and customs would have posed a new form of threat. Herod the Great, and the various Roman prefects and procurators often showed themselves to be insensitive towards Judean religious-cultural sensibilities. We discussed the growing importance of food to Judean self-understanding from the Maccabean period onwards. In the Roman period we amongst other things encounter the growing importance of ritual immersion and the use of stone vessels. And what Cohen here fails to appreciate it would seem is that "rainfall and harvests," or the economic and social viability of the *family on its land*, something which came under severe threat under the Romans, had everything to do with theology and religion (see further below). As Horsley (1995:34) points out, "religion was inseparable from the political-economic dimensions of life."

Since Judeanism was a wholly integrated system of thought, it provided an interesting dynamic between the sectarians, the priesthood, and the rest of the population. Collectively, however, the sectarians and priesthood formed a small minority of the population. The sectarians in particular might have been more devoted to what they thought it meant to be Judean, but this kind concern did not exclusively characterize them. For the vast majority of Judeans, being true to your identity meant living on and working the ancestral land, while being concerned with how the traditional way of life was threatened with the "foreigner being in the house."

Palestine Under Herod the Great

It was during rule of the last Hasmonean king-priests that Herod the Great manoeuvred to become king over the Judeans (ruled 37–4 BCE). It is also here, where the impact of Hellenism was felt. Herod, who simply loved to build, gave the Judeans something to be really proud of by constructing the magnificent temple complex. Josephus boasted that the temple was renowned and world famous, and was a feast for the eyes (*War* 5.222). Herod was in a way sensitive to Judean cultural requirements for the predominant floral motif used in decorating the temple was the vine with clusters of grapes, symbolic for blessing, happiness and productivity (Shanks 1990:13). Otherwise the temple also boasted other floral and geometrical motifs (Ritmeyer & Ritmeyer 1990:44–47). But overall, the temple complex drew heavily on Greek and Roman design principles. The temple was located on a large terrace or esplanade. A temple located on a large terrace was a typical feature of late Republican and early Imperial Roman architecture. A further Roman feature was the colonnades that surrounded the esplanade that were integrated into a triple-aisled basilica (or "Royal Stoa") along the southern end. There are also the Corinthian capitals of the columns, and the geometrical principles used in the design, all which came from the Roman architecture of the period (Jacobson 2002).

Unfortunately, the temple in Jerusalem was not the only temple that Herod built. He also built temples dedicated to Caesar Augustus—known as Augusteums—in Caesarea, Sebaste in Samaria, while archaeologists have claimed to have found the third at Omrit in far northern Galilee (Overman et al. 2003; cf. Jacobson 2002:22). Josephus notes that Herod built none of these temples in Judean territory (*Ant.* 15.328–30, 363–64; *War* 1.403–7). From the Herodian period Gentile games were also occurring in Palestine. In Jerusalem itself, Herod built a theatre, amphitheater (*Ant.* 15.268–76) and a hippodrome, and similarly to Caesarea, introduced games held in honor of Caesar every four years (Ben-Dov 1990:24). Some people were not happy about the theatre as it was decorated with human busts (*Ant.* 15.277–79). Greek music was performed at festivals in Jerusalem under Herod, as well as games of amusement and chance, such as the throwing of dice—the latter was by rabbinic tradition condemned (Schürer et al. 1979:60).

Other cities were also part of Herod's ambitious building plans. Especially Caesarea saw a dramatic transformation, as it was transformed from a small fishing village originally known as Strato's Tower, to the largest port in the Mediterranean basin (Ben-Dov 1990:24). The city was inaugurated in 13/12 BCE. Here Herod built a large palace, a system of aqueducts, and an amphitheatre.[13] The temple dedicated to Rome and Augustus that faced the harbor contained a colossal statue of the emperor (cf. Bull 1990; Schürer et al. 1979:46). Other Hellenistic

---

13. The hippodrome found by archaeologists has been dated to the second century (Bull 1990:114).

building projects occurred in Jericho, Ptolemeis, Damascus, Tiberias and Tarichaea (Magdala). Jericho supposedly possessed a theatre, an amphitheatre and a hippodrome (*Ant.* 17.161, 178, 194; *War* 1.659, 666). Herod built a gymnasium in Ptolemeis, and both a gymnasium and theatre in Damascus (*War* 1.422). Mention is made of a stadium in Tiberias (*War* 2.618; 3.539; *Life* 92; 331) and Tarichaea (Magdala) apparently had a hippodrome (*War* 2.599; *Life* 132; 138). Josephus himself described the theatre and amphitheatre as things alien to Judean custom (*Ant.* 15.268). It should come as little surprise that the opponents of Herod the Great called him a "half-Judean" because he was a descendent of the Idumeans, who were in the time of the Maccabees forcibly converted to Judeanism (Cohen 1987:54), but this was more a statement of cultural opposition.

Even Herod's descendents continued to some degree in the spirit of their father. Antipas' newly built Tiberias was named after the emperor, and he introduced pictures of animals in the palace (*Life* 12.65). Apparently Antipas built the largest synagogue in Palestine in Tiberias (the prayer house?) (*t. Sukk.* 4:6). He also allowed the city to mint its own coins, and have a Greek constitution with a *boule* under the leadership of an *archon* (Hengel 1989:39). Philip (4 BCE—34 CE) renamed Bethsaida as Julias, most probably after the wife of Augustus,[14] and his new capital was called Caesarea (Philippi). He was the first Judean ruler to mint coins bearing an image of himself, while the reverse depicted a temple which he maybe built in Julias and dedicated to Augustus (Brenner 2003:49; Jacobson 2002:20–21). Agrippa I, who for a period ruled over all of Palestine (41–44 CE),[15] combined a Judean piety with a liberal attitude where he allowed for the worship of himself outside Judean territory. He further sponsored festivals in honor of Caesar as well as theatrical and gladiatorial entertainment (*Ant.* 19.330–37, 343–52; Acts 12:21–23). The coins minted outside of Judean territory bore his image or that of the emperor. He also put up statues of his daughters in Caesarea (*Ant.* 19.357)

The political situation under Herod and his successors therefore facilitated the advance of Roman-Hellenistic influence in Palestine.

---

14. Josephus (*Ant.* 18.28) says that Philip renamed the city after Augustus' daughter, Julia. She was banished in 2 BCE and died in 14 CE. Augustus' wife died in 29 CE so Philip most likely renamed the city after her a year later (Chancey 2002:106).

15. Agrippa received from the Emperor Claudius both Judea and Samaria, in addition to Galilee he had already received from Caligula. Thus all of Palestine was under a Herodian ruler as it had been under Herod the Great (*War* 2.215; *Ant.* 19.274).

Naturally this represented more the interests and political inclinations of the ruling elite.

Language

Aramaic

It is the basic scholarly convention that the principal language of Judeans in Palestine was Aramaic, at one time being the *lingua franca* of the Persian empire. Traces of it can be found in transliterated words of the New Testament[16] and Josephus, and sayings of early Tannaitic figures in the Mishnah. Additional archaeological findings have confirmed this conclusion. Aramaic is found in the Dead Sea Scrolls, ossuary inscriptions, and contracts and archival documents and letters found at Murabba'at, Masada, and Naḥal Ḥever (Schürer et al. 1979:20–25). Scripture readings from the Torah, which was in Hebrew, was followed by a translation into Aramaic. This translation was done by a person known as the *meturgeman*, the "translator." In time these translations were written down and are known as *targumim* (singular, *targum*) (Fitzmyer 1992).

Hebrew

Hebrew, the language of the Torah, might have been the tongue of creation (*Jub.* 12:26), but the common use of Hebrew does not seem to have been widespread in our period (Fitzmyer 1992). At the same time, however, it seems that biblical Hebrew enjoyed resurgence in literary works (e.g., Sirach, Tobit, *Jubilees*, *Testament of Naphtali*) and the Essenes seem to have tried to resurrect the "sacred language" since most of the material at Qumran was written in Hebrew (Fitzmyer 1992). The first coin to be minted by a Judean government in Jerusalem, issued by John Hyrcanus I, had a legend in paleo-Hebrew script (along with Greek). Later revolutionary Judean authorities, be it at the time of the Great Revolt (66–70 CE) or the Bar Kokhba Revolt (132–135 CE), issued their own coins exclusively using paleo-Hebrew script (Brenner

---

16. For example when Jesus raised Jairus' daughter he spoke: *Talitha kum*, "Get up my child" (Mark 5:41), where the noun (literally meaning 'little lamb') is attested only in the *Palestinian Targum*. The word *mamona* (money), used in the Sermon on the Mount (Matt 6:24) also mostly appears in the targums. Then there is another targumic parallel when Jesus healed the deaf man near the Decapolis, and said in Aramaic: *Ephphatha*, 'Be opened' (Mark 7:34). Lastly, there were Jesus' last words on the cross: *Eloi Eloi lama sabachtani*, "My God, my God, why have you forsaken me?" (Mark 15:34–35) (Vermes 1973).

2003:48, 50–51; Schürer et al. 1979:26–27) thereby making a strong political statement (Porter 1994:137–38). In Gamla, during the revolt of 66–70 CE, coins were minted using both paleo-Hebrew and square Aramaic script (Syon 1992). Mishnaic Hebrew is said to have been used by Judeans as a secondary language in addition to Aramaic, and was occasionally used at Qumran and more frequently by those associated with Simeon Bar Kokhba during the 132–135 CE war. Mishnaic Hebrew eventually became the official language of the Galilean academies in the second half of the second century CE (Schürer et al. 1979:27–28).

Greek

It was once supposed that knowledge of Greek of the people would have been incomplete—a rough familiarity was widespread, even in Galilee, while the more educated classes used it without difficulty (Schürer et al. 1979:75, 77). Hengel (1989:7–8) points out, however, "that in the time of Jesus Greek had already been established as a language for more than three hundred years ... Judaea, Samaria and Galilee were bilingual (or better, trilingual) areas. While Aramaic was the vernacular of ordinary people, and Hebrew the sacred language of religious worship and of scribal discussion, Greek had largely become established as the linguistic medium for trade, commerce and administration." The epigraphic and literary evidence does suggest that the use of Greek was relatively widespread in Palestine, including Galilee. The evidence consists of coins, papyri and literary texts, and inscriptions, especially funerary inscriptions in the case of the latter (Porter 1994:137–47).

Already in the time of Alexander Jannaeus (103–76 BCE), bilingual coins were issued, using both Greek and paleo-Hebrew script (Brenner 2003:48). Bilingual coins were also issued by the last Hasmonean king, Mattathias Antigonus (40–37 BCE). Herod the Great only used Greek in his inscriptions on Judean coins and weights, as did his sons and the Roman prefects/procurators (Hengel 1989:8; Porter 1994:137).

The influence of Greek can also be seen in the loanwords that appear in Judean texts. This is applicable to the musical instruments (lyre, harp, and pipes) in Daniel (3:5, 10, 15) and the drachmae in Ezra 2:69 and Neh 7:69–71. Greek loan words are attested in the Copper Scroll (3Q15) and the papyri of Murabba'at and Naḥal Ḥever. There is also a notable amount of Greek non-biblical texts (e.g., *Ezekiel the Tragedian*), and additional sections to Daniel (Prayer of Azariah, Song of the Three Children, Susanna, and Bel and the Dragon) and Esther were composed in Greek. First Esdras and 2 Maccabees are thought to have been written in Greek in Palestine. The translations of 1 Maccabees, Esther, 2 Esdras (Ezra-Nehemiah), Lamentations, Qoheleth, Judith, Tobit, Chronicles, and the Song of Songs may have been done in Palestine, and one can also mention the Greek Minor Prophets Scroll found at Naḥal Ḥever. *Jubilees,* although written in Hebrew, demonstrates extensive knowledge of Greek geographical literature. One can add to the above the Palestinian and/or Judean authors who composed in Greek. These include Justus of Tiberius, Josephus, Eupolemus, and Jason of Cyrene (2 Maccabees), 3 and 4 Maccabees, while others may be added if their origins were in Palestine (Porter 1994:140–42; Lieu 2002:297).

Hengel (1989:25–26) points out it is inappropriate to distinguish between "Judean-Hellenistic" literature of the Diaspora and "genuine Judean" literature of Palestine. There were connections in both directions and a constant interchange. Porter (1994:142) suggests: "That Greek was used not only in the Diaspora but also in Palestine, even for composition by [Judeans] of distinctly [Judean] literature including much religious literature, indicates that Greek was an important and widely used language by a sizable portion of the Palestinian [Judean] population."

Galilee itself was surrounded by Hellenized territories. The Gospels take for granted that Jesus could speak to the centurion in Capernaum, Pilate, and the Syro-Phoenician woman (Ἑλληνίς; Mark 7:26) (Hengel 1989:17; cf. Porter 1994:148–53). Many Judeans were also given Greek names: some high priests (Jason and Menelaus in Maccabean period; Boethus and Theophilus in Herodian era); Hasmonean and Herodian rulers (Alexander, Aristobulus, Antigonus, Herod, Archelaus, Philip, Antipas, and Agrippa); also followers of Jesus (Andrew and Philip) and in the circle of rabbinic masters (see Hengel 1989:9; Schürer et al. 1979:73).

The papyri found in the Judean Desert are also instructive that dates to the period between the two revolts. These documents include letters, marriage contracts, legal documents and literary texts (Fitzmyer 1992). One of these letters is addressed to a Judas at Masada, one of the last survivors of the first revolt. There are also two letters found that date to the time of the second revolt (132–135 CE). Probably from Bar Kokhba himself, or written by one of his associates, these letters were surprisingly written in Greek and it is even stated that the "impulse/desire" was not found to write Ἑβραϊστὶ (Porter 1994:138).

Inscriptions are also often bilingual or only in Greek, but we will focus on evidence dating to no later than the first century. The ossuaries in Jerusalem and its environs testify to Greek being used on around 40 percent of them (van der Horst 1992; Hengel 1989:10). In a first-century tomb near Jericho, a Judean family nicknamed the Goliaths used Greek in more than half of the epitaphs. In Beth-Shearim/Scythopolis (south of Galilee), most of the epitaphs were inscribed in Greek. Porter (1994:147) says that the earliest evidence (first and second century CE) are *all* in Greek, but most of the inscriptions, however, date to the late second-century CE and thereafter (van der Horst 1992; Chancey & Meyers 2000:33). Nevertheless, the use of Greek in burial sites is significant as funerary inscriptions are the best evidence for the everyday language of the people. "At the most private and final moments when a loved one was finally laid to rest, in the majority of instances, [Judeans] chose Greek as the language in which to memorialize their deceased . . . [Greek] took precedence over the [Judean] sacred language, even at a moment of highly personal and religious significance" (Porter 1994:147). Porter is here commenting on the overall evidence for funerary inscriptions available across several centuries, yet there is enough evidence to suggest that even in the first century at least some Judeans spoke Greek as their everyday language. Other evidence for Greek includes the Theodotus Inscription of Jerusalem, referring to three generations of synagogue-rulers. The warning to Gentiles not to enter the inner courts of the temple was in Greek, although this was mainly aimed at outsiders. There is also an inscription in Jerusalem honoring a man named Paris who sponsored a stone pavement on or around the temple—presumably, there were residents in Jerusalem who were able to read it (Porter 1994:144–45).

Evidence in the New Testament also suggest that many Judeans who lived in Judea had Greek as a mother-tongue. Greek-speaking Judean communities had their own assemblies in Jerusalem. Acts 6:9 speaks of "the synagogue of the Freedmen (as it was called), and of the Cyrenians, and the Alexandrians, and Cilicia, and Asia" (συναγωγῆς τῆς λεγομένης Λιβερτίνων καὶ Κυρηναίων καὶ Ἀλεξανδρέων καὶ τῶν ἀπὸ Κιλικίας καὶ Ἀσίας). In Acts 6:1, Luke distinguishes between the Ἑλληνισταί and Ἑβραῖοι, and so distinguishes between the Greek and Aramaic speaking communities of the early Messianists. All of the "Seven" men appointed to serve the Hellenist community had, not surprisingly, Greek names (Acts 6:5). Greek speaking Judeans also made pilgrimages to the holy city and real Greeks (or proselytes?) as well (John 12:20ff). The festival games which Herod held in Jerusalem would also have brought in Greek-speaking foreign spectators (*Ant.*

15.267ff.). But the use of Greek was not reserved for Jerusalem alone. Hengel (1989:14) explains:

> a substantial [Judean] population lived in the Hellenized cities of the coastal plain from Gaza to Dor or Ptolemais-Acco: in Caesarea they made up almost half the population, and in Jamnia certainly and Ashdod probably they outnumbered the Hellenized Gentile population ... That Greek was the principal language in these cities is again confirmed by [Judean] epitaphs and synagogue inscriptions.

Religious Influence

It becomes obvious that Hellenism influenced the people of Palestine in various ways, be it through architecture, governmental forms, or the use of the Greek language. The adoption of Gentile forms of religion, however, was in general strongly resisted, yet Judeanism did not remain immune to Hellenistic influence. The Tanak was translated into Greek starting ca. 250 BCE, and so, quite ironically, the "constitution" of the Judean symbolic universe became available in the language representative of the ideological enemy. Judean religious leaders in Palestine itself were probably well exposed to Greek philosophy and culture (Glasson 1961:5–6).[17] The four metals of Daniel 2 (gold, silver, bronze, and iron), representing ages of world history, are exactly the same as the metals in Hesiod's *Work and Days* (eighth century BCE), which also represent successive ages of world history. Therefore a measure of Greek influence in Daniel is evident, although the symbolism using four metals may originally have been Persian (Hengel 1989:46).

Quite striking is the Greek influence on the Judean notions of the afterlife. In the period of 200 BCE to 200 CE, from obscure origins, a belief in life after death emerged dramatically in Judeanism (Bauckham 1998:80–95). Judeanism also began to share with Hellenism an increasing awareness in this period in the importance of the individual, and that individual choice brings about a better hope for life after death (Hengel 1989:48–50). This value of the individual developed into the glorification of the martyr, where "dying for" the Torah and the people—already an established feature in Greek tradition—saw its ap-

---

17. Glasson also points to a saying of Rabban Simeon b. Gamaliel: "There were a thousand young men in my father's house, 500 of them studied the Law, while the other 500 studied Greek wisdom." The father in question was Gamaliel II who became Nasi in 80 CE.

pearance in Judeanism for the first time in the Maccabean period (e.g., 1 Macc 2:50; 6:44; 2 Macc 6–7) (Hengel 1989:50). Elements of Greek teaching about Hades are likewise well attested in Judean apocalyptic writings of the period, such as visions of the beyond (e.g., *1 Enoch*), postmortem discrimination with rewards and punishment in the afterlife, and divisions in Hades or the yonder world for the "good" (or initiated) and the "bad." Generelly, beliefs about life after death found its expression through a belief in the resurrection of the dead, and thereto related speculation about the current state of the departed emerged as well. In contrast to the older view, it was now seen that personality could be expressed in terms of discarnate soul (Russell 1980:359). The souls or spirits of the departed are therefore represented as fully conscious, possessing form and recognizable appearance as well.

Glasson (1961:8) makes mention that in Greek antiquity, outstanding figures were often said to have visited the realm of the dead. In Homer's *Odyssey* (book 11), it speaks of the hero going into the underworld to meet the shades. Also in Virgil's *Aeneid* (book 6), Aeneas does the same. This kind of Greek tradition was so familiar that it had a special name attached to it, *Nekuia*. The word *nekuia* (from νέκυς, dead body) originally meant a magical rite through which the dead were called up and questioned about the future. It eventually became a familiar title for the eleventh book of the *Odyssey* and was applied to all similar accounts of visits to the realm of the dead. This tradition according to Glasson seemed to be the inspiration for the author of *Ethiopic Enoch* to write about the famous biblical figure doing the same and disclosing divine secrets. Genesis 5:24 indicated Enoch was specially adapted for this purpose. *First Enoch* 1–36 can thus be described as a *Judean Nekuia*.

Some Judean writings also understood that the righteous dead immediately entered the presence of God after death. Hellenistic philosophical ideas and language were freely borrowed as evidenced by 4 Maccabees and the Wisdom of Solomon. They sound Greek in the way they speak of the righteous as not dying but only seeming to die (WisSol 3:1–4; 4 Macc 7:18–19; 16:25; cf. *Jub.* 23:31). Yet, in these writings the Greek notion of life after death was qualified by Judean elements. In 4 Maccabees, the martyrs become immortal at death, but this was given to them by God and is not explained as an inherent quality of the soul. The Wisdom of Solomon also speaks of the future of the righteous within the context of a cosmic and collective eschatology (WisSol 3:7–8), a notion quite alien to Greek thinking (Bauckham

1998). But overall, the cultural contact with Hellenism allowed for the Judean symbolic universe to become a bit more "populated" and cosmologically complex, the souls of the departed being conceived as being somewhere "above" or "below," or places that defy explanation.

Summary

As can be seen from the above, Judeans did undergo a measure of Hellenization, but as Hengel (1989:54) points out, what is meant by "Hellenistic" should be defined more precisely; for example, does it refer to oriental syncretism, or does "it refer to technology, art, economics, politics, rhetoric and literature, philosophy or religion?" What was impossible was a Judean pagan cult, the denial of monotheism, the failure to observe the Torah and the desecration of the temple (Hengel 1989:54).

The Maccabean revolt drew the battle lines between "Judeanism" and "Hellenism." Any forms of Gentile worship were banned. Particularly from the Maccabean period, the Judean approach to food was characterized by a strict avoidance of anything Gentile. Sectarian movements began to flourish, however, as the Hasmonean rulers made various accommodations to foreign influences. Under the Herodian rulers, Roman-Hellenistic influence was present through architecture, theatres, gymnasiums and hippodromes, and Gentile games and festivals. Various cities were renamed after the emperors and their wives. Tiberias had a Greek constitution with a *boule* under the leadership of an *archon*. The most profound form of Hellenization was the Judean adoption of the Greek language. Various Judean texts were produced in Greek, while the translation of the Hebrew scriptures and apocryphal texts made the Judean worldview available in another language. The Judean understanding of the afterlife was also influenced by Greek thought, although it was qualified by Judean elements. But generally, if one wants to speak of *Hellenistic* Judeanism, it should be properly qualified to avoid misrepresentation.

Religion and Covenantal Praxis

Sanders (1992:48) suggests that there were three focal points of religion: the temple, the synagogue, and the home. Meier can be paraphrased here by saying that there were three focal points of Judean ethnicity. Below we will trace some historical developments relevant to our period, and give an overview of prevalent covenantal praxis that gave Judeans their unique identity in each sphere.

The Judeans were certainly a unique people. Greco-Roman civilization was quite successful in removing the identity and memories of the people that came within its orbit. The same cannot be said for Judeans. They remembered where they came from, and covenantal nomism ensured they acted accordingly (cf. Hengel 1989:19). Their distinctive identity was maintained through covenantal praxis relevant to the temple, to the synagogue (or assembly), and lastly, to the home. Smith (1994:716) also explains that in

> pre-modern eras, a distinctive religion or vision of a world religion appears to be the most potent source of ethnic persistence; but it is the social rather than the doctrinal aspects of a religion—its community-forming propensities such as rites, ceremonies, liturgy, script-and-language, sacred texts and clergy, and the value systems they transmit—that are crucial for ethnic survival in the long term.

Indeed, religion and covenantal praxis combined to make Judeanism a tenacious social entity with distinct values and which fostered a strong consciousness of difference in relation to outsiders. As a result it is required that the cultural features of *religion* and *covenantal praxis* (or *customs*) be treated together. In similar vein it should be noted that the Pentateuch does not make a distinction between ritual and ethics. It is the wisdom literature (Job, Proverbs, Ecclesiastes) that places more emphasis on ethics and universal virtues (Sanders 1992:50; Cohen 1987:76). We will first have a look at how the temple, its symbolism and its rites, helped to foster a Judean consciousness.

The Temple—A Focal Point of Judean Identity

In Leontopolis in Egypt there was the unique phenomenon of a Judean temple built outside Jerusalem.[18] About 165 BCE, Onias IV, son of Onias III, built upon an earlier shrine on the pattern of the temple in Jerusalem but on a smaller and less grand scale. Evidently there was sufficient number of priests to establish formal Judean temple worship, which was continuously in operation until the Romans destroyed it in 73 CE (Schürer et al. 1986:145–46; cf. *War* 7.420–36; *Ant.* 13.62–73). Besides the reality of a Judean temple in Leontopolis, during our pe-

---

18. There was also a temple built on the island of Elephantine in Egypt that was destroyed around 410 BCE (Schmidt 2001:122–23).

riod, Judeanism understood that there should be only one temple and one place of sacrifice (*Apion* 2.193). This was in contrast to the Greeks and Romans who had countless temples and sacrifices could also be made where no temples were present (Sanders 1992:49). The Egyptian Judeans, like other members of the Diaspora, therefore maintained contact with Jerusalem and went there on pilgrimage and paid their tithes and taxes due to the temple.[19] Josephus states that Judeans from Mesopotamia made "dedicatory offerings" to the temple in addition to the half-shekel (two drachmas) temple tax (*Ant.* 18.312; cf. Exod 30:13; Neh 10:32). Philo describes Jerusalem as the "mother-city" of the Judeans and went there on pilgrimage at least once (see *Flaccus* 7.46; *Embassy* 36.281; *Providence* 2.64), and writes of the zeal that Judeans had for the temple (*Embassy* 210–12). The *Letter of Aristeas* (ca. 170 BCE), written in Alexandria, also gives evidence for devotion to the temple in Jerusalem. Acts 2:5–11 mentions that Judeans from various parts of the world were in Jerusalem. What occurred in Jerusalem, affected Judeans in all parts of the ancient world.

The temple required the services of priests. Josephus testifies that in the Diaspora priests took care in assuring the purity of the priestly line (*Apion* 1.32) while Philo suggests that priests held onto their leading positions in the Diaspora (*Hyp.* 7.12–13). Overall, Judeanism had a large hereditary priesthood that was supported by the populace. For the Greeks and Romans priests were often taken from the elite—the priesthood was not a profession or a caste (Sanders 1992:49). So besides criticisms against the Temple and the priesthood (e.g., *Pss. Sol.* 8; 1QpHab 12.8; CD 4.17—5.11; 6.15–16), support for them both was very strong, and generally people made the required gifts and offerings.[20]

The temple evidently had lots of wealth, sometimes being the target of looting by Romans (Evans 1992:235–41; Sanders 1992:52, 83–85), or even a source of finance for Herod the Great and his ambitious building plans (Schmidt 2001:37–38). The temple also enjoyed Gentile patronage. Ptolemy III; Antiochus III Sidetes; Herod's patron, Marcus Agrippa; the governor of Syria, Vitellius; and Gaius Caesar, the grandson of Augustus, brought their sacrifices or forms of Gentile piety. At times Gentiles also made votive offerings. It is said that at the siege of Jerusalem John of Gischala melted sacred vessels that were

---

19. Cf. Philo, *Spec. Laws* 1.133, 141–44, 153; 1.77–78; *Embassy* 156; Josephus, *Ant.* 14.245.

20. Although Philo does acknowledge that there were some priests who were poor (*Spec. Laws* 1.154).

given by Augustus and his wife Julia, as well as other emperors (Schürer et al. 1979:310–12). Josephus explains that when the temple was being destroyed, the Romans found enormous amounts of money and other valuables in the treasury chambers. The priests handed over to the victors various lampstands, tables, bowls and platters of solid gold, and other treasures and sacred ornaments (*War* 6.282, 387–91). The wealth of the temple has even led Feldman (2001) to suggest that the Colosseum in Rome was funded by the booty taken by the Romans from the Jerusalem temple. The first three tiers of the Colosseum were built during the reign of Vespasian (69–79 CE).

THE HIGH PRIESTHOOD

The high priest was the principle mediator between God and the people. The present day realities, however, also necessitated that he play a mediating role between the people and the Roman authorities. According to Josephus (*Ant.* 14.29–60), Judeans petitioned Pompey not to appoint a king over them, since it was customary for them to be ruled by the priests. This was in response to the Hasmoneans who while being the high priests as well, acted much like Hellenistic kings, ruling with absolute power. As Sanders suggests (1992:37), these Judeans preferred things to be how it was in the Persian and Ptolemaic periods: "a distant monarch, no close supervision of daily life, and local government by the high priest and his council . . . the state would again become a theocracy . . . ." A similar request was made after Herod's death where Judeans requested Augustus not to give power to Herod's descendents, and that while the country will fall under Syria, local government will be decided upon by the Judeans themselves (*War* 2.80, 91). The Judeans wanted to get rid of the high priest appointed by Herod in favor of someone "more lawful and pure" (*Ant.* 17.207–8; *War* 2.7). No doubt, the people were annoyed with Herod's appointment and constant change of high priests who did not have the appropriate pedigree. This also illustrates that at this time, it was more important for the Judeans to live according to the Law and for an appropriate high priest to assume responsibilities. Without an acceptable high priest, the Judean symbolic universe will be dysfunctional.

Even after the death of Herod it must have been annoying that the later Herodian rulers, Agrippa I, Herod of Chalcis, and Agrippa II were entrusted with the authority over the temple, the temple vessels and high-priestly robes, and/or appointment of the high priests (*Ant.* 19.274–75, 297, 313–14; 20.15–16, 179, 203, 213). In the period from

6 to 65 CE, 18 high priests were appointed and dismissed. During the period of Agrippa II in 50–65 CE alone, 6 high priests from different families filled the high priestly office (Schmidt 2001:36).

Jerusalem, the Holy

Living according to the Law meant that the sanctity of the priesthood, the temple, and Jerusalem itself had to be protected. "The more vigorous and persistent the pressure of paganism on Palestine, the more energetic was the resistance offered by [Judeanism]" (Schürer et al. 1979:81). Two points in particular came into emphasis: idolatry, and the levitical laws of purity. To avoid any association with idolatry, the Mosaic prohibition of idols was stressed (Exod 20:4–5; Deut 4:16ff.; 27:15). The following incidents are used as illustration.

In the last year of Herod's reign (5 BCE), he erected over the great gate of the temple a golden eagle. Knowing that Herod's death was near, two men, Judas and Matthaias, who had the reputation of being learned and unrivalled in the interpretation of Judean laws, encouraged young men to take the eagle down. On hearing about this, Herod had the protestors and their teachers arrested, tried and burned alive. Herod also held the high priest as partially responsible for the incident, and so had him deposed from office (*War* 1.651–55; *Ant.* 17.149–67). The eagle, besides being an impure animal, also reminded Judeans of Roman domination. Putting up an eagle over the gate of the temple is a bit like hoisting the American flag over an entrance to the mosque in Mecca. Here idolatry and politics intermingled.

Judeans experienced more insults to their holy city and the temple. After the death of Herod in 4 BCE, the Roman financial administrator Sabinus plundered the treasury (*War* 2.45ff.; *Ant.* 17.261ff.). When Pontius Pilate became prefect in 26 CE, he ordered that Roman troops enter Jerusalem with standards which had the bust of Caesar on them. A number of Judeans followed Pilate back to Caesarea and sat outside his residence for five days and nights as a means of peaceful protest. Pilate had them summoned and surrounded by troops. On drawing their swords the Judeans responded by falling to the ground and extending their necks, choosing rather to die than to transgress the Law. Pilate capitulated and had the standards removed from Jerusalem (*War* 2.169–74; *Ant.* 18.55–59). Yet Pilate took money from the temple treasury as well to finance the construction of an aqueduct, but this time he brutally suppressed any protests (*War* 2.175ff.; *Ant.* 18.60ff.).

It was not that Judeans had complete paranoia over images.[21] The theatre that Herod built had human busts. Some objected but it was not torn down (*Ant.* 15.277–79). The Judeans further did not mind the use of floral motifs, particularly the vine, for the decoration of the temple-complex, for besides being symbolic for blessing, happiness and productivity (Shanks 1990:13), the Judeans would also have recognized a deeper significance. They themselves as a people were identified as the vineyard planted by God (Jer 2:21; cf. Ps 80:9–12; Ezek 17:5–8). The front of the Sanctuary was adorned with golden vines, from which were hung grape clusters the height of a man (*War* 5.210). Herod also minted coins with images of wreaths, palm branches, anchors and cornucopias on them, as did the Hasmoneans. During the revolt, the rebels minted coins, depicting vines, vessels and lulavs (Sanders 1992:243). Strangely enough, according to the Mishnah, the temple demanded the Tyrian shekels as currency, whose silver content was high and consistent, even though they had the head of the god Melqart engraved on them (*m. Ber.* 8:7). Coins with an image of the emperor also circulated freely (e.g., Mark 12:13–17), but these did not lead to riots. According to Josephus the curtain in front of the doors of the sanctuary had the stars depicted on them (*War* 5.214).

A serious crisis faced the Judeans when the emperor Gaius (Caligula) decided to erect a statue of himself in the temple. At the time when the Alexandrian embassy was in Rome to see Caligula, trouble brewed for Palestinian Judeans due to events in Jamnia, a city that was mainly inhabited by Judeans. The Gentile inhabitants set up a crude altar to the emperor and to annoy the Judeans, who then immediately destroyed it. The procurator of the city, Herennius Capito, reported this incident to the emperor. He responded by ordering that a statue of himself be set up in the temple in Jerusalem (*Embassy* 30.203). The governor of Syria, Publius Petronius, was also commanded to proceed to Palestine with half of his army to make sure that the emperor's wishes are fulfilled. Petronius did so reluctantly. The statue was being prepared in Sidon, and news of what was about to occur spread across Palestine. Masses of people ("tens of thousands"; *Ant.* 18.261–72; 18.305–9) came to see Petronius in Ptolemais sometime between Passover and Pentecost in 40 CE, and later in Tiberias towards the end of that same year, pleading

---

21. Although an interesting story in the Mishnah relates that Gamaliel II visited the bath of Aphrodite at Acco (Ptolemais) based on the premise that the image of the god was there to decorate the bath—a view that did not have widespread appeal (*m. A.Z.* 3:4).

with him to stop the desecration of the temple. Petronius eventually withdrew his troops back to Antioch and entreated the emperor to stop his plans. In the meanwhile, Agrippa I went to Rome to see the emperor knowing as yet nothing of the emperor's plans. After the shock of finding out—Agrippa we are told fainted and only recovered the evening of the next day—Agrippa endeavored to persuade Caligula to change his mind. Caligula it seems listened and a letter was sent to Petronius instructing that nothing must be changed in the temple, but ordered that there should be no interference if an altar or temple to the emperor was to be erected outside Jerusalem (Schürer et al. 1973:396).

Caligula later regretted his decision, and ordered a new statue to be made at Rome. It was to be put ashore on the coast of Palestine while on his journey to Alexandria, and secretly sent to Jerusalem (*Embassy* 42.331–37). It was fortunate from a Judean perspective that Caligula was murdered soon thereafter (*Ant.* 18.307)—in January 41 CE—and so the Judeans of Palestine were spared, for the moment, from a major confrontation with Rome. It was eventually the procurator, Florus, who contributed to the outbreak of the Great Revolt when he took money from the temple treasury.

The Judeans would have been particularly sensitive to the religious claims made on behalf of the emperor. Herod built his temples dedicated to the emperor cult. Both he and his descendants named cities after the emperors and their wives. The residents of Palestine "were thus living in a landscape with constant reminders of the emperor's power and glory, if not divinity ... The Roman impact on Galilee and Judea was cultural-religious as well as political-economic, and it focused on the lordship of Caesar in a way that conflicted in a particular poignant way with traditional Israelite loyalties" (Horsley 1995:122).

Many Judeans, accepting the reality of Roman dominance, reluctantly accepted the status quo as long as there was no outside interference with their religion and customs. Generally any overt incursion of the emperor cult into Jerusalem invited strong opposition. Those who protested against the Roman standards in Jerusalem and Gaius' plans to erect a statue in the temple illustrated, however, that they did not threaten war, "but were prepared to die passively rather than have the holiness of the city and the sanctuary defiled" (Sanders 1992:41). "Zeal for God's law and his worship was one of the principal motives of the actions of many [Judeans], and belief in an afterlife encouraged people to follow the law even if it meant death" (Sanders 1992:42–43). Of course, this kind of zeal or commitment was also about their own ethnic identity in opposition to Roman religious-cultural influence. Primordial sentiments flourished since important aspects of Judean culture—the temple, monotheism, ritual purity—came under threat. Josephus in *Against Apion* (2.234, 271) places emphasis on the Judean willingness to remain faithful to the Law, something that is not found in other nations. The Torah was a guide to life, eternally valid and meaningful. Josephus remarked that Judeans were willing to die for their Torah (*Apion* 1.44–45; 2.232–34, 271–77; *Ant.* 15.248), but what Greeks were prepared to die for classical Greek literature? Philo expressed similar sentiments (*Hyp.* 6.9; *Embassy* 192). The Gentile author Dio Cassius, also commented on the passion which Judeans had for their religion; in fact, he said it was well known (*History of Rome* 37.17.4). Overall, one can say that the Judeans had passion for their own ethnic identity.

THE TEMPLE AND RITUAL PURITY

The notions of the sacred and the profane, of the pure and impure, were important elements of the Judean symbolic universe. It was especially the role of the priests to distinguish (*badal*) between the two (Lev 10:10) and which had to be taught to the people (Ezek 44:23). Impurity could be acquired through transgressing the Law, but essentially had to do with the changes of status. So before we continue, what exactly did ritual purity entail? According to the Judean symbolic universe, there was a certain order to Creation; everything had its proper place.

> What is at one and the same time intact and in its place is pure, *ṭahor*. Conversely, what is impure, *ṭame*, presupposes mixture and disorder. Hence the attention given to extreme situations, to the margins, to beginnings and ends, to the frontiers of otherness in all its forms ... Thus the margins of the body are dangerous. The skin diseases, bodily secretions, the emissions of sperm and blood, excrement, by blurring the frontiers between the interior and the exterior, threaten physical integrity. (Schmidt 2001:91)

The purity laws are found mainly in Leviticus 12 (childbirth), Leviticus 13–14 ("leprosy"), Leviticus 15 (bodily emissions), Numbers 19 (death), and Leviticus 11; Deuteronomy 14 (food). A more detailed discussion is reserved for later, but for example, after childbirth a woman was impure for either forty days (after the birth of a son) or eighty days (after the birth of a daughter). She was not allowed to enter the temple or touch holy things. After menstruation, women were impure for a week—anybody touching a menstruant, her bed, or chair was impure for a day, the same length required for purification after contact with semen. Unnatural discharge of blood (for women) and semen (for men) was considered as leading to a high degree of impurity (Sanders 1992:71–72). Death was the most severe form of "change of status." One contracted corpse impurity through physical contact, or just by being in the same room. In our period you could even contract it by "overshadowing" the corpse (by walking over a grave) or by being "overshadowed" by one. Here purification required seven days. Especially the priesthood and the temple had to be protected from contracting corpse impurity. Even the high priest was not allowed to contract corpse impurity when his father or mother died (Lev 21:1–11).

In order to remedy impurity, ritual immersion and sacrificial rituals were put in place to bring about a change from one status to another. As such, they were a means by which the Judean community was restored to its integrity and where everything could be established in its right place in conformity with the order of Creation (Schmidt 2001:93–94; cf. Schürer et al. 1979:476–77).

The notion of pure and impure, however, also extended to other aspects of Judean life (Schmidt 2001:94). For example, clothing could not be made of hybrid fabrics, woven from wool and linen, in order to prevent the mixing of animal with vegetable (Lev 19:19; Deut 22:11). Similarly the farmer must preserve the perfect order of the Creation by not mating two different species of his livestock (Lev 19:19), by not yoking together the ox and the donkey (Deut 22:10), by not sowing different seeds together on his agricultural land (Lev 19:19; Deut 22:9). The production and consumption of food also played an important part, but this will be discussed later.

The entire system of purity naturally focussed on, and was analogous to the rules for the temple. According to Leviticus and Numbers, anyone who enters the "camp," or God's abode, must be pure. It was mainly the temple that organized the natural and supernatural world, from which the perfect order of Creation could be regulated in every day life. The temple would therefore play a primary role in the identity and thinking of Judeans.

> The symbolic and classificatory system that is proper to [the Temple], which is internalized by each group according to the place it occupies in the social hierarchy and the bonds that unite it to the Sanctuary, is shared by the whole community. This sharing and this internalizing lay the foundation for [Judean] solidarity. (Schmidt 2001:95–96)

Since much of the purity system focussed on the temple, a description of the centre of the Judean symbolic universe is in order (cf. Sanders 1992:54–69; Ritmeyer & Ritmeyer 1990). Preparation to enter the temple-complex already began outside. To the south opposite the main entrances was a ritual bathhouse for ritual purification, where many *miqva'ot* cut into the bedrock have been found. After immersion, Judeans could enter the temple-complex. The outer wall had several gates, but most visitors would have approached the temple from the south, gaining entry through the triple gate, also known as the "Beautiful Gate" (Acts 3:2). The double gate located alongside was for exiting the temple-complex—collectively these two gates were known as the Huldah Gates, so named after the prophetess (2 Kgs 22:14; 2 Chr 34:22). Once through the gate, a tunnel leads you upwards and exits on the plaza or esplanade above. Now you are standing in the Court of Gentiles, which made up most of the area enclosed by the walls. To the south was the Royal Stoa that ran along the southern edge of the temple complex. Anybody—subject to purification—was allowed entry into the Court of Gentiles, except for menstruating women. To the north was the temple area proper. The Court of Gentiles was separated from the area reserved exclusively for Judeans by a chest-high balustrade (1.5 m or three cubits), or *soreg*. Next to the gates, notices in Greek and Latin were placed warning Gentiles not to go further. Here the Roman authorities respected Judean wishes and even allowed the death sentence to be applied to Roman citizens (*Ant.* 15.417; Philo, *Embassy* 212; cf. Acts 21:27–31). The notice read:

> No foreigner may enter within the railing and enclosure that surround the Temple. Anyone apprehended shall have himself to blame for his consequent death! (see Millard 2003:41; Sanders 1992:61)

Enacted around 10 BCE (Schmidt 2001:108), this is quite different from the edict of Antiochus III, the oldest attestation of the ban (dated to 200 BCE), where guilty foreigners had to pay a fine of three thousand drachmas of silver to the priests (*Ant.* 12.145–46). Since the "foreigner is in the house," Schmidt (2001:109) explains that on the political level, "the strengthening of the *soreg* seems to be a withdrawal and focusing within the Sanctuary of the distinctions between [Judeans] and foreigners that otherwise, in the territories and on its frontiers, are blurred." For Josephus, these warnings were about the laws of purification (*Ant.* 15.417; *War* 5.194). But what Judeans could not achieve politically and territorially, was symbolized by the soreg of the temple, which became a representation of what the ideal Judean symbolic universe required. Judeans are in. Gentiles are out. As such, the strengthening of the *soreg* also "indicates the strengthening and extension of the purity laws to the daily life of all Israel ritually separated from foreigners" (Schmidt 2001:110). Although purity laws were mainly aimed at regulating access to the temple, it is difficult to agree with Sanders (1992:71) that it affected daily life relatively little. In our period, purity requirements broadened in its scope and application and it came to prominence in our period. The system of the sacred and the profane, of the pure and impure, was no longer applicable just to direct relations with the temple, the pilgrimages and sacrificial meals, but was extended to concern every aspect of daily life away from the temple (Schmidt 2001:231; Poirier 2003). Philo states: "The Judean nation is to the whole inhabited world what the priest is to the State" (*Spec. Laws* 2.163). Especially the pious and the sectarians placed emphasis on maintaining a high degree of purity.

From the Court of Gentiles, one would eventually have to pass through the Court of Women, the Court of Israelites, coming to those areas reserved for the priests alone, namely, the Court of Priests and the temple building proper: *'ulam, hekal, debir*. Josephus counts seven degrees of purity from the Court of Gentiles to the Holy of Holies (*War* 1.26). The temple area surrounded by the inner wall was orientated from east to west, end entered from the eastern side. Having passed through the balustrade, you would have gone up a flight of fourteen steps, crossed a terrace and gone up another five steps and came to the inner wall which had ten gates. From east to west was the Court of Women, the Court of Israelites, the Court of Priests, and the sanctuary building itself. The Court of Women was open for all Judeans, subject to ritual purity of course, and according to the Mishnah it provided a gallery so that the women could see into the Court of Priests. Judean men could proceed westwards, ascend fifteen more steps, going through the Nicanor Gate in a wall that separated the Court of Women from the Court of Israelites. Here they could see the priests doing their sacred tasks, but they were separated from the Court of Priests by a low stone parapet, about half a metre high (a cubit). In the Court of Priests were the altar, the shambles (where the animals were butchered), and the laver (for priests to wash their hands and feet). This area was exclusively reserved for the priests—not even the Levites could enter this area. Then came the sanctuary itself, where twelve steps led to the temple entrance. Inside the front chamber was a lampstand, a table for the showbread and an altar for burning incense. The Holy of Holies located beyond it, and separated by a curtain, was empty and was entered by the High Priest only once a year on the Day of Atonement.

As can be seen from the above, as one progressed from the Court of Gentiles to the Court of Priests, the courts became more and more exclusive, all related to the required degrees of purity (*War* 5.227; *Apion* 2.102–4). Purity was so important that strict measures were put into place to uphold its requirements. Only priests were allowed to build the inner area of the temple complex. Herod had 1,000 priests trained as masons and carpenters (*Ant.* 15.390). This is clear change from Ezra 3:10, where ordinary builders lay the foundation for the second temple. The temple was a special place for the presence of God, and anyone who approached it had to do it with the necessary sanctity. Anything impure could not approach God's special dwelling place. The temple-complex was as a result heavily guarded. Philo explains that Levites were placed as guards at the entrances to the temple-complex, and at the entrances of the temple itself to see that the requirements of purity were met. Guards also patrolled the Court of Israelites and the area around the Sanctuary day and night (*Spec. Laws* 1.156). Josephus explains that during the tenure of Coponius (6–9 CE) the watch was intensified after some Samaritans scattered human bones in the temple (*Ant.* 18.30).

It is not just that the "ideas of holiness and separation, which allowed only what was most pure to come near, informed the entire arrangement of the temple and its rites" (Sanders 1992:70), but also the "Temple and the symbolic system of which it is the architectural expression at the same time separate, integrate and organize into a hierarchy" (Schmidt 2001:246). The Judean temple both shapes, and is shaped by Judean notions of purity. For our present purposes, however, in the first century CE the whole of Judean society was graded according to the purity system as symbolized by the temple architecture. First was the division of priests, Levites, and Israelites, legitimate descendents of the twelve tribes and who preserved their genealogies through strict marriage regulations. On the other end of the spectrum are people tainted with defilements, such as the illegitimates, foundlings, or eunuchs, who were prohibited from marrying into a legitimate family. In between these extremes were a category consisting of proselytes, the illegitimate children of priests, and freed slaves (Schmidt 2001:32–33).

Gentiles were initially not classified according to the purity system. The Tanak allows for Gentiles to bring their sacrifices as did the Israelites

(Num 15:14–16). This situation changed however by the late third or early second century BCE. Here Gentiles (along with impure Israelites) were not allowed to enter the temple enclosure (cf. the proclamation of Antiochus III in *Ant.* 12.145–46). The same situation prevailed in Herod's temple—Gentiles were not to go beyond the balustrades that surrounded the temple enclosure. So although the Judean purity laws did not initially apply to Gentiles, in our period Gentiles were treated as impure (they were excluded from the temple proper) and contact was avoided as far as possible because they were tainted by idolatry. They were allowed access to the Court of Gentiles as compared with Judean "lepers" who were expelled from the city, and Judean menstruants who were forbidden to enter any part of the temple-complex (implied in *War* 5.226). Roman troops were allowed to keep guard on the roofs of the temple porticoes.

The schools of Shammai and Hillel apparently debated the issue of Gentile impurity. The School of Shammai (prevailing over the school of Hillel) decided on eighteen measures with regards to the impurity of foreigners, and amongst others, placed a ban on Gentile bread, wine, cheese, oil, their daughters, and their sperm and urine (Schmidt 2001:240). The Shammaites placed Gentiles on the level of Judean semen impurity, while the Hillelites believed that the Gentiles permanently had corpse impurity—an uncircumcised male was the equivalent of being a corpse (*m. Pes.* 8:8)! Generally, there seems to have been no consensus at the time on the issue of Gentile impurity (cf. Sanders 1992:72–76), although according to Schmidt (2001:241), the Sages considered the impurity of the foreigner as equivalent to that of a person with discharge.

The Sacrifices/Offerings

According to Sanders (1992:43), animal sacrifice was the simplest and most fundamental aspect of any ancient religion. Sanders gives an overview of the entire temple operation but here we are indebted to his work on sacrifices (Sanders 1992:103–45). It may come as a shock to us moderns far removed from slaughtering animals that the priests in the temple were expert butchers, from slitting the animals throat, to taking off the hide and removing the inward parts, to cutting the carcass into its designated parts. Generally sacrifices could consist of meal flour, wine, birds (doves or pigeons), and quadrupeds (sheep, goats and cattle). Every day the priests on duty would perform community sacrifices such as the *tamid*, sacrificing a male lamb in the morning and evening along with flour, oil, and wine (Exod 29:40; cf. *L.A.B.* 13:2–3). These were burnt sacrifices, where the entire animal was burnt on the altar. Such sacrifices increased in number on the Sabbath and to mark the new moon, as well as the major festivals and the Day of Atonement. Apart from these community sacrifices there were individual sacrifices brought by ordinary Judeans themselves. It is on these individual sacrifices we will focus. Most Judeans of Palestine would probably have sacrificed only once or a few times per year. A lot of preparation would have gone into making a sacrifice and so the whole process would have been sacred. Worshippers had to be in a state of purity—seven days of purification would be required in the case of corpse impurity. The right victim had to be selected, the majestic temple-complex had to be approached, and you had to make your way to the altar. All of this would have been profoundly meaningful. Importantly, the act of sacrifice was also the last moment whereby guilt and some forms of impurity were removed. Here follows a brief overview of the main sacrifices which Judeans would have brought to the temple.

Individual burnt offering. Leviticus 1:4 states that the individual burnt offering was for atonement. A quadruped was used (*Ant.* 3.226). In our period, however, these offerings were thought to be gifts to God (*Ant.* 3.243, 251; 6.121; 7.389; 11.137; 15.419) or to honor God (*Spec. Laws* 1.195–97). It was all for God including the hide, but the hide went to the priest (Lev 7:8). The man who offered the burnt sacrifice had to kill the animal (Lev 1:5; *Ant.* 3.226–27).

Sin offerings and guilt offerings. These are closely related, and in both cases the priest would receive the meat and the hide of quadrupeds. The meat was to be eaten in the temple, on the same day, sharing it with other priests on duty (*Ant.* 3.231; 4.75; Lev 6:29; 7:6–7). The term "sin offering" is a bit misleading, and in certain cases might be understood as a "purification offering," such as that offered by a women after childbirth. She committed no sin, but through her ritual status she deviated from the norm (= the Hebrew conception of sin) and so through her sacrifice was restored to "normality." In other words, her "citizenship" to the Judean symbolic universe was restored.[22] Other "sin offerings" were divided into sacrifices for transgressions committed in ignorance (Lev 4:27–35) and for those committed being fully aware that it is a sin (Lev 6:2–7; *Spec. Laws* 1.226, 235). The latter are the biblical guilt offerings.

---

22. The sin and guilt offerings, as well as ritual immersion, can be understood as "rites of passage," and it is "particularly in rites of passage that one finds highly emotional symbolic reinforcement of ethnic patterns" (De Vos 1975:26).

Sin offerings made use of a lamb and a kid, and for those who could not afford it two birds could be used. If birds cannot be afforded Lev 5:7, 11 allow their substitution with grain, some of which would go to the priest who presumably turned it into bread. Birds were required for the purification of a man or woman who had an abnormal "discharge" (Lev 15:14, 29). Here one bird was entirely burnt, while the other was used as a sin offering. The priest would wring the neck, sprinkle some blood on the side of the altar, and after it was drained, would cook the bird and eat it (Lev 5:8–9). The guilt offering required a ram (Lev 6:6). Here the offender was also expected to repay what he has taken wrongly, add a fifth to its value, and only then go to the temple for the remission of his sin (Lev 6; *Spec. Laws* 1.234–8). A male worshipper was required to put his hand on the victim and tell the priest (or "confess") what the sacrifice was for (Lev 5:1–5; Num 5:7). The male worshipper also killed the animal (Lev 4:29, 33; cf. *Ant.* 3.230). A woman would tell the priest or more probably a Levite what the sacrifice was for, who would in turn carry it to the altar area, but it is not clear whether the woman also laid her hand on the animal's head and "confessed" as the men did.

The shared sacrifice (or "peace/welfare offering"). The shared sacrifice, or "communion sacrifice" (Schmidt 2001:212) had to be a quadruped (*Ant.* 3.228; cf. Lev 3:1–16). It was shared between the altar, the priest and the person who brought the offering, who in turn shared it with family and friends. The fat was burned on the altar, while the blood was sprinkled and poured on or around the altar. The right thigh and the breast went to the priest, which was "waved" by the devotee before the altar. The priest would take his portion home to eat it with his family (Lev 7:30–32; Num 18:11). The devotee would take his portion, neatly butchered by the priest, and carry it out of the temple to enjoy red meat with his friends and family. There were also sub-divisions of the shared offering: the thankoffering that had to be eaten the same day (Lev 7:12); the votive offering in order to fulfil a vow; and the freewill offering. The latter two could be eaten over two days (Lev 7:16–17; 22:21–23). The sacrifices had to be accompanied by cakes and wafers, with some leavened and some not (Lev 7:12–13). One cake went to the priest while the offerer took the rest to be enjoyed with the meat. Both the priest and the offerer along with his family and guests had to eat the shared offering in purity (Lev 7:19–21).

The Annual Festivals

Sanders (1992:127–28) speculates that if about half of the Palestinian Judean population attended the Passover festival—which was the most popular (*Ant.* 17.214)—and when combined with pilgrims from the Diaspora, around 300,000 to 500,000 people would have been present. Other estimates place the number of pilgrims at around 80,000 to 100,000, to which must be added the Jerusalem population of about 150,000 to 200,000 people (Ben-Dov 1990:23). We cannot be sure about the numbers, but it is plausible that tens-of-thousands of Judeans would have participated in the major festivals, and they would have been enthusiastic in doing so (cf. *L.A.B.* 13:4–7). It was to solve this logistical nightmare that contributed to Herod rebuilding the temple area, and the esplanade covered the size of twelve soccer fields, stands included (Ben-Dov 1990:24).

People traveled to Jerusalem in groups. Large caravans came from Babylonia, bringing with them the temple tax as well (*Ant.* 17.313). Other caravans and ships brought pilgrims from Syria, Asia Minor and North Africa (*Spec. Laws* 1.69). Galileans and Idumeans made the pilgrimage journey in groups as well (*War* 2.232). As Sanders (1992:128) explains, the Judeans festivals were like Christmas, "a blend of piety, good cheer, hearty eating, making music, chatting with friends, drinking and dancing. While the festive atmosphere started on the road, the true feast came in Jerusalem." The pilgrims would also have had their "second tithe" money (see below) to spend. According to Deut 14:26:

> Use the silver to buy whatever you like: cattle, sheep, wine or other fermented drink, or anything you wish. Then you and your household shall eat there in the presence of the LORD your God and rejoice. (NIV)

Some of the pilgrims would have found accommodation in Jerusalem itself, while many brought their own tents and stayed outside the city (*Ant.* 17.217). The Tanak requires that all males attend each of the major festivals (Exod 23:17; 34:23; Deut 16:16). Naturally, this would only be possible for those that lived in or close to Jerusalem. Whatever males did go on pilgrimage, no doubt brought their wives and children as well. Both Josephus (*Ant.* 4.203–4) and Philo (*Spec. Laws* 1.70) testify to the sense of community that was engendered by these pilgrimages. This sense of community and sharing would have been taken back to their respective homes, be it in Palestine or the Diaspora. Here follows a brief discussion of the three major festivals (cf.

Sanders 1992:132–41), all of which would have contributed to fostering a strong Judean ethnic identity. As Sanders (1992:144) points out correctly, "group identity and devotion to God went together."

Passover (Hebrew, *pesaḥ*). Also known as the feast of Unleavened Bread (*maṣṣot*), it recalled the exodus from Egypt. Originally there were two festivals, Passover and Unleavened Bread, that with time merged into one forming an eight day festival (cf. Lev 23:4–8; Deut 16:1–8). On the 14th of Nisan the Passover lamb was sacrificed, while on the fifteenth (beginning at sundown) the feast of Unleavened Bread began lasting seven days (*Ant.* 3.248f.; *Spec. Laws* 2.149–50, 155). One lamb was seen as adequate for ten people (*War* 6.423) so presumably one of the ten would have made the sacrifice in the temple. The worshipper, however, would have been required to be in a state of ritual purity. Whoever entered the temple-complex was required to stay outside the temple for seven days in the case of corpse impurity. He had to be sprinkled with ashes on the third and seventh day, ritually immerse himself in the immersion pools located towards the south of the complex, and only then could he enter to sacrifice the Passover lamb (*Spec. Laws* 1.261).

The sacrifices were made between the ninth and eleventh hours of the day (around four to six o'clock in the afternoon) (*War* 6.423) accompanied by the full compliment of priests and Levites numbering thousands. According to the Tosefta (*t. Sukk.* 3:2) the Levites sang the Hallel (Psalms 113–118), which centred on praise and thanksgiving for personal and national deliverance. The man who brought the sacrifice slaughtered the animal and the priest caught the blood, which was passed on for the blood to be thrown against the base of the altar (*m. Pes.* 5:5–6). The priest then took the lamb and hung it on a hook on one of the walls and flayed it—or alternatively, staves were supported on the shoulders whereupon the lamb could be hung and flayed. This means the process could take place throughout the large temple-complex, or the priests stayed inside the balustrade where pilgrims and animals continuously flowed by (see Sanders 1992:133–37, who does not see the description of the Mishnah as likely, where the worshippers come in three different groups). In whatever way it happened, it is worth to comment that it must have required exceptional organization and experience on the part of the priests. The priest involved removed the main fatty portions and returned the lamb and its hide to the offerer, while the fat was burned on the altar (*m. Pes.* 5:9). He returned to his fellow pilgrims with the whole lamb, which was roasted on a skewer after nightfall (Exod 12:8–9; cf. *m. Pes.* 7:1–2). The roasted lamb was eaten with unleavened bread and bitter herbs (Exod 12:8). One also had to be properly attired. The loins had to be girded, with sandals on the feet and staff in hand to remember that the Israelites fled from Egypt in haste (Exod 12:11). The children also had to be instructed on the meaning of the Passover festival—God "passed over" the houses of the Israelites when he killed the Egyptians (Exod 12:26–27).

Not surprisingly, as the feast had to do with national liberation, it was often accompanied by Judean riots. It was the usual practice of the Roman prefect or procurator, stationed in Caesarea, to come to Jerusalem with additional troops to maintain order. Guards were posted on the roofs of the porticoes that surrounded the entire complex. There was one incident in 4 CE when Archelaus was ethnarch of Judea. While he was standing in the temple court, some Judeans made use of the opportunity to protest against the execution of the two Pharisees who encouraged their students to take down the eagle that stood above the entrance to the temple. Archelaus sent in troops to arrest them but the crowd threw them with stones killing a few in the process. When further troops were sent in, 3,000 Judeans were supposedly killed, the rest fled and the sacrifices were canceled (*War* 2.10–13). During the time of the procurator Cumanus (48–52 CE), as per usual, Roman troops were on guard on the roofs of the porticoes. Josephus describes that one of them "stooped in an indecent attitude, so as to turn his backside to the Judeans, and made a noise in keeping with his posture." The consequences of this insensitive behavior are predictable. The riot that ensued we are told cost the lives of thousands (*War* 2.224–27; *Ant.* 20.112).

The Feast of Weeks (Hebrew *šavu'ot* or *'atseret*, "concluding feast"). Also called "Pentecost" or the "Day of First Fruits," it celebrated an agricultural festival. Occurring fifty days after Passover, it was identified mainly by the offering of new wheat. Two loaves of bread were made from the first wheat of the harvest, and offered as "first fruits" (Lev 23:15–21; cf. Num 28:26–31). This inaugurated the period where Judeans brought their offerings of first fruits to the temple. Here God's ownership of the land was declared, as well as his grace that allowed the land to bring forth food. In addition, it was a time to remember and give thanks for God's deeds on behalf of Israel: the election, the covenant and the exodus (cf. Deut 26:1–15).

In 4 BCE the Feast of Weeks saw a fight between Romans and Judeans. Sabinus, the procurator of Syria attempted to take for Rome (and himself) some of Herod's treasure after his death. Thousands of

Judeans began an attack on Sabinus' troops and many lost their lives on both sides (*Ant.* 17.221–268; *War* 2.42–44). Even here, the smallest of pilgrimage festivals, there was opportunity for riots where many Judeans were present.

The Feast of Booths/Tabernacles (Hebrew, *sukkot*). It is an autumn festival that began five days after the Day of Atonement, being second to Passover with regards to the number of pilgrims. It is prescribed that for seven days Israelites will live in booths (Lev 23:42). One more festival day (where work was forbidden) was added, making it in effect an eight day festival (Lev 23:33–36). The booths or tabernacles were made of "branches from olive and wild olive trees, and from myrtles, palms and shade trees" (Neh 8:15). The residents of Jerusalem probably built them on the roofs of their houses, while pilgrims built them outside the city walls. Also an agricultural festival, it marked the conclusion of the harvest season. It was "a showy and happy occasion with something of a carnival spirit. Worshippers carried *lulavs*, made of branches from palm, willow and myrtle trees, to which a citron (a citrus fruit) was attached ... There was flute playing and dancing by night" (Sanders 1992:139; cf. Lev 23:40; *Ant.* 3.245; *m. Sukk.* 5:4). The Hallel was apparently sung on each of the eight days and during the singing the worshippers shook their *lulavs* (*m. Sukk.* 3:9; 4:8). A plethora of community sacrifices were made (Num 29:12–34; *Ant.* 3.246), while study of scripture was probably an important element during the festival (Deut 31:10–11; Neh 8:17–18). Leviticus also connects this festival to the exodus (Lev 23:42–43).

Some famous events are connected with the Feast of Booths/Tabernacles. While the Hasmonean Alexander Jannaeus (103–76 BCE) was serving at the altar, the on-lookers threw citrons at him. They accused him of being a descendent of captives, thus implying he was illegitimate and not eligible to serve as a priest. Once the troops were called in some 6,000 Judeans were killed according to Josephus (*Ant.* 13.372–73). It was also during this festival that a Jesus son of Ananias proclaimed a message of doom over the temple and the Judean people. Even after being punished and scourged before the procurator, he continued lamenting for seven years and five months, being most vocal at the festivals. He was eventually killed by a Roman missile during the Great Revolt (*War* 6.300–309).

Tithes, Offerings, and the Temple Tax

The Tanak, particularly the Torah, has no uniform prescription on tithing and offerings. What was tithed and how much developed over time, and here again we are indebted to Sanders (1992:146–57) and will follow his reconstruction of the tithing and offering system that was in place in the first century. All these contributions existed to support the priests and Levites who were not allowed to "inherit the land" (Num 18:20–31; Deut 18:1–2), although evidently there were those who did own land but refrained from working it themselves. But the onus was on ordinary Israelites to support their priests and Levites who were to serve in the Temple (*T. Levi* 9:4; *Jub.* 14:25; 32:10–15). There were strict biblical requirements for the priests and their families when they ate the tithes and offerings. They had to be in a state of ritual purity (Lev 22:4–7; Num 18:13), while ordinary Israelites were also expected to handle and eat second tithe in purity (Deut 26:13–14).

The tithe literally means "one-tenth." In our period the requirements of Deuteronomy 14; Leviticus 27 and Numbers 18 (cf. Neh 10:37–39) were combined to form what Sanders calls the fourteen tithe system in a seven-year cycle. Every seventh year, the sabbatical year, no tithes were offered as the land was given an opportunity to rest. In the other years there were at least two tithes, the tenth of all agricultural produce—not animals—that went to the Levites (who then gave a tenth of what they received to the priests), and the so-called "second tithe," money that had to be spent in Jerusalem especially during pilgrimage festivals. Every third and sixth year there was a third tithe, which was given to benefit the poor. Josephus understands that Moses required the two tithes per year and the third tithe every third and sixth year (*Ant.* 4.69, 205, 240), illustrating that the fourteen tithe system was used. Priests and Levites collected the tithes themselves (Neh 10:37–38; *Life* 63), so farmers every year expected that the religious clergy would come to ask for the tithes. This also implies that there were sufficient storage facilities for grain (and wine and oil), which in turn could be distributed amongst the recipients.[23] Based on the debate of the Pharisees, not all people were necessarily enthusiastic about giving the Levites their portion, although the ordinary people were inclined to give the priests the one tenth of the first tithe as required.

First fruits. This category involves food (first produce and firstlings), money (redemption of non-edible firstlings) and fleece. In the case of *firstlings*, the requirements of Exodus 13 and Numbers 18 prevailed, where all male firstlings of animals belonged to God, that is, it went to the priests. All the firstlings of impure animals (donkeys,

---

23. Beneath the esplanade, there were three stories of vaults that provided a lot of space for storage (Ben-Dov 1990:28–29).

horses, camels etc.) were redeemed for one and a half shekels, while a first born son was redeemed by the father for five shekels (*Ant.* 4.71; cf. Num 18:15–16). The *first fruits of produce* required the first of everything that the land produced (*Ant.* 4.70). First fruits involved both primary and secondary produce: "both raw food (grain, grapes, olives, and the like) and the first things made from it (cakes, wine, and oil); both the first-born lamb and the first of the year's wool" (Sanders 1992:152). In our period the distinction of Leviticus 23 was followed, where the offering of the first fruits of the harvest occurred on the second day of Unleavened Bread (where a sheaf of barley was waved before the altar), and where the first cakes or loaves were offered at the Feast of Weeks around fifty days later (*Ant.* 3.251–52). Since the Feast of Weeks was not that popular, it probably worked out that most people offered their first fruits at the feast of Booths. Those who brought their first fruits had a required avowal to say that concerns God's gift of the land and the exodus (Deut 26:1–11).

Sanders also discusses the *heave offering*, or terumah. Neither Josephus nor Philo mentions it, and in Num 15:20 and 18:11 the noun terumah is used to refer to the primary offerings, the shared sacrifice and first fruits. The LXX usually translated the heave offering as "first fruits," nevertheless, terumah may be a separate offering in Neh 10:37, 39, and this is the way that the rabbi's understood it (*m. Ter.* 4:3).

The *temple tax*. This contribution did not go towards the priests, but was used to pay the Temple costs, especially the community sacrifices. According to Exod 30:13–16, every Israelite male twenty years old and above was required to pay a half shekel in support of the tabernacle, a tax that was required to be given only once in a lifetime. Nehemiah 10:32 requires an annual tax of one third shekel. Eventually it was understood that that the Tanak requires an annual tax of one half shekel (= two drachmas), payable by each adult Judean male. The preferred currency was the Tyrian half-shekel. The money was stored in the treasury located in the vaulted rooms beneath the esplanade (cf. *Ant.* 19.294; Mark 12:41; John 8:12, 20). The Mishnah also speaks of thirteen trumpet-shaped collection boxes in the Court of Women (*m. Sheq.* 6:5–6). On them was written (in Aramaic) their purpose. For example, "New Shekel" was for the temple tax of that year; "Old Shekel" for the tax not paid for the previous year. Others were for burnt offerings and freewill offerings and so on. As Stegemann & Stegemann (1999:122) point out, this is perhaps the place where the story of the poor widow took place (Mark 12:41–44; cf. Luke 21:1ff.). After the temple was destroyed, the *didrachma* or half-shekel was changed into a Roman tax, the humiliating *fiscus Judaicus*, but the tax base was broadened to include women and children as well. All Judean men and women between the ages of three and sixty-two were taxed. To add insult to injury, the money was paid to the temple of Jupiter Capitolinus in Rome (*War* 7.218; Dio Cassius 66.7). This tax was eventually abolished under Nerva (96–98 CE).

Now did all of these tithes and taxes impose a serious economic burden on the people? This is the view of Horsley (1987:232–56). The tithes and taxes when combined with the Roman tribute added up to over 40 per cent of production. This double taxation led to an increased cycle of indebtedness, and eventually, loss of land, which led to increased poverty, unemployment and finally, banditry.

Sanders (1992:157–69) seriously questions such an understanding. He argues that the system in place under the Romans was nothing new, as the Judeans had supported the Temple staff and paid foreign tribute (or Hasmonean taxes) for centuries. The numbers of the unemployed are exaggerated by scholars, and Josephus' use of "brigand" and "bandit" is apologetic, demonstrating that only these Judeans were rebellious. In addition, the use of these two terms does not prove that the rebels were landless and unemployed. The situation for the farmers were no doubt difficult, but they evidently had enough to attend the festivals and were able to survive the sabbatical years. Sanders estimates that the average total tribute would have been less than 28 percent (cf. Fiensy 1991:103, who estimates the total tribute at 25 percent). For Sanders (1992:168–69) the "social and economic situation was not very remarkable ... What wa*s peculiar* to the situation was not taxation and a hard-pressed peasantry, but the [Judean] combination of theology and patriotism" (emphasis original).

Sanders, however, is here guilty of oversimplification. Although we do not know exactly what the ratio between freeholders and tenant farmers was, and what the burden of taxation involved, there is enough evidence that at least *some* peasant farmers were indebted, or even had lost their land. For example, at the beginning of the Great Revolt, the debt records in Jerusalem were burned (*War* 2.427). The Gospels take for granted the reality of debt and the existence of tenant farmers (e.g., Mark 12:1–12; Matt 18:23–35) (cf. Fiensy 1991; Stegemann & Stegemann 1999:100, 110–25, 134; Horsley 1995:216). The issue of land will be discussed in further detail below, but for the average Judean peasant farmer, indebtedness, poverty and loss of land was just as important as the desecration of Jerusalem or the Temple (if not more so?) and thus had everything to do with theology and patriotism as well.

The Synagogue

In Hebrew, the term for synagogue is *beth knesset*, "house of assembly." Generally there is no certainty about the history of the synagogue, yet it is regarded as an important element in Judean life and worship in the first century. According to Richardson (2004:111–221) synagogues most likely had their origins in the Diaspora, and their development took place within the broader context of associations. He refers to the Roman toleration of Judean communities and the decrees of Julius Caesar and Augustus in particular which allowed for them to gather while other *collegia* were prohibited. The Roman authorities according to Richardson nevertheless viewed the synagogues as *collegia*, while the Judeans also adopted architectural forms for their places of meeting that were similar to other associations. On the other hand, some have questioned the synagogue's prevalence or existence as a building, especially in Judea and Galilee. Below the textual and archaeological evidence will be reviewed before any conclusions are drawn.

The Synagogue: A Building or Assembly of People?

Let us first review the textual evidence. The Gospels speak of a συναγωγή in Nazareth (Matt 13:54; Mark 5:2; Luke 4:16) and Capernaum (Mark 1:21; Luke 7:5; John 6:59). The amounts in larger cities were apparently greater, such as Jerusalem (Acts 6:9; 24:12), Alexandria (Philo, *Embassy* 132) and Rome (*Embassy* 155–8). Philo makes specific mention of Essenes who gather at places they call "synagogues" (*Omnis Probus* 81). Most often Acts makes use of συναγωγή for assemblies in the Diaspora, while it describes that Paul found Judean synagogues everywhere on his travels in Asia Minor and Greece (Acts 13:14; 14:1; 16:13, 16; 17:1, 10, 17; 18:4, 7, 19, 26; 19:8), Cyprus (Acts 13:5) and Damascus (Acts 9:20). Josephus mentions a synagogue in Caesarea (*War* 2.285–290), Dora (*Ant.* 19.300), on the Phoenician coast (*War* 2.185–90) and a magnificent synagogue in Antioch (*War* 7.44–5) suggesting that there was more than one.

A related term is προσευχή, or "prayer-house." Προσευχή appears in Josephus (*Life* 277, 280, 290–303; in Tiberias) and Philo (*Embassy* 132, 155–56; in Alexandria and Rome), 3 Macc 7:20 and in the New Testament (Acts 16:13, 16). Philo also speaks of people attending "schools"[24] on the Sabbath (*Spec. Laws* 2.62–63) where Judeans received instruction in the Law. Alternatively, these two Greek terms are used for Judean assemblies of people and/or places of meeting in the Diaspora and in Palestine. The earliest evidence comes from Egypt, where documents and inscriptions dating from the third century BCE and onwards make mention of προσευχαί, although συναγωγή in the Diaspora initially did not have this meaning. It signified the congregation (of people) and not the building. It is supposed that it was in Palestine where συναγωγή was first used for a "meeting house"—although it is also claimed that there is no realistic distinction between these two Greek terms (Schürer et al. 1979:425, 439–47). It is thought that in view of the importance of Sabbath meetings, "it must be assumed that at least one synagogue stood in every town of Palestine, even in the smaller places" (Schürer et al. 1979:445), a view similarly held by Sanders (1992:198).

Horsley (1995:222–27; 1996:131–53) has rejected the usual scholarly construct of synagogues in Palestine and argues that συναγωγή, or the Hebrew *knesset* refers more to the assembly of people than a structure. In the Diaspora προσευχή denotes a building wherein the congregation meets. Josephus does use the term συναγωγή to refer to buildings in Dora, Caesarea and Antioch, but these cannot be used to argue for the existence of "synagogue" buildings in Judean or Galilean villages. These structures clearly also have a socio-political dimension as a centre for the local community in addition to its religious dimension, as does the prayer-house in Tiberias. The brunt of Horsley's argument seems to be that there is no justification for the standard reading of συναγωγή, in the New Testament as a religious *building*. The places of meeting were according to him the local village or town square. "It is increasingly clear from critical examinations of archaeological findings ... that we cannot identify *buildings* to which the term *synagogue* could

---

24. According to later tradition, Jesus ben Gamla, probably a high priest who flourished in 63–65 CE, ordered that school teachers be appointed in every province and town, and that children ages six or seven be brought to them (*b. B.B.* 21a). Both Josephus (*Apion* 1.60; 2.178; 2.204) and Philo (*Embassy* 115, 210) say that children were educated in the matters of the law, or even taught to read (cf. Evans 2001:17). Other texts say that fathers must teach their children to read to know the Law of God (*T. Levi* 13:2; *L.A.B.* 22:5–6). Schürer (1979:418) argues there can be no doubt "that in the circles of traditional [Judeanism] a boy was familiarized with the demands of the Torah from earliest childhood." This duty was primarily that of parents but "it seems that already by the time of Jesus the community also provided for the instruction of the young by establishing schools."

have referred," to which Horsley adds: "What were claimed as 'synagogue' buildings in the towns of Magdala and Gamla turned out to be private houses ..." (Horsley 1995:224, emphasis original). Horsley also questions that the rooms at Masada and Herodium can be identified as synagogues.

One can agree that the synagogue (be they buildings or merely assemblies of people) did not purely perform a religious function. A political meeting was even held in the great προσευχή of Tiberias (*Life* 280). Shanks (2001:52–53) states that before 70 CE "a synagogue was more like a community center. It was a place where groups of [Judeans] assembled for social functions and political matters, where they kept their money, where they collected and dispensed charity, where they judged disputes—and especially, where they studied the sacred texts. Probably not where they prayed, however" (but cf. Matt 6:5). Otherwise the New Testament makes mention of punishment being administered in the συναγωγή, (Matt 10:17; 23:34; Mark 13:9; cf. Acts 22:19; 26:11). Besides punishment, members could also be excommunicated from the assemblies. Supposedly "this punishment was nothing less than vital to post-exilic [Judeanism]. In continuous contact with a Gentile environment, the [Judean] communities could only preserve themselves by constantly and carefully eliminating alien elements" (Schürer et al. 1979:431). These kind of expulsions are testified to in the time of the New Testament (Luke 6:22; John 9:22; 12:42; 16:2). Clearly then, the first Messianists were seen as undermining the Judean symbolic universe, posing a threat to the integrity of Judean ethnic identity.

In addition, Horsley's argument above is to a degree ignoring or dismissing the available evidence. There is of course the Theodotus Inscription found near the Temple Mount, which refers to a synagogue that could have been built as early as 100 BCE (Shanks 2001:51). The inscription itself dates to the first century CE and reads in part: "Theodotus son of Vettenus ... *rebuilt this synagogue* for the reading of the Law and the teaching of the commandments...." Clearly some or other *building* is referred to. According to Kloppenborg (2006:251–79), both the provenance and the palaeography of the inscription point to a Herodian or early Roman dating (i.e. prior to 70 CE). There is also the Benghazi inscription (in Cyrenaica), dated to 55/56 CE, where συναγωγή refers to *both* the congregation and a building (Kloppenborg 2006:245–46). But as Kloppenborg (2006:278) argues, the Theodotus Inscription confirms that συναγωγή "was used of buildings not only in Egypt and Cyrenaica but also in early Roman Palestine." Other archaeological evidence for Palestine is meagre, but it does exist. Synagogue buildings have been identified at Masada and Herodium, the two desert fortresses that were built by Herod the Great, and at Gamla in the Golan Heights. The Masada structure was probably converted to a synagogue by the Sicarii during the First Revolt. None of the sources consulted identify these structures or rooms as "houses." In addition there is a synagogue at Capernaum (cf. Luke 7:5) and Chorazin (Strange & Shanks 1990), and a house-synagogue in Caesarea (Bull 1990:115). Archaeologists have also suggested that they have found synagogue buildings at Jericho and at Migdal (or Magdala), both dating to the first-century BCE. The structure at Jericho boasts a *mikveh* and an *otzar* (reserve), while at least four *miqva'ot* have been located around the structure at Migdal. Whether the structure at Migdal was in fact a synagogue is disputed, however. It is suggested that the structure rather served as a springhouse where the city's residents came to draw water (Shanks 2001).[25]

According to Cohen (1987:114), "the synagogue is an amalgamation of a prayer-house, which apparently originated in the diaspora in early Hellenistic times; a study house or school, which apparently originated in Israel also in early Hellenistic times; and a meeting-house, which served the different needs of diaspora and Palestinan [Judeans]. By the first century these diverse elements had not yet united to form a single type." But another process is also likely. The various buildings/assemblies already had various functions, as suggested by the evidence, and only much later did they develop to have a more "religious" purpose with recognisable architectural features. In summary the evidence is meagre, but there is evidence for synagogue buildings, while we will take note of Horsley's objection in that συναγωγή in some cases, particularly in small villages and towns, could rather have referred to an assembly of people. Beyond the family, the assemblies/synagogues would have formed the most important social and cultural form of the local community, and so would have promoted a strong group identity of being Judean.

Teaching the Law and the Prophets

In post-exilic Judeanism the custom of Sabbath readings in the assembly took shape. These Sabbath meetings were not religious worship in the

---

25. We may add to this list Kiryat Sepher, Modi'in, and Horvat 'Ethri, also identified as synagogues by archaeologists, or referred to as public assembly halls by Kloppenborg (see Kloppenborg 2006:248–49; Richardson 2004:219).

narrow sense, but also contained instruction in the Torah. By the first century CE obedience to the Torah was an essential part of Judeanism (cf. *Apion* 2.276–77; 1.43). Besides instruction in the Torah, Luke 4:17 gives evidence of the *haftarah*, or reading of the prophets. Both Josephus (*Apion* 2.175–78) and Philo (*Creation* 128) testify that there were regular Sabbath services in the assemblies and it was an important means of maintaining the ancestral religion. The Law and the prophets were read and elaborated upon every Sabbath wherever Judeans lived in the Diaspora, the normal liturgical language most probably being Greek (Schürer et al. 1979:424; 1986:142). The reading from the Torah and the prophets is also in evidence in the New Testament (Luke 4:17; Acts 13:15). In Palestine a reading from the scriptures was sometimes accompanied by a translation, or *targum*, an ongoing rendering into Aramaic (cf. Schürer et al. 1979:452–53).

Part of the proceedings was a spiritual sermon, which in Philo appears as almost the most important aspect of the gathering (*Spec. Laws* 2.62; *Moses* 2.216; Eusebius, *Pr. Ev.* 8.7.12–13). Here Bible passages were expounded and given practical application. This teaching function of the assemblies is corroborated by the New Testament (Matt 4:23; Mark 1:21; 6:2; Luke 4:15, 4:20ff.; 6:6; 13:10; John 6:59; 18:20; Acts 15:21 et al.), where it was the primary activity of Jesus and Paul. Josephus (*Apion* 2.175) also makes reference to the teaching function of the assemblies. Prayer is mentioned in Matt 6:5. Study of scripture in the assemblies was therefore common to Judeans, both in Palestine and in the Diaspora (Cohen 1987:113).

According to Cohen, with the development of the synagogue it meant the Temple was not the only place where people could communicate with God. The development of prayer and Torah study was an alternative means for reaching God. The emergence of scribes and sages meant that the priesthood no longer had the monopoly on religious truth. This means that during the Second Temple period Judeanism was "democratized." It was far more concerned with the piety and fate of the individual than the pre-exilic Israelite religion was (Cohen 1987:75).[26] Sanders (Sanders 1992:181) has a different approach. There

---

26. Cf. Oppenheimer (2005:106), who speaks of the proliferation of synagogues in Jerusalem in the Second Temple period based on the Babylonian Talmud. They were used for prayers, Torah study and raising the hands in blessing. The synagogues "included an expansion and deepening of religious experience by making possible the participation of every man in the worship of God without the mediation of a priest." Although this did not apply to every individual while the Temple stood: "it was probably the preserve of elite groups, including *havurot* in general and those in Jerusalem

were approximately 18,000 to 20,000 priests and Levites, as opposed to 6,000 Pharisees. There were thousands of priests and Levites that probably lived in Jerusalem, while the rest lived in other cities of Judea and Galilee. Since the priests and Levites were only on duty one week in every twenty-four (as they were divided into twenty-four "courses"), plus during the pilgrimage festivals, they were free most of the time to conduct their own affairs. Thus it is likely that they served in their towns and villages as teachers and magistrates. So in most parts of Palestine they would have assumed their traditional leading roles, which included teaching of the Law and serving as judges. In these tasks they were assisted by the Levites (Neh 8:7–9; 1 Chr 23:2–6; 2 Chr 17:7–9; 19:8–11). "Priests and Levites were often scribes, a title that covers a range of activities: copying texts, drawing up legal documents and serving as experts on the law ... The post-exilic biblical evidence uniformly points to the fact that the priests (and Levites, at least a few of them) were 'scribes' in the sense of studying, teaching and enforcing the law" (Sanders 1992:170–71). Deuteronomy places the responsibility of the Law into the hands of the priests (Deut 17:18; 31:9), and Ben Sira regarded the priests as the nation's teachers (Sir 45:17). Josephus regarded the priests as the nation's rulers and judges (*Ant.* 4.304; 14.41; *Apion* 2.165)—the system was a "theocracy" (*Apion* 2.184–87).

Sanders' (1992:173) basic argument is that the priests maintained their traditional roles but they no longer had a monopoly over them. Nevertheless, Sanders seriously questions that the Pharisees, with scribal leaders, took over the responsibility as legal experts, teachers and magistrates. Inscriptional evidence supports the textual evidence that priests maintained their traditional roles. Sanders refers to the Theodotus Inscription that mentions a third-generation priest and "ruler of the synagogue" (ἀρχισυνάγωγος)[27] who built a synagogue "for the reading of the Law and for the teaching of the commandments." Here three generations of priests were rulers of the synagogue (Sanders 1992:176). Philo informs us that Sabbath instruction was led by a priest or elder (*Hyp.* 7.12–13). Overall Sanders concludes

in particular."

27. Mark 5:22, 35–38; and Acts 13:15; 18:8, 17 and others also refer to an ἀρχισυνάγωγος—is it likely that they were priests as well? It is a distinct possibility. Compare Horsley (1995:232), however, who speaking of Galilee, suggests that local governance of village and town were provided by local assemblies (and courts) "operating more or less democratically" with the local ἀρχισυνάγωγος and ὑπηρέτης managing the affairs. Horsley does not identify these officials as priests, but neither does he identify Galileans as Judeans for that matter.

> that it is unreasonable to suppose that the small number of Pharisees, most of whom probably worked from dawn to dusk six days a week, also served their communities as lawyers and scribes, while the large number of priests and Levites, who were on duty in the temple only a few weeks a year, who could not farm, and who were educated in the law, did nothing. It is much more likely that ordinary priests and many of the Levites put their learning to good use and served as scribes and legal experts ... Priests and Levites were the employees of the nation for the purposes of maintaining the worship of God in the temple, and teaching and judging the people. (Sanders 1992:181–82)

The understanding of the Pharisees may be a bit questionable so far as their work hours is concerned (cf. Baumgarten 1997:51), but one can agree with Sanders (1992:201) that the priests were likely to be involved in community study and teaching in the synagogue (cf. Stegemann & Stegemann 1999:140). If this was the case, which is very likely, the temple and its symbolic meaning and ability to shape identity would also extend to outlying Judean communities. The priests and the temple were not as sidelined as Cohen suggests. Similarly Schmidt (2001:263) argues that already before 70 CE

> the synagogal institution is a bearer of the thinking of the Temple. Far from being a sign of a decline of the Temple, it is one of the principal vehicles of the extension to the whole of [Judean] society of the ritual prescriptions expressing the categories of the sacred and the profane, of the pure and the impure, as well as the mode of classification proper to the thinking of the Temple. As such, the synagogal institution appears as a manifestation of the extension—in the strongest sense of the term—of the Sanctuary.

Indeed, the synagogue or assembly would have been a perfect tool for the maintenance of the Judean symbolic universe. The temple and its "thinking" was the focal point, but it was complimented by instruction in the Torah, correction, and even excommunication. Here we must be reminded of the social function of religion, and its ability to shape communities (Smith 1994:716). Communal solidarity would have been engendered and of course, a shared ethnic identity.

The Household

Everyday life for the Judean was regulated by requirements of the Torah. They shaped mutual relationships, the rhythm of every day life, the Sabbath and feasts, and work. "In particular, the consciousness of [Judean] identity was reinforced through the religious structuring of time, daily prayers, the study of the Torah, and, not least of all, purity and food regulations, as well as endogamous marriage strategies" (Stegemann & Stegemann 1999:142). Matters pertaining to kinship will not be discussed here, as for now we will concentrate on the issue of religion and covenantal praxis at home, the primary place of worship or the place used most frequently (Sanders 1992:197; cf. Sanders 2002:121). Horsley (1995:129) points out that

> Religious formation and expression operated at more than one level, that of family and local village community being at least as important as that of the Jerusalem Temple for the vast majority of people, who lived in outlying towns and villages.

We must therefore always bear in mind the close association that exists between the family and the local community, but the home would be the primary area of early socialization and where "habitual dispositions" (cf. Jones 1997:87–105; Bourdieu 1977:72) will be formed and "categorization" (we know who we are because other people tell us; see Jenkins 1997:166) will take place. So for the average Judean child of the first century, what would he/she be socialized into?

THE *SHEMA*, DRESS, AND PRAYERS

The saying of the *Shema*, the biblical passage in Deut 6:4–9, was fundamental to Judean life and worship. It began with the confession: "Hear [*shema*], O Israel: The LORD our God, the LORD is one. Love the LORD your God with all your heart and with all your soul and with all your strength" (vv. 4–5). The *Shema* encouraged Israelites to place the commandments of God upon their heart, hand, forehead and on the doorpost and the gate. The commandments should also be taught to children and be remembered before sleep and on waking up (Deut 6:6–9). The commandments to be remembered was especially the Ten Commandments of Deuteronomy 5, but all the commandments are referred to. The mishnaic rabbis simply took it for granted that Judeans recited the *Shema* (along with daily prayers) twice a day, at morning and at evening (*m. Ber.* 1:1–3).

The importance of the *Shema* is highlighted by other Judean customs. Some of the instructions contained therein were taken literally by the second century BCE and gave rise to the custom of wearing *tefillin* (phylacteries) and fixing *mezuzot* to doorposts (Cohen 1987:74). The *tefillin* are prayer straps that every male Judean had to put on at morning prayer (except the Sabbath and holy days), their use based on Exod 13:9, 16 and Deut 6:8; 11:18. There was a hand *tefillah* and an arm *tefillah*. The latter was a small cup-shaped hollow case made of parchment, which contained a small parchment scroll with Bible passages written upon them (Exod 13:1–10; 11–16; Deut 6:4–9; 11:13–21) that was fastened to the left upper arm with a strap. The head *tefillah* worked on the same principle, but the case was divided into four compartments that contained the biblical passages written on four scrolls. It was attached by a strap to the middle of the forehead just beneath the hairline. The *mezuzah* is an oblong box that was fixed to the right-hand doorpost of the house and every room. It contained a small scroll of parchment on which was written in twenty-two lines Deut 6:4–9 and 11:13–21. It was meant to turn one's thoughts towards thanksgiving to God and was also believed to keep evil spirits at bay.

According to Sanders (1992:123) Judeans would have dressed as other people did in the Greek-speaking world. Yet they could be distinguished by them wearing *tefillin* as discussed above, and also by tassels (Schürer et al. 1979:479–81). The tassels (*ṣiṣit*) were attached to the hem of garments (on the four corners) and were made of blue or white wool, and is mentioned in Num 15:37–41 and Deut 22:12.[28] This is to be worn by every Israelite and it had the purpose of when looking upon them, to remember the commandments and to do them. The hem of a garment in ancient society was indicative of a person's rank and authority. In addition, wool dyed blue was very expensive. The presence of a blue cord (*petil tekelet*) in the tassel gave the wearer a mark of nobility. But within a Judean context, it had special religious significance. Normally their was a general prohibition against cloth mixing linen and wool (Deut 22:11; cf. Lev 19:19), but *Tg. Ps-J.* on Deut 22:12 shows this combination was required in priestly garments (cf. Exod 28:6; 39:29). Thus ordinary Israelites could not wear a combination of linen and wool as it was reserved for the priests and the sanctuary (Exod 26:1). But by combining linen and wool in the tassel, the ordinary Israelite was to a degree wearing a priestly garment. Israel as a whole is a "kingdom

---

28. Cf. *L.A.B.* 16:1; Matt 9:20; 14:36; 23:5; Mark 6:56; Luke 8:44; and LXX and *Tg. Num.* 15:38.

of priests and a holy nation" (Exod 19:6), so the tassel was not only a reminder of the commandments, but by observing the commandments, they also strive for a life of holiness (Milgrom 1983).

The Pharisees were accused of making their phylacteries broad and their fringes long (Matt 23:4). "Pharisees wore the same clothes as everyone else, with only the minor statement of special identity expressed through *broad* phylacteries and *long* fringes" (Baumgarten 1997:102, emphasis original). The *Letter of Aristeas* testifies to these Judean customs and the importance of the *Shema*. Accordingly God commanded the following:

> ... in our clothes he has given us a distinguishing mark as a reminder, and similarly on our gates and doors he has commanded us to set up the "Words," so as to be a reminder of God. He also strictly commands that the sign shall be worn on our hands, clearly indicating that it is our duty to fulfil every activity with justice ... He also commands that "on going to bed and rising" men should meditate on the ordinances of God ... (*Let. Aris.* 158–60)

Accompanying the saying of the *Shema*, *daily prayers* were also offered. Josephus states that Moses required thanksgiving prayers when waking up and going to sleep (*Ant.* 4.212). It is said of Judeans: "at dawn they lift up holy arms toward heaven, from their beds, always sanctifying their flesh with water" (*Sib. Or.* 3:591–94). Washing of hands during prayers is mentioned in the *Letter of Aristeas* 305–6. Some offered evening prayers during the time of the last sacrifice in the Temple (e.g., Jdt 9:1). The pseudepigrapha depict the biblical heroes as praying often (see Sanders 1992:202). There were also thanksgiving prayers (*berakhoth*) before and after meals (Deut 8:10). It is also argued that the *Shemoneh Esreh*, the prayer required from every Israelite three times a day, though more recent, is fundamentally still very old, the foundation of the prayer preceding 70–100 CE (Schürer et al. 1979:455–63). Prayer was also at times accompanied by the practice of fasting[29] (cf. Schürer et al. 1979:481–84, 455).

The *Shema* further requires that the commandments of God be taught to children. Together with theoretical instruction went training in religious practice. "For although children were not obliged to fulfil the Torah, they were nevertheless habituated to it from the earliest years"

---

29. Cf. *T. Levi* 9:4; *Jub.* 14:25; 32:10–15; Matt 6:5; 9:14; 15:7–8; Mark 2:18; 7:6; 12:40; Luke 5:33; 20:47.

(Schürer et al. 1979:420). Rabbinical writings explain that parents were obliged to make their children keep the Sabbath rest. Children were gradually accustomed to keep fasts, such as on the Day of Atonement. They were further required to recite the *Shemoneh Esreh* and grace at table. Young boys were to go to the Temple at festivals and were also required to observe the Feast of Booths/Tabernacles. As soon as the first signs of manhood appeared, he had to keep the whole Law (the expression *bar-miṣwah* is attested in the Talmud; *b. B.M.* 96a). Later it was standardized and the young Judean reached legal majority at the age of thirteen (Schürer et al. 1979:421).

SABBATH OBSERVANCE

Josephus (*War* 4.580–83) informs us that a priest stood on one of the Temple Mount towers to blow a trumpet in order to announce the start and the end of the Sabbath. An inscription has been discovered on what may have been the corner stone of the south-western tower that has led archaeologists to conclude that this tower was the place where the Sabbath period was begun and ended by the trumpeting priest (Ben-Dov 1990:29–30; Ritmeyer & Ritmeyer 1990:40–43). This was Jerusalem at the Sabbath period. Celebrated by all Judeans wherever they were, the Sabbath was to be kept as a day of rest (Exod 20:8–11; Deut 5:12–15). The Maccabean crisis ensured its growing status for Judean self-understanding (1 Macc 1:43; *Jub.* 2:17–33; 50:6–13; *L.A.B.* 11:8). It was one of the most recognisable and unusual customs of Judeanism, sometimes even imitated by Gentiles, who like Judeans, marked the day by abstaining from doing work and having lamps burning (*Apion* 2.282). According to Jubilees in particular, divine election went hand in hand with the requirement to keep the Sabbath (*Jub.* 2:19), a right that was granted to no other nation (*Jub.* 2:31). Transgressors must die (*Jub.* 50:7–8, 12–13).

In the Pentateuch there is a short ban on work on the Sabbath that enters almost into no detail (Exod 16:23–30; 20:8–11; Lev 23:3; Num 15:32–6; Deut 5:12–15). The later rabbis felt obliged to be more exact and specified thirty-nine activities that were not allowed on the Sabbath (*m. Shab.* 7:2; cf. *Jub.* 50). In the Pentateuch, for example, ploughing and reaping are forbidden (Exod 34:21), but evidently by the time of Jesus, even the gathering of a few ears of corn was regarded as reaping (Matt 12:1–2; Mark 2:23–24; Luke 6:1–2; cf. Philo, *Moses* 2.4.22). The boiling and baking of food was also forbidden (Exod 16:23) so the hot meals had to be prepared before the Sabbath and be kept warm. It was also not permissible to light a fire (Exod 35:3). The rabbinnic prohibition of carrying anything from one domain to another was inspired by Jeremiah 17:21–23, although the idea could be stretched to mean a lot of things (cf. *Jub.* 2:29–30; 50:8).

Other rulings included the restriction on how far one may journey on the Sabbath (Exod 16:29; cf. Acts 1:12). Even the Romans did not recruit Judean soldiers because of the incompatibility between the Sabbath and Roman military requirements (*Ant.* 14.226). There was a basic rule that the saving of life took priority over Sabbath rulings. This was already in place from the time of the Maccabean revolt when a group of Hasideans were attacked by Gentiles, but rather chose to die than to fight on the Sabbath (1 Macc 2:34–8; *Ant.* 12.274). As a consequence, it was decided that the sword could be taken in defence on the Sabbath (1 Macc 2:39–42), but this ruling was only followed in extreme cases (Schürer et al. 1979:474).

The Day of Atonement

This special day on the Judean calendar is treated here since for most Judeans it was a day spent in and around the home. The Day of Atonement (Hebrew, *yom kippur*) is the only fast prescribed by the Tanak. It was not a time for pilgrimage, but a communal day of worship, in thought and spirit being connected to what took place in the Temple. It was a day for the atonement of sin, and the sacrifices made by the High Priest in Jerusalem was made for all (Lev 16). The goat "for Azazel" was brought in, whereupon the high priest laid his hand and confessed the sins of Israel as a whole. An appointed person then took this "scapegoat," which carried the sins of Israel, out of the city and into the wilderness (Lev 16:15–22).

The Purity of Food

As we investigated already, the issue of food became an important factor in Judean life from the Maccabean revolt onwards. In comparison with the holy food (*teruma*) of the priests and their families, the food of lay Israelites were made from *ḥullin* (or profane) products, which nevertheless, had to conform to the rules of the *kashrut*, that is, the prohibition of unclean animals (land and marine hybrids, wild animals, vultures or predators), the prohibition of blood, the ritual slaughter of clean animals, and separation of milk and meat (Schmidt 2001:217).

Regulations were already in place to distinguish food that was allowed for consumption from "impure" food that was disallowed

(Lev 11:1–23; Deut 14:3–21). Judeans were allowed to eat only a few animals, while the fatty parts and blood was forbidden. It was a strict requirement that the blood be drained (from the meat of clean animals) in accordance with the requirements of the Torah (Lev 3:17; 7:26–27; 17:10–14; Deut 12:16, 23–24; 15:23; *Jub.* 6:7–10; 21:6, 17–18; *Sib. Or.* 2:96). Quadrupeds that could be eaten were those that chew the cud and have cloven hoofs (Lev 11:3–7; Deut 14:6–8). This includes cattle, sheep and goats, as well as wild goats and deer. Pork was forbidden, a well known Judean characteristic in the ancient world. Fish with fins and scales could be eaten (Lev 11:9), as well as several birds, but birds of prey were prohibited (Lev 11:13–17). Insects and "swarming things" (serpents, lizards, weasels etc) were likewise forbidden, but locusts, crickets and grasshoppers, who have their legs above their feet were allowed (Lev 11:20–45). It is also probable that by our period it was prohibited to cook or serve red meat (and fowl) together with milk and cheese (Sanders 1992:217). These regulations naturally had profound implications for social life. Josephus says that food is the starting point of the Law and connects directly to social relations (*Apion* 2.173–74).

Processed food was in a similar way imprinted with the social order. Drawing on the work of anthropologists, Baumgarten (1997:92) explains: "A person or group expresses crucial aspects of their identity and of their relationship to other components of society through the regulations which govern their behavior in accepting processed food from others. Commensality is the other side of the same coin ... Those with whom one eats are friends of a special sort, and those with whom one refuses to eat marked as foes." Unclean food, or the food of Gentiles must be avoided, because it was not slaughtered properly or offered to idols (*Jos. Asen.* 7:1; 8:5; 3 Macc 3:4, 7; 4 Macc 1:34; *Sib. Or.* 2:96). The production and consumption of food was another way in which the Judeans maintained their symbolic universe. It determined who was in and who was out. Regulations concerning food were therefore primary boundary markers in Judeanism, even more so in the sects whose members began to regard fellow Judeans as "outsiders." Second Maccabees 5:27 speaks of food *defiled by Gentiles*. But when the new Maccabean leadership "disappointed and did not sufficiently reinstate the old borders, under the new purity distinctions of the sects—treating insufficiently observant [Judeans] as outsiders of a new sort—wild food was the only alternative to food *defiled by other* [*Judeans*] when food prepared under the auspices of the sect was unavailable" (Baumgarten 1997:92, emphasis original). One can also add that according to Josephus, Bannus only ate things that grew in the wild. Even his clothing—that trees provided—showed concern for purity (*Life* 11). John the Baptist ate locusts and honey. His clothing was a garment of camel's hair with a girdle made of leather (Matt 3:4). John refused to eat bread and drink wine—two foods that were central to the Judean diet—hence people thought he was possessed (Luke 7:33). So the diet of Bannus and John the Baptist "is a critical indication of a high degree of tension between themselves and the rest of [Judean] society of their day" (Baumgarten 1997:93). The Pharisees' restrictions on food were less stringent than those of Bannus, John the Baptist and the Qumran Covenanters/ Essenes. Yet they maintained boundaries around themselves through their food regulations—in the hierarchy of purity, they placed themselves above normal Judean society (Baumgarten 1997:97).

Hand in hand with type of food you ate was the issue of how you stored, prepared or served it. Generally, regulations governed the use of eating utensils (cf. Matt 15:2; 23:25–6; Mark 7:2–5; Luke 11:38–39), and the type of water to be used, all elaborated upon in the twelve tractates of Seder Tohoroth in the Mishnah (Schürer et al. 1979:476–77). Jars, cooking pots, jugs, plates, bowls and cups had to satisfy the laws of purity. Stone vessels were widely used, as it was believed to be impervious to contracting impurity (cf. *m. Kel.* 10:1; *m. Par.* 3:2). Pottery vessels, on the other hand, had to be destroyed after it came into contact with an impure substance or object (Avigad 1990). Metal and glass vessels could be repurified, however, which brings us to the matter of ritual immersion.

Ritual Immersion

Ritual immersion (and washings) developed to be quite a distinctive trait of first-century Judeanism, particularly so among sectarians. The Sadducees carried on with the biblical tradition. The Essenes transferred to their community the requirements of the Jerusalem temple. It is argued that the Pharisees "centred the laws of purity on the table, with the idea of eating their everyday meals in the same state of purity as that required of the priests in the Temple" (Schürer et al. 1979:475 n. 63; cf. Neusner 1973), a position with which Sanders (1992:380–451) disagrees.

Mark 7:3–4 relates directly to Pharisaic eating practices (Baumgarten 1997:97). Mark 7:3 (cf. Matt 15:1–20) says: "The Pharisees and all the Judeans do not eat unless they give their hands a ceremonial washing, holding to the tradition of the elders." This requirement in the time of Jesus is said to be only really applicable to the *ḥaberim* or associates,[30] and Schmidt (2001:235) suggests that this rite was not simply to achieve purity as an ideal, but marked a passage to enter a space or time of a greater or lesser holiness. Thus the *ḥullin* food is not necessarily seen as "holy," but the time in which it is consumed is, separated from profane space and time. Otherwise Mark 7:4 continues: "When they come from the marketplace they do not eat unless they wash [or *immerse*, βαπτίσωνται; other mss read 'purify']. And they observe many other traditions, such as the washing of cups, pitchers and kettles." Here to wash/immerse themselves when they come from the marketplace involves a purification of the whole body, not just the hands as in v. 3. Immersion is also mentioned in Luke 11:38. A Pharisee invites Jesus to eat with him. He is surprised that Jesus did not first *immerse* (ἐβαπτίσθη) himself before the meal (the text has got nothing to do with the *washing of hands:* ὁ δὲ Φαρισαῖος ἰδὼν ἐθαύμασεν ὅτι οὐ πρῶτον ἐβαπτίσθη πρὸ τοῦ ἀρίστου). This presupposes that the Pharisee thought Jesus belonged to the same group, or at least was willing to conform to Pharisaic purity standards. Baumgarten states that it is fair to conclude that such "immersion was deemed necessary because Pharisees believed that they had contracted impurity while in the market, from 'bumping into' people of indeterminate status, [Judeans] and/or [non-Judeans]. Eating could only take place after the elimination of this impurity, and in the company of others who were also pure (lest an impure person present reintroduce the impurity which had just been removed by immersion, which would then start the cycle going again, and prevent the Pharisee from eating)" (Baumgarten 1997:99).

If the above is correct, Pharisees could only eat with other Pharisees, or with those who maintained their standards, even if only temporarily (Baumgarten 1997:100). Cohen (1987:130) similarly explains that "the laws of purity prevent normal social intercourse between those who observe them and those who do not. Those who observe the laws cannot share the table, utensils, or food of those who do not. They must avoid physical contact . . . with those who are impure." Even so, we need to draw attention to the suggestion of Schmidt (see above) in that the washing of hands before the eating of profane food served a purpose in that the participants entered a sacred space or time period. Although

---

30. Cf. Schmidt (2001:232–34), who explains that the "Associates are mainly lay persons organized in associations in which they commit themselves to respect scrupulously the purity regulations and the tithes as they have been decreed, already before the destruction of the Temple, by the Sages of proto-rabbinism."

Schmidt does not make this connection himself, the same might have been part of the intention when it came to ritual immersion of persons and their eating utensils before meals. Maybe it was not simply just for the sake of achieving purity for its own sake.

Overall, there was a development in some Judean quarters with regards to the way you eat your food. The old table system, which prevailed during the Hasmonean period, was bipartite; the common meal of the priests was separated from that of the common meal of lay persons.

> In the Roman period, with the entry of the foreigner into the house, a new table system is introduced. For the *haberim* and more broadly those who put into practice the new prescriptions of the Sages as regards tithes and ritual purity, the frontier that separates the order of priests from that of the laity tends to get blurred. Set apart from the profane activities, the *time* of the daily meals of the laity is regarded as sacred. (Schmidt 2001:236–37; emphasis added)

How did all this preoccupation with purity and sacredness affect ordinary Judeans? Maybe Mark 7:3–4 as both interested in personal purity and a sacred time period had wide application, but for now the focus will shift onto the ritual status of the individual alone. According to Cohen for most Judeans of the second temple period "the sanctification of daily life was not implemented to such a radical degree. They felt ... that 'the camp' included only the temple and the temple mount. [Judeans] who wished to enter the temple or bring a sacrifice purified themselves[31] ... Away from the temple, however, most [Judeans] saw no need to observe the purity laws since they were no longer in the 'camp'..." (Cohen 1987:130). But as already mentioned, in contrast to Israelite religion, one of the hallmarks of Judeanism was the extension of purity laws to the laity away from the Temple (Schmidt 2001:231; cf. Schürer et al. 1979:475). In the Second Temple period there is evidence of ritual baths or *miqva'ot* (singular *miqveh*), found all over Palestine and not only in priestly contexts. It was one important or essential means to maintain a life of purity (cf. Sanders 1992:222–29). Sanders (1992:218–24, 228–29) therefore has a different view. Many people, he

---

31. Ritual immersion for participation in the temple cult is already attested for the Maccabean period: "Before you enter the sanctuary, bathe; while you are sacrificing, wash; and again when the sacrifice is concluded, wash" (*T. Levi* 9:11). A similar instruction is given in *Jub.* 21:16 (cf. *Let. Aris.* 106). Generally, ordinary Judeans would have required immersion only before entering the temple or when eating holy food (Passover, the second tithe, and the shared sacrifice).

argues, regarded purity as a positive good. It could have been that the first part of Num 19:20 was seen as a positive commandment: "remove corpse impurity." This is based on *Ant.* 3.262 where remaining corpse-impure for longer than seven days required the equivalent of a sin offering. So remaining impure was seen as a transgression. Ritual immersion was also extended to be applicable to women. According to Leviticus, contact with semen only required the passage of time for the purification of women, while it requires both the passing of time and bathing for men. But in our period it was agreed that both men and women had to bathe, or rather, immerse themselves for purification.

Ritual immersion, however, did not only revolve around the issue of avoiding transgression. Stegemann & Stegemann (1999:143) also point to another reason why Judeans ritually immersed themselves. Because of the presence of Gentiles in Palestine and the pagan or semi-pagan governing structures "the urgency of an identity-preserving delineation was not exactly small." Schmidt (2001:239) also points out that due to the proximity of Gentiles after the Hasmonean period it lead to a "transformation and reinforcement of that separation [i.e. between Judean and Gentile]. It was spatial; it becomes ritual. Because, established in the house, the foreigner is declared 'impure.'" Certainly, ritual immersion and washings would have been a meaningful way of maintaining your own position within the Judean symbolic universe and separating yourself from alien elements. What the *soreg* in the Temple symbolized became concrete in ritual immersion. Schmidt (2001:244) explains it succinctly:

> In the old system, the categories structuring the thinking of the Temple had as their first function to determine the sphere of holiness *within* the [Judean] community. While retaining this function, the new system thus modified acquires a new one: that of keeping the foreigners *outside* the community by establishing a hedge between [Judeans] and [non-Judeans]. Being no longer either territorial or political, the necessary separation between [Judeans] and [non-Judeans], that allows the community to protect itself from the danger of profanation that they impose on it, is henceforth symbolic and ritual. (emphasis original)

So what did immersion pools involve? According to Sanders, Lev 15:16 requires that a man who had a nocturnal emission to bathe "his whole body." The question of *where* was answered by the development of Lev 11:36: not even dead swarming things can make a spring or fountain or cistern holding water impure. Leviticus 15:13 prescribes that a man with discharge bathe in "living" (= "running") water. All the above verses, when combined, "led to the view that one should immerse in spring water or in a large pool, large enough for the entire body; if the water was not actually running, it should originally have been running water, and therefore it should have collected in the pool naturally" (Sanders 1992:222). What Sanders says here needs some change. "Living water" refers exclusively to water flowing directly from a natural spring or lake, and the water used in a *miqveh* need not originally have been "living/running" water. Sometimes rainwater was used, which flowed in from a roof or courtyard, although it is not "living/running water." The water could also in small quantities be replenished by drawn water, since *miqveh* water had the power to purify (Reich 2002:51–52).

On the odd occasion, a *miqveh* was accompanied by pool called an *otzer*. The latter served as a reserve pool wherein "living water" or rainwater was gathered. A pipe connected the two pools, and as needed, the water from the *otzer* could be transferred to the *miqveh*. As already mentioned, ritual immersion required the whole body to be immersed. Immersion was usually performed naked. The pools were cut into bedrock with steps leading down and usually covered with several layers of plaster to prevent water seepage. The water used usually remained in the pool from one rainy season to the next. For this reason *miqva'ot* were normally located in dark basements, thereby preventing the penetration of light and the growth of algae in the water. Some pools had a double entrance and/or a partitioned staircase (where a single staircase was divided into two by a low partition)—one staircase was for going into the pool and the other for coming out (Reich 2002; Eshel 2000; Meyers 2000).

Specific Impurities

Other dimensions of the purity system need to be discussed. The Tanak of course informed purity regulations. In what is to follow, we will do an overview of the "change in status" that affected ordinary life, and how "deviance" from the perfect order of Creation, and indeed, of Judean ethnic identity, was restored to normality.

Corpse impurity is treated in Numbers 19 and it describes a ritual for purification as well. A red heifer was slaughtered and burned by a priest outside the Temple. The ashes were then mixed with water. Those who had corpse impurity were sprinkled with the mixture on the third day and the seventh, remembering this impurity required seven days of purification. Also on the seventh day those concerned immersed and washed their clothes, and so the impurity was removed. Also the room where the corpse had lain and all the objects within it had to be sprinkled. It is difficult to see how this law applied to those living far from Jerusalem. According to Josephus, a person who remained corpse-impure for more than seven days was required to sacrifice two lambs. One was burned while the other went to the priest (*Ant.* 3.262). The Tanak does not prescribe this requirement. Sanders (1992:218) suggests that for those who lived far away from the temple it was thought that they transgressed the purity laws "inadvertently," which required a sin offering (Lev 4:27–35) at the first occasion of visiting Jerusalem.

Childbirth resulted in a long period of impurity that was divided into two stages. The first stage lasted for a week if the child was a boy, and two weeks if a girl. The mother was understood to be impure as if she was menstruating, thus sexual relations were forbidden. It may well be that the mother underwent ritual immersion at the end of the first stage.[32] The second stage lasted for thirty-three or sixty-six days, depending on the child's gender. Here she was not allowed to touch "holy things" (Lev 12:4), that is, food that was destined for the Temple. The impurity ended with the presentation of either a lamb as a burnt offering and a bird (pigeon or dove) as a sin offering, or alternatively, two birds if she could not afford a lamb (Lev 12:1–8).

Menstruation resulted in a seven day state of impurity. After the seven days the menstruant immersed. Anything she touched like her bed or chair would also become impure, which also required washing. As for those who touched her bed or chair, they had to immerse and wash their clothes and were impure until sunset (Lev 15:19–23). According to Sanders (1992:229), the Pharisees were of the opinion that the ordinary people were not that reliable to avoid this secondary (or *midras*) impurity. Sexual intercourse during menstruation was strictly forbidden, but if it was inadvertent, the man also became impure for seven days (Lev 15:24). Both parties owed a sin offering in this scenario (Lev 4:27—5:13).

Irregular discharges concerned discharges from male and female genitalia (Lev 15:1–15, 25–30). These impurities were equivalent to menstruation in the way that impurity was transferred, but as it was more severe than menstruation, purification also required sacrifices, the passing of seven pure days, and immersion.

---

32. Laws of purification after childbirth are mentioned in *Jubilees* (*Jub.* 3:8–14), but here is no mention of ritual immersion. Ritual immersion is evidently expected of males who bring offerings to the Temple, however (*Jub.* 21:16).

A man who had a *nocturnal emission* had to immerse and wash everything that came into contact with the semen. Impurity ended at sunset (Lev 15:16–17). After sexual intercourse, both man and woman were impure. Here purification required immersion, and impurity ended at sunset (Lev 15:18).

Carcasses of animals (including "swarming things") also resulted in impurity. Impurity ceased at sunset without immersion (Lev 11:29–30). *Dead swarming things* (e.g., rodents, weasels, lizards, and crocodiles etc.) rendered moist food, liquids, vessels and ovens impure (Lev 11:32–8).

The main category remaining is *leprosy*. This did not only refer to leprosy as such, but also to any kind of skin condition (Lev 13–14) —impurity was transferred to clothing and houses (Lev 13:47–59; 14:33–53). Purification required the inspection of a priest and sacrifices. To turn our modern conception of purity on its head, if a person was entirely covered in "leprosy," a priest would pronounce the "leper" *pure* (Lev 13:13)! His "change of status" ended, or his skin no longer suffered an improper mixture (Sanders 1992:220).

Because of semen impurity and menstrual impurity, many adults would have been impure a lot of the time. How individuals observed purity laws must have varied from person to person, but many Judeans, however, probably thought it necessary to be pure (Sanders 1992:228–29). As can be seen from the above, it was not just people that immersed themselves, but objects like clothing, house furniture and eating vessels had to be immersed as well.

Summary

Paul lamented that most of his fellow Judeans had rejected the Messiah, nevertheless, he still admitted that they had zeal for God (Rom 10:2). This of course translates into a zeal for their own ethnic identity. This was demonstrated through their zeal for the Temple and their devotion to covenantal praxis. One must be wary of romanticising first century Judeanism, but overall, they constituted a unique identity in antiquity. Being grounded in the *habitus* or "Israel," the combination of religion and covenantal praxis involved the objectification of religious-cultural practices in the recognition and communication of affinity *and* difference vis-à-vis other peoples. This occurred in the three primary domains of the Temple, synagogue, and the home.

Attention was brought to the Temple as a focal point of Judean identity. Besides the criticism that was levelled against the Temple and priesthood, support for them as Judean institutions was widespread as is evidenced by the wealth of the Temple. The people persistently chose to be ruled by a high priest, of the appropriate pedigree, to make the Judean nation what it should be—a theocracy. This ideal was undermined through the constant change and appointment of high priests by the Herodians. Connected to this is the particular sensitivities which Judeans had in terms of the holiness of Jerusalem. Particularly the presence of the emperor cult in its various forms in Jerusalem drew strong opposition. The Temple was the focal point of the Judean symbolic universe. It regulated the supernatural and natural world, in terms of the sacred and the profane, the pure and the impure. In other words, it regulated the perfect order of Creation.

It also was an architectural expression of the ideal Judean symbolic universe. Most poignantly expressed by the *soreg*, only the pure, Judeans could proceed to have an encounter with God. The Gentiles and the impure must stay out. The *soreg* also symbolized the ritual separation between Judean and Gentile which could not be achieved territorially. The pure could bring their sacrifices, and the major pilgrimage festivals would have engendered a strong sense of community. Tithes, offerings and the temple tax were paid by the people and in support of the priesthood. Overall, the temple and the priesthood as institutions operated pretty well.

The synagogue, whether referring to the assembly of people or to a building, was a primary means whereby the Judean symbolic universe was maintained. It was the place where the Torah and the prophets was read and expounded. Presided over mostly by priests, it became an extension of the "thinking" of the temple.

In the household, the primary locus of identity formation, Judeans were socialized into saying the *Shema*, wearing *tefillin*, tassels on the hem of garments, fixing *mezuzah* on the doorposts, and saying daily prayers. It was where Judeans kept the Sabbath day rest, fasted on the Day of Atonement, and prepared food according to the laws of the *kashrut*. For those who wanted to maintain their position within the privileged Judean symbolic universe, and separate themselves from Gentile contamination, ritual immersion would have been performed regularly. Home was further the place were various forms of impurity—most often semen and menstrual impurity—would have been contracted. Ritual immersion, the passing of time and a visit to the temple in some instances was the means by which various forms of impurity were removed.

In Pursuit of the Millennium

There can be little doubt that Judeans of the first century CE were in pursuit of the millennium.[33] The pursuit of the millennium involved many things, but a primary feature involved corporate Israel's right to the *land*; for indebted or landless Judean peasants even more so. The importance of the land to Judean ethnic identity can hardly be overemphasized. Brueggemann (2002:3) even contends that land "is a central, if not *the central theme* of biblical faith" (emphasis original). Israel's history is a recurring cycle, moving from land to landlessness, from landedness to land. The land for which Israel yearns

> is always *a place with Yahweh*, a place well filled with memories or life with him and promise from him and vows to him. It is land that provides the central assurance to Israel of its historicality, that it will be and always must be concerned with actual rootage in a place that is a repository for commitment and therefore identity ... It will no longer do to talk about Yahweh and his people but we must speak about Yahweh and his people *and his land*. (Brueggemann 2002:5; emphasis original)

The myth of divine election is an important feature in legitimating a community's "title-deeds" or land charter (Smith 1994:712). From an Israelite or Judean perspective, this all began with God's promise to Abraham: God will give him the land and he will become a great nation (Gen 12:1–3; 15:7–21; 17:1–8). This promise was fulfilled (in part) with the conquest, but the dream was shattered through the exile. Yet the exile or the situation of landlessness was the setting for hope and a reaffirmation of God's faithfulness to the covenant (Isa 43:18–21; Jer 31:17–18; Ezek 37:5–6), and there were the promises of restoration as well.[34] The returning exiles came to believe that the land could

---

33. Baumgarten speaks specifically of millennial expectations, in that they "are a sub-group of eschatological ones. They set forth the belief in the *imminent* commencing of the eschatological era, leading to ultimate collective salvation" (Baumgarten 1997:154, emphasis original). Duling (1994:132) describes millennialism in a slightly different but complimentary manner: "Millennialism describes a social movement of people whose central belief is that the present oppressive world is in crisis and will soon end, usually by some cataclysmic event, and that this world will be replaced by a new, perfect, blissful, and trouble free world, often believed to be a restoration of some perfect time and place of old; so intense is this hope that those who accept it engage in preparing for the coming new age, or even try to bring it about, especially by some political activity."

34. Jer 30:18–19; 31:2–5; 33:6–11, 25–26; Ezek 36:22–28, 33–36; 37:12, 14; Isa 49:8–13.

be kept through the rigorous obedience of God's commandments (Brueggemann 2002:12, 145–50). They confessed the sins of their royal forefathers (Neh 9; Ezra 9). Rigorous obedience to Torah entailed the observance of the Sabbath (Neh 13:15–22), the ending of mixed marriages in the cause of purity (Neh 9:12; 13:23–27; Ezra 10:10–11, 44), and the right of the peasantry to retain their land (Neh 5:5–11). All of these obligations were sworn to by an oath (Neh 10:29–31). Yet Israel persistently remained under the control of foreigners. The relationship to the land was highly frustrated.

Quite relevant to our purposes, Smith distinguishes between two processes in ethnic ideology when it comes to the land:

> on the one hand, towards and extension of the *ethnie* in space at the cost of any social depth, and on the other hand, a social "deepening" of ethnic culture at the cost of its tight circumscription in space. The former process leads to what may be termed "lateral" *ethnie*, the latter to "vertical" *ethnie*. These are pure types; in practice, ethnic communities often embody contradictory trends. Yet, at given stages in the history of particular *ethnie*, one or other of these processes may predominate, presenting a close approximation to either the "lateral" or the "vertical" type. (Smith 1994:713)

Now one can say that Judeanism essentially represented the more "vertical" type that laid emphasis on the deepening of ethnic culture. Yet, the "lateral" ideology also comes into play during the period of Hasmonean expansion that will be discussed below. Ezekiel 40–48 has a vision of an Israel with a much enlarged territory, which is echoed by the fragments of Eupolemus, Josephus (*Ant.* 1.134–42, 185; 2.194–95; 4.300), and the *Genesis Apocryphon* from Qumran (Freyne 2001:293–97).[35] Strangely enough, Ezekiel and Eupolemus endorse the presence of foreigners within the enlarged territory, but the Maccabeans forcefully converted Gentiles to Judeanism in (re)conquered territories or forced them to leave. So any "lateral" ideology was still "vertical" at its

---

35. The "Greater Israel" ideology is also in evidence in rabbinic literature. Oppenheimer explains that the Babylonian *amoraim* drew their boundaries for genealogical purposes. The Euphrates served as the western boundary (the Tigris as the eastern boundary), while at the same time, the Euphrates served as the eastern boundary for burial purposes, and so as the eastern boundary of the greater Land of Israel as promised (*gevulot ha-havtahah*). People buried west of the Euphrates were therefore considered as buried in the Land of Israel (Oppenheimer 2005:339–55).

core.[36] That is, for the Hasmoneans, the deepening of ethnic culture in the (re)conquered territories was of primary importance, even though they spearheaded a "conquering empire" of sorts. Eventually this policy did not succeed in all its aims as Gentiles and Samaritans still lived as culturally distinct groups within the Israelite ancestral land—even more so when the Romans took control of Palestine. At the same time, the ideal boundaries of an enlarged Israel as espoused by Ezekiel were never acquired, although Judean territory was greatly increased.

The Hasmonean Expansion

Sirach 36 wishes for the annihilation of Israel's enemies (Sir 36:1–17)—but this will happen in some unspecified time in the future. The situation changed radically at the forced Hellenization of Judeans which eventually prompted strong resistance and territorial expansion. As Hellenization was essentially an urban phenomenon, Jerusalem in particular would have been a likely candidate to succumb to its influence. "Obviously such a transformation called into question every claim and effort of Ezra to make Jerusalem the locus of covenant, and to define [Judean] sensitivities in terms of Torah and covenantal obedience" (Brueggemann 2002:151). The wealthy urban citizens would have benefited, while Hellenization had little sympathy for the rural peasantry, who clung to the Ezra-shaped notion of Judeanness, "committed to historical particularity and traditional rights of inheritance" (Brueggemann 2002:152). Connected to this is that a more "vertical" ethnie that is more territorially bounded and compact can be associated with the tendency of popular mobilization against outsiders. "At these times," Smith explains, "we find a crusading and missionary quality not confined to aristocratic knights, but embracing the lower classes who may be engaged in battle and in ritual or cultural renewal of the community." Such groups are ethnically unified from top to bottom, their "'verticality' often presenting problems for the 'lateral' *ethnie* that dominate polyethnic states or empires . . ." (Smith 1994:714). This de-

---

36. Cf. Freyne (2001:292–93), who has his own take of the "vertical" and "lateral" ideologies discussed here. He sees the above two ideologies as present in Ezekiel (Ezek 40–48), but in a way where emphasis is placed on the importance of Jerusalem and the temple, and the holiness and separateness it entails, even from the other tribal territories, while on the other hand emphasis is also placed on an enlarged territory based on tribal and boundary traditions. "In the fractured circumstances of the Hasmonean and Herodian periods both aspects of Ezekiel's vision of restoration can be shown to have been operative within different circles" (Freyne 2001:293).

scription fits the situation of Judea quite well. During the Maccabean revolt (and the First Revolt of 66–70 CE), it is the peasantry (under religious-political style leadership) that fights for the land and cultural renewal (cf. Brueggemann 2002:153). In this regard 1 Macc 2:19–22, 27 sees the battle in terms of fidelity to the covenant, or one can say, of fidelity to Judean ethnic culture. The close connection between land, culture and covenant is evident in *Jub.* 15:34, where to perform epispasm is to leave the covenant, making the guilty Judeans like Gentiles, and they are "to be removed and uprooted from the land." The land theology of Ezra and Nehemia thus continues. First Maccabees further explains how Judas reminded the people how God had saved the ancestors at the Red Sea, and urged them to cry out for help and that God would remember his covenant with the forefathers and defeat the enemy (1 Macc 4:8–11).

The Book of Daniel, written during the time of Antiochus' persecutions, looks forward to imminent redemption, which will occur with the defeat of Antiochus IV and eternal reward for the righteous (Dan 11:40—12:3). The Hasmoneans or Hasideans are described as "a little help" during the time of persecution (Dan 11:33–34), but they have no role to play when the Great Prince, Michael, will arise and deliver the faithful (Dan 12:1). A more pro-Hasmonean stance is found in 1 Enoch 90, written around the same time as Daniel 7–12, that is, during the Maccabean revolt. It also looks forward to a glorious future, as the Temple will be rebuilt to its true and grand proportions (*1 En.* 90:28–29). Humans do play a part in bringing this about. The "great horned ram" (= Judas Maccabees) fights on behalf of the cause of good (the sheep) (*1 En.* 90:9–12), and a white cow is born later, as well as a great beast with black horns (*1 En.* 90:37–39). These passages are messianic in a sense but these animals do nothing to redeem the world. Yet *1 Enoch* 90 gives testimony that some saw the successes of the Hasmoneans as leading to the fulfilment of millenarian hopes (Baumgarten 1997:171).

It is when the Hasmoneans gained control of Judean society that the expansionist or more "lateral" ideology mentioned above came to the fore. At the time of the Maccabean revolt, Judea was no larger than a day's walk in any direction from Jerusalem. From the time of Jonathan (161–143 BCE) onwards, Judean territory was greatly increased. Fragments of the historian Eupolemus, clearly expresses expansionist ideals. In interpreting Judean history he portrays David as leading a conquering army against the Idumeans, Ammonites, Moabites, the Itureans and the Nabateans, and Phoenicia, who he forced to pay tribute to the Judeans (in Eusebius, *Pr. Ev.* 9.30.3–5). According to Horsley (1995:37) a "principal motive of Hasmonean expansion may have been to establish Judean rule in the rest of Palestine as had the prototypical Judean king David." Jonathan himself gained control of a part of the coastal plain and a large part of Samaria. Simon (143–134 BCE) seized the Acra in Jerusalem and also extended the borders of Judea in a number of campaigns. For example, access to the coast would be important for economic reasons. Simon set up a Judean garrison at Joppa (1 Macc 12:33–4) and drove out its Gentile inhabitants (1 Macc 13:11). He captured Gazara (Gezer) after a siege and also drove out its inhabitants, replacing them with people who observe the Torah (1 Macc 13:43–8). The territorial expansion was also accompanied by ritual purifications, as was performed in the Temple, where idolatry was removed from the land. The expansion was therefore reinforced with rituals so that the land becomes an extension of the holiness and purity of the temple in opposition to anything that is Gentile (cf. Schmidt 2001:127). But Simon declares that the land they have taken was not foreign property, "but only the inheritance of our fathers" that was taken away by Israel's enemies (1 Macc 15:33).

The territorial expansion must have been widely popular amongst Judeans, recalling the ancient Exodus and conquest of the land (cf. WisSol 12:3, 7; Sir 46:8; 1 Bar 1:20). Frequent mention is made in Judean literature of our period to the land as an inheritance or as promised to the forefathers.[37] It is the land of the fathers (1 Macc 10:55, 67), the land that God gave to the descendants of Jacob (*T. Levi* 7:1), or in short, the promised land (*T. Mos.* 1:8; 11:11; *L.A.B.* 7:4). In *Jubilees* 8 the portion of Shem is described as in the "middle of the earth" to be a possession for "eternal generations," and that Mount Zion is in the midst of "the navel of the earth," indeed, the center of the Judean symbolic universe. In fact, in Jubilees repeated attention is drawn to the covenant and God's promise of the land to Abraham, where he will be established as a great and numerous people (*Jub.* 12:22–24; 13:3, 19–21; 14:18; 15:9–10; 22:27; 24:10; 25:17; 27:11, 22). God even says to Jacob that "I shall give to your seed all of the land under heaven and they will rule in all nations as they have desired" and eventually will inherit the earth forever (*Jub.* 32:19). Israel will also be purified from all sin and

---

37. Cf. 1 Macc 2:56; 15:33; 2 Ezra 8:83, 85; Tob 4:12; Sir 44:21; 46:1, 9; 1 Bar 2:34–35; *L.A.B.* 12:4; 14:2; 15:4; 19:10; 20:5; 21:9; 23:1, 5; *Pss. Sol.* 9:1.

defilement (*Jub.* 50:5; cf. *1 En.* 5:7 [and 10:18–19] where it is stated that the elect will inherit the earth).

Afterwards John Hyrcanus (134–104 BCE) invaded the Transjordan and conquered Medeba located on the Via Regis. Hyrcanus then destroyed the Samaritan temple on Mount Gerizim in 128 BCE, an event that would have caused strong resentment between Samaritans and Judeans. The idea was for one people to worship the one God in one temple. The Samaritans were not impressed. John Hyrcanus attacked again in 108/7 BCE and devastated the city of Samaria and probably Shechem as well (*Ant.* 13.249, 254–56; *War* 1.61–63). The Samaritans had to wait until 64 BCE to be liberated from the Judeans when Pompey arrived on the scene. After John Hyrcanus' initial campaign in Samaria he turned south and defeated the Idumeans and forced them to undergo circumcision and follow the Judean law (*Ant.* 13.255–8; *War* 1.63). From then on, Schürer (1979:3, 7) argues, the Idumeans were Judeans ("Jews"), and appeared as such even during the war in 67/68 CE (cf. *War* 4.270–84) but as Horsley (1995:59) points out their conversion could hardly have been substantial. Along with Samaria, Hyrcanus conquered Scythopolis and the Great Plain (*Ant.* 13.275–81; *War* 1.64–66), so his control reached to the frontier of Galilee. The secular nature of these wars of Hyrcanus are demonstrated by the fact that he used foreign mercenaries, and not a Judean army (*Ant.* 13.249). For many Judeans, however, the expansion of Judean territory would also have had religious and a broader cultural significance. The Judean symbolic universe was taking shape on a territorial level.

Hyrcanus was succeeded by Aristobulus I (104–103 BCE). This supporter of Hellenism nevertheless forced the Itureans, located in southern Lebanon (and Upper Galilee?), to be circumcised and to convert to Judeanism (*Ant.* 13.311; *War* 1.78ff.). The incorporation of Galilee and possibly any northern based Israelites into the body-politic of the Judeans will be discussed in further detail in the next chapter.

Alexander Jannaeus (103–76 BCE) continued the expansionist policy and undertook a campaign east of the Jordan and captured Gezer and other places. Here Hebrew and Greek boundary markers were erected around the city to identify the surrounding territory as Judean (Reed 2000:42). Alexander Jannaeus also captured Gaza and a temple of Apollo is mentioned when he destroyed the city (*Ant.* 13.364); this was followed by various Greek cities in the Transjordan, most of which were part of the Decapolis (*War* 1.103–5; *Ant.* 13.393–98). By the end of his rule, the entire region from Lake Merom to the Dead Sea, and the whole coastal plain except for Ashkelon was under Judean rule. The inhabitants of the Greek cities went over to Judeanism except for the people of Pella. Alexander demanded that the local Gentiles accept Judean customs but after they refused he destroyed the city (*Ant.* 13.395–97). After this campaign Alexander returned to Jerusalem where he was given a hero's welcome by many people because of his successes. The extent of the Hasmonean kingdom was now virtually the same as that of Solomon centuries earlier (Horsley 1995:38; cf. Jagersma 1986:84; Schmidt 2001:27). Certainly the Hasmonean expansion would have been informed by popular expectations.

One can see that although the Hasmonean rulers followed a "lateral" land ideology, their overall approach was "vertical," that is, they focussed on the deepening of ethnic culture in the (re)conquered territories.

Millenarian hopes are also encountered at the end of the second letter that is attached to 2 Maccabees (2 Macc 2:18). The exiles will be gathered in because God has purified Jerusalem/the temple. The gathering of exiles was a strong motif for events during the final redemption (e.g., Isa 66:19–20; Sir 36:11; Tob 14:5). Based on the successes of the recent past, the author had reason to believe that salvation for the Judeans lay in the immediate future, although 4Q471a attacks its rivals—the Judean leadership—who think that salvation is under way (Baumgarten 1997:172). The idea of redemption might have been sponsored by the Hasmonean house itself. Based on a tradition in the Talmud (*b. Kid.* 66a) and Josephus (*Ant.* 13.288–98), King Hyrcanus won a battle in the desert in Kohalit, where after a celebration was held. Sages were invited and they enjoyed mallows (a desert food, cf. Job 30:4) served on golden tablets. The exiles from Babylon who rebuilt the temple also ate mallows. This time of salvation is surpassed, however, since Hyrcanus and the sages are eating mallows in a period of triumph—this salvation will be even greater (Baumgarten 1997:173).

In the Qumran community (4QMMT), it was believed that the end of days has arrived since some of the *blessings and curses*, spoken of in Deut 4:40 and 30:1 (C20–22), were believed to have come about (Baumgarten 1997:174–75). Although, this intense eschatological fervor subsided with time (cf. 1QpHab 7.5–14) since it was later believed that the end time has been delayed. Nevertheless, those who remained faithful to the community will be vindicated (Baumgarten 1997:178–79). Millenarian hopes may at times lead to anarchy, but at times also to live according to strict moral/religious principles. This is most evident at Qumran (4QMMT), where an expectation of imminent salvation required a scrupulous observance of the law (C32–34). As a result, millenarian hopes also contributed towards the formation of Judean religious sects. Members will also endeavor that others adopt their understanding of the Law, and "messianism and sectarianism marched inexorably hand in hand in the Second Temple period" (Baumgarten 1997:185). So the Judean sects who flourished during the Second Temple period "acquired their agendas, formed around these platforms and their leaders, and set out to change themselves and/or the world as a result of their millenarian convictions" (Baumgarten 1997:188).

Millenarian Hopes under Roman Rule

The character of Palestine changed dramatically under Roman rule. After a prolonged strife between Hyrcanus II and Aristobulus II the Romans finally decided to stake their claim on Palestine. Besides, it was made easier for them since some Judeans, tired of the civil war, asked the Romans to intervene. Both Hyrcanus II and Aristobulus II also attempted at securing support from Pompey, but in the end he decided to take control of Jerusalem. Hyrcanus opened the city gates to the Romans whereas many—the supporters of Aristobulus— were massacred after a long siege of the Temple mount (*War* 1.124–51). Pompey even entered the Holy of Holies, a serious desecration as even the Judean High priest only entered it once a year (*War* 1.152). As Tacitus (*Hist.* 5.9) explained, Pompey found nothing in the Holy of Holies, testifying to the imageless worship of the Judeans. When Pompey took over Palestine for the Romans in 63 BCE (although it would take another twenty years to have full control of the area), he also delivered the Hellenistic cities from Judean domination and were incorporated into the province of Syria. Josephus lists these cities as Hippos, Scythopolis, Pella, Samaria, Jamnia, Marisa, Azotus, Arethus, Gaza, Joppa, Dora, and Strato's Tower (*Ant.* 13.74–76; *War* 1.155–57). The proconsul Gabinius set out to rebuilt Hellenistic cities around 57–55 BCE some of which were entirely destroyed by the Hasmoneans; these include Raphia, Gaza, Anthedon, Azotus, Jamnia, Apollonia, Dora, Samaria, and Scythopolis (Schürer et al. 1979:92). All that eventually remained of the Hasmonean kingdom was Judea, Galilee, Idumea, and Perea.

So Israel was back to where it was before the Maccabean revolt in the sense that foreign rule was again a reality. The expansionist ideology of the Hasmoneans came to a halt as well. It was time again where the emphasis shifted to the "vertical" land ideology, or the deepening of ethnic culture, a culture often regarded with contempt as demonstrated by Pompey, and by the insensitivities of the Roman governors that followed. Yet there was hope for God's deliverance. For example, the Psalms of Solomon were written after the Romans made their unwelcome claim on Judean territory, one of which exclaimed on behalf of Israel:

> See, Lord, and raise up for them their king . . . Undergird him with the strength to destroy unrighteous rulers, to purge Jerusalem from gentiles who trample her to destruction . . . He will gather a holy people . . . He will distribute them upon the land according to their tribes; the alien and the foreigner will no longer live near them . . . And he will have gentile nations serving him under his yoke . . . And he will purge Jerusalem . . . (for) nations to come from the ends of the earth to see his glory, to bring as gifts her children who had been driven out. (*Pss. Sol.* 16:21–31)

Israel will be cleared of all Gentiles, especially Gentile rulers, the tribes will be restored and the nations who took the Judeans into exile will restore them to their homeland (cf. Isa 2:2–4). The messiah will rule and the Gentile nations will serve him. This was the hope. But in 40 BCE the Romans made Herod the Great of Idumean stock the client king over the Judeans. As we saw his whole policy was strongly orientated towards Rome and the Emperor. Even here there were messianic hopes present, this time among Pharisaic circles. Josephus relates that the Pharisees gave outrageous guarantees to members of Herod's court, in that the messianic king would grant them special favors (*Ant.* 17.41–44).

The concern for the land and ethnic culture can also be seen in the non-violent resistance of Judeans to Roman interference already reviewed above. Judeans objected to Pilate bringing in Roman standards into Jerusalem and his plunder of the temple treasury. Caligula attempted to have a statue of himself erected in the temple. Only his assassination prevented Judea and surrounds to be plunged into war. Yet, the first century saw other forms of unrest and protests as well. Banditry, royal pretenders, sign prophets and insurrectionary groups were characteristic traits of Judeanism leading up to and during the Great Revolt (66–70 CE). Before we have a look at these groups, however, we first need to understand the plight of the Judean peasant farmer.

The Peasant Farmer

In our period, Palestine was an agrarian society that mostly consisted of peasant farmers.[38] The economy as a whole rested primarily on agriculture (Stegemann & Stegemann 1999:104). The peasant farmers themselves, however, worked their land for subsistence, not for profit, and they normally worked their land as a family unit. Thus three things were important for the peasant farmer: God, the family, and the land. As we already saw above, they were expected to give various tithes and the firstfruits of the land, but any other surplus went to the elite (Fiensy 1991:vi–vii). "Tribute, tithes, taxes, rents, interest in debts—all involved certain claims on the produce of the land" (Horsley 1995:207). Horsley even goes on to argue that these "claims were the major factor determining the lives of villagers in ancient Galilee or Judea." In the Tanak there are various attitudes to the land,[39] but peasant farmers as part

---

38. In *T. 12 Patr.* the following instruction is given: "Bend your back in farming, perform the tasks of the soil in every kind of agriculture, offering gifts gratefully to the Lord" (*T. Iss.* 5:3).

39. Habel (1995) has identified six land ideologies in the Tanak, although there is a degree of overlap between them. Habel (1995:134–35) has conveniently put the ideologies in summary form: (1) Land as a source of Wealth: A Royal Ideology; "In the royal ideology, land is a source of centralized wealth and glory for the monarch and the empire, the monarch being the earthly representative of YHWH located in heaven; the people are the monarch's labor force in the land." (2) Land as Conditional Grant: A Theocratic Ideology; "In the theocratic ideology of the book of Deuteronomy, Canaan is a land grant, an unearned gift from YHWH, its owner and custodian; the people of Israel have conditional entitlement to the land by treaty." (3) Land as Family Lots: An Ancestral Household Ideology; "In the ancestral household ideology of the book of Joshua, land is a cluster of promised entitlements in Canaan allotted by YHWH to ancestral households who are to undertake the conquest and settlement of their allotments." (4) Land as YHWH's Personal nahalah: A Prophetic Ideology; "In the prophetic ideology of the book of Jeremiah, land is YHWH's own pure and precious *naḥalah*; the land suffers great anguish when defiled by the people who YHWH has chosen to plant in the land; the landowner, YHWH, suffers with the land." (5) Land as Sabbath Bound: An Agrarian Ideology; "In the agrarian ideology of the book of Leviticus 25–27, land is YHWH's personal sanctuary and garden, worked by Israelite families as tenant farmers on their traditional properties, and bound by the principles of a sabbath economy." (6) Land as Host Country: An Immigrant Ideology; "In the immigrant ideology of the Abraham narratives, land is a host country where immigrant ancestors find God at sacred sites, discern promises of future land, and establish peaceful relations with the indigenous peoples of the land." From the viewpoint of the peasant farmer, ideologies (3) and (5) are particularly relevant here. Of course, Brueggemann's understanding of the land issue in Ezra and Nehemiah (see above) may be added as a seventh, perhaps "A Covenanting for the Land" ideology. It has close associations with ideologies (2), (4) and (5), however.

of the "little tradition" (the low or folk culture) would have existed by the belief that the land belonged to God (Lev 25:23) and "was given in trust to Israel as inalienable family farm plots. Land is not capital to be exploited but the God-given means to subsist" (Fiensy 1991:3). So the land is Israel's inheritance and the promised gift of Yahweh. Yahweh is the landlord and the Israelites his tenants. Possession of the land brought about responsibilities as well. Apart from the tithes, the poor (Lev 19:9–10; 23:22; Deut 24:19–21) and the passers by (Deut 23:25–26) also had to benefit from the land. In honor of the Sabbath the land must lie fallow every seventh year, debts must be forgiven and all Israelite slaves must be released (Lev 25:2–7; Exod 21:2–6; 23:10–11; Deut 15:1–18). The law of Jubilee (Lev 25:10–17, 28, 30, 40) required that all land be returned to its original owners every fifty years. Of course, the Jubilee legislation would have ensured that the farm plot remained in the hand of its original owners and that the land was evenly distributed. There is little evidence that the Sabbath and Jubilee laws were enacted in our period. We do find evidence, however, for the exploitation of the peasantry by the urban elite. Taxation also seems to have been burdensome, although we do not know exactly what the level of taxation was. This resulted in landless people, indebtedness, tenant farmers, day laborers (although not all were landless), and banditry.

As already noted, we do not know how many peasants had lost their land, but to a degree more and more land became concentrated in the hands of a rich few. Large estates were owned by the Herodians, their officials and the Judean aristocracy, including some priestly families. Josephus himself owned land near Jerusalem (*Life* 422). The lands of Judean aristocracy were sometimes enlarged by stealing the plots of small freeholders (Fiensy 1991:21–60; Stegemann & Stegemann 1999:110–11). Sometimes the land was gained by the aristocracy in Jerusalem and Galilee by foreclosure on a farm when a debt could not be repaid, or alternatively, threats and violence could be used to force the small farmer to sell or abandon his land (Fiensy 1991:78–79). At least some Judean peasant farmers were affected (cf. Horsley 1987; Fiensy 1991:4–15; Oakman 1986; Stegemann & Stegemann 1999:110–25). A problem was also the shortage of agriculturally usable land per capita of the population. This means that more and more people worked for subsistence from less and less land (Stegemann & Stegemann 1999:112). Not helping were the severe famines and drought in Palestine, in 29 BCE and one during the reign of Claudius (41–54 CE). The farmer also had to contend with locusts, other pests, destructive winds, earthquakes, the plunder of troops and bandits, all of which had economic impact (Fiensy 1991:98).

Josephus also informs us that during the 50s and the 60s, the ruling priests engaged in theft, violence and bribery, amongst others, taking the tithes from the threshing floors intended for the ordinary priests (*Ant.* 20.180–81, 206–7). The high priestly families had a notorious reputation (*b. Pes.* 57a). Certainly from the perspective of the indebted or landless peasant Judean farmer, his right to the land was undermined by corrupt high priests and their elite associates who cooperated with Roman rule.

Banditry, Rebellion, and Royal Pretenders

When we look at the above, the socio-economic situation was such that at least some Judeans peasants got involved in banditry and/or insurrectionary activities, whether these be motivated by the Jubilee legislation or not. There were uprisings after Herod's death in 4 BCE. Pilgrims who had come to Jerusalem for the feast of Pentecost rebelled (*Ant.* 17.254–55; *War* 2.42–44). Similarly a Judas, son of Hezekiah the bandit led a revolt in Galilee. He led a mob to Sepphoris where they attacked the royal arsenal and armed themselves. Order was restored in Palestine after the intervention of Varus, the Roman legate in Syria (*War* 2.39–79; *Ant.* 17.271–98, 369–70) who in the process burned many villages and crucified thousands of rebels. East of the Jordan a Simon, a former slave of Herod the Great, revolted in Perea. He plundered the royal palace in Jericho and the country villas of the rich, also burning them down. There was also Athronges the shepherd, who attacked Roman troops. What these three figures have in common is that all three were social bandits, and all three had royal pretensions. Simon and Athronges were even addressed by some as "king" (Stegemann & Stegemann 1999:177–78).

Archelaus, the son of Herod, was appointed as "ethnarch" over Judea, Samaria, and Idumea after his father's death. He was not that effective as his father and was eventually deposed and exiled. Augustus sent Coponius, the first Roman prefect, to govern Judea directly. In 6 CE, Quirinius, the legate of Syria, initiated a census of the Palestinian population that meant only one thing—a better stronghold on the exaction of taxes. The census was to help assess the population for land and head tax (*tributum soli* and *tributum capitis*). All male members of a household fourteen and older and all female members twelve years old and above had to pay tribute, which probably involved the payment of one denarius per head annually (Stegemann & Stegemann 1999:117). In response, Judas of Galilee and Zaddok the Pharisee spearheaded a rebellion (*War* 2.117–18; *Ant.* 18.1–10), as they and their followers resisted this further encroachment of Roman rule. The slogan was "no Master but God," which also adopted by the later Sicarii. But who enjoys paying taxes, even more so to a foreign oppressor?

Banditry itself continued to be a problem, and at times ordinary Judeans were punished as their accomplices or sympathizers (cf. Stegemann & Stegemann 1999:175–77). The bandits, however, not only stole from the rich, but also from the poor (*War* 2.253, 581–82; 4.135; *Ant.* 14.159; 17.285; 20.185).

The Sicarii

In the 40s/50s, a new type of rebel appeared, the Sicarii ("dagger men"), who in particular mixed with the crowds in Jerusalem and stabbed to death those who collaborated with Roman rule. According to Josephus, they were descendents of the "fourth philosophy" founded by Judas the Galilean and Zaddok the Pharisee (*Ant.* 18.3–10; *War* 2.117–18). There was a family connection in that Menachem and Eleazar ben Jair, the leaders of the Sicarii, were related to Judas. Menachem commanded his forces, recruited from rural social bandits (*War* 2.434), in Jerusalem at the beginning of the revolt (see below).

The Sign Prophets

The first century also saw the appearance of various would-be prophets that led protest movements in opposition to the oppression of Israel. Under the procurator Cuspius Fadus (44–46 CE), a certain Theudas led a crowd to the Jordan (400 according to Acts 5:36), claiming the water will part through his command. Roman troops were sent out killing many while capturing others—the head of the would-be prophet himself was brought to Jerusalem (*Ant.* 20.97–9). Other "exodus-type" prophets also appeared during the procuratorship of Felix (52–59 CE). Prophets lead many into the desert, promising that God will give them signs of deliverance. Again many died at the hands of Roman troops (*War* 2.258–60; *Ant.* 20.167–68). In the same period, another prophet pretender, the so-called "the Egyptian," led many (Josephus, 30,000; Acts, 4,000) in an attack on Jerusalem. He marched them up from the wilderness to the Mount of Olives, hoping to force his way into Jerusalem. He also claimed that the walls of Jerusalem would come down at his command. The Roman troops were again pressed into service, killing and capturing many, but the Egyptian escaped (*War* 2.261–63; *Ant.* 20.169–72; Acts 21:38). Other prophets also appeared during the Great Revolt, but these will be discussed below. Not to be forgotten is John the Baptist and Jesus of Nazareth that appeared around the 30s CE. They were prophets of a different kind, however, as they had no overt religio-political agenda as the prophets discussed here.

The Great Revolt

According to Sanders (1992:40), the "events that actually led to the revolt were not connected with prophets and crowds of followers, were unforeseen, and took everyone by surprise." Yet the revolt was the result of a culmination of events. In Caesarea, Greeks built next to a synagogue, the result of which was that the synagogue was partly blocked off. Tensions between Judeans and Greeks increased and exploded in 66 when Judeans arrived at the synagogue on the Sabbath only to discover that a prankster was sacrificing birds outside the synagogue entrance. Street fighting broke out in the city. At the same time in Jerusalem the procurator, Florus, took seventeen talents from the temple treasury. This lead to protest and Florus was insulted in public. Florus responded by killing many, followed by scourgings and crucifixions and so the first revolt got underway (*War* 2.284–308). These events were a catalyst, however, that brought into relief other social tensions that existed within Palestine. The rural peasantry, no doubt some of which were landless or indebted, combined with bandit leaders and they along with other insurrectionary groups made their way to Jerusalem to vent their anger at the Judean aristocracy. The revolt was a culmination of both religio-political and socio-revolutionary forces comprising both the urban population and the rural peasantry. While some directed their wrath against the Romans for disrespecting the temple, other Judeans, while wanting to fight the Romans, also had an axe to grind with the Judean aristocracy in Jerusalem. The revolt became in part a class war (Fiensy 1991:14).[40]

Present were the Sicarii. Their leader, Menachem, apparently entered Jerusalem like a king (*War* 2.434), and so like Judas, Simon and

---

40. Cf. Horsley (1995:73): "It is increasingly clear that the hostilities that erupted in the summer of 66 C.E. were primarily between groups of ordinary Judeans and their high-priestly and Herodian rulers and creditors, with the Roman troops called in to suppress the insurrections." But why then, did the "ordinary Judeans" stay on in Jerusalem to fight the Romans?

Athronges had royal pretensions. In 66 CE the Sicarii burned the public archives where the debt records were kept (*War* 2.427)—no doubt some Judean peasant farmers would have been delighted. Galileans at the outbreak of the war also tried to burn down Sepphoris, where their debt records would have been kept at the time (*Life* 38, 375). The Sicarii murdered the high priest Ananias (*War* 2.423ff.), burned the palace of Agrippa II and that of the High Priest, and chased after other wealthy Judeans in the city sewers of Jerusalem (*War* 2.426–28). Menachem was eventually killed and his followers were expelled from Jerusalem by other Judeans. Under the leadership of Eleazar, a relative of Menachem, they escaped to Masada (*War* 2.433–48) which they defended up to the point of committing suicide (*War* 7.323; cf. Netzer 1991). According to Cohen (1987:166), the Sicarii were motivated by religious goals, to hasten or bring about the messianic age, to fight for God, the Torah and the holy land and to rid Israel of foreigners. Yes, but these were not "religious" goals only, as they can be seen (along with other Judeans) as participating in a broader pattern of ethnicism (cf. Smith 1986:50–56).

During the revolt, the Zealots emerged, who like the Sicarii set their aim at attacking and killing the Judean aristocracy and the chief priests.[41] In 67–68 they selected a high priest by lot, a country priest named Phineas who was of a high priestly family (*War* 4.147ff.). The Zealots ended up fighting other Judean revolutionary groups, but also chose to defend Jerusalem to their deaths (*War* 2.651; 4.160—6.148; 7.268). According to Cohen (1987:165) the Zealots consisted mostly of peasants who fled to Jerusalem as Romans came through the country from Galilee. Horsley (1995:66) identifies them as a coalition of villagers from northwest Judea. Josephus (*War* 5.443) speaks of them in derogatory language (they are "slaves," "rabble," "bastards"), perhaps suggesting (at least from Josephus' point of view) they were of the lower rural classes (Fiensy 1991:169). Stegemann & Stegemann (1999:180–81) suggests, however, that they were a group of radical priests. The appointment of Phineas does illustrate that the Zealots were interested in temple purity and this "also places the Zealots in the tradition of the anti-Hellenist battle over the purity of the temple at the time of the Maccabeans" (Stegemann & Stegemann 1999:182).

Bandit leaders also made their way to Jerusalem. John ben Levi from Galilean Gischala (Gush Halav) was a Levite, although accord-

---

41. Horsley (1995:213) suggests that the Herodians, Saul, and Costobar were attacked by the Zealots because they owned land in northwest Judea. They did manage to flee from Jerusalem (*War* 2.418; *Ant.* 20.214).

ing to Josephus, he did not keep the food and purity laws (*War* 7.264). Probably he became a bandit as a result of the socio-economic decline and he recruited his followers from the peasantry of upper Galilee and refugees from the region of Tyre (*War* 2.587–89; *Life* 372). John made his way to Jerusalem after the Romans took control of Galilee by the end of 67. On arrival he initially got the support of the Zealots and took over the leadership of the rebellion. There was also a Simon bar Giora, however, the son of a proselyte. He came from Gerasa in the Decapolis and in the Judean border region attacked the houses of the wealthy large landowners and had an intense dislike of the rich (*War* 2.652; 5.309). He came to Jerusalem in 69 when he and his followers were driven out of Idumea. He attempted (successfully) to gain control of the rebellion and like others, was a royal pretender (*War* 4.510, 575). He held on to his royal claim until the end but was eventually executed in Rome.

Lastly, prophets also had their part to play during the Great Revolt. Towards the end, there were still those who had hoped that God would intervene on their behalf, as did the others who were led by the self-styled prophets into the wilderness to enact the Exodus and the conquest of Canaan (Sanders 1992:286). Roman troops set fire to the last of the Temple porticoes, burning many ordinary people alive, as they followed a prophet who claimed that God commanded them to go to the temple, also to receive signs of deliverance. Others according to Josephus also encouraged the people to wait for God's help (*War* 6.283–87).

Fighting also raged in the rest of the country, particularly in cities of mixed Judean and Gentile population (Jagersma 1986:140). But the Roman military machine lead by Vespasian, and eventually his son Titus, slowly but surely regained control of Palestine—the last city to fall was Jerusalem. But as we can see from the above, the revolt that eventually focussed on the holy city was from a Judean perspective incoherent and undermined by factionalism. Participants mostly came from the lower social stratums of Judean society (cf. Stegemann & Stegemann 1999:184–86).

Israel Without a Temple and Its Land

Little information is available about the events between the first and second revolts (Soggin 1993:359). We will focus on some texts and also look at the archaeological evidence, however. The Romans obviously knew what great importance the city of Jerusalem had for Judeans. On the so-called "Shekel of Israel," minted by the revolutionary authorities during the revolt, was engraved "Jerusalem the Holy" (Brenner 2003:50). Even in far away Gamla, located in the Golan Heights, coins were minted during the revolt with inscriptions that read: "For the redemption of Jerusalem the H(oly)" (Syon 1992). Needless to say, the consequences of the war were devastating (cf. *4 Ezra* 10:21–23). So it is ironic that archaeological evidence illustrates that Jerusalem, along with the temple, was practically destroyed. The Romans evidently wanted any future nationalist aspirations of a restored Jerusalem focussed on the temple suppressed. Many Judeans were crucified outside Jerusalem. In addition, Titus held gladiatorial contests and animal-baiting in the amphitheatre of Caesarea to celebrate his victory wherein hundreds of Judean prisoners were killed (Bull 1990:110). Josephus claims that about 97,000 Judeans were taken as prisoners during the war (*War* 6.420). Those over the age of seventeen were sent to work in Egypt, while those under seventeen were sold as slaves (*War* 6.418).

Judea became a Roman imperial province, and a detachment of the Tenth Roman Legion (Legio X Fretensis) was stationed in the city. Judeans were generally forbidden to enter (Geva 1997). Much land was given to Romans or favorites of the emperor. For example, Emmaus became a fortress with 800 war veterans (Jagersma 1986:147). The land, however, still belonged to Yahweh (*4 Ezra* 9:7–8). Hopes for the rebuilding of the Temple and Jerusalem prevailed, even though the symbolic universe of Judeanism was in tatters. For *2 Baruch*, the destruction of the Temple meant that the "order of human, social and cosmic relations appear to be definitively disturbed by this sacrilegious defilement . . . the function of the Temple is to maintain the order of creation, as the Divinity set it up in the first week of the world" (Schmidt 2001:88). Judeans were again without the land, their mother city, and their Temple; no more sacrifices and offerings; no more pilgrimages. The symbolic centre and heartbeat of Judeanism was no more. The sense of perplexity and frustration that must have existed is captured by various texts in *4 Ezra*. Fourth Ezra laments to God: "[you] have destroyed your people, and have preserved your enemies . . . Are the deeds of Babylon [i.e. Rome] better than those of Zion? Or has another nation known you besides Israel? Or what tribes have so believed your covenants [cf. 5:29] as these tribes of Jacob." Ezra is perplexed, for the nations "are unmindful of your commandments" (*4 Ezra* 3:30–33). Later Ezra asks "why Israel has been given over to the gentiles as a reproach; why the people whom you loved has been given to godless tribes, and the Law of our fathers has been made of no effect and the written covenants no longer exist" (*4 Ezra* 4:23–24). God has chosen Israel as his special people, from all the peoples of the world he loved them and gave them his Law (*4 Ezra* 5:23–27). Why be destroyed by the Gentiles? "If you really hate your people," Ezra tells God, "they should be punished at your own hands" (*4 Ezra* 5:30). The other nations are nothing before God, but

> we your people, who you have called your first-born, only begotten, zealous for you, and most dear, have been given into their hands. If the world has indeed been created for us [something confirmed in 7:11], why do we not possess our world as an inheritance? (*4 Ezra* 6:56–59)

It was also asked: "How can we sing to you, being in a foreign land" (*4 Bar.* 7:35; cf. Ps 137:3–4). Besides the above, the typical tenacity of the Judean spirit prevailed as it was informed by its rich ethno-symbolism. Zion remains "the mother of us all" (*4 Ezra* 10:7). The Messiah will come (*4 Ezra* 7:28–29; 12:32; 13:32–52; 14:9) so there is hope: "Take courage, O Israel; and do not be sorrowful, O house of Jacob; for the Most High has you in remembrance, and the Mighty One has not forgotten you in the struggle" (*4 Ezra* 12:46–47). Similarly the Testament of Moses 3:9 (cf. 4:4:5–6) makes the following plea: "God of Abraham, God of Isaac, and God of Jacob, remember your covenant which you made with them, and the oath which you swore to them by yourself, that their seed would never fail from the land which you have given them." *First Baruch* 2:35 on the other hand has God promising: "And I will make an everlasting covenant with them to be their God, and they shall be my people: and I will no more drive my people of Israel out of the land that I have given them." This land theology, similar to Ezra and Nehemiah, is also encountered in *4 Ezra* 14:28–32 (cf. *4 Bar.* 4:7), where it was Israel's sinfulness that was the reason for Israel's fate. Even in the Diaspora there was still hope for a restored and glorious Jerusalem in that

> the divine and heavenly race of blessed [Judeans], who live around the city of God in the middle of the earth, are raised up even to the dark clouds, having built a great wall round about, as far as Joppa... No longer will the unclean foot of Greeks revel around your land but they will have a mind in their breasts that conforms to your laws. (*Sib. Or.* 5:249–66)

God's love for Judea is mentioned in *Sib. Or.* 5:328–32 and Jerusalem will be restored with the aid of a heavenly savior figure (*Sib. Or.* 5:414–27).

The Second Revolt against Rome (132–135 CE) proved to be inevitable[42] and commenced under the leadership of a Simon who was known as Bar Kokhba ("son of the star"). According to rabbinic sources he was even hailed as the "star of David" (cf. Num 24:17) and "king Messiah" by Akiba (Jagersma 1986:157). The Bar Kokhba revolt was probably inspired by Hadrian's plans to establish a Roman colony, named Aelia Capitolina, where Jerusalem once stood (Oppenheimer 2005:243–55). This is supported by numismatic evidence. A coin was discovered in a cave in the Judean desert that illustrates the ceremony of the founding of Jerusalem as a Roman colony. The Emperor Hadrian is depicted as ploughing the boundary of the city with an ox and cow. The coin was found in the cave with other coins from Gaza, which commemorated Hadrian's visit in 133/4 CE, which suggest that Aelia Capitolina must have been founded at least by 133/4 CE, a year or so before the end of the revolt (Eshel 1997).

During this revolt, silver *didrachma*, *sela*, and *tetradrachma* coins and bronze coins, variously bearing the facade of the temple and clusters of grapes and leaves were minted, no doubt recalling the decorations and glory of Herod's temple while looking forward to its restoration. It was the institution that symbolized Judean unity and perpetuity. Coins were the best or the only means of propaganda in antiquity (Schmidt 2001:38). One inscription around the grapes read: "First Year of the redemption of Israel" (Patrich 1990:67, 72; Brenner 2003:51). Over 80 per cent of the Bar Kokhba coins mention Jerusalem, while it also depicts other ceremonial objects related to the temple, such as amphorae, jugs, lyres, trumpets, and harps (Meshorer 1978).

Alas, the revolt failed. Judeans were forbidden to enter the city on pain of death. The Romans apparently built two temples in Jerusalem. Dio Cassius relates that a temple for Jupiter was built on the site of the destroyed Judean temple, although this can not be corroborated. Judean religious practices were also forbidden according to rabbinic sources, but all we know for certain is that circumcision was prohibited, as this prohibition was stopped under Antoninus Pius (138–161 CE) (Jagersma 1986:160).

---

42. There was also the so-called Quietus War (115–117 CE) wherein Judeans of the Diaspora participated. It started in Cyrene and from there spread to Cyprus, Egypt, and Mesopotamia.

Summary: The Hope for the Restoration of Israel

Sanders (1992:289–90) states that the "chief hopes were for the re-establishment of the twelve tribes; for the subjugation or conversion of the Gentiles; for a new, purified temple, or renewed and glorious temple; and for purity and righteousness in both worship and morals." Sanders (1992:291–94) does an overview of Judean literature based on these main themes which he identified for the future of Israel, summarized in the table on the following page.[43] What is not that explicit in Sanders' approach and what has been emphasized here throughout was the Judean hope to fully reclaim the *land*, the *sine qua non* of restoration. Sanders (1992:41) also explains the Judean religio-political sentiment as follows:

> With regard to foreign rule: many bitterly resented it. The Hasmonean revolt was widely supported, and so was the revolt against Rome . . . The general desire for "freedom" cannot be doubted. On the other hand, foreign rule was not judged bad by everyone all the time . . . It is probable that many would have been willing to remain obedient had the Romans always respected [Judean] sensibilities and institutions.

The latter part of Sanders' statement points to a pragmatism in the best of circumstances, but as things worked out many did bitterly resent foreign rule. And the Judeans "felt that the rule of aliens in the land of Israel constituted a glaring contrast between ideal and reality. The land was the property of the chosen people. Only Israelites could own territory there" (Schürer et al. 1979:84). This was even more acute for those Judean peasant farmers gripped by indebtedness, or tenant farmers who lost all claims on their traditional heritage. But overall, the reality

---

43. More texts can be added the list of Sanders: 1) For the restoration of the 12 tribes: *T. Benj.* 9:2 (who along with all the nations will gather around the latter Temple); 2 Macc 2:18; 4 Ezra 13:39–48; 2) The Gentiles will be destroyed: *4 Ezra* 13:37–38; will receive God's vengeance: *T. Mos.* 10:7–8; 3) The temple will be made glorious: *T. Benj.* 9:2; Jerusalem will be made new: *T. Dan* 5:12.

	1 The twelve tribes of Israel will be assembled	2 The Gentiles will be converted, destroyed, or subjugated	3 Jerusalem will be made glorious; the temple rebuilt, made more glorious, or purified	4 Worship will be pure and the people will be righteous
a) Pre-Roman era literature	Sir 36:11; 48:10; 1 Bar 4:37; 5:5; 2 Macc 1:27–28; *Jub.* 1:15; cf. 2:18	The Gentiles will be destroyed: Sir 36:1–9; *Jub.* 24:29–30; *1 En.* 90:19	Tob 13:16–18; 14:5; *1 En.* 90:28–29; 91:13; *Jub.* 1:17; cf. 1:27; 1:29; 25:21	*Jub.* 33:11, 20
b) Palestinian literature of the Roman era	*Pss. Sol.* 11:2–3; 17:28–31; cf. 17:50; 8:34; 1QM 2:2–3; cf. 2:7–8; 3:13; 5:1; 11QTemple 8:14–16; 57:5–6	They will be destroyed: *Pss. Sol.* 17:24, but not all according to *Pss. Sol.* 17:31; 1QM, although CD 14:6 allows for proselytes. They will be punished: *T. Mos.* 10:7	11QTemple 29:8–10; *Pss. Sol.* 8:12; 17:30	cf. *War* 2.7; 1QSa 2:3–10; 1QM 7:5–6; 11QTemple 45:11–17; *Pss. Sol.* 17:26–27
c) Diaspora literature	Philo, *Rewards* 164–65	They will be destroyed: *Sib. Or.* 3:670–72. They will be converted: *Sib. Or.* 3:616–17; 3:710–20 (after some are destroyed in 3:709); 3:772–73	*Sib. Or.* 3:657–709; 5:420–5	*Sib. Or.* 3:756–81 (incl. the Gentiles)

of the day was in conflict with what Judeans thought was theirs by right by virtue of the covenant. Indeed, ownership of the land was one of the primary reasons for the existence of the covenant in the first place. It was therefore part and parcel of Judean ethnic identity. It should not come as a surprise that millennial hope "was to remain an active force, sometimes perhaps even a driving one in the lives of [Judeans] from the Maccabean era down to the Bar Kochba revolt ... Imminent expectations of redemption did not really begin to wane until after the failure of the Bar Kochba revolt" (Baumgarten 1997:181–82).

To summarize, above the historical processes that were influenced by the Judean claim and attitude to the *land* were investigated. After the Maccabean Revolt, the vision of a greater Israel influenced the "lateral" ideology of the Hasmonean expansion, yet the "vertical" element or the deepening of ethnic culture always predominated. The idea was that Gentiles in the (re)conquered territories convert to Judeanism or leave the land altogether. The ideal Judean symbolic universe was also taking shape on a territorial level so naturally this gave rise to millennial expectations, although not all supported the Hasmoneans and had millenarian convictions of their own. The pursuit of the millennium continued into the Roman era. The presence of the foreigner and foreign rule was yet again firmly established within the ancestral land. The emphasis shifted to a deepening of ethnic culture and the expansionist ideology came to a halt. Roman insensitivities and the exploitation of the peasant farmer by the urban elite was characteristic of this period. So was banditry, rebellion, and the emergence of sign prophets and an intense longing for divine deliverance. All these factors contributed towards the outbreak of the Great Revolt. The results were devastating, as the focal point of the Judean symbolic universe, Jerusalem and the Temple, was destroyed, and the Judean claim on the land regarded with disdain. The covenant appeared to be in tatters; "How can we sing to you" it was asked, "being in a foreign land" (*4 Bar.* 7:35), echoing the experience of the Exile. But even here, millennial hopes remained and came to a head during the Bar Kokhba revolt as Hadrian planned to re-establish Jerusalem as a Roman colony.

Yahweh, the people, and the land were cultural elements that to the Judean mind were inseparable. Millennial expectations were not driven by purely "religious" motivations alone, but primarily by the need for Judeans to re-establish the perfect contours of their ethnic identity. It was an identity that ideally could only become realized by living on the ancestral land. They were God's people that needed to live on God's land.

Kinship

This is the last cultural feature that will be investigated in further detail. The importance of the family is already evident in the Mosaic covenant (Exod 20:12–17), where the regulations aimed at the male head of households, protect the continuing viability of the household. With the development of the Deuteronomic legal code, which would have overlaid the earlier traditions, the father of the household lost some of his authority in favor of the centralized authority of the king (Horsley 1995:196–197). Overall, a three-tiered structure formed a series of nested households (King & Stager 2002).

First, on the ground level was the ancestral or patriarchal family, the "house of the father" (*bet 'ab*; Gen 24:7; Josh 2:12, 18; 6:25). As a social unit, the joint or extended family, not a purely biological family, often contained three generations. The ultimate authority was the father, who had control over his wife (or wives), his sons and their wives, grandsons and their wives, unmarried sons and daughters, slaves, servants, non-kin (*gerim*) who were included in the protective framework, aunts, uncles, widows, orphans and Levites who may have been members of the household. According to King and Stager (2002:44) the *bet 'ab* was "the basic unit of Israelite society" and "was the focus of religious, social and economic spheres of Israelite life and was at the center of Israel's history, faith and traditions." Wright argued very much the same, and represents the position of the household within the pattern of relationships between Israel, Yahweh, and the land as follows (Wright 1990:105, adapted):

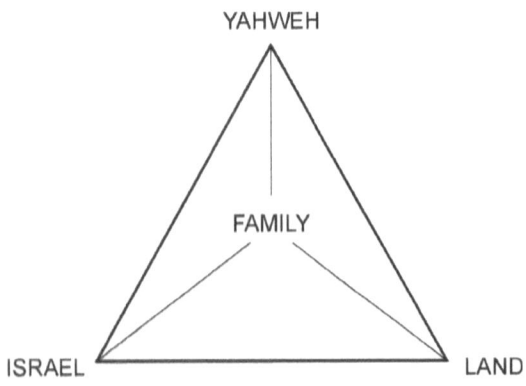

Not to be missed in this is the family's close attachment to the land, as the family was the basic unit of Israelite culture and society, the basic unit of Israel's stewardship of the land which belonged to God, and the basic unit "in the experience and preservation of the covenant relationship with Yahweh" (Sanders 2002:121). Overall, kinship relationships were largely organized around the land and agriculture. If one traced back the ancestry, the household becomes larger. Very large families formed the *mispaḥah* or "clan."

Second, on the level of the state, the king functioned as the paterfamilias who presided over his "house" (*bayit*). Third, Yahweh was the supreme paterfamilias, and the "children" of Israel were bound to him through the covenant as his kindred (*'am*) or kindred-in-law. In our period, some things remained the same while some aspects of the household changed. What was characteristic of the first-century family and kinship arrangements will be focussed on next.

The Patriarchal Family

In our period you find the virtual disappearance of the clan or tribe, and the emergence of the nuclear family—consisting of about six people—that constituted the household. Most families lived in small villages or towns, and their agricultural lands would have been located in the surrounding fields (Fiensy 1991:119–46). Guijarro on the other hand, has identified four different family types for non-elites in the Roman empire, and states that the situation in Galilee, which we can extend throughout all of Palestine as well, was little different. These were extended families, multiple families, nucleated families and scattered families, all of whom strived for the following ideal characteristics: 1) to be patriarchal, pointing to the dominating role of the paterfamilias; 2) having patrilineal descent, where the bloodline is traced through the sons of the male descendents of a common ancestor; 3) to be patrilocal, where marriage consisted of the woman being transferred from her original home to the home of her husband; 4) and to have productive resources held collectively (Guijarro 1992:224–26). In all of the families

> the authority of the paterfamilias was the axis which underpinned and gave unity to the family group; in all of them descent was by the male line ... and residence was patrilocal; possessions and honor, although in short supply, were held in common, and although most families were very small and did not have rela-

tives to call on, the bonding to the kinship group and to the extended family were the ideal. (Guijarro 2001:226)

Descent, as it was traced through the male line, also had a religious function, especially for the caste of priests and their wives, but it also regulated the cultic membership for the laity (Phil 3:5). Kinship thus had a religious-cultural dimension in terms of purity. There were regulations on intercourse (John 7:53—8:11) and the status of spouses (Deut 7:1–4; Luke 1:5). Genealogies, whether oral or written, also organized relatives into appropriate relationships based on generation and parentage. Genealogies were an important feature in the various Judean literature[44] and functioned amongst other things, to defend a claim to honor, social status, and rights of inheritance (Hanson 1994:183, 187). A very important feature of ancient Mediterranean culture "is that status in the form of ascribed honor derive from one's family [cf. Matt 13:54–57; Mark 6:3; John 7:40–44]" (Hanson 1994:185).

Generally, families strived to be self-sufficient. The family was "the basic social unit, of production and consumption, of reproduction and socialization, of personal identity and membership in a wider community. And because, in an agrarian society, families could not survive without land on which they have at least some rights, the two went together. Thus, the purpose of both production and reproduction was to perpetuate the family on its land" (Horsley 1995:195–96). Indeed, it would be difficult for any Israelite family to give identity to its members without possession of and living on their portion of the ancestral land, Israel. As we saw above, Brueggemann regarded the land as a primary, if not the primary category of faith. The land would be important for the production of food and families were involved in "polycropping," that is, raising various crops such as grain, olives for oil and grapes for wine. Most Judean men would have been occupied with agriculture. They would have "sheared the sheep and carded the wool, as well as ploughing and harvesting" while "much of the work involved in feeding and clothing the family was done by women" (Sanders 1992:122). According to Horsley (1995:200), however, all able bodied persons, men, women and children will help at harvest time while men and women were involved in the production of textiles; there was no strict separation in the roles. We can also add that the income of the household would have been

---

44. E.g., Gen 5:4–32; 2 Sam 5:13–16; 1 Chr 3:10–24; Ruth 4:18–22; 1 Macc 2:1–5; Matt 1:1–17.

supplemented in most cases by developing a craft or working as day laborers (Fiensy 1991:135).

The standard house where the family lived generally consisted of a small room or two, which was arranged around a central courtyard shared with other families. The courtyard allowed for shared use of the oven, cistern and millstone—on a village level common use was made of a wine-press and olive-press (Horsley 1995:192; 1996:89; Fiensy 1991:124–26). Strange & Shanks (1990:196) give a slightly different description, as they describe a standard house as consisting of a series of rooms situated around two courtyards, used variously for domestic chores and keeping animals. The courtyard-house was linked to others through the alley, all of which combined to form the village, the largest social unit for peasants.

Generally Judeanism espoused a very positive family ethic. The love of brother (*T. Reu.* 6:9; *T. Sim.* 4:7; *T. Gad* 6:1–7; *T. Jos.* 17:2–3; *T. Benj.* 7:5—8:2; *Jub.* 36:8; 4 Macc 13:19–27), or the love of God and brothers (*T. Dan* 5:3) features in various texts. Brothers are encouraged to love one another and not calculate the wrong done to each other, "This shatters unity, and scatters all kinship" (*T. Zeb.* 8:6). One must honor the parents (*Let. Aris.* 228, 238; *Jub.* 7:20; *L.A.B.* 11:9) and appreciate the value of family (*Let. Aris.* 241–42), and the worst form of neglect is the neglect of children (*Let. Aris.* 248). The Tanak especially gave regulations that protected the family as a unit (Hanson 1994:183). Laws aimed at countering deviance covered issues such as incest (Lev 18:6–19), rape (Deut 22:23–29), adultery (Lev 20:10), marriage (Lev 21:7; Deut 25:5–10), divorce (Deut 24:1–4), and inheritance (Num 27:1–11; Luke 12:13).

Marriage

Since "the foreigner was in the house," we will first have a look at Judean attitudes towards intermarriage. In the post-exilic period intermarriage was prohibited. According to Cohen (1987:51), it was believed that intermarriage leads to religious disloyalty and so was a threat to the religious community. One can rather say that it was believed that intermarriage posed a threat to the integrity of Judean ethnic identity. So generally, marriage or sexual intercourse with Gentiles was abhorred,[45]

---

45. Cf. *T. Levi* 9:10; cf. 14:6; *Jub.* 20:4; 22:20; 25:1, 5; 27:10; 30:11; *L.A.B.* 9:5; 18:13–14; 21:1; 30:1; 44:7; 45:3; Tob 4:12; 2 Ezra 8:70, 92; 9:9; *4 Bar.* 8:1–8; Theodotus in Eusebius, *Pr. Ev.* 9.22.4–6.

something also noticed by Tacitus (*Hist.* 5.5)—never mind the fact that the sons of Jacob took Gentile wives (*Jub.* 34:20–21)! For example, the apocryphal Addition to Esther (14:15; LXX 4:17) states that Judean women should avoid having intercourse with uncircumcised men. Both Josephus (*Ant.* 18.345) and Philo (*Spec. Laws* 3.29) also express sentiments that the Law does not allow marrying someone from another nationality. Overall the major issue was the protection of boundaries (cf. Lieu 2002:308, on *T. Jud.* 23:2), and some quarters even took extreme views on the question of intermarriage. It is said that a man who gives his daughter or sister in marriage to a Gentile must be stoned to death, along with the bride (*Jub.* 30:7). Those who marry foreigners defile the nation, hence they are to be excluded from the Temple, and no sacrifice, fat or other offering must be accepted from them (*Jub.* 30:16). The offering of fat was normally the prerogative of the priest (e.g., Ezek 44:15), and only the faithful—those who keep the boundary between Judean and Gentile secure—will be allowed to minister to God (cf. CD 6.1–2). Intermarriage for the lay Judean was possible where the foreigner converted to Judeanism, however (see below). But generally, marriages were mostly endogamous, that is, marriage occurred with close kin (Hanson 1994:188).[46]

Hanson (1994:188) explains that in "traditional societies, the marriage of a male and female is seldom (if ever) an arrangement between individuals. It is a social contract negotiated between families, with economic, religious and (occasionally) political implications beyond the interests of sexuality, relationship, and reproduction." Divorce would, therefore, have had serious social ramifications (cf. Mark 10:2–9; Matt 5:31–32; 19:3–9; cf. *m. Git.* 9:10a). "It potentially affected the disposition of the woman's dowry, the change of residences, the ability to find another spouse, and the honor of the families" (Hanson 1994:188).

In terms of residence, we saw above that the traditional family was patrilocal, where marriage consisted of the woman being transferred from her original home to the home of her husband. With this came a transfer of authority from that of her father to her husband as well. He would manage her property or dowry that was provided by the bride's family. She retained ownership, however, which passed on to her children, distinct from the property of the husband, his kin-group and his children from other marriages. The dowry—which was often used as a public display of wealth and honor—was actually the full or partial payment of the family inheritance given to the daughter at the time

---

46. Cf. Jdt 8:2; Tob 1:9; 3:15–17; 4:12–13, and *Jubilees*, that retells biblical stories.

of marriage (cf. Gen 31:14–16; Josh 15:18–19; *m. Ket.* 6:6) (Hanson 1994:189).

Besides the above, the reproduction of the family unit was of paramount importance. Women played an important role as they obviously were the main source for a family's reproduction. Crass as it may sound, in a patriarchal society, "a woman was basically a regenerative-sexual being . . . It was the man's family she was committed to multiply when getting married" (Sanders 2002:118). The wife's sexuality was subject to the husband's exclusive use and authority as she was vital for the perpetuation of his family (Horsley 1995:199–200). But the children would also fulfil another important function—they continue the existence of the twelve patriarchs (cf. Sanders 2002:118). In Genesis, Tamar may have seduced her father-in-law, Judah, to have sexual intercourse with her, but this was in order to carry out the custom of Levirate marriage. The focus of the story is Tamar's determination to provide progeny for her deceased husband (Sanders 2002:118). The survival of the family is also encountered in other examples of womanly "heroism."

> The stories of Tamar, Ruth, Esther, Hannah, Abigail and many other women in the Bible, heroic as each was in her own right, are built around the family heritage theme of God's fulfillment of the divine promise of progeny and land God had made to Abraham and Sarah in Genesis 12. All had consciously or subconsciously sinned in some way that the family might survive, and the Bible honors them all. (Sanders 2002:119)

The Father-Son Relationship

Despite the potential fertility of the daughter, she was of less value than a son (Sir 22:3; 42:9–14). For example, the daughter would be sent out as a debt-slave to help pay off debts, while the son would remain to ensure the continuity of the household (Horsley 1995:199). Overall, the values of Judean society, pretty much like others in antiquity, gave prominence to the father-son relationship—even the husband-wife relationship is modified and in part suppressed to accommodate it. It also afforded intrinsic attributes to the father-son relationship that defined the roles and status of each party. For now we will concentrate on the role and status of the father (Guijarro 2001:227–28).

The father exercised control over his son throughout his entire life. The father decided whether the new born son is accepted into the family and the father later welcomed him into the family by giving him a name. The father also had to give his consent in everything that the son did, like getting married, performing an economic transaction or accepting a public office. The authority of the father was such that he could legally sell his son or even condemn him to death (Philo, *Spec. Laws* 2.232, 243–48; Josephus, *Ant.* 4.260–64; 16.365; *m. Sanh.* 7:4).

The father also had a series of obligations to fulfil towards his son. This included the elementary tasks of feeding him, education, protection, economic assistance and giving him a job. Particularly the task of education or instruction was important (Prov 4:1–4; Tob 4; *Spec. Laws* 2.228; *b. B.B.* 21a). The son amongst other things had to learn how to run the house and family property. "An important aspect of domestic education consisted in telling and learning the great deeds of the ancestors, those deeds which had brought prestige and honor to the house. The illustrious ancestors' example was used to model the character and lifestyle of those who would one day have the responsibility of continuing the house's name" (Guijarro 2001:227; cf. *Apion* 2.204). Guijarro states further that during the years of education the father had to treat his son with severity, whereby his authority was imposed by means of punishments—this was typical of agrarian societies. In this manner the order of the house was preserved and the future paterfamilias learned how to exercise his authority (Sir 30:1–13; Prov 13:24; 22:15; 23:13–14; *Spec. Laws* 2.240). We can add here that in order to maintain the family on its land as a viable social and economic unit, the Tanak emphasized patrilineal inheritance, where the first-born son inherits twice as much as any brothers (Deut 21:17; cf. *m. B.B.* 8:3–5). If there was no first-born son, the daughter would inherit, followed by the brother and the father's brother (Num 27:8–11).

The father also had the responsibility to teach his son the religious traditions. The Tanak in various passages (Exod 12:26–27; 13:14–15; Deut 6:20–24; Josh 4:6–7, 21–23) specifies that the father must explain an event, memory or institution. So the exodus, the conquest and the gift of the land, and their common history (Tob 4; 4 Macc 18:10–19; Philo, *Spec. Laws* 4.150; Josephus, *Apion* 1.60; *m. Pes.* 10:4) would be explained via the privileged father-son line of communication.

Besides the roles and obligations of the father, the son had his own towards the father (Guijarro 2001:228–29). This had great relevance for the continuity of the household depended on it. For example, the son was obliged to honor and obey his father as long as he lived (Exod 20:12; Deut 5:16). He also had to assist and care for him in his old age (Prov 1:8; 4:1; 19:26; 20:20; 23:22; 30:17; Sir 3:3–16; Ps 126:3–5;

Philo, *Decal.* 111–20, 165–67; *Spec. Laws* 2.223–62).[47] So anyone who despised his father was cursed and cut off from blessing. He who did not take care of his father in old age was a blasphemer and disobedience was deserving of death (Deut 21:18–21; 27:16; Sir 3:8–9; *Apion* 2.206). The law of the rebellious son (Deut 21:18–21) was still in force in the Hellenistic-Roman period (Philo, *Spec. Laws* 2.232, 243–48; Josephus, *Ant.* 4.260–64; 16.365) attesting to the importance that was attached to the responsibilities of the son. It was at the moment of the father's death where the son showed his respect in the most visible way. The son had to give a proper burial and carry out the necessary funeral rites (Gen 25:9–11; 35:29). At death the father became a family ancestor and in the burial rite the son was recognized as the new paterfamilias

> and from then on one of his principal functions would be to venerate the remains of the ancestors to whom the living still felt themselves bound as members of the same family. This obligation was one of the most sacred that a son had towards his father, and it did not finish on the day of burial but was prolonged in a series of funeral ceremonies after the burial and in the annual commemorations whose celebration was also entrusted to the son. (Guijarro 2001:229)[48]

Now archaeological evidence illuminates the burial customs of Judeans in our period. Burial sometimes took place in decorated wooden coffins, as is demonstrated by the tomb-caves near Jericho. These wooden coffins date to the late-Hasmonean period through to 6 CE (Hachlili 1979). But during our period a distinctive burial custom developed in Judeanism, referred to today as ossilegium. After initial

---

47. It must also be remembered, however, that in the Greco-Roman world, death was a grim reality, so not too many would have reached an "old age." According to Bolt (1998), Roman tombs suggest an average life expectancy of about twenty-two years for men and twenty years for women, with Egyptian tombs indicating a figure of around thirty years for both. Bolt also indicates that alternative estimates based on comparative populations studies claim that most people of the Greco-Roman world had an average life expectancy of around twenty to twenty-five years; that only 40 percent of the population reached that age; and that only 50 percent of children made it to their tenth birthday. The precariousness of life in the first-century was due mainly to three key factors. There was the brutal influence of Roman military power, malevolent magic, where the curses of such magic aimed at bringing suffering or death to its victims, and lastly, human illness, the ancients not having access to modern medicine and health measures.

48. Cf. Gen 49:29–32; 50:25; Jos 24:32; Tob 4:3–4; 6:15; 14:9, 11–12; *Jub.* 23:7; 36:1–2, 18; 2 Macc 5:10; *War* 5.545; *T. Reu.* 7:1; *T. Levi* 19:5.

burial, where the body was placed on a shelf or placed in long cavities carved in a burial cave (called *loculi*), Judeans, about a year later, performed a secondary burial, where the bones of their dead were gathered into ossuaries or bone boxes. It was mainly practiced in and around Jerusalem from just before the turn of the era until 70 CE. Ossuaries were usually made of limestone and on occasion, clay. The usual practice was when more space was needed in the cave, the bodies were exhumed, and the bones were placed in charnel piles where bones of a similar type of various persons were stacked together (Fine 2001:39–40). Fine (2001:41–43) has connected the use of ossuaries with the emergence of the local stone-carving industry, which was given strong impetus by Herod the Great's building programs in Jerusalem and the city's prosperity. The Temple mount, the Temple itself and Herod's palace were constructed largely of stone. It is also in this period that we see the emergence of stone tables and dinnerware.

In addition we can mention that in the tomb-caves near Jericho, two inscribed ossuaries (one in Hebrew and one in Greek) with an inscribed bowl (in Hebrew) were found in one loculus. The two ossuaries naming the deceased persons within were stacked on top of each other. The funerary bowl found with them refer to the persons in the ossuaries, and it indicates that an Ishmael, a third generation son, commemorated his father and grandfather (Hachlili 1979).

Thus in antiquity the father-son relationship was the closest and most lasting of all relationships. Its importance was based on the need for the continuity of the family. Guijarro (2001:229) explains that from

> his father the son inherited the house with its properties, its honor and its worship, and in order to preserve this heritage he received authority over all those persons who formed part of the household. The value attributed to this continuity shows that what mattered was not individuals but the household. It was the household which perpetuated itself in time; the head of the family was only its representative and guardian at any specific time. Because of this, fathers saw in their sons another "I," one more link in the chain of succession who would guarantee the continuity of the household and who would honor them as ancestors. (Sir 30:4; 44:10–11; 46:12)

Summary

In our period the family was the basic social unit, of production and consumption, of reproduction and socialization, and personal honor and identity. All family types basically strived to be patriarchal, patrilineal, patrilocal, and to have productive sources held collectively. Also striving for self-sufficiency, the family as a unit, being part of an agrarian society, had an inseparable relationship with the land. It was the family's source of food, and the means by which the family line and inheritance could be perpetuated. Most families lived in small villages and towns, which were surrounded by their agricultural fields. The family house consisted of a room or several rooms arranged around one or two courtyards. Judeanism espoused a positive family ethic, and various regulations in the Tanak ensured the continuance of the family as a unit.

Marriage strategies were predominantly endogamous, and was basically never arranged by the two individuals concerned, having economic, religious and political implications as well. The authority over the wife was transferred from that of her father to that of her husband, to whose home she is also transferred. The women played a vital role in the perpetuation of her husband's family, but also to provide a progeny in fulfilment of God's promises to Abraham and Sarah in Genesis 12.

Lastly, Judeanism, much like other societies of antiquity, gave prominence to the father-son relationship. It was the closest and most lasting of all relationships. The son came under the complete authority of the father, who had the responsibility of educating his son on how to run the household and family property. The father also had to teach his son the religious traditions. The continuity of the household was dependent on how the son fulfilled his obligations. He had to be obedient, and take care of his father in old age, and venerate him as a family ancestor through burial rites and annual commemorations. It was also upon the father's death that the son, the link in the chain of succession, would be recognized as the new paterfamilias.

What of the Gentiles?

A Clash of Cultures

The Judeans certainly had a consciousness of difference vis-à-vis other peoples. In addition to the various texts already referred to in this chapter, others may be added. It is said that because of exile, "Everyone will be offended at your customs" (*Sib. Or.* 3:271–72). In *Sib. Or.* 4:35–36 it is said that men will never imitate the piety or customs of those who love God, because they desire shamelessness. Good views of Gentiles were generally few and far in between.[49] Contact with Gentiles had to be avoided (*Liv. Pro.* 10:5; *4 Bar.* 7:37) and the most frequent criticism against Gentiles focussed on idolatry and sexual immorality.[50] The Greeks are "overbearing and impious" (*Sib. Or.* 3:171). There is the warning not to "become involved in revolting gentile affairs" (*T. Jud.* 23:2; cf. *T. Dan* 5:5, 8). The Gentiles are "abominable and lawless" (*3 Macc* 6:9, 12). *Psalms of Solomon* 17:15 laments that "the children of the covenant" living among Gentile rabble adopted foreign customs. Jubilees use the solar calendar (and the Sabbath) as a distinguishing mark between Judeans and Gentiles. As far as the author is concerned, the lunar calendar is associated with the error of the Gentile nations (Baumgarten 1997:85). The deeds of Gentiles are "defilement and corruption and contamination; and there is no righteousness with them" (*Jub.* 21:21); they are sinners (*Jub.* 23:24). In contrast, the Judeans are "a race of most righteous men" (*Sib. Or.* 3:219); "For to them alone did the great God give wise counsel and faith and excellent understanding" (*Sib. Or.* 3:584–85). Judeans are from "a chosen and honored race from the seed of Jacob" (*T. Job* 1:5). *Jubilees* 15:31 states that God caused for spirits to rule over the Gentiles to led them astray and it is hoped for Jacob: "May the nations serve you, and all nations bow down before your seed" (*Jub.* 22:11; cf. 26:23).

49. All nations will worship and bless God in *1 En.* 10:21. The discerning nations must receive Enoch's books so they may fear God (*2 En.* 48:7 [J]). The *T. 12 Patr.* in particular expresses favorable views towards Gentiles. God will save all the Gentiles when the 2 Messiah's arrive (*T. Sim.* 7:2), although traditional and current enemies will be destroyed (*T. Sim.* 6:3–4). A king will arise from Judah and he "will found a new priesthood in accord with the gentile model and for all nations" (*T. Levi* 8:14). The salvation of the Gentiles seems to be implied in *T. Jud.* 24:6—this accords with *T. Naph.* 8:2–4, which says that the future king from Judah will bring salvation to Israel, but he will also "assemble the righteous from among the nations" and *T. Ash.* 7:3: God will save Israel and the nations; cf. *T. Benj.* 11:1–3; *T. Gad* 7:2.

50. It is said to the Gentiles: "You neither revere or fear God, but wander to no purpose, worshipping snakes and sacrificing to cats, speechless idols, and stone statues of people; and sitting in front of the doors at godless temples you do not fear the existing God who guards all things" (*Sib. Or.* 3:30–34). Idolatry is also attacked in *Sib. Or.* 3:545–54; 5:276–80, 484–500; *T. Job* 2:2—3:3, 5:2; *T. Mos.* 2:8–9; *Let. Aris.* 134–35; *Jub.* 12:2–5; 20:7–9; 21:5; 22:18, 22. It is also said that Judeans do not commit adultery and "do not engage in impious intercourse with male children, as do Phoenicians, Egyptians, and Romans, spacious Greece and many nations of others, Persians and Galatians and all Asia, transgressing the holy law of immortal God" (*Sib. Or.* 3:596–600; cf. *Sib. Or.* 4:33–34; 5:430).

Not surprisingly, to maintain identity, most Judeans of the ancient world sought to separate themselves from their Gentile neighbors. In the East, they formed their own autonomous ethnic communities, and in cities such as Rome and Alexandria there were neighborhoods largely inhabited by Judeans. Following Ezra, Judeans in this period also increasingly had little tolerance for marriages with Gentiles. They also buried there dead separately. In the polyethnic Hellenistic and Roman empires, the Judeans "carried their separateness to unusual lengths," and their refusal to participate in Gentile religious activities was unparalleled (Cohen 1987:46). Mainstream Judeanism rejected the Hellenistic idea that all men are brothers and equal before God and this "theoretical and practical ἀμιξία, which ran counter to the whole tendency of Hellenistic times, was a constant and particular reproach against the [Judeans]" (Schürer et al. 1986:614).[51]

Negative views of Gentiles were just one part of a mutual exchange. For educated men of the period the Judean religion was a *barbara superstitio* (Cicero, *pro Flacco* 28.67). A fictitious tale developed concerning the Exodus from Egypt, the foundations being laid by Manetho (*Apion* 1.227–53). In the course of time the story developed but the essence of the story is thus: A number of lepers were banished by the Egyptian king and were sent into the quarries or the desert. One of them was a priest of Heliopolis named Moses (Manetho said his real name was Osarsiph). Through his influence the lepers apostasized from the Egyptian gods and gave them a new religion. Under his leadership they left the country and eventually came to Jerusalem, which they conquered and occupied for a long time (Schürer et al. 1986:151). The Alexandrian grammarian Apion said that the Judeans paid divine honors to the head of an ass (*Apion* 2.80). Tacitus picks up this story and links it to the fact that the Judeans in the desert were made aware of many springs of water by a herd of wild asses (*Hist.* 5.3–4).

Juvenal says Judeans will show the way only to fellow Judeans, and will direct only the circumcised to a well (*Sat.* 14.103–4). In Alexandria it was apparently said that Judeans took an oath not to be well-disposed to any Gentile, and that they offered a Greek in sacrifice on a yearly basis (*Apion* 2.121–24; 2.89–96). Apollonius Molon claimed that Judeans were the most incompetent of barbarians, and contributed no useful invention to the general culture (*Apion* 2.148).

---

51. Cf. Hecataeus (300 BCE) in Diodorus 40.3.4; *Ant.* 13.245, 247; *Apion* 1.309; 2.121, 148; 2.258; Tacitus, *Hist.* 5.5; Juvenal, *Sat.* 14.103–4.

Much fun was made of three points in particular by the educated world: abstention from pork, strict observance of the Sabbath and imageless worship. Juvenal (*Sat.* 6.160; 14.96–106) speaks of the land where "customary kindness bestows on pigs a ripe old age" and where "pork is accounted as precious as human flesh." In the Sabbath observance he sees "nothing but indolence and laziness, and in [Judean] divine service only worship of clouds and the sky" (Schürer et al. 1986:152). Similarly Seneca (in Augustine, *City of God* 6.11) accuses the Judeans of laziness and of wasting one-seventh of their lives in idleness through their observance of the Sabbath.

So much of the Judean literature that attacked Gentile ways also had an apologetic purpose. Most of the apologetic literature was "directed towards strengthening the confidence of a [Judean] audience in their own heritage, and it is doubtful whether a gentile audience was ever intended to read it" (Schürer et al. 1986:609). In a similar yet somewhat different way Gruen (2002) argued that in Judean literature we do not find a struggle for identity, apologetics for strange customs and beliefs, nor propaganda to convince Gentiles. The literature was for internal consumption and to boost Judean self-esteem. Josephus argues that the Judeans were not inferior with regards to their antiquity compared with other nations. He discounts the story that Judeans originated from Egyptian lepers. Judeans were originators of all civilization. In the process Josephus also used material of Eupolemus, Artapanus and Aristobulus. He further answers the charges of atheism, religious and social segregation, and Judean peculiarities (e.g., circumcision) (Schürer et al. 1986:610–16). Judeans may have been accused of being bad subjects by not worshipping the emperor, but a daily sacrifice was offered for the emperor in the Temple (*Apion* 2.73–77; *War* 2.197).

The authors further placed emphasis on the humane regulations of the Law, especially to foreigners (*Apion* 2.209–14; Philo, *Virtues* 12.88; cf. *Apion* 2.255–75). The stipulations of the Law are pure in every respect and most ideal (*Apion* 2.188–219). The Law has excellence and is of great antiquity (2.154, 156), and in terms of character Moses was blameless (2.158–61). Philo also concentrated on the excellence and humanity of the Law and its moral strictness in general, but he was also concerned to demonstrate that circumcision, unclean animals and Sabbath observance were reasonable and purposeful (*Spec. Laws* 1.2–7; 4.125; *Hyp.* in *Pr. Ev.* 8.7.10–20). Pseudo-Aristeas and Aristobulus before him had done much the same (*Ps.-Aris.* 128 ff., 142–69; Aristobulus in *Pr. Ev.* 13.12.9–16).

In addition, Judeanism had a problem with the relationship between universalism[52] and particularism. The tension is that God is both Lord of all and also the national God of Israel. The Messianists (at least some of them) "resolved the tension between these conceptions by affirming the universality of God and denying all doctrines that bound God to a particular nation or land. For most [Judeans], however, this was not a viable option" (Cohen 1987:81).

The Judeans enjoyed special privileges in the Diaspora (and Palestine), thanks especially to the decrees of Julius Caesar and Augustus, whereby the Judeans could manage their own affairs. They could practice their religion and send contributions to the Jerusalem Temple (Schürer et al. 1986:114–21). Despite this legal protection, however, the "otherness" of Judeans combined with their protected rights often led to friction with local Gentiles—this kind of situation is mirrored in the territory of Palestine. In Caesarea Gentiles and Judeans were repeatedly involved in bloody conflict. Judeans protested after a soldier had torn up a Torah scroll and thrown it into the fire. The protest it caused only ceased after Cumanus had the soldier executed (*War* 2.228ff.). In addition, there was disagreement between Greeks and Judeans over access to a synagogue in a Gentile district in Caesarea. It led to open conflict and the desecration of the synagogue. Soon thereafter, the Judeans of Caesarea heard that the local garrison of Roman troops plundered the Temple treasury in Jerusalem, and consequently attacked them. The Roman troops responded, and the events contributed towards the outbreak of the Great Revolt (Bull 1990:110). Gentile hostility towards Judeans broke out in particular at the outbreak of the Judean war. For example, the residents of Scythopolis massacred the Judeans in the city as the Judean revolt erupted in the summer of 66 (*War* 2.466–68; *Life* 26). The effects of the revolt were also felt in Alexandria (*War* 2.457–98) and other places. "While the triumph of the revolution was thus being decided in Jerusalem, bloody battles were taking place in many other cities inhabited by both [Judeans] and Gentiles. Where the [Judeans] were in the majority, they massacred their Gentile fellow-citizens, and where the latter had the upper hand they struck down the [Judeans]" (Schürer et al. 1973:487). Philo says that the people of Ascalon bore

---

52. We can bring attention here to Second Isaiah which states that God had chosen Israel to be his servant, to whom he first gave the Law and Judgement. But Israel must proclaim this to the nations (Isa 42:1–4; 49:1–6); Israel must become a light to the Gentiles (Isa 42:6; 49:6); the religion of Israel must become a world religion and then the Gentiles will also be accepted by God (Isa 56:1–8; cf. Rom 3:28–9).

relentless hostility towards Judeans (*Embassy* 205). Of the Phoenicians, the Tyrians were, according to Josephus, especially hostile in their attitude to Judeans (*Apion* 1.70). The mutual hostilities at this time are also demonstrated by the following incident. At the outbreak of the revolution in 66 CE, the head of the temple police, Eleazar, son of the high priest Ananias, convinced the other priests to abolish sacrifices for Gentiles, including the one offered for the emperor (*War* 2.408–21).

God-Fearers and Proselytes

The irony of the above is that besides the mutual hostility, there were those Gentiles that in some form or another attached themselves to the Judean way of life, even becoming proselytes. Three points have been suggested regarding the success of Judean propaganda: 1) Judeanism was represented in a form that would have been acceptable to Greeks and Romans. The peculiar and unpalatable was left in the background with main emphasis placed upon the concept of God, the one Lord and Creator who rewards according to moral conduct; 2) there was the practical direction of Judeanism towards training conduct in ordinary life; 3) the possibility that Judeanism fulfilled the potential needs of monotheism, expiation of sins and ritual purification, and the reward of a happy afterlife—these elements maybe being present in pagan, or rather, Gentile religions in some form or another (Schürer et al. 1986:153–58).

Seemingly there were many Gentiles in the Hellenistic-Roman period "who attached themselves more or less closely to [Judean] communities, took part in the [Judean] divine service and observed [Judean] precepts sometimes more, sometimes less completely" (Schürer et al. 1986:160–61). According to Dunn (1991:125), "there can be no disputing the fact that many Gentiles were attracted to [Judeanism] and attached themselves to the local synagogues in varying degrees of adherence . . . *Ioudaizein*, 'to live like a [Judean]', was already a well established term to indicate the adoption of [Judean] practices."

Plutarch (*Cicero* 7.6.5) refers to a freedman of the first-century BCE who was suspected of Judeanising. Seneca (in Augustine, *City of God* 6.11) speaks of many who adopted the custom of the Judean Sabbath. Other writers that refer to Gentiles adopting some Judean customs are Epictetus (quoted by Arrian, *Dissertationes* 2.19–21), Petronius (fragment 37), Suetonius (*Lives of the Caesars* 12.2) and Juvenal (14.96–99). Josephus reports that every city in Syria had Judeanizers (τοὺς

Ἰουδαΐζοντας; *War* 2.463); in Antioch many Greeks were attracted to Judean religious ceremonies and were in some measure incorporated into the Judean community there (War 7.45); in Damascus almost all women were devoted to Judeanism (*War* 2.560), and women of high social standing often too (*Ant.* 18. 81–4; cf. Acts 13:50; 17:4). He also distinguishes between God-fearers and Judeans who from various parts of the empire brought gifts to the temple (*Ant.* 14.110). Josephus explains that many Judean customs were adopted in Gentiles cities, especially the abstinence of work on the Sabbath, the observance of the fast days and the lighting of Sabbath lamps (*Apion* 1.166–67; 2.282). Philo refers to those Gentiles who have not undergone circumcision. They are "sympathizers," for they honor the one God, but they are not converts (*QExodus* 2.2). Later rabbis referred to such a person as a *ger tošab* and they also spoke of "Heaven Fearers" (*yirei šamayim*) (Feldman 1986; Tannenbaum 1986). Philo also claims that Judean institutions, especially the Sabbath and the Day of Atonement, have won the attention of the whole inhabited world (*Moses* 2.4.20–24) and he speaks of pious men and those who practice wisdom in Grecian and barbarian lands (*Spec. Laws* 2.42–44) which must refer to Gentiles attracted to the spiritual or ethical aspects of Judeanism.

Acts speak of φοβούμενοι τὸν θεόν ("fearers of God": Acts 10:2, 22; 13:16, 26) or σεβόμενοι τὸν θεόν ("worshippers of God": Acts 13:43, 50; 16:14; 17:4; 17:17; 18:7), while θεοσεβεῖς ("God worshippers") is found on inscriptions as well. For example, in Pisidian Antioch Paul is said to have addressed those who fear God, distinct from Israelites (Acts 13:16, 26) and afterwards Judeans and devout proselytes followed him (Acts 13:43). In Thessalonica Paul converted Judeans and God-fearing Greeks (Acts 17:4) and in Athens he preached in the assembly to the Judeans and God-fearing Greeks (Acts 17:17). It is possibly from these groups that there came the Greeks who went up to worship in the Temple during Passover (John 12:20). It was the Sabbath and dietary laws that these Gentiles observed most strongly, but they must be distinguished from full proselytes.

But MacLennan & Kraabel (1986) have argued that the "God-fearers" in Acts were a literary and theological invention. Excavated synagogues of Diaspora communities (dating from the first century BCE to the seventh century CE) have uncovered over one hundred inscriptions. None of them use φοβούμενος or σεβομένος, and θεοσεβής appearing about ten times, refers to "Jews." There is one possible exception, the inscription at Aphrodisias (Asia Minor), yet it should not necessarily be understood that these Gentiles were interested in Judean religion. Also θεοσεβής did not have a single meaning, as it could also apart from referring to Judeans, also refer to Gentiles and Gentile Messianists.

"God-fearer" may not be a technical terms for a specific group of Gentiles that are attached to the synagogue, but neither can the term exclude those Gentiles genuinely interested in the culture of the Judeans. "God-fearer" seems to have been an umbrella term that referred to Gentiles who were in various ways in a relationship with Judeanism, be it for religious, political or social reasons (Lieu 2002:31–47; Feldman 1986; Tannenbaum 1986). Even Acts betrays a "broader" understanding of the term as it speaks of "God-fearing proselytes" (σεβόμενοι προσήλυτοι: Acts 13:43).

Judeans were seemingly eager to accept and retain Gentile converts. Some of the anti-Judean literature of the time was to discourage conversion to Judeanism. Tacitus (*Hist.* 5.5) offers a measure of truth when he said that Judean proselytes "learned nothing so quickly as to despise the gods, to abjure their fatherland, and to regard parents, children and kindred as nothing" (cf. Schürer et al. 1986:153). Horace (*Satires* 1.4.142–43) alludes to the Judeans as if they characteristically encourage Gentiles to join them; "we, like the Judeans, will compel you to make one of our throng." This attests to the fact that Judeanism held a powerful attraction for some. The New Testament also makes reference to proselytes (Acts 2:11; 6:5; 13:43; Matt 23:15). Israel felt itself to be a teacher of the peoples of the world. Justin's Dialogue with Trypho (121–22) indicates that Isaiah 49:6 was understood this way. *Sibylline Oracles* 3:195 says Judeans "will be for all mortals leaders to life," and we may draw attention to Paul's self-awareness in this regard (Rom 2:19–20). According to Cohen (1987:57) some Judeans engaged themselves in "missionary" work—referring to Matt 23:15 and the story of the house of Adiabene—but there is "no evidence for an organized [Judean] mission to the gentiles, but individuals seem to have engaged in this activity on their own" (cf. MacLennan & Kraabel 1986).

The conversion of Asenath requires rejection of idolatry and avoidance of meat sacrificed to idols or the meat of strangled animals (*Jos. Asen.* 9; 10:12–13; 11:4ff.; 12:5ff; 13:11; 21:13–14). This goes without saying, but during the existence of the Temple, three main demands were made according to the rabbis for the acceptance of proselytes into the Judean community: 1) circumcision; 2) baptism, or a ritual purification; and lastly, 3) an offering in the Temple (*Sif. Num.* 15:4; *m. Ker.* 2:1;

m. Pes. 8:8; *m. 'Eduy.* 5:2; *b. Ker.* 9a; *b. Yeb.* 46a).[53] For women only the last two were relevant.

Judith, written or redacted in second century BCE, describes conversion of an Ammonite general (Jdt 14:10). It has essential aspects of conversion: belief in God, circumcision, and joining the house of Israel. The Greek version of Esther (114 BCE) understands "and many from the peoples of the country declared themselves Judeans" (Esth 8:17) to mean the Gentiles "were circumcised" (Cohen 1987:52–53). Josephus also reports that foreign male rulers who wished to marry into the Herodian household had to be circumcised (*Ant.* 20.1, 3; cf. 16.5). Josephus also writes of the Roman general, Metilius, who at the outbreak of the Great Revolt, begged for his life and promised to become a Judean by being circumcised (*War* 2.10). He also related how Izates, king of Adiabene, wished to become a Judean, but he was advised by his mother (herself a Judean convert) and Ananias, a Judean merchant, not to undergo circumcision in order for him to keep his crown (*Ant.* 20.34–46). Eventually, Izates was circumcised (cf. *Ant.* 13.1; 16.6; *War* 1.10), however.

Philo stresses the moral meaning of circumcision, and refers to Alexandrian Judeans who dismissed physical circumcision in favor of its allegorical meaning. Philo himself, however, affirmed its physical necessity as well (*Mig. Abraham* 92). This represented the majority opinion, but according to Saldarini (1994:159), the discussions show that in the Talmudic period, and certainly in the first century, the practice of circumcision was local and varied. Nevertheless, in most cases circumcision was required of converts (Sim 1996:175–76; Schürer et al. 1986:169).

Based on the importance of ritual immersion in our period, it must be agreed with the view that it formed part of the conversion process. Cohen (1987:53) is a bit more cautious as he argues that "it seems most likely that baptism/immersion was part of the conversion process in at least some [Judean] circles in Palestine by the first century of our era" although not all Judeans "of the first century recognized baptism/immersion as a ritual of conversion." A saying of Epictetus (reported by Arrian, *Dissertationes* 2.19–21) is best understood as referring to proselyte baptism: "But if a man adopts the manner of life of a man who has been baptized and has made his choice, then he really is, and is called, a Judean."

---

53. Later rabbinic traditions indicate that both immersion and circumcision was required for full conversion (*b. Yeb.* 46b).

For Gentile woman, marriage with a Judean man was a de facto equivalent of conversion (Cohen 1987:54). Conversion to Judeanism at times also entailed taking on a Hebrew name (*Jos. Asen.* 15:7). Proselytes were regarded in important matters as equals to born Israelites with regard to duties and rights by the rabbis. But there could be a suspicion that they might laps in halakhic matters (*m. Nid.* 7:3) although for the greater part rabbinic statements is positive with regards to converts (Schürer et al. 1986:176). Philo encouraged accepting proselytes as brothers (*Virtues* 20.103) and placed emphasis on the welcome and equality of rights extended to full proselytes (*Spec. Laws* 1.51–53). A proselyte, however, was not equal in every sense. He/she might not call on the ancestors of Israel as his/her fathers (*m. Bik.* 1:4), and in the theocracy ranked second from last: priest—levite—Israelite—*mamzer*—*nathin*—proselyte—freed slave (*m. Hor.* 3:8). Thus overall, Judeanism could accept converts into the fold but without sacrificing its ethnic identity (Sim 1996:177).

CHAPTER 4

Who Were the Galileans?

Introduction

IN THE previous chapter, we had an overall look at what Judean identity entailed in the first century. Now the question must be asked, how does Galilee fit into this overall picture? This question is important as the eventual focus of the study, the hypothetical source Q, has been plausibly located in Galilee, in particular along the north-western shore of the lake in Capernaum. It is for this reason that the cultural characteristics of Galilee be treated separately. The attempt will be to demonstrate that there was a fundamental continuity between the people of Galilee and that of Judea. There was a continuity in terms of that both shared the same cultural heritage, and importantly, both occupied the ancestral *land* of Israel. Although geographically it was separated from Judea (only by a few days walk) and was at times ruled politically separate from Judea, culturally, first century Judeanism was not some foreign import into Galilee.

The focus will here, as in the previous chapter, be on the question of ethnic identity, hence the investigation is not aimed at doing a detailed historical reconstruction of the region. It can be mentioned that the situation of Galilee was very different in the early history of Israel. Originally it was the territory of the tribes of Naphtali, Zebulun and probably Issachar as well (Judg 5:7–21). In time they became subordinated to the monarchy and Temple in Jerusalem, and after Solomon's death (931 BCE), became part of the northern kingdom of Israel (1 Kgs 12), although there was persistent rebellion against kingly rule (Horsley 1995:23–25). What is of critical importance is what happened to these tribes after the conquest of the Assyrian king Tiglath-pileser in

733/2 BCE. Did many of these Israelites remain behind and survive across the generations until the first century CE?

The Galileans as Descendants of Northern Israelites

Horsley is one scholar in particular who understands the people of Galilee in our period as descendants of northern Israelites. He is aware of surface surveys that seem to demonstrate that after the campaigns of Tiglath-pileser III, Lower Galilee was devastated and that virtually the entire population was deported. "Yet continuity of the Israelite population seems far more likely, despite the fragmentary evidence and often inferential interpretation on which the hypothesis is based" (Horsley 1995:26). So Horsley argues that the vast majority of the peasantry would have been left behind.

Horsley continues by tracing the separate historical development of Galilee from Judeans in the south and Israelites in the central hill country until it came to be part of the Hasmonean, and eventually Roman political system (Horsley 1995:27–157). Throughout this period the Israelites of Galilee would have cultivated their own oral traditions. Josephus also ordinarily distinguishes between "the Galileans" and "the Judeans," and in certain instances he even indicates that the Galileans were a separate *ethnos* from the Judeans (*War* 2.510; 4.105).[1] In the time of the Hasmonean expansion, they were subjected "to the laws of the Judeans," but even long after this annexation there is evidence that the distinctive Galilean traditions and customs continued. But kinship and shared traditions would have been factors in the incorporation of Galileans under the Hasmonean-Judean Temple state.

> As descendants of northern Israelite tribes the inhabitants of Galilee would have shared with the Judean temple-state traditions such as the exodus story, the Mosaic covenant (including the sabbath), stories of independent early Israel prior to the Solomonic monarchy and its temple, and certain traditions akin to some of those subsumed in the Judean Torah and early sections of the Deuteronomic history (including circumcision, ancestor legends, victory songs)... Nevertheless, even as descendants of Israelites, the Galileans would have found "the laws of the Judeans" different from their own indigenous customs and

---

1. In his other major work on Galilee, Horsley (1996:27) actually states that ordinarily "Josephus makes clear distinctions between the Galileans and Idumeans and Judeans as separate *ethnoi* or peoples."

traditions ... [T]hey had undergone more than eight centuries of separate development. (Horsley 1995:50–51)

So the Judean Temple, its dues, and the role of the high priest was something foreign to the Galileans and was superimposed on their own customs. This means that for the Galileans to have been incorporated into the Judean Temple-state, it would have required an intense program of social engineering. "For that to have happened, the officers or retainers of the Hasmonean government ... would have had to undertake a program of resocialization of the Galileans into the Judean laws as well as a detailed application of the Judean laws to local community life." But Horsley continues; "A survey of the subsequent history of the Hasmonean regime and its governing activities suggests that little such effort could have been made in Galilee" (Horsley 1995:51, 52). Indeed, even the period after Hasmonean rule would not have been conducive for "the law of the Judeans" to take a firm hold over Galileans. The Galileans continued to assert their independence from the principal institutions of Jerusalem rule such as the revolt that occurred after Herod's death. Even during the Great Revolt, high priestly-Pharisaic council in Jerusalem through Josephus commanded little authority in Galilee. Horsley (1995:156) basically concluded that there is little evidence to indicate that either the Judean temple-state, or the temple and Torah "established a defining importance for life in Galilee during the time of Jerusalem rule."

Galilee After the Assyrian Conquest

The critical issue is what happened in Galilee after the campaigns of the Assyrian king Tiglath-pileser III in 733/2 BCE. Were there indeed some northern Israelites that continued living in the area? Second Kings 15 claims that Tiglath-pileser III conquered Hazor, as well as Gilead, Galilee and the land of Naphtali, and led the population into exile in Assyria (2 Kgs 15:29). Fragmentary Assyrian texts offer the complete names of Hannathon and Merom, and give four numbers of people being exiled from Galilee (625, 650, 656, and 13,520) (Reed 2000:28). This evidence in itself is ambiguous,[2] but a recent surface survey of Lower Galilee, "when coupled with the results of stratigraphic excavations in Upper and Lower Galilee, paint a picture of a totally devastated and

---

2. It is said in 2 Chr 30:10–11 that in the time of Hezekiah (ca 727–699 BCE), members of Asher, Manasseh and Zebulun humbled themselves and came to Jerusalem. This may suggest that some northern Israelites in Galilee remained in the area.

depopulated Galilee in the wake of the Assyrian campaigns of 733/732 B.C.E" (Reed 2000:29; cf. 1999:90–95). The survey of Lower Galilee found no evidence of occupation from the seventh to sixth centuries (Iron Age III)[3] at any of the eighty or so sites inspected. Surveys also illustrate that even Upper Galilee was not spared by the Assyrians. This leads to the conclusion that Galilee was depopulated in the wake of the Assyrian conquest. Horsley's objection (1996:23) that the sites where the surface surveys have been conducted were not subjected to systematic excavations is legitimate, although other stratigraphic excavations conducted confirm that Galilee was abandoned in the seventh and sixth centuries. Conflagration layers dated to the end of the eighth century are found at many sites in and around Galilee. A few sherds have been found at Gush Halav, otherwise the evidence is limited to a few structures in Hazor (the Huleh Valley) and Tel Chinnereth (north-western shore of the Sea of Galilee) which were probably Assyrian military or administrative buildings. But there is no evidence for a surrounding population (Reed 2000:30–31). An Assyrian-style decorated bronze cup further points to an Assyrian presence in Kefar Kanna (Chancey 2002:33). Generally, however, there

> was simply an insufficient amount of material culture in Galilee following the campaigns of Tiglath-pileser III for serious consideration of any cultural continuity between the Iron Age and subsequent periods . . . There are no villages, no hamlets, no farmsteads, nothing at all indicative of a population that could harvest the Galilean valleys for the Assyrian stores, much less sustained cultural and religious traditions through the centuries. (Reed 2000:32)

The above picture is in keeping with Assyrian policy which often deported all classes of people to Assyria or other regions for agricultural

3. The chronological periods employed by archaeologists and historians are as follows (cf. Reed 2000:21):

Iron II	1000–733/32 BCE
Iron III	733/32–586 BCE
Persian	586–332 BCE
Early Hellenistic	332–167 BCE
Late Hellenistic	167–63 BCE
Early Roman	63 BCE–135 CE
Middle Roman	135–250 CE
Late Roman	250–363 CE

labor. Reed (2000:34) concludes that the position of Horsley that an Israelite village culture spanned the Iron Age to Roman periods "must be abandoned." Chancey (2002:34) refers to various texts that assume the presence of Israelites in Galilee (2 Chr 30:10–11; 34:6; 2 Kgs 21:19; 23:36) in addition the archaeological evidence for Assyrians, but he too concludes that for the most part Galilee was unpopulated. Claims of a continuity between the pre-Assyrian conquest and Second Temple population "are difficult to maintain" (Chancey 2002:34). Archaeological evidence further illustrates that Galilee was resettled during the Persian and Early Hellenistic periods, but even here the evidence is limited and the ethnic identity of the people is difficult to determine (Reed 2000:35–39). Josephus' description of Hyrcanus' defeat of Scythopolis describes that Galilee was open for resettlement, which implies that no other major defensible Gentile sites were present in Galilee, or alternatively, that it had a small population (*Ant.* 13.28; *War* 1.64). Chancey (2002:36) similarly argues that the interior of Galilee "was still relatively sparsely populated on the eve of the Maccabean campaigns."

The Settlement of Galilee in the Late Hellenistic Period

We now move ahead to the history of Galilee during the Hasmonean period. According to 1 Maccabees, news came from Galilee that Galilean Israelites were persecuted by people from Ptolemais, Tyre, Sidon and πᾶσαν Γαλιλαίαν ἀλλοφύλων, "all Galilee of the foreigners" (1 Macc 5:14–22).[4] Based on the archaeological evidence reviewed above, it should not be assumed that these people were descendants of northern Israelites. In fact, it is said that the Judeans deliberated on how they should help "their brothers" (τοῖς ἀδελφοῖς αὐτῶν; 1 Macc 4:16), thus implying that these Galileans were Judeans themselves. First Maccabees explains that Simon went to help these Galileans and so de-

---

4. Γαλιλαία ἀλλοφύλων also appears in LXX Joel 4:4. Along with 1 Macc 5:15, this phrase refers to the coastal regions that surrounded Galilee which were dominated by Gentiles. In the LXX, ἀλλόφυλος is frequently used to translate "Philistine," although literally it means "foreigner," and was later used for "Gentile" (e.g., *Ant.* 1.338; 4.183; *War* 5.194; Acts 10:28) (Chancey 2002:37-39). This phrase is probably an allusion to *galil ha-goyim*, "circle of the peoples," in Isa 9:1 (Γαλιλαία τῶν ἐθνῶν in LXX Isa 8:23). According to Horsley (1995:20), "circle of the peoples" was likely "a reference to the 'peoples,' 'city-states,' and other rulers who surrounded and competed for political-economic domination in the area." When it comes to the region of Galilee itself, the Hebrew term *ha-galil* was probably a shortening of *galil ha-goyim*. "Galilee of the Gentiles" occurs very rarely in ancient literature and the single word "Galilee" was the region's common name (Chancey 2002:170-72).

feated the Gentiles with three thousand men. The people of Galilee, but evidently not all of them (cf. Chancey 2002:41), were brought back to Judea (1 Macc 5:23), although Horsley (1995:40; but see 243) expresses doubt as to the historical veracity of this incident. It could well be that these Galileans settled in the area sometime after the Babylonian exile. Gamla, located in the Golan Heights, was resettled in 150 BCE after being uninhabited for centuries. Syon (1992) conjectures that the settlers of Gamla were Judeans ("Jews") from Babylon and we may infer a similar situation for the people of Galilee (Josephus, however, speak of Gamla's conquest by Alexander Jannaeus; *War* 103–5; *Ant.* 13.393–97).

First Maccabees 11:63–74 and Josephus (*Ant.* 13.158–62) relate that later on Demetrius III encamped at Kedesh in the western part of Upper Galilee (ca. 144 BCE). Josephus (*Ant.* 13.154) specifically says that it was Demetrius' intention to draw Jonathan to Galilee, as the latter would not allow the Galileans, "who were his own people, to be attacked." So not all the people of Galilee were evacuated by Simon, and importantly, Josephus understood the Galileans to be Judeans. Jonathan in response attacked the forces of Demetrius twice; once in the plain of Hazor in Upper Galilee pursuing them back to Kedesh, and at Hammath in Lebanon (1 Macc 11:24ff).

It was much later when the Hasmoneans took actual control of northern Palestine. The account of Josephus does not make explicit reference to Galilee. It is said that Aristobulus I (104–103 BCE) "made war on the Itureans and acquired a good deal of their territory for Judea and compelled the inhabitants, if they wished to remain in the country, to be circumcised and to live in accordance with the law of the Judeans." This is according to Strabo (who follows Timagenes) who is used by Josephus (*Ant.* 13.318–19). According to Horsley (1995:41), in this scenario the "territory acquired for Judea" must have been (part of) Galilee. But were there Itureans based in northern Galilee? Josephus does not specify Galilee as the locale and the archaeological evidence does not support the presence of Itureans in Upper Galilee, their settlements being limited to the Hermon Range and the Lebanon Range and the northern Golan. According to Reed (2000:38–39, 54) this means that the conversion of the Itureans is not an important factor for assessing the ethnicity of the Galileans. In this scenario Horsley suggests an alternative interpretation, however, in that Josephus might be "correcting" his source(s) Strabo-Timagenes who assumed that Galilee was Iturean because it was ruled by Itureans. "Josephus' 'correction' distinguishes between 'the inhabitants ... in the land' (*chora*) and their previous rulers, 'the Itureans,' on whom Aristobulus made war and from whom he wrested territory for Judea" (Horsley 1995:41). Building on the supposition that the Galileans were basically descendents of northern Israelites, Horsley subsequently understands the passage of Josephus (*Ant.* 13.318–19) in that the Galileans were "subjected" in a political-economic-religious sense to the Hasmonean high priesthood in Jerusalem. The requirement of (re-)circumcision—what this means is not clear—for Galileans "is comprehensible as a sign of being joined to the [Judean] 'body-politic'" and so the Hasmoneans "were now requiring peoples of subjected areas to accept new laws, the laws of the Judeans" (Horsley 1995:48, 49).

It is hard to detect any "correction" on the part of Josephus to his source(s), although it might well be that the passage of Josephus was relevant to some *Gentiles* that lived in Galilee (cf. Horsley 1995:243–44). Chancey (2002:43–47), who states that no archaeological finds indicate a massive influx of Itureans into Galilee, suggests that the Galilean population was a mixture of some Itureans, Phoenicians, and "Jews" (be they northern Israelites or more recent immigrants). Based on his analysis, it is possible that the already circumcised Itureans who chose to remain behind subjected themselves to Hasmonean rule. Phoenicians and peoples of other Gentile stock were compelled to undergo circumcision, though many, based on the archaeological evidence chose to leave. The "Jews" presumably welcomed Hasmonean rule.

The above text of Josephus and the various interpretations that are offered is not very helpful. Simplifying matters is that who the original population was in Galilee is probably not that important as what occurred when the Hasmoneans took over the region. As already mentioned, Galilee was only thinly resettled during the Persian and Early Hellenistic periods after it was virtually depopulated. When the Hasmoneans took control of the region it began to experience an increase in sites and an overall population growth during Hasmonean rule.

> The vast majority of stratigraphically excavated sites from the Roman-Byzantine Period contain their earliest recoverable strata, that is to say the earliest architecture and first significant pottery assemblage, from the Late Hellenistic Period or first century B.C.E. This is the case at Capernaum, Hammath Tiberias, Horvat Arbel, Yodefat, Khirbet Shema, Meiron, Nazareth, and Sepphoris . . . The population of Galilee continued to increase through the Early Roman period, and several stratigraphically

excavated sites reveal initial settlement around the turn of the millennium or in the first century C.E. This is the case at Beth Shearim, Nabratein, Chorazin, and of course, Herod Antipas's Tiberias. (Reed 2000:40–41)

The numismatic evidence is also quite instructive in that beginning in the early first century BCE, a significant amount of Hasmonean, particularly Jannaean, coins were used by the people of Galilee, in addition to Tyrian coinage. This means that Galilee was economically and politically orientated towards Judea and that Galilee's population growth was connected to Hasmonean policies (Reed 2000:41–43; Chancey 2002:46).

Overall, the Hasmonean expansion northwards to Galilee must have been part of restoration hopes and the "greater Israel" ideology as referred to in the previous chapter. The Tanak relates that the northern tribes failed to occupy the territories allotted to them (Josh 11:8; 13:4–5; cf. Judg 3:3). When Jonathan campaigned in the north against Demetrius, he went as far as Hammath, situated on the ideal border of the "greater Israel." Freyne (2004:79) explains: "What the northern tribes had failed to accomplish, Jonathan, like a new Joshua, was achieving by military prowess in the name of reclaiming the allotted land." We saw that Eupolemus, akin to Ezekiel, held hopes for an enlarged land. Combined with the military exploits of the Maccabeans as set out in 1 Maccabees, Freyne (2004:79) argues that these samples of writers "indicate that the notion of 'the land remaining' was highly pertinent to the thinking and ideological legitimation of the Hasmonean expansion . . . ." The Phoenicians to the north, and Rome's advance in the east, however, made it impossible to realize the ideal boundaries as articulated by Ezekiel (Freyne 2001:301; 2004:80). But this land ideology, combined with the archaeological evidence for a depopulated Galilee, has led Freyne (2004:62) himself to abandon his earlier position (Freyne 1988:170) of a continued northern Israelite presence in Galilee, and says that by

> the first century CE the successors of these Hasmonean settlers constituted the bulk of Galilean [Judeans], even if other elements, [Judean] and [non-Judean], had entered the mix as a result of the conquests and rule of Herod the Great and his son, Antipas. It is important to acknowledge, therefore, contrary to several modern claims about Galilean opposition to Jerusalem, that there was a strong attachment to the mother-city, its temple

and customs, among Galilean [Judeans] of Jesus' day. (Freyne 2004:82)

The Cultural Continuity between Judea and Galilee

This attachment, as described by Freyne, to Jerusalem, its Temple and customs, is verified by the archaeological record. The "thinking" of the Temple extended to Galilee as well, as will be seen in the investigation to follow. Apart from that, Galilee did experience a measure of Hellenization as well, although it was mostly limited to public architecture, forms of government and the use of the Greek language. No Gentile cultic sites or shrines were present in Galilee during the Late Hellenistic Period. This means that the Hasmoneans did not tolerate Gentile culture, and even the Herodians later showed a general sensitivity to the local people as no "religious" elements characteristic of Roman-Hellenistic culture were present during their tenure.

So what do the archaeological excavations in Galilee tell us about its people's ethnic identity? Importantly, the "Galilean's ethnic identity in the first century can be best determined by examining the material culture inside domestic or private space, since it indicates the populace's behavior and selection of artefacts." Reed (2000:44) continues by saying that the "archaeological artifacts found in Galilean domestic space are remarkably similar to those of Judea." Indeed there are four indicators pointing to a Judean religious, or rather, ethnic identity: 1) the chalk or soft limestone vessels, 2) stepped pools or *miqva'ot*, 3) secondary burial with ossuaries in *loculi* tombs, and 4) bone profiles that lack pork (Reed 2000:44–51; 1999:95–102). The stone vessels indicate a concern for purity as the Mishnah prescribes that vessels made of stone can not contract impurity (*m. Kel.* 10:1). Stone vessels are ubiquitous in Jerusalem and Judea, in Galilee and the Golan. Reina, a village north of Galilee, has also been identified as a centre of production for limestone measuring cups and other vessels (Chancey 2002:68). The stepped pools similarly indicate a concern for ritual purity.[5] As already mentioned in the previous chapter, of the 300 plus *miqva'ot* discovered so far in Palestine,

---

5. According to Kloppenborg (2000:257), *miqva'ot* in Galilee were restricted to places of priestly settlement, a few private homes, and sites identified with oil production. Galileans resisted or ignored an extension of purity practices. Chancey (2002:118) lists Sepphoris and Jotapata as places where *miqva'ot* have been found. Reed (2000:49–51) speaks of *miqva'ot* at Sepphoris, Tiberias, Yodefat, Nazareth, Gamla, Chorazin, Beit Yinam, Beth-Shearim, Har Arbel (?), Khirbet Shema, and Sasa.

they are most frequent in Judea, Galilee and Golan, but only a few have been found along the coast and are basically absent in Samaria. These two indicators, along with secondary burial in *kokhim* or *loculi* tombs were distinctively Judean. The absence of pork in the bone profile is not evidence for Judean (as opposed to northern Israelite) ethnicity in itself, but when combined with the other indicators they form strong evidence for Judean ethnic identity as is also well established for Jerusalem and Judea in our period. The archaeological profile of private space of sites outside Galilee and Golan also lack the four ethnic indicators discussed above. The conclusions for the ethnic identity of Galileans seem to be self-explanatory. So the settlement of Galilee during the Hasmonean period in the first century BCE and the Galilean material culture which match that of Judea

> essentially rules out the possibility that Galileans were descendants of either [northern] Israelites or Itureans. Because of the evidence within domestic space, Hasmonean rule in Galilee should not be construed as a political-economic or administrative veneer over an indigenous Galilean population; wherever archaeologists have excavated, [Judean] religious indicators permeate Galilean domestic space in the Early Roman period. (Reed 2000:53)

This archaeological profile corroborates the understanding that it is more likely that Judeans colonized the Galilee during the Hasmonean expansion (cf. Freyne 2001:299) and/or overwhelmed the few prior inhabitants, regardless of who they were, but the point is that Galilee's population "adhered to or adopted patterns of behavior in private space that is also found in Jerusalem and Judea, so that in terms of ethnicity, the Galileans should be considered [Judean]" (Reed 2000:53). Also the view that Galilee had many Gentiles (e.g., Fitzmyer 1992) must be abandoned. Any significant Gentile presence in the first century is not attested by the archaeological record (Chancey 2002:117–19). This stands in glaring contrast to the surrounding regions.

> Literary sources and archaeological data corroborate each other in the images they suggest of the surrounding regions. These areas were predominantly gentile, though all had [Judean] minorities. The unanimity and clarity of the remains of paganism in these territories starkly contrast with the minimal evidence for paganism within the interior of Galilee itself. (Chancey 2002:165)

Galilee and Judeanism: Other Evidence

Other textual evidence, supplied to us mainly by Josephus, only compliment the understanding that Galileans were ethnic Judeans. For example, the attack of Ptolemy Lathyrus on Asochus, as it is described by Josephus (*Ant.* 13.337–38), suggests that the Sabbath was already observed in Galilee at the beginning of the first century BCE. For now we will only concentrate on some relevant evidence applicable to the first century CE.[6] The examples discussed below have been used by Horsley to show that Galilean behavior was rooted in Northern Israelite traditions, but it will be argued here that they make more sense when seen within the context outlined above.

First, Judas the Galilean, in collaboration with Zaddok the Pharisee, spearheaded a rebellion in response to the requirement of Roman taxes (*War* 2.117–18; *Ant.* 18.1–10), using the slogan "no Master but God." It would be strange for a Pharisee, one who is wholly committed to Judeanism, to cooperate with a Galilean who was not.

Second, a Judean (Ἰουδαῖος) of Galilee by the name of Eleazar, who had a reputation of being very strict when it came to "the ancestral laws," required the circumcision of the king of Adiabene after the latter converted to Judeanism (*Ant.* 20.34–48).

Third, Gischala was evidently the location of the production of olive oil that satisfied the demands of ritual purity. Judeans of Ceasarea-Philippi was supplied as they wanted to avoid Gentile food production (*Life* 74; *War* 2.591–93). This should not be seen as some foreign cultural import into Galilee from the south. When combined with the presence of *miqva'ot*, the stone vessels found all over Galilee, and the fact that Reina was a centre of production for limestone vessels, it demonstrates that purity concerns were a common aspect of life in the region.

Fourth, when Gaius wanted to erect a statue of himself in the Temple in Jerusalem, Judeans and supposedly Galileans as well (Chancey 2002:54) protested by leaving their lands unsown, and so no harvest and payment of tribute would be possible (*Ant.* 18.263–72; *War* 2.192–93). Evidently, the Galileans showed concern for the sanctity of the temple, and certainly far more is involved here than merely making common cause "with the Judeans when faced with a threat to the basic covenantal principles they shared from ancient Israelite tradition"

---

6. Not all the doings of Galileans will therefore be discussed. For example, Antipas' palace was attacked in 66 that contained pictures of animals, but the mob responsible were not necessarily motivated by religious concerns (*Life* 65–66).

(Horsley 1995:71). According to Kloppenborg (2000:227), whose understanding of the Galileans is similar to that of Horsley, Tob 1:6–8 suggests that most Galileans did not participate in pilgrimages. But Josephus takes for granted that a priest representing the temple would have status among Galileans at the outbreak of the revolt, especially so if they have outstanding credentials. Josephus also states that he refused priestly tithes offered to him by the Galileans (*Life* 63, 80, 195–98) (cf. Freyne 2001:300; Chancey 2002:55–56). In addition, Josephus writes that the Galileans visited the temple, "as was their custom" (*Ant.* 20.118; *War* 2.232), suggesting the visits were regular enough from this region. Here Josephus is speaking of some Galileans, or alternatively, only one, that was killed by Samaritans while en route to Jerusalem. It must also be taken into account that a trip from Galilee to Jerusalem would have taken around seven to eight days. A pilgrim staying about a week in Jerusalem would then require a three week period away from home (cf. Sanders 1992:130). Purely for logistical reasons pilgrimage from Galilee on a regular basis would not have been practical. Yet some Galileans did go on pilgrimage,[7] even if they only came "by the hundreds" (Horsley 1995:145), which is being conservative.

We can also add to this that nowhere do the ancient texts suggest that Galileans and Israelite Samaritans ever made common cause against a common ideological enemy, namely, the "Judeans." The hostility between Galileans and Samaritans is properly explained if cultural and ethnic continuity existed between Judea and Galilee.

Fifth, when two renegade royal officials from Agrippa II sought to remain in Sepphoris in 66–67, "the Judeans" (τῶν Ἰουδαίων) demanded that they be circumcised and so conform to the customs of their hosts (*Life* 112–13; 149–54).

Sixth, Josephus dismissed his soldiers for the Sabbath in Taricheae (*Life* 159), in order not to cause offence for the city's residents.

Seventh, Jesus son of Sapphias, the magistrate of Tiberias, took "the laws of Moses" (a Torah scroll) into his hand whom he accused Josephus of betraying. Josephus himself states that he was suspected that his ultimate intention was "to betray the country to the Romans," and that some Galileans attempted to kill him (*Life* 132–48; *War* 2.598–610). Here Galileans were accusing Josephus of betraying "covenantal nomism," or of not being truly Judean. Naturally, the main focus

---

7. The Gospels assume that the Temple was a natural place of worship and pilgrimage for Jesus the Galilean. Luke also mentions some Galileans who were killed by Pilate in Jerusalem (Luke 13:1).

would seem to be that the Roman control of the land is in opposition to the "laws of Moses," an opposition which Josephus is recognised not to uphold.

Eighth, Tiberias boasted a "prayer-house," which was a regular feature of Judean communities in the Diaspora (*Life* 277, 280, 290–303), and to this may be added the existence of a synagogue at Capernaum (Chancey 2002:104).

Horsley's (1995:152–55, 172; cf. Kloppenborg 2000:223–34) subtle hermeneutics in order to illustrate that the above texts of Josephus are not indicative of Galilean Torah observance, that is, of "the laws of the Judeans," is difficult to accept. Rather than merely attesting to basic covenantal traditions common to Israel in general, when seen in conjunction with the overall archaeological profile of Galilee, these texts make perfect sense in that the Galileans shared the same symbolic universe as Judeans to the south. There is a concern for ritual purity, for Judean religion and covenantal praxis, and of course, the land. Also conspicuous by its absence is Horsley's inability to rally any evidence where "the Galileans" give any concrete opposition to the Judean Temple or Torah as religious-cultural institutions. Reed (2000:540) also states that "Josephus's ambiguous use of Galileans contrasts with his unequivocal description of Idumeans, Itureans, and Samarians as non- or half-[Judeans]." As we saw above, Josephus on occasion even refers to Galileans as *Judeans*. And we must also remember that Josephus refers to Judeans as Galileans, Idumeans and Pereans and distinguishes them from Judeans who were born and lived in Judea itself (*War* 2.43ff; cf. *Ant.* 17.254).[8] So even if Josephus refers to the Galileans as an *ethnos* (cf. Horsley's argument above), it does not mean they were not Judean (cf. Esler 2003:72–73).

In addition, as we shall see in the next chapter, the Q source that probably originated in Galilee often freely makes use of Isaiah, Daniel, and the Wisdom traditions that originated in the "south." There was no ideological conflict between Galilee and Judea on a religious or cultural level during our period and the interpreter superimposes it upon the evidence.

Woe to Chorazin, Bethsaida, and Capernaum

We will concentrate on these three towns because they have been plausibly identified as the location for the Q community, Capernaum in

---

8. See introduction, pp. 3–4.

particular (Reed 1995; 1996; 2000). Most of our information is available for Capernaum since it has been subject to extensive archaeological excavations, and is often referred to in the Gospels as the basis of Jesus' ministry.

Chorazin is identified with the site of Khirbet Karaze located in the foothills that rise above the north-eastern shore of the Sea of Galilee. Archaeological excavations performed in the 1980s uncovered next to nothing of the first-century village (Yeivin 1987). It is claimed that a first century *miqveh* and synagogue has been found there (Reed 2000:51, 158; Strange & Shanks 1990), but according to Chancey (2002:105), all finds post-date the time of Jesus. The earliest pottery finds are dated to the late first or early second century CE.

Today Bethsaida is located by archaeologists on et-Tell (the Mound), about two and a half km from the shore of the Sea of Galilee. Luke places the feeding of the five thousand at Bethsaida (Luke 9:12–17). According to Mark Jesus cured a blind man there (Mark 8:22–25) and the location where Jesus walked on water happened close by (Mark 6:45–51). According to John 1:44 (cf. 12:21), Peter, Andrew, and Philip came from Bethsaida. The city was refounded by Herod Philip as the *polis Julias* around 30 CE most probably in honor of the wife of Augustus, Julia-Livia, the mother of Emperor Tiberius (cf. *Ant.* 18.28, which says that Philip renamed the city after the daughter of Augustus). It would have been more Hellenized than the surrounding villages. It is suggested that a Roman style temple has been found there which may have been constructed as part of the renaming ceremony. Two incense shovels have been found near the temple, and combined this evidence suggests that Bethsaida could have been a centre of the Roman imperial cult (Arav & Freund 1997; Arav et al 2000; Hengel 1979:16). Chancey (2002:108) questions this identification as incense shovels can be found in buildings other than temples and states that no cultic objects, altar or dedicatory inscriptions have been found. Generally, archaeological excavations have illustrated that Bethsaida was far more modest in stature and wealth than other Herodian cities, including Philip's own Caesarea located at the springs of the Jordan River. According to Chancey (2002:108), the archaeological finds do not tell us much whether the city's inhabitants were Judean or Gentile. The Gospel texts infer that many Judeans were resident in Bethsaida and its surrounding villages and were culturally orientated towards Galilee. One must therefore consider that a lot of interaction took place between the Judeans of Bethsaida and Galilee, in particular Capernaum (Reed 2000:146, 184).

Capernaum, also known as Kefar Nahum ("village of Nahum"), appears frequently in the Gospels and is portrayed as the centre of Jesus' ministry. In Q (7:1), it is the only named place where a saying or act of Jesus takes place. In Mark, it is the scene of Jesus' first miracle (Mark 1:21), and thereafter it describes Jesus as being "at home" in Capernaum (Mark 2:1; 9:33). Matthew similarly states that Jesus "settled down" there (Matt 4:13) and calls it "his own city" (Matt 9:1). In Luke, Capernaum is recognized as an important center for Jesus' miracles (Luke 4:23), while the Gospel of John has Jesus stay in Capernaum for a few days after the miracle in Cana (John 2:12). He further healed the centurion's child there (John 4:46), withdrew to it and was sought by the crowds in Capernaum (John 6:17, 24), and John also has Jesus teaching in the synagogue (John 6:59). Other than this the Gospels say that fishermen lived there (Matt 4:12–22), suggest that a tollhouse was there (Mark 2:13–14; see with Mark 2:1), and make it the location of a "centurion" (Q 7:1–10; John 4:46–54).

Archaeologically there is no evidence of occupation for the site in the Iron II—Iron III Ages (1000–587 BCE), and the first significant evidence date to the Late Hellenistic Period, at the end of the second century BCE. This coincides with the rise in settlements during the Hasmonean expansion or colonization of Galilee. Capernaum, along with other Judean villages, formed a bridge of settlements ranging from Galilee, across the Jordan into the Golan, which was surrounded by Gentile settlements and cities. "To the north, Itureans inhabited the mountainous regions of the Hauran and at the foot of Mount Hermon, and Syro-Phoenicians (Tyrians) had settled in the Huleh Valley and north of Upper Galilee; on the eastern shore of the lake were the territories of the Decapolis cities of Hippos and Gadara" (Reed 2000:145). During the reign of Herod the Great these diverse ethnic groups and cities to the north and east of the lake were united into a single political kingdom. Thereafter Philip, with the exception of the Decapolis cities, inherited the multi-ethnic area, including Judeans, to the east of the Jordan while Antipas received the Judean Galilee (*War* 2.94–100). The Jordan so formed both a natural and political boundary between the territories of Philip and Antipas. Capernaum was therefore the closest site to Philip's territory, located about 4 km from the Jordan River and the residents must have interacted often with Judeans from Philip's territory (see above).

Interregional traffic through Capernaum, including Gentiles, would have increased with the founding of Tiberias in 18 CE and Bethsaida in 30 CE, so enhancing its role in the regional economy (Reed 2000:146–48). Laughlin (1993) points to the possibility of a first-century bathhouse, which may confirm the existence of a Roman centurion and garrison at Capernaum. He also argues that the village, of about 1,000 people, was quite prosperous while being home to Judeans as well as Gentiles. It is not clear whether the Gentiles are the Romans already mentioned or others. But overall the archaeological evidence does not support the presence of Roman troops or many Gentiles in Capernaum, especially in the first century. The Roman-style bathhouse has been dated to the second century CE, and evidence for Roman Legionnaires at Capernaum dates to long after the First Revolt (Reed 2000:155–56).

Overall Capernaum lacks centralized planning, illustrating organic growth. Reed (2000:152) estimates that it would have had a population of between 600 to 1,500 people. The little evidence available for the archaeology of public and private space suggests that the inhabitants of Capernaum were Judean (Reed 2000:152–60). Most of the houses are clustered by threes or fours around a central courtyard utilising crude construction with local basalt stones and boulders and the roofs would have been made of thatched reeds (cf. Mark 2:5). There are no buildings typical of a Roman-Hellenistic city and no evidence for expensive decorative elements. Neither are Gentile artefacts found connected to shrines and temples. The pottery is mostly common and each and every domestic unit revealed stone vessels, indicating concerns for purity. No *miqva'ot* have been found at Capernaum, but according to Reed (2000:50, 157–58) this can be attributed to the fact that the lake could be used for suitable immersion (*m. Mik.* 1:1; 1:6)—indeed, with the exception of Tiberias, there is virtually a complete absence of immersion pools around the shore of the lake (Reich 1990). Also, where *miqva'ot* have been found in homes, they are restricted to the more wealthier urban homes in Jerusalem and Sepphoris. In the villages or rural areas immersion pools are more public in nature, sometimes attached to synagogues (e.g., Gamla and Chorazin) or near olive press installations (e.g., Mansur el-Aqeb, Gamla and Yodefat) (cf. Kloppenborg 2000:231–34), indicative of the socio-economic status of the resident Judeans. One may also suspect that with the lake providing suitable water for ritual immersion, "the arduous task of digging through basalt ground would diminish a family's interest in having a private [*miqveh*]" (Reed 2000:158). Besides the scholarly scepticism that exists, it is accepted here that Capernaum had a synagogue building as well (cf. Strange & Shanks 1990; Chancey 2002:104; Luke 7:5).

Sepphoris and Tiberias

In this section various aspects of these two cities will be discussed. Sepphoris and Tiberias had both a religio-political and socio-economic impact on Galilee, and both led to tensions that flared up before and during the Great Revolt.

Sepphoris had already been Galilee's most important city. When the Romans took control of Palestine, Gabinius, the Roman proconsul of Syria, made it a centre for one of the five Judean councils in 63 BCE. Located in Lower Galilee it was perched on a hill "like a little bird" (Hebrew, *Zippori*; *b. Meg.* 6a). After the death of Herod the Great, whose reign was met with fierce resistance in Galilee (*War* 1.315–16; *Ant.* 14.432–33),[9] Judas the Galilean, the son of the bandit leader Hezekiah (who was killed by Herod the Great), led an insurrection against Roman-backed rule. Judas armed his group with weapons from Sepphoris' armory (*Ant.* 17.271; cf. *War* 2.56).[10] Judas' revolt was widely supported in Galilee and in retaliation, the Roman legate Varus destroyed the city and sold its inhabitants into slavery in 4 BCE for their role in the rebellion (*Ant.* 17.288–89; *War* 2.68–69). The archaeological evidence, however, does not support Josephus' claim that the city was destroyed and burned (Meyers 1999:114). Herod Antipas (4 BCE—39 CE), the new ruler of Galilee,[11] then rebuilt Sepphoris as the "ornament of all Galilee" and renamed it Autocratoris ("Imperial/Capital City") and made it his capital (*Ant.* 18.27). The Greek word for ornament (πρόσχημα) does not only imply beauty, but also has a military connotation, suggesting a fortification or impregnable city. Antipas then built a new capital, Tiberias, on the site of a graveyard on the western shore of the lake in 18 CE (*Ant.* 18.37–38). Josephus explains that Antipas

9. Even those who went over to Herod (*Ant.* 14.395), probably Hasmonean officers, were drowned by the Galileans in the lake (*Ant.* 14.450) (Horsley 1995:139).

10. Some Galileans also went to Jerusalem during the festival of Pentecost to join the protests in Jerusalem after Herod's death (*Ant.* 17.254–55; *War* 2.42–44).

11. After Herod Antipas, Galilee was ruled by Agrippa I (39–44 CE), where after a series of Roman governors followed: Cuspius Fadus (44–45); the Alexandrian Judean Tiberius Alexander (46–48); Cumanus (49–52); Felix (52–59); Festus (60–62); Albinus (62–64); Florus (64–66). But Nero transferred eastern Galilee around Taricheae and Tiberius to Agrippa II in 54 CE.

forced peasants from the surrounding villages and countryside to live in the new capital or otherwise offered people land. This also illustrates that the local population was Judean as they did not desire to be in a constant state of ritual impurity. These two cities were quite foreign culturally as the client ruler of the Romans demonstrated his cultural orientation by building them introducing Roman city planning as well as Roman-Hellenistic architecture—this is something that Galilee never experienced before. In Sepphoris, two main perpendicular streets have been uncovered, the north-south *cardo* (colonnaded main street) and the east west *decumanus*. The *cardo* in Tiberias is also indicative of Roman city planning (Reed 2000:90–91). The buildings and decorative elements used within the cities also represented Roman-Hellenistic culture. Since more information is available for Sepphoris, the investigation will focus on this city.

First of all, we will look at its public architecture in further detail. Sepphoris had a basilical building, and perhaps a bathhouse. Some interiors of buildings were decorated with frescoes. Yet at the same time some typical features of a Roman city are entirely absent (Reed 2000:95, 117–24; Chancey 2001:136; 2002:77). There is no evidence in the first century for a hippodrome, amphitheatre or circus, stadium, gymnasium, odeons, nymphaea, statues, monuments and temples typical of Roman cities. In relation to this it can be mentioned that the coins that were minted at Sepphoris in 68 CE to illustrate its peaceful intentions during the revolt bear no pagan, or rather, Gentile motifs. This is similar to the coins that were minted by Antipas in Tiberias (Chancey 2002:91). The theatre probably dates to the late first or early second century CE (Chancey & Meyers 2000:24; Chancey 2002:75). Aqueducts brought water to Sepphoris, but this was of the more humble type, which were cut into the bedrock (Tsuk 2000). As can be seen from the above, Jerusalem, the geographical centre of the Judean symbolic universe, was far more Hellenized architecturally than Sepphoris.

Public architecture is of course more instructive as to the ruler's cultural orientation than that of the ordinary people (Reed 2000:43). That is why the archaeology of private space needs to be investigated. Archaeological investigations have revealed that Sepphoris was overwhelmingly inhabited by Judeans (Chancey 2001; 2002:79–80).[12] The

---

12. Cf. Horsley (1995:168) who argued that there is "little concrete evidence for Judean presence and culture in Sepphoris in the first century." But rabbinic traditions also preserve memories of Sepphorean priests that participated in the temple cult (*t. Yom.* 1:4; *t. Sot.* 13:7; *m. Yom.* 6:3).

four religious indicators found all over Galilee are also present in the excavations conducted in Sepphoris. The inhabitants avoided eating pork, *miqva'ot* have been found,[13] as well as stone vessels, and burial was in *kokhim* or *loculi* tombs with ossuaries. Objections have been raised that the pools in Sepphoris be identified as *miqva'ot* (Eshel 2000), but it seems to be generally accepted that the pools are such (Meyers 2000; Reich 2002).

Batey (1992) points out correctly that the setting of Jesus' upbringing and ministry was more urban and sophisticated than previously thought, but he was incorrect to say that Sepphoris was cosmopolitan with a mixed population of Judeans, Arabs, Greeks and Romans. Contrary to this opinion held by some earlier, Sepphoris was a Judean city, although it did have some Roman-Hellenistic features especially in its public architecture and forms of government. So in terms of religious and ethnic indicators, although the people of Sepphoris would have been more "Hellenized" than rural Galileans, cultural continuity existed between the villages and the city (Reed 2000:117–38).[14]

Besides their religio-political impact, the construction of Sepphoris and Tiberias had quite a dramatic socio–economic affect in Galilee. Traditionally, Galilee was made up of small villages and hamlets from which peasant families worked their land. As with the rest of Palestine, Galilee was therefore a traditional agrarian society (*Apion* 1.60). With the construction of these two cities the demographics of Galilee changed dramatically over the course of a single generation. As consumer cities, Sepphoris and Tiberias centred agriculture onto themselves, and as bases for the ruling and social elite, exacted rents or taxes from the countryside.[15] Reed (2000:80, 82) estimates that Sepphoris had a popu-

13. Cf. Sawicki (2000:99), who suggests that the presence of *miqva'ot* in Sepphoris may suggest that the residents "routinely incurred ritual impurity every day when they visited the municipal baths, but just as routinely grounded themselves in the right kind of water when they returned home to a Jewish house." Intriguing is her suggestion that Judean water architecture was a response to Roman water architecture such as aqueducts, public baths and decorative pools. As such the *miqveh* was a technology of symbolic resistance, "designed to correct the disruption of the circulation patterns for 'fluids' (water, food, caste, labor, ethnic identity) and 'containers' (women, men, pots) that the Romans had wrought..." (Sawicki 2000:99–101).

14. According to Reed (2000:135) theories of Greek education or Cynic philosophical schools at Sepphoris are therefore implausible since the city was not home to a significant number of Romans or Greeks.

15. Horsley (1995:218–19) suggests the Galileans were subject to pay tribute to three layers of rulers (tithes and offerings for the priesthood in the temple, Herodian taxation, and Roman tribute) which together amounted to over one-third of their crops.

lation of around 8,000 to 12,000 inhabitants; Tiberias that of between 6,000 to 12,000 inhabitants. Self-sufficiency and subsistence of peasant farmers had to give way to paying tribute and taxes to support the administration, construction and population growth of these cities. Not having enough food left until the next harvest, at least some peasant farmers had to make loans and so became gripped by indebtedness. With time they were increasingly controlled by their creditors, some becoming their tenants, or they lost their land entirely, with some becoming day laborers, beggars or even bandits. But the extent should not be exaggerated, for Richardson (2004:26) points out that rural towns and villages increased in number and size during this period of urbanization. In a similar vein Freyne (1988:165–66) has argued that the level of oppression in Galilee was not on the level of that in Judea, and banditry, located on the border regions, was not a dominant feature of Galilean life in the first century. Neither do we hear of a destruction of debt records at Sephhoris such as occurred in Jerusalem.[16] Even so, tense urban-rural relations did exist which flared up during the Great Revolt, which will be further discussed below (Reed 2000:66–93; Horsley 1995:215–21). As with the Judean peasant farmers in the south, the economic control of the land and its produce by the Galilean urban elite must have been a violation of what impoverished Galilean peasants thought was theirs by virtue of the covenant. No wonder the imperial granaries were a source of dissatisfaction (*Life* 71, 118). Acts 12:20 also mentions that Agrippa I sold food to the coastal cities of Tyre and Sidon. These Roman-Hellenistic style cities, regardless of their Judean inhabitants, then much like Jerusalem symbolized social and economic control by the elite in collaboration with the Romans.

Hellenization and the Use of Greek in Galilee

In addition to the architectural character of Sepphoris and Tiberias, Hellenization would have occurred due to the fact that Galilee was completely surrounded by Hellenistic cities. Acco-Ptolemais, Tyre and Sidon was located to the west and north-west, Panias-Caesarea Philippi, Hippos and Gadara to the north-east, east and south-east, and Scythopolis and Gaba to the south (cf. Hengel 1989:14–15). It is even claimed that Galilee had a "genuinely cosmopolitan flavour" based

---

For more on this, see the previous chapter.

16. Although it could have been part of the intention of the Galileans when they tried to burn down Sepphoris at the beginning of the Great Revolt (*Life* 38, 375).

on its supposed economic ties with these regions (Porter 1994:135), but based on the analysis above, such a view is questionable. Several of these cities were recently founded or refounded in the Early Hellenistic period. Ptolemeis, Galilee's nearest port, was refounded as a *polis*. On the periphery of Galilee several *poleis* were founded, including the Decapolis cities of Scythopolis, Hippos and Gadara. Naturally Gentile religion and customs came with it. For example, Scythopolis (Beth Shean) had two altars, one dedicated to Dionysus and the other to Serapis (Tsafrir 1990). Once part of the Hasmonean kingdom, which did not tolerate most aspects of Gentile culture, these cities were restored to their Gentile inhabitants when the Romans invaded Palestine. As such, the Hellenistic culture of these cities again surrounded Galilee in the first centuries BCE and CE. These cities, however, and in particular Scythopolis had sizeable Judean minorities, therefore living in a dominant Gentile culture. Horsley (1995:161–63) suggests that these surrounding cities had little cultural influence on Galilee, which came more from the local two cities which came to prominence during the rule of Antipas. But even in Chabulon, so Josephus suggests, there were houses that imitated the Hellenistic style of Tyre, Sidon, and Berytus (*War* 2.504).

Based on the broader pattern identified in the previous chapter, however, the adoption of the Greek *language* by Judeans in Galilee must have also been in progress, and certainly the Gentile cities on the periphery of Galilee, and the two major cities located in Lower Galilee itself played their part in this process. Porter (1994:133) argues that "the evidence supports the idea that, besides their being a sizable number of first-language Greek speakers, there were a large and significant number of bilingual Palestinians especially in Galilee who had productive (not merely passive) competence in Greek and may even on occasion have preferred their acquired language, Greek, to their first language, Aramaic." Porter bases his argument firstly on the geography of Galilee that was surrounded by Hellenistic culture. Second, the epigraphic and literary evidence points to the widespread use of Greek in Palestine, including Galilee (see previous chapter). Greek would have been the language of administration in Sepphoris and Tiberias. The centre of the fishing industry in Galilee had a Greek name, Taricheae (the Judean Magdala). Reed (2000:134) suggests that the more "Hellenized" Judeans of Sepphoris (we can add Tiberias as well) would have operated in a more bilingual atmosphere and so much of their life would have operated in Greek, while the rural areas would have tended to be pronouncedly Aramaic.[17] According to Chancey & Meyers (2000:33), however, there is very little evidence for the use of Greek before and during the time of Jesus. The first century evidence is as follows: (1) the Greek inscriptions on coins minted by Antipas, Agrippa I, and at Sepphoris during the Great Revolt; (2) inscriptions in Greek on two market weights, probably from Tiberias; and (3) an inscription near Nazareth, dating to the mid-first century CE, which warns against grave robbing. The hundreds of Greek inscriptions found at the Judean tomb complexes of Beth Shearim in south-western Galilee date mostly to the third-century CE and later. In fact, Chancey (2002:109) states that "only a few of the village's tombs date to the first century CE, and these do not contain inscriptions." Horsley states that recent surveys of inscriptions at seventeen sites along the western shore of the lake and in southern Lower Galilee found around 40 per cent in Greek, 40 per cent in Hebrew, and more than 50 per cent in Aramaic, suggesting "that some people of Lower Galilee were bilingual, knowing some Greek as well as Aramaic and/or Hebrew" (Horsley 1995:248). Otherwise very few inscriptions in Upper Galilee have been found in Greek, where Aramaic and/or Hebrew must have been more dominant.

From the above it may be concluded that Greek did penetrate Galilee to varying degrees. This is true for the interior, especially Lower Galilee. The same can be inferred for the towns and villages on the outskirts of Galilee. For example, Beth Shearim, compared with other Galilean sites, was in close contact with Hellenistic cities such as Ptolemais. A similar situation is true of Capernaum, a likely location for Q, which was most probably written in Greek (see next chapter).

Galilee During and After the Great Revolt

It is noticeable that the same religio-political and socio-revolutionary dynamics identified in the previous chapter that centred on Jerusalem also affected Galilee during the Great Revolt (66–70 CE). Once can say that Galilee was almost a dress rehearsal for what happened later in Jerusalem. Josephus was sent to Galilee by the council formed in Jerusalem to organize the region's defences, or more likely, to convince

17. Evidently the Galileans had a peculiar Aramaic accent (Matt 26:73), something also hinted at in the Talmud (Vermes 1973). According to the Talmud, a Galilean went to the marketplace and asked for something called *amar*. The merchants ridiculed him by replying: "You stupid Galilean, do you want something to ride on (a donkey = $ḥ^amār$)? Or something to drink (wine = $ḥ^amar$)? Or something for clothing (wool = $ʿ^amar$)? Or something for a sacrifice (lamb = $ʾimmar$)?" (*b. ʿErub.* 53b).

them to cease their rebellion. As a result, he was an eye witness to many of the events that transpired in Galilee, taking into account possible exaggerations and his self-serving interests in his various accounts.

First, the tense urban-rural relations that existed came to a head in this period. Sepphorites and (upperclass) Tiberians were prime targets for rural Galileans (*Life* 384). Sepphoris was attacked twice who even hired the bandit Jesus and his followers for protection (*Life* 104–11). Besides the negative economic impact that Sepphoris had, the city was probably also attacked for its pacifist stance during the revolt (*War* 2.574–75; 3.61–62; *Life* 348, 373–80). Early on, the city admitted a garrison of Caesennius Gallus' soldiers (*War* 2.511; *Life* 394), and later it accepted troops of Vespasian (*War* 3.31; *Life* 411). Coins minted during this period describes Sepphoris as a "City of Peace" (Chancey & Meyers 2000:33), which concurs with Josephus' statement that the city's people "thinks peace" (*War* 3.31). Josephus also states that the people of Sepphoris failed to defend the temple "common to us all" (*Life* 348).

At Tiberias, the local residents, some sailors and the poor, joined forces with Galileans under the leadership of Jesus son of Sapphias, the city magistrate, and burned and looted the royal palace and killed "all the Greeks"—probably Syro-Phoenicians from the coast or Tyrian Plain. Afterwards Jesus and his followers led the active resistance at Tiberias and then at Taricheae, whose inhabitants we are told did not want to fight (*War* 3.492, 500–501).

Gischala, located in Upper Galilee was attacked by the people from Gabara, Sogane, Tyre and Gadara, who attacked them in return (*Life* 44). Later Gabara and Gischala formed an alliance. Presumaby Gabara had similar problems with the peasants in their district as had Sepphoris and Tiberias (Horsley 1995:80). Gischala was under the leadership of John ben Levi, who later became Josephus' most important rival for control of Galilee. It must be remembered that Josephus describes John as a not so observant Levite (*War* 7.264), which nevertheless, still makes him a Judean!

As with the situation in Jerusalem later on, internal conflict had to refocus on the advance of the Roman army. Galilee was the first area of reconquest for the Romans during the first revolt. First on the Roman path of destruction were places like Chabulon (*War* 2.503–5; *Life* 213–14) and Gabara and the surrounding villages. At Gabara there was no one who offered armed resistance, but Vespasian killed all the men and burned all the surrounding villages and towns (*War* 3.132–34). When the Romans finally sent troops to protect Sepphoris, it was used as a basis to subdue the surrounding villages and countryside. Roman infantry and cavalry enslaved and killed many in the process (*War* 3.59–63, 110). Jotapata, after a long siege, fell around June/July 67 CE. It should also be noted that Josephus describes the defenders of Jotapata as Ἰουδαῖοι (Chancey 2002:88). The inhabitants were killed or taken into slavery while the city itself was destroyed (*War* 3.141–288, 316–408). At Japha close to Nazareth, the Galileans even advanced to meet the Romans (*War* 3.289–306). Tiberias opened its gates to the Romans, who then took Taricheae (*War* 3.492–502), Gamla, located in the Golan Heights (*War* 4.1–83), and Gischala (*War* 4.84–120), who surrendered peacefully after John of Gischala escaped from the city. At Mount Tabor many offered resistance to the Roman reconquest (*War* 4.54–61) but to no avail. Vespasian had control of Galilee by the end of 67 (Jagersma 1986:141).

Horsley (1995:87–88) places great stock in the fact that the Galileans were continuously suspicious of Josephus and that the high priestly-Pharisaic council in Jerusalem could not assert their authority in Galilee during the Great Revolt. This can not be used as evidence, however, that the Galileans were not Judeans and were striving for independence. Even those of Judea were suspicious of some of their priests in Jerusalem and even killed them. It is also noticeable that nowhere are there reports in Josephus' accounts that "the Galileans" attacked any local "Judeans."They attacked the Greeks in Tiberias and also participated in conflicts with Gentiles in the regions surrounding Galilee (Chancey 2002:56, 132). After Galilee was taken by the Romans, some Galileans even went to Jerusalem to join the resistance there. It is difficult to see how in all of this that there was any attempt to assert independence from Jerusalem or Judeanism ("the laws of the Judeans"). In addition, based on the account given by Josephus, there were no extensive struggle between Galileans and Gentiles within Galilee, undermining any hypothesis that many Gentiles were present within Galilee itself. As already mentioned, there was fighting between Galileans and Gentiles in the surrounding territories (Chancey 2002:132). In addition, the cities of Scythopolis, Hippos, Gadara, and Damascus killed many of their own Judean inhabitants while Gerasa refrained from doing so (*War* 2.457–80). We can assume that a lot of ethnic tension lurked beneath the surface that exploded in indignation during the revolt. Can we extrapolate from the review of the evidence that Galileans were also in pursuit of the millennium? It would seem to be the case, although some, such as the people of Sepphoris, the "city of peace," preferred a more pragmatic approach to the revolt.

After the revolt, the western part of Galilee continued to be governed directly by the Romans as part of the province of Judea. The region around the lake was given back to Agrippa II, but after his death it also came under Roman jurisdiction. Evidently much of the land remained in the hands of Galilean peasants that remained, as it appears that Galilee was not taken as imperial land after the revolt of 66–67 (Horsley 1995:90–91). The Sixth Legion (Legio VI Ferrata) was reassigned from Syria to Galilee from around 120 CE and cohorts were stationed at Tiberias, Sepphoris, and Legio. Rome was to make its unwelcome control of the region permanent. The pacifist stance of Sepphoris during the revolt was rewarded with close relations with Rome and by the time of Hadrian or Antoninus Pius it adopted the official name Diocaesarea (i.e. dedicated to the imperial Zeus, or "City of Zeus-Caesar") (Horsley 1995:93, 165; Reed 2000:101; Chancey 2002:59–60).

After the assembly of Judean sages and priests at Yavneh, Lydda and Joppa in the wake of the Great Revolt (66–70 CE), some rabbinic schools appear to have taken shape at Usha and Beth Shearim in western Lower Galilee after the Bar Kokhba Revolt. Thereafter, around 200 CE, they established themselves more prominently in Sepphoris and Tiberias. With time Galilee became the centre of rabbinic activity, and eventually, the nucleus of rabbinic Judaism. But even when the Mishnah was compiled (200 CE), the rabbis did not provide leadership or did not have any substantial influence over the region (Horsley 1995:90–99, 181).

Conclusions

Based on the overview, it seems clear enough that the overwhelming majority of first century Galileans would have operated within the exclusive realm of covenantal nomism. They shared the same symbolic universe as those Judeans that lived within Judea. Some evidently adopted the Greek language, yet their consciousness of difference vis-à-vis other peoples were objectified in the same religious and cultural practices. Based on Josephus, they observed the Sabbath, practiced circumcision, and went to Jerusalem on pilgrimage and were committed to the Torah. Tiberias had a prayer-house while it is accepted that Capernaum had a synagogue building. Otherwise Galilean religion and covenantal praxis are concretely expressed by the archaeological profile of private space, which is similar to that of Jerusalem and Judea. A concern for purity is evident in the discovery of *miqva'ot*, while stone vessels are ubiquitous throughout Galilee. Secondary burial with ossuaries is a further marker of distinct Judean religious practices, which is complimented by the bone profile that lacks pork. This profile is applicable to both the urban and rural areas of Galilee, although the cities of Sepphoris and Tiberias were more Hellenized in terms of its public architecture. But overall, the "thinking" of the temple was also operating in Galilee.

When it comes to the land, the Hasmonean expansion to the north coincided with the "greater Israel" ideology. With the northern Israelite population deported after the conquest by Assyria, the increase in settlements and overall population growth during the Hasmonean period suggests that most of the first century Galileans were descendants of Judeans that moved to the region during the period of Hasmonean expansion. Importantly, Galileans, like their co-ethnics to the south, lived on the same ancestral land of Israel. The Galileans would therefore have had the same ancestry and historical memories as those living in Judea dating back to the Maccabean revolt, including the rule of the Diadochoi, the Babylonian Exile and beyond. They lived under the same "sacred canopy," which would have given rise to hopes of restoration. Overall, the evidence combines to suggest that from the Hasmonean annexation of the territory, Judeans dominated the region (Chancey 2002:62). "Galilean [Judeans] had a different social, economic and political matrix than [Judeans] living in Judea or the Diaspora ... but they all were [Judean]" (Reed 2000:55).

CHAPTER 5

Judean Ethnicity in Q

Introduction

IN THE first chapter the attempt was made to demonstrate that scholarship on the historical Jesus fails to place Jesus' Judeanness into an overall interpretive framework. What kind of Judean Jesus was cannot be answered comprehensively. In chapter two a model was developed that attempts to correct this shortcoming, and in the process to set some guidelines for a common Judeanism, where Judeanism was also primarily understood as an ethnic identity. In chapter 3 we did an overview of what Judean identity involved in the first century, and discussed some historical developments that led up to it. In the overview of Galilee in chapter 4, I drew the conclusion that there was a fundamental continuity between the people of Galilee and that of Judea. The Galileans were ethnic Judeans, and so would also have operated within that exclusive realm of covenantal nomism.

The previous chapters therefore served as preparatory, yet essential work for what we will attempt to accomplish here. We need to answer the question: What kind of Judeans were the Q people? Studies into Q, however, are complicated by proposed redactional stages and what to include in its overall reconstruction. It is therefore necessary to first establish the approach to Q before we can proceed with the investigation.

The Approach to Q

The most commonly accepted solution for the Synoptic Problem is the Two Document hypothesis.[1] The solution proposes that Matthew and

---

1. There have been recent objections to the Q hypothesis (Goodacre 2002; Goodacre & Perrin 2004; cf. Kloppenborg's [2003] response). Alternatives to the Two

Luke independently made use of Mark, and a source mostly consisting of sayings of Jesus. This latter source is referred to as "Q" (from the German "*Quelle*," "source"). The content of Q is therefore determined mostly by (1) material only found in Matthew or Luke (the double tradition), and by (2) material that has triple attestation but where the agreement of Matthew and Luke over and against Mark is substantial (Kloppenborg 2000:92). Some material found also in Mark has been suggested to be part of Q^2, and lastly, also some traditions that are singly attested (*Sondergut*) in either Matthew or Luke.[3] What of these expansions should be included, however, varies amongst scholars. Kloppenborg (2000:99–100) argues that a judicious and rigorous application of principles to determine inclusion in Q would expand Q from 235 to 264 verses, although Kloppenborg himself regards some of these expansions to Q as doubtful. Here follows the generally proposed content of Q as taken from Kloppenborg:

The Content of Q (with Expansions)

Sigla: 3:7b–9 = Highly Probable;
3:(3) = Probable;
<3:21–22> = Doubtful

3:(3) Setting of John's Preaching	11:33–35 (36) Lamp; Sayings on Light
3:7b–9 John's Preaching of Repentance	11:39–44, 46–52 Woes against Pharisees and Lawyers
3:16b–17 The Coming One	12:2–12 Fearless Confession
<3:21–22> <The Baptism of Jesus>	12:(13–14, 16–21) Divider; Rich Fool
4:1–13 The Temptations	12:22b–31, 33–34 On Anxiety over Life

Document hypothesis are the Griesbach, "Augustine," and Farrer-Goulder hypothesis. The Griesbach (Two Gospel) hypothesis suggests that Luke is directly dependent on Matthew, and Mark is a conflation of both. The "Augustine" hypothesis suggests that Matthew is the earliest gospel, with Luke being dependent on both Matthew and Mark. The Farrer-Goulder solution (revived by Goodacre) agrees with Markan priority, but also that Matthew and Luke used Mark, and that Luke used Matthew (Kloppenborg 2000:38–43; Tuckett 1996:1–7).

2. Luke 3:2–4; 3:21–22; 4:16–30; 10:25–28; 12:1b; 17:2; 17:31 (Kloppenborg 2000:93).

3. E.g., Luke 15:8–10; Matt 5:41.

4:(16a) Reference to Nazara	12:<35–38>, 39–40 <Watch for the Son of Man>
6:20a Introduction to Sermon	12:42b–46 Faithful and Unfaithful Servants
6:20b–23 Beatitudes	12:49, 51–53 On Divisions
6:(24–26) Woes	12:54–56 Weather Signs/Signs of the Times
6:27–33 On Retaliation; Generous Giving; Golden Rule	12:58–59 Settle with a Creditor
(Q/Matt 5:41) Go the Second Mile	13:18–19, 20–21 Parables of the Mustard Seed and the Leaven
6:(34–35b), 35c Conclusion	13:24, (25), 26–27 The Two Ways; Closed Door
6:36–37b, 38c On Mercy and Judging	13:28–29, 30 Many Will Come from East and West
6:39–45 On Self-Correction	13:34–35 Lament Over Jerusalem
6:46 Why Do You Call Me Lord?	14:<5> <A Sheep Who Falls into a Pit on the Sabbath>
6:46–49 The Two House Builders	14:11/18:14 Exalting the Humble
7:1b–2, 6b–10 The Centurion at Capernaum	14:16–24 The Feast
7:18–19, 22–23 John's Question	14:26–27; 17:33 Three Discipleship Sayings
7:24–28 Jesus' Eulogy of John	14:34–35 Savorless Salt
7:(29–30) John, Tax Collectors, and Prostitutes	15:4–7 The Lost Sheep
7:31–35 Children in the Agora	15:(8–10) The Lost Drachma
9:57–60, (61–62) Two (Three?) Volunteers	16:13 God and Mammon
10:2–16 Mission Instructions	16:16 The Kingdom Suffers Violence
10:21–22 Thanksgiving for Revelation	16:17–18 The Torah; Divorce
10:23b–24 Commendation of Disciples	17:1b–2 On Scandals
<Matt 10:5b–6, 23> <Limiting the Mission to Israel>	17:3b–4 Forgiveness

The Content of Q (with Expansions) (*continued*)

<10:25–28> <The Great Command>	17:6b Faith like a Mustard Seed
11:2–4, <5–8> The Lord's Prayer, <Midnight Friend>	17:<7–10> <Unprofitable Servants>
11:9–13 Sayings on Prayer	17:(20–21) (The Kingdom and Signs)
11:14–20 The Beelzebul Controversy	17:23–24, 37b The Coming of the Son of Man
11:(21–22) Binding the Strong Man	17:26–27 The Days of Noah
11:23 Whoever Is Not Against Me	17:(28–29), 30 The Days of Lot
11:24–26 Return of the Evil Spirit	17:34–35 Two in a Field; Two at the Grindstone
11:(27–28) A Woman in the Crowd	19:12–13, 15b–26 The Entrusted Money
11:29–32 Request for a Sign	22:28–30 Judging the Twelve Tribes

It has basically been accepted that Q was a written document based on three observations: "(1) the near-verbatim agreement between Matthew and Luke in certain double tradition pericopae; (2) the significant amount of sequential agreement between Matthew and Luke in some portions of the double tradition; and (3) the use by Matthew and Luke of the same unusual phrases or words" (Kloppenborg 2000:56). This "written document" or "oral-derived text" (Horsley & Draper 1999), now embedded in Matthew and Luke, and the community it presupposes, will be the focus of study into the question of ethnic identity. It must be mentioned, however, that an investigation into the history and complexities of Q's reconstruction will not be conducted here. The literature is vast and will divert us from the principle aim where we seek to answer the following: What can the Q document tell us about the Judean ethnicity of the people for whom it was written? So the use of the hypothetical Q source will—in addition to the work of Kloppenborg—also be heavily reliant on the work of the International Q Project (IQP) (Robinson, Hoffmann & Kloppenborg 2002), and all Q texts referred to and quoted here are indebted to their important work that represents some form of broad consensus.

So the principle aim of the work on Q is to investigate the Judean ethnicity of the Q people. What kind of Judeans were they? Before we can answer this question in detail, however, we first will have a look at the issue of Q's compositional history, investigating in particular the proposed stratification of Kloppenborg. This is necessary in order to define the approach to Q and to see whether a diachronic approach to the analysis is necessary, as opposed to a more "simple" synchronic analysis. Secondly, the proposed date of composition (or various stages of redaction) and Q's provenance will briefly be investigated.

A Stratified Q?

There are a number of scholars that propose that Q was edited over various stages of its history before it made its way into Matthew and Luke. Kloppenborg likewise conceives of Q as consisting of various stratums, that is, texts were added to the original document at various stages of redaction. For now the focus will be on his stratigraphy since it seems to have been the most influential. This "stratigraphy" as Kloppenborg notes can be a bit misleading, since "the analogy of archaeology is not completely apposite." Kloppenborg (2000:117) clarifies:

> To be sure, the archaeologist discerns the history of the tell by proceeding from the top down, reconstructing the history of the tell by proceeding from its most recent stages of occupation to its most ancient, rather than working upwards from its earliest to its latest strata. Yet with literary documents we are not dealing with physically discreet layers but rather with the incorporation of smaller literary units or stages into larger ones.

Of course, to view the Q document as consisting of various layers or stratums, it presupposes an underlying diachronic approach to the text. In essence, Kloppenborg views Q as an *expanded instruction*. He achieves this result by working "backwards," from the macro structural features of Q to the smaller sayings complexes and sayings clusters. Kloppenborg (2000:143 cf. 118–22) at first identifies major redactional themes, and argues that Q was framed by motifs of judgement, polemic against "this generation," a Deuteronomistic understanding of history, and allusions to the story of Lot.[4] These motifs appear both at the beginning and

---

4. Apart from the allusions to the story of Lot, the main redactional themes listed here were already incipient or explicit in Kloppenborg's (1987) earlier work. But when seen in combination with Kloppenborg's socio-rhetorical analysis of Q (see below), there appears to be a shift in emphasis in his approach. Kloppenborg's earlier analysis of Q's stratification revolved around three features: projected audience, forms and motifs. Concentrating on the main redaction, the *projected audience* Kloppenborg argued consists of the impenitent and the opponents of community preaching. Thus the material of the main redaction is directed at the "out-group," while it also functions to strengthen

ending of Q, but they are also the founding principles in four, or maybe five blocks throughout Q:

1. Q 3:(2–3), 7–9, 16b–17 contains allusions to the story of Lot (Gn 19); John announces the coming judgement; it issues a call to repentance; and it challenges the security of Israelite identity;

2. Q 7:1–10, 18–28, 31–35 uses a Gentile to shame Israel; it describes the rejection of John and Jesus as the prophets and envoys of Sophia;

3. Q 11:14–15, 16, 17–26, (27–28), 29–32, 33–36, 39b–44, 46–52 contains a number of examples where Jesus is not recognized; it has announcements of judgement; it represents the prophets as envoys of Sophia; it calls for recognition and repentance; and it uses Gentiles to shame Israel;

4. Q 17:23–24, 37b, 26–30, 34–35; 19:12–27; 22:28–30 has allusions to the story of Lot; it announces the coming judgement; it challenges prevailing apocalyptic scenarios; and contains the judgement of Israel.

Possibly, the following might be added:

5. Q 12:39–40, 42b–46, 49, 50–53, 54–59 that contains an announcement of coming judgement; admonitions

---

the identity of the "in-group." In terms of *forms*, chriae are typical of the main redaction as well as prophetic sayings. They are there to criticize the response of "this generation" and to encapsulate various sayings of Jesus and John. Lastly, in terms of *motifs*, there are various motifs related to the theme of judgement. This includes the imminence of judgement, the parousia, and the negative response of Israelites as compared to that of the Gentiles (Kloppenborg 1987:166–70). Horsley (1999:62–75) has offered a critique of Kloppenborg's (1987) approach and based on his own analysis of the texts argues that the "common features" used as criteria for Kloppenborg's main redaction is difficult to find or it does not appear consistently enough across the various clusters. "Strictly speaking, only two short passages in Q, 11:29–32 and 11:49–51, actually attest the three common features used as criteria for the secondary, judgmental layer" (Horsley 1999:65). But it must be said that Horsley questionably downplays the polemical or judgmental aspect of Q "against Israel/this generation" while *also the rhetorical tone of these clusters* played an important part in Kloppenborg's literary analysis. Otherwise, Horsley (see also 1999:74, 81) exaggerates the "apocalyptic" element in Kloppenborg's analysis since the major motif for Kloppenborg is judgement.

to preparedness; and a call to recognition (and repentance?).

Kloppenborg proposes these redactional themes represent the perspective of the main redaction of Q. These themes tend to cluster together in the four or five subcollections listed above, and overall, Kloppenborg assumes the presence of 14 subcollections.[5] Other clusters according to him are untouched or minimally influenced by such themes (e.g., Q 6:20b–49; 9:57—10:24; 11:2–4, 9–13; and 12:2–7, (8–9), 11–12; and 12:22b–31, 33–34). "What unites these subcollections," Kloppenborg (2000:144) explains, "is not only that they lack features of the main redaction; they also evince an interlocking set of concerns which have to do with the legitimation of a somewhat adventuresome social practice—including debt forgiveness, the eschewing of vengeance, and the embracing of an exposed and marginal lifestyle." Kloppenborg also draws on the work of Piper (1989), who has shown that these clusters share a common rhetoric, namely, the rhetoric of persuasion, instead of prophetic pronouncement or declamation. "This rhetoric focuses not on defending the ethos (character) of Jesus or those associated with him or on attacking opponents; that is the rhetorical strategy of the main redaction" (Kloppenborg 2000:144; cf. 193–96). In addition, these subcollections have a common structure, beginning with programmatic sayings, continued with second person imperatives, and concluding with a saying that underlines the importance of the instructions. "In other words," Kloppenborg (2000:145) concludes, "in terms of thematic organization, rhetorical posture, and structure, the six ... clusters show themselves to cohere as a group and, in all likelihood, as a discrete redactional stratum." The six clusters Kloppenborg (2000:146) speaks of actually looks as follows:

1. Q 6:20b–23b, 27–35, 36–45, 46–49

2. Q 9:57–60, (61–62); 10:2–11, 16, (23–24?)

---

5. Kloppenborg's (2000:115) 14 subcollections are set out as follows: **(1)** 3:3, 7–9, 16–17; **(2)** 4:1–13, (16); **(3)** 6:20b–23, (24–26), 27–33, (Q/Matt 5:41), (34–35b), 35c, 36–37b, 38c, 39–45, 46–49; **(4)** 7:1b–2, 6b–10, 18–19, 21–23, 24–28, 31–35; **(5)** 9:57–60, (61–62); 10:2–16, 21–24; **(6)** 11:2–4, 9–13; **(7)** 11:14–20, (21–22), 23–26, (27–28), 29–35, 39–44, 46–52; **(8)** 12:2–12; **(9)** 12:(13–14, 16–21), 22–31, 33–34; **(10)** 12:39–40, 42b–46, 49, 51–53, 54–56, 58–59; **(11)** 13:18–21; **(12)** 13:24, 26–30, 34–35; 14:11/18:14; 14:16–24, 26–27; 17:33; 14:34–35; **(13)** 15:4–7, (8–10); 16:13, 16–18; 17:1b–2, 3b–4, 6b; **(14)** 17:23–24, 37b, 26–27, (28–29), 30, 34–35; 19:12–13, 15b–26; 22:28–30.

3. Q 11:2–4, 9–13

4. Q 12:2–7, 11–12

5. Q 12:22b–31, 33–34 (13:18–19, 20–21?) and probably

6. Q 13:24; 14:26–27; 17:33; 14:34–35.

These clusters are united by paraenetic, hortatory, and instructional concerns. These sub-collections Kloppenborg argues constituted "the formative stratum" (Q¹), while the material of "the main redaction" (Q²) was added thereafter. Kloppenborg (2000:146) further suggests that Q 15:4–7, 8–10; 16:13, 16, 18; 17:1–2, 3–4, 6 also belongs to the earliest level of Q. Besides the above, Kloppenborg (2000:120–21, 128, 147–150 cf. Tuckett 1996:70, 72) points to several instances which are regarded as interpolations, commentaries or glosses to the formative stratum (Q 6:23c; 10:12, 13–15; 12:8–10; 13:26–27, 28–29, 34–35; 14:16–24) since they cohere with elements of the main redaction. Lastly, the temptation narrative (Q 4:1–13) and Q 11:42c and 16:17 are seen by Kloppenborg (2000:152–53) as additions subsequent to the main redaction and are treated together, since they share the view on the centrality of the Torah, a theme supposedly not encountered in other parts of Q.

We will now continue by doing an overview of Kloppenborg's understanding of Q, which was derived at through what he describes as a sociorhetorical approach.[6] This approach looks at how the text as a whole is constructed to commend itself to its hearers/readers and thus it can help identify the social location/world that lies behind the text.

The Formative Stratum

Kloppenborg at first has a look at the formative stratum's genre and rhetoric. He argues that Q¹ is a good example of instructional literature. It offers topically organized instructions on several themes. Like instructions, Q contains sayings on the relationship between masters and students (Q 6:40, 46–49; 10:16; 14:26–27); on the importance of good guidance (Q 6:40, 41–42), good speech (Q 6:43–45), and good examples (Q 17:1–2). God and Jesus are held up us mimetic ideals (Q

---

6. Kloppenborg (2000:196; cf. 177–78) explains "sociorhetorical approaches ask what the genre of the text and the method of organization imply about its intended audience; how the author diagnoses the situation addressed; and how arguments are constructed [i.e. the selection of metaphors, the choice of evidence, the conduct of the arguments] so as to be persuasive."

6:35, 36; 9:58; 11:13; 12:3; 14:26–27). Q 12:2 is interested in those things hidden, and sees the process of revelation as grounded in the relationship of God to the world (Kloppenborg 2000:197–98).

Many sayings of Q^1 indicate a measure of disenfranchisement with local judicial mechanisms (e.g., 6:27–36 (+ Q/Matt 5:41), 37–38; 12:58–59[7]), some of which are juxtaposed with concerns about subsistence (Q 11:2–4, 9–13; and 12:4–7, 11–12, 22–31) (Kloppenborg 2000:193–95, 198). The bulk of the first stratum is concerned with local conditions: managing conflict (Q 6:27–28, 29; 12:2–7, 11–12, 17:3–4); lending and borrowing (Q 6:30); corvée (Q/Matt 5:41); divorce (Q 16:18); solidarity and reconciliation (Q 15:4–7, 8–10; 17:1–2, 3–4); attitudes toward wealth (Q 12:33–34; 16:13); and the conduct and support of "workers" (Q 9:57–62; 10:2–11, 16). So these sayings presuppose the audience to be on a low social level. The concern for subsistence and the assumption of Q/Matt 5:41 that Q's community members are susceptible to forced labor suggest that they include smallholders or handworkers. Q 6:30 implies community members might make loans, but when money is mentioned, the denominations are small: a Roman *assarion* is mentioned (Q 12:6) and the Parable of the Lost Drachma (Q 15:8–10) apparently concerns the life savings of a woman. The Parable of the Lost Sheep describes a medium sized flock (Q 15:4–7) and the wealthy are held up as negative examples (Q 12:16–21); even nature can outdo their splendor (Q 12:27) (Kloppenborg 2000:198–99).

Kloppenborg then proceeds by looking at the construction of Q's arguments or style of rhetoric. Proofs are drawn from the observation of nature and ordinary human transactions: these include the coming of rain (Q 6:35); cultivation of figs and grapes (Q 6:44); housebuilding (Q 6:47–49); parents providing for their children (Q 11:9–13); small purchases (Q 12:6–7); survival of birds (Q 12:22–24), field flowers (Q 12:26–27) and grass (Q 12:28); shepherds (Q 15:4–7) and poor widows (?) (Q 15:8–10); and simple planting and bread making (Q 13:18–21). What is absent is reference to "higher" forms of culture (e.g., major political and public institutions, kings, palaces, the agora, the gymnasium, the theatre, the assembly). There is no appeal to Israel's epic history apart from the appeal to Solomon's proverbial wealth (Q 12:27). Yet, the environment of Q^1 is largely Israelite—Q can easily give Gentiles as examples from whom one does not expect good behavior (Q 6:33–34; 12:30). What is also absent from Q's repertoire of arguments is that the

---

7. Kloppenborg refers to Piper's (1995) research that includes 12:58–59 here, although Kloppenborg himself allocates these verses to the main redaction of Q (Q^2).

priesthood, Temple, purity distinctions, or the Torah is not the basis of argumentative appeals. Q^1 also lacks oracular appeals or prophetic speech and the mode of argumentation is predominantly persuasion (cf. Piper 1989).[8] According to Kloppenborg (2000:199), "Q^1 is full of confidence in divine providence, in God's loving surveillance, and the possibility of transformed human relationships; but there is no indication whatsoever that this is mediated by Torah[9] or the Temple or the priestly hierarchy, or that it is based on oracular disclosures or commands."

Based on the above Kloppenborg (2000:198, 200) draws some conclusions on the formative stratum's social location. The literary organization of Q^1 does not display sophisticated or learned characteristics (repeated formula, sorites, chiasms, alphabetic acrostics, numeric patterns). This suggests that the authors of Q^1 were of limited skill, not coming from the upper reaches of the scribal establishment. They were probably village and town notaries and scribes. In the life of a village they were most keenly aware of the issues that are contained in Q—debt (Q 6:30; 11:4; 12:58–59), divorce (Q 16:18), lawsuits (Q 6:29)—since they wrote loan contracts, petitions, and bills of divorce. Q^1 is also framed as an instruction (a typical scribal genre) and it reflects the interests of scribes in the process as well as the content of learning. Kloppenborg maintains the first stratum of Q was formulated to address people living near or at subsistence level.[10] They experienced conflict endemic to town and village life as well as occasional outside pressure in the form of corvée, the courts and other demands.

As an aside, it can be mentioned that there are some scholars who have compared this stratum—which they have modified in their own way—with a Cynic-like Jesus movement, particularly drawing atten-

---

8. Contrast Tuckett (1996:348–51) who questions Piper's (1989) description of (1) sayings allocated to Q^1 (Q 11:9–13; 12:22–31; 6:37–41; 6:43–45) as "aphoristic wisdom," functioning to persuade and not to coerce; i.e. it does not operate in prophetic or eschatological categories; and (2) Piper's analysis of isolated aphorisms (e.g., Q 3:9; 6:43–45; 13:24; 17:37). Tuckett argues these texts are eschatologically determined, or alternatively, when viewed in its Q context, are forced into an eschatological mould (e.g., see 6:43–45 with 6:46, 47–49).

9. Here one cannot entirely agree with Kloppenborg. As the analysis will show, particularly Q 6:20–49 engages in the reconstruction of the Torah.

10. Contrast Tuckett (1996:360, 365–66), who, when speaking of some passages Kloppenborg assigns to Q^1, argues the people addressed are, if not well off, at least not destitute. For example, the missionaries can expect to receive hospitality (Q 10:7–8); there are warnings about storing treasures on earth (Q 12:33–34) and serving mammon (Q 16:13); and there are exhortations to lend without expecting a return (Q 6:30).

tion to the mission charge (Q 10:2–16) and various sayings that are claimed to be similar to a Cynic ethos and ideology. According to them, the Q people were not interested in a program of renewal or reform, but like the Cynics, merely offered social critique (Vaage 1994; Mack 1993). Scholars, such as Tuckett (1989; cf. 1996:368–91), for example, have questioned this idea. Vaage (1995a:228) in turn has responded that most of Tuckett's "concerns and arguments against a 'Cynic' Q derive from the generalized confusion ... of comparison with genealogy, understood as a statement about origins." Tuckett (1996:372, 385) evidently is aware of this methodological pitfall, but apparently seems to be concerned with possible attempts where the analogies between Cynicism and Q *are* interpreted to point to genealogical derivation, or as he puts it as "indicating a common background of thought." According to Kloppenborg (2000:431), although there are some interesting and puzzling parallels with Cynicism, the "case for a cynic-like Q has yet to be made effectively." Later on, however, Kloppenborg argues that "the cynic hypothesis underscores the possibility that at Q's earliest layer the early Jesus movement adopted postures that were significantly deviant and socially experimental." At the level of Q^2, Jesus, John and the Q people were aligned with the important figures of Israel's past—the prophets—to defend the novelty of Q^1. "Even in this alignment," Kloppenborg (2000:442) continues, "a memory of deviance is preserved, for the prophets themselves were remembered as similarly uncooperative persons, opposing kings, objecting to political strategies, and decrying the exploitation of the poor and dispossessed."

Even if the Q people were Cynic-like (they were deviant or "countercultural" to a degree) we need not presume that they were anything other than Judeans and understood themselves as such. Kloppenborg (2000:256) asserts at all the redactional levels, "the document presumes a largely or exclusively Israelite audience."[11] Q^1 takes for granted that the people addressed will know of Solomon's proverbial wealth (Q 12:27). Q makes use of the Aramaic words Gehenna (γέεννα, Q 12:5) and mammon (μαμωνᾶς, Q 16:13) without the need to translate it. Gentiles are twice referred to by what ethnicity theory describes as a "we-they" *oppositional* self-definition (Q 6:33–34; 12:30). They evidently were not part of Q's "in-group," or rather, co-ethnics. At the level of Q^2 numerous references are made to Israel's epic history. Q's

---

11. It must be understood that Kloppenborg's "Israelites" will be approached here as Judeans, and the need for a third stratum is questioned, thus it is proposed to limit Q to two redactional layers (see arguments below).

spatial world has Capernaum, Chorazin and Bethsaida at its centre, and Jerusalem is a significant point on Q's horizon. Gentiles, whether actual or imaginary make their appearance, but in Q's rhetoric they are mainly used to shame a principally Israelite audience (Q 7:1–10; 10:12–15; 11:31–32; 13:28–29). Q also makes use of the Torah as a basis for argument (Q 4:1–13), and affirms the ongoing validity of the Torah (Q 11:42c; 16:17). These texts relating to the Torah Kloppenborg assigns to a *third* stratum (or Q^3), but the need for a third stratum will be questioned, however. Q also nowhere challenges circumcision (unlike Paul) or Sabbath observance (unlike Mark), and along with certain dietary requirements would have regarded these as principal distinguishing marks of Israelite identity (Kloppenborg 2000:256).

The Main Redaction

Regarding the main redaction of Q (Q^2), Kloppenborg (2000:201) again begins by having a look at the stratum's genre and rhetoric. He argues that "there is a noticeable shift in formal characteristics of the collection as well as the types of rhetorical appeals" and the "changes are more likely due to a new rhetorical situation—the need to defend the practice of Q^1 and the character of Jesus in the face of challenges—than they are the result of a change in audience." The most obvious formal shift are the increased density of chriae, that is, sayings furnished with a brief setting (e.g., Q 3:7a; 7:18–19, 24a; 10:21a; 11:14–15, 16, etc.). What becomes important here is the characterization of the speaker or of his interlocutors. It is at this stratum "that we first encounter allusion to the prophets and Sophia and Israel's epic history, both in connection with the positive characterization of Jesus and John, and in connection with the Deuteronomistic theme of killing the prophets" (Kloppenborg 2000:201). Also here polemic against "this generation" appears in the rhetoric, referring to a group or type of persons that are opposed to the Q group.

The main redaction also contains woes, warnings of judgement and prophetic correlatives (e.g., Q 11:30; 17:24, 26, 30). It further includes chriae occasioned by a healing (Q 7:1–10), a question from John the Baptist (Q 7:18–23, 24–28, 31–35), and two challenges to Jesus (Q 11:14–23, 29–32). Although prophetic forms are present and the examples of prophets are called upon (Q 6:22–23; 7:26; 10:23–24; 11:32, 49–51; 13:34–35), and while an Elijah-like figure is described in Q 3:16–17; 7:22, most sayings of Q^2 are framed as chriae rather than as direct oracles.[12] Here we also find a development from an instruction to a *bios*, as initial chriae are extended by additional chriae or sayings. So biographical elements are introduced to underline the reliable character (*ethos*) of Jesus. Jesus is placed in situations where he is able to defeat critics with a few well-chosen sayings (Q 7:31–35; 11:14–23, 29–32). He is quick to commend others (Q 7:1–10, 24–28; 10:21–22, 23–24) or rectify misplaced praise (Q 11:27–28). The inferiority of opponents is underlined (Q 7:31–35; 10:12–15; 11:39–52). Other sayings warn of potential dangers (Q 3:7–9, 16–17; 12:39–49, 51–59; 17:23–37; 19:12–27), or implicitly connect Jesus with the Elijah-like "Coming One" (Q 7:18–23 cf. 3:16–17; 13:34–35) and Heavenly Wisdom (Q 11:49–51). Other sayings explicitly assert divine authorization both for Jesus (Q 7:35; 10:21–22) and John (Q 7:26, 27; 7:35) (Kloppenborg 2000:202–3).

By contrasting the ethos of John and Jesus over and against their competitors, it indicates that at this stage the rhetorical situation required a defence or legitimation of the Q people's existence. Opponents are attacked and Jesus and John are associated with Sophia, prophetic figures, and characters of Israel's epic history. Q^2 draws a sacred map of "Israel" (Q 7:9; 22:30), naming Abel (Q 11:51), Abraham (Q 3:8; 13:28), Noah (Q 17:26–27), Lot (Q 17:28–29 cf. 3:3; 10:12), Isaac (Q 13:28), Jacob (Q 13:28), Solomon (Q 11:31), Jonah (Q 11:32), Zechariah (Q 11:51), and the prophets (Q 6:22–23; 11:49–51; 13:34–35). The authors of Q thus situated themselves within this company whereas their opponents are seen as the persecutors and killers of the prophets (Q 6:22–23; 11:49–51; 13:34–35). In Q this is used against opponents who could regard themselves as representatives of the "great tradition," and it brings out the irony that the forbears of those who now claim to honor the prophets actually killed them (Kloppenborg 2000:205–6, 210). Q also employs the strategy of shaming, saying that Gentiles have responded (or would respond) better to Solomon, Jonah and the Patriarchs than their opponents. The evil cities of Sodom, Tyre, and Sidon will be better off at the judgement than Israelite towns that reject the Jesus movement. In addition, it "is perhaps significant that neither Moses[13] nor

---

12. Cf. Sato (1995), who argues that Q witnesses a prophetic movement and that Q as a whole is very similar to an Old Testament prophetic book.

13. Here we cannot entirely agree with Kloppenborg. Moses may not be explicitly mentioned, but he is a figure whose presence is taken for granted. He lurks behind the figure of Jesus who is the new Moses and leader of the new Exodus. See the analysis of the main redaction below.

David—associated with Torah and learning and kingship—appears in Q's list of heroes" (Kloppenborg 2000:203).

Kloppenborg also draws upon the work of Reed, who has suggested that Q^2 was associated with a larger population centre such as Capernaum. The authors of Q made frequent use of urban (Q 10:8, 10; 7:25; 7:31–35; 11:43; 13:26; 14:21; 12:3; 12:58–59; 13:24; 14:16–24; 19:23) and agricultural imagery but they had little first-hand experience of agricultural practices (Q 10:2, and based on the impersonal plural *they* in 6:44; 14:35), and most of the urban imagery used by Q has a negative cast and the city is viewed with suspicion (Reed 1995:26–29; 2000:189–95). Kloppenborg does not endorse Reed's suggestion of Capernaum itself, but he says that

> it is appropriate to conclude with Reed that the Q people are associated with towns sufficiently large to have markets and a small scribal sector, and sufficiently proximate to the larger centers of Tiberias and Sepphoris to come into periodic contact with Pharisees and other representatives of the Judaean hierocracy. Q's cultural allegiances, however, are with the Galilean country side and against the city, which is regarded with distrust and suspicion. In defense of the Jesus movement, the framers of Q construct a notion of Israel and its epic heroes which stand in opposition to Jerusalem,[14] the Herodian dynasty, the Pharisees and lawyers, and the unbelief that is encountered in the marketplaces. (Kloppenborg 2000:204)

The issues behind the apologetic stance of Q^2 are complaints about nonrepentance (Q 3:8; 10:13; 11:32) and accompanying threats of judgement. Failure to repent means a failure to recognize in Jesus and the Q people the presence of divine activity and authorization—it does not seem to refer to a change in one's interior disposition. It has to do with the adoption of certain patterns of behavior and group allegiance (Q 7:9–10; 7:22; 7:31–35; 10:10–12; 11:19–20; 11:29–32; 13:25–27). Jesus and the Q people are being attacked or ignored, but this serves an apologetic strategy since a few sayings in Q^2 continue to promote the ethos of Q^1 as it criticizes the rich and those of high social standing (Q 7:25; 7:22; 10:21–24; 11:43, 47; and indirectly in 14:16–24).

This stratum of Q also illustrates a struggle for influence and "place" in Galilean society. The Q people's opponents (particularly

---

14. Q 13:34–35, however, rather presupposes a positive attachment to the temple and Jerusalem. The "opposition" of Q is conditional, and will disappear once the Temple establishment accepts Jesus as Messiah. Again, see the analysis of the main redaction.

Pharisees and lawyers) already have influence or are seen as likely to obtain it (Q 11:43; 11:46 cf. 11:52; 11:47–51). Q's lack of appeal to Moses may be due to the Pharisees and lawyers who claimed Moses as their authority—Q² looks to the memory of the prophets to counter. In the first-century Galilee, the Pharisees, understood as "retainers," were a minor and new presence, and represented the interests of Jerusalem and its priestly rulers. At the same time, they placed emphasis on tithing and practices that promoted Judean identity. Kloppenborg (2000:205) argues that "Q's conflict with the Pharisees and their hieratic practices (purity and tithing) thus represents a struggle between indigenous Galilean piety and an incursion of Judaean and priestly influence." Q's selection of figures from epic history also deliberately excludes Jerusalem. The Patriarchs, Noah and Lot date to before the priesthood, the monarchy, and the centralization of the Temple cult. David is ignored, Solomon is mentioned once as a negative example (Q 12:27), the sacrificial system is ignored and so is the Decalogue. Kloppenborg refers to Reed's work who writes: "Indeed, in terms of Q's temporal views, law has given way to the kingdom of God" (Q 16:16) (Reed 1996:137; cf. 2000:209). Kloppenborg also follows Reed who adduced evidence of a late first-century tradition that Jonah, a northern prophet, spoke an oracle against Jerusalem—it would be destroyed (see *Liv. Pro.* 10:10–11). Galileans would probably have known about such local traditions and the Sign of Jonah (Q 11:29–30) "referred not just to the preaching of Jonah but contained a barb aimed at Jerusalem and its representatives" (Reed 1996:138–39; and see 2000:211).

As far as the second stratum's social location is concerned, Kloppenborg again assumes that the framers of Q² are scribes but their interests did not coincide with the scribes and literati of Jerusalem. Q's authors were not from the highest scribal levels or high on the social ladder, that is, from the urban retainer class—although Q² does illustrate a sophisticated level of organization and makes use of repeated themes. When Q employs urban images it is in a negative manner. In its arguments against the Pharisees and lawyers Q² does not make use of the Torah. The strategy is rather one of burlesque and ridicule, something that may indicate that the authors of Q were not in a position to confront the Pharisees directly. Tithing and purity distinctions are matters for ridicule (Q 11:42ab, 39–41). The Temple is the place where the prophets are killed (Q 11:49–51; 13:34–35). Also, the people addressed we know little about, but it is likely that they are not on a higher social level than the scribes that framed Q. Kloppenborg understands the Q people as a network of local groups and leaders, maybe household heads, and that the itinerant workers were dependent upon the households for food and lodging and for the legitimation of their roles (Q 10:6–7). But according to Kloppenborg, the role of these itinerants should not be exaggerated—they did not establish groups and neither were they in leadership positions (Kloppenborg 2000:209–11).

The Final Redaction of Q

Kloppenborg argues that it is only at Q^3 that the Torah and the temple appears in a positive light. In the temptation story (Q 4:1–13) Jesus and the devil refer to the Torah and the Psalms as if this was the appropriate way to make an argument. Q 11:42c and 16:17, which Kloppenborg regards as secondary intrusions, also take the validity of the Torah for granted. Q 11:42c insist on the importance of tithing; it is an obligation required by the Torah. Q 16:17 is a qualification and limitation of any possible antinomian interpretation of 16:16 ("The law and the prophets were until John"). An earlier antinomian meaning was probably not the case, but "the addition of 16:17 betrays the hand of a 'nervous redactor' who is worried about any apparent rejection of Torah" (Kloppenborg 2000:212). With regard to the Temple, where Q 11:49–51 and 13:34–35 view the Temple and its ruling elite in a negative light, the second temptation (Q 4:9–12) understands the Temple as a place where angels might be present to assist holy persons—compared with Q^2 the Temple is now again a holy place.

The three temptations also serve to exemplify and legitimate the ethics of the earlier strata. Jesus refuses to produce bread from stones—this picks up the language of Q 11:11 (bread/stone) and represents Jesus as one who, like Q 12:30–31 advises, does not seek food as a first priority. Jesus refuses to call on angelic support in a public display of power and self-protection—this mirrors Q's avoidance of demonstrative signs (Q 11:29–30; 17:23–30) and the advice to fear God rather than those who can kill the body (Q 12:4). Jesus resists power, privilege and wealth—this mirrors the markarism concerning the poor (Q 6:20) and Q's attitude that wealth becomes an obstacle to the service of God (Q 16:13). Thus the temptation story legitimates some aspects of Q's praxis.

The use of Torah quotations in argument and the concern for the enduring validity of the Torah strongly suggests for Kloppenborg (2000:212–213) that scribes were responsible for its production. The

Judean Ethnicity in Q 273

level is somewhat higher and more learned than Q^1 and Q^2, but it is not a matter of discontinuity, but of a different scribal practice. Not enough evidence is available, however, to judge anything further about the addressees of the final stage of Q. It is similar to the letter of James, which shows important contacts with the Jesus tradition but also regards the Torah as a legitimate starting point in argumentation.

Refining the Approach to Q

The above, in abbreviated form, constitutes Kloppenborg's understanding of Q through a sociorhetorical analysis. It is a development based on his overall understanding of Q's stratification, which is represented in the following table (interpolations, glosses and commentaries added during the main redaction (Q^2) are written with emphasis):

Kloppenborg's Stratification of Q

Q^1	Q^2	Q^3
	3:3 Setting of John's Preaching	
	3:7–9 John's Preaching of Repentance	
	3:16–17 The Coming One	
		4:1–13 The Temptations
4:(16) Reference to Nazara (?)		
6:20b–23ab Beatitudes		
	6:23c Reference to Prophets	
6:(24–26) Woes		
6:27–33 On Retaliation; Generous Giving; Golden Rule		
(Q/ Matt 5:41) Go the Second Mile		

Kloppenborg's Stratification of Q (*continued*)

Q¹	Q²	Q³
6:(34–35b), 35c Conclusion		
6:36–37b, 38c On Mercy and Judging		
6:39–45 On Self-Correction		
6:46–49 Why do You Call Me Lord?; The Two House Builders		
	7:1b–2, 6b–10 The Centurion at Capernaum	
	7:18–19, 21–23 John's Question	
	7:24–28 Jesus' Eulogy of John	
	7:31–35 Children in the Agora	
9:57–60, (61–62) Two (Three?) Volunteers		
10:2–11 Mission Instructions		
	10:12, 13–15 Reference to Sodom; Woes on Chorazin and Bethsaida; Humiliation of Capernaum	
10:16 Mission Instructions		
	10:21–24 Thanksgiving for Revelation; Commendation for Disciples	
11:2–4 The Lord's Prayer		

Kloppenborg's Stratification of Q (*continued*)

Q¹	Q²	Q³
11:9–13 Sayings on Prayer		
	11:14–20 The Beelzebul Controversy	
	11:(21–22) Binding the Strong Man	
	11:23–26 Whoever Is Not Against Me; Return of the Evil Spirit	
	11:(27–28) A Woman in the Crowd	
	11:29–35 Request for a Sign; Lamp; Sayings on Light	
	11:39–42ab Woes against Pharisees	
		11:42c Tithing
	11:43–44 Woes against Pharisees	
	11: 46–52 Woes against Lawyers	
12:2–7 Fearless Confession		
	12:8–10 *Reference to Son of Man*	
12:11–12 Fearless Confession		
12:(13–14, 16–21) Divider; Rich Fool		
12:22–31, 33–34 On Anxiety over Life		
	12:39–40 Watch for the Son of Man	

Kloppenborg's Stratification of Q (*continued*)

Q¹	Q²	Q³
	12:42b–46 Faithful and Unfaithful Servants	
	12:49, 51–53 On Divisions	
	12:54–56 Weather Signs/Signs of the Times	
	12:58–59 Settle with a Creditor	
13:18–21 Parables of the Mustard Seed and the Leaven		
13:24 The Two Ways		
	13:26–27 *Closed Door*	
	13:28–30 *Many Will Come from East and West*	
	13:34–35 *Lament Over Jerusalem*	
14:11/ 18:14 Exalting the Humble		
	14:16–24 *The Feast*	
14:26–27; 17:33 Three Discipleship Sayings		
14:34–35 Savorless Salt		
15:4–7 The Lost Sheep		
15:(8–10) The Lost Drachma		
16:13 God and Mammon		

Kloppenborg's Stratification of Q (*continued*)

Q¹	Q²	Q³
16:16 The Kingdom Suffers Violence		
		16:17 Torah
16:18 Divorce		
17:1b–2 On Scandals		
17:3b–4 Forgiveness		
17:6b Faith like a Mustard Seed		
	17:23–24, 37b The Coming of the Son of Man	
	17:26–27 The Days of Noah	
	17:(28–29), 30 The Days of Lot	
	17:34–35 Two in a Field; Two at the Grindstone	
	19:12–13, 15b–26 The Entrusted Money	
	22:28–30 Judging the Twelve Tribes	

Although Kloppenborg's stratification has been widely influential, all scholars have not accepted it. For example, Allison (1997:3–8) offers a critique of Kloppenborg's stratification and then proceeds to propose a different stratification of Q after a section by section analysis. Allison assigns 9:57—11:13; 12:2–12, 22–32 to the earliest stratum of Q (Q¹) because it is addressed to itinerant missionaries. Allison then claims that 12:33—22:30 was added at the second stage (Q²), and finally supplemented by 3:7—7:35 and 11:14–52 (Q³). Kloppenborg (2000:117) in response argues that Allison "provides no grounds for his assertion that 12:33—22:30 was added second or for 3:7—7:35 being added third, and no grounds for his initial choice of 9:57—11:13 as the starting point. It is not even clear that 11:2-4, 9–13, or 12:2-12 or 12:22-31 were addressed to itinerants. On the contrary, these materials speak of 'debts' (11:3) and parental relations (11:11–13), neither of which are relevant to homeless 'missionaries.'" Thus Allison's arguments, Kloppenborg claims, are weakened by an arbitrary construction of his compositional history.

There are also scholars who are totally against the idea of a stratified Q. Meier (1994:179) states that when it comes to Q's community, geographical provenance, different stages of redaction and its theological vision "that exegetes are trying to know the unknowable." Dunn (2003:156, 157) for example, argues that Kloppenborg "does not actually demonstrate that Q^1 ever functioned as a single document or stratum" and there is no reason "why this material [Q^1] should be taken as a single document," and lastly that the "evidence is fully satisfied by the alternative hypothesis of a single compositional act." Tuckett is another one of those scholars who is sceptical about a proposed stratification for Q. He argues that Kloppenborg's "isolation of a specific strand stressing the threat of judgement against 'this generation' [Q^2] is well taken" but the "postulated sapiential strand [Q^1] may be rather less secure ... [T]he question arises whether it is justified to regard the 'Q^1' material as a literary unity, existing as a self-contained entity at some stage in the pre-history of Q" (Tuckett 1996:71). In addition, Tuckett questions the need to separate a Q^3 from a Q^2, since a strong nomistic outlook is more widespread in Q than Kloppenborg allows. Tuckett (1996:73–74) argues that if

> it is unnecessary to postulate a Q^3 subsequent to Q^2, and if the pre-Q^2 material is perhaps rather more disparate, and the alleged 'Q^1' stratum not necessarily capable of being shown to have existed as a literary unity in its own right before Q^2, then we may have a rather simpler model, viz. a Q-editor taking up and using (possibly a variety of) earlier material.

So both Dunn and Tuckett express doubts over Kloppenborg's Q^1 in that it ever functioned as a single document/literary unity and both of them favor a simpler single compositional act for Q.

It must be added, however, that scholars have often misconstrued Kloppenborg's analytical approach to Q. For example, Tuckett (1996:71) alludes to the fact that the sections dominated by the polemical character of the Q² material (e.g., Q 3:7–9, 16–17; 7:18–35) had a long pre-history—something that Kloppenborg's own analysis may suggest[15]—hence the pre-Q² material clearly consisted of more than "sapiential" speeches. Also, Kloppenborg argues that it has been wrongly assumed, particularly by Collins (1993) and Horsley (1989:109–10), that he had piled the Q material into supposedly incompatible "sapiential" and "apocalyptic/prophetic" materials and based his stratigraphy on these theological themes. Also Sato (1995:140) contends that Kloppenborg's stratums "seems to follow a rather schematic conception." Kloppenborg (1987:244–45; 2000:150–51) has always insisted that the stratigraphical analysis of the *literary history* of the *Q document* must not be confused with the tradition history or age of the materials. Also, the stratification of Q is based on *literary*—not theological or thematic—observations on how the various subcollections relate to one another. Thus one must not confuse the results of his stratigraphical analysis with the initial criteria.[16] "The tracing of a compositional history of Q is not a matter of placing its sayings into two or more 'piles,' sorted by form or by supposed theological orientation ... Nor is there any assumption that hortatory materials are necessarily early, or authentic, or that the Jesus movement was originally 'sapiential' or 'apocalyptic' or 'prophetic'" (Kloppenborg 2000:151). Importantly for our purposes is the fact that scholars do not seem to appreciate enough that part and parcel of Kloppenborg's *literary approach* is the primary *rhetorical tone* of the two major strata, something that was already present in his earlier analysis (Kloppenborg 1987:168–69, 238–39, 322). Kloppenborg's approach focuses just as much on *how* things are said than on what is being said. The formative stratum consists of a large number of sayings that are sapiential[17] admonitions. Also present are beatitudes, proverbs

---

15. Tuckett (1996:71) writes: "Kloppenborg's own analysis makes clear that the source material used by any Q² redactor is more complex than a monolithic Q¹ and nothing more."

16. In fairness, Horsley (1995:39–40; 1999:62–67) has recently looked at the *criteria* of Kloppenborg's stratigraphy. See also note 4 above.

17. A characterization that has drawn strong criticism. Horsley (1999:67, 81) argues that much of the material in both the main strata would be described as prophetic, and questions the division into different "sapiential" and "apocalyptic" layers. Tuckett criticizes the use or description of texts allocated to Kloppenborg's first stratum (Q¹) as "sapiential" or as examples of "aphoristic wisdom" (e.g., Q 11:9–13; 12:2–9; 12:22–31; 6:37–41; 6:43–45) (cf. Piper 1989). Tuckett argues that wisdom is a term that is used too loosely and which can mean almost anything in the work of scholars. He understands wisdom based on Von Rad's definition of wisdom as "a practical knowledge of

and wisdom sayings. The tone is hortatory and instructional, and it employs the rhetoric of persuasion, instead of prophetic pronouncement or declamation (although it is suggested here that prophetic elements are

the laws of life and of the world based upon experience" (von Rad 1962:418). Tuckett (1996:333–34) himself writes that above all "there is a belief in the regularity and order of the created world and that the task of wisdom is to discover that order . . . the basis for understanding is human experience, to be communicated and taught to others." Based on this, Tuckett argues the mission instructions (Q 10:2–16) can hardly be called "sapiential." The warnings at the end of the Q Sermon (Q 6:47–49) have far greater affinities with the warnings and threats of future judgement found in the main redaction (Q²) than Kloppenborg allows—in addition, Q 6:43–45 placed just before Q 6:46–49 becomes a warning backed up with threats of future judgement, thus context is determinative. Q 11:2–4, 9–13 and 12:22–31 is determined by a futurist eschatology and the latter's exhortation *not* to work and *not* to make provisions for the future contrasts with the Judean wisdom tradition (cf. Catchpole 1993:35), as does Q 9:60 and 14:26 in relation to the family. In addition, primary Wisdom texts (Q 7:35; 11:49) are found in the main redactional stratum (Q²) (cf. Jacobson 1992:51). Overall, the Q material cannot simply be described as an "instruction" and the use of Wisdom in Q is there to stress the *prophetic* aspect of Q much more, although Tuckett does agree that material in Q does contain "sapiential" material (e.g., Q 6:39; 14:34; and perhaps Q 6:31, 38, 40; 11:34; 12:25) (Tuckett 1996:72, 152, 346–54). Some of these criticisms are relevant, as Kloppenborg's literary approach may tend to under appreciate the prophetic element in Q, and as Horsley (1999:195–227) indicates, the material of the formative stratum is also engaged with the Torah and covenant renewal, an element missing from Kloppenborg's analysis. But as the above criticisms indicate, at times scholars such as Tuckett, thinking in primarily theological terms, can much like Collins (1993) and Horsley (1989; 1995; 1999) miss the point of (or ignore) Kloppenborg's *literary* analysis. To put it differently, when scholars, grounded in theological, thematic or social-scientific approaches criticize Kloppenborg's work, they are not on the same (literary-analytical) wave-length. The critique is not fully appropriate to the argument it opposes. The point is, Kloppenborg's characterization of the formative stratum as "sapiential" points just as much as to *how* things are said than what is being said. Thus the "sapiential" material of the formative stratum must be seen in conjunction with its hortatory and instructional rhetorical style—"sapiential" here does not merely denote form, or theological or schematic content. Most of the above criticisms are as a result misplaced. Kloppenborg does admit that the mission instructions (and Q 12:11–12; 14:26–27; 17:33) go beyond sapiential admonitions; they are seen with the sapiential speeches since they cohere with the radical lifestyle and ethic of the admonitions and build on the theme of God's providential care. It may be added that these instructions in rhetorical tone are not polemical or threatening, apart from the interpolations in Q 10:12–15. In addition, Kloppenborg (1987:239) does admit that proverbs and wisdom sayings are found in the main redaction of Q (7:35; 11:17b–18, 21–22; 11:33, 34a; 12:54–55; 17:37): "these function not to reinforce ethical imperatives, but to undergird the pronouncements of judgment." Thus the rhetorical tone of this wisdom material has determined its position in the main redaction and here one can therefore say that they are present to stress the prophetic aspect of Q (which *pace* Kloppenborg and agreeing with Tuckett can be extended to Q 6:47–49).

certainly present). The main redaction, on the other hand, is dominated by chriae and prophetic words,[18] where the tone is primarily polemical and judgmental, and the Q material demonstrates the need to defend the character of Jesus.

It would seem, however, that there is reasonable agreement among scholars on other issues, particularly when it comes to the nature of the main redactional moment of Q. Jacobson (1992:76, 183, 253), although he proposes (with caution) his own stratigraphy for Q, argues that at the basic, compositional stage, the dominant theological perspective is the deuteronomistic (and wisdom) tradition.[19] Dunn (2000:152–53) states that "the case for seeing Q as structured round the motif of coming judgment and on the lines of Deuteronomistic theology is impressive." Tuckett (1996:71) as we have seen, thinks along similar lines. Uro (1995:245) specifically states that "Q research has largely accepted the judgment of impenitent Israel as representing a significant and clearly recognizable redactional motif in the composition of the document." Tuckett, however, seems to even create common ground with Kloppenborg by making observations that presuppose a more literary approach to Q in terms of its compositional history and the rhetoric it entails. To explain, Tuckett (1996:353) argues that "it would seem that any *sapiential elements* in the tradition *have been overlaid by a powerful eschatological/prophetic element* . . . In one sense this might support Kloppenborg's thesis of a prophetic Q^2 succeeding a sapiential Q^1. I am however sceptical about how successfully we can reconstruct layers of the tradition behind our Q with such accuracy." Nevertheless, he continues by saying that it "*would seem therefore that most of the sapiential elements in Q lie in the background for Q. The interest of Q (i.e. the 'final' form of Q) seems to have left behind the wisdom category and focuses more on prophetic warnings and eschatology*" (emphasis added). This view seems to focus more on *how* things are said and may lend support for the

---

18. Jacobson (1992:51) argues that there are a number of sayings in Kloppenborg's first stratum which are commonly identified as prophetic (Q 10:2–26; 12:2–12), and chriae, also supposed to be characteristic of the second stratum, are also found in the formative stratum (Q 9:57–62). One can agree that Kloppenborg downplays the prophetic element in Q^1 (esp. Q 6:47–49), but Kloppenborg (1987:240), however, does admit to the presence of chriae in the formative stratum (Q 9:57–58, 59–60, 61–62 and 12:13–14).

19. Jacobson (1992:76) identifies the Deuteronomistic-wisdom tradition in the following texts: most explicit in Q 11:47–51; 13:34–35, but also found in Q 6:23b; 7:31–35; 10:13–16; 11:29–32; 12:49–53, 54–56; 13:18–19, 21–22; 14:16–24, 26–27; 17:33; 14:34–35.

existence of two main stratums (or strands of material or tradition) in Q akin to Kloppenborg's own approach. Kloppenborg's own understanding of Q's compositional history is basically that pre-existing polemical material or tradition was incorporated or added to a more "sapiential" document which came to be known as Q.

In connection with this both Tuckett (1996:71, 184, 410, 422) and Dunn (2000:153) support Kloppenborg's view which is also shared by others that earlier materials contain secondary additions or interpolations (Tuckett: Q 10:13–15; 11:42c; 16:17; Dunn: Q 6:23c; 10:12–15 12:8–10). In particular Q 6:23c; 10:12–15 and 12:8–10 Kloppenborg (2000:150) has been earmarked for its *"interruptive character"* and is identified as "stratigraphic markers," which along with Q 13:26–27, 28–29, 34–35 and 14:16–24 are seen as interpolations into the formative stratum. Tuckett and Dunn may not support a stratified Q, but in various ways they do say that the Q material has at least undergone some redactional development.

Considering all of the above, Kloppenborg's proposal of Q consisting of two main redactions appears to be a viable working hypothesis. Particularly convincing is the attention that Kloppenborg places on the predominant rhetorical tone of the material that has contributed towards its stratification and the interpolations or "stratigraphic markers" into the earlier material. One can hypothesize that as the sense of alienation between the Q people and their fellow Judeans increased, the more polemical material or tradition would be called upon more regularly in the Q group's assemblies, and eventually justified its inclusion into an already existing written document. Here there is also no necessary contradiction between Kloppenborg's literary approach and Horsley's (1999) argument for Q being an oral derived text.[20] In fact, Horsley's argument could lend better support to Kloppenborg's hypothesis of the literary development of Q, than the Q^2 (and Q^3) material already having existed in written form (cf. Tuckett's suggestion above that the Q editor could have taken up a variety of earlier and disparate (written?) material). The literary history of Q may broadly coincide with the most regular oral performances of the tradition, which with time, developed a strong polemical edge as the Q people found themselves ostracized, rejected or ignored. But it is important to mention in this regard that the history of the *literary document* Q itself must not be confused with the

---

20. Of course, caution should also be taken on whether the Q discourses were orally regularly performed or even at all as they now exist in Q. According to Vaage (1995b:90–92), this is not likely as oral performances varied.

tradition history of the Q community. The relationship here is between the Q document, and most regular oral performance of the tradition as the circumstances required. Regular oral performances would have been written down, but the texts themselves were written to facilitate oral performances in itself. So to recapitulate, the more "sapiential" Q^1 that focuses on the teaching of Jesus, the sending of itinerant missionaries and so on, could reflect an earlier stage in the Q people's history. This more instructional material was derived from the oral tradition most regularly performed at that stage. The more polemical tradition (Q^2) that places emphasis on judgement, polemic against "this generation," a Deuteronomistic understanding of history and alludes to the story of Lot was then incorporated into and framed this existing written document (Q^1).[21] This more polemical material was likewise derived from the oral tradition most regularly performed at this later stage, and the redactional interpolations were added as the Q editor(s) saw necessary.

The above "oral-derived" Q is a possible scenario, but the main point of reference, however, is Kloppenborg's hypothesis on the stratification of Q, particularly with regards to the two main redactions and their rhetorical character. If there is one major modification that will be made, it is that the necessity for a Q^3 is questioned, since Q shows more interest in the Torah and Moses than Kloppenborg allows, and the material assigned to Q^3 fits very well with the rhetorical character of the material found in the main redaction. Q 4:1–13 for example, as the analysis will show, plays an important part in Q's Christology and it serves more than merely to legitimate Q's praxis. It also forms part of the polemical and apologetic strategy of the main redaction that seeks to defend the character of Jesus and to legitimate the Q people's existence. It explains that Jesus as the "Coming One" has passed the test of a prophet, and indeed, has initiated the new Exodus within which the Q people are participating. This Moses and exodus typology is also present in other parts of Q (Allison 2000). So although Moses may not be explicitly referred to in Q, he is certainly present in the form of Jesus, the new law giver. That is why Q also in many respects presupposes the Torah or takes it for granted—this is not merely applicable to the texts that Kloppenborg has assigned to Q^3 (Q 4:1–13; 11:42c; 16:17). For example, Q 16:17 that attests to the ever abiding status of the Torah

21. It needs to be mentioned here that the presentation of Jesus as the eschatological prophet, and the Moses and exodus typology encountered in the main redaction can be added as other important redactional motifs. See the analysis of the main redaction below.

coheres well with Q 13:27 where Q distances itself from those who do "lawlessness." Again, this constitutes and apologetic strategy where the character of Jesus and the Q people are defended. Overall, the main redaction (Kloppenborg's $Q^2 + Q^3$) we will propose serves *another* apologetic purpose as well—*it defends the Judean ethnic identity of Jesus and his followers;* but the attempt will also be to demonstrate, that *Jesus and his followers were Judeans of a different kind.* A fuller explanation of this and the incorporation of the Q^3 material into the main redaction will be treated below.

Lastly, it must be mentioned that here it is not agreed with Kloppenborg's understanding of the *Israelite identity* of the Galileans, and therefore the Q people. Kloppenborg (2000:221, 223, 229) similarly to Horsley understands the Galileans primarily as descendents of northern Israelites, and that Galilee had a substantial Israelite population before the period of the Hasmonean conquest. These Galileans would have had their own traditions and practices, and would not have been compliant in paying the Temple tax, their observance of tithing was irregular and they did not participate much in pilgrimage to Jerusalem. Centuries of separation of Galilee from Judea would also have led to a different understanding of the Torah, although it is likely that they observed basic practices such as circumcision of males, Sabbath and some purity distinctions. Thus their historical connections to the second Temple were tenuous and the Galileans were in essence not a Judean "Torah-true" people (Kloppenborg 2000:218–34).

Kloppenborg reads this religious and cultural separation of Galilee from Judea into the Q text. The critical points of Q's rhetoric is aimed at issues such as purity distinctions (Q 11:39–41), tithing (Q 11:42), and the role of Jerusalem and the Temple in the social and religious economy of Galilee (Q 11:49–51; 13:34–35). What we have here is a form of resistance to the extension of Judean forms of Temple-orientated practices to Galilee. The Q people did not reject purity distinctions entirely (cf. Q 11:44) or reject tithing in principle, but the "topics of woes in 11:39–44, purity and tithing, are rooted in the economy of the Second Temple ... Q's woes lampoon the highly specific purity practices of the Pharisees who adopted the articulated purity regime of the priestly caste in Judaea" (Kloppenborg 2000:257). This concern for a further articulation of purity distinctions and tithing requirements in reality translated into an increased symbolic (or actual) control of agricultural produce from the south, which the Galileans and people of Q resisted. Overall Q is thus engaged in a struggle "in support of local forms of Israelite religion in the face of pressures from the hierocratic worldview of Judaea" (Kloppenborg 2000:261).

It is argued, however, that this understanding of the Galilean/Q people is not correct. Evidence from archaeology is especially useful in this regard. As we saw in the previous chapter there is no archaeological evidence for an indigenous population in Galilee in the centuries after 733/2 BC. During the period of Hasmonean rule, however, Galilee experienced an overall growth in settlements and population. Combined with this is the cultural continuity that Galilee shows with Judea in terms of stone vessels, *miqva'oth*, lack of pork in the bone profile, and secondary burial with ossuaries in *kokhim* or *loculi* tombs. This strongly suggests that the inhabitants of Galilee during our period were Judeans (Reed 1999:95–102; 2000:23–55), and any reason for the ideological and cultural separation between the Q people and Jerusalem as such must be sought somewhere else.

So the Q people themselves were Judeans, but they were evidently Judeans of a different kind. According to Allison (1997:53), "we are looking at Jewish Christianity," or rather, Judean Messianism. Whether the deviant Q group saw themselves as Messianist Judeans, as part of "eschatological" Judeanism, or whether they adhered to any form of (re)constructed covenantal nomism will be addressed later.

The Date and Provenance of Q

Date

As Kloppenborg (2000:81) explains it, one of the usual ways to set a *terminus a quo* for a document is to find a reference to the First Revolt. This we find in both Matthew (Matt 22:8) and Luke (Luke 21:20–23). The mention of Zechariah in Q (11:51), however, probably does not refer to Zechariah ben Barachiah who was murdered in 67/68 CE (*War* 4.335)—the way it is used in Matthew (Matt 23:35)—but probably refers to the murder of Zechariah ben Jehoida in 2 Chr 24:20–22, who was killed in the courtyard of the temple. Kloppenborg (2000:87) argues that the late 50s or early 60s is a possible date for his proposed second redaction of Q that constitutes the bulk of the document. He further argues that the temptation story (Q 4:1–13) and two glosses (Q 11:43c; 16:17) are later additions, so Q did not reach its final form until slightly after the events of 70 CE. Allison argues along similar lines that Q does not exhibit knowledge of the war against Rome in 66–73 CE. Based on his understanding of Q's stratification, Allison (1997:49–54) conjectures that Q^1 dates to the 30s (aimed at missionaries) and $Q^1 + Q^2 + Q^3$ to the 40s or 50s, with $Q^1 + Q^2$ dated to somewhere in-between. Tuckett's (1996:102) more cautious approach leaves a possible date for Q within a broader time span of c. 40–70 CE. So based on the above, we can generalize and say that the bulk of Q or perhaps the entire document dates to around the 50s or 60s CE.

Provenance

The location of Q was already touched upon when Kloppenborg's understanding that the Galileans (and therefore the Q people) were descendents of northern Israelites was questioned, but in this regard there seems to be reasonable consensus that Q was located somewhere in Galilee. In the very least, due to Q's lack of a Gentile mission, its use of place names, allusions and metaphors, it may be concluded that Q was probably produced somewhere in Palestine (Allison 1997:52–53). Tuckett (1996:103) argues that Q may possibly be located in Galilee/Syria, but more than that we cannot say. Reed has suggested that the social map (i.e. the use of place names and spatial imagery) of Q points to a Galilean setting for the community, particularly Capernaum, but with first hand knowledge of urban centres such as Sepphoris and Tiberias. Reed brings attention to the centrality of Capernaum, Chorazin and Bethsaida (Q 10:13–15). The nine different places named in Q Reed argues form a set of three concentric circles converging on Capernaum (Q 10:15). Within a short radius are Chorazin and Bethsaida; the second concentric circle is formed by Tyre and Sidon in the north (Q 10:13–14) and Jerusalem in the south (Q 13:34); the third and final concentric circle forms the mythical boundaries of the Q people's map made up of Sodom to the far south (Q 10:12) and Nineveh the far north (Q 11:32). Capernaum, Chorazin and Bethsaida "are not only geographically at the center of the place names in Q, the vehemence of their condemnation points to their centrality and distinguishes them from the other six places in Q" (Reed 2000:183; cf. 1995; 1996). These three cities are thus of great importance to the Q community, but Capernaum in particular is singled out for special condemnation. This can be explained by the fact that Capernaum remained an important centre for Jesus' followers and the Q community (Reed 2000:184).[22]

---

22. Richardson (2004:86) argues, however, that the lack of references to lakes, fishing and boats (only slightly present in Q 17:2, 6; 11:11) suggests that the Sea of Galilee is outside Q's field of vision. Further, the Q community presupposes house-holders in towns and villages or as small landowners. Q "was part of an agriculturally

Kloppenborg's basically concurs with Reed's analysis but is cautious to identify Q's origin specifically with Capernaum. "The unlikelihood of a Jerusalem provenance for Q,[23] combined with the focus of Q's map on the Lower Galilee and the local knowledge that Q assumes on the part of its addressees form the best basis for the assumption of a Galilean provenance for Q" (Kloppenborg 2000:175). Also, although itinerants may still have been present when Q was edited, they no longer were the controlling influence over the document or the group. The work reflects mostly that of a settled community (Kloppenborg 2000:183–84).

Summary

The Q document, now embedded in Matthew and Luke, was probably produced, or at least the bulk of it, in Galilee (perhaps Capernaum) somewhere in the 50s or 60s CE. Following the hypothesis of Kloppenborg, the Q document consists of two major strata. The formative stratum was instructional in nature. It consists of a large number of sayings that are sapiential admonitions, and also present are beatitudes, proverbs and wisdom sayings. The tone of this material is hortatory and instructional, and it employs the rhetoric of persuasion, instead of prophetic pronouncement or declamation, while not denying that prophetic elements are present, however. The main redaction, on the other hand, is dominated by chriae and prophetic words, where the tone is primarily polemical and judgmental, and the Q material here demonstrates the need to defend the character of Jesus. At the same time the need for a third stratum is questioned since it will be demonstrated that it properly belongs to the theological, polemical and apologetic strategy of the main redaction. Thus the main redaction will presently become the focus of study.

---

orientated community involved in grain farming and related pursuits in lower Galilee or Gaulanitis. It was set in a town, one in competition with those towns condemned by Jesus [cf. Q 10:13–15], possibly walled, and in a location where Tyre and Sidon were within the situational horizon. Houses and householders were a dominant factor in the town. There was a synagogue, which may have been used for the group's ritual activities: eating and drinking, prayer, baptism, and ritual purity" (2004:89). Exactly where the Q community was located Richardson is not willing to say, but he prefers a location in lower Galilee.

23. Cf. Pearson (2004:493), who suggests that Jerusalem may have been the location for the tradition in Q and further argues "there is absolutely no evidence to suggest that [Q] should be assigned to Galilee." In light of Reed's analysis Pearson's objections are open to questioning.

Judean Ethnicity in Q

Having done the preliminary investigation into Q, we will now shift our focus to the particular cultural features that are present in Q, but with each stratum analysed on its own. The investigation into the two strata is done to help clarify: What kind of Judeans were the Q people? At the end, we will draw a comparison between the two strata to trace noticeable developments within the Q document, which will more or less reflect the developments within the Q community, particularly relating to the Q group's ethnic identity. We will start the analysis concentrating on the main redaction.

The Main Redaction (Q²)

The *Habitus*/Israel

Let us begin by saying that based on the archaeological profile of Galilee and the literary evidence, the Q people would have found themselves in an environment that was essentially primordialist. The interrelationship between the *habitus* (the "habitual dispositions" of Galileans and the internalization of the "sense of self" through categorization) and the more tangible cultural features, would have been dominated by the endeavor to maintain covenant status or Judean ethnic identity ("staying in"). Galilean society, as it was informed by the same "Sacred Canopy," also constituted a highly integrated and uniform system of dispositions. For this reason, their ethnicity was highly congruent with the habitus and established cultural practices. But how did the Q people compare?

Name

Although the Q people were Judeans, Reed (2000:189) notes that "['Ιουδαῖοι] never appears in Q, where instead 'Israel' is cited ... [I]t is conspicuous that this term with southern connotations was avoided, and that the old term used also for the descendants of Abraham and later the Northern Kingdom was preferred." It must be said, however, that it was not a matter of Q avoiding the term Judea/Judeans since it was pre-occupied with a religious-cultural agenda. "Israel" represents an insider perspective related to the history of the covenant people and the land promised by God to their ancestors, and "Israel" with its symbolism and religious connotations was the almost universal self-designation for Judeans of our period (Dunn 2000:263–64; Schmidt 2001:30–31). "Israel" therefore most certainly also had "southern connotations."

Evidently the Q people identified themselves with this symbolic usage and saw themselves as part of Israel, and as heirs of the ancestral land.

There are two instances where "Israel" appears in Q. When Jesus enters Capernaum a centurion demonstrates remarkable faith by requesting that Jesus heal his boy from a distance. Jesus replied: "Not even in Israel have I found such faith" (Q 7:9b). The centurion, although in geographical Israel, is evidently not part of "Israel" as a people. But the exceptional and unusual quality of his faith is emphasized, something that would normally be expected of the traditional people of Israel. The second and last appearance of Israel in Q is used in an eschatological context. The followers of Jesus are promised that they will sit on thrones to judge/liberate/establish justice for the "twelve tribes of Israel" (Q 22:30). So the people of Israel and the geographical area the name presupposes plays an important part even in the future perspective of the Q people.

Overall, when it comes to the name "Israel" the Q people fit in with the general usage and self-understanding of Judeans of our period. They occupy the geographical territory of Israel and saw themselves as part of its cultural and symbolic paradigm. It is within this ancestral land where a Gentile centurion showed remarkable faith, and where the Q people at some time in the future will play a role in its restoration. And restoration implied only one thing: it must be occupied by the kind of people that God always intended. It is only in such a context, where land and people come together, where the name "Israel" can have legitimate meaning.

Language

What does the language of the Q document itself tell us about the Q people? Allison argues that the final form of Q was Greek but there is the presence of translation Greek in all the three strata (70 percent in what he assigns to Q^1; 58 percent in Q^2; 60 percent in Q^3). Dependent on the work of Raymond A Martin (1987), Allison thus argues that Q in its entirety was strongly Semitic and must at all three stages have drawn on materials that were originally composed in Aramaic. Particularly Q^1 has the strongest Semitic flavor—although Q 9:57–60; 12:22–32 according to Martin's statistics (1987:100–101; cf. 1995:136) do not qualify as translation Greek, but Allison (1997:47–49) argues they contain Semitic features. So the possibility exists that his Q^1 was originally a collection of Aramaic traditions.

Kloppenborg (2000:73, 77–78) replies by saying since Q 9:57–60 and 12:22–31 (part of Allison's Q¹) is outside the translation Greek frequency it undermines Allison's case for assigning these pericopae to his possibly original Aramaic Q¹. Kloppenborg also refers to the work of Martin (1995), and Kloppenborg argues that Martin recognizes that Aramaic speech patterns did influence Q's language but he falls short of concluding that Q as a whole was translated from Aramaic. This observation Kloppenborg uses in favor of his own view that Q was originally *written* in Greek. Kloppenborg (2000:80) admits that Q contains Aramaisms but argues that the "thesis of an Aramaic original of Q is extraordinarily weak." A similar view is also held by Tuckett (1996:92). Reed (2000:179) also suggests that the Q document was originally written in Greek and Q must therefore be located in an area "where at least some level of Greek literacy existed."

Kloppenborg (2000:168) asserts that due to the low rates of literacy in the ancient world it "meant that if the documents of a group were to be known at all, they had to be performed." The audience was present already at the time of composition, and ancient "rhetorical practice itself ensured a strong correlation between the values and interests of the audience and the shape of the text" (Kloppenborg 2000:169). A related issue is Horsley's suggestion that most texts from antiquity are "oral-derived" literature. This means that most ancient texts "originated in oral performance and continued to be recited or performed after they were written down. Literary texts were written and used primarily for the purpose of facilitating oral communication. Texts were transcripts of and/or aids to oral performances" (Horsley & Draper 1999:144).[24] In addition, this performance was a communal experience, and "recited discourses or communally read texts [Q being an example] were embedded in communities and their particular historical and social circumstances" (1999:147). So if Q was originally written in Greek as an oral-derived text, if a text at the moment of composition had a strong correlation between itself and shared values and interests of the audience, and if the performance was a communal experience, this all implies that the Q people had to understand Greek (or required the services of a translator into Aramaic?), or even, that they exclusively spoke Greek. Jacobson

---

24. Cf. the results of Mournet's study. "We illustrated that texts were often heard rather than read silently, composition was typically by means of dictation, and oral performance was an integral part of the process of writing a text. Oral traditions served both as a source for texts, and often served as the impetus for the initial inscription of the text itself" (Mournet 2005:289).

(1992:87) draws attention to the biblical quotations in the temptation narrative (Q 4:1–13), and says that these are remarkable for they "come from the LXX and so presumably from a primarily Greek-speaking community" and that "the use of the LXX is typical for Q." Pearson (2004) has argued that Q cannot be easily placed in a Galilean setting for the reason that we know it only in Greek. The lingua franca of Judeans in first-century Palestine was Aramaic, the language in which Jesus' teachings were handed down. Pearson (2004:492) thus suggests, that "the Jesus traditions of the Aramaic-speaking 'Hebrews' led by the twelve 'apostles' [Acts 6:1; 8:1] were translated in Jerusalem for the benefit of the Greek-speaking 'Hellenists' led by the group of seven named in Acts [6:5]. That could very well be the origin of what we know as Q. As to the provenance of Q as we now have it, a good argument could be made that it, too, originated in Jerusalem, though Antioch is also a strong possibility." It must be said, that a Galilean provenance for Q is far more persuasive. And was Aramaic the predominant language of Judeans in Palestine, and in particular, Galilee, as Pearson believes?

We saw in the previous two chapters that use of the Greek language did penetrate into Galilee. Of course, this milieu would also have affected the Q group. Archaeological excavations have shown that the cultural character of Galilee at this period was predominantly Judean (Reed 2000; Chancey 2002), but there seems to have been a relatively widespread use of the Greek *language* throughout Palestine, including Galilee (Porter 1994; Fitzmyer 1992; Batey 2001). So it is important to emphasize that the use of Greek language by Judeans should not be confused with them adopting aspects of Hellenistic culture. Q's probable location in Capernaum or immediate surrounds in any event places it in an area where at least some of the community's people could speak both Aramaic and Greek. Capernaum was the gateway to the Golan Heights (Gaulanitis) that illustrates it would have had linguistic and cultural contact with a far more Hellenized territory (cf. Porter 1994:135–36). A Greek speaking (or bilingual) community in Capernaum should therefore not come as a surprise. Either the Q people's preferred everyday language was Greek, or in the very least, they were bilingual (Porter 1994:133).

If the Q community was exclusively Greek speaking, this could have contributed towards the sense of alienation from their Aramaic speaking brethren. But taking into consideration the widespread use of Greek in Judea and Galilee, not too much must be made of Q and the

Q people's language. Language was hardly a critical issue for Judean ethnic identity in our period.

Religion and Covenantal Praxis

Religion and covenantal praxis in Judeanism manifested itself in three primary areas: the Temple, the synagogue, and at home. It must be said from the outset that Q does not give much explicit information in this regard. We can assume that they shared much with their co-ethnics hence traditional covenantal praxis is not in dispute, and so was part and parcel of everyday life. There is one outstanding exception, however; the issue of immersion/baptism.

Q begins with the fiery preaching of John the Immerser (Q 3:7–9, 16b–17) who offers his listeners the rite of immersion in view of the imminent eschatological crisis.[25] According to Tuckett (1996:114), the prime object of John's attack are those who refuse to accept his preaching and baptism,[26] so the "fruit" his audience must produce refers to baptism itself. This view is not likely. John calls the Judeans to turn to God that will be evidenced by "fruit," that is, practical action, as will be elaborated in Jesus' sermon (Q 6:20b–49) (Jacobson 1992:81).

What was the source of John's immersion? According to La Sor (1987), it is Judean ritual baths, or *miqva'ot*, that undoubtedly provide the background for John's baptism. John the Immerser was a Judean. "No person seeking to influence [Judeans] in any matter concerning religion would introduce something new ... [M]uch stress was laid by [Judeans] on the continuity of tradition. We may therefore reasonably conclude that John's baptism was not something new. It was something that grew out of [Judean] ritual immersion in *miqva'ot*" (La Sor 1987). According to La Sor, it may be possible that John and other immersers did not administer the rite, but rather witnessed it. Such was the case with immersion in the *miqveh*, since Judean law required for the rite to be witnessed, and it is clear that the person immersed him or herself (*m.*

---

25. Q may have mentioned the immersion of Jesus (Q 3:21b–22), but the IQP places the pericope in square brackets to indicate uncertainty, while Kloppenborg regards its inclusion in Q as doubtful.

26. Tuckett (1996:116) argues that a significant portion of Q may be taken up with polemic against "Pharisees" and/or lawyers (11:39ff), thus it is possible that the Pharisees mentioned in Matt 3:7 who come out to see John may reflect the original Q wording. The IQP has "the crowds" coming to be baptized (in square brackets to indicate a level of uncertainty).

Mik. 2:1, 2; 7:6). Q seems to imply, however, that John did administer the rite himself: "ἐγὼ μὲν ὑμᾶς βαπτίζω [[ἐν]] ὕδατι" (Q 3:16b).

Of course there is a difference between ritual immersion and the water rite in a Q/Messianist context. Judean ritual immersion is purificatory, while Messianist immersion was initiatory—it was a one-time ritual that initiated you into the Messianist movement. This was probably the meaning in Q as well. Now this initiatory immersion, according to La Sor (1987), had its parallel in Judean proselyte immersion. Immersion in the *miqveh*, along with circumcision and the offering of a sacrifice in the Temple were required of proselytes to Judeanism (cf. Schürer et al 1986:173–74). After the destruction of the Temple, and after the expansion of the movement to Gentiles where circumcision was abrogated, ritual immersion in the *miqveh* was left as the only Judean requirement of conversion, and so became the central Messianist initiatory rite. In the end, La Sor (1987) suggests that Messianist immersion most probably derived from Judean proselyte immersion. But La Sor's analysis is ambiguous in various respects. Was the background of proselyte immersion also applicable to *Judean* Messianists? And why can John's rite not be the background for Messianist immersion which seems more likely (cf. Acts 18:25; 19:3–4)? And is there any connection between John's rite and proselyte immersion?

It is suggested here that if immersion in the Q group was still performed, it was John's immersion—not proselyte immersion—that formed the immediate background. It is also accepted as historically plausible that John's rite was derived from Judean ritual immersion. The thing is, how did John's rite develop in a Q context? The initial context according to Q was repentance (Q 3:7–9). Now according to Acts, Messianists were immersed "in the name of Jesus Messiah" (Acts 2:38), or "in the name of the Lord Jesus" (Acts 8:16). In Matthew 28:19, immersion was "in the name of the Father, the Son and of the Holy Spirit." Paul also asks the Corinthians, "Were you immersed in the name of Paul?" (1 Cor 1:13). Now similar kind of developments could have occurred within the Q group, or did they still think of the rite as "the immersion of John"? (Matt 21:25; Mark 11:30; Luke 7:29; Acts 1:22; 18:25). We are not told anything in this regard.

Besides the above, what did John's immersion mean in a Q context? Horsley (1999:95) explains it as a "prophetic covenantal exhortation to Israel to repent in the face of judgement." At the same time, however, it clearly also had to do with the redefinition of God's people (Uro 1995:243). Uro argues that Q 3:8bc interrupts the flow from v. 8a ("So bear fruit worthy of repentance . . .") to v. 9 and is likely to be a later addition. The criticism of the appeal to Abraham as father in v. 8bc, which appears to be a rejection of baptism altogether, compliments the redactional layer of Q dominated by the deuteronomistic motif "and by the conviction that Israel has lost her prerogative as covenant people [cf. Q 13:28–30; 14:16–24]" (Uro 1995:244). For Q the appeal to Abraham has been replaced by repentance and baptism, and merit must now be required individually. Maintenance of covenant status requires something not ordinarily expected. The fact that immersion was an *initiatory rite* for the purpose of salvation, a *covenantal praxis* previously unheard of, indicates the Q people participated in a process where covenantal nomism was in (re)construction. Traditional covenantal nomism is left behind. Immersion therefore clearly separated the Q people from other Judeans. We clearly have an ideological conflict between "orthodox" Judeans and the Q people who have redefined Judean ethnicity.

When it comes to other matters of *covenantal praxis* Catchpole (1993:256) suggests that wherever legal material illustrates a conservative coloring (e.g., Q 11:37–52; 16:17), it "necessarily presupposes an appreciative attitude to the temple and its cult." This may well be, but for the Q people the Temple is now "forsaken" (Q 13:35a). Q does not tell us whether the Q people participated in pilgrimages but it is certainly possible. In the very least, they hoped for the restoration of the Temple in its attitude towards Jesus (Q 13:35b) and the Temple still appears to benefit from the Q people's tithing (Q 11:42). Matters of ritual purity are also presupposed (Q 11:39, 41, 44), so the Q people seem to be ordinary Judeans when it comes to traditional covenantal praxis. Here they shared the traditional aspects of the Judean symbolic universe, but more will be said when Q's attitude towards the Torah is discussed.

Kinship

There are various issues that affect kinship, hence the investigation will be conducted by looking first at the Q people's relationship with fellow Judeans in general, and secondly, their relationship with family members.

The Q People and Broader Israel

One of the main themes that Kloppenborg has recognized in the main redaction of Q is polemic against "this generation" (ἡ γενεὰ αὕτη), appearing seven times. In Q 7:31–35, the ascetic John and sociable Jesus, both envoys of Wisdom, are rejected. "This generation" has thus showed itself not to be the true children of Wisdom (v. 35), since the acceptance of Jesus and John's message is the acceptance of Wisdom (Tuckett 1996:178–79). Q 11:29 speaks of "this generation" as evil for it requests for a sign, but the Son of humanity/man will be a sign to "this generation," as was Jonah to the Ninevites. In Q 11:31–32, "this generation" is unfavorably compared with Gentiles, the Ninevites and the queen of the South. The Ninevites repented at the preaching of Jonah, the queen of the South listened to the wisdom of Solomon, yet "this generation" has rejected a message that is qualitatively greater—the preaching of Jesus (and the Q group). Lastly, Q 11:50–51 says the blood of all the prophets, from Abel to Zechariah, will be required of "this generation."

The phrase "this (evil) generation" occurs only twice in the Tanak, speaking about the generation of Noah (Gen 7:1) and once of the time of Moses (Deut 1:35). These two generations became types of the last generation (*Jub.* 23:14, 15, 16, 22; *1 En.* 93:9; 1QpHab 2:7; 1QpMic), so "this generation" in Q recalls the stories of primordial sins. Specifically Q 11:29–32 that speaks of this *evil* generation, compliments the exodus typology encountered in Q (the *evil* generation in the wilderness is referred to in Deut 1:35; Num 32:13; cf. Pss 94:10 and 78:8). Jesus, the prophet like Moses has initiated the new Exodus. The Q people are following. But in Q 11:29–32 the contemporaries of Jesus and the Q group have not heeded their message, so they resemble the generation of the wilderness "which grumbled and rebelled in the wilderness despite God's mighty salvific acts" (Allison 2000:59).

In agreement with Tuckett (1996:199) "this generation" refers to unresponsive Judeans. It does not just refer to the Pharisees alone (*pace* Horsley 1995:49). But in agreement with both Tuckett and Horsley, "this generation" does not refer to Israel as a whole. It was the unresponsive contemporaries of Jesus and John, and of the Q community.

The tension that exists over and against "this generation" is reflected in Q 11:23: "The one not with me is against me, and the one not gathering with me scatters." This saying is the counterpart of Mark 9:40, yet it is far more exclusive. In Mark, it is only those who actively oppose Jesus who are rejected. In Q 11:23, neutrality is taken as opposition (Tuckett 1996:290). Tuckett further suggests that the polemic of several texts, which is assigned here to the main redaction (Q 12:8–10, 51–53; 13:26–29; 14:16–23; 17:22–37; 19:12–29) is concerned to fight neutrality. The Q people are in a situation where those addressed are doing *nothing* in response to the Q people's message. The Q people are surrounded by *apathy* (Tuckett 1996:296). This negative response is understood as "persecutions" (Q 6:22–23; 6:27–35; 11:47–51; 12:4–5; 12:11–12; 13:34–35; 14:27). According to Tuckett (1996:322):

> Yet when we press the details, it seems hard to see the persecution as involving anything very systematic. There may have been hostility, taunts, verbal abuse, social ostracism. But there is no direct evidence of sustained physical attacks, nor of any deaths. The hostility may have become violent at times, but so much of the polemic in Q seems to presuppose a situation of silent ignoring.

There was certainly apathy towards the Q people's message, but it is questionable that the Q people were predominantly the targets of silent ignoring (cf. Horsley & Draper 1999:274; Kloppenborg 2000:193–95, 198). One can accept that the Q people at times experienced active opposition, discrimination and repression (e.g., Q 6:22–23; 11:39; 12:4–5, 8–9, 11–12, 58–59; 14:27; 17:33). This would explain the harsh tone of Q's polemic. For example, "this generation" will also be held accountable for the death of the prophets (Q 11:49–51). The ἵνα ("so that") in Q 11:50 probably denotes purpose, which means that Wisdom sends prophets to Q's opponents ("them" in Q 11:49; "this generation" in Q 11:50–51) for the sole purpose of making them responsible for the blood of all the murdered prophets. If this is the case, "we would seem to have the perspective of a group radically alienated from its [Judean] heritage. Israel's God has vanished in the darkness of a terrible necessity that lies upon 'this generation'" (Jacobson 1992:180). It is assumed that the prophets—now members of the Q community—will be killed and persecuted. The reason for this is that "this generation" is no different from its prophet-murdering forefathers (Q 11:47–48).

The Q community's rejection and persecution is also seen through the experience of John and Jesus, both identified as envoys of Wisdom (Q 7:31–35; 11:49–51). Based on their failure to convert Israel, the Q people had recourse to the myth of Divine Sophia to provide a solution to their problems. "This generation," reflecting the wider community of the people of Israel, has rejected Jesus, and his rejection "is a paradigm for the rejection of the Q community" (Hartin 1995:158–59).[27]

---

27. Although Hartin (1995:159), speaking in reference to Q 10:21–22 and 11:49–51, states that "Sophia opposes those who hold authority [i.e. religious leadership] in Israel." So in these passages "this generation" acquires a narrower frame of references for him. Particularly Q 11:49–51 holds Jerusalem, which represents the religious leadership, as responsible for the rejection of Sophia's emissary (Jesus). But is such a narrower

This rejection has serious consequences for the future. Kloppenborg (1987:148) suggests that very little if anything in Q 11:14–52 "holds out to 'this generation' an opportunity for repentance and rehabilitation ... [N]othing remains but the inevitability of judgment and eschatological punishment." According to Catchpole (1993:262), Q 11:52 "presupposes that entry into the kingdom, which is synonymous with 'sharing in the age to come' [*m. Sanh.* 10:1], is not the automatic assumption for all Israelites ...."

Also relevant here is the harsh polemic we find against the Galilean towns in Q 10:12, 13–15. This is quite relevant since Capernaum and its environs were perhaps the location of the Q community itself. In Q 10:12, the towns are warned that on the day of judgement, Sodom will fare better. In Judean tradition, Sodom was viewed as an extreme example of corruption and wickedness (Gen 13:13; 18:20; 19:13; Jer 23:14), and the typical example of what provokes God's fiery judgement (Deut 29:23; Isa 1:9; 13:19; Jer 50:40; Amos 4:11). "To affirm that any town will fare *worse* than Sodom in the eschatological judgement is truly astonishing" (Catchpole 1993:175; emphasis original). According to Catchpole (1993:176) the towns are not accused of Sodom-like offences (Catchpole lists adultery, lying, pride, approval of evil, gluttony, prosperous ease, idolatry and a failure to help the poor and needy; cf. Jer 23:14; Ezek 16:49; Jude 7; *T. Levi* 14:6; *T. Naph.* 3:4; *T. Benj.* 9:1) but merely the rejection of the message of Jesus. But the dominant exegetical tradition identified arrogance and inhospitality as the Sodomites' gravest sins—particularly affected were the poor.[28] According to Allison (2000:82), Q 10:12 in a similar fashion refers to the sin of inhospitality. This message along with Q 10:13–15 belongs to a mission exclusively aimed at Israel, but clearly these passages illustrate a bitter resentment towards the towns for their inability to respond positively to the Q group's message. Tyre and Sidon it is said will fare better in the judgement, yet these cities were frequently singled out for condemnation[29] and were seen on various occasions as enemies of Israel.[30] It becomes evident that the Q people did not think much of their Judean neighbors!

---

definition justified?

28. Gen 19; Isa 3:9–17; Ezek 16:49–50; WisSol 19:13–14; Josephus, *Ant.* 1.194; *Sif. Deut.* 11:13–17; *b. Sanh.* 109a-b; *P.R.E.* 25.

29. Isa 23; Jer 25:22; 29; 47:4; Ezek 26; 27; 28:11–12, 22–23; Zech 9:2–4; Amos 1:9–10; Joel 3:4–8.

30. Ps 82:8; Amos 1:9–10; 3:11 (LXX); Joel 4:4–8; 1 Macc 5:15.

The Q people's conflict with their co-ethnics is also evident in the polemic against the Pharisees and the lawyers. These Judean groups had influence over the people, and so act as representatives of the people and their spiritual state as well. Particularly the Pharisees—seen by Tuckett as part of the "retainer class"—pre-occupied themselves with issues of ritual purity and tithing (Tuckett 1996:442). Josephus testifies to the supposed popularity the Pharisees had amongst the populace (*Ant.* 18.15, 17), although they did not seem to have much political influence in the first half of the first century. The Pharisees "more likely constituted a group that continually jockeyed for power and tried to gain power, though with varying degrees of success at different periods in history" (Tuckett 1996:444). Whatever their political influence, Q represents them as having considerable influence on the people. Now according to Tuckett, Q illustrates a strong concern to uphold the Pharisaic interpretation of the Law, and draws attention to the speculation that Jesus and his disciples had close links with the Pharisees.[31] However, coupled with this is an intense hostility to non-Messianist Pharisees and/or (non-Messianist) scribes/lawyers (Tuckett 1996:424). Nevertheless, the accusations against the Pharisees never question their practice or rulings (Q 11:39–42). Purity laws and tithing are affirmed, and it is only in Q (as opposed to Mark) where Jesus is represented as affirming these links positively. Tuckett (1996:447) thus argues it would appear that "the community which preserved the Q material may also have preserved positive links with the Pharisaic movement in a way that most other primitive [Messianist] groups about which we have any evidence did not." The woes in Q 11:39–42 suggest that the Q Messianists and the Pharisees they encountered shared a large degree of overlap. Both groups were "reform" or "renewal movements," which sought to influence others. So Tuckett (1996:449) suggests that the Q people may have been claiming to be a genuine part of the Pharisaic movement. The desire of the Q people was *not* to separate, but Q perhaps represents an early stage (earlier than Matthew) in the separation of Messianist communities from their Judean neighbors.

Such a view, however, is difficult to accept. There is obviously a degree of overlap—the Q people were Judeans after all—but there is no claim that the Q community is a part of the Pharisaic movement (Catchpole 1993:277). In Q 10:21 for example, which follows immedi-

---

31. Cf. Mark 7:2; 7:15; 2:15–17; 2:18–20, where it is expected that Jesus and his disciples should obey Pharisaic rules, or alternatively, the stipulations of the associates/*ḥaberim* (Schmidt 2001:235).

ately after the missionary instructions, Jesus thanks the Father that he had kept "these things" from the "sages and the learned." As Jacobson (1992:149) has noted, the bitter denunciations (Q 10:12–15) are followed by joyful praise, and anger and disappointment is followed by the view that God intended the failure of the mission. This actually contradicts the deuteronomistic motif, for nowhere in that tradition is their place for thanksgiving about Israel's unbelief. In addition, it is said that Israel—under the spiritual guidance of the Pharisees and the lawyers—has no knowledge of God. This belongs exclusively to the Son and his followers (Q 10:22). According to Jacobson (1992:149), this "appears to be the expression of a radically sectarian group whose alienation from their own people exceeds anything found anywhere else in Q." Covenantal nomism is in this context obliterated. The corporate notion of Israel as an elect people is denied, for how can you maintain your status within the covenant if you have no knowledge of God? Maintenance of status, it is implied, belongs to those who have responded positively to the message of Jesus.

"This generation" is clearly quite alienated from the Q group (or the Q group alienated itself). This might be taken as support that the Q group had given up hope on Israel in favor of the Gentiles. In connection with this, in Q 13:28–29, mention is made of the many that will come from "Sunrise and Sunset" to eat with the patriarchs in the kingdom of God, while Jesus' (and therefore Q's) unrepentant Judean contemporaries will be excluded. Tuckett understands this to refer to the many Gentiles that will replace the Judeans. He writes the saying (following the Matthean order of the verses: Matt 8:11–12; as does the IQP) "clearly contrasts the future fate of [Judeans] with that of Gentiles in the kingdom of God and claims that Gentiles will not only come into the kingdom but will actually replace [Judeans]" (Tuckett 1996:194). Tuckett (1996:194) argues this saying fits well with other sayings in Q where Gentiles are favorably compared with Judeans, and where Judeans are warned that Gentiles will receive better treatment than they (Q 10:13–15) and will even judge them (Q 11:31–32).

With regards to Q 13:28–29, Allison (1997:117; cf. 2000:166–69) argues that it "has nothing to do with Gentiles. It proclaims rather God's judgment upon unfaithful [Judeans] in the land of Israel and the eschatological ingathering of [Judeans] from the Diaspora." The directions from "Sunrise/East and Sunset/West" occur in Judean texts in connection with the return of Judeans to the land of Israel (Zech 8:7–8; 1 Bar 4:37; 5:5; *Pss. Sol.* 11:2; *1 En.* 57:1). Also, Allison (1997:179–

80) states that his research has not turned up a single text where the expression refers to the eschatological ingathering of Gentiles. There are parallel expressions where it is described that the exiles will return from Assyria/Babylon and Egypt (Isa 27:12–13; Hos 11:11; Zech 10:10).[32] It is not that all in Israel will be cast out of the kingdom. There are sayings that presuppose the presence of Judeans in the eschatological kingdom (Q 6:20; 13:28–29; 22:28–30). But many Judeans of the first century, including the Q people, looked forward to the future ingathering of scattered Israel, including the ten lost tribes.[33] Josephus gives evidence of speculation as to the number and whereabouts of the lost ten tribes (*Ant.* 11.133). So Q looks forward to a blessed future for those in the Diaspora, while the Judeans resident in the land who refuse to accept their message will face eschatological punishment and exclusion. Parallels to this eschatological reversal are also found in the Tanak's prophetic literature (Jer 24:1–10; 29:10–32; Ezek 11).

Q's attitude towards fellow Judeans is typified by Q 13:34–35. Here mention is made of the Coming One, and Kloppenborg suggests that he is described in similar language found in Mal 3:1–2: he will "come" with judgement to Jerusalem and its temple (Kloppenborg 2000:123). This understanding of Q 13:34–35 is not likely, however. Admittedly, Jerusalem is accused as one who kills the prophets. As a result, she is told: "Look, your house is forsaken!" (Q 13:35a; cf. Jer 12:7: God says, "I have abandoned my house . . ."). Yet, v. 35 continues: "I tell you, You will not see me until [[<<the time>> comes when]] you say: Blessed is the one who comes in the name of the Lord" (λέγω .. ὑμῖν, οὐ μὴ ἴδητέ με ἕως [[ἥξει ὅτε]] εἴπητε· εὐλογημένος ὁ ἐρχόμενος ἐν ὀνόματι κυρίου). According to Allison (1997:193), in the LXX and especially in Ps 117:26 that is cited in our Q text, εὐλογημένος (along with εὐλογεῖν and εὐλογημένος in the NT) "are often expressions of joy, and they consistently have a very positive connotation: 'to praise,' 'to extol,' 'to bless,' 'to greet.'" He also suggests that v. 35 can be understood as a conditional sentence. "Until you say" means that when the people of Israel bless the Messiah, the Messiah will come. "In other words, the redemption will come when Israel accepts the person and work of Jesus" (Allison 1997:196). The Jerusalem and the temple is "forsaken" precisely

---

32. For Luke's longer version that includes "from north and south" cf. Isa 43:5–6; Zech 2:10 (LXX); *Pss. Sol.* 11:2–3.

33. Cf. 2 Macc 1:27–28; 2:18; Tob 13:13; *Pss. Sol.* 8:28. On the ten lost tribes, see Sir 36:11; 48:10; 1QM 2:1–3; 4QpIsa[d] line 7; 11QTemple 57:5–6; *4 Ezra* 13:32–50; *2 Bar.* 78:1–7; *Sib. Or.* 2:170–73.

for the reason that those in the temple do not bless Jesus (cf. LXX Ps 117:26b: "We bless you from the house of the Lord"). Allison explains that ἕως can function to express contingency in Greek sentences; "the state in the first half of the sentence lasts only until the state depicted in the second half is realized. In such cases the meaning of ἕως is often not simply temporal ('until') but properly conditional, and thus close to 'unless'" (Allison 1997:198). So a glimmer of hope is present for Jerusalem and the temple. Q is saying that Jerusalem will be forsaken only until such a time when the people bless Jesus as the coming one and accept him as Messiah. So Q 13:35b functions similarly to Amos 9:11–15: an oracle of doom is followed by hope of restoration. This is in line with other Q texts that look forward to the restoration of Israel (Q 13:29; 22:30). So Q 13:35b and its "optimism" is an integral part of the strong language used in Q to speak against "this generation" in order to arouse a positive response, and to warn of the severe consequences if it does not (Tuckett 1996:206).

So Q does entertain hopes for the restoration of Israel, even though it is only occasionally hinted at (Jacobson 1992:248). Jacobson says that Q 22:28–30 points to a ruling function and not the administration of justice. In this regard Horsley (1987:201–207; 1995:38; 1999:69, 105, 263) has persistently argued that the "judging (κρίνοντες) of the twelve tribes of Israel" in Q 22:30 has a positive meaning. Like the Hebrew *šapaṭ*, the Greek points to grace and deliverance. So in Q 22:28–30 the Twelve/Q people (?) are portrayed not as judging (negatively) but as "liberating or establishing justice" for the twelve tribes (cf. *Pss. Sol.* 17:28–32; 1QS 8:1–4; *T. Jud.* 24–25). "In Israelite tradition, God does not 'judge' but 'delivers' ('liberates/saves/effects justice for') the orphan, widow, poor, oppressed" or "even the whole people."[34] In agreement with Horsley (1995:39; 1999:69), based on an appropriate reading of Q 22:28–30, "Q envisages a renewal or restoration of Israel." In relation to this stands Q 13:28–29, which refers to the restoration of the twelve tribes, "one of the principal images of the future renewal of Israel" (Horsley & Draper 1999:106).[35]

But clearly it will only be the Diaspora and those local Judeans who respond to Q's message that will be part of this Israel and one cannot agree with Horsley (1995:46–51) that Q's polemical texts (e.g., Q 11:39–52; 13:28–29, 34–35; 14:16–24) are primarily aimed at the

34. Cf. Judg 2:16; 3:10; 4:4; Pss 9; 10:18; 35; 58; 72:4; 76:9; 82:1–4; 94; 96:13; 98:9; 103:6; 140:12; 146:7; Isa 42:1.

35. Cf. Isa 49:6; Sir 36:13; 48:10; *Pss. Sol.* 17:26–28.

priestly leaders in Jerusalem and their supposed representatives (the Pharisees and scribes). The "you" these Diaspora Judeans will replace in Q 13:28–29 is therefore not just the Judean rulers or those who thought themselves to be the premiere families in Israel (*pace* Horsley 1995:47; 1999:119), but unresponsive Judeans in general. The principal conflict in Q is not that between the people and their rulers, but between the Q group and their co-ethnics in general who have refused to follow Jesus. As we saw, the lament over Jerusalem ends with a ring of hope, and it hints at the possibility that even Jerusalem *and its leaders* may participate in salvation if they accept Jesus and the Q people's message. Jerusalem and the temple should rather be seen as representative of non-responsive Israel as a whole, who like Jerusalem persecute God's prophets, something which the Q people themselves experience from their local communities (Q 6:22–23; 12:10).

One last example also gives us insight into the Q people's relationship with fellow Judeans. In Q 13:24, Judeans are admonished to enter by the narrow door. In the succeeding verses (Q 13:25–29), it is spelled out what will happen if people do not. "Thus the eschatological polemic in Q," Tuckett (1996:204) goes on to argue, "may not be due to 'this generation' having been written off entirely, nor to the Q community strengthening its own group boundaries with a rigid 'us/them' sect mentality—rather, it is simply a way of reinforcing the seriousness of the call to 'this generation' to respond to the [Messianist] message, a call which may still be continuing." But does Q 13:24–27 have to do with "this generation"? This does not seem likely. The Q people (or their scribes?) want to disassociate themselves from those who do "lawlessness" (Q 13:27; cf. Ps 6:8). In Q 13:26 it is explained that they ate and drank in Jesus' presence, and Jesus taught in their streets.[36] But these Judeans will be told to get away from Jesus, reason being they do "lawlessness." We can paraphrase this sentence as follows: "You are not being Judean!" *Who* are these Judeans? What *kind* of "lawlessness" are they guilty of? They did not enter the "narrow door" (Q 13:24), which evidently at the stage of the main redaction, means they did not illustrate obedience to the Torah, or the Judean way of life. Here is evidence that there "seems to be division within the Q community or within the Jesus movement. At issue is the question of the boundaries of the movement—who is in and who is out" (Jacobson 1992:208). It is sug-

---

36. According to Tuckett (1996:192), it is widely agreed that Luke 13:26, which refers to Judean contemporaries of Jesus, is more original than Matt 7:22, which refers to charismatics and prophets acting in Jesus' name.

gested here that it is probable that these Judeans were Messianists that had given up performing some aspects of traditional covenantal praxis (the community of Mark or a Pauline-like movement?). These apostates evidently are followers of Jesus themselves. The interesting corollary of all this is that the Q people might be engaged in fierce polemic with non-responsive Judeans, and might be alienated from them, but the Q people also apologizes for the sins of other Messianists. These apostates may have contributed towards the Q group—law-abiding as they are (see below)—being rejected. They are guilty by association. Thus the Q group through this association might have been seen as undermining Judean ethnic identity, something which Q's polemic aims at addressing.[37] So in turn, the Q group rejects this sort of "lawlessness" and affirms their ethnic status as Judeans.

In concrete social terms, the Q people must have appeared to insiders and outsiders as a distinct group within Judeanism based on their focus on Jesus and his teaching. Although, the Q group like any Messianist group would have shown continuity with Judeanism as well. The fierce polemic in Q shows that a large amount of social and ideological overlap existed between Messianist Judeans and their "unrepentant" neighbors (Tuckett 1996:427). Tuckett further suggests that "we hear nothing in Q suggesting boundary creation by separate social or cultic practices."[38] There is no explicit mention that the rite of baptism should be repeated by the Q group (it would be surprising if it was not) and it *may* be significant that there is no mention of the Eucharist (Tuckett 1996:435). Tuckett (1996:434–35) further suggests that based on this community consciousness of Q's sayings, the divisions between the Messianists behind Q and the Judean community were not that deep. From the Q group's side, it would appear that on the social level the split was as yet not that severe. They had not given up hope for Israel and they did not regard themselves as a separate community. In terms of their self-understanding, the important social divisions was Israel as a whole separated from the Gentiles—the Q Messianists placed themselves within the boundary of Israel, besides the tensions and the differences that existed. The Q people were striving to be "Messianist Judeans," not "Judean Messianists"; there is "no indication

---

37. See Tuckett (1996:427), who for other reasons argue that from the Judean side, the hostility shown towards the Messianists can be seen as based on the belief that the Messianists "constituted a threat from within to [Judeanism's] self-identity."

38. But see Pearson (2004:488) who argues that Q 6:46 (cf. 1 Cor 16:11; *Did.* 10:6) may reflect something of the cultic life of the community.

that Q [Messianists] are being encouraged to separate themselves from the social and religious life of their [Judean] neighbours," thus there is "little evidence of a specifically [Messianist] community consciousness or social self-awareness" (Tuckett 1996:435). So Q represents a stage prior to that of Matthew,[39] since it would seem that they have not reached that state of self-conscious "sectarian" differentiation from their Judean contemporaries. This is difficult to accept, however, for Q does give evidence of a strong us/them outlook—the followers of Jesus, as opposed to "this generation," have secured for themselves participation in the kingdom of God. *They* are destined to be part of eschatological Israel. Their opponents are headed for damnation. The eschatology and Christology of Q (see below) is quite telling in this regard. It is indirectly claimed in Q 10:22 that those who do not follow Jesus—the Son of God—have no knowledge of God. Within the context of the Judean symbolic universe, this is a very pretentious and dismissive claim indeed! Their intention was not to break with Judeanism as such, but commitment to Jesus engendered a strong consciousness of difference vis-à-vis other *Judeans* (Q 10:12–15, 22; 11:49–52; 12:8–9; 13:34–35). The polemical attitude shows that the Q people are different kind of Judeans, but they are shaking their co-ethnics by the scruff of the neck trying desperately to make them as "different" as they are.

The Q People and the Family

In addition to the tension that existed between the Q people and their co-ethnics, obvious tension also existed within their families. One text in the main redaction is relevant for our discussion here. Family divisions were understood as signs of the coming end.[40] Q 12:49–53 implies the end is here, but note the apologetic introduction to this saying:

> ... [[Do you]] think that I have come to hurl peace on earth? I did not come to hurl peace, but a sword! For I have come to divide son against father, [[and]] daughter against mother, [[and]] daughter-in-law against her mother-in-law.

According to Cotter (1995a:127), in Q 9:59–62 it is the social system's expectations that are challenged, but in Q 12:49–53 "the ex-

---

39. Tuckett (1996:438) makes reference to Matt 21:43; 22:7; 27:25. Matthew also speaks of "their" or "your" synagogues/scribes (Matt 4:23; 9:35; 10:17; 12:9; 13:54; 23:34; 7:29). There is clearly an element of self-awareness, where the Matthean Messianists distinguish and distance themselves from their Judean contemporaries.

40. Mic 7:6; Isa 19:12; Zech 13:3; *Jub.* 23:16; *1 En.* 100:1; 4QTest 15–17.

amples suggest that the disciples is still at home or nearby, and the saying justifies the rifts that occur right within the larger family complex." Here the household is the primary focus of attention and the conflict is between the generations, and the source of the conflict is Jesus. Importantly, it is something he intended! According to Jacobson (1995:365), the saying may reflect "a situation in which it was the young who were most attracted to the Jesus movement, and this led to dissension." Guijarro (2001:216, 221–22) is more cautious regarding whether it is the children who cause the division in Q[41] (certainly implied in the IQP reconstruction of Q 12:53 and in Q 9:59–60); but generally the sayings in Q imply that following Jesus disrupts the family, and that the family conflict was mainly between the parents and their children. So Jesus it is said, intentionally undermined the structure of the patriarchal family, but more about this when the relevant texts of the formative stratum are investigated.

Summary

There is a strong sense of alienation between the Q people and "this generation" who are seen as guilty of primordial sins (Q 7:31–35; Q 11:29–51). This refers to unresponsive Judeans from whom the Q community is experiencing opposition, discrimination and repression. God/Wisdom will send them prophets to make them responsible for the death of all the prophets—the prophets will not be sent for their salvation. In fact, the Gentiles will fare better than them in the judgement. They are under the spiritual leadership of the Pharisees and lawyers, the blind guides, whereby their knowledge of God is denied (Q 10:21–22; 11:39–42). Even neutrality is seen as a sign of opposition (Q 11:23). The Diaspora will replace local Israelites (Q 13:28–29), yet there is a glimmer of hope that the Q people's fellow Judeans will accept Jesus and so participate in the restoration of Israel (Q 13:34–35). At the same time, Q disassociates itself from those who do "lawlessness" (Q 13:27), presumably from those Messianists who have given up aspects of covenantal praxis. Jesus also came to divide the family, especially causing separation between the parents and their children (Q 12:49–53).

41. Guijarro believes that Luke has best preserved the form of Q here where the conflict is in both directions. Guijarro's study is more relevant to the historical Jesus, nevertheless, it is argued that the sayings in Q (along with Mark 1:16–20; 10:28–30) seem to indicate that the origin of the family divisions lay in the attitude of the children and that these sayings could have been aimed at the younger generation. This, we suggest, could also be relevant to Q 12:53.

Overall, Q does not reject kinship relationships with fellow Judeans, but clearly has a strong consciousness of difference in opposition to fellow Judeans and family members—also from those guilty of "lawlessness." The relationship of the Q people with their co-ethnics is therefore highly frustrated and one can hardly speak of a feeling of communal solidarity. Q is negotiating the position of its people within Israel but is clearly situated on the periphery. From Q's perspective, however, they properly belong within the Judean symbolic universe where kinship patterns are (re)constructed because of commitment to Jesus.

Land

After Catchpole's (1993) analysis of Q's attitude towards tradition and the temple, he concludes that the Q community shows a continuing commitment to the covenant, the law and the temple, but at the same time, had the expectation that Jerusalem and the temple would be abandoned by God sometime in the future. Overall, as the temple still stood in the present, "we have a picture of a community whose outlook was essentially Jerusalem-centred . . . whose worship was temple-centred, and which saw . . . no incompatibility between all of that and commitment to Jesus" (Catchpole 1993:279). But the lament over Jerusalem in Q 13:34–35 suggests that God has already abandoned the temple, by implication the city as well: "Look, your house is forsaken!" (v. 35a). As Reed (2000:187) suggests, "the Q community's social map envisions Jerusalem as forsaken and deserted." Otherwise it can be agreed that the Q community was Jerusalem and temple-centred, although evidently that relationship was frustrated as well. Jerusalem is forsaken, yes, but v. 35b still clings on to hope for the city's salvation: "You will not see me until [[the time comes when]] you say: Blessed is the one who comes in the name of the Lord!" And also the twofold "Jerusalem, Jerusalem" in v. 34 and the disappointment it presupposes is more understandable if it continued to play a central role in the hopes and expectations of Jesus' earliest followers (Freyne 2001:308–9). As Freyne hints at, a north/south polarity, or Q's supposed inherent anti-Jerusalem stance, is unwarranted. But what are the implications for Q's relationship to the *land*?

As already indicated above, Q 13:35b suggests an attachment to Jerusalem (and its temple), and by implication, to the territorial land of Israel itself. This suggestion is supported by two other passages of the main redaction. The eschatological pilgrimage, where many will come from Sunrise/East and Sunset/West (Q 13:28–30) has territorial Israel as the locus of the coming Age. In Q 22:28–30, the followers of Jesus are promised that they will sit on thrones judging the twelve tribes of Israel. Q 22:28–30 presupposes the reconstitution of the twelve tribes, thus the restoration of Israel. Freyne (2001:310) argues this tribal symbolism is not related to geography at all as in the expansionist tendencies of Ezekiel 40–48. His argument is based on the opinion that Q demonstrates an "openness" to outsiders. Freyne (2001:310) states that the Q group

> saw that Israel was different from the gentiles and that a greater holiness was called for [Q 6:27–35], but this did not preclude an openness to outsiders, as the story of the healing of the centurion's servant demonstrates [Q 7:1–10] . . . Rather than expanding territorial boundaries, the sense of inclusion is represented by the arrival of the nations at the eschatological banquet [Q 13:28–30].

Freyne (2001:311) argues further that in Q we encounter a group who are deeply aware of their Judean identity but their openness to outsiders led to conflict with other Judean groups of a separatist bent. So what can be said for Gentile participation in the eschatological blessings of Israel? There seems to be widespread agreement that the Q group did not engage in a mission to Gentiles (see below), thus Q's "openness" to Gentiles must be approached with caution. Some sayings presuppose the presence of "righteous" Gentiles at the judgement (e.g., Q 11:31–32), but as to their further status nothing is said. As will be discussed later, Gentile faith is recognized, but the Gentiles are primarily present in Q as a polemical device to shame non-responsive Judeans. Gentile participation in the eschatological future is not a primary concern for Q. Nothing is said of contemporary Romans, Greeks and Samaritans. It is preoccupied with the restoration of Israel, with Jerusalem and the temple welcoming Jesus, with the eschatological pilgrimage of Diaspora Judeans, and all these sayings presuppose some geographical area. What Q exactly envisions for this geographical "Israel," however, is uncertain. So whether Q endorsed an expansionist ("lateral") ideology or not cannot be established with certainty.

In sum, the sayings in Q evidently look forward to the restoration of Israel, and the ancestral land—of uncertain magnitude and scope—will feature prominently in the Age to come. But certainly the Jerusalem and the temple will continue to play a central role, on the condition that it accepts Jesus. The Diaspora Judeans will return, and the Q people will sit on thrones to act as judges over the twelve tribes as in the days of old. Gentile participation in the land is at best ambiguous, since Q is preoccupied with the future destiny of eschatological Israel. Here a more primordialist approach to ethnicity is in evidence. Q shares the millennial dream of common Judeanism, yet it is redefined around the eschatological significance of Jesus.

The Sacred Canopy

It needs to be remembered that Judean ethnicity based on the model outlined in chapter 2 is also dependent on the interrelationship between the *habitus* and the "Sacred Canopy." This dialectical interrelationship primarily has to do with the belief that Yahweh established/prescribes Judean ethnicity ("getting in"). So again the question must be asked: How did the Q people compare?

The treatment of Q with regards to the "Sacred Canopy" needs some immediate modification and will be approached by looking at three primary features that are present in Q, namely, its Christology, the relationship between the Torah and the kingdom/reign of God, and its eschatology. Eschatology is very similar to the millennial aspect of the model, while the notion of Christology and the Kingdom of God, are of course, new elements. This adaptation to the Sacred Canopy of Q already suggests an element of (re)construction, yet, it is required by the evidence as set out below.

The Christology of the Main Redaction

The term Χριστός/Messiah does not appear in Q, so it may seem quite inappropriate to speak of Q's "Christology." But especially Q 13:34–35 seems to suggest that Q understood Jesus as the Messiah (Allison 1997:192–204), and in the very least, Jesus is clearly understood by Q as the eschatological prophet, and a prophet like Moses who has initiated the new Exodus.[42] Q 7:22–23 presupposes the anointed figure of Isaiah, so it does not seem inappropriate to speak of the Christology of Q.

As Tuckett (1996:210) notes, "the era of eschatological fulfilment is clearly seen in Q as inextricably linked with the person of Jesus." Through Jesus' actions, various Isaianic prophecies are fulfilled (Q 7:22;

---

42. Q 10:5 may also suggest that the Q people understood Jesus to be the Davidic Messiah. See 1 Sam 25:6, where David sends men to Nabal with a peace greeting, in the hope of receiving some food, motifs also found in Q 10:5, 7–8 (Allison 2000:147).

cf. Isa 29:18–19; 35:5; 61:1–62); Jesus also asserts that in the person of John the Baptist, the Tanak has been fulfilled (Q 7:27; cf. Mal 3:1; Exod 23:20); the longed for future, looked forward to by the prophets, is now being experienced in the present (Q 10:23–24); the eschatological kingdom is present in Jesus' exorcisms (Q 11:20); the parables of the mustard seed and the leaven at a pre-redactional stage already implied that the future kingdom of God is already present (Q 13:18–21; 16:16); something greater than Jonah and Solomon in the form of Jesus is present (Q 11:31–32); and eschatological turbulence in the form of family divisions are mentioned in Q 12:51–53 (cf. Mic 7:6). Already at a pre-redactional stage, in the Great Sermon, a warning was issued that to ignore Jesus' teaching will have severe eschatological consequences (Q 6:47–49). More examples can be called upon, but it is evident that for Q "Jesus has central significance" (Tuckett 1996:212). What did this significance entail?

Jesus, the Eschatological Prophet

In Q 3:16 the reader/audience is introduced to the "Coming One." The identity of this figure is not revealed, but the temptation narrative (Q 4:1–13) that sets Jesus over and against the temptations of the devil gives a hint of who this figure might be. More is involved here than just a defence of the ethos of the Q group in that "Jesus provided an example of the absolutely dependent, non-defensive and apolitical stance of his followers." More is involved here than a test to demonstrate Jesus' virtue and to legitimate Jesus' authority as a sage who has endured temptation, thus to "legitimate and guarantee the reliability of his teachings or revelations" (Kloppenborg 1987:256, 261, 327). It is all that but what we also have here is a "testing of an Israelite prophet being commissioned to lead the people, patterned after that of Moses and Elijah" (Horsley & Draper 1999:96). Prophets of Israel were also tested in the wilderness for forty days before their missions. Draper explains:

> Moses spent two forty-day fasts on Mount Sinai. In the first, before the giving of the Torah and the renewed covenant in Deut. 9:9–11, his prophetic status was confirmed and he was prepared for his authoritative presentation and interpretation of the word of God inscribed in text. Again in Deut. 9:18–19, after the disobedience of Israel with the golden calf, Moses lay prostrate and fasted for forty days and nights to avert the wrath of God against Israel. The paradigmatic prophet of Israel's renewal, Elijah, moreover, was tested and commissioned in the wilder-

ness in 1 Kings 19:1–18 ... If Jesus is to succeed as a prophet, he must successfully complete the forty days of testing.[43] (Horsley & Draper 1999:256)

In addition, Q recounts a new exodus. According to Josephus, there were a few Moses and Joshua-like figures that emerged in the first century that led their followers into the wilderness (*Ant.* 20.97–98; 169–71; *War* 2.261–63). Q's representation of Jesus fits this same pattern. Allison (2000:26) explains:

> If Israel was in the wilderness for forty years (Deut 8:2), Jesus is there for forty days (Q 4:2; forty days symbolizes forty years in Num 14:34 and Ezek 4:56). If Israel was tempted by hunger and fed upon manna (Exod 16:2–8), so is the hungry Jesus tempted to turn stones into bread (Q 4:2–3; manna, one should recall, was spoken of as bread).[44] If Israel was tempted to put God to the test, the same thing happens to Jesus (Exod 17:1–3; Q 4:9–12). And if Israel was lured to idolatry (Exodus 32), the devil confronts Jesus with the same temptation to worship something other than Israel's God (Q 4:5–8).

Q 4:4 quotes Deut 8:3, and the context (Deut 8:2–5) has elements similar to the temptation narrative, "being led, the wilderness, the number forty, temptation, hunger and sonship ... Q 4:1–13 appears to present Jesus as one like Moses" (Allison 2000:27). There could be more allusions, as Jesus is taken up to a mountain (Q 4:5–7), so Moses went to the top of Pisgah (Num 27:12–14; Deut 3:27; 32:48–52; 34:1–4). But a clearer allusion to Moses is present in Q 11:20: "But if it is by the finger of God that I cast out demons, then there has come upon you God's reign." The phrase "the finger of God" appears three times in the Tanak (Exod 8:19; 31:18; Deut 9:10) and they have to do with the miracles of Moses before Pharaoh and God giving the law to Moses on Mount Sinai. So in Q 11:20 the miracles of Jesus are set beside the miracles of Moses (Allison 2000:53). As Allison explains, in Judeanism the idea developed that the latter things will be as the first. The future

---

43. Draper (Horsley & Draper 1999:259) sees the Q discourses as dedicated to different aspects of Jesus as the prophet spearheading the renewal of Israel in the following sequence: "the announcement of the prophet, the testing of the prophet, the prophet enacting the covenant renewal, the confirmation of the prophet's authority, the prophet fulfilling the age-old longings for renewal, and the prophet commissioning envoys to broaden the movement of renewal of Israel."

44. Exod 16:4; Deut 8:3; Neh 9:15; Ps 78:25; 105:40; WisSol 16:20; John 6:31–34; and other texts.

redemption will be like the redemption from Egypt.[45] For some the idea developed of an eschatological prophet like Moses based on Deut 18:15, 18, as well as the idea that the Messiah might be like Moses. Q 11:20 is an illustration of such kind of typology (Allison 2000:56). In addition, John has according to Q fulfilled the prophecy of a messenger preparing the way for a new Exodus (Q 7:18–35; cf. Exod 23:20; Mal 3:1).

The temptation narrative only hints at the identity of the "Coming One." What is implicit becomes explicit in Q 7:18–23, where John's envoys ask Jesus whether he is this expected figure spoken of in Q 3:16–17. Jesus' answer is indirect but affirmative, and gives a list of events that constitute God's reversal of status for the disabled and the poor that recall elements from the Psalms (146) and Isaiah (26:18–19; 29:18–19; 35:5–6; 42:7, 18; 49:1–2; 61:1–2). A text from Qumran (4Q521) which in some respects are similar to Q 7:22 has a list of deeds ascribed to the messiah.[46] In a similar manner the 11QMelch text illustrates that Isa 61:1–2 was used in the first century to refer to an "eschatological prophetic figure" (Tuckett 1996:221). So Q firmly stands within an exegetical tradition (cf. Allison 2000:109–14). In Q itself, the poor are being evangelized (Q 7:22), indicating in particular that the anointed figure of Isa 61:1–2 is also finding its fulfilment. So Q's Jesus connects John's Coming One with the anointed prophet of Isa 61:1–2. The reference to Jesus raising the dead and cleansing the lepers in Q 7:22[47] may also have been influenced by the prophetic tradition. In the Tanak it is the prophets Elijah (1 Kgs 17:1–24) and Elisha (2 Kgs 4:18–37) who raised the dead and the prophet Elisha (2 Kgs 5:8–10) who also healed leprosy. So these traditions of raising the dead and healing may have been mentioned here to show that Jesus, the eschatological prophet, is

---

45. Isa 40:3–5; 41:17–20; 43:1–3, 14–21; 48:20–21; 51:9–10; 52:11–12; Jer 16:14–15; Ezek 20:33–38; Hos 2:14–16; 11:10–11; Mic 7:14–15.

46. Q 7:22 refers to the blind seeing (cf. Isa 29:18; 35:5; 42:7, 18; 61:1), the lame walking (Isa 35:6), the cleansing of lepers, the deaf hearing (cf. Isa 29:18; 35:5; 42:18), the dead being raised (cf. Isa 26:19), and the poor being evangelized (cf. Isa 29:19; 61:1). Parts of 4Q521 read: "... [the hea]vens and the earth will listen to His Messiah ... Over the poor His [i.e. the Lord] spirit will hover and will renew the faithful with His power. And He will glorify the pious on the throne of the eternal Kingdom. He who liberates the captives, *restores sight to the blind* ... For he will heal the wounded, and *revive the dead* and *bring good news to the poor* ..." (Vermes 1998:391–92; emphasis added).

47. The cleansing of lepers has no parallel in Isaiah, but Tuckett (1996:222) refers to Isa 26:19, which may possibly have influenced Q's reference to the dead being raised. See also Allison (2000:110).

also continuing in the line of the prophets Elijah and Elisha (Tuckett 1996:222–23). In Q 6:20–21 (formative stratum) this prophetic theme is similarly present. In the Beatitudes, the "poor," the "mourners" and the "hungry" are a single group who receive divine promises couched in the language of Isa 61:1–2, whereby Jesus is implicitly represented as the eschatological prophet (Tuckett 1996:226).[48]

Forming part of this prophetic representation of Jesus is where he is understood as an envoy of Wisdom (Q 7:31–35; 11:49–51; 13:34–35). The "figure of Divine Sophia developed within the Hebrew writings as reflection upon Wisdom and her relationship to God developed. Proverbs 1–9 seems to have initiated this reflection" (Hartin 1995:151). Ben Sira and the Wisdom of Solomon continues this tradition. It is probable that behind this is an idea of Wisdom as a kind of personified being, who, being rejected, fails to find a home in Israel. Several Judean texts (Prov 1, 8; Sir 24; Job 28; *1 En.* 42) speak of σοφία not just as an attribute of God, but almost as if she had a being of her own. An important part of this tradition speaks of Wisdom calling people to obedience, but they reject the call (e.g., Prov 1:20ff). In Sirach 24, Wisdom seeks a home in Israel, finding such in the Torah. In *1 Enoch* 42, Wisdom is unable to find a home and so withdraws. "There seems then to have been a strand in [Judean] thought which could talk of Wisdom appealing to men and women to follow the ways of Yahweh, but experiencing only rejection and rebuttal" (Tuckett 1996:170). This theme is evidently very similar in substance to the idea of the rejected prophets.

In Q 7:31–35 Jesus alongside John is portrayed as those to whom Divine Sophia has communicated herself in this generation. But like the prophets of old, both are rejected. In Q 11:49–51, Wisdom's role in salvation history is explained (cf. WisSol 7:27; 10:1–4). She sends her messengers to Israel, but these envoys are rejected, persecuted and even killed. "Noticeable here is the theme of the rejection of God's messengers, whereby the Deuteronomistic understanding of history has been joined together with the Sophia motif" (Hartin 1995:157; cf. Tuckett 1996:170). Q 13:34–35 is identified as an oracle of Wisdom where she wails her inability to "gather" the children of Jerusalem through the sending of prophets. This "gathering" is a call to repentance, something which Jesus himself, like the prophets of old, was involved with and is

---

48. Tuckett (1996:226–37) also argues that a substantial portion of Luke 4:16ff—the rejection scene in Nazareth where Isaiah 61 is explicitly quoted—was originally part of Q.

now being accomplished through the Q community (Q 11:23; 14:16–24) (Jacobson 1992:212–13). Tuckett (1996:175) also says that Q may have regarded the lament over Jerusalem in 13:34–35 as a Wisdom saying with the final sayings clause (v. 35b) being a secondary addition, it not being clear whether the latter saying requires a different speaker (in the form of Jesus) or not. Whatever the original reference, however, this addition with its allusion to LXX Ps 117:26 now refers to Jesus as "the one to come" (ὁ ἐρχόμενος; cf. Q 3:16; 7:19).

Jesus is *the* representative of Wisdom, or alternatively, its eschatological emissary (Hartin 1995:159). Tuckett and Pearson (2004:488) notes that Q implicitly takes note of Jesus' death since it seems to be the case that his death is placed on par with the death of the prophetic messengers sent by Wisdom down the ages—Jesus is the final envoy of Wisdom, however, so it is appropriate to think of Jesus as an "eschatological prophet" (Tuckett 1996:220–21).

Jesus the Son of humanity/man

Jacobson (1992:123) understands the "son of man" in Q 7:34 as a circumlocution for "I." It cannot refer to an apocalyptic figure for in the apocalyptic texts it refers to a future figure, not one who "has come," and mundane activities such as eating and drinking are inappropriate for an apocalyptic figure. Similarly in the apocalyptic/eschatological discourse of Q 17:23–37b, the "son of man" does not necessarily refer to an individual figure or his parousia, or his involvement in the "rapture." Jacobson (1992:235) sees Q 17:23 with v. 37b, and the latter as a "sardonic comment on the suppression of [Judean] freedom movements by the Romans." Thus an attempt was made to separate the Q community from eschatological excitement in the Judean community at large. The "son of man" sayings were added later, but the connection of Q 17:24, 26–27, 30 with Dan 7:13–14, Jacobson argues, is tenuous. The "son of man" in Q is not a redeemer figure, only a judgement figure and he will be "revealed" for the destruction of the heedless (Q 17:30). Nothing is said of the exaltation of the "son of man" or how he would rescue the righteous. Jacobson consequently proposes that the "son of man" is a symbol of the faithful people of God, amongst which the Q people would number themselves. This indicates a new sense of identity and a sharpening of group boundaries. This implies they participate in judgement, a corporate image possibly also found in Q 11:31–32 and 22:28–30 (Jacobson 1992:237–38). The sayings of the "son of man" like

Q 17:23, 37b reject apocalyptic watching and waiting, for the kingdom is present (something implied in Q 17:26–27, 30), and the level of messianic excitement has subsided, or even disappeared (Jacobson 1992:236, 238). In a similar vein Horsley (1999:65, 70–71) argues that "(the day of) the son of man" in Q 12:40; 17:24, 26, 30 is not a reference to an individual figure of redemption/judgment or his "coming" but is a symbolic reference to the judgement. This appears to be similar yet different to Daniel 7 where "the people of the saints of the Most High" (= "son of man") appears at the divine judgement of the beastly empires. And when Jesus referred to himself with "the son of man" (Q 6:22; 7:34; 9:58; 11:30) it is not a title.

The above arguments are questionable, however. It is arbitrary how the Son of humanity/man sayings are categorized as being nothing more than a circumlocution for the speaker's self-reference ("I/me") on one hand, while in others it refers to the Q community or is merely a symbolic reference to the judgement. The fact of the matter is the Q text, when seen as a whole, strongly suggests that for Q the Son of humanity/man does refer to an individual, future apocalyptic figure, and that it does refer to Jesus in view of an imminent eschatological scenario. Jesus is identified as the Son of humanity/man in Q (6:22; 7:34; 9:58; 11:30; 12:8), even if it only serves there as a circumlocution for "I/me." Particularly Q 12:8–9 probably refers to Daniel 7:13–14 and its context (Allison 2000:130–31). Both texts involve the last judgement, the central figure of the Son of humanity/man before the divine court, the presence of angels, and both texts involve persecution. So Q 12:8–9 may indirectly refer to the coming of Jesus as the Son of humanity/man and his role as judge before the divine court.[49] In the support of this connection with Daniel, Tuckett (1996:276) argues that both "the prophetic/wisdom category and the [Son of humanity/man] terminology are rooted in the idea of suffering and hence it is no coincidence that both appear together in Q." So the Son of humanity/man, as the persecuted righteous sufferer, could be a reference to Daniel 7, where the usage of Q would fit in with Daniel 7 and related texts (*1 En.*

---

49. Duling states that as Q now stands, it is dominated by apocalyptic, especially the return of Jesus as the Son of Man with power to execute the final judgement (in reference to Q 12:8–9). "In characteristic fashion, eschatological hopes in a time of alienation drew on prophetic and apocalyptic ideas and images from other apocalyptic and prophetic literature. It seems likely that the developing Q community was led, at least in part, by Spirit-filled, eschatological prophets who spoke for the now departed, but soon to return, Jesus" (Duling 2003:120).

62; cf. WisSol 2–5) as it was used in first century Judeanism (Tuckett 1996:276).

If Q 12:8–9 refers indirectly to the coming of Jesus, Q 12:40 is explicit with regards to the "coming" of the Son of humanity/man. Jesus has already been identified as the "Coming One" in Q 7:18–23, who in Q 3:16b–17 is given the task of a *future* immersion, be it in Spirit or in fire. When the Son of humanity/man is revealed, the eschatological separation of the elect will occur (Q 17:30, 34–35) (Kloppenborg 1987:163), and one is reminded of the Coming One's function in Q 3:16b–17 who will gather the wheat and burn the chaff.[50] Q 7:18–23 where the Coming One's identity is affirmed as Jesus, also anticipates Q 13:35 where the returning Jesus will be addressed as follows: "Blessed is the one who comes in the name of the Lord!" (Allison 2000:109). The point is that Jesus is identified in Q as both the Son of humanity/man and as the Coming One—it only makes logical sense that the "coming" or future role of the Son of humanity/man in Q 12:40 and 17:23–37 is relevant to Jesus himself.

In Q 17:24, the coming of the Son of humanity/man is associated with lightning, implying this figure's appearance will be sudden and visible to all and Q 17:30 speaks of the day that he will be "revealed"—this imagery can hardly be applicable to the Q community! Kloppenborg (1987:161) argues that Q 17:24 serves as a positive counterpart for Q 17:23 in terms of Son of humanity/man eschatology: "do not attend to earthly messianic figures; the Son of Man will come as a heavenly figure!"[51] In the very least it clearly refers to a heavenly figure who is described as "coming" at an unexpected hour (Q 12:40; cf. Q 17:26–30). According to Pearson (2004:488), references "to the coming of the 'Son of Man' [Q 12:40 cf. 12:37, 43; 17:23–37] clearly presuppose the resurrection and exaltation of Jesus." He may have a point, for were the Q people merely expecting the return of a martyr?

---

50. With regards to the eschatological separation of the elect, Allison (2000:83–84) suggests that Q 10:12 expects the resurrection of the just and the unjust. The same can be said for Q 10:14.

51. Kloppenborg (1987:160) also draws attention to the similarity between Q 17:24 and the fragmentary Daniel apocryphon (4Q246) where it speaks of a "Son of God" and "Son of the Most High"—although it is not clear whether the text speaks of a Gentile pretender or an heir to the Davidic throne—and the mention of a kingdom that will like comets flash into sight.

Jesus the Lord/Master

Already at a pre-redactional stage (Q 6:46), Jesus is identified as Lord or Master (κύριε). This idea comes to fuller expression in the main redaction. Surprisingly, the Gentile centurion addresses Jesus as Lord/Master in Q 7:6. In the parables of Q 12:42–46 and 19:12–27, the Lord/Master is the one who gives instructions to his servants, goes away and upon his return, requires an account of how his instructions were obeyed. The κύριος figure in these parables has been identified in Q 12:39–40 as the coming Son of humanity/man (Catchpole 1993:99).

Jesus the Son of God

Lastly, Q also contains an explicit "Son" Christology in Q 10:21–22, which is similar to the sonship language of Wisdom 2–5, where the righteous sufferer, and perhaps the follower of Wisdom, is the son of God (WisSol 2:16; cf. Sir 4:10). This son also claims to have knowledge of God (WisSol 2:13). It may therefore be that Q 10:21–22 must be seen as similar to other Q texts already mentioned that represent Jesus as an envoy of Wisdom (Tuckett 1996:279–80). Jacobson (1992:149) has a different but related view, as he argues that "the wisdom tradition here functions to absolutize the status of Jesus. Moreover, rather than being an emissary of Wisdom, Jesus is here said to mediate revelation directly." So here we have the identification of Jesus with Sophia, and the "new status of Jesus is clearly reflected in the 'father/son' terminology, which is not found elsewhere in Q." This high Christology is evidence for Jacobson that Q 10:21–22 is quite separate from the rest of Q. It is worthwhile having the text in front of us, especially v. 22:

> Everything has been entrusted to me by my Father, and no one knows the Son except the Father, nor [[does anyone know]] the Father except the Son, and to whomever the Son chooses to reveal him.

This text need not to be separated from the rest of Q as Jacobson sees no connection between this text and the traditional status of Moses, a role we have already identified to be fulfilled by Jesus as the leader of the new Exodus. Jesus is represented as the exclusive revealer of divine knowledge, and must be seen against the backdrop of Exod 33:11–23 and other traditions (e.g., Num 12:6–8; Deut 34:40) where this privilege is afforded Moses. It was Moses who knew God "face to face" (Deut 34:10), and the tradition also refers to the reciprocal knowledge between God and the lawgiver (Allison 2000:43–48). Jesus has received "everything," or the whole revelation from the Father, which is another Mosaic trait, "for the Moses of the haggadah came to enjoy practical omniscience" (Allison 2000:47). The second-century BCE *Exagoge* of Ezekiel has Moses saying:

> I gazed upon the whole earth round about;
> things under it, and high above the skies.
> Then at my feet a multitude of stars
> fell down, and I their number reckoned up (*Ezek. Trag.* 77–80)

It is later on explained to Moses that he will see things present, past and future (*Ezek. Trag.* 89). Other traditions also attest to supernatural knowledge of the lawgiver.[52] According to Allison (2000:48), Q 10:22 makes the same claim for Jesus, thus "it is setting him beside Moses." Setting him *beside* Moses or rather, is Q 10:22 not placing Jesus, the new lawgiver, *above* Moses? When seen in conjunction with Q 6:27–45 where Jesus reconstructs Lev 19, Q 10:22 seems to suggest that Jesus, the Son of God, is afforded a higher status than Moses in the Q community.

Q 10:21–22 can also be an implicit reference to the heavenly status of Jesus. The tragedy of Ezekiel also has Moses saying the following, when speaking of a throne he sees atop Mt. Sinai:

> Upon it sat a man of noble mien,
> becrowned, and with a scepter in one hand
> while with the other he did beckon me.
> I made approach and stood before the throne.
> He handed o'er the scepter and he bade
> me mount the throne, and gave me the crown;
> then he himself withdrew from off the throne (*Ezek. Trag.* 70–76)

Here evidently God vacates his throne for Moses! In a sense, Moses is conceived of as divine (cf. Philo, *Moses* 1:55–58) (Collins 1997:89). There is a resemblance here to the divine exaltation of the son of man in Daniel 7. It has been argued here that the Son of humanity/man in Q is Jesus, a heavenly figure whose coming is anticipated. Is Q 10:22 in reference to the usual status of Moses another indication of the heavenly status of Jesus?

In the very least, the comparison between Q 10:21–22 and traditions about Moses reveal that Jesus had immense status for the Q

---

52. *Jub.* 1:4; *Let. Aris.* 139; *2 Bar.* 59:4–11; *Sifre* 357 on Num 12:8; *b. Meg.* 19b; *Midr. Ps.* 24:5; *Memar Marqah* 5:1.

people. This high valuation of Jesus must be seen in connection with
Q 12:8–10. The members of the Q community are expected to confess
the Son of humanity/man presumably in the context of a trial before
Judean elders (?) where they must renounce Jesus or admit that they are
his followers (Jacobson 1992:188). Kloppenborg (1987:201) argues that
Q 12:8–9 "makes confession *of Jesus* the definitive measure of salvation"
(emphasis original). In this regard Q seems to be on par with general
Messianist Judeanism. What is particularly relevant here is what Paul
writes in Galatians. Paul writes that "we who are Judeans by birth," that
is, Judean Messianists, "know that a man is not justified by observing the
law, *but/except* (ἐὰν μὴ) by faith in Jesus Messiah" (Gal 2:16a).[53] Here
Paul is appealing it would seem to common ground between himself
and Peter, and Messianist Judeans in general. Faith in Jesus is a *qualification* to justification by works of the Law. The works of the Law are not
rejected, so faith in Jesus is one identity marker—indeed the primary
identity marker—next to the works of the Law. The works of the Law,
however, will have no effect if faith in Jesus is not in place (cf. Dunn
1990:195–96). Covenantal praxis takes a backseat to the significance of
Jesus. Of course, Paul continues by placing faith in Jesus and the works
of the Law as antithetical opposites (Gal 2:16b), a position rejected by
the main redaction of Q (Q 13:27; 16:17). Nevertheless, Q displays
similar thinking to other Messianist groups—salvation is dependent on
confession of/faith in Jesus, the Son of humanity/man, in addition to
the works of the Law.

Jesus is also recognized as God's Son in the temptation narrative
(Q 4:3, 9). It is interesting to note that it occurs within the context where
Jesus is represented as the prophet like Moses—this compliments the
connection to Moses identified in Q 10:22. Jacobson (1992:93–94) has
also seen the connection between the second temptation (Q 4:9–12)
and the Wisdom of Solomon 2:17–20, where it is assumed that God's
son can expect divine protection.

Summary

For Q the arrival of Jesus inaugurated the eschatological age, already
partly fulfilled, in part still expected to come to its full consummation. In the main redaction Jesus is at first identified as the "Coming
One." This figure is developed in two ways in Q. He is represented as

---

53. Or should it be translated "by the faith *of* Jesus Messiah" (διὰ πίστεως Ἰησοῦ
Χριστοῦ)? (cf. Hooker 1990:165–86). If this is the case, then the parallel to Q fails.

the prophet like Moses who has initiated the new Exodus, and as the anointed prophet of Isaiah—overall, the Coming One is the eschatological prophet. Within this prophetic tradition Jesus is also understood as the final emissary of Wisdom. Secondly, the Coming One is the heavenly Son of humanity/man, whose future coming in judgement is still expected. Jesus is the Lord/Master who expects that his instructions be adhered to in his absence. As the Son of God, Jesus is placed on par or even above Moses—the Son has received the whole revelation of the Father. Jesus as an envoy of Wisdom, as the eschatological prophet, as the Son of humanity/man, and as a Son of God, all have in common the idea of conflict leading to rejection and suffering (Tuckett 1996:282). Knowledge of the suffering and death of Jesus (and his resurrection?) is presupposed throughout. We can see that the Christology of the main redaction of Q is naturally analogous to the main redactional themes of judgement, polemic against "this generation," a Deuteronomistic understanding of history, and allusions to the story of Lot.

In a context where the Q document was orally performed, "the performer assumes the voice of the prophet himself" (Horsley & Draper 1999:168). Yet this was no ordinary prophet. Contrast Q's high estimation of Jesus with Q 11:29–30 where "this generation" puts in a request for a sign (cf. Mark 8:11–12; John 6:30). Jacobson (1992:169) understands that the dispute over the "signs" (and Jesus' authority) were questions put to the early followers of Jesus, and not to Jesus himself. Most likely they originated from the religious leaders, and the general consensus that Jesus was no authentic religious authority, a view that reflected popular sentiment. What clearly separates the Q community from their co-ethnics is the heavenly status they afforded Jesus, his eschatological significance, and his rank which is on par or even higher than Moses. Although the Torah and traditional covenantal praxis plays an important role in Q's covenantal nomism, it is *confession of Jesus that gives eschatological salvation.* Jesus in fact has become part of the Q people's Sacred Canopy, being afforded a status that is only second to God. Q's covenantal nomism is in (re)construction, and in quite a dramatic way.

The Torah and the Kingdom of God

According to Horsley (1999:87), the "principal, unifying theme of the whole document is clearly 'the kingdom of God.' Featured prominently at crucial points in most speeches (6:20; 7:28; 10:9, 11; 11:2, 20; 12:31;

13:18–21, 28–29; 16:16; 22:28–30), the kingdom of God is virtually assumed or taken for granted as the focus of Q discourses as well as the comprehensive agenda of preaching, practice, and purpose in Q." Following a scheme of two main redactional strata for Q, it can be seen that where the kingdom of God is mentioned explicitly it has strong representation in both strata. Thus overall it is clear that the kingdom of God—be it in a hortatory or polemical context—was a prominent religious identifier for the Q people, "virtually assumed or taken for granted" throughout the document, and supposedly the oral performances thereof as well. At the same time, it is quite obvious that some tension exists between the kingdom of God and the Torah, or rather, Jesus' interpretation of it. So the validity of the Law or the covenant itself is never questioned, what is questioned by opponents and defended by Q is Jesus' eschatological status and his Torah interpretation, the latter being the equivalent of the requirements of the kingdom of God.

Kloppenborg, as we have seen, assigned the temptation narrative, Q 11:42c and 16:17 to his third stratum since it is pre-occupied with the Torah. Tuckett (1996:423) argues the temptation narrative and the redactional additions in Q 11:42c and 16:17 more probably belong to the same (single) redactional moment hence a Q^3 stage is not necessary. Catchpole (1993:229) refers to Q 7:27 and the temptation narrative (Q 4:1–12) where both use the introductory formula γέγραπται, then proceed to cite scripture,[54] suggesting that they belong to the same stratum in Q. Q 13:27 (part of Kloppenborg's Q^2) also suggests that Q^3 can comfortably belong to the main redaction. Here Jesus' Judean contemporaries—which I have argued refers to Judean Messianists in Q—are accused of doing "lawlessness" (ἀνομίαν). In this regard Tuckett (1996:406) says that "almost certainly the [Q 16:17] saying is asserting the abiding validity of the Law in the present." It is suggested here that Q 13:27 makes the same assumption. But Q 16:17 clearly modifies Q 16:16, correcting any possible reading that the (traditional) Law was no longer to be applied (Tuckett 1996:407). Both Q 13:27 and 16:17 can be said to modify any misunderstanding that could have been caused at a pre-redactional stage (Q 16:16). So the main redaction is engaged with correction and apologetics. The Law is strongly affirmed, and Q attempts to create distance between its community and law-

---

54. Other examples of scripture being cited are Isa 14:13, 15 in Q 10:15; Mic 7:6 (modified) in Q 12:53; Ps 6:9 in Q 13:27; Ps 118:26 in Q 13:35. All of these Q texts are allocated by Kloppenborg to the main redaction of Q.

less Messianists.[55] So their own and Jesus' Judean identity is recovered. Catchpole (1993:94) argues in reference to Q 11:42 and 16:17 that "the Jesus of Q is through and through orthodox." But there are certainly instances where Jesus is not *that* orthodox, hence the need for this corrective and apologetic strategy.

In the temptation narrative, we encounter the testing of a prophet and the demonstration of his proficiency in the sacred tradition (Horsley & Draper 1999:257), but within the context of the main redaction, it also serves an apologetic purpose along with the other passages already identified. Jesus is portrayed as obedient to scripture (Tuckett 1996:422). Jesus is tempted by the devil in various ways. After he had nothing to eat, the devil told Jesus to turn stones into bread. Jesus answers by citing Deut 8:3: "It is written: A person is not to live only from bread" (Q 4:4). In the second temptation, the devil (citing LXX Ps 90:11–12) tempts Jesus to throw himself down from the temple. Jesus retorts citing Deuteronomy 6:16: "It is written: Do not put to the test the Lord your God" (Q 4:12). In the last temptation, the devil takes Jesus to a high mountain and says he will give all the kingdoms of the world to Jesus if he bows down before him. The reply is emphatic citing Deuteronomy 6:13: "It is written: Bow down to the Lord your God, and serve only him" (Q 4:8).

Specific matters pertaining to the Law are mentioned in Q. In Q 11:42, the tithing practices of the Pharisees are spoken of. Catchpole (1993:264) argues that it does not attack Pharisaic teaching or principles, and it is widely agreed that there is no question of an attack on the Law (Lev 27:30–33; Num 18:12; Deut 14:22–23). The final clause ("But these [i.e. tithing] one had to do, without giving up those [i.e. justice, mercy, faithfulness]") appears to be a secondary comment, correcting any possible understanding that tithing was not important or necessary (Tuckett 1996:410; Kloppenborg 1987; 2000, who assigns v. 42c to his Q³). Although the principle of tithing may not be in doubt, the meaning of the initial part of v. 42 is not that clear. The Matthean version ("tithing mint and dill and cumin") is normally accepted as representing Q (also IQP), as it fits our knowledge of Judeanism bet-

---

55. Here we want to draw attention to what Tuckett (1996:83–92) suggests. One must perhaps be aware of the distinction that must always exist between any text's author and the people it addresses. They might not have shared the same views, and it may be in the case of Q that the "person(s) responsible for producing Q intended the ideas expressed not only to articulate the views *of* the community but also to speak *to* the community, perhaps to change existing ideas (Tuckett 1996:82; emphasis original). Was Q here speaking *to* (a part of) the community?

ter (cf. *m. Maas.* 4:5; *m. Dem.* 2:1, which mention dill and cumin).⁵⁶ Alternatively, it simply refers to the Pharisees and their obsession to observe the Law correctly.⁵⁷ If Luke 11:42 is original ("mint, rue and every herb"), it suggests that the Pharisees voluntarily do more than what the law requires (Tuckett 1996:412). Whatever the first part of v. 42 meant, for Q, justice, mercy and faithfulness should not undermine the principle of tithing. So at level of the main redaction, the Q people were like the Pharisees expected to continue the practice of tithing—the ceremonial law is just as important as the rest (Tuckett 1996:410, 412).

A second matter pertaining to the Law referred to in Q is ritual purity (Q 11:39–41, 44). The Pharisees are accused that they "purify the outside of the cup and dish," while inside "[[they are]] full of plunder and dissipation" (Q 11:39b). Woes about the cup in Q presume a Shammaite distinction that was dominant before the First Revolt—it was to be replaced by the Hillelite position thereafter (Neusner 1976; Kloppenborg 2000:175). Based on Neusner's analysis (cf. *m. Kel.* 25:1, 7–8; *m. Ber.* 8:2; *y. Ber.* 8:2), the Shammaites understood that impurity could be transferred to the entire cup by unclean hands touching liquid on the outside of the cup. For the Hillelites, this was irrelevant in one respect, for they deemed that the outside of the cup was in a permanent state of impurity, implying that the outside of the cup does not affect the status of the inside. So it was the status of the inside of the cup that was decisive—the inner part determines the state of the cup as a whole. That is why the polemic in Q coheres with the position of the Hillelites: "first cleanse the inside," so that the whole cup will be in a state of cleanness; the outer part can never be clean anyway.

If a metaphorical understanding is followed, the Q saying points only to the bad character traits of the Pharisees. Catchpole (1993:266–67) argues that the imagery is not metaphorical at all. The food and drink satisfies Judean food laws, but it has been obtained by ἁρπαγή (plunder, robbery) and so have made the vessels "unclean." So the cleanness of the vessels is not just dependent on ritual law, but also on the conduct that produced the food. In a similar manner, Q 11:44 attacks the moral character of the Pharisees. They are like unmarked graves,

---

56. The items mentioned by Luke (mint, rue, and every herb) do not cohere with later rabbinic tradition. In *m. Sheb.* 9:1, for example, rue is excluded from liability to tithing and mint is never mentioned in *m. Maas.* 4:5; *m. Dem.* 2:1.

57. Although the Tanak itself only specifies that farm and garden produce, especially corn, wine, and oil be tithed.

who transfer "corpse" impurity[58] to others, which may be using another Hillelite tradition, this time in relation to the purity classification of Gentiles (*m. Pes.* 8:8). Based on Catchpole's (1993:268) approach, however, here the same kind of (moral) impurity may be referred to which existed in their eating vessels.[59] The term ἁρπαγή and its cognates is often used in Judean literature "as a vivid metaphor for the predatory activities of wolves and lions,[60] and in a transferred sense for injustice done by the rich and powerful to the poor and vulnerable. It represents the unprincipled grasping of the self-seeking who prosper, enjoy good food and high living, and do not give priority to 'judgment and mercy'" (Catchpole 1993:267). This concurs with Q 11:43, where the Pharisees are attacked for their love of high social standing; they "love [[the place of honor at banquets and]] the front seat in the synagogues and accolades in the markets." Catchpole also draws attention to the ἅρπαξ word group (Q 11:39; 16:16) where it is used to describe the opposition to the kingdom-centred mission and to where the Pharisees alienate themselves from the principles of the covenant. So Q 10:3 + 11:39 + 16:16 must be seen in combination and they indicate the context of religious polarization; the envoys of Jesus and the Pharisees are engaged in conflict. But this conflict evidently has led to the financial exploitation or opression of the Q people.

Q 11:39–44 therefore goes beyond a mere mockery of the Pharisees' concern for cultic purity (Horsley & Draper 1999:114). Horsley (1995:47–49; Horsley & Draper 1999:114–15) argues that Q's Jesus is indicting the Pharisees and the scribes for contributing towards the exploitation of the people. Q 11:39–52 focuses on their political-economic-religious role, part of it being their insistence that the people pay tithes to Jerusalem and its ruling priestly aristocracy in addition to the taxes that the Galileans were paying Antipas or Agrippa or to Caesar. Horsley (1995:42) understands the Pharisees to be "legal-clerical retainers" for the interpretation and application of official Judean laws initially delegated by Hasmonean rulers who from then on continued to impose these laws on behalf of Jerusalem. Here the Q people

---

58. Cf. Kloppenborg (1987:141): "The accusation that the Pharisees are 'unmarked graves'... portrays them as a source of ritual defilement."

59. Cf. Matt 23:27: "Woe to you, teachers of the law and Pharisees, you hypocrites! You are like whitewashed tombs, which look beautiful on the outside but on the inside are full of dead men's bones and everything unclean." (NIV)

60. Cf. Gen 49:27; Pss 7:2; 22:13; 104:21; Ezek 19:3, 6; 22:25, 27; Hos 5:14; Mic 5:8; *T. Dan* 5:7; *T. Benj.* 11:1, 2; Matt 7:15; John 10:12.

are understood to be Judeans themselves, however, and the Pharisees exploiting the Q people coheres well with Baumgarten's understanding of Judean sects. He suggests that members of sectarian groups were more likely to have come from the economic, social and educational elite, who could afford the "luxury" to be heavily involved in spiritual affairs. Members of sects would have regarded themselves as standing above society as a whole (Baumgarten 1997:47, 51, 66). "Ancient [Judean] sectarians ... were *not* lower class dissidents, shunned by the ruling powers. They were not an alienated and underemployed intelligentsia, searching for a place in society," they were, however, "elitist" (Baumgarten 1997:51). This, according to him, raises a question over the understanding of Pharisees as a retainer class in service of the ruling groups (cf. Saldarini 1988). The rapacity of the elitist Pharisees (Q 11:39–43) seems to be somehow self-serving, rather than them acting on behalf of the temple or Jerusalem aristocracy.

When reviewing the above the practice of tithing is taken for granted and even protected. Tuckett (1996:412–23) says that there is no affirmation of purity rituals (as there is of tithing in Q 11:42c) but neither are they condemned. One must concur that Q never questions aspects of ritual law (cf. Kloppenborg 1987:140). Matters of tithing and ritual purity (also presupposed in Q 11:44) are conveniently used to attack the Pharisees, and are not the target of the attack itself. What is at issue here is that obligations of justice, mercy (Mic 6:8; Hos 4:1; 12:7; Zech 7:9) and concern for the poor are seen as primary and aspects of ritual law should be subordinated to those primary concerns (Catchpole 1993:275; Horsley & Draper 1999:97). This forms part of an inner-Judean debate, and the "validity of the Law is assumed, and the only issue is its correct interpretation" (Jacobson 1992:177). This is also relevant to Q 11:46 where we find mention of "burdens" that are loaded onto people by the lawyers and their multiplication of the rules. What is at issue here is the scribal interpretation of the Law that is brought into question (Kloppenborg 1987:141). It is these scribes or "exegetes of the Law" that prevent people from entering the kingdom (Q 11:52).

Certainly at the stage of the main redaction, it is agreed that a new era ("the kingdom of God") has dawned, but some of the traditional demands of the Law that shape and define Judean ethnic identity are still valid. The new era is to be lived within the confines of the Judean symbolic universe, where the requirements of purity, for example, are still taken for granted. Yet, there is also another dimension to the Law present in the main redaction. The Torah and the Kingdom of God are not that mutually complimentary in all respects. Here it is agreed with Tuckett (1996:418)[61] who argues that Q "shows a deep concern that the Law should be maintained; it is aware that Jesus could be seen as antinomian, *and Q appears to represent a strong movement to 'rejudaise' Jesus*" (emphasis added).[62] Jesus and the Q people could have been accused of undermining Judean ethnic identity, since they are associated with a movement where "lawlessness" does happen (Q 13:27), and Jesus' own behavior and teaching is at times suspect for it contradicts Moses in some respects (e.g., Q 7:34; 16:18). But any tendencies "in the tradition which might be interpreted in a way that would challenge the authority of the Law are firmly countered" (Tuckett 1996:424). This is the apologetic strategy of the main redaction where Jesus—and therefore the Q community—on one level are represented as unwaveringly obedient to the Torah (Q 4:1–13; 11:39–44, esp. 11:42c; 13:27; 16:17). Judean ethnic identity is strongly reclaimed or affirmed. In the main redaction Q therefore sends the following intended message: "We *are* Judean!" And so the Q people's citizenship in the Judean symbolic universe is restored. Jesus is also a model Judean, for he can quote scripture at will, illustrates unwavering obedience to God, and so is a true son of God. Since Jesus quotes from Deuteronomy 6, it can be seen that Jesus takes his stand on the central Judean confession, the *Shema* (Jacobson 1992:92).

Even so, this does not stop Q from representing Jesus as equal to, or even greater than the law-giver of old himself. Q's Christology places Jesus in tension with Moses, for Jesus is a prophet like him who has initiated the *new* Exodus. As the Son of God, he has authority and alone has received the whole revelation of God (Q 10:22). If so, then what room is left for Moses? The Mosaic covenant was one of the main reference points in the life of Israel (cf. Horsley & Draper 1999:201). So Q wants to have its cake and eat it. It is adamant: Jesus is a law-abiding Judean, and so are its people. It is also adamant, Jesus, the eschatological prophet, has divine authority and is a law-giver like Moses. It therefore becomes clear that tension exists between the Torah of the Q people, and the Torah derived from Moses. More will be said about this when the treatment of the Law in the formative stratum is discussed.

---

61. Tuckett (1996:414–18) argues that behind Luke 14:5 // Matt 12:11 and Matt 22:34–40 // Luke 10:25–28 lies a Q source.

62. *Pace* Catchpole (1993:277) who argues that there is no tendency to "re-Judaize" in Q.

Shared "Historical" Memories

As Allison's (2000) intertextual analysis indicates, there are numerous examples in Q that can qualify as pertaining to *shared "historical" memories* as Q in its language and biblical allusions persistently draws on the Tanak. For this we reason we will be selective, and concentrate on some examples which are important to Q. Also at times not all relevant examples are treated here, since they are touched upon in other parts of the current investigation. This is to avoid repetition as far as possible, so it must be understood that the *shared "historical" memories* present in Q is by no means exhausted in this section of the work, and in fact, can be found in every cultural feature investigated here.

The first *shared "historical" memory* that will be investigated as part of the main redaction is the temptation narrative (Q 4:1–13) and its allusion to Moses and the exodus. Jacobson (1992:88) is sceptical whether Q 4:1–13 clearly alludes to the exodus tradition. Similarly Reed (2000:209) argued that Moses, as well as the Mosaic covenant and the Mosaic laws, the Law in general including the Decalogue, is not appealed to or found in Q. But what Jacobson and Reed state cannot be accepted as is. We saw that in terms of Q's Christology and apologetic strategy that it shows more than a passing interest in the Moses traditions and the Torah, by implication, the covenant as well—often these are background references simply taken for granted. Particularly relevant here, is where Jesus in the temptation narrative is identified with Moses and as the new Exodus (Allison 2000:26–28). So Moses and the exodus are present in Q, and this historic figure and event serves as a foil to explain the eschatological role and status of Jesus. This Moses/Exodus typology is also found in other parts of Q (e.g., 7:26–27; 10:21–24; 11:20).

As already alluded to, Kloppenborg suggests that the story of Lot is one of the motifs of the main redaction. The opening of Q probably placed John in "all the region/circuit of the Jordan" (Q 3:3). This phrase in the Tanak occurs mainly in connection with the story of Lot (Gen 13:10–12; 19:17, 25, 28). Kloppenborg (2000:119) explains this may be insignificant "were it not for the fact that the oracle of John that follows speaks of 'fleeing' the coming wrath, warns against reliance on kinship to Abraham, threatens a fiery destruction, and inverts the story of Lot's wife by declaring God's ability to fashion people out of stones or pillars." It is questionable that John's preaching has particularly Lot's wife in view, but the Lot story recurs when it is threatened that it would be easier for Sodom than those towns not receptive to the Q people's mission (Q 10:12). The destruction of Sodom is also represented as an example for the unexpected day of the Son of humanity/man (Q 17:28–30). This motif continues in Q 17:34–35 where coworkers will be separated, one being "swept away" (παραλαμβάνεται) and the other "spared" (ἀφίεται). The same pair of verbs is found in Genesis 18:26 and 19:17 where it describes the destruction of the wicked and the sparing of Lot's family. Kloppenborg (2000:119) explains that the story of Lot "already had a long history of exegetical use in the Tanak and the literature of Second Temple [Judeanism], being employed as the archetype of a divine judgment that was total, sudden, and enduring, and which occurred without human instrumentality." The dominant exegetical tradition identified arrogance and inhospitality as the Sodomites' gravest sins. Proud Sodom did not share its available food with the poor and needy (Ezek 16:49) and Isa 3:9–17 intimates that its inhabitants arrogantly oppressed the poor. "When Q threatens the 'children of Abraham' with Sodom's judgment," Kloppenborg (2000:120) elaborates, "it continues the tradition of Isaiah and when it suggests that Sodom will fare better in the judgement, it elaborates the exegetical tradition of Ezekiel [16:49–52]." The return of the Son of humanity/man is also compared to the days of Noah (Q 17:26–27, 30). The story of the flood and the destruction of Sodom (Q 17:28–29) were frequently brought together as examples of divine judgement (Tuckett 1996:159).

Q also employs other historical examples of divine judgement. Q 10:13–14 contains woes directed at the Galilean towns of Chorazin and Bethsaida, and is compared unfavorably with the Gentile cities of Tyre and Sidon. Tyre is denounced in Isaiah 23; Amos 1:9–10 and Joel 3:4–8, and both cities are assured of divine judgement in Ezekiel 28. Elsewhere in the Tanak the prophets speak of Tyre and Sidon "as surpassing embodiments of wickedness headed for destruction"[63] (Allison 2000:124).

Another motif of the main redaction pertaining to *shared "historical" memories* is the employment of Deuteronomistic theology. According to this theology "the history of Israel is depicted as a repetitive cycle of sinfulness, prophetic calls to repentance (which are ignored), punishment by God, and renewed calls to repentance with threats of judgment. Common in this schema is the motif of the rejection of the prophets and even of their murder ... [T]he prophets are represented primarily as preachers of repentance and, generally speaking, as rejected preachers"

63. Jer 25:22; 47:4; Joel 3:4; Zech 9:1–4.

(Kloppenborg 2000:121). Q several times recalls the rejection, persecution and murder of the prophets (Q 6:23c; 11:47–51; 13:34–35). For Q Jesus' followers and their fate are of a piece with the prophets (Q 6:22–23). Tuckett (1996:180) also sees 6:23c as an addition to the earlier form of the beatitude for the persecuted (6:22–23b) and says "the suffering and hostility experienced by those addressed in the beatitude is said to be similar in kind to the hostility experienced by the rejected prophets of the past. The experience of the Q [Messianists] is thus equated with the experience of rejected prophets and their 'suffering' is interpreted as specifically prophetic suffering." John is represented primarily as a repentance preacher (Q 3:7–9), and he, along with Jesus, is rejected by "this generation" (Q 7:31–35). Jesus' role is also implicitly connected with repentance (Q 10:13–15; 11:29–32). The story of the prophet Zechariah who was murdered in the courtyard of the Temple (2 Chr 24:20–22) is mentioned (Q 11:51). Continuing the Deuteronomistic theology there is the threat that the Israelites will be expelled (Q 13:28–29) and a woe is spoken over Jerusalem (Q 13:34–35). Also present is the Parable of the Great Supper (Q 14:16–24), which functions as a commentary on Israel's rejection of God's spokesmen, and their eventual reception by others (Kloppenborg 2000:121).

According to Reed (1999:106; 2000:209), in contrast to the prophet, the priest and king as types became localized in Jerusalem. The prophets traditionally served as a moral and social critic of priests and kings, even of their centralization in Jerusalem (Mic 3:9–12; Jer 26), so "the prophet as a model was the natural choice for a religious community in a Galilean setting" (Reed 2000:209). This may well be, but the Q community was critical of fellow Israelites in general (e.g., Q 10:12–13!), so not too much must be made their critique of Jerusalem, be it explicit (Q 13:34–35) or as Reed (2000:210–11) suggests, implicit in the sign of Jonah (Q 11:29–32; cf. *Liv. Pro.* 10:10–11), or the critique of the Pharisees and the lawyers (Q 11:39–52). The fact of the matter is, be it inside or outside Jerusalem, God's prophets experience suffering and rejection. It is this paradigm that the Q people remember and identify themselves with.

Fitting in with the employment of a Deuteronomistic theology is Q's allusion to the Elijah tradition. In Q 7:18–23, Jesus, in response to the messengers of John, lists a series of events that occur in his ministry. The events listed in Q, particularly the raising of the dead evoke expectations associated with an Elijah-like figure (cf. 1 Kgs 17:1–24).[64] John's

64. Of course, Elijah's successor, Elisha, also raised the dead (2 Kgs 4:18–37) and

scenario of the future (Q 3:7–9, 16b–17) recalls Malachi's "coming day" (Mal 3:19) when Elijah will appear to bring repentance (Mal 3:22–23) and a figure associated with Elijah will "come to his temple" and "purify" the sons of Levi with fire, burning evil doers like stubble, where neither root nor branch will remain (Mal 3:19). John himself, however, is a preacher of repentance (Q 3:7–9) and even identified as Elijah (Q 7:27), and Jesus does not exactly fit John's picture of the "Coming One," that is, as a judge (Q 3:16–17). Nevertheless this role for Jesus is reserved by Q for the future. Thus in various ways both John and Jesus are associated with Elijah.

In connection with another main redactional theme, namely, the polemic against "this generation," reference is made to the Jonah and the Ninevites (Q 11:16, 29–30, 32). This is particularly relevant here as Jonah was a Galilean prophet. According to Reed (2000:208), drawing upon rabbinic and early church traditions, it "seems probable that upon the resettlement of Gath-Hepher at the beginning of the early Roman Period, its [Judean] inhabitants revived the tradition linking Jonah's hometown with theirs as recorded in 2 Kgs 14:25, and at some point began to nurture traditions of his burial there." So it is likely that Jonah was venerated in Lower Galilee as a local hero. Gath-Hepher (in late antiquity called Gobebatha) was reportedly located on the road between Sepphoris and Tiberias, which today is identified as the modern village el-Meshed, where to this day visitors are shown the tomb of Jonah (Reed 2000:206). Thus Jesus and the Q community are related to an earlier Galilean prophet, Jonah, a preacher of repentance from Israelite epic history. Also within the context of polemic against "this generation," the Queen of the South who came to listen to the wisdom of Solomon is mentioned (Q 11:31; cf. 1 Kgs 10:1–13; 2 Chr 9:1–12). According to Josephus (*Ant.* 8.165) she was the queen of Egypt and Ethiopia.

It is at once obvious, that figures and events of the past, as compared with the formative stratum, are ubiquitous in the main redaction. Mention is made of Abraham (Q 3:8; 13:28), Isaac and Jacob (Q 13:28), Jonah (Q 11:30, 32), the Queen of the South (Q 11:31), Solomon (Q 11:31), Abel (Q 11:51), Zechariah (Q 11:51), Noah (Q 13:26–27; 17:26–27) and Lot (Q 17:28), and the persecuted prophets (Q 6:23c; 11:47–51; 13:34–35). Reference is made to "this (evil) generation" (Q 11:29, 31–32) which alludes to the generation in the wilderness and in the time of Noah. Reference is made to the Twelve tribes of

healed leprosy (2 Kgs 5:8–10), another miracle listed in our Q text.

Israel (Q 22:28–30) and Q 13:28–29 presuppose their reconstitution. Also present but implicitly so is Moses and the Exodus (Q 4:1–13; 7:26–27; 10:21–24; 11:20), the anointed figure of Isaiah (Q 7:18–23) and Elijah (Q 3:7–9, 16b–17; 7:27). Particular Gentile cities, such as Sodom (Q 10:12; 17:28–30, 34–35), Tyre and Sidon (Q 10:13–14) and the Ninevites (Q 11:16, 29–30, 32) are recalled as well. According to Cotter an important issue for the Q^2 stratum was the prestige of antiquity, that is, the community invoking its continuity with Judean religious tradition. Cotter (1995a:132) argues the

> cultural values and perspectives which are disposed to recognize the credibility of religions and institutions depending on their rootedness in antiquity seems fully engaged in the Q^2 stratum. The clear, constant and various references to [Judean] sagas, [Judean] patriarchs and the prophets as well as the appeal to [Judean] scriptures for verifications plainly demonstrate that the community has consciously identified itself with an ancient recognized religion in a most deliberate and indeed necessary manner ... It is only in Q^2 where the deliberate identification of the community with Israel's tradition becomes not only prominent but indeed takes control of the document.

We can agree with Cotter that Q aims at ratifying "the authenticity of the community and its heroes," but it is questioned whether Q was interested in gaining the prestige of antiquity or prestige "through their identification with a religion publicly known and recognized within the Greco-Roman world" (Cotter 1995a:133). It rather appears that Q was not interested in the "antiquity" of its religion and also felt little for the opinion of the broader Greco-Roman world. The rhetoric of the main redaction is exclusively aimed at Judeans. Q is definitively rooted in the past, but is primarily concerned with the eschatological present and future, and its use of past traditions is aimed at affirming the eschatological status of Jesus and the community and denouncing non-responsive Israel. It must be recalled that ethnicity is a commitment that is primarily, not exclusively though, orientated towards the past (De Vos 1975). Q does not fit this profile, for its primary commitment lies elsewhere. So other apologetic and polemical concerns are at work here. To elaborate, on the one hand, the Q community is *defending its Judean ethnic identity* or the "authenticity" of its identity *as eschatological Israel*. And Q represents its hero Jesus as the anointed figure, the Moses-like prophet who has initiated the new Exodus. The Q community encapsulates (re)constructed Judean ethnic identity, since it lives and breathes eschatological newness, in short, the founding event of the Kingdom of God. Jesus and the Q community is replaying the Exodus and the giving of the law (Q 6:27–45). By no means is what the Q people stand for entirely new and the past is not rejected, but *based on recent events*, the "antiquity" of traditional covenantal nomism has fulfilled its purpose and has been left behind (cf. Q 3:8; 16:16). On the other hand, the *shared "historical" memories*—often involving Gentiles—are used *negatively* in most cases! The Q people associate themselves with the persecuted and rejected prophets, and past traditions are exploited in various ways in service of the motifs of the main redaction identified by Kloppenborg, all in some way related to judgement.

So the *shared "historical" memories* in Q are used to defend the eschatological identity of Jesus and his followers. Q actually flaunts its newness but it is a newness that can only be appreciated and communicated within a Judean context. The past is also used to denounce non-responsive Israel; it is threatened with judgement and is accused of rejecting God's prophets. Thus Q is not pre-occupied with the prestige of antiquity. Q is more interested in the eschatological present and future than the past, and has little sympathy for nostalgic ethno-symbolism where the privileged status of Israel is affirmed. Call the Q people deviant, or counter-cultural, since for them the epic history of Israel only has meaning and is qualified by the newness of the Kingdom of God. Unfortunately for the Q people, this newness is not recognized by some of their Judean contemporaries.

Myths of Common Ancestry

At the beginning of Q, John the Immerser (Baptist) touches on the cultural feature of common ancestry in his preaching and rite of water immersion (the latter is discussed above). As Tuckett (1996:115) makes mention of, based on Q 3:8b John's preaching is aimed at Judeans alone. He is warning them not to claim Abraham as their forefather, for God can produce children for Abraham from the rocks at their feet. John's rejection of Judean pleas to the ancestor Abraham is quite significant. John rejects "any special exemption from divine judgement which can be claimed by [Judeans] *qua* [Judeans]. Something more is now required and anyone failing to produce that 'more' is threatened with destructive judgement" (Tuckett 1996:114). Verse 8b does not reject all value to Judeanness, "it simply says that appeal to [Judean] birth alone is in itself insufficient to escape what is coming soon" (Tuckett 1996:115).

According to Jacobson (1992:82–83), Q 3:8 is a redactional addition, providing a new assessment of what is wrong with John's audience, "not failure to produce fruits, but presumption upon their ancestry." Although Israel's election is not denied, it might be suggested that others might be created as children of Abraham. In the context of Q, "we are bound to think of instances in which non-Israelites are used to put Israel to shame. That is also what seems to be implied here" (Jacobson 1992:83). It does not seem likely, however, that Gentiles are here in view, or that John's audience is not failing to produce fruits. The Judeans *are* failing to produce fruits, that is exactly why John is subverting their appeal to Judean birth, or rather, the presumption attached with that ancestry.

What is this special link Judeans had to their ancestor Abraham that gave them a (now false) sense of security? According to Horsley (Horsley & Draper 1999:118–19, 253), Abraham had become a very important symbol from Hasmonean (3 Macc 6:3; 4 Macc 6:17, 11; 18:23; cf. 2 Chr 20:7) and Herodian times as the Jerusalem elite emphasized their descent from Abraham. According to his interpretive paradigm that Q reflects a conflict between the rulers and the ruled, Horsley (Horsley & Draper 1999:119) argues that Q 3:8 (much like Q 13:28–29) "would have been understood as a sharp rejection of the Jerusalem elite and other pretentious wealthy and powerful families who, in the common people's eyes, would have been the worst violators of the covenantal principles of nonexploitative economic social relations." This interpretation is difficult to accept. Q 3:8 is relevant to *all* Judeans, all of whom were children of Abraham, and all of whom would have claimed the glorious status of being Judean (cf. Esler 2006). This would have been part of the common stock of knowledge and self understanding. In this regard attention must be drawn to Isa 51:1–2:

> Listen to me, you who pursue righteousness and who seek the LORD: Look to the rock from which you were cut and to the quarry from which you were hewn; look to Abraham, your father, and to Sarah, who gave you birth. When I called him he was but one, and I blessed him and made him many. (NIV)

Abraham is compared to a rock, and his descendents are cut out of this same rock.

Now compare Q 3:8b:

> ... do not presume to tell yourselves: We have as <<fore>>father Abraham! For I tell you: God can produce children for Abraham right out of these rocks!

In certain ways, the Judeans had a special kind of ancestry. Allison has here drawn attention to the concept of "merit" (*zekhut*). The Judeans benefit because of the merit of their ancestors (Ezek 33:24; Jer 9:24–25), who in Judean tradition were often associated with rocks or mountains.[65] We may also draw attention to other texts that make similar claims:

> And unless you had received mercy through Abraham, Isaac, and Jacob, our fathers, not a single one of your descendants would be left on the earth. (*T. Levi* 15:4)

> But he [God] will have mercy, as no one else has mercy, on the race of Israel, though not on account of you but on account of those who have fallen asleep. (*L.A.B.* 35:3)

> [The Judeans plea for deliverance]—And if not for their own sakes, yet for the covenants he had made with their fathers ... (2 Macc 8:15)

The Q text, however, denies that any benefit will be derived because of the ancestors and asserts that merit must now be earned individually by each person in his or her own life, and only then can they claim to be children of Abraham (Allison 2000:101–3). This shares with the Hellenistic spirit of individual decision (Hengel 1989:48–50) but this de-emphasis on the corporate selection of Israel and the individualization of salvation was already an established feature of Judean apocalypticism (cf. Stegemann & Stegemann 1999:146).[66]

Nevertheless, it becomes clear that John's eschatological message of judgement is subverting, or alternatively, is (re)constructing covenantal nomism. What covenantal nomism has guaranteed up and to that moment—to be part of God's elect and saved people—can no longer be given. Maintenance of status as (righteous) Judeans has become an individual responsibility while the privileges of corporate Israel, which derives benefit from the ancestors, is de-emphasized, if not refuted.

---

65. *Mekilta* on Exod 17:12; *Tg. Cant.* 2:8; *Frg. Tg.* P on Gen 49:26; *Tg. Neof.* 1 on Num 23:9.

66. Cf. *1 Enoch*, esp. chaps 1–36 and 83–90; 91–107; *2 En.* 41:1; 71:25 [J] (on Adam and ancestors)—parts of apocalyptic literature see Israel's history as a recurring cycle of sin and punishment, only the elect will be saved (cf. *Jub.* 1:29).

The second issue that affects ancestry is in Q 11:47–48 where the lawyers are associated with their "forefathers" who are said to have killed the prophets. The Deuteronomistic view of Israel's history is thus employed, a major motif of the main redaction. Their guilt and association comes about, quite sarcastically, by them building the tombs of the prophets. But the real issue at stake is the opposition of the lawyers to the Q group's message. As the "forefathers" persecuted and killed the prophets, in a similar manner their descendents, the lawyers, are currently in opposition to the prophetic message of the Q people (Q 11:52). Here the aristocracy or retainers of the exegetical tradition is in view, and not the Israelite people as a whole.

In summary, while the value of Judean ancestry and birth is not denied, it receives a rather negative treatment in Q. Ancestry and birth is here connected with a false claim to privilege and presumption on the one hand, and with the persecution of the prophets on the other. In response Q constructs an ancestry emphasising individual religious, ethical and prophetic characteristics while de-emphasising corporate peoplehood and biological links. First, there is no claim to privilege or no presumption on the part of the Q people since they no longer claim to derive benefit from their ancestors, particularly Abraham, since they work on acquiring merit for themselves individually. It is through this individual effort that the Q people feel that they are the true descendents of Abraham. Second, the Q people align themselves with the persecuted prophets of the past, since they are persecuted themselves by the descendents of the prophet killers. It is because the Q community now finds itself within the orbit of the Kingdom of God. "The key factor for the community is repentance from sin, faithful vigilance and a confession of Jesus 'before people.' The works of righteousness and not the state of being [Judean] take precedence" (Cotter 1995a:130). Thus overall, Judean ethnic identity is (re)constructed. Again, any form of ethno-symbolism where Israel's privileged status is affirmed is absent. Here is nothing like the notion of the "covenant of our (fore)fathers." The corporate and biological link with the ancestors, and the merit attached therewith is de-emphasized; the link can only be maintained through individual merit, that is, through response to the Immerser (and Jesus' preaching), baptism, and righteousness.

The Eschatology of the Main Redaction

Judgement

One of the important themes of the main redaction is the theme of a coming judgement. This section is analogous to the *shared "historical" memories* and *kinship* already discussed, and Q's Christology with reference to the coming of the Son of humanity/man (see further below), so the treatment here will be brief. At the beginning of Q, John warns of an imminent and fiery judgement and admonishes his listeners to repent (Q 3:7–9) in view of a "Coming One" spoken of thereafter (Q 3:16–17). Tuckett (1996:114) explains that the call to his countrymen "must be to change their ways, to accept the validity of John's call to repentance in the face of a coming potential catastrophe and to undergo the rite that makes visible their commitment to his cause." John challenges their sense of national security (Q 3:8), and "every tree not bearing healthy fruit is to be chopped down and thrown in the fire." Whether John's message is aimed at the unresponsive in Israel, or those coming to be immersed, one can agree that clearly "one is in the thought world of [Judean] eschatology, with a vivid expectation of an imminent End culminating in some judging process" (Tuckett 1996:115).

John proclaims that a "Coming One" βαπτίσει ἐν πνεύματι [[ἁγίῳ]] καὶ πυρί (Q 3:16b). According to Jacobson (1992:84) the baptism with πνεῦμα does not refer to the "holy spirit," but simply "wind," which like fire, is an agent of judgement. Kloppenborg (1987:106–7) argues along similar lines, in that it seems unlikely that "spirit" and "fire" refers to alternative baptisms and Q's main interest lies in the destructive side of the Coming One's role. It is rather agreed with Tuckett (1996:122–23), however, that this passage refers to the Coming One who will give a two-fold baptism/immersion; a Spirit-immersion for those who respond, and a fire-immersion for those who do not. Those who were baptized by John will not undergo the destructive or "fire"-immersion, but the Coming One will immerse them in the Spirit. Q's John clearly is speaking of two groups: the wheat that will be gathered into the granary, and the chaff that will be burnt in the fire, imagery typical of divine judgement.[67]

The threat of judgment runs throughout the main redaction. Galilean towns are threatened with a more severe judgement than Sodom and the Gentile cities of Tyre and Sidon (Q 10:12–14). Capernaum is

---

67. Isa 17:13; 29:5; 33:11; 41:15; Jer 13:24; Dan 2:35; Hos 13:3; Mic 4:12; Zeph 2:2.

especially lampooned with a text from Isa 14:13, 15—instead of being exalted to heaven the town will be brought down to Hades (Q 10:15). But judgement has already in a sense begun. Jerusalem and its temple are declared as "desolate" (Q 13:34–35; cf. Jer 12:7). According to Allison (2000:149–51) Q 11:49–51 + 13:34–34 draws heavily on 2 Chr 24:17–25 that pertains to the stoning of Zechariah, and God forsaking Judah and Jerusalem in consequence. In a similar vein, the rejection of Jesus means the rejection of Jerusalem—although it is conditional, since Q still hopes for Jerusalem to accept Jesus (Q 13:35b), just as 2 Chronicles 24 looks forward to a restoration at the end. Threats of judgement are also directed at "this generation" (Q 11:31–32, 49–51) or "you" (pl.), who stand in contrast to "the many" that will "come from Sunrise/East and Sunset/West" that will sit down at table with the patriarchs (Q 13:28–29). The rebellious generation that seeks a sign will only be given the sign of Jonah (Q 11:16, 29–30), which refers to his preaching of judgment[68] (Jacobson 1992:165; Kloppenborg 1987:133). The eventual judgement will be sudden and will come without warning (Q 12:39–40; 17:23–34) having terrible results (Q 12:42–46; 19:12–27).

The End Has Arrived!

There are various passages in the main redaction that understands the End has arrived. In the investigation into Q's Christology we saw that the End is inextricably bound up with the person of Jesus. The "Coming One" it is said will immerse people in the Spirit (Q 3:16b). The Spirit may be seen in connection with Joel 2:28–29 that promises that God will pour out his Spirit onto all people in the last days. The fire-immersion is evidently in the future in Q's perspective, but based on Q 12:10, it may well be that the Spirit-immersion was in part a matter of experienced fulfilment on the Q-group's part (Tuckett 1996:124). Certainly this was the case with Jesus. In the fulfilment of various Isaianic texts (e.g., Isa 35:5–6; 61:1–2) in Q 7:22, Jesus identifies himself with the final End-time prophet of Isaiah 61 who has been anointed by the Spirit (Tuckett 1996:222). A sense of realized eschatology is present in Q 7:22 in other ways as well. The emissaries of John "hear and see" what was looked forward to by the prophets. Q 7:18–23 therefore continues the thought of Q 3:16, and John's prediction of a Coming One is confirmed, this figure being none other than Jesus himself who is "fulfilling" the Old

---

68. Cf. *Lam. Rab.* Proem 31; *Mekilta Pisha* 1.80–82.

Testament dispensation by the eschatological events that are occurring (Kloppenborg 1987:108; Tuckett 1996:128).

John himself also has eschatological significance, since he is identified as the Elijah *redivivus* in Q 7:27, where Jesus quotes both Exod 23:20 and Mal 3:1 in relation to the Immerser. Thus the new age inaugurated by John is the "kingdom/reign of God," which at a preredactional (or Q¹) stage was already recognized as a present reality (Q 16:16). John is therefore regarded as more than a prophet (Q 7:26), since he is the inaugurator of the new age forecast by Malachi. Yet, in Q 7:28 his significance is placed in perspective: "the least significant in God's kingdom is more than he." He is now placed outside of the kingdom. Overall, John's relationship to the kingdom is ambivalent, as he is sometimes placed within its orbit (Q 7:27; 7:31–35) and sometimes placed without (Q 7:18–23; 7:28) (Kloppenborg 1987:109, 115). But importantly, the kingdom/reign of God has arrived. Jesus himself says in Q 11:20:

> But if it is by the finger of God that I cast out demons, then there has come upon you God's reign.

Q 12:51–53 alludes to the breakdown of the social order expected as part of end-time events (Mic 7:6 cf. *1 En.* 100:1–2; *Jub.* 23:19; *4 Ezra* 6:24). Here is also an implicit claim that the events of the Endtime have already started. Similar ideas are expressed in Q 12:54–56; those who have eyes to see can see the signs of the times, being none other than the signs of the End (Tuckett 1996:158). As Kloppenborg (1987:153) says, "Q repeatedly implies that there is little time left, since the signs of the end are already in evidence."

The Coming of the Son of humanity/man

Horsley (1999:71) is of the view that "there appears to be no basis whatever in Q itself for positing the concept of 'the parousia' in Q, let alone to believe that two whole sections of Q (12:39–59; 17:23–37) deal with it." His argument is difficult to accept since Q shows clear interest in the coming of the Son of humanity/man, which is understood here as referring to Jesus (see above).

The parables in Q 12:39–46 aim at arousing a belief in an imminent "coming" of the Son of humanity/man, whether such a belief had waned or never existed at all (Tuckett 1996:156–57). According to Kloppenborg (1987:153) Q 12:39–59 "is unified by the motifs of the nearness and unexpectedness of the parousia and of judgment." In particular Q 12:40 (cf. Q 12:43) warns:

> You ... must be ready, for the Son of Humanity is coming at an hour you do not expect.

The theme of the return of the Son of humanity/man is taken up again in Q 17:23–37. In Q 17:23–24 the image of lightning is employed, a recurrent theme of judgement, and often divine *theophany* is involved as well (Exod 19:16; Deut 32:41; Pss 18:14; 144:6). Catchpole (1993:254) also brings attention to traditions in Josephus (*Ant.* 1.203) and Philo (*Abraham* 43; *Moses* 2.56) which import lightning into the events of the flood and the judgement of Sodom, two themes taken up in Q 17:26–30. Q 17:37 speaks of vultures that will gather around a corpse (cf. Job 39:30). Vultures/eagles are used in the Tanak as images of divine judgement (Prov 30:17; Jer 4:13; Hos 8:1; Hab 1:8), and the saying in Q becomes a metaphor for the parousia (Kloppenborg 1987:162).

When the Son of humanity/man will be revealed it will be as in the days of Noah and Lot (Q 17:26–30).[69] Ordinary and everyday activities are referred to such as eating, drinking and marrying. This may refer to gluttony and the questionable marriages of the Giants to the daughters of men (Gen 6:1–4) but such a view is questioned by Catchpole (1993:250). He points to traditions in Josephus (*Ant.* 1.374), Philo (QGenesis 1.91; 2.13) and the targums[70] that testify that the days of Noah and Lot were days of opportunity for repentance. The flood in particular became a prototype of the last judgement and the end of the world.[71] In this regard Allison argues that Q 17:26–27 could help explain Q 17:34–35, where it explains that one will be taken (παραλαμβάνεται) and another left (ἀφίεται). "This probably envisages, not the wicked being removed and condemned, but rather the righteous being taken to meet Jesus in the air" (Allison 2000:94). Allison also refers to ἀφίημι in Q 9:60 and 13:35, which means "abandon" or "forsake." "If this is the correct interpretation, then those left behind (ἀφίεται) are like the people who were left behind to perish in the flood" (Allison 2000:94). As we saw already, Kloppenborg had a different approach to the text. He understands that in Q 17:34–35 the co-workers will be separated, one being "swept away" (παραλαμβάνεται) and the other "spared"

---

69. The IQP does not include Q 17:28–29 that refers to Lot.

70. *Tg. Onq.* on Gen 6:3; 7:4, 10; *Tg. Ps.-J.* on Gen 19:24; *Tg. Neof.* on Gen 18:21.

71. Isa 24:18; *Jub.* 20:5–6; *1 En.* 1–16; 67:10; 93:4; *2 En.* 70:10 (J); *Apoc. Adam* 3:3; Sir 16:7; 2 Macc 2:4; *L.A.B.* 3:1–3, 9–10; 49:3; Josephus, *Ant.* 1.72–6; 2 Pet 2:5; 3:6–7.

(ἀφίεται). The same pair of verbs are found in Genesis 18:26 and 19:17 where it describes the destruction of the wicked and the sparing of Lot's family. The interpretation of Q 17:34–35 is not easy, since both verbs can either have a positive or a negative import. Q 17:34–35 is in closer proximity to Q 17:28–29 that refers to the story of Lot, so Kloppenborg may have the better approach. Q 17:27 also speaks of the unrighteous that the "flood came and *took* them all," while Q 13:28 speaks of the unresponsive Judeans that will be *thrown out* of the kingdom. When also seen with Q 22:28–30, this seems to be the better solution. The Q people looked forward to a *this*-worldly kingdom where Israel will be reconstituted. Those who will not participate in the Kingdom will be "swept away," and the Q people themselves will be "spared," that is, they will remain within Israel.

Thus the situation points to an imminent crisis. The Q people are, as in the days of Noah and Lot, in a position of safety as compared to their compatriots. If the latter do not use this opportunity to repent and divorce themselves of complacency, unrepentant Israel will be overcome with a sudden and disastrous judgement when the Son of humanity/man finally comes. The Q Apocalypse brings emphasis to the visible and swift nature of the return of the Son of humanity/man (Q 17:23, 24, 37b) and its unexpectedness (Q 17:26–27, 28–30) (Kloppenborg 1987:164).

Summary

The eschatology of Q is focussed on the imminent judgement of Israel (Q 3:7–9, 16–17; 10:12–15; 13:34, 28–29; 11:16, 29–51) that will be sudden and without warning (12:39–40; 17:23–34). It will have terrible results for Israel (Q 12:42–46; 19:12–27). The Q people also find themselves in an area of eschatological fulfilment, for John the Immerser has inaugurated the new age (Q 7:27) and Jesus, the "Coming One" has arrived (Q 7:18–23). The kingdom has arrived through his exorcisms, and the End is here for those who can recognize it. Family divisions and the Spirit, assumed to be present in some way, are all evidence of this (Q 12:10, 51–53, 54–56). Q is also waiting for the coming of the Son of humanity/man who will bring judgement (Q 12:39–59; 17:23–37). The Q people are in a position of safety for they have made use of this opportunity for repentance.

Overall it can be agreed with Tuckett (1996:163) that "large parts of Q are dominated by ideas of a futurist eschatology." Here it is particularly relevant to the main redaction, but it also gives examples of realized eschatology, especially when it comes to the activities and teaching of Jesus.

The Gentiles

Participation in the Judean symbolic universe naturally also influenced the Q people's relationship to the Gentiles. There are passages in the main redaction that appear at first to have a positive of view of Gentiles. The centurion had a faith which could not be matched anywhere in Israel (Q 7:1–10). Tyre and Sidon would have repented if the signs performed in Chorazin and Bethsaida had taken place there (Q 10:13). The Queen of the South listened to Solomon's wisdom (Q 11:31) and the Ninevites repented at Jonah's preaching (Q 11:32), and they will rise to judge "this generation" for their non-repentance since something greater than Solomon or Jonah is here.[72] In Q 10:12–14 it says that Sodom, Tyre and Sidon will fare better in the judgement than the unresponsive Galilean towns. Thus in Q, the Queen of the South, the Ninevites, the cities of Sodom, Tyre and Sidon, all with Gentile associations, are in various ways compared favorably with Judeans. According to Reed (2000:188), the

> use of distant ethnic groups to shame one's own group is a common *topos* in literature of the Greco-Roman period. Many geographical writers in antiquity envisioned an "inverse ethnocentric" scheme, in which peoples were more virtuous in proportion to their distance from the author's place of writing, with the author's audience the target of moral shame.

It must be said, however, that in Q it is not that the other ethnic groups are more virtuous; it is rather assumed that they will hypothetically respond to the preaching of repentance.

Other texts have also been identified that may involve the Gentiles (Tuckett 1996:397–98). The image of the "harvest" (Q 10:2) may refer to the judgement of Gentiles (cf. Joel 3:13–14; Isa 27:11; Hos 6:11), so missionaries sent to gather the harvest may point to the existence of a Gentile mission. The parable of the Great Supper (Q 14:16–24) could point to the failure of the Judean mission, with threats that the mission will be sent to the Gentiles instead (cf. Kloppenborg 1987:230). The parable of the mustard seen, where all the birds will find a home

---

72. Cf. *T. Benj.* 10:10, where it is stated that God will judge Israel by the chosen Gentiles, just as God tested Esau by the Midianites.

in the tree could maybe refer to Gentiles coming into the kingdom (Q 13:18–19). Both these parables, however, are ambiguous. If the association is pressed, the birds nesting in the tree could point to the eschatological future, and not a present reality. In the case of the parable of the Great Supper, the emphasis may be on those refusing to repent, not on possible Gentile replacements. It has also been argued that Luke 10:8b ("eat what is set before you" cf. Q 10:7) was in Q—this instruction makes sense in an environment of a Gentile mission where Judean food laws are not followed (see Tuckett 1996:398). A crucial factor is whether Matthew 10:5–6 at a pre-redactional stage was originally part of Q. This is the argument of Catchpole (1993:165–71) and Horsley (1999:244), but they are representative of a minority position. It is probably better not to make judgements based on these texts.

Catchpole (1993:280–308) has argued that in Q 7:1–10 the centurion does not necessarily refer to a Gentile (since ἑκατοντάρχης in the LXX and Josephus often does not); rather, he is ethnically neutral. So the story does not intend to draw a contrast between Gentile faith and Judean faith. The centurion is merely an example of extraordinary faith within the setting of the mission of Jesus to Israel. Jacobson (1992:109) sees it quite differently, as he says "on one important point there is no disagreement: the figure in the story is a gentile centurion." One must agree, for the reference to "Israel" in v. 9 is hard to explain if no Judean/Gentile distinction ever existed. The ἑκατοντάρχης functions as other Gentiles do in the main redaction—he is a useful way to launch a rebuke at unresponsive Judeans (Tuckett 1996:396). But this was no Roman centurion, as evidence for Roman Legionnaires stationed at Capernaum dates to well after the First Revolt. In the first century, the Legio X Fretensis was stationed in Syria, and it is not until the second century CE that Roman troops were stationed in and around Galilee. Herod Antipas adopted common Greek terms used for Roman officials, thus the centurion was likely an official in Antipas' administrative and military apparatus, "which apparently also included non-[Judeans]" (Reed 2000:162).

Reed also brings attention to a possible significance in the connection between Jesus and the prophet Jonah, that is, their openness to Gentiles. According to Reed (2000:211),

> Q 11:29–32 clearly is designed to shame Israel, this generation, with the positive response of both the Ninevites and the Queen of the South. That Gentiles recognized what is here, their repentance and quest for wisdom respectively, is contrasted with this

generation's obstinacy. In Q's perspective, the gentile centurion is beyond anyone's faith in all Israel (Q 7:1–10), the gentile cities of Tyre and Sidon would have reacted more favorably than the Galilean villages (Q 10:11–13), and people from the ends of the earth will replace the supposed heirs at the in-gathering (Q 13:28–29).

The question, therefore, is: exactly "how open" were the Q people to the Gentiles? According to Kloppenborg, the story of the centurion's servant emphasizes both the *fact* of the centurion's faith, and its *exceptional quality*. "Such a narrative undermines the notion that Gentile participation in the kingdom is restricted to an eschatological pilgrimage and would undoubtedly serve as useful ammunition in support of the Gentile mission ... It may be that 7:1–10 by itself does not evidence the involvement of the Q community in the Gentile mission, but the frequency with which the theme of Gentile response and faith occurs in Q [cf. Q 7:9; 10:13–15; 11:31–32; 13:29, 28; 14:16–24] suggests that such faith was no longer regarded as quite so unusual as the story by itself suggests" (Kloppenborg 1987:119). Overall, Kloppenborg (1987:236) argued that Q 13:28–29 when seen in conjunction with Q 7:1–10 and 11:31–32, which speaks of actual Gentile belief, and Q 10:13–15 that predicts potential Gentile belief, has in view an actual Gentile mission. Cotter (1995a:126) in reference to Q 12:8–9 and 22:28–30 argues that "it is clear that the community of Q^2 is open to Gentile membership," and she even speaks of the "displacement" of Israel by Gentiles in reference to Q 3:8 and 22:28–30 (1995b:137–38). Cotter (1995a:126) also argues that there "is no exclusivity on the basis of either [Judean] birth or observance of laws. The Law is recognized (Q 16:17) but Q^2 does explain how it is observed."

Tuckett (1996:399) approaches this issue from another angle and argues that the Gentiles mentioned "are generally not people who are present for Q." The people mentioned are either in the past (e.g., Q 11:31–32) or in the future (Q 10:13–15; 13:28–29). The story of the centurion's servant has a Gentile reacting to Jesus positively, but this occurred in Jesus' own day. This was certainly also relevant for Q's present (Gentiles reacting positively), but the centurion is evidently an exceptional case. The centurion is used to put faithless Israel to shame (cf. Jacobson 1992:110) and nothing "indicates that the centurion stands at the head of a long line of other Gentiles who are responding positively, either to Q's Jesus or to later Q [Messianists]" (Tuckett 1996:399). As can be seen, Q 13:28–29 and 22:28–30 is often seen in connection with the displacement of Judeans with Gentiles. As the analysis here already argued above, these texts have nothing to do with Gentiles. Q 13:28–29 refers to the eschatological pilgrimage of Diaspora Judeans, and the "judging" of the Q people over the twelve tribes of Israel in Q 22:28–30 has a positive meaning. Q demonstrates it is pre-occupied with the fate of ethnic and territorial Israel—the conversion of the Gentiles is not a primary concern.

According to Meyer (1970), Q uses the Gentile mission to urge Israel to repent, but does not engage in such missionary activity itself. The natural inclination of the Q group—evident at a pre-redactional level (Q 6:34; 12:30)—is that the Gentiles are the "others." There is no discussion it would seem of how a Gentile mission would create problems with regards to the Law or how far Gentile Messianists are expected to obey the Law—although, it is suggested that Q 13:27 does indicate that Q disassociates itself from those Messianists who have Gentile associations and have given up aspects of covenantal praxis. In addition, the redactional woes on the Galilean towns (Q 10:12–15) indicate a (failed) mission to Israel alone (Catchpole 1993:171–76) since they are not willing to convert (Uro 1987:172–73). Overall, we must agree with the position that Q was not engaged with a Gentile mission (Tuckett 1996:404; Jacobson 1992:256). The Gentiles are used in a polemical strategy to intensify the appeal to other Judeans.[73] In addition, based on the polemical and apologetic strategy of the main redaction in general, Q is far too busy to affirm their own status as Judeans which any contact with Gentiles would undermine. Allison (1997:121) also notes that Isaiah is often quoted or alluded to in support of the Gentile mission,[74] but Q, which interacts often with Isaiah,[75] never uses the prophetic book in such a way.

---

73. In Matt 10:5–6 the mission of the disciples is restricted to Israel, while in Matt 28:19 the mission is to both Judeans and non-Judeans. Did Matthew derive his universal mission from the rhetorical strategy of Q^2 (Van Aarde [2005] 2007)?

74. Matt 4:12–16 (Isa 9:1–2); Matt 12:18–21 (Isa 42:1–4); Matt 21:13 = Mark 11:17 = Luke 19:46 (Isa 56:7); Luke 1:79 (Isa 9:1); Luke 2:30, 32 (Isa 42:6); Acts 13:47 (Isa 49:6); Acts 26:18 (Isa 42:7); Rom 10:20–21 (Isa 65:1–2); Eph 2:17 (Isa 57:19); etc.

75. Q 3:8 (Isa 51:1–2); Q 6:20–23 (Isa 61:1–2); Q 6:29–30 (Isa 50:6, 8); Q 7:22 (Isa 26:19; 29:18–19; 35:5–6; 42:18; 61:1–2); Q 10:15 (Isa 14:13, 15); Q 10:23–24 (Isa 6:9–10); Q 12:33–34 (Isa 51:8); Q 17:26–27 (Isa 54:9–10).

The Formative Stratum (Q¹)

THE *HABITUS*/ISRAEL

Religion and Covenantal Praxis

There is not much in the formative stratum that concerns *religion* and *covenantal praxis*. Catchpole (1993:152, 176–78) argues that Q did not contain the instruction to eat whatever food is provided (Luke 10:8b). It encourages conduct that is not restricted by Judean food laws so it belongs to context of the Messianist mission expanding into the Gentile world. In Matthew (Matt 10:7–13) no such instruction is given. The IQP accepts Luke 10:7 as part of Q while Q10:8b ("eat what is set before you") is placed in brackets to indicate a level of uncertainty. If the instructions were in Q, it does not have to presuppose a mission to the Gentiles anyway. It probably had to with the fact that the missionaries should not pre-occupy themselves with purity concerns at the meal table. After all, Jesus himself came "eating and drinking," at times with Judean "tax-collectors and sinners" (Q 7:34). Lastly Q 6:46, where Jesus is addressed as "Lord, Lord," may have to do with the cultic life of the community (Pearson 2004:488). No firm conclusions can be reached in this regard, however. But here we will conclude the survey of the formative stratum that does not reveal much. At best, the evidence suggests that the Q people were willing to sacrifice aspects of ritual purity to bring the kingdom into the homes of others.

Kinship

The Q People and Broader Israel

The first element we will investigate with regards to kinship is the sermon (Q 6:20b–49—the markarisms will be discussed later). Jacobson (1992:95–97) argues that the sermon is drawing on the Wisdom tradition. Similarly Kloppenborg's (1987:189) analysis argued that the sermon was "overwhelmingly sapiential." Catchpole (1993:101–34) has a different approach, as he argues that at the heart of the discourse is an explanation of Lev 19:17–18:

> Do not hate your brother in your heart. Rebuke your neighbour frankly so you will not share in his guilt. Do not seek revenge or bear a grudge against one of your people, but love your neighbour as yourself. (NIV)

Allison (2000:29) agrees that Lev 19, part of the Holiness Code, is the chief intertext for Q 6:27–45. Horsley argues that the discourse is aimed at covenantal renewal, engaged with socio-economic matters in village communities. The sermon in Q 6:27–49 utilizes traditional covenantal exhortation and popular wisdom (Horsley & Draper 1999:88, 195–227). Therefore it is not denied here that the wisdom element is present, but this instructional discourse is engaged with the requirements of the covenant (or Torah), particularly with what the covenant requires in terms of social relationships between Israelites. In any event, for Judeans Wisdom and Torah were virtually synonymous, as in Sir 24:23 Wisdom is identified as the "book of the covenant of the most high God, even the law which Moses commanded."

Catchpole treats the entire section of Q 6:27–35 under the rubric of "love your enemies" (Q 6:27). He argues that Q 6:27–28, 35 by general consensus, has as the underlying thought Lev 19:18b: "You shall love your neighbour as yourself." In fact, Lev 19:18 is the underlying text for Q 6:27–35 as a whole (cf. Tuckett 1996:431). The three elements of Lev 19:18b ("You shall love // your neighbour // as yourself") can be related to all of Q 6:27–35 (Catchpole 1993:115; Allison 2000:31).[76] Catchpole and the IQP reconstructs Q 6:27–28, 35 differently, but in general the thrust of the message encourages the love of enemies, and to pray for them so that they may receive God's blessing in imitation of God's own benevolent behavior. Here is the IQP reconstruction of Q 6:27–28, 35:

> Love your enemies [[and]] pray for those [[persecuting]] you, so that you may become sons of your Father, for he raises his sun on bad and [[good and rains on the just and the unjust]].

Catchpole (1993:107) maintains that this love is one that should be extended to fellow members of the community of Israel, who have become estranged and hostile—this is an intra-Israel situation. In Q 6:32-33 the sense of Israelite community continues. It encourages loving and lending without expecting anything in return. The Q group's behavior should not be like the tax-collectors and the Gentiles, so the

---

76. Kloppenborg also acknowledges that the core of Q 6:27–35 is the love command, but according to him it does not obviously recall Lev 19:18: "It is much closer in form and content to a host of admonitions from sapiential sources and from Hellenistic popular philosophy" and it is far from obvious that "these sayings are intended as reinterpretations or radicalizations of the Torah" (Kloppenborg 1987:178, 179). The closest parallels according to Jacobson (1992:97) in Judean texts are found in the wisdom tradition (e.g., Prov 24:29; 25:21–22; cf. Sir 7:1–2; 31:15; Tob 4:15; *Let. Aris.* 207).

editor and his readers "are primarily conditioned by their [Judeanness] and their sense of separateness from other nations. They share a concern to live according to the covenant" (Catchpole 1993:109). Q 6:30 encourages similar behavior; one should give without asking back (cf. Sir 4:3–5; Tob 4:7–8). This may point to the Sabbath year legislation found in Deut 15:1–11, which lays down the cancellation of debts within the community of Israel. The there is the golden rule (Q 6:31), and the teaching to experience shame and mistreatment at the hands of others (Q 6:29, 30; Q/Matt 5:41). So the teaching of Jesus is not there to bring about a separation within the Israelite community, although it provoked serious opposition, since the Q people confessed Jesus as the Son of humanity/man. Nevertheless, Catchpole (1993:115–16) states it is a "confession which must be maintained *within* the ancient community. Every effort is made therefore to be faithful simultaneously to the confession of Jesus and the command of Moses" (emphasis original). The latter part of Catchpole's statement is a bit suspect since Jesus and the Q community was not in all respects faithful to the command of Moses. It is agreed with him, however, that Q was interested to live within the confines of the Israelite community.

This sense of community continues in Q 6:36–45 that Catchpole (1993:116–33) treats under the rubric "reproof in mercy." Here the underlying text according to him is Lev 19:17 where it encourages "You shall not hate your brother in your heart, but you shall reason with your neighbour." There is the injunction to be merciful in imitation of the Father (Q 6:36 cf. Exod 34:6; Lev 19:2). For Catchpole "mercy" is the keynote of the entire discourse. The persons addressed have responded to Jesus' message of repentance and the offer of divine mercy in forgiveness, and the call to exercise compassion towards others. This must be seen in conjunction with the teaching not to pass judgement (Q 6:37–38) that builds on the "mercy" theme. In Q 6:41–42 (cf. *b. Arak* 16b) it is encouraged to rather throw out the beam from your own eye before looking at the faults of your neighbor.[77] It is what lies in your heart that comes to expression, for it is from the good treasure that good things are produced and from an evil treasure that evil is

77. Jacobson (1992:103–4) here sees a connection between Q 6:39 and 6:41–42. Q 6:41–42 was given a polemical character by Q. They took up the polemical stance of defiant Judeans who refused rabbinic instruction (*b. Arak.* 16b). These leaders are themselves blind (Q 6:39) and in need of instruction. But see Kloppenborg (1987:184) who questions that Q 6:39 was anti-Pharisaic polemic. "Q 6:39–45, of course, takes particular aim at teachers ... who do not follow Jesus in his radical lifestyle and ethic" (Kloppenborg 1987:185).

produced (Q 6:43–45). Overall Jesus' teaching continues the familiar theme of this discourse, in that "the persons being addressed should bring to realization the existence of Israel as the covenant intended . . . They are enabled, indeed obliged, to act mercifully because they have experienced in the past, and they know they will experience in the future, that mercy by which, as adherents of Jesus and members of the community of Israel, they bring to effect what it means to be the community of God" (Catchpole 1993:117, 134). But the community of God, as will be demonstrated later, should illustrate allegiance to Jesus' teaching of what the covenant required.

The Q sermon is concerned with renewing relationships between the covenant people. But what it intended, and what actually happened, is glaringly different. There is clearly at the level of the formative stratum enough evidence that tension existed between the Q people and fellow Judeans. Q 6:22–23 speaks of those who are persecuted (cf. Q 6:28) and experience verbal abuse because of the Son of humanity/man. Catchpole (1993:94) understands that the opposition is due to the conviction that the Son of man is Jesus, an identification made with care elsewhere in Q (7:18–23). This identification points to the heavenly status that was afforded to Jesus, and his future coming in judgement. He also argues that Q 6:22–23ab which echo's the deuteronomistic motif of the persecution of the prophets, indicates that there was a strong sense of estrangement between the Q people and their fellow Judeans, but as yet, no separation has yet occurred (Catchpole 1993:94). But the evidence in Q does suggest that a form of separation has already occurred (Q 6:22–23; 12:2–12; 14:27; 16:16; 17:33). Horsley (Horsley & Draper 1999:274) says that "it seems difficult to conclude that the trials anticipated are utterly imaginary. The situation of the community hearing this speech appears to be one of actual repression or the threat of repression." In disagreement with Horsley (Horsley & Draper 1999:272–73), however, this repression does not come from the rulers as such, but from fellow Judeans. In addition, there are also sayings that show the local judicial systems cannot be trusted, "each of its component parts concerns institutionalized or ongoing violence and exploitation" (see esp. 6:22–23, 27–36 (+ Q/Matt 5:41), 37–38; 12:4–7, 11–12, 22–31, 58–59) (Kloppenborg 2000:193–95, 198).

This division between the Q people and their co-ethnics is also evidenced in the mission charge (Q 10:2–16). Uro (1987:208–9) argues that Q 10:2 illustrates an optimism which is difficult to explain if it was aimed at Judeans at the time of the writing of Q. Comparing it with

Acts 13:1–3, he argues for a Hellenistic setting, thus Q 10:2 points to a later Gentile mission, while Q 10:3, 12–16 represents an earlier stage of the tradition. But Q 10:2 should rather be seen in conjunction with Q 10:3–16 that clearly as a whole refers to a mission to Israel. The Q missionaries, however, are sent out as "lambs in the midst of wolves" (Q 10:3). This saying implies an element of danger, possibly because of the rejection of their message. According to Tuckett, here may be also an element of sarcastic inversion in the imagery employed, a rationalization of what is already happening, or has happened, in the experience of the Q missionaries. In some Judean texts (e.g., *1 En.* 89:13–27; 90:1–27), the imagery of lambs and wolves is used to characterize the position of Israel surrounded by a hostile Gentile world. In Q, the wolves refer to unresponsive cities in Israel, and Q 10:3 "now ascribes to these [Judean] groups the derogatory image (of wolves threatening lambs) previously applied to Gentiles" (Tuckett 1996:185; cf. Kloppenborg 1987:194). It is suggested that the saying is rather a metaphor for vulnerability (Jacobson 1992:146) but as already mentioned above, Catchpole draws attention to the ἅρπαξ word group (Q 11:39; 16:16). It involves opposition to the kingdom and to the rapacious behavior of the Pharisees. Q 10:3 + 11:39 + 16:16 must be seen in combination and they point to religious polarization between the envoys of Jesus and the Pharisees. Thus the warning in Q 10:3 has fellow Judeans or particularly the Pharisees in view, not Herod Antipas (*pace* Horsley 1999:245), and "in the context of bringing to Israel a disturbing call not to presume on the covenant as the sure and sufficient basis for security and the enjoyment of the grace of God, sober realism would dictate the need to be prepared for rejection" (Catchpole 1993:163). Overall the ethnic horizon in Q 10:2 does not go beyond Israel, and from the context of the formative stratum of Q, Q 10:3 implies that rejection was already experienced, be it a past or present reality. The imagery of Judeans being "wolves" indicates that the Q group's view of their co-ethnics, particularly the Pharisees, left a lot to be desired, as wolves "habitually feature in contexts which highlight rapacity, destruction and devastation" (Catchpole 1993:180).[78]

Nevertheless, when it comes to the issue of ethnic identity, the Q people are not estranged from their Judean contemporaries. When the

---

78. Cf. Gen 49:27; Prov 28:15; Jer 5:6; Ezek 22:27; Zeph 3:3; *T. Gad* 1:3; *T. Benj.* 11:1–2; Matt 7:15; John 10:12; Acts 20:29. See also Jacobson (1992:146, n. 50): "... the image can also be used to speak of the treachery of leaders"; and Horsley (Horsley & Draper 1999:245): "... the standard image was one of oppressive, predatory rulers" (cf. Ezek 22:23–27; Zeph 3:1–3; Prov 28:15).

Q people uses an outside group to contrast the behavior expected of them, it is the "Gentiles," not Judeans who are used (Q 6:34; 12:30). In these two texts, Q uses what ethnicity theory describes as a "we-they" *oppositional* self-definition. "Thus in terms of social boundaries, Q's consciousness seems much more determined by the distinctiveness of Q [Messianists] from Gentiles than from [Judeans]" (Tuckett 1996:202). Yet, as argued before, the Q people also had a strong consciousness of difference in relation to fellow Judeans. This is also evident in the formative stratum. The Q people experience repression and verbal insults, and according to Q 10:16, it is only those Judeans who receive Jesus who receive God.

The Q People and the Family

Other tensions are in evidence, such as the Q people's relationship towards their families. This aspect is downplayed by Arnal (2001) who argues that the missionary discourse (treated below) was not aimed at homeless itinerant missionaries, but constituted the program of disenfranchised scribes who lost their local status in the villages due to the construction of Tiberias. They took their program, aimed to counter the influence from the city or the outside, from village to village by making contact with other scribes who are seen to represent the village as a whole. In support of his argument, Arnal dismisses the idea of "homelessness" and family divisions as present in Q. For example, Q 9:59–60 "is not an exhortation literally to leave one's parents unburied," but the would-be follower is to "value his commitment to Jesus over basic filial responsibility" (Arnal 2001:93, 176). Similarly, Q 9:57–58 has more to do with absolute commitment than with literal homelessness. The saying is opaque and when detached from its literary context, the point of this "Wisdom saying" is that all human beings have no natural sanctuary (Arnal 2001:176–77). Overall Q 9:59–62 and 14:26 actually suggests the opposite of an antifamilial ethos: "the texts work in a rhetorically effective way only on the supposition that family relations continue within the group to whom Q is addressed" (Arnal 2001:174). These texts illustrate that following Jesus requires unconditional commitment, and family connections are of less importance, but the rhetoric of these sayings imply that the Q people have close family relationships and persist in maintaining them.

It is reasonable to accept that there probably were those who refused to break with their families, but the sayings also presuppose that there were examples (at least for some) where family relationships had broken asunder and where homelessness was an issue. According to Kloppenborg (1987:192) in Q the "Son of Man" came to be used as a Christological title, and in Q 9:57–58 he is used as a pattern for Messianist discipleship. This appears to be correct, but one must wonder, however, whether this saying does not also relate to family tensions in addition to the issue of discipleship. The "Son of humanity does not have anywhere he can lay his head," so was the historical Jesus asked (to put it politely) to leave home? If this is the case, then Q's Jesus might be telling the would-be follower yes, you can follow me, but be prepared for rejection at home.[79] This interpretation makes sense when seen in conjunction with the other sayings on the family. In Q 9:59–60 Jesus is asked by the potential disciple if he could first bury his father (cf. Elisha's request to Elijah in 1 Kgs 19:20). Jesus refuses and answers quite bluntly: "Follow me, and leave the dead to bury the dead." Thus commitment to Jesus and the kingdom carries priority over family obligations, particularly here, the father, and inevitably, one must be prepared to lose the support structure of family as a consequence of following Jesus. This mirrors the "Ego-centred network faction" model developed by Duling (2001:135, 145, 159–60) where personal recruitment by an Ego, and where total commitment is required as well, will more likely involve a stranger or casual acquaintance and takes place in public or directly. Duling, commenting on Q 9:57–60 (61–62), also states that Q clearly "emphasizes a sharp break with family." This is particularly relevant to the "intimate network" that formed around the Ego, Jesus. Thus overall, Q 9:59–60 constitutes a radical break from traditional kinship patterns, as the family was "the firmest pillar of Israelite society" (Guijarro 2001:216).

When seen in context of the first century society and the importance that was attached to the father-son relationship, one can appreciate the radical nature of this saying even more. As was discussed already, based on the intrinsic attributes (that define the roles) of the father-son relationship, it came to be the dominant relationship. The father saw in their sons another "I," and in antiquity "the relationship between father and his male offspring was the closest and most lasting

---

79. It is important to realize that in antiquity religion was embedded in kinship and politics. According to Duling (2001:144–45) "those ancients who affiliated with a deviant movement, especially one considered by the state as subversive, experienced a much greater break with trusted family, friends, and work associates, thus a more immediate social, not to mention political, risk than in modern Western society."

of all relationships because the whole continuity of the family was based on it" (Guijarro 2001:229). The father exercised his authority over his son throughout his life. In turn, the son had responsibilities towards his father. The son was expected to "honor and obey [cf. Exod 20:12; Deut 5:16] his father as long as he lived, to assist and care for him in his old age and to give him burial and carry out the funeral rites when he died" (Guijarro 2001:228). It was at the father's death where the son demonstrated his respect towards his father in the most visible way, and he was supposed to bury him according to the established rites (Gen 25:9–11; 35:29). At burial the deceased father became one of the family ancestors (Sir 30:4; 44:10–11; 46:12), and the heir's role was important here to insure the continuity of the household. Guijarro (2001:229) explains:

> In the burial rite the heir was presented and recognized as the new paterfamilias and from then on one of his principal functions would be to venerate the remains of the ancestors to whom the living still felt themselves bound as members of the same family. This obligation was one of the most sacred that a son had towards his father, and it did not finish on the day of burial but was prolonged in a series of funeral ceremonies after the burial and in the annual commemorations whose celebration was also entrusted to the son.[80]

Also in Mishnaic law, filial obligations towards one's deceased parents took precedence over the recitation of the *Shema* or the *Shemoneh Esreh* (*m. Ber.* 3:1) (Kloppenborg 1987:191). In Q 9:59–60 Jesus places requirements of the kingdom above standard filial piety, and the son's request to bury his father may have also referred to his responsibility to feed and take care of the aged father (Guijarro 2001:230). And for the son not to bury his father would be an act of impiety that would stain the family honor, and it would have had economic consequences as Jesus' request would threaten the continuity of the household.

Burial it would seem took place as soon as possible (cf. Acts 5:6, 7–10; 8:2), and leaving a body unburied through the night was regarded as sinfully disrespectful. Jacobson (1995:362) explains:

> Among the various tasks a son was expected to perform was that of obligatory grief and mourning and the rending of garments. But the call of Jesus would require the son to trample on all of

---

80. Cf. Gen 49:29–32; 50:25; Josh 24:32; Tob 4:3–4; 6:15; 14:9, 11–12; *Jub.* 23:7; 36:1–2, 18; 2 Macc 5:10; Josephus, *War* 5.545; *T. Reu.* 7:1; *T. Levi* 19:5.

these family pieties, including the most solemn one of all, the duty of burying one's father ... Jesus' call is, in any context but especially that of first-century Palestine, utterly insensitive. It is an insult to the most inviolate of all bonds, those of the family.

Fletcher-Louis (2003) explains that Q 9:60 has to do with the redefinition of the people of God. Apostates and Gentiles, based on various texts, were regarded as "spiritually dead." Related to this, non-burial of family members or fellow Judeans (those who could be regarded as "dead") was also a declaration of divine punishment and excommunication. In Q, Jesus labels those who are not his followers as "dead." But Jesus says "*leave* the dead to bury their own dead." He does not advocate non-burial as such, but a detachment from the "dead" (both literally and figuratively), that is, from those who do not follow him.

The second important anti-family saying in the formative stratum is Q 14:26. It is worth having the text in front of us:

> [[<The one who>]] does not hate father and mother <can>not <be> my <disciple>; and [[<the one who>]] <does not hate> son and daughter cannot be my disciple.

Q assumes that both men and women left home and family for the sake of following Jesus. "Q 14:26 is not just radical; it would have been profoundly offensive" (Jacobson 1995:363). "Hate" is here not a prerequisite for following Jesus, however, and here probably refers to a willingness to "sever one's relationship with" the family. Jacobson (1995:364) explains that "love" and "hate" can mean something like "recognise one's obligation to someone" or refusing to do so. Similarly Guijarro (2001:230) explains that "love" and "hate" are "attitudes coupled with behaviour which expressed group, rather than individual, values and were related to belonging and fidelity (love) or division and infidelity (hate)" (cf. Deut 21:15–18; Gen 29:31–33; Mal 1:2; Josephus, *Ant.* 6.255–56, 324; 7.254). The Q people, therefore, illustrate a scant regard for the continuity of the traditional household and the household economy and the continuity from generation to generation. There is no concern over issues of inheritance, for the veneration of the deceased father and family ancestors, nor a concern that a son take up his role as the new paterfamilias. The importance of biological ancestral links are denied. And so much for the role of "categorization" by the most important "person-sustaining" group, the family. The "sense of self" is rather determined by a spiritual kinship.

Tension with the family by following Jesus also existed because following Jesus required imitating his lifestyle, and his lifestyle by the standards of the day was scandalous and invoked rejection from his co-ethnics. Some traces are present in Q. By enacting the Kingdom of God, Jesus had no fixed abode (Q 9:58); his exorcisms it was said were performed by Beelzebul, the ruler of demons (Q 11:15); he was called a "glutton and a drunkard" (cf. Jer 5:21–24; 11QTemple 64:5), and his inclusive approach made him a friend of "tax-collectors and sinners" (Q 7:34). Particularly by being accused as a "glutton and a drunkard," in Israelite tradition reference could be made to the rebellious son that through his behavior brought dishonor to his family and who should be stoned to death (Deut 21:18–22).[81] "To follow Jesus, imitating his lifestyle, meant for his disciples acquiring this bad name which not only affected those who had decided to follow him, but also the rest of the family" (Guijarro 2001:234). This association is present in Q 11:19–20, where Jesus is accused of casting out demons by Beelzebul. Jesus retorts: "... if I by Beelzebul cast out demons, your sons, by whom do they cast <<them>> out?," thereby turning the accusations of the parents against themselves.

The reference to the πτωχοί, is also relevant here (Q 6:20). Catchpole interprets it as referring to those who are poor economically. He also argues that the first three markarisms concerning the poor, hungry and the mourning (Q 6:20b–21) should not be seen as three different statements aimed at three different groups, but as a "single declaration which was amplified or paraphrased by two others" (Catchpole 1993:86). In Judean tradition, the poor in all times experience what others know in time of bereavement (Sir 4:1–2; 7:32–34; 38:19) and struggle to obtain food (Prov 22:9; Sir 4:1; 34:25). For these people, the God of the covenant's concern has not changed. But is there not another dimension to the poverty in question? Guijarro argues convincingly that these poor could also refer to disciples of Jesus who had been rejected by their parents. Those who lacked family support was πτωχός, a person who could not survive without begging. Guijarro (2001:235) explains that in "Hellenistic society poverty was not defined principally by economic criteria but rather by kinship because kinship was the main way of accessing economic resources and all other goods." This argu-

---

81. Allison (2000:40–41) notes that Deut 21:18–21 is found just before vv. 22–23, that instructs that bodies of executed criminals are to be hung on a tree, a penalty which at the time was associated with crucifixion. Thus Q's allusion here to Deut 21:20 might have had implicit reference to Jesus' crucifixion (cf. Q 14:26).

ment is convincing when seen in connection with the fourth markarism (Q 6:22–23) that describes the social ostracism and repression of the disciples. Jesus also gave instructions that are proper to beggars. The disciples are encouraged to make requests with confidence (Q 11:9–13); they should not be concerned with material things (Q 12:22–32); and not to store up earthly treasures (Q 12:33–34). "The foundation for this confidence is a God who is father, not family, which was then the social institution that supplied all these things" (Guijarro 2001:235).

According to Jacobson (1992:222–24), the cross saying (Q 14:27) points to suffering entailed in the division of families and loss of community. The cross is a metaphor for rejection and alienation and in a similar manner to Q 14:26, it functions as a principle for exclusion (cf. Mark 8:34 where the saying is formulated as a principle for inclusion). In Q 17:33 "life" is to be found where it seems to be lost, that is, in following Jesus. So following Jesus is not in vain—it justifies the loss of one's family and community and finding life in a new community.[82]

It is not clear whether the cross saying refers to family divisions as such, but overall the formative stratum has sayings that represent a strong attack on the traditional (patriarchal) family, that is, if following Jesus becomes a problem. According to Guijarro (2001:215–16, 222) in the original tradition the split was between parents and children, but caused by the latter—Q represents the first stage of the tendency where the divisions between family members are widened, but the Q sayings do not specify who cause the division. It is quite possible, however, that in Q it is the children who are the cause of the family divisions (see Q 9:59–60; 12:53). But similar to the analysis of Q 12:49–53 (the main redaction), the sayings in the formative stratum imply that following Jesus disrupts the family, and that the family conflict was mainly between the parents and the children. This is not to say this happened in all instances since the itinerants on their mission were sent to house-

---

82. Jacobson (1995:367–73) also discusses Q 16:13 and 16:18 as anti-family sayings. He argues that Q 16:13 probably stood just before Q 12:22–31 so Mammon in this context was probably intended to refer to "money," "property," or "making a living," not amassing wealth as such. Since the "economy" of the first-century was primarily an economy of the household, the saying seems to imply that serving God must be preferred over serving the household economy (whether based on agriculture, crafts, fishing and so on). As far as Q 16:18 is concerned, Jacobson argues the saying primarily concerns *remarriage*. People that might have left their families might now wish to marry a "believer," and Q 16:18 Jacobson suggests, stigmatizes any who would do that. The saying prohibits the formation of new families within the new community to facilitate communal life.

holds (Q 10:5–7). Where all family members accepted Jesus' message of the kingdom, no divisions were caused. The family remained intact in these circumstances, but at the same time, they formed a fictive kinship group with other followers of Jesus, including those who needed support since they had to abandon their homes. According to Jacobson (1995:375), evidence "of fictive family formation is not strong, but not entirely absent . . . Religious symbolism in Q is consistent with fictive family formation." But the evidence for fictive family formation is sufficient, and this is especially true for the first stratum. God is addressed as "Father" (Q 6:36; 11:2, 13; 12:30). The Q people are "sons" (Q 6:35) and addressed each other as "brothers" (Q 6:41–42; 17:3). These fictive kinship patterns could easily have been accommodated in first-century Galilee. The primary locus of religious life outside of the temple and synagogue/assembly was the household. The architecture of our period indicates that the courtyard house was the dominant style, where several rooms were arranged around internal courts. The courtyard house could be expanded or contracted according to need, so "it would have been ideal for communal living, with individual rooms for sleeping and for cooking and so on" (Jacobson 1995:379). The early Messianist movement was a "house-church" movement, Q being no exception. But the Q people were now part of the household of God, where the Divine Patriarch will look after their needs.

Summary

The Q sermon is aimed at covenant renewal whereby relationships within the Israelite community can be restored (Q 6:27–45). Yet, the Q people's association with Jesus had the opposite effect. They themselves are persecuted (Q 6:22–23); they are the targets of ongoing violence and exploitation from their co-ethnics (Q 6:22–23, 27–36 (+ Q/Matt 5:41); 12:2–12, 22–31, 58–59; 14:27; 17:33) where the Pharisees seem to be singled out (Q 10:3; 11:39; 16:16). The Q mission itself did not go beyond Israel (Q 10:2), but evidently it failed. It is the Gentiles whom are identified (Q 6:34; 12:30) as the "others" from whom the Q people primarily distinguish themselves, yet, a certain distance also existed between them and fellow Judeans.

Tension also existed between the Q people and their families (Q 9:57–60; 14:26), although this was not the intention (Q 10:5–7). The main division was between parents and their children. Jesus himself is regarded as a "glutton and a drunkard" (Q 7:34; main redaction), associating him with the tradition of the rebellious son. What we find as a result is a fictive family formation. God is the Divine Patriarch (Q 6:36; 11:2, 13; 12:30); the Q people are his sons (Q 6:35) and they are brothers (Q 6:41–42; 17:3). This "spiritual" family is no longer characterized by blood or ethnic ties, but by positive response to Jesus and imitating his lifestyle. This new household will provide what is needed, and is a substitute for the traditional patriarchal family. Evidently, the Q people were not that concerned over the continuity of the household and the household economy, matters of inheritance, or maintaining biological ancestral links to the family forefathers. It was a matter of leaving the dead to bury the dead. In this respect, Q has "emigrated" from the Judean symbolic universe in a radical way.

The Sacred Canopy

The Christology of the Formative Stratum

When it comes to the Christology of the first stratum, Arnal (2001:167–68) contends that here we find the complete absence of Christological reflection (in consequence it points to an early dating). Q 6:46, where Jesus is addressed as "Lord, Lord," it does show interest in the significance and status of Jesus, but Jesus is simply a wise man with no reflection on his supernatural significance or his relationship to God. When it comes to the Son of humanity/man in Q 6:22–23, Jacobson argues that it is embedded in material that is rooted in the tradition of the suffering of the righteous. "The association of 'son of man' with the suffering of the righteous may indicate that the Q community did not understand the title 'son of man' as a reference to an apocalyptic figure of judgment" (Jacobson 1992:101).

It is argued here, however, that the Christology of the main redaction is already present in the formative stratum. The difference here is that the Christology is assumed—it needs little defence and no overt apologetics are involved as we encounter in the rhetorical strategy of the main redaction. Jesus is already represented as the eschatological prophet in Q 6:20–21. In addition, the Moses typology, encountered regularly in the main redaction, is already present in the formative stratum; Jesus reconstructs Lev 19 (Q 6:27–45), inverts Moses' instructions to the Israelites (Q 10:4), and on one occasion even contradicts Moses by disallowing divorce (Q 16:18).

As we saw earlier, Catchpole (1993:94) understands that the opposition to the Q people (Q 6:22–23) is due to the conviction that the Son of humanity/man is Jesus (see also Q 9:58). This identification referred to the heavenly status that was afforded to Jesus, and his future coming in judgement. In Q 6:46 Jesus is addressed as "κύριε κύριε," a context which demands absolute obedience (see with Q 6:47–49).[83] Pearson (2004:488) argues that Q 6:46 may reflect something of the cultic life of the community, with Jesus being addressed as the exalted lord (cf. 1 Cor 16:11; *Did.* 10:6). Catchpole (1993:100) argues that the Q sermon is both deliberately designed and Christologically controlled. Only on two occasions does explicit Christology make it appearance, at the start (Q 6:22) and at the end (Q 6:46). It exists to articulate the conviction that the coming "son of man" is the authoritatively speaking Jesus. Catchpole identifies both texts as expressing an intense longing for the coming of the "son of man." In addition, he argues that from Q 6:46 onwards that κυρίος becomes the dominant Christological category. Thus in Q 10:2 for example, ὁ κυρίος τοῦ θερισμοῦ may refer to the "exalted and returning one who during the present interval authorizes those who continue and expand upon his own mission" (Catchpole 1993:161). Catchpole also argues that Q 10:2 demands a functional equivalence between God and Jesus (see with Q 10:3). God's authority is experienced in the authority of Jesus, and God's harvest is experienced in Jesus' harvest. So the meaning is the same as that found at the conclusion of the mission charge where it states that those who receive (or reject) Jesus receive (or reject) God himself (Q 10:16).

It is questionable that Jesus as Lord/Master is the dominant Christological category in Q, for it stands alongside the others. But Catchpole is right to bring attention to the authority of Jesus. In the parable of the houses built on rock or sand (Q 6:47–49), it is interesting to note how much emphasis is placed on the authority of Jesus' teaching. It is hearing and doing (Q 6:46) Jesus' teaching (no reference is made to the Torah as such) that secures stability in the present and the eschatological future. A similar motif is found in Q 10:16:

> Whoever takes you in takes me in, [and] whoever takes me in takes in the one who sent me.

---

83. Based on the analysis above, Q 6:47–49 must be understood in an eschatological context, that is, Jesus' teaching has eschatological consequences. This calls for an implicit Christology being present in this pericope. It is therefore disagreed with Jacobson (1992:106) who argues that the emphasis here is on doing Jesus' words; "there is no reference here to confessing Jesus before people or to any christological assertion."

It is indirectly said that those who reject Jesus reject God. This is analogous to Q 10:22 where it is implied that those who do not hear Jesus have no knowledge of God. It is analogous to Q 12:8–9, where confessing Jesus is the definitive requirement for eschatological salvation. But overall the authority and eschatological status of Jesus is assumed—not defended—in the formative stratum. It required the polemical and apologetic requirements of the main redaction to come to fuller expression.

The Torah and the Kingdom of God

The kingdom/reign of God and its nearness is an important religious theme in the formative stratum (Q 6:20; 9:60, 62; 10:9, 11; 11:2; 12:31; 13:18–21; 16:16). But similarly to the main redaction, the kingdom/reign of God stands in tension with the received Torah. Horsley (Horsley & Draper 1999:96) argues that Q 6:20–49 "makes numerous allusions to Israelite traditions, particularly to Mosaic covenantal laws and teachings in 6:27–36."[84] As we saw already, Lev 19 is the chief intertext of the sermon, but it is important to bring attention to the fact that some of the teaching we encounter in the sermon modifies or runs counter to the Torah. Here are the examples.

The love of enemies (Q 6:27), for example, runs counter to the "measure for measure" principle, although a precedent does exist in the way that Joseph treated his brothers (Gen 50:15–19; cf. *T. Zeb.* 5:3; *T. Gad* 4:2; *T. Benj.* 3:3–4) (Catchpole 1993:107–8). This love of enemies ran contrary to the general ethos of both the Greco-Roman world and Judeanism. Reiser (2001:426), while taking note of other texts, limits the background of Q 6:27 to Lev 19:18: "Jesus, who, taking [Lev 19:18] as a starting point, is the first to preach a general *commandment* to love one's enemies" (emphasis added). The love of neighbor also requires that the disciples do more than the tax-collectors and the Gentiles, who only love their own (Q 6:32–33). Q 6:36 has the instruction: "Be full of pity" or "be merciful," "just as your Father is full of pity." This is close to Lev 19:2 that places emphasis on holiness in imitation of God's holiness. If Q 6:36 is a reformulation of Lev 19:2, then Q places mercy above holiness, or alternatively, it is explaining that mercy is the true meaning of holiness. Either way, Lev 19:2 "is being reconstructed" (Allison 2000:30). Holiness within the context of first-

---

84. Horsley refers to Q 6:27 cf. Lev 19:17–18; Exod 23:4–5; Deut 22:1–4; Sir 29:1; to Q 6:29 cf. Exod 22:25–26; Deut 24:10–13; Amos 2:8; to Q 6:36 cf. Lev 19:2.

century Judeanism was the equivalent of having the status of ritual purity. Q 6:36 is similar to Q 11:39–44 of the main redaction in that it places ethical concerns above requirements of the ritual law. Interestingly, the "mercy" above holiness theme is complimentary to Q 6:35; God makes the sun rise on the good and bad and gives rain to both the just and the unjust, an idea which runs contrary to evidence found in the Hebrew scriptures where God does not necessarily provide sunshine and rain for the wicked (Catchpole 1993:105).[85]

Q 6:37–38 instructs the disciples not to judge (but cf. Q 6:42 and 17:3!), which stands in contrast to Lev 19:15 that commands: "you will judge your neighbor." So Q 6:37–38 is qualifying Lev 19:15 or "at least dissenting from a common application of it" (Allison 2000:33). If one reads Q 6:27–38 with Lev 19 in view,

> Jesus is modifying and adding to the Mosaic demands. He substitutes mercy for holiness, enjoins his hearers not to judge, uses a positive form of the golden rule instead of a negative one, speaks of love of enemy rather than love of neighbor, and says it is not enough to have right fraternal relations (the subject of [Lev] 19:17), for even Gentiles do that.[86] (Allison 2000:33–34)

There are other examples where Jesus revises the holiness code. In Q 17:3–4, Jesus supports the injunction of Lev 19:17 that instructs that one should reprove your brother. But the emphasis of Jesus in Q lies on forgiveness, not reproof. What Jesus demands "is not repeated rebukes but repeated acts of forgiveness" (Allison 2000:67).

The demands of the kingdom also place the followers of Jesus in tension with what the Torah expects in terms of family relationships. In Q 9:60 there is the injunction that a potential disciple should "leave the dead to bury their own dead." Q 9:59–60 "contravenes most radically the norms of the law, of moral conduct and of standard religious practice" (Guijarro 2001:214). But the emphasis of the teaching is on discipleship and commitment to Jesus, not about Torah observance as such. According to Tuckett (1996:424), far reaching implications can be drawn, but Q does not suggest that it has consequences for Torah

---

85. Catchpole draws attention to various biblical passages; especially relevant are Job 8:16; Sir 12:2; Is 13:10; Ezek 32:7; WisSol 5:6 (on sunlight); and Isa 5:6; 1 Kgs 17–18; Amos 4:7–8 (on rain).

86. Allison (2000:34) also points out, however, that this kind of provocative inversion of Mosaic Law is also found in the Tanak. Isaiah 56:1–8, for example, rewrites Pentateuchal language (Num 16:9; 18:2–6) to promote a new idea in that foreigners and the physically maimed may serve in the Temple of the future.

observance or that any such issues are at stake. Even so, also the injunction to "hate" father and mother (Q 14:26) runs contrary to the fourth commandment (Exod 12:12; Deut 5:16). Allison (2000:63) treats Q 14:26 within a context where certain circumstances do not require the deconstruction of Torah but the subordination of one commandment to another, so the Jesus of Q 14:26 remains under the parental roof of the Law. The same is relevant for Q 9:60.

Another text quite relevant to our investigation is Q 16:18. The text has difficulties of its own. The total ban on divorce (cf. Mic 2:16) could either be seen as an attack on Deuteronomy 24:1–4, or as a stricter demand, hence a more rigorous obedience to the Law is required (Tuckett 1996:408; Catchpole 1993:237). The primeval will of God was for a union between a man and a woman (Gen 2–3), so Deut 24:1–4 could be seen as a divine concession to or compromise for human sin (Allison 2000:65). Jesus rejects it, and it is not just a matter here of Jesus requiring more rigorous obedience. What should be emphasized here is that Jesus disallows what Moses allowed. Allison (2000:65) asks appropriately: "what is Jesus doing to Moses?" Here is another example where Jesus is not that "orthodox." Jesus contradicts the great law-giver in this one instance and freely reconstructs the holiness code. Q 16:16 offers an explanation:

> ... The law and the prophets were until John. From then on the kingdom of God [that is already present] is violated and the violent plunder it.

It seems to suggest that in some sense the era of the Law and the prophets has come to an end. In the discussion of the sermon when treating kinship, it was seen that Catchpole argued that Jesus' teaching (based on Lev 19) emphasizes what the people of the covenant should live like. This is true, but it was illustrated above that the kingdom/reign of God requires a reconstructed Torah or covenant, given by the eschatological prophet, Jesus. Similarly in Q 16:16 it is simply assumed that a new era has surpassed the old. No defence or apologetics are required here. It is not that the Torah is entirely abandoned, but certainly there is a depreciation of the Law and the prophets (*pace* Catchpole 1993:237)—it is part of the "old" system. Allison approaches the issue from another angle. He argues that the rewriting or contradiction of the Torah in Q should not be seen that Q has abandoned the Torah:

> Such an inference would fail to recognize that many [Judean] interpreters felt the independence and freedom not only to re-

write Scripture, but also to turn it upside down and even contradict it ... [Q's] intertextual irony is not an example of Messianist antinomianism but an illustration of the interpretive freedom of [Judean] rhetoric. (Allison 2000:194, 197)

Horsley (Horsley & Draper 1999:115–16) argues that if "the law and the prophets" was a standard phrase for the Israelite tradition among both the people and scribal circles, "the kingdom of God means realization and practice of just covenantal relations, moreover, 'the law' not only is of enduring validity but is the authoritative guide for societal life, as stated in Q 16:17." Alternatively, and an interpretation Horsley prefers, if "the law and the prophets" referred to the great tradition of the rulers and their representatives (the rich), then there is a polemical edge to Q 16:16.

One can rather agree that the kingdom of God means the realization and practice of just covenantal relations. But Q 16:16 clearly implies that a level of tension existed between the new and the old, hence the corrective strategy of Q 16:17. The freedom of Judean rhetoric may play a role here, but more so Jesus—a teacher with divine authority—has given his followers an eschatological identity and frame of reference. It is the kingdom/reign of God, which requires a reconstructed Torah, and this new combination forms part of Q's sacred canopy.

As an aside, the rhetorical tone of Jesus' teaching in the formative stratum, aimed at covenant renewal, is instructional. The authority of Jesus is simply taken for granted and no apologetic stance towards the Torah is present. The lack of a developed Christology in the formative stratum should not therefore be seen that it lacked Christological reflection, or that the Q people merely saw Jesus as a "wise man." Jesus' reconstruction of the Torah is not challenged, indicating that Jesus' eschatological status and authority was common knowledge and accepted by the Q people.

In summary, in the formative stratum Jesus freely reconstructs the Torah, even contradicts Moses on one occasion, and it is stated that a new era, the kingdom/reign of God has surpassed the old (the Law and the prophets). It is not that the Law has been left behind entirely, but what is important is the newness of the kingdom. There is no defence offered of this position in Q^1, it is a matter taken for granted. This is closely related to the rhetorical tone of Jesus' teaching about the kingdom and covenant renewal. It is instructional. This hortatory tone also tells us much about the Christology of the formative stratum. The authority of Jesus and his eschatological status is assumed—Q^1 requires no apologetics, hence its hortatory nature. It is because of Jesus that the Q people are living according to eschatological Torah, or one can say that for Q covenantal nomism is in (re)construction. It is somewhat like a hypothetical group of patriotic Americans coming together, and acting as founding fathers by writing a new declaration of independence—somewhat the same, somewhat different from the original—for a renewed America. Q's sacred canopy now boasts a heavenly Jesus, a reconstructed Torah, and the kingdom/reign of God. This eschatological identity later on required the polemical and apologetic strategy of the main redaction whereby the Q people were given affirmation and legitimation of their (re)constructed Judean ethnic identity.

Shared "Historical" Memories

Most examples that recall traditions of the past in the formative stratum are implicit, rather than explicit. As we shall see later, the Moses typology encountered in the main redaction is also encountered in the formative stratum. This is relevant, for example, to Jesus reconstructing the holiness code of Lev 19 in Q 6:27–45. What will be discussed here is that the Moses and the new Exodus typology is probably also present in the mission instructions. The IQP reconstructs Q 10:4 as follows:

> Carry no [[purse]] [presumably for money], nor knapsack [presumably for bread], nor shoes, nor stick; and greet no one on the road.

Now some of these elements also appear when the Israelites departed from Egypt. Exodus 12:11 explains that Moses instructed the Israelites to eat the Passover in a hurry, with sandals on their feet and staff in hand, while Exod 12:34–36 (cf. Gen 15:14; 1 Sam 4–6) recalls that they left Egypt with bread, silver and gold, and with clothing. Allison (2000:42–43) considers the text of Q 10:4 as uncertain, although based on the IQP reconstruction, the text there seems to be an inversion of Moses' instructions to the Israelites. In line with this prophetic typology are the markarisms (Q 6:20–21) where Jesus is represented as the anointed eschatological prophet of Isa 60:1–2.

Q 9:61–62 alludes to Elijah calling Elisha (1 Kgs 19:19–21), but in addition, it may also recall the story of Lot's wife. Those who look back are not fit for the Kingdom of God. Lot's wife "looked back" (Gen 19:26) in disobedience to the divine command not to do so (Gen 19:17). The targums suggest that she looked back "because she was sentimentally attached to her family and past" (Allison 2000:80).[87] Thus in similar fashion the disciple of Q 9:61–62 is attached to his old life—this disqualifies him from being a disciple of Jesus.

The only explicit example relevant to *shared "historical" memories* in the formative stratum is when reference is made to Solomon and his "glory" in Q 12:27. "Glory" (δόξα) was often associated with Solomon's reign.[88] Also the κρίνον usually translated as "lilies" appears twenty-two times in the LXX, with more than half having to do with Solomon (cf. Allison 2000:153–54).

Based on the above it can be seen that *shared "historical" memories* is not an important cultural feature of the formative stratum. Probably most important here is not what is explicitly being said, but what is assumed. Jesus stands within the prophetic tradition. As a prophet like Moses, he is reconstructing Lev 19 (discussed above) in Q 6:27–45, and inverts Moses' instructions to the Israelites (Q 10:4). In Q 6:20–21 Jesus is identified with the eschatological prophet of Isaiah. Elijah and Elisha is present as well, but not in an important way (Q 9:61–62). These themes, as we saw, were further developed in the main redaction.

The Eschatology of the Formative Stratum

The first area of investigation into the eschatological character of the formative stratum is the sermon (Q 6:20b–49). Kloppenborg (1987:188), although he laid emphasis on the sapiential nature of the beatitudes he also stated that "they are proclamations of eschatological salvation." Alternatively he described them as "radical wisdom of the kingdom" or as "sapiential forms infused with eschatological content" (1987:189). Tuckett (1996:141) argues that the beatitudes (Q 6:20–23) as a whole are eschatologically orientated: the poor, hungry and the mourning in the present are promised future reversal of their present and less than desirable state in an eschatological future. For Catchpole (1993:86), the future reversal predicted in χορτασθήσονται (IQP: χορτασθήσεσθε) and παρακληθήσονται (IQP: [[παρακληθήσεσθε]]) enables the verb ἐστίν in Q 6:20b to be interpreted as a Semitic future-type present and ἡ βασιλεία τοῦ θεοῦ as the totality of God's design for the poor. This draws on the vision promoted by apocalyptic, specifically Isa 61:1–2, as Jesus' answer to John in Q 7:22 indicates.

---

87. *Tg. Ps.-J.* on Gen 19:26; *Tg. Neof.* 1 on Gen 19:26; cf. Philo, *Abraham* 164.
88. 1 Chr 29:25; 2 Chr 1:12; 5:13, 14; 7:1–3; Josephus, *Ant.* 8.190; *T. Sol.* 5:5.

It was argued previously that "the poor" is also applicable to Jesus' followers who had lost the support of their families. They are promised eschatological reversal, and this is something verified in Q 6:22–23 where they as the "persecuted" and "insulted" are promised a great reward in heaven. At the end of the Sermon (Q 6:47–49; see also Q 12:4–5) the listeners are warned "of the (eschatological) consequences which will result from their attitudes to the teaching of Jesus as just set out: those who hear and obey Jesus' teaching will be secure against the onslaughts of flood and storm; those who do not will perish" (Tuckett 1996:142). In Q 6:47–49 a contrast is made between houses built on rock (cf. Ps 27:5; 40:2; Isa 22:16; 33:16) or sand (cf. Sir 18:10; Gen 13:16; Ps 78:27; Jdt 2:20). With the onset of a severe storm, they either collapse or stand. In contrast with Tuckett, Jacobson (1992:96–97 cf. Kloppenborg 1987:186) argues that the sermon is predominantly sapiential in character. The parable of the two builders/houses has its closest parallels in the wisdom parables of the rabbinic tradition (*m. Ab.* 3:22; *A.R.N.* 24). Also, the parable conforms to the typical practice of the wisdom tradition, where a "ruined house" occurs at the end of a number of collections (Prov 1–9; 10–15; 22:17–24:22; Job 3–27). Catchpole (1993:96–97) agrees with Tuckett's eschatological interpretation, however. The parable when viewed in isolation is concerned with how to live in the present. By listening to Jesus and by doing what he says, you will have firm stability or security and will be ready for any threat. But based on Q 6:46, which displays an intense longing for the return of the Son of humanity/man (cf. Q 6:22),[89] the parable of the builders/houses following immediately thereafter now had to be read eschatologically. "In Q, and only in Q, its imagery would as a result have recalled the imagery of theophanic texts in the biblical tradition" (Catchpole 1993:100). These texts referred to rain (Ps 68:9) and flood (Job 22:16; Pss 93:3; 98:8; Hab 3:10) and wind (Is 17:13; 57:13; 64:6) to warn about "the ultimate storm-like appearance of God in judgment."[90] So the "coming of the Lord and Son of man" must be anticipated in a spirit of obedience and must be a time of "dedicated 'doing'" (Catchpole 1993:100–101).

Likewise the parables of the mustard seed and the leaven (Q 13:18–21) also refer to an eschatological future (Tuckett 1996:143). But Tuckett, in his attempt to make some Q material *un*-sapiential, also

---

89. Cf. Jacobson (1992:95–96) who argues that it is by no means clear that Q 6:46 is a "prophetic saying."

90. Catchpole (1993:100) also refers to other texts related to this idea: WisSol 4:19; Sir 43:16; 5:22–23; Jdg 5:5; Pss 18:7; 77:17–18; 97:4; Mic 1:4; Jdt 16:15.

seems prone to read eschatology in some traditions where its presence is questionable. On the teaching about anxiety (Q 12:22–31), Tuckett (1996:152) argues it is "thoroughly impregnated with a powerful eschatological awareness and expectation." Here Tuckett claims to draw on the view of Catchpole, who is understood to argue that this material involves a strong clash with wisdom literature's expectation that human beings should work to sustain themselves (e.g., Prov 6:6–8; 10:21; 12:24, 27). The situation this Q material belongs to is special in character and short in duration and is "conditioned by the expectation of an imminent eschatological crisis" (Catchpole 1993:35). But Tuckett fails to take notice that Catchpole was here commenting on these sayings with regards to their original life setting (viz. charismatic itinerants), and not on their function in Q. In addition, Tuckett (1996:152–55) also argues that Q 11:2–4, 9–13, a possible unit devoted to prayer, is dominated by the prayer for the kingdom in an eschatological sense. The Lord's Prayer itself has a dominant theme of eschatology and the kingdom of God. The Q people are then assured their prayers will be answered: they may ask, search and knock. The "good things" that will be given in Q 11:13 by the Father are gifts of the Eschaton. Overall, the Q people, Tuckett (1996:155 cf. 347–54) maintains, "are exhorted to work and strive for the establishment of the kingdom of God," a concern which overrides a concern for material needs. The urgency of the appeals are explained by the rationale that the kingdom will arrive in the *near* future (Q 12:39–46; 17:23–37).[91] Catchpole (1993:211–28) does not agree, and he suggests that Q 11:2–13 (incl. Luke 11:5–8) *in association with Q 12:22–31* refers to a situation where although they proclaimed the imminence of the kingdom of God, the Q people were in socio-economic need (cf. Kloppenborg 1987:220–21), since they needed insistent teaching about the Father's provision of food and clothing. Both Tuckett (1996:360, 365–66) and Kloppenborg (1987:251), however, also rightly refer to other passages where it suggests that the people addressed are not destitute and where it seems to imply that possessions were real options (Q 6:30; 9:57–62; 10:7–8; 12:29–31, 33–34; 16:13). Thus Q must have consisted of members who were on various levels of the socio-economic scale. In fact, Q 12:31 might be an instruction to join/remain with the Q community where the necessary provisions can be provided in the new spiritual household.

The formative stratum also contains elements of realized eschatology. Q 6:20–21 implies the anointed one of Yahweh has arrived.

---

91. These two texts are assigned by Kloppenborg to the main redaction of Q.

Jacobson (1992:144, 147) argues that eschatology is clearly present in the mission charge. This is present in the idea of the harvest metaphor (Q 10:2; cf. 3:9, 17) since it is frequently used to refer to judgement/the End (cf. Catchpole 1993:164).[92] Similarly Kloppenborg (1987:125) argues that Q 10:2 describes missionary work as eschatological gathering. Even the parables of the mustard seed and the leaven imply that the future kingdom of God is already present (Q 13:18–21). This is supported by Q 16:16, for the kingdom is already violated and plundered, implying it is already here. When curing the sick, the envoys of Jesus must tell them that the kingdom/reign of God has reached them (Q 10:9). Jesus' followers are encouraged to seek the Father's kingdom (Q 12:31). If the Holy Spirit is mentioned in Q 12:12, it is promised that he will help those who face interrogation before the assemblies.

In summary the formative stratum looks towards an eschatological future. They are expecting the arrival of the kingdom (Q 6:46; 11:2; 13:18–21) and judgement (Q 6:47–49; cf. 12:4–5). The future, as opposed to the main redaction, is couched in positive language in hope of a blessed future existence (Q 6:20–21, 22–23). It also makes the claim that the kingdom is present through the teaching and presence of Jesus and healing (Q 6:20–21; 10:9; 12:31; 13:18–21) and suggests that judgement is already in progress (Q 10:2). It is interesting to note that in the formative stratum there is a reasonable balance between futurist and realized eschatology, and a few texts contain both ideas at the same time. In the main redaction, where judgement on unrepentant Israel predominates, there is a shift in emphasis towards a more futurist eschatology.

The Reconstruction of Judean Ethnicity in Q

Now it is time to review the analysis above by comparing the two stratums. One will see that in the formative stratum the main issues that occupy Q are *kinship*, and relevant to the Sacred Canopy, the eschatological identity of the Q people because of the teaching of Jesus, and the tension that existed between the "old" system (the Law and the prophets) and the newness of the kingdom/reign of God. In the main redaction basically all the relevant cultural features identified by ethnicity theory are represented. This shows that the issue of ethnic identity

---

92. Cf. Isa 18:3–6; 24:13; Jer 51:33; Joel 3:13; Mic 4:11–13; *4 Ezra* 4:28–32; *2 Bar.* 70:2.

was given more attention in the later development of Q. We will no do a review of how this development took place.

The *Habitus*/Israel

Name

Primordialist tendencies: The name "Israel" does not feature in the formative stratum. One can accept that it was the accepted self-identification of the Q people, however, and it appears on two occasions in the main redaction. They regard themselves as part of Israel and identify themselves with its cultural and symbolic usage. They are heirs of the ancestral land and are part of a privileged people. It is within Israel that a Gentile's faith is acknowledged. Nothing like it was found in Israel (Q 7:9). The Q people look forward to the future restoration of Israel when they will judge/liberate/effect justice for the twelve tribes of Israel (Q 22:28–30). Thus Israel will finally become what it is supposed to be, where God's people and God's land will come together and where the eschatological kingdom will become a full reality. Israel, both as a geographical region and as a people is therefore part and parcel of the Q people's vision for the future.

Language

(Re)constructionist tendencies: Not much can be said for the cultural feature of language. Accepting that Q was most probably written in Greek, perhaps in or near Capernaum, it implies that Q was written for a primarily if not exclusively Greek-speaking community. This may have contributed towards the Q people and their separation from other Aramaic speaking Judeans, but based on the widespread use of Greek in Judea and Galilee, not too much must be read into Q's use of the Greek language. Here the Q people shared in the (re)construction of Judean ethnicity along with other Judeans.

Religion and Covenantal Praxis

Q¹

(Re)constructionist tendencies: The formative stratum does not reveal much concerning these cultural features. Q 10:7–8 instructs that the missionaries should eat whatever is set before them (cf. Q 7:34). This suggests that they should not be concerned over matters of ritual purity

at the meal table through which the message of the kingdom can be jeopardized.

Q²

Primordialist tendencies: In the main redaction the Q people are in some respects represented as normal Judeans. Tithing and matters pertaining to ritual purity are accepted as a valid part of the Law (Q 11:39–44). Q hopes that the temple will accept Jesus, therefore it hopes for its future restoration, although for now the temple is "forsaken" (Q 13:35).

(Re)constructionist tendencies: It is with John's rite of immersion where a radical discontinuity with Judean rites is present. This is an *initiatory* rite necessary for eschatological salvation (Q 3:7–9), something previously unheard of. Here we have the redefinition of God's people, and the divine election of corporate Israel is denied. Covenantal nomism, therefore Judean ethnic identity, is in this one instance radically (re)constructed. Covenant status is no longer a birth right, but must be individually earned through immersion and response to the message of the kingdom.

KINSHIP

Q¹

Primordialist tendencies: The Q sermon (6:27–45) is aimed at covenant renewal and the rehabilitation of relationships between Judeans. The people of the covenant should be characterized by forgiveness, love, mercy and justice, and so on. Q's mission was only aimed at Israel (Q 10:2), and Gentiles are clearly the primary outside group from whom the Q people distinguish themselves (Q 6:34; 12:30).

(Re)constructionist tendencies: Following Jesus often brought about a rift between his disciples and their co-ethnics and family. The followers of Jesus, also identified as "the poor" (Q 6:20), since they no longer enjoy family support, are insulted and experience opposition. The Q people are also the victims of ongoing violence and exploitation and the local judicial systems are regarded with suspicion (Q 6:22–23, 27–36 (+ Q/Matt 5:41); 12:2–12, 22–31, 58–59; 14:27; 16:16; 17:33). They seem in particular to be the targets of the rapacity of the elitist Pharisees (Q 10:3; see with Q 11:39; 16:16).

In the formative stratum severe tension with the family is already evident. Following Jesus and imitating his lifestyle may bring about rejection at home (Q 9:57–58). A son is refused permission to bury his father, and must immediately follow Jesus (Q 9:59–60). Here we have the redefinition of the people of God, as those who do not follow Jesus are regarded as (spiritually) "dead." Q 14:26 instructs that belonging and fidelity to the Jesus movement is more important than belonging and fidelity to the patriarchal family—although it was not the intention of the Q mission to divide the family, since Q itinerants are sent on their mission to households (Q 10:5–7). Nevertheless, the Q mission did bring about division, and the split was mainly between the parents and the children. If the choice must be made, Q shows little sympathy for the continuity of the traditional household and household economy, and the continuity of generation to generation. There is little concern for issues of inheritance, for the veneration of the family ancestors, and for the new paterfamilias to take up his role. The "sense of self" is no longer dependent on the most important "person-sustaining group," that is, the family. So much for the traditional role of "categorization." As a result we find the formation of fictive kinship patterns. Loss of traditional family is replaced by a spiritual household bonded by a commitment to Jesus and the kingdom/reign of God. At the head of the household is the Divine Patriarch, reverently addressed as "Father" (Q 6:36; 11:2, 13; 12:30). The household members are sons (Q 6:35) who address each other as brothers (Q 6:41–42; 17:3).

Q²

(Re)constructionist tendencies: It is noticeable in the main redaction that *kinship* indicators in Q shifts in emphasis towards the Q people's frustrated relationship with broader Israel. One can accept that family divisions were already an established fact, but presumably still going on (Q 12:49–53). Here it is actually said that it was the intention of Jesus to bring about family division, justifying the actions of those who had left home, while probably also aimed at those who had difficulty in staying away from their homes or who had difficulty leaving. It should come as no surprise that Jesus is called a "glutton and a drunkard," where he is associated with the tradition of the rebellious son (Q 7:34). Following Jesus and imitating his lifestyle negatively affects the family honor, something which Jesus exploits in Q 11:19–20.

The main redaction's focus is on Q's attitude towards broader Israel. It is negatively referred to as "this (evil) generation," which refers to unrepentant Israelites (Q 7:31–35; 11:29–51). They are guilty of the primordial sins of the generations in the times of Noah and Moses, and when the time comes, they will be judged by the Gentiles who responded to Jonah's preaching and the wisdom of Solomon (Q 11:31–32). Evidence of active opposition and repression of the Q people is also evident in the main redaction (Q 11:39; 12:8–10, 58–59; 17:33). Opposition is even present in the form of neutrality (Q 11:23). The alienation between the Q group and their co-ethnics is evident in Q 11:49–51, where it is explained that God/Wisdom will send them prophets only to make "this generation" guilty for their death. The Galilean towns are denounced (Q 10:12–14), and it is said that Gentiles will fare better than them in the judgement. Israel, under the spiritual guidance of the so-called wise and learned (Pharisees and lawyers) (Q 10:21), has no knowledge of God (Q 10:22; 11:39–442; 11:46–52). It is Jesus who has received the whole revelation of the Father and communicated it towards his followers. Also, the Diaspora Judeans will replace non-responsive local Israelites (Q 13:28–29) at the time when the Q people will help with Israel's restoration (Q 22:28–30). The attitude of Q towards broader Israel is typified by Q 13:34–35, where an oracle of doom is followed by the hope of restoration. Q has as yet not written off Israel and a glimmer of hope is present for Jerusalem and the temple (and broader Israel) to accept Jesus and join the Q community. Also, and this is important, the Q people disassociate themselves from those Messianists who presumably have given up aspects of traditional covenantal praxis (Q 13:27). The Q people's ethnic status as Judeans is confirmed, as Q walks a tightrope between broader Israel and that branch of the Jesus movement that appears to have Gentile associations.

Overall, Q demonstrates a strong consciousness of difference vis-à-vis other Judeans. Non-responsive Judeans are headed for destruction (cf. Q 10:16; 12:8–9). Although Q hopes for a restored Israelite community, as things now stand, one can hardly talk of a feeling of communal solidarity with co-ethnics. Q on the other hand feels that it properly belongs to the Judean symbolic universe, where kinship patterns are (re)constructed around commitment to Jesus and the resultant kingdom/reign of God.

LAND

Primordialist tendencies: Insight into Q's attitude towards the *land* may be implied in Jesus' teaching aimed at covenant renewal (Q 6:27–45), but it is only in the main redaction where we are given some explicit information of Q's position. Overall, the scant evidence suggests that Q had a positive attitude and relationship with territorial Israel, and it formed the locus of the eschatological kingdom. They had hope for Jerusalem and the temple's future restoration, that is, if they accepted Jesus as the Coming One (Q 13:35b). In a similar vein Q 22:28–30 has in view the restoration of Israel and the eschatological ingathering of the scattered Israelites, or the twelve tribes (13:28–29). So Q shows strong attachment to ethnic and territorial Israel, and the land plays an important role in Q's vision of the future kingdom, although we are given no information as to its magnitude and scope. But it is particularly the *land*, in combination with the Q people's self-identification as part of Israel (*name*), where an essentially primordialist approach to ethnicity is evident.

The Sacred Canopy

CHRISTOLOGY

Q¹

(Re)constructionist tendencies: The present era of eschatological fulfilment and the future is inseparable from the person of Jesus. The Christology of the formative stratum is largely assumed, however. There is no explanation or background to it. Jesus is the eschatological prophet (Q 6:20–21), and the Moses typology is suggested by Q 6:27–45 where Jesus reconstructs the Torah; by Q 10:4 where Jesus appears to invert Moses' instructions to the Israelites; and by Q 16:18 where Jesus contradicts an instruction of Moses by disallowing divorce. Jesus is addressed as "Lord, Lord" in Q 6:46, and is referred to as the "Lord" of the harvest in Q 10:22. He is identified as the Son of humanity/man in Q 6:22–23, which may indirectly refer to Jesus' heavenly status. The high status Jesus had for the Q people is evidenced by Q 10:16; those who receive (or reject) Jesus receive (or reject) God himself.

Q²

(Re)constructionist tendencies: Where the Christology of the formative stratum is assumed or implicit, it comes to fuller expression within the polemical context of the main redaction. Taking the analysis above into account, the Christology of Q must be read in close association with its attitude towards the Law as well, but more will be said about this later. The Christology of the main redaction serves both a polemical and apologetic purpose. It is there to defend and explain the eschatological status and authority of Jesus. Jesus is strongly identified with the Judean

prophetic tradition, whereby the Q people attest to their own Judean ethnic identity as well. This is especially so when Jesus is identified as the prophet like Moses who has initiated the new Exodus. The Q people identify themselves with the first founding event of Israel, and with the first law-giver, Moses.

How is this prophetic motif developed with regards to Jesus himself? Jesus is at first referred to as the "Coming One" (Q 3:16). This coming figure is developed in two ways. First, this coming one is the eschatological prophet, the prophet like Moses who has initiated the new Exodus (Q 4:1–13). He, as in the days of old, has passed the test of a prophet by rebuking the temptations of the devil in the wilderness. Jesus, like Moses, performs miracles by the finger of God (Q 11:20). John himself was the messenger who had prepared the way for the new Exodus (Q 7:18–35). In Q 7:18–23 the identity of Jesus as the "Coming One" is affirmed, and the fact that he raised the dead and cleansed the lepers also places him within the prophetic tradition of Elijah and Elisha. Lastly, Jesus as a prophet is also an envoy of Wisdom. Indeed, he is the final emissary of Wisdom who like the prophets of the past was rejected and persecuted (Q 7:31–35; 11:49–51; 13:34–35). Second, Jesus as the "Coming One" also points forward to the coming of the Son of humanity/man in judgement who already now enjoys heavenly status (Q 12:8–9, 40; 17:23–37).

Jesus is also the Lord/Master, who expects that his instructions will be obeyed in his absence (Q 12:42–46; 19:12–27). Even a Gentile—who demonstrated extraordinary faith—addressed Jesus as Lord/Master (Q 7:6). For the main redaction Jesus is also the Son of God (Q 4:3, 9; 10:22). This is complimentary to the Moses typology in Q, for this identification appears where Jesus enacts a new Exodus, and where it is said that Jesus alone has received the whole revelation from the Father, a privilege that was reserved for Moses in Judean tradition. Based on Q 10:22, it can also be seen that for Q, Jesus enjoyed a higher status than Moses. The absolute status of Jesus is affirmed in Q 12:8–9, where it is explained that confession of Jesus is the definitive measure of salvation (cf. Q 10:16). So Jesus has become part of the Q people's Sacred Canopy, and in terms of importance, ranks second to God. Jesus dominates all the other aspects of the traditional Sacred Canopy. Covenantal nomism is being (re)constructed in a radical way. This high regard for Jesus separated the Q people quite sharply from other Judeans. They must have been baffled: how can this person with questionable authority, who seems to undermine the Torah, a glutton and a drunkard, a friend of tax-collectors and sinners be afforded the eschatological and heavenly status afforded to him by the Q community? Q responded by designing the polemical and apologetic strategy reviewed above.

The Torah and the Kingdom/Reign of God:

Q¹

(Re)constructionist tendencies: The kingdom/reign of God and its nearness is an important religious theme in the formative stratum (Q 6:20; 9:60, 62; 10:9, 11; 11:2; 12:31; 13:18–21; 16:16). Yet, tension with the Torah is already evident. Jesus freely reconstructs the holiness code of Lev 19 (Q 6:27–45), where for example, mercy is regarded as more important than holiness or as the proper meaning of holiness. Jesus' teaching on the relationship with the family (Q 9:59–60; 14:26) also has implications for perfect Torah obedience—children in some respects need not honor their parents, for the kingdom carries greater priority. On one occasion Jesus even contradicts Moses—divorce is not allowed (Q 16:18). Note should be taken of the rhetorical tone of this material, particularly Q 6:27–45. Jesus freely reconstructs the Torah without any defence being offered. The tone is hortatory and instructional. This gives evidence that Jesus' eschatological authority was already assumed by Q, and generally recognized by the Q people. In a similar vain the kingdom is simply assumed to be present—it has replaced the "old" era of the Law and the prophets (Q 16:16).

Q²

Primordialist tendencies: In the main redaction, the kingdom of God appears primarily in a polemical context (Q 7:28; 11:20; 13:28–29; 22:28–30) and Jesus' eschatological status and Q's attitude towards the Law requires explanation. Q apologizes for the sins of other Messianists who are guilty of "lawlessness" (Q 13:27), in other words, it apologizes for those Messianists who are not being so Judean anymore. Q also affirms its allegiance to the Torah (Q 16:17). Even Jesus himself is a model Judean, for he demonstrates an unwavering obedience to scripture (Q 4:1–13). Tithing and various aspects of ritual purity is accepted as part of the Law although it was a helpful tool to criticize the questionable character of the Pharisees (Q 11:39–44). So Q explains, its community has not abandoned the Torah. By recognising the everlasting validity of the Law, Q reclaims or affirms the Judean ethnic identity of the community and of its hero, Jesus. Their citizenship in the Judean symbolic universe is restored. At the same time, however, Q is living according to the Torah given by the eschatological prophet like Moses, Jesus. What is also at stake is the correct interpretation of the Law (Q 11:46b, 52), for more ethical concerns such as justice, mercy and faithfulness is more important than the ritual law (Q 11:39–44).

(Re)constructionist tendencies: Q's approach to the Law in the main redaction is not that simple as the polemical and apologetic approach aimed at achieving, and must be qualified by its Christology. Jesus as the eschatological prophet has the status and authority to teach what the Law within the context of the kingdom requires. The Q people are participating in the newness of the kingdom/reign of God, a new Exodus, led by Jesus, the new law-giver. In Q 12:8–9 it is explained that confession of Jesus is the definitive measure of salvation. So confessing Jesus qualifies any traditional Torah observance (therefore traditional covenant status as well). The Q people might not have abandoned the Torah, but they live according to (re)constructed or eschatological Torah. So what room is left for Moses? He is there, but the (re)constructed Torah of Jesus only points to one thing: the kingdom/reign of God requires the (re)construction of covenantal nomism. There is both continuity and discontinuity with what has gone before.

Shared "Historical" Memories

Q¹

In the formative stratum, this cultural feature does not play a prominent role and for the most part is implicit. Moses typology is present (Q 6:27–35; 10:4) and Jesus is placed within the context of the Judean prophetic tradition (Q 6:20–21). Q 9:61–62 alludes to Elijah calling Elisha and possibly to Lot's wife who looked back to her past. The only explicit example is where reference is made to Solomon and his glory (Q 12:27).

Q²

(Re)constructionist tendencies: In the main redaction *shared "historical" memories* are quite prevalent. It is used to affirm and explain the eschatological status of Jesus. In the temptation narrative (Q 4:1–13), allusion is made to Moses and the exodus. This typology is also present in other parts of Q (7:26–27; 10:21–24; 11:20). Jesus is also connected to the anointed figure of Isaiah (Q 7:18–23). Both Jesus and John are

associated with Elijah. Jesus raised the dead (Q 7:18–23) and John himself is identified as the coming Elijah (Q 3:7–9, 16b–17; 7:27).

Apart from the above, traditions of the past are predominantly used negatively to denounce non-responsive Israel. They are referred to as "this (evil) generation," recalling the primordial sins of the generation in the wilderness and the time of Noah (Q 7:31–35; 11:29, 31–32; 11:50–51). The evil Gentile cities of Sodom, Tyre and Sidon are called upon—they will fare better in the judgement than the Galilean town who have not responded to Q's message of the kingdom (Q 10:12–14). Particularly Tyre and Sidon, it said, would have responded positively to the working of miracles. The Ninevites and the Queen of the South is similarly favorably compared—the Ninevites repented at the preaching of Jonah, the Galilean prophet; the Queen of the South listened to the wisdom of Solomon (Q 11:16, 29–32), while Q's contemporaries failed to listen to something that was qualitatively greater, the message of the kingdom. The days of Noah and Lot are also held up as examples future judgement (Q 17:26–30), when the eschatological separation of the elect will occur (Q 17:34–35). The region of the Jordan—also associated with the Lot story—is the setting of John's fiery preaching of repentance and judgement (Q 3:3). Q employs the Deuteronomistic theology and so recalls the rejection and persecution of the prophets (Q 6:23c; 11:47–51; 13:28–29; 14:16–24). Particularly Abel—regarded as a prophet in Q—and Zechariah are mentioned (Q 13:28–29). Abraham, Isaac and Jacob will be present in the future kingdom, along with the reconstituted twelve tribes (Q 13:28–29; 22:28–30), but unrepentant Israelites will be thrown out (Q 13:28).

One can see that within the polemical context of the main redaction, Q illustrates little or no sentimental attachment to the past. Ethno-symbolism is not employed to affirm Israel's privileged status. Q is pre-occupied to use the past traditions in service of the eschatological present and future. The past is qualified or only has meaning when you participate in the eschatological newness of the kingdom.

MYTHS OF COMMON ANCESTRY

(Re)constructionist tendencies: This cultural feature is prominent only in the main redaction of Q and it is used rather negatively. It is accepted that Abraham, Isaac and Jacob will be present in the future kingdom (Q 13:28). Otherwise, Q attacks the presumption attached with Judean ancestry. It is denied that Judeans benefit from the merit of Abraham (Q 3:8). Now it is time where merit must be required by each individual

in his/her own lifetime. Maintenance of covenant status is no longer the prerogative of corporate Israel and the notion of divine election is denied. The lawyers are said to be just like their forefathers, who have killed the prophets (Q 11:47–48). So where ancestry is used in Q, it is used to attack the now false claim to privilege attached therewith, and lastly, the murder of the prophets.

Eschatology

Q¹

(Re)constructionist tendencies: The eschatological character of the formative stratum is not that pronounced as in the main redaction, but it is present. The Q people look forward to the arrival of the kingdom, and their future is couched in positive language (Q 6:20–23, 46; 11:2; 13:18–21). Accepting or rejecting the teaching of Jesus will have eschatological consequences (Q 6:47–49 cf. 12:4–5). But the present is also a time of eschatological fulfilment. The ingathering of the harvest and judgement is already underway (Q 10:2). The Holy Spirit will teach those what to say if brought before the assemblies (Q 12:12). The kingdom/reign of God has arrived (Q 12:31; 13:18–21), present through the activity and healing of Jesus (Q 6:20–21; 10:9).

Q²

(Re)constructionist tendencies: This era of eschatological fulfilment is also represented in the main redaction. Sin against the Holy Spirit will not be forgiven (Q 12:10), implying he is present in some way. The emissaries of John "hear and see" what was looked forward to by the prophets of old in the person of Jesus (Q 7:22), and if present in Q, those who have eyes to see will recognize in the signs that the End has arrived (Q 12:54–56). In Q 7:18–23 Jesus is identified as the "Coming One" through the activities of his ministry. The kingdom/reign of God is also present through his exorcisms (Q 11:20). That the End has arrived is also supported by the fact that families are experiencing divisions (Q 12:49–53). John himself is recognized as the Elijah *redivivus* who has inaugurated the new time period (Q 7:27).

The main redaction, however, is dominated by a futurist eschatology and often speaks of the judgement of non-responsive Israel (Q 3:7–9, 16–17; 10:12–15; 11:16, 29–32, 49–51; 13:28–29, 34). This judgement will be sudden and without warning (Q 12:39–40; 17:23–34), and will have dire consequences (Q 12:42–46; 19:12–27). Closely related to this is the future coming of the Son of humanity/man in judgment (Q 12:39–59; 17:23–37). The Q people are in a position of safety and security since they have made use of the current opportunity for repentance. Broader Israel, if it remains unrepentant, is facing serious judgement and punishment.

The Gentiles

Although not strictly a part of the model, some remarks are in order in terms of Q's relationship to the Gentiles. In the formative stratum the Gentiles are identified by what ethnicity theory describes as a "we-they" *oppositional* self-definition (Q 6:34; 12:30). In the main redaction the Q people's relationship to the Gentiles does change, but mainly to form part of the polemical rhetoric characteristic of that stratum. Some passages have been identified that may suggest a mission to the Gentiles (e.g., Q 10:2, 7–8b; 13:18–19; 14:16–24), but the evidence is not strong enough to suggest that the Q people were participating in such a mission, although that such a mission exists is implicitly acknowledged. Rather, the Gentiles are used as a polemical device to shame Israel and to bring it to repentance. The faith of a Gentile centurion is contrasted with the lack of faith in Israel (Q 7:1–10). The Ninevites and the Queen of the South will judge "this generation" for its inability to respond to the message of the kingdom (Q 11:31–32). The Gentile cities of Sodom, Tyre, and Sidon will fare better in the judgement than the Galilean towns—also, it is assumed that they would have responded positively if the miracles of the kingdom were performed there (Q 10:12–14). Gentiles are either in the past or future perspective of Q, and Q generally is pre-occupied with the fate of ethnic and territorial Israel. Any contact with Gentiles would also have undermined the polemical and apologetic strategy of the main redaction where Q affirmed its allegiance to the Torah, hence, reaffirming the Judean ethnic identity of its community. Overall, the Gentiles do not properly belong to Q's symbolic universe.

So What Kind of Judeans Were the Q People?

In chapters 1 and 2 I analysed *interpretations* of the historical Jesus. Here, an interpretation of the Q source attempts to improve our understanding of the Judean ethnic identity of the *community* it presupposes. Thus again, no claims are made with regards to the historical Jesus, although admittedly, the results may have implications for historical Jesus research.

Overall, where does the Q community fit on the scale mentioned by Holmén (see chapters 1 and 2) from the commonly Judean to the marginally Judean? In a few respects, the Q people appear to be profoundly Judean, while being different kind of Judeans in others. Based on the above overview, there is both continuity and discontinuity between the Q people and established Judean ethnic identity. Their essentially primordialist tendencies are restricted to the cultural features of *name* and *land*. They identify themselves as part of Israel, and look forward to its restoration. Other features of primordialism are also present, however. Ironically the polemic of the main redaction shows that Q is concerned over the eschatological future of all Israel, including Jerusalem and the temple. They claim to be Torah obedient and accept tithing and ritual purity as part of everyday life. The Gentiles are still seen as "the others." In some respects, the Q people fit in comfortably within the Judean symbolic universe. But *apart from* name *and* land, *all the cultural features in Q are essentially (re)constructionist as they display strong elements of discontinuity with traditional covenantal nomism.*

The *Habitus*/Israel

The Q people, but as the many Judeans around them, are speaking the Greek *language*. Eschatological salvation requires the new initiatory rite of water immersion. All traditional *religion* and *covenantal praxis* must be qualified by this rite and commitment to the message of Jesus. The Q people are alienated from their co-ethnics, for are as things now stand, they are headed for destruction. The continuing viability of the patriarchal family is undermined through alternative *kinship* patterns where God is Father.

It must be remembered that Judean ethnicity is grounded in the *habitus*, the shared habitual dispositions of Judean social agents, or in short, "Israel," which shape and are shaped by objective common cultural practices. Within the *habitus* the "sense of self" is also internalized through "categorization." The dialectical interrelationship between the *habitus* and the more tangible cultural features is dominated by the endeavor to respond to God's divine election and to maintain covenant status or Judean ethnic identity ("staying in"). In Q therefore, noticeable developments are taking place. Here the interrelationship between the *habitus* or "Israel," and the immediate cultural features, were not successful in regenerating traditional covenantal nomism. In other words, in the Q community Judean ethnicity was not that congruent with the *habitus* and established cultural practices, even though they found themselves within a highly integrated system of habitual dispositions. Evidently, they were "jolted" out of a primordialist mode by accepting the message and eschatological status of Jesus, which demanded a (re)construction of the *habitus* and common cultural practices. The latter (re)construction, in its turn, set new requirements for the maintenance of covenant status or Judean ethnic identity ("staying in"). Their identity as individuals, and sense of belongingness and self-esteem, were determined by finding a place within the eschatological Judean symbolic universe, in short, the kingdom/reign of God.

The Sacred Canopy

Again, discontinuity with traditional covenantal nomism dominates. Jesus has become part of the Sacred Canopy, their cosmic and all-embracing frame of reference. It is no longer the notion of divine election, the covenant, and the gift of the Torah that gives salvation. Confession of Jesus gives eschatological salvation, and serves as a qualification to the other aspects of the Sacred Canopy. The *shared "historical" memories* are used predominantly to speak of the future judgment of Israel. Otherwise it is their as a foil to explain the prophetic and eschatological status of Jesus and the community. The Q community is more concerned with the present and future than to create a positive link with the past. The Q people now find themselves within the orbit of the kingdom/reign of God, partly fulfilled, partly to be completed. The End has arrived. All of this was due to the person of Jesus, the eschatological prophet, who is afforded a higher status than Moses, and who has given a (re)constructed Torah. Israel should also no longer claim to benefit from the merit of Abraham (*myths of common ancestry*). You only become a child of Abraham by individual acceptance of the message of Jesus, who as the heavenly Son of humanity/man, will return in judgement to separate the wheat from the chaff.

The *habitus* not only shape, and are shaped by common cultural practices, but they also shape and are shaped by Israel's common beliefs; i.e. the "Sacred Canopy." Here the role of "categorization" must not be forgotten. The dialectical interrelationship here primarily has to do with the belief that Yahweh established/prescribes Judean ethnicity ("getting in"). Here also, noticeable differences are present as the Q community's theological identity was not that congruent with the *habitus* or common beliefs. As already stated above, the Q people were "jolted" out of a primordialist mode by accepting the message and eschatological status of Jesus. This also required the (re)construction of the *habitus* and common beliefs. This (re)construction involved the Divine Patriarch, who through Jesus, established/prescribes eschatological Judean ethnicity ("getting in"). Covenant status as a result moved beyond traditional Judean ethnic identity. For the Q people therefore, the interrelationship between both the *habitus* and the immediate cultural features on the one hand, and the interrelationship between the *habitus* and the Sacred Canopy on the other, *produced eschatological Judean ethnic identity*, which involved the objectification of cultural practices in the recognition and communication of affinity with fellow Judeans, *and* difference vis-à-vis the Gentiles *and* fellow Judeans.

A Last Word

The evidence is therefore conclusive: *the covenantal nomism or symbolic universe of the Q people was in (re)construction*. The effect was that on the social level *the Q people were Judean ethnicity in (re)construction*. On that scale of Holmén they were Judeans of a different kind, or marginal, given their identity by their commitment to Jesus and the requirements of the kingdom/reign of God. Although this was never their intention, the Q people were part of a reform movement *within* Judeanism that was *destined from the start* to become a movement *outside* of Judeanism. The Q community, although their scribes argued to the contrary in the main redaction, undermined Judean ethnic identity, which in the historical context of the first century was *essentially* primordialist. Other reasons, of course, can also be given for the failure of the Messianist mission to Judeans. But it would seem that the question of ethnic identity was a primary factor for determining the success (or failure) of that mission. The Judean attachment to the land, religion, covenantal praxis, family, the traditions that linked it to the past and which inspired hopes of future restoration, and the attempt to maintain the Judean symbolic universe in the face of Roman-Hellenistic intrusion, all these factors were not conducive for the Messianist mission, even those of a more conservative nature, to succeed. The fundamental difference between the Q group and other Judean sects and renewal movements was that Q (and other Messianist groups) participated in eschatological renewal that (re)constructed covenantal nomism, while the other Judean movements had an eschatological vision that aimed at the renewal of traditional covenantal nomism.

Bibliography

Allison, Dale C. 1997. *The Jesus Tradition in Q*. Harrisburg, PA: Trinity.
———. 2000. *The Intertextual Jesus: Scripture in Q*. Harrisburg, PA: Trinity.
Arav, Rami, and Richard A. Freund. 1997. "Prize Find: An Incense Shovel from Bethsaida." *BAR* 23.1:32.
———, and John F. Shroder, Jr. 2000. "Bethsaida Rediscovered." *BAR* 26.1:44–56.
Arnal, William E. 2001. *Jesus and the Village Scribes: Galilean Conflicts and the Setting of Q*. Minneapolis: Fortress.
Avigad, Nachman. 1990. "Jerusalem Flourishing—A Craft Center for Stone, Pottery and Glass." In *Archaeology in the World of Herod, Jesus and Paul*, edited by Hershel Shanks and Dan P. Cole, 78–95. *Archaeology and the Bible: The Best of BAR*, vol. 2. Washington, DC: Biblical Archaeology Society.
Avruch, Kevin. 2003. "Culture and Ethnic Conflict in the New World Disorder." In *Race and Ethnicity: Comparative and Theoretical Approaches*, edited by John Stone and Rutledge Dennis, 72–82. Malden, MA: Blackwell.
Barth, Fredrik, editor. 1969. *Ethnic Groups and Boundaries*. Boston: Little, Brown.
———. 1994. "Enduring and Emerging Issues in the Analysis of Ethnicity." In *The Anthropology of Ethnicity: Beyond 'Ethnic Groups and Boundaries,'* edited by Hans Vermeulen and Cora Govers, 11–32. Amsterdam: Spinhuis.
Batey, Richard A. 1992. "Sepphoris—An Urban Portrait of Jesus." *BAR* 18.3:50–63.
———. 2001. "Sepphoris and the Jesus Movement." *NTS* 47:402–9.
Bauckham, Richard. 1998. "Life, Death and the Afterlife in Second Temple Judaism." In *Life in the Face of Death*, edited by Richard N. Longenecker, 80–95. Grand Rapids: Eerdmans.
———. 2000. "All in the Family: Identifying Jesus' Relatives." *BR* 16.2:20–31.
Baumgarten, Albert I. 1997. *The Flourishing of Jewish Sects in the Maccabean Era: An Interpretation*. JSJSup 55. Leiden: Brill.
BDAG 2000. *A Greek-English Lexicon of the New Testament and other Early Christian literature*. 3rd ed of Bauer, Arndt, and Gingrich, revised by Frederick W. Danker, Chicago: University of Chicago Press.
Becker, Jürgen. 1998. *Jesus of Nazareth*. Translated by James E. Crouch. New York: de Gruyter.
Ben-Dov, Meir. 1990. "Herod's Mighty Temple Mount." In *Archaeology in the World of Herod, Jesus and Paul*, edited by Hershel Shanks and Dan P. Cole, 21–30. *Archaeology and the Bible: The Best of BAR*, vol. 2. Washington, DC: Biblical Archaeology Society.

Bentley, G. Carter. 1987. "Ethnicity and Practice." *Comparative Studies in Society and History* 29:24–55.
Berger, Peter L. 1973. *The Social Reality of Religion*. Penguin University Series. Harmondsworth: Penguin.
———, and Thomas Luckmann. 1966. *The Social Construction of Reality: A Treatise in the Sociology of Knowledge*. Garden City, NY: Doubleday.
Bolt, Peter. G. 1998. "Life, Death, and the Afterlife in the Greco-Roman World." In *Life in the Face of Death*, edited by Richard N. Longenecker, 51–79. Grand Rapids: Eerdmans.
Borg, Marcus J. 1983. *Conflict, Holiness and Politics in the Teachings of Jesus*. SBEC 5. New York: Mellen.
———. 1987. *Jesus: A New Vision: Spirit, Culture, and the Life of Discipleship*. San Francisco: Harper & Row.
———. 1994. *Jesus in Contemporary Scholarship*. Valley Forge, PA: Trinity.
Bourdieu, Pierre. 1977. *Outline of a Theory of Practice*. Translated by Richard Nice. Cambridge Studies in Social Anthropology 16. Cambridge: Cambridge University Press.
Brenner, Sandy. 2003. "Spending Your Way through Jewish History." *BAR* 29.3:46–51.
Brueggemann, Walter. 2002. *The Land: Place as Gift, Promise, and Challenge in Biblical Faith*. 2d ed. Minneapolis: Fortress.
Bull, Robert J. 1990. "Caesarea Maritima—The Search for Herod's City." In *Archaeology in the World of Herod, Jesus and Paul*, edited by Hershel Shanks and Dan P. Cole, 106–22. *Archaeology and the Bible: The Best of BAR*, vol. 2. Washington, DC: Biblical Archaeology Society.
Campbell, Jonathan G. 1996. *Deciphering the Dead Sea Scrolls*. London: Fontana.
Catchpole, David R. 1993. *The Quest for Q*. Edinburgh: T. & T. Clark.
Chancey, Mark A. 2001. "The Cultural Milieu of Ancient Sepphoris." *NTS* 47:127–45.
———. 2002. *The Myth of a Gentile Galilee*. SNTSMS 118. Cambridge: Cambridge University Press.
———, and Eric M. Meyers. 2000. "How Jewish Was Sepphoris in Jesus' Time?" *BAR* 26.4:18–33, 61.
Charlesworth, James H., editor. 1992. *Jesus and the Dead Sea Scrolls*. New York: Doubleday.
Chilton, Bruce, and Jacob Neusner. 1995. *Judaism in the New Testament: Practices and Beliefs*. London: Routledge.
Cohen, Shaye J. D. 1987. *From the Maccabees to the Mishnah*. Library of Early Christianity 7. Philadelphia: Westminster.
———. 1990. "Religion, Ethnicity, and Hellenism in the Emergence of Jewish Identity in Maccabean Palestine." In *Religion and Religious Practice in the Seleucid Kingdom*, edited by Per Bilde, 204–23. Studies in Hellenistic Civilization 1. Aarhus: Aarhus University Press.
———. 1999. *The Beginnings of Jewishness: Boundaries, Varieties, Uncertainties*. Hellenistic Culture and Society 31. Berkeley: University of California Press.
Collins, John J. 1993. "Wisdom, Apocalypticism, and Generic Compatibility." In *In Search of Wisdom: Essays in Memory of John G. Gammie*, edited by Leo G. Perdue et al., 165–85. Louisville: Westminster John Knox.

———. 1997. "Jewish Monotheism and Christian Theology." In *Aspects of Monotheism: How God is One*, edited by Hershel Shanks and Jack Meinhardt, 81–105. Washington, DC: Biblical Archaeology Society.
Cotter, Wendy. 1995a. "Prestige, Protection and Promise: A Proposal for the Apologetics of Q2." In *The Gospel behind the Gospels: Current Studies on Q*, edited by Ronald A. Piper, 117–38. NovTSup 75. Leiden: Brill.
———. 1995b. "'Yes, I tell you, and more than a prophet': The Function of John in Q." In *Conflict and Invention: Literary, Rhetorical and Social Studies on the Sayings Gospel Q*, edited by John S. Kloppenborg, 135–50. Valley Forge, PA: Trinity.
Crossan, John Dominic. 1991. *The Historical Jesus: The Life of a Mediterranean Jewish Peasant*. San Francisco: HarperSanFrancisco.
———. 1999. *The Birth of Christianity: Discovering What Happened in the Years Immediately after the Execution of Jesus*. New York: HarperCollins.
———, and Jonathan L. Reed. 2001. *Excavating Jesus: Beneath the Stones, Behind the Texts*. San Francisco: HarperSanFrancisco.
Denzey, Nicola. 2002. "The Limits of Ethnic Categories." In *Handbook of Early Christianity: Social Science Approaches*, edited by Anthony J. Blasi, Jean Duhaime, and Paul-André Turcotte, 489–507. Walnut Creek, CA: AltaMira.
De Vos, George. 1975. "Ethnic Pluralism: Conflict and Accommodation." In *Ethnic Identity: Cultural Continuities and Change*, edited by George De Vos and Lola Romanucci-Ross, 5–41. Palo Alto, CA: Mayfield.
Duling, Dennis C. 1994. "BTB Readers Guide: Millennialism." *BTB* 24:132–42.
———. 2001. "Recruitment to the Jesus Movement in Social-Scientific Perspective." In *Social Scientific Models for Interpreting the Bible: Essays by the Context Group in Honor of Bruce J. Malina*, edited by John J. Pilch, 132–75. BibIntSer 53. Leiden: Brill.
———. 2003. *The New Testament: History, Literature, and Social Context*. 4th ed. Belmont: Wadsworth.
———. 2005. "Ethnicity, Ethnocentrism, and the Matthean *ethnos*." *BTB* 35:125–43.
Dunn, James D. G. 1990. *Jesus, Paul and the Law: Studies in Mark and Galatians*. Louisville: Westminster John Knox.
———. 1991. *The Partings of the Ways between Christianity and Judaism and Their Significance for the Character of Christianity*. Philadelphia: Trinity.
———. 2003. *Christianity in the Making: Jesus Remembered*. Grand Rapids: Eerdmans.
Du Toit, David S. 2001. "Redefining Jesus: Current Trends in Jesus Research." In *Jesus, Mark and Q*, edited by Michaael Labahn and Andreas Schmidt, 82–124. JSNTSup 214. Sheffield: Sheffield Academic.
Eller, Jack David, and Reed M. Coughlan. 1993. "The Poverty of Primordialism: The Demystification of Ethnic Attachments." *ERS* 16:185–202.
Elliott, John H. 2002. "Jesus Was Not an Egalitarian: A Critique of an Anachronistic and Idealist Theory." *BTB* 32:75–91.
———. 2003. "The Jesus Movement Was Not Egalitarian but Family-oriented." *Biblical Interpretation* 11:173–210.
Enslin, Morton S. 1961. *The Prophet from Nazareth*. New York: McGraw-Hill.
Eshel, Hanan. 1997. "Aelia Capitolina: Jerusalem No More." *BAR* 23.6:46–48.
———. 2000. "They're Not Ritual Baths." *BAR* 26.4:42–45.
Esler, Philip F. 2003. *Conflict and Identity in Romans: The Social Setting of Paul's Letter*. Minneapolis: Fortress.

———. 2006. "Paul's Contestation of Israel's (Ethnic) Memory of Abraham in Galatians 3." *BTB* 36:23–33.
Evans, Craig A. 1992. "Opposition to the Temple: Jesus and the Dead Sea Scrolls." In *Jesus and the Dead Sea Scrolls*, edited by James H. Charlesworth, 235–53. New York: Doubleday.
———. 2001. "Context, Family and Formation." In *The Cambridge Companion to Jesus*, edited by Markus Bockmuehl, 11–24. Cambridge Companions to Religion. Cambridge: Cambridge University Press.
Feldman, Louis H. 1986. "The Omnipresence of the God-fearers." *BAR* 12.5:58–69.
———. 2001. "Financing the Colosseum." *BAR* 27.4:20–31, 60–61.
Fenton, Steve. 2003. *Ethnicity*. Key Concepts. Cambridge: Polity.
Fiensy, David A. 1991. *The Social History of Palestine in the Herodian Period: The Land Is Mine*. SBEC 20. Lewiston, NY: Mellen.
Fine, Steven. 2001. "Why Bone Boxes?" *BAR* 27.4:38–44, 57.
Fishman, J. 1996. "Ethnicity as Being, Doing, and Knowing." In *Ethnicity*, edited by John Hutchinson and Anthony D. Smith, 63–69. Oxfordreaders. Oxford: Oxford University Press.
Fitzmyer, Joseph A. 1992. "Did Jesus Speak Greek?" *BAR* 18.5:58–63, 76, 77.
Fletcher-Louis, Crispin H. T. 2003. "Leave the Dead to Bury Their Own Dead": Q 9.60 and the Redefinition of the People of God." *JSNT* 26:39–68.
Freyne, Sean. 1988. *Galilee, Jesus and the Gospels: Literary Approaches and Historical Investigations*. Philadelphia: Fortress.
———. 2001. "The Geography of Restoration: Galilee-Jerusalem Relations in Early Jewish and Christian Experience." *NTS* 47:289–311.
———. 2004. *Jesus, a Jewish Galilean: A New Reading of the Jesus-Story*. London: T. & T. Clark.
Geertz, Clifford. 1963. "The Integrative Revolution: Primordial Sentiments and Civil Politics in the New States." In *Old Societies and New States: The Quest for Modernity in Asia and Africa*, edited by Clifford Geertz, 105–57. New York: Free Press.
Geva, H. 1997. "Searching for Roman Jerusalem." *BAR* 23.6:34–45, 72, 73.
Glasson, T. F. 1961. *Greek Influence on Jewish Eschatology*. London: SPCK.
Goodacre, Mark S. 2002. *The Case against Q: Studies in Markan Priority and the Synoptic Problem*. Harrisburg, PA: Trinity.
———, and Nicholas Perrin, editors. 2004. *Questioning Q: A Multidimensional Critique*. London: SPCK.
Grosby, Steven. 1996. "The Inexpungeable Tie of Primordiality." In *Ethnicity*, edited by John Hutchinson and Anthony D. Smith, 51–56. Oxfordreaders. Oxford: Oxford University Press.
Gruen, Erich S. 2002. *Heritage and Hellenism: The Reinvention of Jewish Tradition*. Hellenistic Culture and Society 30. Berkeley: University of California Press.
Guijarro, Santiago. 2001. "Kingdom and Family in Conflict: A Contribution to the Study of the Historical Jesus." In *Social Scientific Models for Interpreting the Bible: Essays by the Context Group in Honor of Bruce J. Malina*, edited by John J. Pilch. 210–38. BibIntSer 53. Leiden: Brill.
———. 2004."The Family in the Jesus Movement." *BTB* 34:114–21.
Habel, Norman C. 1995. *The Land Is Mine: Six Biblical Land Ideologies*. Overtures to Biblical Theology. Minneapolis: Fortress.
Hachlili, Rachel. 1979. "Ancient Burial Customs Preserved in Jericho Hills." *BAR* 5.4:28–35.

Hahn, Ferdinand. 1965. *Mission in the New Testament.* Translated by Frank Clarke. SBT 1/47. London: SCM.
Hanson, K. C. 1994. "BTB Readers Guide: Kinship." *BTB* 24:183–92.
———. 1997. "The Galilean Fishing Economy and the Jesus Tradition." *BTB* 27:99–111.
———, and Douglas E. Oakman. 1998. *Palestine in the Time of Jesus: Social Structures and Social Conflicts.* Minneapolis: Fortress.
Harnack, Adolf von. 1962. *The Mission and Expansion of Christianity in the First Three Centuries,* vol. 1. Translated by J. Moffat. New York: Harper.
Harrington, Daniel J. 1985. "Pseudo-Philo." In *The Old Testament Pseudepigrapha,* edited by James H. Charlesworth, 2:297–377. Garden City, NY: Doubleday.
———. 1987. "The Jewishness of Jesus: Facing Some Problems." *CBQ* 49:1–13.
Hartin, Patrick J. 1995. "'Yet Wisdom is Justified by Her Children' (Q 7:35): A Rhetorical and Compositional Analysis of Divine Sophia in Q." In *Conflict and Invention: Literary, Rhetorical and Social Studies on the Sayings Gospel Q,* edited by John S. Kloppenborg, 151–64. Valley Forge, PA: Trinity.
Hengel, Martin. 1989. *The 'Hellenization' of Judaea in the First Century after Christ.* Translated by John Bowden. Philadelphia: Trinity.
Hjelm, Ingrid. 2000. *The Samaritans and Early Judaism: A Literary Analysis.* JSOTSup 303. Sheffield: Sheffield Academic.
Holmén, Tom. 2001. "The Jewishness of Jesus in the 'Third Quest.'" In *Jesus, Mark and Q: The Teaching of Jesus and Its Earliest Records,* edited by Michael Labahn and Andreas Schmidt, 143–62. JSNTSup 214. Sheffield: Sheffield Academic.
Hooker, Morna D. 1990. *From Adam to Christ: Essays on Paul.* Cambridge: Cambridge University Press.
Horsley, Richard A. 1987. *Jesus and the Spiral of Violence: Popular Resistance in Roman Palestine.* Reprinted, Minneapolis: Fortress, 1993.
———. 1989. *Sociology and the Jesus Movement.* New York: Crossroad.
———. 1995. "Social Conflict in the Synoptic Sayings Source Q." In *Conflict and Invention: Literary, Rhetorical and Social Studies on the Sayings Gospel Q,* edited by John S. Kloppenborg, 37–52. Valley Forge, PA: Trinity.
———. 1995. *Galilee: History, Politics, People.* Valley Forge, PA: Trinity.
———. 1996. *Archaeology, History and Society in Galilee: The Social Context of Jesus and the Rabbis.* Valley Forge, PA: Trinity.
———, and Jonathan A. Draper. 1999. *Whoever Hears You Hears Me: Prophets, Performance, and Tradition in Q.* Harrisburg, PA: Trinity.
Hutchinson, John, and Anthony D. Smith, editors. 1996. *Ethnicity.* Oxfordreaders. Oxford: Oxford University Press.
Jackson, Glenna S. 2002. *"Have Mercy on Me": The Story of the Canaanite Woman in Matthew 15.21–28.* JSNTSup 228. Sheffield: Sheffield Academic.
———. 2003. "Enemies of Israel: Ruth and the Canaanite Woman." *HTS* 59:779–92.
Jacobson, Arland D. 1992. *The First Gospel: An Introduction to Q.* Reprinted, Eugene, OR: Wipf & Stock, 2005.
———. 1995. "Divided Families and Christian Origins." In *The Gospel behind the Gospels: Current Studies on Q,* edited by Ronald A. Piper, 360–80. NovTSup 75. Leiden: Brill.
Jacobson, David. 2002. "Herod's Roman Temple." *BAR* 28.2:18–27, 60–61.
Jagersma, Henk. 1986. *A History of Israel from Alexander the Great to Bar Kochba.* Translated by John Bowden. Philadelphia: Fortress.

Jenkins, Richard. 1994. "Rethinking Ethnicity: Identity, Categorization and Power." *ERS* 17:197–223.
———. 1996. "Ethnicity Etcetera: Social Anthropological Points of View." *ERS* 19:807–22.
———. 1997. *Rethinking Ethnicity: Arguments and Explorations*. Thousand Oaks, CA: Sage.
———. 2003. "Rethinking Ethnicity: Identity, Categorization, and Power." In *Race and Ethnicity: Comparative and Theoretical Approaches*, edited by John Stone and Rutledge Dennis, 59–71. Malden, MA: Blackwell.
Jeremias, Joachim. 1967. *Jesus' Promise to the Nations*. Translated by S. H. Hooke. SBT 1/24. London: SCM.
———. 1971. *New Testament Theology*. Vol. 1. New York: Scribner.
Jones, S. 1997. *The Archaeology of Ethnicity: Constructing Identities in the Past and Present*. London: Routledge.
King, Philip J., and Lawrence E. Stager. 2002. "Of Fathers, Kings and the Deity." *BAR* 28.2:42–45, 62.
Kloppenborg, John S. 1987. *The Formation of Q: Trajectories in Ancient Wisdom Collections*. Philadelphia: Fortress.
———. 2000. *Excavating Q: The History and Setting of the Sayings Gospel*. Minneapolis: Fortress.
———. 2003. "On Dispensing with Q?: Goodacre on the Relation of Luke to Matthew." *NTS* 49:210–36.
———. 2006. "The Theodotos Synagogue Inscription and the Problem of First-century Synagogue Buildings." In *Jesus and Archaeology*, edited by James H. Charlesworth, 236–82. Grand Rapids: Eerdmans.
LaGrand, J. 1995. *The Earliest Christian Mission to "All Nations" in the Light of Matthew's Gospel*. Atlanta: Scholars. Reprinted, Grand Rapids: Eerdmans, 1999.
Laughlin, John C. H. 1993. "Capernaum: From Jesus' Time and After." *BAR* 19.5:55–61.
Lieu, Judith. 2002. *Neither Jew nor Greek? Constructing Early Christianity*. Studies in the New Testament and Its World. London: T. & T. Clark.
———. 2002. "'Impregnable Ramparts and Walls of Iron': Boundary and Identity in Early 'Judaism' and 'Christianity.'" *NTS* 48:297–313.
Mack, Burton L. 1993. *The Lost Gospel: The Book of Q and Christian Origins*. San Francisco: HarperSanFrancisco.
MacLennan, Robert S., and A. Thomas Kraabel. 1986. "The God-Fearers: A Literary and Theological Invention." *BAR* 12.5:46–53.
Malina, Bruce J. *The New Testament World: Insights from Cultural Anthropology*. 3d ed. Louisville: Westminster John Knox.
Manson, T. W. 1964. *Only to the House of Israel? Jesus and the Non-Jews*. Facet Books. Philadelphia: Fortress.
Martin, Raymond A. 1987. *Syntax Criticism of the Synoptic Gospels*. SBEC 10. Lewiston, NY: Mellen.
———. 1995. *Studies in the Life and Ministry of the Historical Jesus*. Lanham, MD: University Press of America.
Meier, John P. 1991, 1994, 2001. *A Marginal Jew: Rethinking the Historical Jesus*. 3 vols. New York: Doubleday.
Meshorer, Yaakov. 1978. "The Holy Land in Coins." *BAR* 4.1. (*BAR* CD Archive: 1975–2001).

Meyer, Paul D. 1970. "The Gentile Mission in Q." *JBL* 89:405–17.
Meyers, Eric M. 1999. "Sepphoris on the Eve of the Great Revolt (67–68 C.E.): Archaeology and Josephus." In *Galilee through the Centuries: Confluence of Cultures*, edited by Eric M. Meyers, 109–22. DJSS 1. Winona Lake, IN: Eisenbrauns.
———. 2000. "Yes, They Are." *BAR* 26.4:46–49, 60–61.
Milgrom, Jacob. 1983. "Of Hems and Tassels." *BAR* 9.3:61–65.
Millard, Alan. 2003. "Literacy in the Time of Jesus." *BAR* 29.4:36–45.
Mournet, Terence C. 2005. *Oral Tradition and Literary Dependency: Variability and Stability in the Synoptic Tradition and Q*. WUNT 2/195. Tübingen: Mohr/Siebeck.
Muthuraj, J. G. 1997. "The Meaning of *Ethnos* and *Ethne* and Its Significance to the Study of the New Testament." *Bangalore Theological Forum* 29:3–36.
Nash, M. 1996. "The Core Elements of Ethnicity." In *Ethnicity*, edited by John Hutchinson and Anthony D. Smith, 24–28. Oxfordreaders. Oxford: Oxford University Press.
Netzer, Ehud. 1991. "The Last Days and Hours at Masada." *BAR* 17.6:20–32.
Neusner, Jacob. 1973. *From Politics to Piety: The Emergence of Rabbinic Judaism*. Reprinted, Eugene, OR: Wipf & Stock, 2003.
———. 1976. "'First Cleanse the Inside': 'Halakhic' Background of a Controversy Saying." *NTS* 22:486–95.
———. 1988. *The Mishnah: A New Translation*. New Haven: Yale University Press.
Oakman, Douglas E. 1986. *Jesus and the Economic Questions of His Day*. SBEC 8. Lewiston, NY: Mellen.
Oppenheimer, Aharon. 2005. *Between Rome and Babylon: Studies in Jewish Leadership and Society*. Texts and Studies in Ancient Judaism 108. Tübingen: Mohr/Siebeck.
Overman, J. Andrew, Jack Olive, and M. Nelson. 2003. "Discovering Herod's Shrine to Augustus." *BAR* 29.2:40–49, 67–68.
Paget, James Carleton. 2001. "Quests for the Historical Jesus." In *The Cambridge Companion to Jesus*, edited by Markus Bockmuehl, 138–55. Cambridge Companions to Religion. Cambridge: Cambridge University Press.
Patrich, Joseph. 1990. "Reconstructing the Magnificent Temple Herod Built." In *Archaeology in the World of Herod, Jesus and Paul*, edited by Hershel Shanks and Dan P. Cole, 64–77. *Archaeology and the Bible: The Best of BAR*, vol. 2. Washington, DC: Biblical Archaeology Society.
Pearson, Birger A. 2004. "A Q Community in Galilee?" *NTS* 50:476–94.
Pilch, John J. 1997. "Are There Jews and Christians in the Bible?" *HTS* 53.1–2:119–25.
Piper, Ronald A. 1989. *Wisdom in the Q-tradition: The Aphoristic Teaching of Jesus*. SNTSMS 61. Cambridge: Cambridge University Press.
———. 1995. "The Language of Violence and the Aphoristic Sayings in Q: A Study of Q 6:27–36." In *Conflict and Invention: Literary, Rhetorical and Social Studies on the Sayings Gospel Q*, edited by John S. Kloppenborg, 53–72. Valley Forge, PA: Trinity.
Poirier, John C. 2003. "Purity beyond the Temple in the Second Temple Era." *JBL* 122:247–65.
Porter, Stanley E. 1994. "Jesus and the Use of Greek in Galilee." In *Studying the Historical Jesus: Evaluations of the State of Current Research*, edited by Bruce Chilton and Craig A. Evans, 123–54. NTTS 19. Leiden: Brill.
Rad, Gerhard von. 1962. *Old Testament Theology*. Vol. 1: *The Theology of Israel's Historical Traditions*. Translated by D. M. G. Stalker. Edinburgh: Oliver & Boyd.

Reed, Jonathan L. 1995. "The Social Map of Q." In *Conflict and Invention: Literary, Rhetorical and Social Studies on the Sayings Gospel Q*, edited by John S. Kloppenborg, 17–36. Valley Forge, PA: Trinity.

———. 1996. "The Sign of Jonah (Q 11:29–32) and Other Epic Traditions in Q." In *Reimagining Christian Origins: A Colloquium Honoring Burton L. Mack*, edited by Elizabeth Castelli and Hal Taussig, 130–43. Valley Forge, PA: Trinity.

———. 1999. "Galileans, 'Israelite Village Communities,' and the Sayings Gospel Q." In *Galilee through the Centuries: Confluence of Cultures*, edited by Eric M. Meyers, 87–108. DJSS 1. Winona Lake, IN: Eisenbrauns.

———. 2000. *Archaeology and the Galilean Jesus: A Re-examination of the Evidence*. Harrisburg, PA: Trinity.

Reich, Ronny. 1990. "Miqvaot (Jewish Ritual Immersion Baths) in Eretz-Israel in the Second Temple Period and the Mishnah and Talmud Periods." Ph.D. diss., Hebrew University Jerusalem [Hebrew with English summary].

———. 2002. "They *Are* Ritual Baths." *BAR* 28.2:50–55.

Reiser, Marius. 2001. "Love of Enemies in the Context of Antiquity." *NTS* 47:411–27.

Richardson, Peter. 1969. *Israel in the Apostolic Church*. SNTSMS 10. Cambridge: University Press.

———. 2004. *Building Jewish in the Roman East*. Waco, TX: Baylor University Press.

Ridderbos, Herman N. 1975. *Paul: An Outline of His Theology*. Translated by John Richard De Witt. Grand Rapids: Eerdmans.

Ritmeyer, Kathleen, and Leen Ritmeyer. 1990. "Reconstructing Herod's Temple Mount in Jerusalem." In *Archaeology in the World of Herod, Jesus and Paul*, edited by Hershel Shanks and Dan P. Cole, 31–61. *Archaeology and the Bible: The Best of BAR*, vol. 2. Washington, DC: Biblical Archaeology Society.

Robinson, James M., Paul Hoffmann, and John S. Kloppenborg Verbin. 2002. *The Sayings Gospel Q in Greek and English with Parallels from the Gospels of Mark and Thomas*. Hermeneia Supplements. Minneapolis: Fortress.

Roosens, Eugeen. 1994. "The Primordial Nature of Origins in Migrant Ethnicity." In *The Anthropology of Ethnicity: Beyond "Ethnic Groups and Boundaries,"* edited by Hans Vermeulen and Cora Govers, 81–104. Amsterdam: Spinhuis.

Rubens, Alfred. 1973. *A History of Jewish Costume*. Rev ed. London: Owen.

Russell, D. S. 1980. *The Method and Message of Jewish Apocalyptic*. Old Testament Library. Philadelphia: Westminster.

Saldarini, Anthony J. 1988. *Pharisees, Scribes and Sadducees in Palestinian Society: A Sociological Approach*. Wilmington, DE: Glazier.

———. 1994. *Matthew's Christian-Jewish Community*. Chicago Studies in the History of Judaism. Chicago: University of Chicago Press.

Sanders, E. P. 1977. *Paul and Palestinian Judaism: A Comparison of Patterns of Religion*. Philadelphia: Fortress.

———. 1985. *Jesus and Judaism*. Philadelphia: Fortress.

———. 1992. *Judaism: Practice and Belief 63 BCE—66 CE*. Philadelphia: Trinity.

———. 1993. *The Historical Figure of Jesus*. Harmondsworth: Penguin.

Sanders, James A. 2002. "The Family in the Bible." *BTB 32:117–28*.

Sato, Migaku. 1995. "Wisdom Statements in the Sphere of Prophecy." In *The Gospel behind the Gospels: Current Studies on Q*, edited by Ronald A. Piper, 139–58. NovTSup 75. Leiden: Brill.

Sawicki, Marianne. 2000. *Crossing Galilee: Architectures of Contact in the Occupied Land of Jesus*. Harrisburg, PA: Trinity.

Schmidt, Francis. 2001. *How the Temple Thinks: Identity and Social Cohesion in Ancient Judaism.* Translated by J. Edward Crowley. Biblical Seminar 78. Sheffield: Sheffield Academic.

Schürer, Emil. 1973–1987. *The History of the Jewish People in the Age of Jesus Christ (175 B.C.—A.D. 135).* 3 vols. in 4 parts. Revised and edited by Geza Vermes, Fergus Millar, and Martin Goodman. Edinburgh: T. & T. Clark.

Scott, George M. 1990. "A Resynthesis of the Primordial and Circumstantial Approaches to Ethnic Group Solidarity: Towards and Explanatory Model." *ERS* 13:147–71.

Shanks, Hershel. 1990. "Excavating in the Shadow of the Temple Mount." In *Archaeology in the World of Herod, Jesus and Paul*, edited by Hershel Shanks and Dan P. Cole, 2–20. *Archaeology and the Bible: The Best of BAR*, vol. 2. Washington, DC: Biblical Archaeology Society.

———. 2001. "Is It or Isn't It—A Synagogue?" *BAR* 27.6:51–57.

Shils, Edward A. 1957a. *Center and Periphery: Essays in Macrosociology. Selected Papers of Edward Shils*, vol. 2, 111–26. Chicago: Chicago University Press.

———. 1957b. "Primordial, Personal, Sacred and Civil Ties." *British Journal of Sociology* 8:130–45.

Sim, David Campbell. 1996. "Christianity and Ethnicity in the Gospel of Matthew." In *Ethnicity and the Bible*, edited by Mark G. Brett, 171–95. BibIntSer 19. Leiden: Brill.

Smiles, Vincent M. 2002. "The Concept of 'Zeal' in Second-Temple Judaism and Paul's Critique of It in Romans 10:2." *CBQ* 64:282–99.

Smith, Anthony D. 1986. *The Ethnic Origins of Nations.* Oxford: Blackwell.

———. 1994. "The Politics of Culture: Ethnicity and Nationalism." In *Companion Encyclopedia of Anthropology*, edited by Tim Ingold, 706–33. Routledge Reference. London: Routledge.

———. 1997. "Structure and Persistence of Ethnie." In *The Ethnicity Reader: Nationalism, Multiculturalism and Migration*, edited by Montserrat Guibernau and John Rex, 27–33. Cambridge: Polity.

Soggin, J. Alberto. 1993. *An Introduction to the History of Israel and Judah.* 2d ed. Translated by John Bowden. London: SCM.

Stegemann, Ekkehard W., and Wolfgang Stegemann. 1999. *The Jesus Movement: A Social History of Its First Century.* Translated by O. C. Dean, Jr. Minneapolis: Fortress.

Stegemann, Wolfgang. 2006. "The Emergence of God's New People: The Beginnings of Christianity Reconsidered." *HTS* 62:23–40.

Stein, S. 2004. "Ethnicity." In *Encyclopedia of Race and Ethnic Studies*, edited by Ellis Cashmore, 142–46. London: Routledge.

Strange, James F., and Hershel Shanks. 1990. "Synagogue Where Jesus Preached Found at Capernaum." In *Archaeology in the World of Herod, Jesus and Paul*, edited by Hershel Shanks and Dan P. Cole, 200–207. *Archaeology and the Bible: The Best of BAR*, vol. 2. Washington, DC: Biblical Archaeology Society.

———. 1990. "Has the House Where Jesus Stayed in Capernaum Been Found?" In *Archaeology in the World of Herod, Jesus and Paul*, edited by Hershel Shanks and Dan P. Cole, 188–99. *Archaeology and the Bible: The Best of BAR*, vol. 2. Washington, DC: Biblical Archaeology Society.

Syon, Danny. 1992. "Gamla: Portrait of a Rebellion." *BAR* 18.1. (*BAR* CD Archive: 1975–2001).

Tannenbaum, Robert F. 1986. "Jews and God-fearers in the Holy City of Aphrodite." *BAR* 12.5:54–57.

Tomson, Peter J. 2001. "Jesus and His Judaism." In *The Cambridge Companion to Jesus*, edited by M. Bockmuehl, 25–40. Cambridge: Cambridge University Press.
Tsafrir, Y., et al., 1990. "Glorious Beth-Shean." *BAR* 16.4:17–32.
Tsuk, Tsvika. 2000. "Bringing Water to Sepphoris." *BAR* 26.4:35–41.
Tuckett, Christopher M. 1989. "A Cynic Q?" *Biblica* 70:349–76.
———. 1996. *Q and the History of Early Christianity: Studies on Q*. Edinburgh: T. & T. Clark.
Uro, Risto. 1987. *Sheep among the Wolves: A Study of the Mission Instructions of Q*. Helsinki: Suomalainen Tiedeakatemia.
———. 1995. "John the Baptist and the Jesus Movement: What Does Q Tell Us?" In *The Gospel behind the Gospels: Current Studies on Q*, edited by Ronald A. Piper, 231–57. NovTSup 75. Leiden: Brill.
Vaage, Leif E. 1994. *Galilean Upstarts: Jesus' First Followers according to Q*. Valley Forge, PA: Trinity.
———. 1995a. "Q and Cynicism: On Comparison and Social identity." In *The Gospel behind the Gospels. Current Studies on Q*, edited by Ronald A. Piper, 199–229. NovTSup 75. Leiden: Brill.
———. 1995b. "Composite Texts and Oral Mythology." In *Conflict and Invention: Literary, Rhetorical and Social Studies on the Sayings Gospel Q*, edited by John S. Kloppenborg, 75–97. Valley Forge, PA: Trinity.
Van Aarde, Andries G. [2005] 2007. "Jesus' Mission to All of Israel Emplotted in Matthew's Story." For publication in *Neotestamentica* 41(2) 2007.
Van der Horst, Pieter W. 1992. "Jewish Funerary Inscriptions—Most Are in Greek." *BAR* 18.5. (*BAR* CD Archive: 1975–2001).
Vermes, Geza. 1973. *Jesus the Jew: A Historian's Reading of the Gospels*. Glasgow: Collins.
———. 1998. *The Complete Dead Sea Scrolls in English*. New York: Penguin.
———. 2001. *The Changing Faces of Jesus*. New York: Penguin.
Wilson, Bryan R. 1973. *Magic and the Millennium*. New York: Harper & Row.
Wright, Christopher J. H. 1990. *God's People in God's Land: Family, Land, and Property in the Old Testament*. Grand Rapids: Eerdmans.
Yeivin, Ze'ev. 1987. "Ancient Chorazin Comes Back to Life." *BAR* 13.5:22–36.

www.ingramcontent.com/pod-product-compliance
Lightning Source LLC
Chambersburg PA
CBHW022226010526
44113CB00033B/512